Cambridge International AS Level

US History since 1877

Gale Deeney
Mara Sankey
Elizabeth Sparey

Endorsement indicates that a resource has passed Cambridge International Education's rigorous quality-assurance process and is suitable to support the delivery of their syllabus. However, endorsed resources are not the only suitable materials available to support teaching and learning, and are not essential to achieve the qualification. For the full list of endorsed resources to support this syllabus, visit www.cambridgeinternational.org/endorsedresources

Any example answers to questions taken from past question papers, practice questions, accompanying marks and mark schemes included in this resource have been written by the authors and are for guidance only. They do not replicate examination papers. In examinations the way marks are awarded may be different. Any references to assessment and/or assessment preparation are the publisher's interpretation of the syllabus requirements. Examiners will not use endorsed resources as a source of material for any assessment set by Cambridge International Education.

While the publishers have made every attempt to ensure that advice on the qualification and its assessment is accurate, the official syllabus, specimen assessment materials and any associated assessment guidance materials produced by the awarding body are the only authoritative source of information and should always be referred to for definitive guidance.

Our approach is to provide teachers with access to a wide range of high-quality resources that suit different styles and types of teaching and learning.

For more information about the endorsement process, please visit www.cambridgeinternational.org/endorsed-resources

Cambridge International Education material in this publication is reproduced under licence and remains the intellectual property of Cambridge University Press & Assessment.

Third-party websites and resources referred to in this publication are not endorsed.

Although every effort has been made to ensure that website addresses are correct at time of going to press, Hachette Learning cannot be held responsible for the content of any website mentioned in this book. It is sometimes possible to find a relocated web page by typing in the address of the home page for a website in the URL window of your browser.

Hachette UK's policy is to use papers that are natural, renewable and recyclable products and made from wood grown in well-managed forests and other controlled sources. The logging and manufacturing processes are expected to conform to the environmental regulations of the country of origin.

To order, please visit www.HachetteLearning.com or contact Customer Service at education@hachette.co.uk / +44 (0)1235 827827.

ISBN: 9781036008994

© Gale Deeney, Mara Sankey, Elizabeth Sparey 2025

First published in 2025 by

Hachette Learning (a trading division of Hodder & Stoughton Ltd.),

An Hachette UK Company

Carmelite House

50 Victoria Embankment

London EC4Y 0DZ

www.hachettelearning.com

Impression number   10 9 8 7 6 5 4 3 2 1

Year   2028 2027 2026 2025

All rights reserved. Apart from any use permitted under UK copyright law, no part of this publication may be reproduced or transmitted in any form or by any means, electronic or mechanical, including photocopying and recording, or held within any information storage and retrieval system, without permission in writing from the publisher or under licence from the Copyright Licensing Agency Limited. Further details of such licences (for reprographic reproduction) may be obtained from the Copyright Licensing Agency Limited, www.cla.co.uk

The authorised representative in the EEA is Hachette Ireland, 8 Castlecourt Centre, Castleknock Road, Castleknock, Dublin 15, D15 YF6A, Ireland

Cover photo © Dom Slike / Alamy Stock Photo

Illustrations by Newgen Knowledge Works

Typeset by Newgen Publishing UK

Printed and Bound in Great Britain by Bell & Bain Ltd, Glasgow

A catalogue record for this title is available from the British Library.

Contents

Introduction	iv
What you will study	iv
Structure of the syllabus	v
About this book	vii
Overview	ix

CHAPTER 1 The Gilded Age and Progressive Era — 1

1.1 What were the impacts of rapid economic growth in the US during the Gilded Age?	2
1.2 What were the main aims and policies of the Progressive Movement?	33
1.3 How successful was the Progressive Movement up to 1920?	56
Study skills	77

CHAPTER 2 American Imperialism, the First World War, and the 1920s — 86

2.1 What were the causes and consequences of US territorial expansion in the late nineteenth and early twentieth centuries?	87
2.2 Why did the US enter the First World War and how did the war impact Americans?	99
2.3 What were the causes and impacts of economic and cultural changes in the 1920s?	114
Study skills	134

CHAPTER 3 The Great Depression, the Second World War, and the Early Cold War — 137

3.1 What were the causes and impacts of the Great Depression and New Deal?	138
3.2 Why and how did US foreign policy evolve between 1935 and 1959?	155
3.3 Why and how far did US society change in the 1940s and 1950s?	174
Study skills	191

CHAPTER 4 The Development of the US in the 1960s and 1970s — 195

4.1 Why and how did US approaches to the Cold War change between 1960 and 1979?	196
4.2 Why and how did politics in the US evolve between 1960 and 1979?	210
4.3 Why and how far did the position of minorities improve in the US between 1960 and 1979?	224
Study skills	242

CHAPTER 5 The Modern US, 1980 to 2008 — 245

5.1 Why and how did the global role of the US evolve between 1980 and 2008?	246
5.2 Why and how did US politics change between 1980 and 2008?	264
5.3 Why and how far did US society change between 1980 and 2008?	279
Study skills	294
Further reading	300
Glossary	302
Index	307
Photo credits	310

Introduction

This book is designed to support your understanding of the key themes, topics and people significant to the period of US history between 1877 and 2008. The Cambridge International AS Level History syllabus (8102) offers an education in understanding the changes that characterized the period. The book has been endorsed by Cambridge International Education and is listed as an endorsed textbook for students studying the syllabus.

This introduction gives you an overview of:
- the content you will study for Cambridge International AS Level US History since 1877
- the structure of the syllabus
- the different features of this book and how these will aid your learning.

1 What you will study

The period from 1877 to 2008 in the United States was marked by transformations that reshaped the nation. Starting with the aftermath of Reconstruction, when the newly granted civil rights of formerly enslaved people were swiftly suppressed, the US evolved into the world's largest economic power, facing issues of industrialization, immigration and inequality. By the mid-twentieth century, the US had expanded its influence, participated in two world wars and emerged as a Cold War power. Economic booms were often followed by downturns like the Great Depression, leading to increased federal intervention. Social movements flourished as marginalized groups sought equality, with the 1960s seeing significant progress in civil rights. US foreign policy shifted from isolationism to a more interventionist stance. This era saw cultural shifts, from the 1960s counterculture to the 1980s conservative resurgence. By 2008, Barack Obama's election highlighted greater diversity. However, debates on equality and government's role continued. These transformations form the core of this book.

This book covers the following topics post-1877:
- Chapter 1, The Gilded Age and Progressive Era, considers the impact of rapid economic change, the aims of the Progressive Movement and the extent to which they succeeded in achieving their aims by 1920.
- Chapter 2, American Imperialism, the First World War and the 1920s, examines the debates about imperialism that followed the US's adoption of an interventionist foreign policy from the 1890s. It considers and the return of isolationism after the First World War. This chapter also discusses how the 1920s brought wealth for some but saw inequality and intolerance persisting, overshadowing apparent prosperity and liberalization.
- Chapter 3, The Great Depression, the Second World War and the Early Cold War, explores the reasons for and impacts of the Wall Street Crash, the effects of involvement in the Second World War on society and the economy, and the threats posed by fear of communism at the start of the Cold War. This chapter also considers the extent to which all Americans shared in post-war prosperity and opportunities.
- Chapter 4, The Development of the US in the 1960s and 1970s, investigates the shift from an era of apparent political and social liberalism in the early 1960s to a growing conservatism. The anti-war movement, civil rights activism, and development of feminism are among the social issues which will be considered. The impact of changes brought about through economic transformation from the post-war economic boom to the stagnation of the 1970s are examined.
- Chapter 5, The Modern US, 1980 to 2008, discusses the end of the Cold War and the US's difficulties in navigating the post-Cold War world. It covers extremism, terrorism, stagflation, Reaganomics, and the impact of globalization and technological advances on society and the economy.

2 Structure of the syllabus

*The information in this section is based on the Cambridge International Education **syllabus**. You should always refer to the appropriate **syllabus** document for the year of examination to confirm the details and for more information. The syllabus document is available on the website: www.cambridgeinternational.org.*

The Cambridge International AS Level History will be assessed through two papers, a Historical Sources Paper and an Outline Study.

- Paper 1: For Paper 1 you need to answer one two-part question on historical sources. This counts for 40 percent of the AS Level. The topic for the Historical Sources Paper is the Gilded Age and the Progressive Era, which is covered in Chapter 1 of this book.
- Paper 2: For Paper 2 you need to answer two two-part questions from a choice of four questions (one on each of the four Paper 2 topics). You must answer both parts of the question you choose. This counts for 60 percent of the AS Level. Chapters 2 through 5 are covered in Paper 2.

Assessment questions

For Paper 1 there will be two parts to the question. For Part (a) you will be expected to compare two sources on one aspect of the material. For Part (b) you will be expected to use all four sources and your knowledge of the period to address how far the sources support a given view.

For Paper 2 you will select two questions from the four options. There will be two parts to each question. Part (a) requires you to explain the causes of events and Part (b) requires you to develop a balanced answer in response to a given question. You will need to answer both parts of the question you choose.

Command words

When choosing the two essay questions, keep in mind that it is vital to answer the actual question that has been asked, not the one that you might have hoped for. A key to doing well is understanding the demands of the question. Cambridge International AS Level History uses key terms and phrases known as command words. The command words are listed below.

Command word	What it means
Compare	Identify/comment on similarities and/or differences
Explain	Set out purposes or reasons/make the relationships between things evident/provide reasons why and/or how and support with relevant evidence

Questions may also use phrases such as:
- How far do the sources support the view ... ?
- How far was ... the key factor/the main reason for ... ?
- How successful/how important was ... ?
- How far do you agree?
- To what extent?

Key concepts

The syllabus also focuses on developing your understanding of a number of key concepts and these are also reflected in the nature of the questions set in the examination. The key concepts for AS Level History are as follows:

Cause and consequence

The events, circumstances, actions and beliefs that have a direct causal connection to consequential events and developments, circumstances, actions or beliefs. Causes can be both human and non-human.

Change and continuity

The patterns, processes, and interplay of change and continuity within a given time frame.

Similarity and difference

The patterns of similarity and difference that exist between people, lived experiences, events, and situations in the past.

Significance

The importance attached to an event, individual, or entity in the past, whether at the time or subsequent to it. Historical significance is a constructed label that is dependent upon the perspective (context, values, interests, and concerns) of the person ascribing significance and is therefore changeable.

The icons above appear next to questions to show where key concepts are being tested and what they are.

Answering Assessment questions

It is important that you organize your time well. In other words, do not spend too long on one question and leave yourself short of time. Before you begin a question, take a few minutes to draw up a brief plan of the major points you want to make and your argument. You can then tick them off as you make them. This is not a waste of time as it will help you produce a coherent and well-organized response with a conclusion rather than a response that lacks coherency and jumps from point to point.

Whoever reads your answers will focus on what you have done right, rather than what you have done wrong.

Answering source questions

For a comparison question you should be able to:
- make a developed comparison of the two sources
- identify both similarities **and** differences in the evidence that two sources give about a particular issue, and develop them with content from the sources
- use contextual knowledge to **explain** the similarities and/or differences.

For questions that ask you to analyse more than two sources you should be able to:
- identify whether sources support or challenge the statement in the question
- use source content to explain how the source supports or challenges the statement
- use your contextual knowledge to help you to understand and analyze the sources
- recognize nuance in the sources if appropriate.

A well written answer for a source question should
- evaluate the sources to reach a considered judgment as to how far the sources support the view stated in the question.

If you are writing a timed essay about sources where you cannot choose a question to answer, you may find it helpful to
- spend ten minutes reading the sources carefully
- identify the key terms and phrases in the question so that you remain focused on the actual question
- underline any quotations you will use to support your arguments.

Answering essay questions

Both the short and long answer questions should:
- be well focused
- be well supported by precise and accurate evidence
- reach a relevant and supported conclusion or judgment
- demonstrate knowledge and understanding of historical processes
- demonstrate a clear understanding of connections between causes.

Your essay should include an introduction which sets out your main points. Do not waste time copying out the question but do define any key terms that are in the question. The strongest essays will show awareness of different possible approaches to the question. You will need to write an in-depth analysis of your main points in several paragraphs, providing detailed and accurate information to support them. Each paragraph will focus on one of your main points and be directly related to the question. Finally, you should write a concluding paragraph. All of these skills are developed throughout the book in the study skills section at the end of each chapter.

If you need to choose multiple questions to answer
- circle the **two** questions you intend to answer
- identify the command terms, keywords, and phrases so you remain focused on them
- then spend a short period of time planning your answers.

3 About this book

Coverage of the course content

This book addresses the key areas listed in the Cambridge International syllabus. The content follows closely the layout and sequence of the Cambridge syllabus with each chapter representing each topic. Chapters start with an introduction outlining key questions they address. Each key question is accompanied by content that you are expected to understand and deploy when addressing the key question. Throughout the chapters, you will find the following features to aid your study of the course content.

Key terms

Key terms are the important terms you need to know to gain an understanding of the period. These are highlighted in the text the first time they appear in the book and are defined in the margin. They also appear in the glossary at the end of the book.

Key figures and profiles

Key figures highlight important individuals and can be found in the margin. Some chapters contain profiles that offer more information about the importance and impact of the individual. This information can be very useful in understanding certain events and providing supporting evidence to your arguments.

Sources

Throughout the book, you will encounter both written and visual sources. Historical sources are important components in understanding more fully why specific decisions were taken, how events and policies were viewed at the time, and the impacts they had on different groups of people. They also help to explain both the causes and consequences of past developments. The sources are accompanied by questions to help you dig deeper into US History since 1877. To help with analyzing the sources, think about the message of the sources, their purpose, and their usefulness for a particular line of inquiry. The questions that accompany the sources will help you with this.

Activities

Activities and tasks throughout the book will help you develop conceptual understanding and consolidate knowledge.

Summary diagrams

At the end of each section is a summary diagram which gives a visual summary of the content of the section. It is intended as an aid for revision. Try copying the diagram into your own set of notes and, using information from the chapter, provide precise examples to develop each point. This will help build your knowledge of the issues that relate to the key question.

Chapter summaries

At the end of each chapter is a short summary of the content of that chapter. This is intended to help you consolidate your knowledge and understanding of the content.

Refresher questions

Questions at the end of each chapter will serve as a useful tool to test your knowledge of what you have read. These serve as prompts and show where you have gaps in your knowledge and understanding.

Study skills

At the end of each chapter, you will find guidance on how to approach writing a successful essay and how to evaluate sources. These pages feature the kinds of questions you may come across in assessment. There are also analyses of and comments on sample answers. These are not full responses to the questions. We have written them to help you to see what part of a good answer might look like.

End of the book

The book concludes with the following sections.

Glossary

All key terms in the book are defined in the glossary.

Further reading

This contains a list of books that may help you with further independent research. At this level of study, it is important to read around the subject and not just solely rely on the content of this textbook. The further reading section will help you with this.

Ebook support

The ebook of this title contains knowledge tests, with ten tests per key topic.

When reading the text of this book, you might encounter terms that feel inappropriate and outdated. This text has been sensitivity reviewed to ensure that any instances of terminology that is out of date are used to reflect historical accuracy. For example, the "National Association of Colored Women" was the formal title of a self-named organization from that period.

Overview

This course is designed to develop an understanding of key events, trends, and developments which shaped America and Americans between 1877 and 2008. It spans the period, starting with the failure of Reconstruction in 1877, when formerly enslaved people were often prevented from exercising civil rights granted through constitutional amendments. The period ends in 2008 with the election of Barack Obama, the first African American President of the United States. Achieving equality in terms of civil rights, political rights, and opportunity for Americans of all racial origins and from all social groups is a key theme in this period. Who could vote for the government, and how accountable to the electorate that government should be, were key concerns.

The American economy developed enormously during this period, and the United States rapidly became the richest country in the world. In 1877, the first transcontinental railroad had recently been completed and railroads, together with mining, steel, and textiles, were growth areas of the economy. By 2008, healthcare, technology, construction, and retail were important. In 1877, most Americans lived in rural areas but by 2008 only twenty percent did so. Periods of rapid growth were often followed by economic downturns and depression, which caused unemployment and social distress. Many Americans believed that the best form of government was that which interfered the least. Nevertheless, from the Progressives onward, there was growing pressure for federal (and state) governments to address the key economic and social problems of the age.

In 1877, white Anglo-Saxon Protestants dominated American politics and culture, and were the socioeconomic elite. By 2008, there was greater diversity in all these areas and at every level. The speed and extent of industrialization encouraged large numbers of immigrants to come to the US to set up a new future in a land that promised endless opportunities. Immigration was a divisive issue: the American economy needed workers, but how to ensure that immigrants developed an American identity presented challenges. Who should be allowed to become American and what should be done to help them assimilate?

The United States was traditionally reluctant to become involved in other countries' wars. The issue of how involved the US should be with other powers was keenly debated and is a key theme. In 1890, the armed forces were far smaller than those of even minor European powers. By 2002, the US spent more on defense than all the member states of the European Union combined. Although there were periods when the US seemed to retreat into isolationism, a more active and globally involved foreign policy developed. The reasons for, and impacts of, this development are traced from Chapter 2 through Chapter 5.

This book explores this period of significant political, social, and economic change, and is divided into five chapters that cover these key themes. This course considers the experiences of a wide range of different social groups. It looks at how political and economic developments changed lives, and examines the issues people faced and the activism that secured a more equal society in the US. This course covers the causes, chronological sequences, and effects of events. It looks at individual topics from 1877 onward to build an overall knowledge and understanding of the factors, people, and developments that shaped America as it entered the twenty-first century.

Chapter 1 The Gilded Age and Progressive Era

By 1877, the US economy was transforming from agricultural to industrial, with the country becoming the world's greatest economic power. In 1873, *The Gilded Age* was written by Mark Twain and Charles Dudley Warner. It was a novel that satirized the greed and corruption of the late nineteenth century, and the name was adopted for the period which covered the 1870s to the turn of the century. It was not a flattering title. In a period of rapid economic growth, the few amassed vast wealth, and these so-called "robber barons" gained political power and influence. Meanwhile, the many occupied poor-quality housing, lacked security of employment, worked in hazardous conditions and, in the case of many immigrants and African Americans, faced racial, religious, and political prejudice. The labor unions, populists and Progressive Movement developed, each aiming to achieve better conditions for workers, create a fairer society, and establish more transparent and accountable business and political practices. Fueled by the work of the "muckrakers," debates raged at all levels of society, and at state and federal level, about whether and how America should change. This chapter considers the impact of rapid economic change, the aims of the Progressive Movement, and the extent to which they succeeded in achieving these aims by 1920.

Chapter 2 American Imperialism, the First World War, and the 1920s

From the 1890s onward, the US developed a more interventionist approach to foreign affairs. There were economic and cultural motives for expansion; however, this was highly controversial. Americans had won their independence from Britain to establish a democracy and be free from external control. Should the US acquire colonial possessions, or would this be a form of tyranny for those who lived there? When the First World War broke out in 1914, most Americans believed it was a European dispute and of little concern to the US. Despite President Wilson's declaration of neutrality, in April 1917 the US declared war on Germany. The reasons for, and impact of, this policy change are considered in this chapter. When the war ended, most Americans favored a return to isolationism and "normalcy."

Social issues and economic concerns dominated most people's thoughts. The 1920s appeared to promise great things; Americans grew wealthy, bought cars, and went to jazz clubs. Housewives coveted labor-saving consumer goods, young women cut their hair, shortened their hemlines and headed to the city. However, this picture was misleading and true for only a few rather than most. The "boom" did not affect all sectors of the economy and apparent liberalization in social attitudes was accompanied by intolerance and suspicion of immigrants, those with different political beliefs, and those of different racial origins.

Chapter 3 The Great Depression, the Second World War, and the Early Cold War

In 1929, the Wall Street Crash brought dramatic change and years of economic depression followed. This chapter explores the reasons why the Great Depression took place at this time. This financial and industrial collapse brought unprecedented levels of unemployment and hardship, and seemed to require a higher level of federal intervention than the United States had encountered or tolerated before. The election of President Franklin Roosevelt led to the New Deal and, although this was widely supported, its introduction, scope, and effectiveness were the subjects of scrutiny and debate.

In 1939, the Second World War broke out in Europe. At first, the US resisted military involvement. However, in December 1941 Japan attacked the US Pacific Fleet at Pearl Harbor and the US declared war. In 1945, peace was restored for a brief time. The Allies attempted to establish a new order in Europe and, through the formation of the United Nations, a mechanism for ensuring world peace. However, by 1949 a "Cold War" had developed between the West and the Soviet Union. It was waged through a series of proxy wars that took place across the world, starting in Korea in 1950.

This chapter considers the impact of involvement in the Second World War on US society and the economy. Fighting in the Second World War involved many Americans, including women and African Americans, both on the home front and in the armed forces. There was a widespread belief that the war was fought for a just cause and for a better future. Many benefited from the post-war economic boom and enjoyed affluent suburban living, full employment, and greater educational opportunities. However, the re-establishment of conservative values left others dissatisfied. The onset of the Cold War encouraged a widespread fear of communism and those with "un-American" political leanings were persecuted. Civil rights were not assured and activism during the 1950s grew more intense. Problems in the cities appeared to threaten the "American dream."

Chapter 4 The Development of the US in the 1960s and 1970s

In the 1960s, the babies of the post-war baby boom became adults. The enactment of civil rights legislation suggested progress towards a more equal society. Two Democratic presidents dominated the early 1960s as the Cold War continued. President Kennedy was praised for avoiding thermonuclear war over Cuba, but his assassination in 1963 left America stunned. Increasing involvement in Vietnam caused many Americans to question whether US policy was correct. The draft was unpopular, the televised Vietnam War had a negative impact on public morale and, worse, the US appeared to be losing. President Johnson's social programs, such as the provision of welfare and housing, were sidelined in favor of military spending which grew increasingly unpopular. Johnson declined to stand for reelection and conservative messaging to the "silent majority" resulted in the election of Republican President Nixon.

What had appeared to be an era of liberalism was replaced by growing conservatism. The development of feminism, more radical civil rights activism, and the counterculture were seen as challenges to traditional authority, and resistance to social change grew. At the same time, the 1970s saw the end of the post-war economic boom. Global issues such as the oil crisis led to stagnation in the economy. Political credibility also faced a crisis. The Watergate Scandal of Nixon's presidency helped to create an air of distrust of politicians.

Chapter 5 The Modern US, 1980–2008

The late twentieth century brought changes to US politics, society and the economy, as issues of national security became increasingly prominent. US politics grew more divided and arguments about economic ideology and cultural issues dominated party politics. In 1980, Reagan became president. His anti-communist, anti-big government and anti-high taxation message was popular and seemed, on the surface at least, to represent what many Americans wanted. Reagan was also influential in bringing the Cold War to an end.

However, the post-Cold War world was difficult to navigate. What global role should the US take, peacemaker or police officer? Could the US maintain its prosperity, freedom, and security? The "evil empire" of the Soviet Union had been the enemy for half a century, but now the enemy was more diffuse and harder to identify. In 2001, terrorist attacks on the World Trade Center and the Pentagon rocked America to its core and this chapter examines their impact on how the US viewed its security.

The 1980s were dominated by stagflation and Reaganomics. In the 1990s, President Clinton succeeded in reducing the federal deficit, but his healthcare reforms failed. Entering the twenty-first century, globalization and technological advances changed economic structures and brought new challenges, as social media came to dominate political engagement.

In 2008, the first African American president was elected. Women, racial, and ethnic groups participated at all levels of state and federal government—a far cry from the situation in 1877. However, inequality remained and the debates continued: how free and equal a society was America by 2008?

1 The Gilded Age and Progressive Era

> ### Introduction
>
> To gild something means to cover it in gold. The "Gilded Age" therefore suggests that the United States was incredibly wealthy during this period. However, contemporaries used this term in a negative way to show that although the US might have looked shiny and rich on the outside, on the inside it was corrupt and rotten. How accurate was this image of America in the late nineteenth century? To be progressive means to be forward-thinking and to have a desire to bring about political, social, and economic reforms that will benefit society as a whole. The word has positive associations and the Progressive Movement certainly aimed to make America a better and fairer place to live. But did the Progressive Movement bring about positive changes for all Americans?
>
> This chapter covers three key questions about the Gilded Age and the Progressive Era from 1877 to 1920.
> - ▶ What were the impacts of rapid economic growth in the US during the Gilded Age?
> - ▶ What were the main aims and policies of the Progressive Movement?
> - ▶ How successful was the Progressive Movement up to 1920?

▶ KEY DATES

1877	Reconstruction ends
1882	Chinese Exclusion Act
1886	Haymarket Affair
1887	Dawes Act
1890	Sherman Antitrust Act
1892	Formation of the Populist Party
1893	Anti-Saloon League founded
1901	Theodore Roosevelt becomes president
1902	Coal Strike
1908	William Taft elected president
1909	National Association for the Advancement of Colored People founded
1912	Woodrow Wilson elected president
1919	Eighteenth Amendment to the Constitution
1920	Nineteenth Amendment to the Constitution

Figure 1.1 Map of the United States of America

1.1 What were the impacts of rapid economic growth in the US during the Gilded Age?

The economy of the United States grew rapidly in the last three decades of the nineteenth century. In 1870, the economy was still largely based on agriculture but, by 1900, the US produced around 30 percent of all the manufactured goods in the world.

Criteria	1860	1900
Value of industrial production	$2,000 million	$13,000 million
Capital invested in manufacturing	$1,000 million	$10,000 million
Number of people employed in manufacturing, mining, construction, and service industries	4 million	18 million

Table 1.1 Overview of economic growth 1860–1900

The reasons for industrial growth include:
- Natural resources: America had a huge expanse of land which could be used for farming, vast reserves of oil and coal which could be used for power, and other resources such as cotton and iron deposits to be used in industry and manufacturing.
- Communications: America was served by an increasingly sophisticated communications network which included rail links from the Atlantic to the Pacific, a reliable postal service, and the beginnings of telegraph and telephone communications.
- Immigration: this provided cheap labor to work in the factories and build the railroads. As **immigrants** poured into the country, the population, and therefore the market for products, grew.

KEY TERM

Immigrant Someone who moves to a country to become a permanent resident.

KEY TERMS

Laissez-faire French, meaning "allow to do." A doctrine where a government has minimal interference in the economy, with few laws controlling businesses.

Migrant Someone who moves to another country temporarily. Also, someone who moves within their own country.

- Government policies: these were known as *laissez-faire*. Republican and Democrat governments opted not to interfere in business but to leave it alone and allow it to flourish. Taxes were low and this allowed excess capital to be invested in developing industry and encouraged higher consumption.
- Development of the steel industry: steel was key to developments in transport and other industries. Output of steel grew from around 1 million tons in 1870 to almost 30 million in 1920.

This rapid industrial and economic development had a range of different impacts:
- A relatively small group of industrialists grew very wealthy and powerful.
- Rapid growth was accompanied by downturns which were equally dramatic and resulted in unemployment.
- There was a population shift from the countryside to the towns.
- Towns and cities developed at a fast pace and this development was largely unregulated. This resulted in overcrowding and unsanitary conditions.
- Between 1870 and 1920 over 25 million immigrants came to America to work in the new factories, mills, and coal mines.

Urbanization and immigration, and their impacts

The scale and speed with which the economy grew meant that large numbers of workers were required in many industries such as steel manufacturing, coal mining, and textile production. Workers needed to live close to their workplaces, so towns and cities developed around centers of industry. On a national level, the change was huge as America's urban population increased sevenfold in the half-century after the Civil War. Locally, changes were also dramatic. Much of the workforce which was needed to keep the economy growing came from the immigrants who poured into the United States between 1870 and 1920.

Reasons for population growth in the cities and the problems caused by it

In the years between 1860 and 1910, the population of the USA almost trebled.

Year	Population (in millions)
1880	50.2
1890	62.9
1900	75.9
1910	91.9
1920	105.7

Table 1.2 Population growth between 1880 and 1920

This was not due to a rise in the birth rate. From 1870 onward, the birth rate declined as people opted to have fewer children. However, at the same time there was a decline in the death rate. People lived longer on account of:
- better medical care
- improved diet
- improvements in housing and sanitation, such as in the provision of clean water.

There was also a shift in where the population was located. In 1860 one-sixth of Americans lived in cities. By 1900 this had increased to one-third, and by 1920 the proportion was over half. As Tables 1.3 and 1.4 show, New York was the largest city, with its population growing from just under 1 million to 4.8 million people in this period. However, there were 40 cities with a population of over 100,000. The increase in city populations was matched by a shift away from the countryside. New England was one of the most affected regions and saw a decline in population during this period.

The most important reason for the growth of cities was the development of industry. Pittsburgh is one example of industrialization promoting rapid urbanization. The development of the iron and steel industry was central to economic development in the

United States. These metals were used to build railroads and their locomotives, the girders for skyscrapers, and all kinds of machinery needed for industrial and agricultural production. Pittsburgh became the heart of this industry. It was surrounded by coal and iron deposits and its position on two rivers meant it was in a prime position for trade. In 1870, the city's population was around 140,000. By 1920, it had quadrupled to just less than 600,000.

However, the main reason for the increase in population was immigration and this will be considered later in this chapter.

Population growth

Where and why was the population growing in the United States in the late nineteenth and early twentieth centuries?

City	Population
New York	942,292
Philadelphia	674,022
Brooklyn, New York	419,921
St Louis	310,864
Chicago	298,977
Baltimore	267,354
Boston	250,526
Cincinnati	216,239
New Orleans	191,418
San Francisco	149,473

Table 1.3 The population of the ten largest cities in the US in 1870

City	Population
New York	4,766,883
Chicago	2,185,283
Philadelphia	1,549,008
St Louis	687,029
Boston	670,585
Cleveland	560,663
Baltimore	558,485
Pittsburgh	533,905
Detroit	465,766
Buffalo	423,715

Table 1.4 The population of the ten largest cities in the US in 1910

ACTIVITY

Working with a partner, use the tables in this section to identify the main trends in population change in the US in this period.

Do you think these trends would have a positive or negative impact?

One of you should write a list of possible positive impacts. The other writes a list of possible negative impacts.

Discuss your ideas. On balance do you think the changes would be mainly positive or negative?

Make two predictions based on these lists about how American could change. Keep a record of your predictions so that you can revisit it at the end of this section.

Problems

Housing and transportation issues

SOURCE 1.1

A photograph of Hester Street, part of Little Italy in New York City, taken around 1903

> What impression does this source give of city life in the early twentieth century?

KEY TERM

Provenance / attribution
All the sources in this book have a provenance or attribution statement like this. The statement shows when and where a source was written or published. It also says who wrote or produced the source. It may explain some of the details or references if it is a textual source. The information in the provenance statement can be used to help analyse or evaluate the source.

KEY TERM

Dumbbell tenement
Sometimes known as Old Law Tenements, these were blocks of housing that were given this name because the indentations of the air shafts created a building shape that resembled a dumbbell weight.

The vast numbers of workers moving to the cities meant that housing stock was in short supply. The housing which was built for the workers was often built quickly, to poor standards and lacked clean water and adequate toilet facilities. In 1879, **dumbbell tenements** started to be built. Typically five or six stories high, these were often dark and damp, with shared toilet facilities and many families crowded on each floor. Although they were designed with air shafts which were supposed to make them better ventilated than earlier tenement buildings, the air shafts were often used for dumping trash, making the housing even more unhealthy and increasing the risk of fires.

What were the advantages and disadvantages of dumbbell tenement buildings?

SOURCE 1.2

A plan of a dumbbell tenement. Blocks like this were built next to each other so the view from the windows would have been of another block

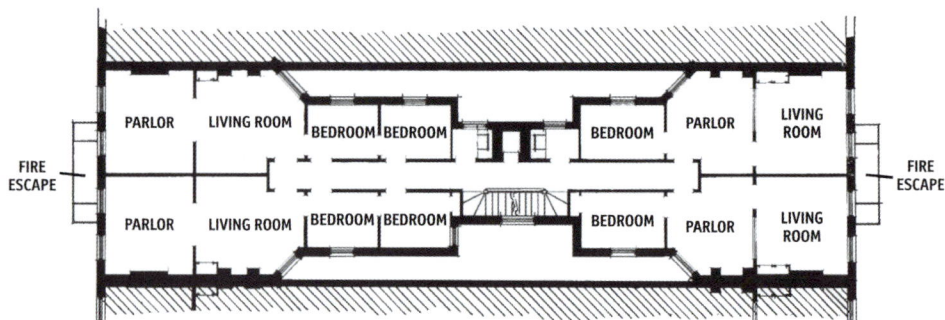

Life in the tenements was hard and unhealthy. Worse, however, were the flophouses that existed for those who had fallen on hard times and others who simply could not afford the rent for an apartment. The photograph below was taken by Jacob Riis, who documented the living conditions of people in the Lower East Side of New York City in a book called *How the Other Half Lives*. His work was partly responsible for the establishment of a Tenement House Commission to ensure housing conditions were improved. Laws were passed in 1901 to improve the quality of tenement buildings but were often restricted by vested interests. Those who owned property were often influential in city government and this enabled them to avoid expensive repairs or upgrades to their existing tenement blocks.

Why do you think this photograph was taken? Think about what Riis intended to happen as a result of its publication.

SOURCE 1.3

This photograph by Jacob Riis was entitled *Five Cents a Spot* and was taken around 1890

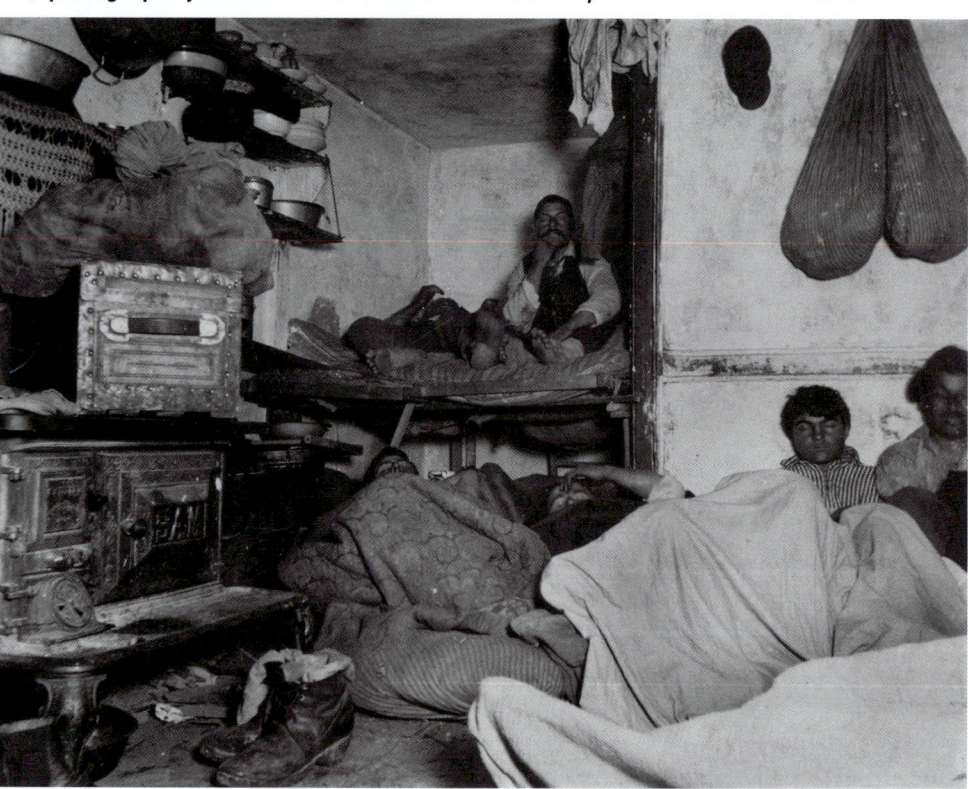

As we can see from Source 1.1, transport in the city was largely horse-drawn. This had several disadvantages for city dwellers. It was a slow method of transport and although there were trolley cars, these could not carry many passengers at a time. It was difficult to commute which meant that workers, even if they could afford to do so, could not move out of the cities to the suburbs. Improvements in road building in the 1880s meant that roads had better surfaces, which eased some of the problems. However, New York City faced a specific issue that increased congestion and that was a lack of good bridges. This was partly addressed by building Brooklyn Bridge in 1883 and then Williamsburg Bridge in 1903. Elevated steam railroads, such as the Chicago "L," were introduced in some cities. These carried passengers above street level in railway carriages. However, they contributed to the poor air quality and often caused cinders to fall onto pedestrians in the streets below. A more effective system was developed in San Francisco, where cable cars were used to cope with the hilly streets. Trolley cars, as these became known, were developed using electricity and by 1890 over 50 cities had adopted them. The trollies and the new subway systems meant that some workers could commute to the city daily and this led to the development of suburbs.

Health and sanitation

Slums, such as New York City's notorious "Lung Block," led to many health problems and outbreaks of disease among their residents.
- Overcrowding meant that contagious diseases such as typhoid and influenza spread easily among the population.
- Poor sanitation and a lack of clean drinking water led to diseases such as cholera which were of pandemic proportions in the mid-1890s and early 1900s.
- Poverty meant many families in the slums had a poor diet and this made them (especially children) susceptible to diseases such as measles, whooping cough, and rickets.
- Poor air quality and overcrowded conditions were also responsible for the spread of tuberculosis which was one of the leading causes of premature death in inner cities in the late nineteenth century.

Arrangements for water supply and the disposal of sewage were often rudimentary. Cities by the sea or on a river often dumped their waste straight into the water. Some cities had open sewers which ran along the sides of the streets and others had a system of cesspools where waste was collected. The smell in the summer months especially must have been horrendous! Things improved slowly and understanding of how diseases such as cholera spread was increasing by the 1850s. Serious fires in Chicago in 1871, where many buildings were made of timber, as is explained in Source 1.4 by **Jane Addams** below, and in Boston in 1873 demonstrated the necessity for towns to have access to a plentiful supply of water.

> ### KEY FIGURE
>
> **Jane Addams** (1860–1935) Addams was a progressive social reformer, sometimes known as America's first social worker. She was one of the founding members of the settlement movement, establishing Hull House in Chicago in 1889 after a visit to a similar project in the East End of London, England. Settlement houses were established in some of the worst slum areas and were intended to help new immigrants settle into American society. Addams also encouraged education and recreation at Hull House. A diverse range of projects included setting up day care for the children of working mothers, a Well Baby Clinic and theatre groups, and building kilns so that recently arrived Mexican immigrants could make their traditional ceramics to sell locally. She was a committed advocate of social reform, arguing in favor of women's suffrage, but also campaigned on diverse issues such as reducing the incidence of tuberculosis and establishing a juvenile court system. By 1910 there were over 400 settlement houses in the US with around 100 of them in Boston, Chicago, and New York City alone. However, many smaller cities, and even rural communities, also established settlement houses.

> **What can you learn from Source 1.4 about the health hazards faced by those living on these streets in Chicago?**

SOURCE 1.4

Jane Addams describes the state of the streets around Hull House in Chicago between 1889 and 1909 in her book *Twenty Years at Hull House*. Rear tenements were additional tenement buildings on land behind buildings that faced onto the street

The streets are inexpressibly dirty, the number of schools inadequate, sanitary legislation unenforced, the lighting bad. The paving is miserable and altogether lacking in the alleys and smaller streets, and the stables foul beyond description.

The houses, for the most part wooden, were originally built for one family and are now occupied by several. They are after the type of the inconvenient frame cottages found in the poorer suburbs twenty years ago. Many of them were built where they now stand; others were brought thither on rollers, because their previous sites had been taken for factories. The little wooden houses have a temporary aspect, and for this reason, perhaps, the tenement house legislation in Chicago is totally inadequate. Rear tenements flourish, many houses have no water supply save for the faucet in the backyard, there are no fire escapes, the garbage and ashes are placed in wooden boxes which are fastened to the street pavements.

Crime

The slums were densely populated, poverty-stricken, and poorly lit. It is not surprising that they became notorious for crime. Areas of New York City were particularly badly affected, earning titles such as "Bandits' Roost" and "Murderers' Alley." Gangs committed crimes such as pickpocketing, robbery, and assault. Gambling dens and prostitution (now referred to as sex work) were also common. The crime wave was particularly bad in the 1880s when the prison population of the United States rose by 50 percent. Although murder rates in Europe were falling in the same period, in New York City the rate increased fourfold between 1881 and 1889.

Law enforcement was inadequate. Police forces were enlarged, often in proportion to the rise in city population; however, corruption was rife. In 1904, an investigation in New York City found evidence of officers buying promotions and of police agents taking a monthly cut from the proceeds of a gambling den in exchange for turning a blind eye to illegal activities.

Immigration from Asia, Eastern and Southern Europe, and Mexico

> What can you learn from Source 1.5 about changes to immigration in the US between 1861 and 1920?

SOURCE 1.5

Immigration to the US between 1861 and 1920

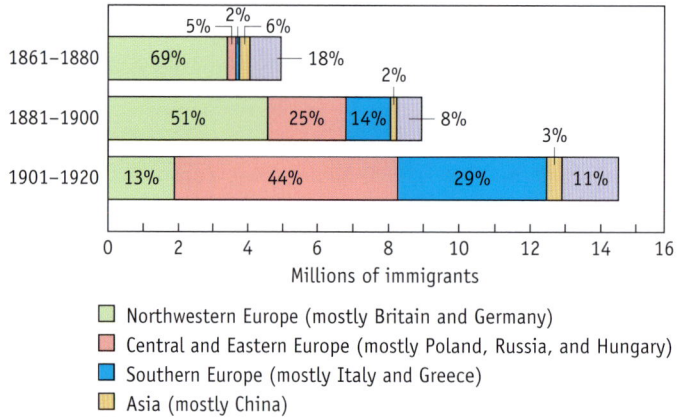

Source: *Historical Statistics of the United States*

KEY TERM

Britain Formally known as the United Kingdom of Great Britain and Northern Ireland (UK). Includes England, Northern Ireland, Scotland, and Wales. In 1922, Ireland left the UK, with the exception of Northern Ireland.

After the Civil War, immigration to the US grew considerably. Between 1865 and 1915 more than 25 million people migrated to America, which was five times more than in the period between 1815 and 1865. Up to the 1880s, most immigrants came from northern and western Europe, such as Scandinavia, **Britain**, and Germany. However, there was a shift toward the end of the nineteenth century with many more immigrants coming from southern Europe, Mexico, and Asia instead. This is sometimes referred to as "new immigration" with people including Russians, Greeks, Mexicans, Japanese, Chinese, and Italians coming to the United States in large numbers.

Many came to the US because of pull factors which included employment opportunities and the promise of a better life and a more secure future. Many already had friends or family in the US and by 1901 as many as 60 percent of immigrants traveled on tickets that were prepaid by friends and relatives who had migrated already. A further 25 percent were what was known as "birds of passage" who worked in the United States for a time and then returned home.

Others came for push reasons such as the fear of persecution—for example, Russian Jews escaping the threat of pogroms (state-sponsored violence against Jews) following the assassination of the Tsar. Many wanted to escape poverty caused by industrialization or economic disasters in their home countries. Some, for example from Hungary, wanted to avoid being conscripted into the armed forces.

Tensions between "New" and "Old" immigrants

Those who emigrated to the United States between 1820 and the Civil War are often referred to as **old immigrants**. They came mainly from Northern and Western Europe, including from Britain and Germany. Many of them were Protestant, except for the Irish who were Catholic, spoke English, were skilled workers and some were wealthy enough to buy land. Often, they moved to rural states and became farmers. For example, many German immigrants settled in Ohio, Wisconsin, and Illinois. Old immigrants had much in common with Americans in terms of their culture, language, and religion. Therefore, they generally found it easier to fit into American culture.

After the Civil War, **new immigrants** began to arrive in much larger numbers. They differed from old immigrants in that they were often from Southern and Eastern Europe, or from Asia, including China and Japan. They were much less likely than old immigrants to be Protestant and religions such as Catholicism, Judaism, and Orthodox Christianity were more prevalent. New immigrants were also less likely to be English-speaking and more likely to be unskilled, illiterate, and poor. They found it much less easy to fit into American life and tended to gravitate toward others from a similar background in the large cities.

Tensions often led to violence between different groups. Chinese immigrants who settled in the West faced persecution, often at the hands of earlier immigrants. Riots in the 1870s and 1880s saw Chinese workers killed and injured. These incidents are discussed in more detail later in this chapter. Those of different religions also faced discrimination. Organizations were set up to restrict the opportunities of Catholics (see below) and Jewish people were often banned from public schools, clubs, and holiday resorts. Such actions made it more difficult for new immigrants to integrate.

> **KEY TERMS**
>
> **Old immigrants** mainly from Northern Europe, many were English-speaking and they are generally considered to have emigrated to the US before the Civil War.
>
> **New immigrants** came to the US in the period from the end of the Civil War up to the 1920s and from a much wider range of countries including those of Southern, Central and Eastern Europe, and Asia.

> What can you learn from Source 1.6 about the changing patterns of immigration in Chicago at this time?

SOURCE 1.6

Jane Addams describes the neighborhood of Hull House in Chicago between 1889 and 1909

Halsted Street has grown so familiar during twenty years of residence, that it is difficult to recall its gradual changes—the withdrawal of the more prosperous Irish and Germans, and the slow substitution of Russian Jews, Italians, and Greeks. Hull House once stood in the suburbs, but the city has steadily grown up around it and its site now corners on three or four foreign colonies. Between Halsted Street and the river live about 10,000 Italians—Neapolitans, Sicilians, and Calabrians*. To the south on Twelfth Street are many Germans, and the side streets are given over entirely to Polish and Russian Jews. Still farther south, these Jewish colonies merge into a huge Bohemian** colony, so vast that Chicago ranks as the third Bohemian city in the world. To the northwest are many Canadian-French, clannish in spite of their long residence in America, and to the north are Irish and first-generation Americans. On the streets directly west and farther north are well-to-do English-speaking families, many of whom own their own houses and have lived in the neighborhood for years.

*Naples, Sicily and Calabria are regions of Italy.

**Bohemia was part of Germany. Both Italy and Germany were only recently unified and immigrants often remained close to people who had come from the same region.

Impacts of nativism and the Americanization movement

The influx of immigrants to the growing cities and towns caused anxiety for native-born Americans and Old Immigrants. As we have seen already, immigrants tended to be concentrated in industrial areas where there was work and gravitated toward people of the same origin. This gave some cities a feeling of being dominated by foreigners who did not speak English and were often illiterate. Fear spread among native-born

KEY TERMS

Socialism An ideology that advocates that the economic system should be changed so that major industries are owned by the workers, rather than by private businesses or corporations. It is different from capitalism, the basis of the American economy, where private individuals, such as business owners and shareholders, own the means of production.

Communism An ideology that was growing in popularity in parts of Europe at this time, in which all property should be owned by the community, and each person should contribute and receive according to their ability and needs. There were debates about whether this would be achieved through an evolutionary process or by revolution.

Anarchism An ideology that argues that an ideal society would not have a government of any kind. Many of those who supported anarchist ideas believed that this kind of society could only be brought about through violence.

Nativism An ideology based on the idea that people born in a country are more important than people who have moved there. Applied to policies, ideas, and people as "Nativist."

Americans that they were becoming outnumbered and that New Immigrants were endangering the qualities which underpinned American character and values. It was feared that immigrants:

- increased competition for jobs, which would lead to unemployment among native-born Americans
- brought down wages, with some arguing that immigrants had been brought to the US by employers for the precise purpose of lowering wages
- threatened the traditional Protestant basis and values of American society by introducing different religions, such as Catholicism
- brought with them dangerous political ideologies such as socialism, communism, and anarchism
- had a negative impact on the towns where they settled in large numbers (they were blamed for crime, industrial unrest, and spreading un-American ideas).

Such concerns led to some groups demanding that immigration be restricted. Anti-foreignism or "nativism" had already existed in the 1840s and 1850s and was mainly directed against Irish and German immigrants. The influx of immigrants in the years following the Civil War meant nativism gained strength again. However, nativists did not argue that immigration should be halted completely. Instead, they argued that certain groups of people should be allowed in and others should be kept out.

Anti-foreign organizations like the American Protective Association (APA) emerged. The APA campaigned to persuade Americans to vote against Roman Catholic candidates and published anti-immigration literature which was designed to promote suspicion of immigrants.

However, there was also a movement that favored a more educative approach based on the idea that foreign-born residents should learn about American values and principles so that they became assimilated and would benefit fully as US citizens. The idea of American society as a place where cultures and ethnicities melted together had existed since the late eighteenth century. However, the term "melting pot" became popular in the early twentieth century. It was used to symbolize the power of the great democracy, where people from every corner of the Earth were fused into a harmonious and admirable blend.

SOURCE 1.7

A poster from a 1908 play entitled *The Melting Pot* which shows an idealized view of how immigration from diverse cultures should work

> What are the similarities and differences between Sources 1.7 and 1.8? Support your answer using details from the sources.

SOURCE 1.8

A cartoon representing a different view of the melting pot was published in the US in March 1919. The figure stirring the pot represents Uncle Sam

KEY TERM

National Society of the Daughters of the American Revolution
A non-profit, volunteer organization founded in 1890 for women who were directly descended from someone who was involved in the American Revolutionary War.

The Americanization movement was formed in the early twentieth century to address issues of assimilation. The movement supported a program of education delivered through schools, voluntary associations, libraries, and businesses. Being involved in helping to educate immigrants became a popular form of public service. Many members of the **National Society of the Daughters of the American Revolution** became involved and this increased with American entry into the First World War.

The sources below highlight the reasons for and the nature of the Americanization movement.

> According to Source 1.9, what are the key purposes of Americanization?

SOURCE 1.9

From a statement by the Cleveland Americanization Council, which was formed in 1915. This council developed from the Cleveland Public Schools Organization, which had been formed to help educate immigrants in the 1830s

Americanization means assimilation into the American life of the community. The keystone to Americanization is learning the language of our country. Americanization is the co-operative process by means of which "many peoples" in our city and in America become "One Nation" united in language, work, home ties, and citizenship, with one flag above all flags, and only one allegiance to that flag. Americanization is a co-operative movement, bigger than America. It is a worldwide movement that all peoples may be united in a "world brotherhood." It is part of the aim of the great war being waged, that the world may be made safe for "democracy" abroad and at home as well. Americanization is carrying democracy to all peoples, first, within the boundaries of America, and second, to all peoples without the boundaries of America, in order that the world may have a greater industrial, educational, economic, and political freedom.

> How far does Source 1.10 agree with Source 1.9 on page 11? Are there any areas where the sources disagree? Support your comparisons with evidence from the sources.

SOURCE 1.10

A statement of objectives of the National Americanization Committee, which was formed in May 1915

The interpretation of American ideals, traditions, and standards and institutions to foreign-born peoples. The acquirement of a common language for the entire nation. The universal desire of all peoples in America to unite in a common citizenship under one flag. The combating of anti-American propaganda activities and schemes and the stamping out of sedition and disloyalty wherever found. The elimination of causes of disorder, unrest, and disloyalty which make fruitful soil for un-American propagandists and disloyal agitators. The abolition of racial prejudices, barriers, and discriminations, of colonies and immigrant sections, which keep people in America apart. The maintenance of an American standard of living including the use of American foods, preparation of foods, care of children. The discontinuance of discriminations in housing, care, protection, and treatment of aliens. The creation of an understanding of and love for America and the desire of immigrants to remain in America, have a home here, and support American institutions and laws.

Anti-immigrant legislation

Choosing to emigrate to the US from Asia was not an easy option as the two details below indicate.
- The phrase "not a Chinaman's chance" emerged during this period. The word "Chinaman" would be considered derogatory today and the phrase symbolized the challenges faced by Chinese immigrants in America.
- Many immigrants from Asia settled on the West Coast. However, according to one contemporary, James D. Phelan, Mayor of San Francisco and later a US Senator, "Chinese and Japanese are not the stuff of which American citizens can be made." Phelan was of Irish immigrant descent and his view here illustrates the tension and prejudice which existed between old and new immigrants in California.

In view of these statements, it is remarkable that immigrants from Asia came to the US at all, let alone decided to stay. Chinese immigrants initially came to work in the goldfields and to build the Pacific railroad in the 1860s. Many remained after the completion of railroad construction, but they encountered considerable difficulties. They were only allowed access to the lowest-paid jobs, such as laundrymen or domestic servants. Without family or community support, they often found themselves isolated in a hostile environment where they faced discrimination and exclusion.

A series of laws was passed to restrict immigration:
- In 1882, Congress passed the first restrictive law, barring entry for paupers (a negative term which was used at the time to describe those who were very poor and depended on charity to survive), criminals, and convicts, requiring their return at the shipper's expense.
- In 1885, Congress responded to labor concerns by prohibiting the importation of foreign workers under contract and often on substandard wages.
- A series of subsequent laws expanded the list to include those considered to be undesirable at the time, including those with serious mental illnesses, polygamists, sex workers, alcoholics, anarchists (people who believed in anarchism, see page 10), and individuals with contagious diseases.
- In 1917, a literacy test long favored by nativists was finally introduced, having been opposed and vetoed over a number of years by three presidents.

The Chinese Exclusion Act, 1882

By 1880, California had a significant Chinese immigrant population of around 75,000 constituting about nine percent of the state's total population. Chinese immigrants came together to form community centers in cities such as San Francisco. These provided a range of services from health and education facilities to social welfare and places of worship. However, many white Americans feared that Chinese workers would compete for jobs and undercut wages. In San Francisco, Denis Kearney, an Irish-born political leader of immigrant stock himself, led violent attacks against the Chinese, inciting his followers to abuse and frighten them in an attempt to make them leave. One example of the negative and derogatory attitudes toward Chinese immigrants was in the formation of the so-called anti-**coolie** clubs.

KEY TERM

Coolie Coolie was a racial slur directed toward people of Asian descent.

These clubs organized boycotts of Chinese products and services. Lobbying by these groups was partly responsible for the new California constitution of 1879, which denied naturalized Chinese citizens the right to vote or hold state employment. Some protests against Chinese immigrants turned violent. In 1885 in Rock Springs, Wyoming, tensions between white and Chinese immigrant miners erupted into a riot, resulting in over two dozen Chinese immigrants being murdered and many more injured.

The Chinese Exclusion Act was approved on May 6, 1882. It was the first significant law restricting immigration into the United States. The Act introduced a ten-year ban on Chinese laborers immigrating to the United States. The justification for the Act was that it was for the good of public order in certain parts of the country.

Non-laborers (such as civil servants) who wanted to enter the United States had to obtain a certificate from the Chinese government to prove that they were qualified to emigrate. However, the 1882 Act defined laborers as "skilled and unskilled, and Chinese employed in mining." This very wide definition made it difficult for anyone from China to emigrate to the US.

The 1882 Act also placed new requirements on Chinese who had already entered the country. If they left the United States, they had to obtain a certificate to re-enter. When the Exclusion Act expired in 1892, Congress extended it for ten years in the form of the Geary Act. This extension was made permanent in 1902 and added restrictions that required each Chinese immigrant to register and obtain a certificate of residence. Chinese immigrants found without a certificate could be deported. The 1882 Act was controversial and attracted comment such as in Source 1.11 below. The cartoon uses racial stereotypes which are reflective of the time in which it was produced.

SOURCE 1.11

A cartoon published in the US in 1882, commenting on the Chinese Exclusion Act. The caption reads: "The only one barred out. Enlightened American Statesman—'We must draw the line *somewhere*, you know'"

> What is the message of Source 1.11? What evidence can you see of the cartoonist using racial stereotypes in this source? "Americans were in favor of the 1882 Chinese Exclusion Act." Does Source 1.11 support or challenge this viewpoint? Explain your answer using details from the cartoon.

Although federal and state courts would not award citizenship to settled Chinese immigrants, the Supreme Court allowed birthright citizenship under the terms of the Fourteenth Amendment, in the case of *US v. Wong Kim Ark* in 1898. This provided a degree of legal protection to Chinese Americans and other immigrant communities.

The Gentleman's Agreement, 1907

Following the Japanese government's easing of emigration policies in 1868, Japanese people began immigrating to the US Pacific Coast, landing primarily in California. An 1894 treaty granted the Japanese immigration rights. Japanese immigrants often worked for low wages as laborers on farms, railroads, and in mines. They soon found themselves as a target for discrimination.

Examples of this discrimination included the exclusion of Japanese workers from the American Federation of Labor, the largest union in the country, and the 1905 launch of the Asiatic Exclusion League, founded with the goal of stopping Japanese and Korean immigration. In 1905, the *San Francisco Chronicle* launched an 18-month anti-Japanese newspaper campaign that warned of an invasion of "little brown men" and headlines like "The Japanese Invasion, the Problem of the Hour."

On October 11, 1906, a regulation passed by the San Francisco Board of Education called for all Japanese and Korean students, along with Chinese students, to be sent to a segregated "Oriental School," even though only 93 Japanese students, 25 of whom were born in America, lived in the district. The Japanese government was furious and President Roosevelt reportedly told Congress "To shut [Japanese students] out from the public schools is a wicked absurdity."

The Gentlemen's Agreement of 1907–08 was brokered to ease the tension. Japan called for Roosevelt to force San Francisco to repeal school segregation. In exchange, Japan agreed to deny emigration passports to Japanese laborers, while still allowing wives, children, and parents of existing immigrants to enter the United States.

Immigration Act, 1917

In 1896, Henry Cabot Lodge made a highly controversial speech in the Senate in favor of a literacy test for immigrants. Cabot Lodge was a member of the Immigration Restriction League. Note that in Source 1.12, below, Cabot Lodge refers to this as an "illiteracy test."

> According to Source 1.12, what are the main reasons for introducing the literacy test? Support your answer using details from the source.

SOURCE 1.12

Extracts from a speech by Henry Cabot Lodge in the Senate in 1896

The illiteracy test will bear most heavily upon the Italians, Russians, Poles, Hungarians, Greeks, and Asiatics, and very lightly upon English-speaking **emigrants**, or Germans, Scandinavians, and French. In other words, the races most affected by the test are those whose emigration to this country has begun within the last twenty years and swelled rapidly to enormous proportions, races with which the English-speaking people have never hitherto assimilated, and who are most alien to the great body of the people of the United States.

It is also proved that the classes now excluded by law—the criminals, the diseased, the paupers, and the contract laborers—are furnished chiefly by the same races as those most affected by the test of illiteracy. The same is true as to those immigrants who come to this country for a brief season and return to their native land, taking with them the money they have earned in the United States.

These facts prove that the exclusion of immigrants unable to read or write … will operate against the most undesirable and harmful part of our present immigration and shut out elements which no thoughtful or patriotic man can wish to see multiplied among the people of the United States.

KEY TERM

Emigrant Someone who has moved away from their home country.

However, despite considerable support for a literacy test, three successive presidents vetoed the proposed legislation.

> In Source 1.13, how does President Cleveland address the arguments made in favor of a literacy test in Source 1.12?

SOURCE 1.13

Extracts from President Cleveland's Veto Message, March 2, 1897

It is not claimed that the time has come for the further restriction of immigration on the ground that an excess of population overcrowds our land. It is said that the quality of recent immigration is undesirable. The time is quite within recent memory when the same thing was said of immigrants who, with their descendants, are now numbered among our best citizens.

It is said that too many immigrants settle in our cities, thus dangerously increasing their idle and vicious population. This is certainly a disadvantage. It cannot be shown, however, that it affects all our cities, nor that it is permanent; nor does it appear that this condition where it exists demands as its remedy the reversal of our present immigration policy. The claim is also made that the influx of foreign laborers deprives of the opportunity to work those who are better entitled than they to the privilege of earning their livelihood by daily toil.

I cannot believe that we would be protected against these evils by limiting immigration to those who can read and write in any language 25 words of our Constitution. In my opinion, it is infinitely more safe to admit a hundred thousand immigrants who, though unable to read and write, seek among us only a home and opportunity to work than to admit one of those unruly agitators and enemies of governmental control who can not only read and write, but delights in arousing by inflammatory speech the illiterate and peacefully inclined to discontent and tumult. Violence and disorder do not originate with illiterate laborers. They are, rather, the victims of the educated agitator.

By 1917, however, the mood had changed and Congress passed a widely restrictive immigration law. The difference in attitude was probably accounted for by concerns over national security which increased considerably because of US involvement in the First World War. The 1917 Act:
- introduced a literacy test that required immigrants older than sixteen to demonstrate basic reading comprehension in any language
- increased the tax paid by new immigrants upon arrival
- allowed immigration officials to exercise more discretion in making decisions over whom to exclude
- banned entry to the United States for anyone born in a geographical area known as the "Asiatic Barred Zone," which stretched from the Middle East to Southeast Asia, except for Japanese and Filipinos. The 1917 Act is sometimes referred to as the "Barred Zone Act."

ACTIVITY

From the information you have read in this section, make a list of the challenges which faced new immigrants.

Your list might include the following, but there are likely to be others.
- racial prejudice
- fear of different religious beliefs
- inability to speak English
- poor living conditions
- dangerous working conditions

In groups, take one feature from the list and explain why this was a challenge for immigrants.

As a class, debate which challenge would be the most difficult to overcome.

Growth of monopolies/trusts, corporations, and robber barons

The rapid development of industry in the United States meant that some individuals who were successful in business development, industry, and commerce amassed great wealth. They would probably have referred to themselves as "captains of industry," individuals who, through their hard work and determination, made America wealthy and who used their vast resources to benefit the public by funding schools, libraries, and museums. However, in the Gilded Age, these men came to be called the "robber barons." They amassed enormous wealth and power by using ruthless methods to create and control monopolies and trusts that dominated entire industries.

KEY TERMS

Robber barons Industrialists who dominated businesses, starting in the railroad industry but spreading from there. They became wealthy and powerful to an unprecedented level.

Monopoly A person or a company having sole control or possession of something, in this context often a commodity such as steel.

Trust An arrangement in which multiple shareholders transfer shares in a business to a named party or group to manage so that they become the single largest body. The members of the trust benefit from the combined earnings of the group. Modern "antitrust" laws work against the monopolies held by Trusts in businesses to preserve competition.

The robber barons created monopolies and trusts by using their wealth to buy out smaller companies. As they bought out competitors, they were able to control the market, set prices, limit competition and maximize profits. By the end of the nineteenth century, trusts dominated a number of major industries. The first was formed on January 2, 1882 by Standard Oil. A board of trustees was established and shares from all the companies which made up Standard Oil were placed in its hands. Every stockholder received twenty trust certificates for each share of Standard Oil stock. All the profits of the component companies were sent to the nine trustees, who determined the dividends which were paid out to the stockholders. The nine trustees elected the directors and officers of all the component companies. This allowed Standard Oil to function as a monopoly since the nine trustees ran all the component companies. Over time, the influence of the trusts grew so that as well as owning the main interest in the oil business the trust also had a controlling interest in other businesses. By 1900, Standard Oil held stock in 41 businesses.

The impact of monopolies and trusts on consumers and workers could be negative. Wages were kept low and this led to economic inequality. This was a long-term trend that had serious implications in the 1920s. Working conditions were often poor with workers facing long hours, little in terms of safety regulation, and dangerous practices. This was one reason for the development of labor unions (see pages 18–20).

During the 1880s, concerns grew about the impact of monopolies on consumers and the Progressive Presidents attempted to address these by beginning to regulate business practices and break up monopolies and trusts. The Sherman Antitrust Act of 1890 (see pages 36–37) was one of the first laws aimed at preventing monopolies and promoting competition.

Vertical and horizontal integration

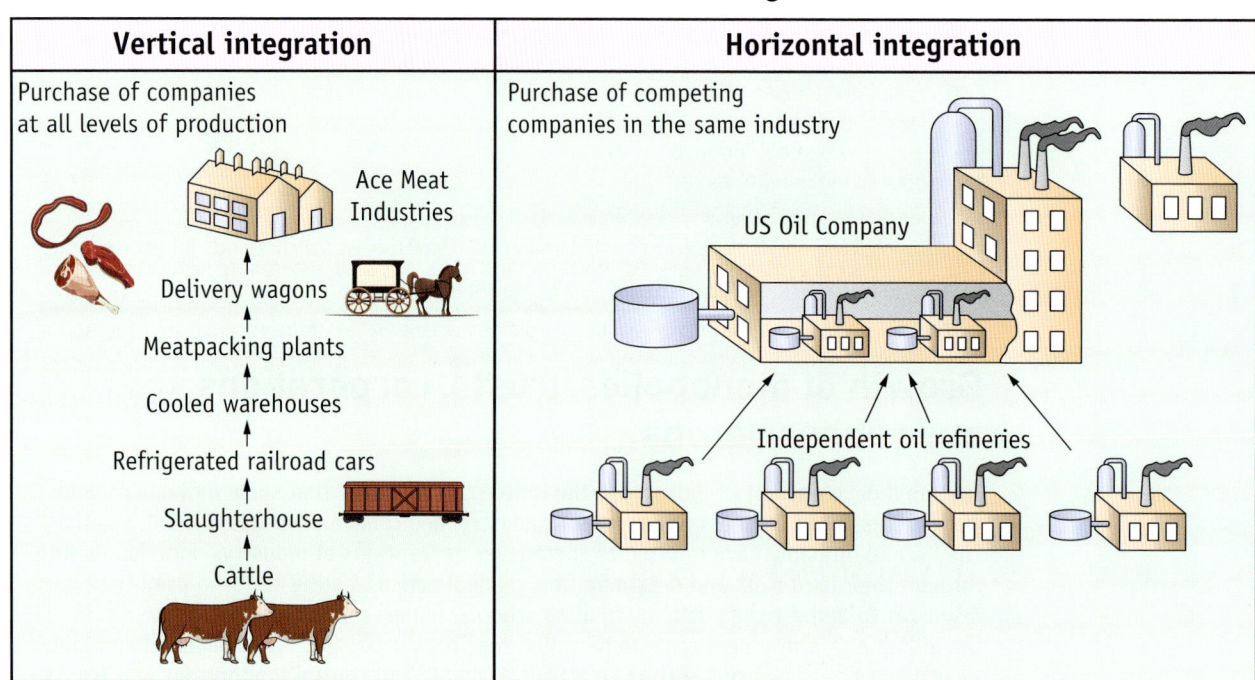

Figure 1.2 A diagram explaining vertical and horizontal integration

KEY TERMS

Vertical integration A top-to-bottom approach to industrial development where the manufacturer owns all parts of the process, from raw materials to distribution.

Horizontal integration The owner of one business buys out its competitors, thus creating a monopoly.

One example of vertical integration was the steel business established by **Andrew Carnegie**. Working with Henry Frick, he set up a business that not only consisted of steel manufacturing mills but which also contained all the component parts for the steel business including:
- coal fields and coke plants for fueling the furnaces
- iron and limestone deposits for making the steel
- ships for transporting the raw materials
- railroads for transporting the raw materials and the finished products.

An example of horizontal integration was the oil business established by **John D Rockefeller**. He created a huge business by buying out smaller oil companies. What this meant in turn was that he had created a monopoly. Standard Oil was the only company anyone could buy their oil from. This meant prices could be fixed and customers had a lack of choice.

How far do you agree that the cartoonist (Source 1.14) supported the concept of horizontal integration/growth of trusts? Use details from the cartoon to support your answer.

SOURCE 1.14

A cartoon published in the United States in 1884

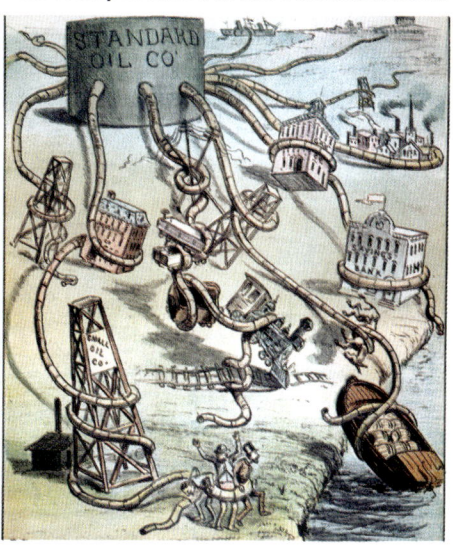

Major industrialists of the period

Andrew Carnegie

Carnegie was the greatest steel master of the age and, unusually for an American industrialist, came from a humble background. He was the son of a Scottish weaver and was taken to the US in 1848 by his parents when he was 13. He worked as a bobbin boy in a cotton mill and then as a telegraph operator before becoming involved in iron manufacturing. Carnegie showed a rare aptitude for business and, even though he was not trained in engineering, quickly understood how important the development and manufacture of steel would be. He built a huge business empire, which earned $40 million in profit in 1900 alone. In 1901, the company he had established merged with others and formed the United States Steel Corporation which controlled 60 percent of steel production in the United States. Carnegie amassed great wealth but he also spent huge sums, well over $300 million, on philanthropic projects such as building schools and libraries.

JP Morgan

John Pierpoint Morgan was the son of a wealthy banker. He co-founded a large New York banking company called Drexel Morgan. In 1895, he reorganized the bank and rebranded it as JP Morgan and Co. He became extremely wealthy and powerful. He bought shares and bonds from businesses and made money by selling these at a profit. By improving the management of the companies, he made them more cost-effective and profitable. In the 1890s, he was partly responsible for rescuing the railroads from bankruptcy. Morgan promoted business combinations, such as the United States Steel Corporation, founded by Carnegie. Some commentators accused him of underhand practices and of being ruthless and greedy. However, like Carnegie, he was a great philanthropist and is credited by some as having played an important role in the growth of US business.

John D Rockefeller

Oil was discovered in Pennsylvania in 1859 and the petroleum business which developed grew rapidly. As it was relatively cheap to drill for oil, many small businesses developed. Rockefeller established the Standard Oil Company in 1872 and quickly came to dominate the oil landscape. He bought out rivals and eliminated his opposition. Standard Oil became the first "trust" and a group of nine trustees from Standard Oil controlled the stock of 77 oil companies, which between them produced 90 percent of the oil drilled in the US. Although Rockefeller was controversial and criticized for his ruthless business practices, like Carnegie, he was also a philanthropist.

KEY TERM

Lobbying Attempts by individuals or associations to influence the decisions of government about future policy. Lobbying has always been part of the US governmental system and is argued to have been protected by the First Amendment, which guarantees Americans' right to free speech.

What can you learn from Source 1.15 about the attitude of the cartoonist towards the influence of US business on the US government? Support your answer using details from the cartoon.

Impacts of business associations and lobbying on US politics

During the Gilded Age, organized trade associations took on the role of **lobbying** politicians in order to influence policies in their favor. Many lobbying organizations were established, two of which were:
- The American Bankers Association (ABA). Established in 1875, the ABA represented the banking industry. It focused on standardizing banking practices, promoting sound financial policies, and lobbying for legislation that would support the banking sector.
- The National Association of Manufacturers (NAM). Founded in 1895, the NAM promoted American manufacturing and industrial interests. It campaigned for protective tariffs to shelter American manufacturers against imports and campaigned to influence labor policies.

SOURCE 1.15

A cartoon by Joseph Keppler published in an American magazine in 1889. The title of the cartoon is "The Bosses of the Senate"

Rise of labor unions and significant strikes

Factory wages were generally low. In 1900, the average factory wage was approximately twenty cents per hour, for an annual salary of barely 600 dollars. This wage meant that roughly twenty percent of the population in industrialized cities was living on or below the poverty line. A typical working week in a factory was 60 hours over six days. In steel mills, it was common for workers to work twelve-hour shifts, seven days a week. Women and children were cheaper to employ than adult males. Mechanization saw the rise of unskilled jobs and women and children were considered well suited to working in the small spaces around the machines. The labor movement developed in response to the poor pay and conditions.

Industrial working conditions

Working conditions were often detrimental to workers' health. In 1884, a study of the Illinois Central Railroad showed that in the period from 1874 to 1884 one in twenty of its workers had been killed or severely injured by an accident at work. Brakemen, who had one of the most dangerous jobs on the railroad, had a much higher incidence of accidents and fatalities. Mining was also extremely dangerous. From the mid-1870s to the mid-1920s on average 2,000 miners were killed each year by explosions and cave-ins. This was often the result of the mining companies' refusal to introduce safety practices.

Mining and the development of factories also damaged the health of people living nearby, by causing pollution in the air and local water courses. Toxic substances, such as mercury and lead, accumulated in the soil and those working in the coal mines often developed terminal illnesses and lung damage from breathing in contaminated air. Although people were aware of the dangers, they continued to work because the alternative was poverty. Pittsburgh's smokestacks (see Source 1.16) spewed out smoke, which caused respiratory diseases but also meant there was employment.

SOURCE 1.16

An engraving showing the blast furnaces of Pittsburgh at night. This picture was published in *Harper's Weekly* in 1885

> Describe what you can see in this picture. From your description, what inferences can be drawn about the challenges of living and working in Pittsburgh in the late nineteenth century?

Significant unions, the composition of their members and their aims

The Knights of Labor

The Knights of Labor was founded in 1869 by a group of tailors from Philadelphia. The purpose of the organization was to unite all workers in one large association, irrespective of their occupation, nationality, or race. Unskilled workers were welcome, as were farmers and more skilled craftsmen. The organization grew slowly until 1879 when Terence Powderly was elected as their Grand Master Workman. He aimed to modernize and popularize the organization. It grew quickly so that by the mid-1880s there were 700,000 members. Source 1.17, below, shows part of the program of the Knights of Labor.

SOURCE 1.17

From the Program of the Knights of Labor, 1878

I. To bring within the folds of organization every department of productive industry, making knowledge a standpoint for action, and industrial, moral worth, not wealth, the true standard of individual and national greatness.

II. To secure to the [workers] a proper share of the wealth that they create; more of the leisure that rightfully belongs to them; more [social] advantages, more of the benefits and privileges of the world.

X. The substitution of arbitration for strikes, whenever and wherever employers and employees are willing to meet on equitable grounds.

XI. The prohibition of the employment of children in workshops, mines, and factories before obtaining their fourteenth year.

XIII. To obtain for both sexes equal pay for equal work.

XIV. The reduction of the hours of labor to eight per day, so that the laborers may have more time for social enjoyment and intellectual improvement.

> Why do you think some business leaders were opposed to the demands listed in Source 1.17?

The Knights had some success. In 1885, affiliated unions forced the Wabash Railway Company to recognize the union and restore wages to their previous level. This boosted membership. However, a similar strike in 1886 failed and the Haymarket Affair (page 22) damaged their reputation.

American Federation of Labor

The American Federation of Labor (AFL) was founded on December 8, 1886. Its predecessor, the Federation of Organized Trade and Labor Unions (FOTLU), was formed by members of the Knights of Labor and leaders including **Samuel Gompers**. After the Haymarket Affair in May 1886 (page 22), and after a dispute over the inclusion of craft unions, FOTLU and trade union leaders met in Ohio. They announced the formation of the AFL, with Samuel Gompers becoming its first president. The organization was formed for skilled workers, such as cigarmakers and stone masons. It was against the formation of one centrally controlled union, which the Knights had aimed to do, and instead was a looser organization. The main focus of the union was to improve working conditions and pay for members. Although the AFL rejected radical political ideas, it was prepared to use strikes and boycotts. Labor unions, which were largely made up of unskilled workers, were excluded. This meant that recent immigrants and other minority groups were not represented, although the Brotherhood of Sleeping Car Porters was included.

> **KEY FIGURE**
>
> **Samuel Gompers (1850–1924)** was a British-born cigar maker who emigrated to New York with his parents in 1863. He founded the American Federation of Labor, and served as its president from 1886 for most of the rest of his life. He supported "craft" unions and wanted to work to improve working conditions within the existing capitalist system. He was instrumental in the formation of the International Labor Organization which was one of the agencies of the League of Nations established at the end of the First World War.

Industrial Workers of the World

The Industrial Workers of the World (IWW) organization (also known as the Wobblies) was founded in Chicago in 1905. The IWW aimed to unite unskilled workers and had strong links to socialist organizations. The Wobblies, unlike the AFL, aimed to attract members from the most discriminated against sections of the workforce such as unskilled workers, immigrants, women, and migrant workers. The IWW hoped to create one big union through which workers would own the means of production and distribution.

> What can you learn from Source 1.18 about the views of the Wobblies on the following issues:
> - relations between the workers and their employers
> - attitudes toward existing trade unions
> - industrial action?

SOURCE 1.18

From the constitution of the Industrial Workers of the World, written in 1908

The working class and the employing class have nothing in common. There can be no peace so long as hunger and want are found among millions of the working people and the few, who make up the employing class, have all the good things of life. Between these two classes a struggle must go on until the workers of the world organize as a class, take possession of the means of production, abolish the wage system, and live in harmony with the earth.

The trade unions foster a state of affairs which allows one set of workers to be pitted against another set of workers in the same industry, thereby helping defeat one another in wage wars. Moreover, the trade unions aid the employing class to mislead the workers into the belief that the working class have interests in common with their employers.

These conditions can be changed and the interest of the working class upheld only by an organization formed in such a way that all its members in any one industry, or in all industries if necessary, cease work whenever a strike or lockout is on in any department thereof, thus making an injury to one an injury to all.

Differing opinions over gender, race, and immigration within labor unions

Labor unions were developed to protect the rights and status of different groups of workers and in many cases, to fight for better pay and conditions.

Although the desire to protect workers united the labor movement, there were areas where labor unions and organizations disagreed. Areas of disagreement included:
- Should the union represent a specific group of workers, such as boilermen on the railroads, or include all those who worked on the railroads?

- Should unskilled workers be allowed to join the union or should it be reserved for those in skilled positions?
- Should women be allowed to join unions which also included men?
- Should new immigrants be granted union membership?
- Should African American workers be allowed to join the union or should they have their own unions?
- Should the union work within the existing political framework, or adopt new ideas and try to bring about wider changes for the working classes?

> What is the attitude of the author toward women working? What arguments does he use to make his point?

SOURCE 1.19

From an article written in 1897 by Edward O'Donnell, an official of the AFL, entitled "Women as Bread Winners—the Error of the Age"

The invasion of crafts by women has been developing for years amid irritation and injury to the workman. The right of the woman to win honest bread is accorded on all sides, but with craftsmen it is an open question whether this manifestation is of a healthy social growth or not.

The rapid displacement of men by women in the factory and workshop has to be met sooner or later, and the question is forcing itself upon the leaders and thinkers among the labor organizations of the land.

Is it a pleasing indication of progress to see the father, the brother, and the son displaced as the bread winner by the mother, sister, and daughter? The growing demand for female labor is not founded upon philanthropy, as those who encourage it would have sentimentalists believe; it does not spring from the milk of human kindness. It is an insidious assault upon the home; it is the knife of the assassin aimed at the family circle.

> How different is Source 1.20 from the other sources in this section?

SOURCE 1.20

Extracts from the constitution of the IWW about membership, written in 1908

It is the aim of the IWW to build world-wide working-class solidarity. The IWW therefore actively opposes bigotry and discrimination on and off the job. No wage or salaried worker shall be excluded from the IWW or barred from holding union office because of race, ethnicity, sex, nationality, creed, disability, sexual orientation, or conviction and charges history.

No unemployed or retired worker, no working-class student, apprentice, homemaker, prisoner, or unwaged volunteer on a project initiated by the IWW or any subordinate body thereof shall be excluded from membership on the grounds that they are not currently receiving wages.

No member of the Industrial Workers of the World shall be an officer of a trade or craft union or political party.

ACTIVITY

Using the sources and information in this section, copy and complete the table below to summarize how views on different types of workers varied between labor organizations.

Groups of workers	Knights of Labor	AFL	IWW
Immigrants			
Women			
African Americans			
Skilled			
Unskilled			

Work with a partner to answer the question

"How far do you agree that all labor unions had the interests of all workers at heart?"

One of you should find evidence to support the statement, and the other should find evidence to challenge it.

Share your ideas and each write a paragraph in response to the question.

Significant events and their impacts

The Great Railroad Strike of 1877 was the first major rail strike in the United States and marked the beginning of a period of serious industrial unrest which was motivated by poor pay and conditions, made worse by the economic depression of the 1890s. It involved clashes between unionized labor and business owners. In some instances, strikes led to violence and presidents intervened, sending in federal troops to break up strikes. However, the coal strike saw the president threaten the business owners, rather than the strikers, with military action.

The Great Railroad Strike, 1877

In 1877, the owners of the northern railroads, still suffering financially after the Great Panic of 1873, began to cut wages to save money. In May 1877, the Pennsylvania Railroad, the largest of the railroad companies, cut wages by ten percent. This was followed in June by another wage cut. In July, the Baltimore and Ohio Railroad cut wages and reduced the working week. Workers faced a difficult situation as wages and hours were being cut but rents and food prices remained the same. At Martinsburg, West Virginia, they walked out in protest. They blocked the railroad lines and refused to allow freight trains through. At the same time, the Pennsylvania Railroad doubled the length of all eastbound trains from Pittsburgh, but no additional crew were employed. Railroad workers seized control of the rail yards and prevented trains from moving.

Violence broke out in several large cities. In ten states, including Maryland, Pennsylvania and West Virginia, state defense forces were called out to break up the strikes. In Baltimore, troops fired on the strikers, killing ten, including a newsboy and a sixteen-year-old student. These shootings sparked further violence, and not just from railroad workers. Passenger cars were burned, fire hoses were cut, and at one point it was estimated that 14,000 rioters had taken to the streets. The Governor of Maryland was so alarmed he telegraphed President Hayes and asked him to send troops.

In Pittsburgh, the governor called in National Guard troops from Philadelphia, knowing that the local troops were sympathetic to the strikers. The troops fired into a crowd, killing more than twenty civilians, including women and at least three children. A newspaper headline read "Shot in Cold Blood by the Roughs of Philadelphia. The Slaughter of Innocents." An angry crowd forced the Philadelphia troops to retreat, and set fire to engines and equipment. The Pennsylvania Railroad claimed that they lost more than $4 million in engines, carriages, and rolling stock.

Eventually, the federal troops prevailed and reopened the railroad in Pittsburgh. However, 40 people were killed there and it is estimated that over 100 died countrywide. By the end of July, the strike was ended and the railroads reopened. Most workers returned to work as they faced destitution if they did not. However, strikes in the rail yards continued through the 1880s.

The Haymarket Affair, May 1886

The Haymarket Affair took place in Chicago. Workers at the McCormick Harvesting Machine Company were involved in a strike that was part of a national campaign by the Knights of Labor to secure an eight-hour workday. On May 3, police intervened to protect strikebreakers. A confrontation between the strikers and the police followed. The next day, a protest against police methods was organized by labor leaders, some of whom were German immigrant anarchists. This took place in Haymarket Square. The Mayor of Chicago attended the protest and declared it peaceful. However, after he and many of the demonstrators had left, the police arrived and demanded that the remaining crowd disperse. At that point, a bomb was thrown by an unknown individual and police responded with random gunfire. Before the violence ended seven police officers and 60 civilians were killed, including people not involved in the strike.

> Do you think the artist who produced the illustration in Source 1.21 supported the union movement? Explain your answer.

SOURCE 1.21

This illustration was produced in 1886 and shows a Methodist pastor speaking to the demonstrators at the same time that the bomb was thrown. In fact, the speeches were over before the bombing and many of the demonstrators had left

The impact of the event was to discredit the Knights of Labor and to create a wave of resentment against immigrants. Eight anarchists were convicted of murder, despite some of them not being present at the demonstration. Four were hanged and another committed suicide in prison. In 1893, Illinois Governor John Peter Altgeld pardoned the remaining three defendants. He concluded that they had not been given a fair trial and that much of the evidence against them had been made up.

The Pullman Strike, May–July 1894

Pullman was a company town near Chicago that had been built by George Pullman who owned Chicago Pullman Palace Car Company. He controlled wages and the rents workers paid for their homes. The Panic of 1893 led to a drop in company profits, and so, during the winter of 1893–94, Pullman cut the wages of his workers by 25 percent. However, Pullman refused to reduce rents and, when some of his employees formed a representative committee to discuss matters, the management of the company refused to talk to them. Some of the committee members were sacked. In response, nearly 4,000 workers walked out on May 11, 1894, shutting down the Pullman factory.

The strike was supported by the American Railway Union (ARU), which was led by **Eugene Debs**. In solidarity with the Pullman workers, the ARU decided to boycott railroads that used Pullman cars. This brought railway traffic in and out of Chicago to a standstill. The strike spread, eventually involving almost a quarter of a million workers across 27 states, disrupting almost all rail travel west of Chicago.

> ### KEY FIGURE
>
> **Eugene Debs** (1855–1926) Debs was a socialist and stood for US President five times. From the age of fourteen, he worked on the railroads, becoming a locomotive fireman. He was involved in the union movement, advocating that they should be organized by industry rather than craft, which would make for bigger and potentially more powerful organizations. In 1893, Debs became the president of the newly established American Railway Union. After the Pullman strike, Debs was convicted of contempt of court for violating the injunction. He spent six months in prison reading radical literature by authors including Karl Marx and emerged more determined than ever to uphold the rights of the unions. In 1897, he formed the Socialist Party of America.

The railway companies called for federal intervention. Under the Sherman Antitrust Act (page 36), a court injunction was issued against the ARU to prevent anyone from interfering with the railroads, impeding the mail or discouraging railroad workers from carrying out their duties. On July 3, President Cleveland sent in federal troops to protect mail deliveries, despite protests from the Governor of Illinois. By the end of the day, the situation had deteriorated to the point that violence broke out between the striking workers, supporters from the ARU, and federal troops. When the violence ended in late July, as many as

30 workers were dead, and millions of dollars in railroad property had been destroyed. Eugene Debs was convicted of contempt of court for violating the injunction. He spent six months in prison but emerged more determined to uphold the rights of the unions.

The Coal Strike, May–October 1902

Conditions for workers in the Pennsylvania coal fields were very poor. The work was hard and dangerous, and many immigrants from eastern and southern Europe were employed. There was a history of tension between the miners and the mine operators. The Depression in 1893 had forced wages down and a strike broke in 1894 which lasted eight weeks and almost destroyed the United Mine Workers union. In 1900, the union and the mine operators went head to head again, this time in the **anthracite** mines of Pennsylvania. Under political pressure caused by the presidential election taking place at the time, the mine operators backed down and increased wages.

In 1902, there was further industrial action. The miners made several demands including an eight-hour workday, a pay increase and that their union should be recognized. However, the mine operators and members of the railroad companies that owned the mines refused to meet with representatives of the union. The strike began in eastern Pennsylvania, where most anthracite coal was mined, on May 12, 1902. As production dropped, coal prices doubled. The strike rumbled on unresolved until the fall. By this time President Theodore Roosevelt began to be concerned that a coal shortage would develop that would bring hardship to many Americans in the winter. He decided to intervene (there is more detail about his involvement on page 54). On October 3, 1902, Roosevelt met with presidents of the mine-owning railroads and union leaders. John Mitchell, head of the United Mine Workers of America union outlined their demands. The mine owners insisted that compromise was not possible. The situation seemed to be in a deadlock and the conference ended without a resolution. However, Roosevelt formed a commission to investigate the strike and, after intervention by JP Morgan and the Secretary of State for War, the railroad leaders agreed to abide by the findings of the commission. The unions also accepted the commission and on October 20, voted to end the anthracite strike.

In 1903, the miners had their pay increased by ten percent (rather than the twenty percent they had demanded), and their working hours were reduced from ten to nine hours.

> **KEY TERM**
>
> **Anthracite** A hard form of coal that contains a lot of carbon and few impurities. This made it ideal for use in industry and for domestic heating.

> Who did the cartoonist support: the miners or the mine operators? Use details from Source 1.22 to support your answer.

SOURCE 1.22

A cartoon published in an Ohio newspaper in 1902. The text on the hammer reads "No concessions, no arbitration, no interference." Uncle Sam can be seen in the background

THE REAL OBJECT OF THE OPERATORS IS TO CRUSH IT.

From the *Ohio State Journal* (Columbus).

> **ACTIVITY**
>
> Work in a group of four to assess the significance of the events in this section. You could take one event each. Decide between you what criteria you will use to assess significance.
>
> Share your ideas with other groups in the class.

Rural reactions to industrialization

Native American resistance to urbanization and industrialization in the West

Although violent conflict had plagued relations between white settlers and Native Americans from the very beginning of European colonization of North America, such violence increased in the mid-nineteenth century as American settlers moved ever farther west across the continent.

In 1851, the US government created the reservation system to keep Native Americans off lands that European Americans wished to settle on. Many indigenous people resisted their confinement to the reservations, and many white settlers continued to settle on reservation lands or migrate through reservations despite both of these being against the terms of reservation treaties. This resulted in a series of conflicts known as the "Indian Wars." Ultimately, the US Army subdued Native Americans and forced them onto reservations, where they were allowed to govern themselves and maintain some of their traditions and culture, albeit under the supervision of often corrupt "Indian" agents and the federal government.

However, the idea that Native Americans should **assimilate** (be completely absorbed) into mainstream white American society gained traction. Sometimes this belief was described in religious terms: many white Christians argued that by abandoning their spiritual traditions and accepting Christianity, Native Americans could be "saved." Others wanted Native Americans to adopt Western ideas about private property, which many indigenous peoples rejected as this went against their beliefs.

In the late nineteenth century, a political consensus formed around these ideas and the result was the 1887 passage of the Dawes Act.

> **KEY TERM**
>
> **Assimiliation** is the complete incorporation of an individual or group of people into an existing society, where they adopt that society's customs and traditions.

Responses to the Dawes Act, 1887

The Dawes Act of 1887, sometimes known as the Dawes Severalty Act or the General Allotment Act, was brought into force on January 8, 1887 by President Cleveland. It authorized the federal government to break up tribal lands by partitioning them into individual plots. Only those Native Americans who accepted the individual allotments were allowed to become US citizens. Those who did not accept the allotments would have their land confiscated and redistributed. Initially, the Dawes Act did not apply to those who were referred to as the "**Five Civilized Tribes**." These tribes were referred to in this way because they had adopted many elements of American society and culture. They were protected by treaties that guaranteed that their lands would remain free of white settlers. However, they were unwilling to accept individual allotments of land, with the result that the Dawes Act was amended in 1898 so that it applied to the "Five Civilized Tribes" as well. Their governments were dismantled and their courts destroyed, and over 90 million acres of their land was sold off to white Americans.

> **KEY TERM**
>
> **The Five Civilized Tribes** A colonial term grouping together the Cherokee, Chickasaw, Choctaw, Creek, and Seminole peoples.

How did the Department of the Interior try to make purchasing land attractive to potential buyers in 1911?

SOURCE 1.23

Poster produced in 1911 by the Department of the Interior

The Wounded Knee Massacre, 1890

By 1890, forced removals, disease, and military campaigns meant that the population of Native Americans had been radically reduced. The bison herds that had once supported these peoples were close to extinction. Those living on the reservations faced starvation. Drought meant their lands were dry, there were few plants to eat and few animals to hunt. However, in the middle of the drought, some buffalo appeared in one of the Lakota Sioux reservations in South Dakota. This miracle led some to believe that the spirits were reaching out to rescue the Native Americans. Wovoka, a religious leader of the Northern Paiute tribe, had a near-death experience in which he had a dream where he saw all the ancestors living happily and forever young. He claimed that he had been given the Ghost Dance in this dream. By performing the dance at regular intervals, for five days at a time, the people could secure a happy future where they would be reconnected with their ancestors and live in peace and plenty. Many tribes joined the dance and Chief Sitting Bull, who led the Lakota Sioux and Cheyenne to victory at the Battle of the Little Bighorn in 1876, embraced the Ghost Dance and helped it to spread throughout the Lakota Sioux Reservation. There was a general concern that the Ghost Dance was the start of an uprising that would be led by Chief Sitting Bull. On December 15, 1890, reservation police and "Indian" agents were sent to arrest Chief Sitting Bull. When others objected to the arrest, a scuffle ensued and Chief Sitting Bull was killed.

Two weeks later, the 7th Cavalry Regiment surrounded an encampment of Lakota Sioux Indians near Wounded Knee Creek on the Pine Ridge Indian Reservation in South Dakota. They attempted to disarm the Lakota Sioux but a shot was fired and fighting broke out. The soldiers opened fire indiscriminately, killing hundreds of men, women, and children.

The few who survived the massacre fled. An army inquiry into the massacre exonerated the 7th Cavalry Regiment.

> **Assess the weight of Source 1.24 as evidence about what happened at Wounded Knee Creek. To do this think about the following questions:**
> - Why was this book published?
> - What impression does Black Elk give of events?
> - Do other sources/information you have support or contradict this account?

▶ SOURCE 1.24

From a book entitled *Black Elk Speaks*, published in 1932. Black Elk was an Oglala Lakota Sioux leader and medicine man

Many were shot down right there. The women and children ran into the gulch [gully] and up west, dropping all the time, for the soldiers shot them as they ran. There were only about a hundred warriors and five hundred soldiers. The warriors rushed to where they had piled their guns and knives. They fought soldiers with only their hands until they got their guns …

It was a good winter day when all this happened. The sun was shining. But after the soldiers marched away from their dirty work, a heavy snow began to fall. The wind came up in the night. There was a big blizzard and it grew very cold. The snow drifted deep in the crooked gulch and it was one long grave of butchered women and children … who had never done any harm and were only trying to run away.

American Indian boarding schools

Indian boarding schools were founded to replace traditional American Indian culture and traditions with mainstream American culture. The first Indian boarding schools were set up by Christian missionaries in the mid-seventeenth century. Some of these were on reservations but later the federal government gave their support, through the Bureau of Indian Affairs, to the opening of off-reservation residential schools. The Carlisle Indian Industrial School, established in 1879, became a model and by 1902 there were 25 federally funded off-reservation boarding schools.

> **What can you learn from Source 1.25 about General Pratt's attitude toward Native Americans?**

▶ SOURCE 1.25

From a speech by General Richard Henry Pratt, founder of the Carlisle Indian Industrial School, 1892

It is a great mistake to think that the Indian is born an inevitable savage. He is born a blank, like all the rest of us. Left in the surroundings of savagery, he grows to possess a savage language, superstition, and life. We, left in the surroundings of civilization, grow to possess a civilized language, life, and purpose. Transfer the infant white to the savage surroundings, he will grow to possess a savage language, superstition, and habit. Transfer the savage-born infant to the surroundings of civilization, and he will grow to possess a civilized language and habit.

Being at boarding school often meant long periods of separation from family and friends. Some children were away from home for over four years at a time. This was intended to distance them from their cultural and linguistic heritage. Traditional dress was not allowed and Indian children were forced to have their hair cut, wear Western-style clothes, and give up their meaningful Native names. They were taught to speak English and punished if they spoke their Native language. In schools that were run under religious management, there was a heavy emphasis on learning about Christianity, which was to replace traditional religious and spiritual practices. The schools were run on military lines with harsh discipline and were, according to many accounts, places of humiliation. Reports from those who went through the school system tell of Native languages and cultures being derided and students being made to feel ashamed of their heritage. Worse, some suffered physical abuse and neglect. The schools damaged the self-esteem of many students and had a detrimental impact on Native languages and cultures.

However, this education system had an impact most likely unintended by General Pratt. In the most influential schools, such as Carlisle School and Hampton Institute, Native American children from different backgrounds and nations met each other and became friends. Many of them went on to become activists in the campaign for the civil rights of Native Americans. This is discussed further in this chapter (page 69) and in Chapter 2, page 126.

Reactions of "cowboys" to increased development in the West

As more people settled west of the Mississippi River, and more towns and villages were established, cowboys came into conflict with farmers and settlers as their freedom to roam on the plains was reduced. Their open-range lifestyle and the need for long cattle drives were diminished by technological changes and by the end of the 1800s the era of the cowboy was over.

- From the mid-1870s, farmers started using industrially produced barbed wire fencing. This made cattle drives more difficult. The open plains were fenced off to prevent cattle from destroying crops.
- The development of railroads meant there was less need for long cattle drives; instead cattle were shipped using freight cars.
- In 1878, an early system of refrigeration was invented. Ice was placed in the freight cars and this kept the meat cool on long journeys. Fresh meat could be transported from cattle ranches to large cities in the North and East of the United States. Although this meant large profits for the ranchers, cowboys continued to be poorly paid.

There were other reasons why the livelihoods of the cowboys came under threat.
- Cattle in Texas sometimes developed a disease called Texas fever, which caused ranchers in other states to prohibit the movement of Texas cows across state lines.
- A bitterly cold winter in 1886–87 killed large numbers of cattle across the West. Many small ranchers went bankrupt. This accelerated the consolidation of the cattle business into the hands of a few large ranchers who had the wealth to survive such problems.

Though smaller cattle drives would continue into the 1900s, many cowboys began working for private ranch owners, giving up their open trail lifestyle.

Reasons for the migration of Exodusters to the West

> Why do you think this poster was printed at this time?

KEY TERM

Exodusters African Americans who left the South in the late 1870s. Many set up home in Kansas.

SOURCE 1.26

A poster published in 1878, advertising land in Kansas

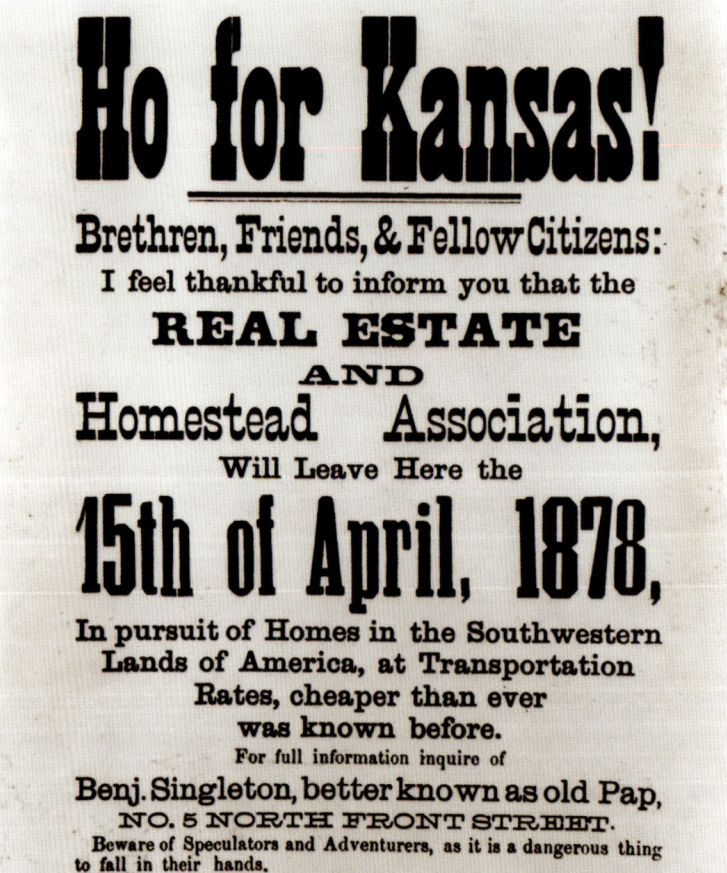

Even before the emancipation of enslaved people in 1863, many African Americans were keen to leave the South, and during the Civil War almost 180,000 joined the Union Army. Once the war was over people continued to leave, as Source 1.26 indicates. Kansas was a popular destination although some also left for Colorado and Oklahoma. However, in the spring of 1879, 6,000 African Americans left the South, becoming known as the "Exodusters." There are several reasons why they were keen to leave the South, why they specifically chose to leave in 1879, and why so many went to Kansas.

- **The Homestead Act:** passed in 1862, this Act gave formerly enslaved people the opportunity to buy land and establish their own independent farms.
- **Economic conditions in the South:** many formerly enslaved people became agricultural laborers. Although they were now paid wages, these were low and few had the necessary skills to adapt to different professions. Although it would be difficult to raise the money needed to move, leaving the South seemed to offer better prospects.
- **Political conditions in the South:** freedmen supposedly had their citizenship and voting rights protected by the Fourteenth and Fifteenth Amendments to the Constitution. However, exercising these rights was difficult and campaigns of intimidation were carried out to prevent African Americans from voting.
- **The end of Reconstruction:** when Reconstruction ended in 1877, federal troops were removed from the South and the little protection they had offered freedmen went with them. There was a dramatic increase in the incidence of violence against African Americans.
- **The impact of the 1878 elections in Louisiana:** formerly enslaved people tended to vote Republican, when they were able, as this was the party that had secured their freedom. However, the white South was staunchly Democrat. In 1878, the Democrats gained many congressional seats and the governorship. Black Southerners were intimidated to prevent them from voting.
- **The Windom Resolution:** in January 1879, a white Republican senator introduced a resolution that encouraged Black migration.
- **Promotion campaigns:** posters such as Source 1.26 encouraged migration and letters from others who had already left were published in newspapers. These often talked up the opportunities and quality of life offered in states such as Kansas.
- **Why Kansas?** Many felt a strong attachment to Kansas because it had been key to the debate about abolition and the activities of abolitionists such as John Brown enhanced its appeal as a liberal state. A more pragmatic reason to move to Kansas was that it was not as far away as California or Oregon and, given the cost of transport, it was therefore a more achievable target.

The Grange Movement and the creation of farmers' alliances

The Grange Movement (which takes its name from a word for granary) developed because of discontent among farmers. After the Civil War, prices for farm produce such as wheat and cotton fell quite significantly. The worst affected areas were the West and the South. Farmers who had borrowed money to buy land, livestock, and equipment found themselves unable to service their debts. They blamed several different factors for the difficulties they were facing.

- The banks were blamed. Although prices, and therefore profits, were falling, interest rates had increased and this made it even more difficult to pay back bank loans.
- The merchants who bought the crops wholesale from the farmers were blamed for exploiting the farmers by paying low prices and taking too much of a cut for themselves.
- The railroad companies were blamed, as transport costs in the South and West were higher than in the Northeast.

Partly in response to these issues, but also to provide social support for isolated farmers and improve farming techniques, Oliver Kelley founded the National Grange of the Order of Patrons of Husbandry organization in 1867. It aimed to promote the establishment of farmer co-operatives that would sell farm produce without the need for merchants or middlemen. However, the main aim of the "Grangers" (as the supporters of "the Grange" became known) was to gain political support to reduce and regulate the prices charged for transport and warehousing.

What is the main message of Source 1.27? Explain your answer using details from the source.

SOURCE 1.27

An illustration produced in Milwaukee, 1875

The membership of the movement grew rapidly and by 1874 the Grangers had won control of eleven Midwestern state legislatures. In five Western states, they passed "Granger Laws" to regulate railroad and storage prices. The movement lost momentum in the 1880s, when there was an increase in farm prices.

However, in the late 1880s, farmers faced further problems, partly due to a drought. In response, the Farmers' Alliance was formed, which had many local organizations that ended up assembling into three large groupings:
- the Northern Alliance, which grew out of the Grange Movement and was strong in wheat-growing areas such as Kansas
- the Southern Alliance, which grew from the Texas State Farmers' Alliance and spread throughout the South and into the West
- the Colored Farmers Alliance, which developed because African American farmers in the South were banned from joining the Southern Alliance.

There was an attempt to merge these alliances into one organization in 1889, but this failed due to tension over Southern attitudes toward African American farmers. However, the alliances had very similar political aims.

The rise of the Populists and the goals of the Populist Party

The People's Party, or "Populists," emerged as a significant political force in 1892. They represented the interests of the farmers and shared many of the aims of the Grange and the Farmers' Alliance. They adopted the ideas of the **Greenbackers** to form a more radical political party.

The common problem facing the farmers was debt and from 1873 farmers began to attack the monetary system, seeing it as the cause of their problems. What they wanted to achieve was **inflation**. This was usually considered harmful for economic growth and had a negative impact on many workers as prices rose. However, for the farmer, inflation meant increased prices which would mean they made greater profits and could pay off their debts.

The Grange, Farmers' Alliances, and the Greenback-Labor Party all had some degree of electoral success.

Some Grangers had been elected to state legislatures but the improvement in the economy in the late 1870s meant they lost momentum.

In 1878 the Greenback-Labor Party had polled over a million votes and fourteen Greenbackers were elected to Congress. However, by the 1880s their popularity had been radically reduced and they polled only 300,000 votes.

KEY TERMS

Greenbacker A member of a political party opposed to a reduction in the amount of paper money in circulation. As part of the Free Silver Movement, the Populists supported Bimetallism and demanded the unlimited coinage of silver at a fixed ratio to gold, aiming to increase the money supply and ease the economic struggles faced by farmers and workers.

Inflation A general increase in prices and fall in the purchasing value of money.

The Farmers' Alliances also had some success, particularly in the Northwest in states such as Kansas, Nebraska, and the Dakotas, and gained control of several state legislatures. Two Senators and nine Congressmen were elected from parties which represented the Alliances in national elections.

Inspired by these successes and struggling to win support from either the Republicans or the Democrats, some thought that forming a third political party would be the best way to represent the interests of the farmers at a national level. With this aim in mind, the farmers' representatives met at St Louis in February 1892. They were joined by the Greenbackers and members of the Knights of Labor. These groups formed the Populist party and at their first convention in July 1892, they established a wide-based political agenda and nominated General James B Weaver, a Greenbacker, as their first presidential candidate.

SOURCE 1.28

Extracts from the Populist Party Platform, 1892

The conditions which surround us best justify our co-operation; we meet in the midst of a nation brought to the verge of moral, political, and material ruin. Corruption dominates the ballot-box, the Legislatures, the Congress … The people are demoralized; most of the States have been compelled to isolate the voters at the polling places to prevent universal intimidation and bribery. The newspapers are largely subsidized or muzzled, public opinion silenced, business prostrated, homes covered with mortgages, labor impoverished, and the land concentrating in the hands of capitalists. The urban workmen are denied the right to organize for self-protection, imported pauperized labor beats down their wages … The fruits of the toil of millions are boldly stolen to build up colossal fortunes for a few … we breed the two great classes—tramps and millionaires.

In an "Expression of Sentiments," the Populist Party Platform also included resolutions demanding the following:
1. secret ballot in all elections
2. graduated income tax
3. fair pensions for ex-Union soldiers and sailors
4. further restriction of undesirable emigration
5. shortening of working men's hours of labor
6. abolition of the Pinkerton private police force
7. legislative system known as the initiative and referendum (see page 34)
8. constitutional provision limiting the office of president and vice president to one term and providing for the election of Senators of the United States by a direct vote of the people.
9. opposition to any subsidy or national aid to any private corporation for any purpose.

ACTIVITY

Having read Source 1.28 (and the "Expression of Sentiments,") copy and complete the table below to show (i) the problems that the Populists wanted to address, and (ii) how they wanted to bring about reform in each of the categories listed. In the third column, you should add evidence from Source 1.28 to support these points.

Problems: economic, social, political	Proposed solutions: economic, social, political	Evidence from Source 1.28

Work in a pair or small group to write a list of the impacts of industrialization on rural areas. Think about the different groups of people (Native Americans, farmers, African Americans, cowboys) and whether they were impacted in a positive or negative way.

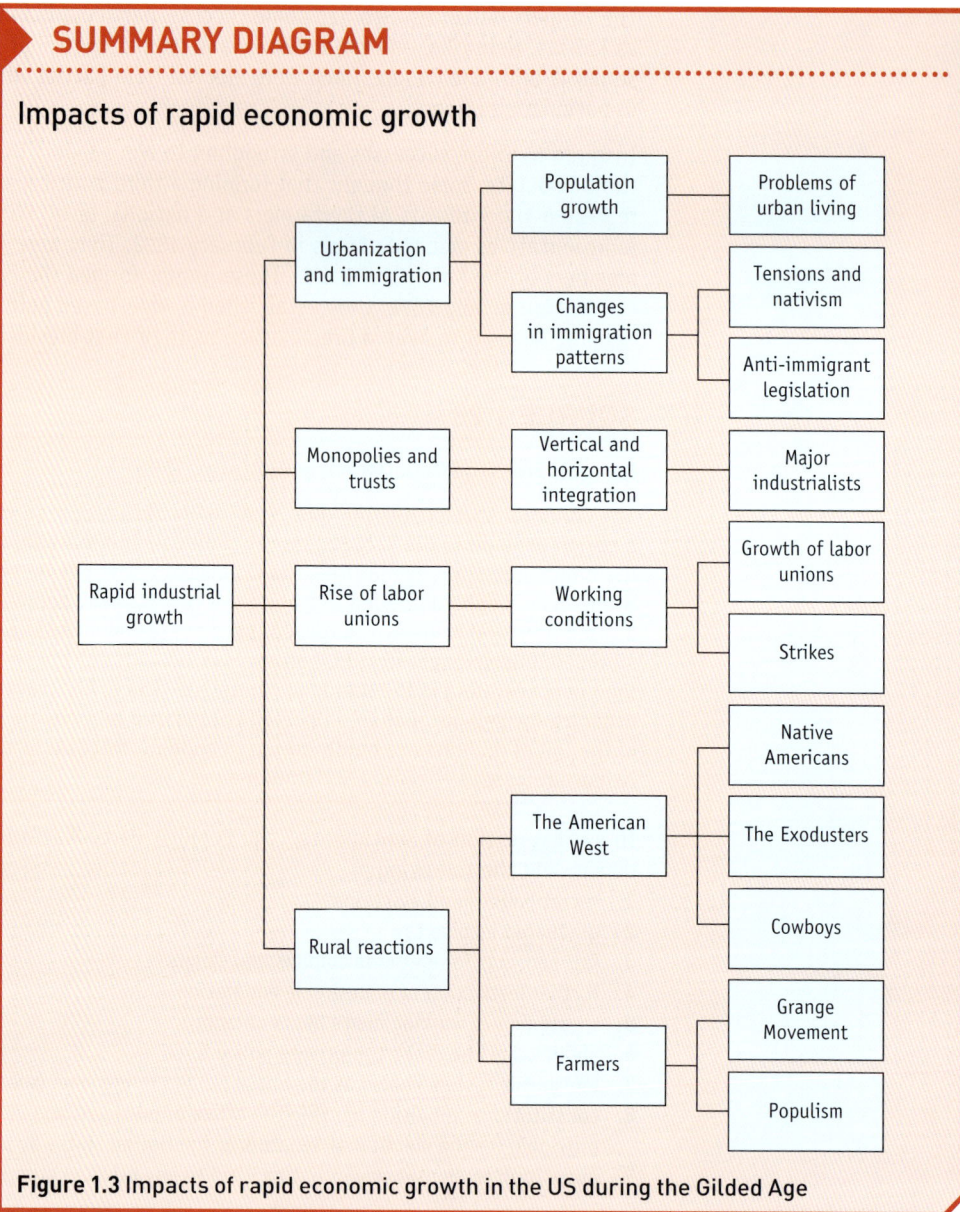

Figure 1.3 Impacts of rapid economic growth in the US during the Gilded Age

1.2 What were the main aims and policies of the Progressive Movement?

The Progressive Movement was not an organized movement or a political party until the 1912 presidential election when Theodore Roosevelt stood for the new Progressive Party. Instead, it was a collection of different movements that wanted to bring about social, economic, and political change. Some Progressives were interested in achieving social justice, others were more motivated to regulate the activities of politicians and capitalists. As seen in Section 1.1 of this chapter, progressivism emerged around 1890 and was, in part, a response to issues that arose because of the surge in industrialization. However, the impact of the Depression of 1893–97 was also a key factor in leading the Progressives to press for state and federal intervention. During this time almost twenty percent of the workforce were unemployed, and it became clear that the welfare support offered by charities was not enough to meet the need. Progressivism often had its roots in local issues, but these developed so that many were addressed at state level and later federal level. In broad terms, there were three main strands to the movement:

- Economic change: the main focus for many Progressives was to control the power of the corporations and, for some groups at least, to bring about a more equal distribution of wealth. The Progressives did not want to turn back the clock and remove big business but rather reduce corruption and what they saw as the undue power and influence of the corporations.
- Social change: the main focus for some Progressives was to achieve social justice. In 1910, Theodore Roosevelt declared that the government should be "the steward of the public welfare" and this sums up what many Progressives wanted to achieve. Providing better living conditions for workers, improving the lives of immigrants, introducing prohibition, and introducing government commissions to investigate child labor or poverty began to be seen as the responsibility of government at state and federal level.
- Political change: different Progressive groups campaigned to make elected government more transparent and accountable to the people, to reduce corruption at all levels, and to achieve equal rights for women and civil rights for African Americans and other minority groups.

Many Progressives were active in a number of areas. For example, Jane Addams (page 7) established settlement houses to help immigrants, but was also active in the Women's Trade Union and the National Association for the Advancement of Colored People (page 67). Progressives sometimes disagreed among themselves about how far reform should go. However, the movement was unusual in that both Republican and Democrat presidents pursued policies that were progressive.

Eliminating political corruption

Although there was debate about what Progressives believed in, and many of them had different opinions from each other, one thing that united them was their belief in democracy. One of their main aims was to make the government more responsive to the people and they thought that this would bring about political reform. State governments adopted a variety of measures to make politics less corrupt and government more efficient, more democratic, and more representative.

Limits on party machines and bosses

At the turn of the century, control over political processes lay in the hands of the party bosses and their highly organized **party machines**. These operated at city and state levels and there were several different features.
- State bosses were often well-educated. Many were US senators and came from old families which were established in American society and part of the political elite.
- City bosses did not seek political office themselves but operated behind the scenes. Many were from recent immigrant families (quite often of Irish descent) so they were less well known.

> **KEY TERM**
>
> **Party machines** Political party organizations headed by single bosses or small groups that held enough votes to maintain political and administrative control of cities, counties, or states.

- Party machines were developed to ensure that their chosen men were elected. They were highly organized and often used bribery and other corrupt methods to help their proposed candidates. Elections were quite frequent and the electorate was large. These factors encouraged the growth of the machines to run campaigns and control the elections.
- Lobbying went hand in hand with the bribery of the machines. Often, business owners tried to control state and city legislatures so that decisions taken, and any policies introduced, favored their businesses. For example, some state legislatures were on the pay roll of railroad corporations.
- At federal level, corruption was less obvious than at state level, but was still widespread and there was also lobbying.

At a local level, many working-class Americans engaged in machine politics. Every citizen belonged to a ward that had an elected **alderman** who spoke on their behalf at city hall. When problems arose, such as the need for paved sidewalks or better street lighting, people could approach their alderman and ask him to find a solution. One response to such issues was to take the problem to city hall and campaign for the necessary funds to complete the work. However, this was a long and bureaucratic process and many aldermen preferred to work within the machine of local politics to solve the problem. The voters wanted a quick solution and, by providing it, the alderman secured their support. To achieve a speedy resolution, the alderman called in favors and this usually involved some sort of payment or kickback for the machine boss.

One example was the Democratic political machine Tammany Hall in New York, run by machine boss William Tweed until 1871. He built a loyal following among immigrant groups by providing jobs and securing housing. Tammany Hall ran New York politics from the 1850s until the 1930s. Other large cities, including Boston and Cleveland, were run in a similar way.

> **KEY TERM**
>
> **Alderman** A member of the governing body of a town or city.

> What can you learn from Source 1.29 about machine politics? Do you agree with Plunkitt that this was honest graft?

SOURCE 1.29

New York City ward boss George Washington Plunkitt defends "Honest Graft" in a speech, 1905

Everybody is talkin' these days about Tammany men growin' rich on graft … Yes, many of our men have grown rich in politics. I have myself but I've not gone in for dishonest graft—blackmailin' gamblers, saloonkeepers … There's an honest graft and I'm an example of how it works … Just let me explain by examples. My party's in power in the city, and it's going to undertake a lot of public improvements. Well I'm tipped off, say, that they're going to lay out a park in a certain place. I see my opportunity and I take it. I go to that place and I buy up all the land I can in the neighborhood. Then the board makes its plan public and there is a rush to get my land, which nobody cared particular for before. Ain't it perfectly honest to charge a good price and make a profit on my investment and foresight?

Another kind of honest graft. Tammany has raised a good many salaries. The Wall Street Banker thinks it shameful to raise a department clerk's salary from $1,500 to $1,800 a year, but every man who draws a salary himself says: "That's all right. I wish it was me." And he feels very much like voting the Tammany ticket on election day, just out of sympathy.

A number of initiatives were introduced to curb corruption and make government more democratic.

Direct primaries

Under the existing system, only a small number of voters attended the local meetings where candidates were selected for county, state, and national conventions. This gave the voters who attended disproportionate influence on the selection of candidates. Under a new system, primaries were held where all party members voted to nominate candidates. South Carolina adopted this system in 1896 and many other states quickly followed.

The three developments below were introduced by William S U'Ren in Oregon. He was the secretary of the Populist Party and was motivated to ensure that power stayed in the hands of the people rather than in back rooms where shady characters made secret deals to control politics. He was also influential in the development of the "Hold-Up Legislature" tactic which was used by Populist representatives when the legislature rejected reform measures, including the initiative and the referendum. The representatives involved refused to attend and this kept the House from being called into session.

- **Initiative:** gave voters the right to raise issues that they wanted to be considered. A minimum of eight percent of the electorate in the state had to agree for the initiative to be put forward.
- **Referendum:** made certain legislative proposals subject to popular vote so long as five percent of the electorate supported the referendum.
- **Recall:** allowed the removal of elected officials by popular vote before the end of their term in office for "poor leadership, malfeasance (dishonesty), or extreme political partisanship."

Senatorial elections

In 1899, Nevada was the first state to consider voter preference in the selection of senatorial candidates. It was made clear that the state legislature would follow voter recommendations. This marked a radical departure from the previous system, which was not transparent and often corrupt. Between 1899 and 1912, 30 states passed laws that required state legislators to accept the popular choice of candidates and in 1913, this was added to the Constitution through the **ratification** of the Seventeenth Amendment (see page 60).

Fostering efficiency in the government

President George Washington based most of his federal appointments on merit, but many of his successors strayed from this policy. By the time Andrew Jackson was elected president in 1828, the **spoils system** was in full swing. In the early nineteenth century, there were approximately 20,000 federal employees. By the mid-1880s there were over 130,000.

The abuses in this system worsened as candidates required political appointees to spend increasing amounts of time and money on political activities. The rapid expansion of the federal bureaucracy meant those seeking federal employment could approach the president and senators in an attempt to secure a position. One Republican party supporter, who wrongly felt that his work during the presidential election campaign entitled him to the position of consul in Paris, was so enraged at being turned down that he assassinated President Garfield in 1881. This acted as a catalyst for political reform efforts, particularly in addressing the spoils system. Chester Arthur, who had been Garfield's Vice President, emerged as a key figure in promoting reform. Congress passed the Pendleton Act (named after reformer Senator George Pendleton) in January 1883. The basic principles of the Pendleton Act were that:

- federal government jobs be awarded on the basis of merit
- government employees be selected through competitive exams
- it be unlawful to demote or fire an employee for political reasons
- employers be forbidden from requiring employees to give political service or contributions
- the Civil Service Commission be established to enforce the Act.

While initially covering only a fraction of federal positions, civil service reform helped curb some of the most shocking forms of political patronage.

> **KEY TERM**
>
> **Ratification** The process of making a policy part of the law.

> **KEY TERM**
>
> **Spoils system** A system in which elected officials reward political friends and supporters with government positions.

Answer both these questions using details from Source 1.30.
- What can you learn from this source about some of the reasons why the Pendleton Act might have been unpopular with some people?
- Do you think the cartoonist was in favor of the Pendleton Act?

SOURCE 1.30

A cartoon by Thomas Nast, published in Harper's Weekly in 1886 entitled "The Pendleton Act Provides Civil Service Reform". The caption reads 'The real lesson of the fall elections; The rascals are still out'

The Act was not popular with everyone. It went too far for machine politicians and not far enough for reformers. President Arthur was the last incumbent president to be denied renomination for a second term by his own party. The Act also had some unintended consequences, including a shift in political fundraising strategies. With access to lucrative federal posts restricted, politicians increasingly relied on contributions from big corporations.

However, the Pendleton Act had a far-reaching impact and transformed the nature of public service. When it came into effect, its reforms covered around ten percent of federal government's 132,000 employees. Today, it applies to most of the 2.9 million positions held in federal government.

Role of muckrakers in exposing corruption

"Muckraker" is a term used to describe Progressive Era journalists who investigated and publicized social and economic injustices. In this context, "raking the muck" means uncovering the unpleasant "muck" of corruption in government and big business. Today, muckrakers would be referred to as investigative journalists. Theodore Roosevelt is credited with adopting this term in a speech made in 1906, an extract of which is below.

Do you think Roosevelt approved of the "muckrakers"? Use evidence from Source 1.31 to support your answer.

SOURCE 1.31

From a speech entitled *The Man with the Muckrake* made by Theodore Roosevelt in April 1906

... my plea is not for immunity to, but for the most unsparing exposure of, the politician who betrays his trust, of the big businessman who makes or spends his fortune in illegitimate or corrupt ways. There should be a resolute effort to hunt every such man out of the position he has disgraced. Expose the crime, and hunt down the criminal; but remember that even in the case of crime, if it is attacked in sensational, lurid, and untruthful fashion, the attack may do more damage to the public mind than the crime itself.

It is because I feel that there should be no rest in the endless war against the forces of evil that I ask the war be conducted with sanity as well as with resolution. The men with the muckrakes are often indispensable to the well-being of society; but only if they know when to stop raking the muck, and to look upward to the celestial crown above them, to the crown of worthy endeavor. There are beautiful things above and round about them; and if they gradually grow to feel that the whole world is nothing but muck, their power of usefulness is gone.

Although Roosevelt's speech above is about muckraking journalism, there were other types of muckrakers and they were not all men. The list below shows some examples of muckrakers and the issues in which they were interested.
- Jacob Riis, a Danish immigrant and photojournalist, published an eighteen-page photo essay called *How the Other Half Lives: Studies among the Tenements of New York*, which first appeared in a magazine in February 1889 (see page 6). Riis' work drew attention to poor conditions in the cities and encouraged campaigns to improve living conditions such as the Tenement House Commission (see page 6). He was also an important influence in campaigns to improve education and to end child labor.
- Ida B Wells was an African American journalist and suffragist (see page 66). She was born into enslavement in Mississippi in 1862 and became involved in anti-lynching activism. In 1892, she published *Southern Horrors: Lynch Law in All its Phases*, which detailed the process of disenfranchisement of African Americans in the South.
- Lincoln Steffens was a journalist who published an article called "Tweed Days" in St Louis in 1902, exposing corruption in the city government. This was followed by a book entitled *The Shame of the Cities* which generated public outcry for changes to the way in which cities were controlled.
- Ida Tarbell was a journalist and writer. In 1902, she began a series of articles in *McLure's* magazine, a well-known muckraking publication, called "History of the Standard Oil Company." She documented the business practices behind John Rockefeller's rise and was influential in legislation that aimed to curb the corrupt practices of trusts and corporations.
- **Upton Sinclair** was a novelist whose work *The Jungle* was influential in tackling corruption in the meatpacking business. This novel follows the story of a character called Jurgis Rudkus, a Lithuanian immigrant who spent time working in a meatpacking factory. It became highly influential in bringing about the Meat Inspection Act of 1906 which is discussed in more detail on page 38.

Regulation of monopolies/private corporations

Section 1.1 of this chapter considered the development of big business, trusts, and corporations. Business owners like Morgan and Carnegie controlled vast business empires and dominated the national economy in a way that was never seen before. Many people shared their belief in rugged individualism and *laissez-faire*. However, there were those who disagreed with Carnegie's ideas that were outlined in his book *The Gospel of Wealth*. Trusts also came under increased scrutiny in the 1880s. Farmers, small business owners, and trade unionists all argued that trusts should be controlled. They were partly motivated by self-interest and feared that prices would be kept artificially high. However, many were also concerned that the trusts represented a threat to democracy and competition, and would prevent other people from making the most of economic opportunities.

Antitrust legislation

In the 1880s, 27 states introduced legislation that banned trusts and other forms of combined companies. In general, these were not very effective, as shown by the example of Standard Oil, which simply moved its headquarters to another state to avoid such laws. However, by this time both the Republican and Democratic parties were committed through their platforms to reducing the power of the trusts.

Sherman Antitrust Act, July 1890

The Sherman Antitrust Act was the first federal act that outlawed monopolistic business practices. It was named after Senator John Sherman of Ohio, a chairman of the Senate Finance Committee and Secretary of the Treasury under President Hayes, although in practice the Senate Judiciary Committee designed the legislation. This Act aimed to regulate interstate commerce, which was beyond the control of individual state legislatures.

> **KEY TERM**
> **Lynching** A form of violence by a mob where someone accused of a crime is murdered without recourse to the law or justice. The victims were often, but not exclusively, African Americans, and those responsible were rarely brought to justice.

> **KEY FIGURE**
> **Upton Sinclair**
> (1878–1968) Sinclair was a muckraker and political activist whose novel *The Jungle* was important in bringing about legislation to improve the standards of cleanliness in meat production and prevent the adulteration of food with poisonous chemicals.

The Act authorized federal government to take legal proceedings against trusts to dissolve them. It declared illegal "every combination in the form of a trust or otherwise, or conspiracy, that was in restraint of trade or commerce among the several states, or with foreign nations." Anyone found guilty of breaking this law faced a fine of $5,000 and a year in prison. Individuals and companies suffering losses because of trusts were permitted to sue in federal court for triple damages.

Although the Act was designed to reinstate competition, historians argue about how serious an attempt it was and there were issues that undermined its effectiveness. Important terms such as "trust," "combination," "conspiracy," and "monopoly" were not defined. In 1895, the Supreme Court appeared to dismantle the act in *United States v. EC Knight Company*. The court ruled that the American Sugar Refining Company had not broken the law even though the company controlled 98 percent of all sugar refining in the United States. The Supreme Court argued that the company's control of the manufacture of sugar was different from having control of trade.

The EC Knight ruling seemed to signal the end of government regulation of trusts. However, President Roosevelt used the Sherman Antitrust Act with considerable success in 1904, when the Supreme Court upheld the government's decision to dissolve the Northern Securities Company. By 1911, President Taft had used the Act against the Standard Oil Company and the American Tobacco Company.

President Wilson suggested a revision of the Sherman Antitrust Act, and in 1914 two related measures were passed to strengthen the powers of the federal government against the trusts.

Federal Trade Commission Act, September 1914

In 1914, the Federal Trade Commission Act was passed, and the Federal Trade Commission (FTC) was established. This was an independent agency of the US government and was formed to promote consumer protection and prevent anti-competitive business practices. It monitored businesses and had the authority to investigate all corporations which carried out inter-state trade. For example, the Commission had the power to investigate possible mislabeling of goods which were inspected under the Pure Food and Drug Act (see below). The act had two main related goals to ensure that there was
- fair competition between businesses
- consumer protection against fraudulent business practices such as false advertising or deceptive marketing.

The establishment of the FTC was important because it represented a change in economic policy and reinforced the responsibility of the Federal government in economic affairs. It altered the relationship between government and business by introducing regulations which protected consumers and reduced corporate power. In effect, this meant businesses had to comply with regulations, could not operate unchecked, and could not avoid regulation by simply moving to a different state.

Clayton Act, October 1914

The Clayton Act extended the power of the Sherman Act in the following ways:
- It was made illegal to carry out price discrimination, which meant that companies could no longer lower prices with the intention of forcing out local competitors.
- Offering discounts to buyers if they only bought from companies that were part of the trust was banned.
- The terms which had been problematic in the Sherman Act were clearly defined.

The Clayton Act also protected labor unions from antitrust regulation. Under previous court judgments, unions could be prosecuted for restraining trade under the Sherman Act. However, the new Act clarified that unions were not considered illegal combinations in restraint of trade, and it allowed peaceful strikes, picketing, and the payment of strike benefits to workers. But this did not mean, as Samuel Gompers had hoped, that unions could not be prosecuted under the terms of the Sherman Act.

Progressives who wanted to eliminate trusts were displeased that the antitrust reforms left many trusts intact. Meanwhile, pro-business conservatives thought that the government should not have interfered at all with businesses. Nevertheless, the moderate reforms that were typical of progressivism produced real benefits for society.

Regulating products

As well as protecting consumers from sharp business practices, the Progressives were also interested to protect public health. Dr Harvey W. Wiley was chief chemist of the Department of Agriculture. He and his team of investigators discovered that harmful preservatives and additives were widely used in food processing. They also established that **patent medicines** were commonly mislabeled and contained dangerous ingredients such as opiates, alcohol, and tar, a derivative of petroleum. Wiley campaigned for a change in the law, but every attempt stalled. In 1905–06, Samuel Hopkins Adams, a muckraking journalist and writer, aroused public rage against patent medicines with a series of articles called "The Great American Fraud." His writing exposed the dangerous ingredients contained in some patent medicines and challenged the false claims they carried about their ability to cure everything from arthritis to cancer and improve conditions such as poor growth in children and hair loss in men.

Pure Food and Drug Act, June 1906

In the 1880s, Harvey Wiley, who was chief of the Bureau of Chemistry, reported that many of the chemicals used to preserve and color processed foods, such as canned meat, were dangerous. The Association of Official Agricultural Chemists (an organization established by Wiley) began to lobby for federal government legislation to address this. An example of the problem can be seen in Source 1.32.

> **KEY TERM**
>
> **Patent medicine** An over-the-counter medicine which could be purchased without a prescription from a qualified doctor. Often these contained dangerous substances and were marketed misleadingly as "cure-alls."

> What can you learn from Source 1.32 about the reasons for introducing the Pure Food and Drug Act?

SOURCE 1.32

Representative James Mann of Illinois's speech to the US House of Representatives, June 21, 1906

I have here a number of adulterated articles. Here is a bottle of cherries, originally picked green, in order that they might be firm, with the green color all taken out with acid until they were perfectly white, and then colored with an aniline dye which is poisonous in any quantity.

The Pure Food and Drug Act was introduced by James Mann and forbade the sale of adulterated or mislabeled food and drugs. It also laid the foundations for the Food and Drug Administration (FDA).

Meat Inspection Act, June 1906

Unsafe practices of the meatpacking industry gained widespread public condemnation in 1898, when the press reported that Armour & Co. had supplied tins of rotten canned beef to the US Army in Cuba during the Spanish-American War. The meat had been packed in tins under a layer of boric acid, which was thought to act as a preservative and was used to mask the smell of the rotten meat. Troops who consumed the meat fell ill, many were too ill to fight and some died. Soldiers accused the Army of feeding them "embalmed beef." They presented so much evidence that the federal government was forced to hold public hearings into the situation and this led to the resignation of the Secretary of War.

Thomas F Dolan, a former superintendent for Armour & Co., signed a document under oath that stated that it was common practice for the company to pack and sell meat that was not fit for human consumption. He also noted the ineffectiveness of government inspections. The *New York Journal* published Dolan's statement in March 1899. In response, the US Senate formed the Pure-Food Investigating Committee which declared that common meat preservatives such as boric acid, salicylic acid, and formaldehyde were "unwholesome."

The spotlight fell on the "Beef Trust," made up of the five largest meatpacking companies and based in Chicago's Packingtown area. Journalists published pieces in radical and muckraking magazines detailing the corrupt practices of Beef Trust businesses, as well as the unsanitary conditions of the packing houses and the tactics they employed to avoid government inspections.

In 1904, Upton Sinclair (page 36) covered a labor strike at Chicago's Union Stockyards where meatpacking took place, for the socialist magazine *Appeal to Reason*. Following this experience, he spent a year investigating the Beef Trust's exploitation of their workforce. The result was his novel *The Jungle* which painted a revolting picture of the working conditions of packing houses and meatpacking practices. Roosevelt, who gained an arguably exaggerated reputation for "trust-busting," was sent a copy of the book. He ordered two commissioners to investigate. They confirmed what Sinclair had claimed and pressure on the government to take action to protect the public began to grow. However, the Beef Trust was a powerful organization and both the proposed Meat Inspection Act and the Pure Food and Drug Act stalled in Congress. Progress was made when Roosevelt threatened to disclose the commissioner's report. Both acts became law on the same day. Although patent medicines continued to be produced after 1906, new regulations demanded that ingredients should be printed on the labels and advertising should be more truthful.

> What impression does this cartoon give of (i) the meatpacking scandal and (ii) President Roosevelt?

SOURCE 1.33

A cartoon published in 1906 showing President Roosevelt attempting to address the meat scandal

A NAUSEATING JOB, BUT IT MUST BE DONE
(President Roosevelt takes hold of the investigating muck-rake himself in the packing-house scandal.)

The Meat Inspection Act prohibited the sale of adulterated or misbranded livestock and derived products as food, and ensured that livestock were slaughtered and processed under sanitary conditions. The law reformed the meatpacking industry, mandating that the US Department of Agriculture inspect all animals before and after they were slaughtered and processed for human consumption. The law also applied to imported products.

Regulating child labor

One of the most infamous aspects of industrialization was the widespread introduction of child labor in textile mills and coal mines. Children worked long hours in dangerous factory conditions for low wages. They were small enough to fit easily between the machines and could be hired to carry out simple tasks for a fraction of an adult man's pay. Between 1870 and 1900, the number of children working in factories tripled. Growing concerns among Progressive reformers over the safety of children in the workplace led to campaigns to end child labor. Socialist and muckraking journalist John Spargo published a book about the horrors of child labor in 1906.

> What can you learn from Source 1.34 about child labor? Find three pieces of evidence from the source that show that the author was against child labor.

SOURCE 1.34

Extracts from *The Bitter Cry of Children* by John Spargo, published in 1906

Work in the coal breakers is exceedingly hard and dangerous. Crouched over the chutes, the boys sit hour after hour, picking out the pieces of slate and other refuse from the coal as it rushes past to the washers. From the cramped position they have to assume, most of them become more or less deformed and bent-backed like old men.

The coal is hard, and accidents to the hands, such as cut, broken, or crushed fingers, are common among the boys. Sometimes there is a worse accident: a terrified shriek is heard, and a boy is mangled and torn in the machinery, or disappears in the chute to be picked out later smothered and dead. Clouds of dust fill the breakers and are inhaled by the boys, laying the foundations for asthma and miners' consumption.

Boys twelve years of age may be legally employed in the mines of West Virginia, by day or by night, and for as many hours as the employers care to make them toil or their bodies will stand the strain. Where the disregard of child life is such that this may be done openly and with legal sanction, it is easy to believe what miners have again and again told me—that there are hundreds of little boys of nine and ten years of age employed in the coal mines of this state.

Several states passed laws to make workplaces safer and lobby groups pressured Congress to create laws against child labor. In the meantime, many working-class immigrants still needed the additional wages that child labor produced, regardless of the harsh working conditions.

Keating-Owen Act, September 1916

The 1900 census revealed that approximately two million children worked in mills, mines, factories, stores, on farms, and on city streets across the United States. The census report helped spark a national movement to end child labor. In 1908, the National Child Labor Committee hired Lewis Hine as its staff photographer and sent him across the country to photograph and report on child labor. His work was important in bringing about the Keating-Owen Act.

The Act, passed in 1916, was based on a 1906 proposal by Senator Albert J Beveridge. It used the government's ability to regulate interstate trade to regulate child labor. It banned the sale of products from any factory, shop, or cannery that employed children under the age of fourteen, from any mine that employed children under the age of sixteen, and from any facility that allowed children under the age of sixteen to work at night or for more than eight hours during the day.

Hammer v. Dagenhart, June 1918

Although Congress passed the Keating-Owen Act and President Woodrow Wilson signed it into law, the Supreme Court ruled that it was unconstitutional in 1918 because it overstepped the purpose of the government's powers to regulate interstate trade. The court ruled that the power to regulate production and trade were two different things. A further attempt to regulate child labor was introduced in 1918 and also found unconstitutional.

Hammer v. Dagenhart was a case brought by employers who were angry about the regulation of their employment practices. Dagenhart worked in a cotton mill with his two sons. They would lose their jobs if the Keating-Owen Act were upheld. Hammer was the US Attorney for Charlotte, NC. In a five to four decision, the Supreme Court ruled that the Keating-Owen Act exceeded federal authority and represented an unwarranted over reaching of state powers to determine local labor conditions. Justice Holmes, on the losing side in this decision, strongly disagreed with the court's decision and pointed out the evils of excessive child labor, arguing, "But if there is any matter upon which civilized countries have agreed—it is the evil of premature and excessive child labor."

Does the cartoonist support the Supreme Court's decision in *Hammer v. Dagenhart*? Use details from the source to explain your answer.

SOURCE 1.35

A cartoon published in 1918 in the *Liberator*, an American magazine that was linked to the Communist Party of America

"Now then, children, all together, three cheers for the Supreme Court!"

Temperance and prohibition

National **prohibition** was introduced through the Eighteenth Amendment to the Constitution, which was signed into law in January 1919. The reasons for this precise timing will be discussed later in this chapter. However, it is important to note that the process by which America went from "wet" to "dry" was piecemeal. By the time the Eighteenth Amendment was introduced, there were already 36 states where alcohol was banned. Some states introduced prohibition through an amendment to their state constitution, such as in Kansas in 1881. Others used a local option whereby counties within a state opted to go dry individually. One example of this process was in Missouri and can be seen in Source 1.36, below.

KEY TERM

Prohibition A ban on the manufacture, sale, and transportation of alcohol.

> Does Source 1.36 support or challenge the idea that prohibition was popular in America? Use details from the source to develop your answer.

SOURCE 1.36

Three maps showing the spread of prohibition across Missouri. Adapted from the Kansas City Star, October 1914. The original caption reads 'How Missouri is shaking out the saloon'

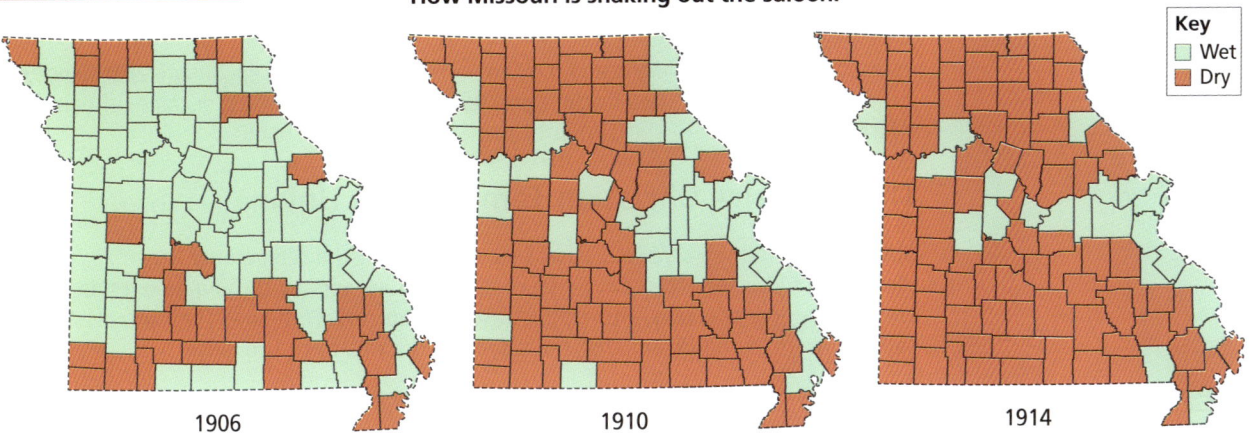

How Missouri is shaking out the saloon.

1906 — 1910 — 1914

Key: Wet / Dry

The idea that drinking alcohol was harmful was not new. Neither was the conviction of some groups that it should be banned. Alcoholism is thought to have been more widespread in nineteenth-century America than it is today. Certain groups of workers, including soldiers, farm workers, and laborers, received part of their wages in whiskey. Records show that in some areas of the West, people even paid their church dues in liquor and there was a widespread belief that drinking alcohol helped to protect against disease. Liquor consumption increased during the Civil War and the taxes raised in revenue from alcohol sales were welcomed by many states, removing any incentive to introduce prohibition laws.

The social status and position of many women meant they and their families could be vulnerable to homelessness, poverty, hunger, and domestic violence if the head of the family drank excessively. Despite changes to the law to protect married women's property, society remained male-dominated. Although educational opportunities for women were improving, few professions were open to women and they were often expected to give up work on marriage. For further discussion of this, see page 48. The day-to-day reality for most women was that if they were married, they had no right to their husband's incomes and, in the case of those who worked, no right to their own earnings. There were few opportunities to escape domestic abuse and the little help that could be found was provided by a small number of charities.

There had been many groups, often but not exclusively church-based, that had tried to tackle alcoholism and drunkenness in the past. They focused on the negative impact of alcohol on the health and well-being of individuals and their families but relied on self-help from individuals to tackle addiction. Although some states had tried to ban alcohol in the 1850s, such as Maine in 1851, laws were often hard to enforce.

In the years following the Civil War, there were renewed and more concentrated attempts to introduce prohibition. There are several reasons why this development took place at this time.
- The rise in alcohol consumption in the Civil War raised concerns about a possible negative impact on "national efficiency."

- Many women had been forced to live differently during the Civil War, taking responsibility for their households and working outside the home for the first time. This experience gave those involved a newfound sense of confidence.
- The Progressive Movement gave new vigor to the Temperance Movement. The brewers and distillers were seen as a source of political corruption, wielding too much influence over federal government. On a local level, saloons promoted drinking, gambling, prostitution, and corruption, all regarded as evils in a society which the Progressives were determined to reform.

In response to these changes and picking up from attempts to encourage abstinence which pre-dated the Civil War, two distinct pressure groups formed which became influential in the effort to reform society and prohibit the manufacture of alcohol.

The Woman's Christian Temperance Union

In Ohio in the fall of 1873, a group of 75 women formed a temperance organization called the Woman's Crusade. They put pressure on saloon keepers by turning up outside their premises to pray and sing. This is illustrated in Source 1.37, below. Their intention was to deter drinkers to the extent that the saloon owner was forced to close.

> **KEY TERM**
>
> **Temperance** Choosing to not drink alcohol.

> What do you think the artist who drew this image thought about the likelihood of the Temperance Movement succeeding? Explain your answer using details from the source.

SOURCE 1.37

This illustration appeared in an Ohio newspaper in February 1874. The caption accompanying it read "The Ohio whiskey war – the ladies of Logan singing hymns in front of barrooms in aid of the Temperance Movement"

In 1874, the Woman's Christian Temperance Union (WCTU) was formed in Cleveland, Ohio. Its formation depended on the growing confidence of some groups of women. Annie Wittenmyer, who became its first president, had developed her organizational abilities through her role as a fundraiser during the Civil War. The WCTU had influential support, including from Lucy Hayes, wife of President Hayes, who famously refused to serve liquor at White House functions. By 1879, there was dissent within the movement with one section, led by Frances Willard, demanding that the union also focus on the issue of women's suffrage. This highlighted the growing realization that to achieve social reform it was necessary for women to have political rights.

> **KEY TERM**
>
> **Suffrage** The right to vote in political elections.

By 1890, there were over 200,000 members of the WCTU; it had over 10,000 local branches (also known as chapters) and was represented in every state. The organization published a journal called *Our Nation* to spread the word and campaigned for prohibition laws to be passed and upheld. It ran education classes for women on everything from hygiene to public speaking and campaigned on a wide range of issues, including demands for the employment of female police officers and prison reform. After the death of Frances Willard in 1898, the movement returned to a stricter focus on prohibition. It still exists as an international organization that aims to "organize the motherhood of the world for the protection and exaltation of its homes."

Role of key leaders

Frances Willard

Frances Willard was born in 1839 in New York State and both her parents were teachers. Willard grew up in a progressive-minded household which included regular family meetings that were run by a "parliamentary" process. She went into teaching in 1860 and became the president of Evanston College for Ladies (later part of Northwestern University) in 1871. After resigning in 1874, Willard became secretary of the WCTU in the same year and president in 1879, a position she retained until her death in 1898. She became known for her "Do Everything" policy.

> What impression do you gain from Source 1.38 about Frances Willard? Are you surprised by this source? Think about who wrote it and what else you know about Frances Willard to help you answer.

SOURCE 1.38

From a description of Frances Willard written in 1884 by fellow founder of the WCTU, Hannah Whitehall Smith

I have named Miss Willard the "Octopus" because she is continually reaching out her great tentacles and dragging us all into her insatiable maw*. I never saw such a head for planning. I tell her I sometimes wish it was cut off—she does hustle a body about so from one thing to another! But, after all, that is the way she has made our Woman's Christian Temperance Union the power it is.

*"Insatiable maw" means the greedy mouth, or jaws of a fierce creature, which is never satisfied.

Although Willard was a strong president, some have argued that "Do Everything" weakened the effectiveness of the WCTU as a temperance organization. Trying to tackle so many issues meant it made limited progress toward prohibition. However, it made an important contribution to public education. In 1881, the WCTU started to campaign for lessons on temperance to be made compulsory in schools. Such lessons were similar to modern-day anti-drug programs and were implemented in public schools and military colleges by 1901.

Carrie Nation

Carrie Nation (also known as Carry A Nation) was born Carrie Moore and was a vibrant and resolute member of the Temperance Movement who divided opinion with her saloon-smashing antics.

Nation was born in 1846 in Kentucky. She became a nurse in the Civil War and her first husband was a physician. Unknown to Moore at the time of their wedding, he was an alcoholic. Carrie soon realized he could not support her and their daughter because of his excessive drinking. She left him and returned home. Her husband died a few months later. This experience shaped her dedication to the cause of temperance. In 1874, she married Daniel Nation, who was a journalist and lawyer. When he became a preacher in 1889, they moved to Medicine Lodge in Kansas where Nation organized a chapter of the WCTU. She engaged in charity work with disadvantaged women and children and became known as "Mother Nation." At first, Nation used similar tactics to the ladies of Logan, campaigning outside saloons until they were closed. However, her methods became more dramatic as she grew frustrated by the failure of the Kansas legislature to enforce its own prohibition laws. In June 1900, she drove her buggy to Kiowa where she smashed up Dobson's Saloon. In the following two years, she attacked numerous saloons using a hatchet given to her by a supporter. She was arrested several times and spent time in jail at Little Rock, Arkansas. Her activities, and the notoriety they brought, put a strain on her marriage and she separated from her husband. In 1903, she abandoned saloon wrecking and took to more peaceful methods of promoting temperance, including education and sharing her home with women escaping domestic abuse, until her death in 1911.

What impression does Source 1.39 give of Carrie Nation?

SOURCE 1.39

A cartoon of Carrie Nation published in New York's *Saturday Globe* newspaper, 1901

"I CANNOT TELL A LIE--I DID IT WITH MY LITTLE HATCHET!"
Mrs. Nation's Reform Crusade in Kansas, as the Globe Artist Understands It From the Press Dispatches.

ACTIVITY

Compare Source 1.39 with Source 1.37 on page 42. How similar are the attitudes of the cartoonists toward the activities of women who wanted to achieve temperance reform?

Think about the following questions:
- Are the sources similar in detail?
- Are the sources similar in message?
- What details of the sources show this?
- What differences are there between the sources?
- Do you think the cartoonists think the women's methods will work?

The Anti-Saloon League

The Anti-Saloon League (later changing its name to the Anti-Saloon League of America) was formed in 1895 as the combination of two leagues founded in Ohio and Washington in 1893. Its motto was "The Saloon Must Go" and it aimed to bring about nationwide prohibition. Like other temperance groups, the League produced huge volumes of propaganda to publicize the cause. A newspaper called the *American Issue* was launched in 1906. In 1909, its publishing company was moved to Westerville, Ohio where it printed 40 tons (equivalent to 89,600 pounds) of anti-alcohol literature a month.

The League had a two-pronged approach which was different from previous temperance organizations.
- It tapped into existing pro-temperance feeling in the churches to raise awareness and funds to support campaigning.
- It lobbied politicians to try to get as many "dry" candidates into office as possible. At first, the focus was on local elections, but the focus shifted in 1903 when the movement became a federation under national leadership. The League did not favor either party but would support Republicans or Democrats if they were "dry."

In 1905, the League had significant success in Ohio. It had been trying to gain support for the Brannock Bill which would allow local option legislation to be passed. The Governor of Ohio, Myron T Herrick, attempted to veto the bill. In the election later that year the League successfully backed a "dry" Democrat candidate, John M Pattison.

The League switched its focus to achieving national prohibition. The Webb-Kenyon Act, passed in 1913 despite President Taft's attempts at veto, forbade the import of alcoholic drinks into areas that had already banned their sale, and this made national legislation seem a more likely prospect. In December 1913, 4,000 members of the Anti-Saloon League marched down Pennsylvania Avenue, singing temperance songs with blood-curdling lyrics such as in Source 1.40, to present a petition to Congress.

> Why do you think the Anti-Saloon League used these lyrics?

SOURCE 1.40

A temperance hymn sung to the tune of *Onward Christian Soldiers*

Onward temperance soldiers;

Children starve and die;

Mothers, loving mothers, bruised and bleeding lie;

Double quick the order, onward then with speed;

Souls in sorrow call us, souls despairing plead;

Onward temperance soldiers, to the holy war;

Jesus Christ your captain trod the way before.

The marchers presented their petition to Congressman Richard Hobson from Alabama and Senator Morris Sheppard from Texas. The League increased its efforts in the elections of 1914, as described in Source 1.41 by Wayne Wheeler, director of the League since 1904.

> What can you learn from Source 1.41 about the methods used by the Anti-Saloon League?

SOURCE 1.41

Wayne Wheeler describes the activities of the Anti-Saloon League in 1914

Word went out from Washington and state headquarters to send letters, telegrams, and petitions to Congressmen and Senators in Washington. They rolled in by tens of thousands, burying Congress like an avalanche. We started off, early in 1914, with about 20,000 speakers, mostly volunteers all over the United States. They spoke at every opportunity to every sort of gathering. As the climax approached, we doubled our forces. Even that wasn't enough, so for a time the world's largest prohibition printing establishment ran three shifts a day, every hour of the 24, grinding out dry literature.

ACTIVITY

Work in a pair or a small group. Consider this question: "Groups which wanted to achieve prohibition employed the same tactics." How far do the sources in this section support this view?

Answer this question by doing the following:
- Make a list of the tactics that are discussed in Source 1.41.
- Make a list of tactics that are discussed in other sources in this section.
- Color code your lists to show support for the idea that groups used the same methods.
- Color code your lists (in a different color) to challenge the idea that they used the same methods.
- Write your answer to the question above.

Although the League gained "dry" seats in the 1914 elections, the Hobson-Sheppard Bill fell short of the two-thirds majority it needed in order to be passed. All was not lost and by 1915, a total of nineteen states had adopted statewide prohibition and others had adopted local option prohibition. This represented roughly two-thirds of the geographical area of the United States and included approximately half of the population.

Women's suffrage

Timeline

1848	Seneca Falls Convention
1869	National Woman Suffrage Association founded
	American Woman Suffrage Association founded
	Wyoming grants full voting rights to women
1890	National American Woman Suffrage Association (NAWSA)
1893	Colorado grants full voting rights to women
1896	Utah and Idaho give women the right to vote
1911	National Association Opposed to Woman Suffrage formed
1913	The Woman Suffrage Procession organized by Alice Paul
1917	Membership of the NAWSA reaches 2 million
	The United States enters the First World War
1919	Congress passes the Nineteenth Amendment granting women the right to vote

The fight to win equality for women and the right to vote pre-dated the Gilded Age. The law discriminated against women in many ways. Until the 1830s, women gave up their individual property to their husbands upon marriage. If the marriage ended in divorce, the husband was entitled to keep this property and was automatically given custody of any children, even if the divorce was his fault. The belief in **separate spheres** meant that women did not generally seek employment outside the home, did not have access to education, and were therefore not able to enter many professions.

However, by the mid-nineteenth century, things were beginning to change. Many women became involved in the movement to abolish enslavement for example, Lucy Stone, Lucretia Mott, Susan B Anthony, and Elizabeth Cady Stanton (pages 49–50). They were all key figures in the woman suffrage movement and had all been active abolitionists. Many male abolitionists were sympathetic to the idea of equality for women, but they were concerned that this should not be allowed to distract attention from abolition. Women were advised to keep quiet about female equality and prevented from speaking in anti-enslavement meetings. In response to this, the Seneca Falls Convention, the first women's rights convention in the US, met in 1848 and issued a declaration that demanded five things for women:

- equal educational opportunities
- entry into the professions
- equal property rights
- an end to double standards in morality
- the right to vote.

After the Civil War, women's role in society began to change. The war itself was partly responsible for these changes. As the men of the household went away to fight, many of the women who had not previously been encouraged to work outside the home found it necessary to do so to support their families. Thousands of women in the North and South joined volunteer brigades and signed up to work as nurses. Others joined fundraising campaigns and honed their organizational skills. During the Gilded Age, industrialization provided women with more opportunities to work outside the home. The number of working women increased fourfold between 1870 and 1910. Many worked in factories, as domestic servants, or became teachers. Inventions such as the telephone and typewriter then opened up further opportunities for women in office work. Better educational opportunities were also available and by 1900 almost 80 percent of colleges and universities were open to women. Women played a significant role in the Progressive Movement (as seen with the campaign for prohibition). There were many clubs for women which were affiliated with the General Federation of Women's Clubs, which was founded in 1890 to promote civic improvements through volunteer service.

> **KEY TERM**
>
> **Separate spheres** An ideology that prescribes gender roles (sometimes referred to as the "Cult of Domesticity" or "Cult of True Womanhood"). It was commonly believed that men were associated with the public sphere, belonging outside of the home in areas such as business and politics, whereas women belonged in the private sphere, doing domestic duties within the home.

> What point is the cartoonist making about women not being able to vote?

SOURCE 1.42

A cartoon published in the US in the early twentieth century. The man about to vote holds a ballot paper in one hand and in his pocket are bribes. The woman also holds a ballot paper and packets labeled "taxes"

Growth of women's suffrage associations in the Gilded Age and Progressive Era

In 1866, Susan B Anthony and Elizabeth Cady Stanton organized the Eleventh National Women's Rights Convention. The convention voted to become the American Equal Rights Association with the purpose of campaigning for the equal rights of all citizens.

However, tensions emerged and the Association began to split into two groups. The issue was whether African American men should be granted the vote before or at the same time as women. In 1869, the following two organizations were founded to further demand equal rights.

- The National Woman Suffrage Association (NWSA) was founded by Elizabeth Cady Stanton and Susan B Anthony. This group opposed the proposed Fifteenth Amendment (see page 63), insisting that voting rights be extended to all women and all African Americans at the same time. The NWSA focused on bringing about a constitutional amendment to give women the vote. The organization also dealt with a range of issues that impacted women, such as divorce reform and equal pay. Stanton proposed that the membership should be limited to women. Although this was not accepted, the majority of NWSA members and officers were women. To support the goal of change at federal level, they held conventions in Washington.
- The American Woman Suffrage Association (AWSA) headed by Lucy Stone and Julia Ward Howe was also formed in 1869. Although Lucy Stone argued that suffrage for women would bring more benefits to the nation than suffrage for African American men, she supported the Amendment and was prepared to accept that African American men

should gain the vote first, in line with the aims of the abolitionist movement. The AWSA worked to bring about change at state level and, unlike the NWSA, focused exclusively on gaining the right to vote. The AWSA's membership included women and men, and its first president was Henry Ward Beecher.

In 1887, a proposed amendment to the Constitution, which would have given women the vote, was rejected by Congress. This was one reason the two movements outlined above merged in 1890 to form the National American Woman Suffrage Association (NAWSA).

> How does Source 1.43 relate to the idea of separate spheres?

SOURCE 1.43

A poster published by the National American Woman Suffrage Association

TO THE MALE CITIZEN

If this is womanly—   *Why not this?*

Housekeeping is woman's work—no man denies that.

Government is public house-keeping—practically everybody agrees to that.

Isn't it foolish, then, to keep out of government the very people who have had most training for a large part of its functions?

Men have never regarded it as unwomanly for women to do the scrubbing and cleaning indoors—even in public places, like office buildings.

Why, then, should they think it unwomanly for women to keep the streets clean?

Be logical and insist that women should no longer shirk their duty as house-keepers. You need their help.

DEMAND VOTES FOR WOMEN!

NATIONAL AMERICAN WOMAN SUFFRAGE ASSOCIATION
505 FIFTH AVENUE   NEW YORK CITY

However, not all women, and certainly not all men, were in favor of giving women the right to vote. Some thought that involvement in politics would undermine family life. Others believed that women did not need the vote as they were represented by the men in their households. A few argued that women were not sufficiently intelligent to understand political issues. The National Association Opposed to Woman Suffrage, founded in 1911, distributed a pamphlet explaining why women shouldn't be allowed to vote.

> Compare Sources 1.43 and 1.44. What are the main differences between these two posters? Support your answer with details from the sources. Are there any similarities between the sources regarding the roles of women?

SOURCE 1.44

A pamphlet produced by the National Association Opposed to Women Suffrage

The pamphlet offered a few tips to housewives such as "Sour milk removes ink spots. There is, however, no method known by which mud-stained reputations may be cleansed after bitter political campaigns."

Leaders in the movement distributed postcards illustrating the gender role reversals they feared would happen if women became enfranchised (were given the vote). Images showed men holding shopping baskets, doing the washing and pushing baby strollers. Others suggested that if women began doing the work of men, they would become uglier, less feminine, and less desirable to men.

Role and influence of leaders

Each of the women discussed in this section campaigned tirelessly, from the 1840s onward, for the abolition of enslavement, the recognition of women's rights, and for women to be granted the right to vote. Their work included education, writing, public speaking, organising conventions and rallies, fund raising, and, most importantly, inspiring others to join the suffrage movement. Some were devastated when the Fourteenth Amendment extended the Constitution's protection to all citizens but defined these as "male," and the Fifteenth Amendment did not include voting rights for women. However, they did not lose sight of their goal and, despite setbacks and divisions within the suffrage movement, continued to fight not to be denied the vote based on their gender.

Although none of the women in this section lived long enough to see the Constitution finally amended in 1919, it is undoubtedly true that they all played a vital part in the achievement of the Nineteenth Amendment.

Lucretia Mott

Lucretia Mott was born in 1793 and became a keen advocate for abolition, women's rights, and female suffrage. In 1840, Mott met Elizabeth Cady Stanton in London, England. She became involved in the women's rights movement and helped organize the Seneca Falls Convention in 1848. In 1866, Mott was elected as the first president of the American Equal Rights Association (AERA), which she helped found with Stanton and Susan B Anthony. However, she disagreed with them over the Fifteenth Amendment and resigned her position when Stanton and Anthony allied themselves with George Francis Train, viewed by many as racist. She died in 1880.

Susan B Anthony

Susan B Anthony became one of the most visible leaders of the women's suffrage movement. She was born in February 1820 in Massachusetts. Her father was a Quaker, and she was inspired by their belief that everyone was equal under God. Anthony taught for many years and, having met William Lloyd Garrison and Frederick Douglass, who were friends with her father, became an activist in the abolition movement. In 1851, Anthony met Elizabeth Cady Stanton. The two women became good friends, with Anthony proving to be a good strategist and capable organizer. They worked together for over 50 years. In 1872, Anthony was arrested for voting. She was tried and fined $100. There was a public outcry and this was one of many ways she secured national attention for the suffrage movement. In 1888, she helped to merge the two largest suffrage associations into the NAWSA. She led the group until 1900 and died in 1906.

Elizabeth Cady Stanton

Elizabeth Stanton was born in 1815 and became a leading figure in the movements for abolition, women's rights, and female suffrage. She played a key role in organizing the Seneca Falls Convention in 1848, where she met Susan B Anthony. Stanton wrote a great deal, sometimes in collaboration with Anthony, and her book *The Declaration of Sentiments* argued strongly that there must be social and legal improvements to the status of women. Along with Anthony, she founded the NWSA in 1869, becoming president of the NAWSA in 1890. Although sometimes eclipsed by Anthony as leader of the female suffrage movement, Stanton was a radical and tireless campaigner. She died in 1902, after a long life of dedicated campaigning.

Lucy Stone

Lucy Stone was born in 1818. From an early age, she was irritated by the restrictions placed on women and girls. After graduating from college in 1847, she became a lecturer for the Massachusetts Anti-Slavery Society, which soon granted her permission to devote part of each week to speaking on her own for women's rights. She helped organize the first truly national women's rights convention in 1850. In 1855, Stone married Henry Blackwell but retained her own name in protest against the unequal laws applicable to married women. In 1866, she helped found the AERA and in 1869 the AWSA. Her daughter, Alice Blackwell, was influential in the formation of the NAWSA. Stone became chairperson of the executive board of the NAWSA and died in 1893.

Carrie Chapman Catt and her "Winning Plan" v. Alice Paul and the Congressional Union

Although the formation of the NAWSA brought together the two main factions of the women's suffrage movement, there were still different opinions on how to go about gaining the political support needed to get the vote. **Carrie Chapman Catt** fully supported the war effort, seeing full participation by women as evidence of patriotic citizenship which could help increase support for women's suffrage. **Alice Paul**, founder of the Congressional Union and later the National Woman's Party (NWP), was solely concerned with suffrage. Her priority was to gain the vote by any means necessary. Her tactics included picketing at the White House, which led to the imprisonment of 168 NWP members.

> ## KEY FIGURES
>
> **Carrie Chapman Catt** (1859–1947) Carrie Chapman Catt became a key figure in the suffrage movement and was a skillful political strategist. She was born in Wisconsin in 1859. After college, she worked as a law clerk, a schoolteacher, and principal. At the age of 24, she became one of the first women to be appointed superintendent of schools. In 1885, Carrie married Leo Chapman, an editor and publisher. After he died, she joined the Iowa Woman Suffrage Association, working for them as a writer and lecturer. In June 1890, Chapman married George Catt. She started to work for the NAWSA and spoke at its Washington DC convention in 1890. In 1892, Susan B Anthony asked her to address Congress on the proposed suffrage amendment. Catt served as president of the NAWSA from 1900–04 and 1915–20. She died in 1947.
>
> **Alice Paul** (1885–1977) Alice Paul's parents were keen supporters of gender equality and education for women and her mother took her to women's suffrage meetings. After leaving university in the US, Paul went to England to study social work. While she was there, she took part in the suffragette movement and learned their militant tactics, which included picketing and hunger strikes. When she returned to the US, she joined the NAWSA. Paul organized parades and pickets in support of suffrage. Her first event was held the day before President Wilson's inauguration when 8,000 women marched down Pennsylvania Avenue to protest for their right to vote. In 1913, Paul formed the Congressional Union for Woman Suffrage and the National Woman's Party (NWP) in 1916. In January 1917, Paul and over 1,000 "Silent Sentinels" began eighteen months of picketing at the White House. She was sentenced to several months in prison.

In 1902, Catt helped to organize the International Woman Suffrage Alliance (IWSA). She resigned from her NAWSA presidency to care for her ailing husband and, after his death, spent time abroad as IWSA president promoting suffrage rights worldwide. By 1916, Catt had returned to the US and, at a NAWSA convention in Atlantic City, New Jersey, unveiled her "Winning Plan" to campaign for suffrage on both the state and federal levels, and to settle for partial suffrage in the states resisting change.

When the United States entered the First World War in 1917, Catt curbed the NAWSA's petitions and instead threw its weight behind the war effort. She hoped this decision would earn favor by turning the NAWSA into a symbol of patriotism. On the other hand, Paul and the NWP did not pause their campaigning because the country was at war. They argued that the war highlighted President Wilson's hypocrisy. He claimed America was at war to make the world "safe for democracy," but half the US population did not have the right to vote. In 1917, the NWP held a constant, silent vigil in front of the White House, protesting throughout the day, regardless of the weather. The Silent Sentinels did not break the law but their picketing attracted criticism that they were disloyal and unpatriotic. The women were sometimes attacked, knocked to the ground, and had their banners shredded. The police refused to intervene in such attacks.

In October 1917, police announced they would arrest the protesters in front of the White House. Paul and members of the Silent Sentinels were arrested and sent either to the District of Columbia prison or the Occoquan Workhouse on charges of blocking traffic. They were treated badly and the conditions they were subject to were appalling. They were kept in freezing rooms in unsanitary conditions, were forced to wear filthy uniforms and shared cells with women suffering from contagious diseases. However, as each group was arrested, more women stepped up to take their place.

Reasons for changing attitudes of politicians to the suffrage campaign

Suffragists hoped to win support from Roosevelt when he became president. In 1883 he introduced a bill to the New York State Assembly supporting severe punishment for men who beat their wives. As president of the New York City Board of Police Commissioners he appointed women to senior positions in the police department. These seemed to be promising signs. However, as President, he opted not to take a firm stand. In a letter written in 1908 he commented that "Personally I believe in women's suffrage, but I am not an enthusiastic advocate of it because I do not regard it as a very important matter."

However, when Roosevelt returned to politics as leader of the Progressive Party in 1912, he needed to appeal to as many voters as possible. This included women in states where they had the right to vote. At the start of 1912 this included California, Colorado, Idaho, Utah, Washington, and Wyoming with Arizona, Kansas, and Oregon added later in the year. The Progressives were far more welcoming to women than either of the major parties. Their Convention in August 1912 was attended by many women, including delegates and potential candidates. Jane Addams was one of two people chosen to second Roosevelt's nomination as a presidential candidate. Later in August 1912, Roosevelt made the party's position official during a speech in Vermont with the comment, "We recognize that there should be equality of right, between men and women, and we are therefore for equal suffrage for men and women."

Although Roosevelt lost the presidential election, the support of the Progressive Party was important. The Progressive-led state legislature in Illinois granted women the right to vote in 1913, becoming the first state east of the Mississippi River to do so.

Wilson became president at the height of the suffrage movement in 1913. Some historians have argued that Wilson was too focused on other significant issues such as war in Europe to pay much attention to female suffrage and he appeared to ignore the campaign for most of his first term. However, in 1915, he voted to support women's suffrage in the New Jersey state election. He made his support public, saying that "I believe the time has come to extend the privilege and responsibility to the women of the State, but I shall vote only upon my private conviction. I believe that it should be settled by the State and not by the National Government." Although this suggested he was not opposed to women voting, it also implied that a Constitutional amendment was unlikely. However, events during 1917 appeared to change his mind.

When America entered the war in April 1917, former NAWSA president Anna Howard Shaw became a driving force in mobilizing American women for the war effort. She founded the Women's Committee of the Council of National Defense to deal with the millions of women who wanted to serve, and to match those who volunteered with specific roles. Women fulfilled many different roles and this undoubtedly helped to make the suffrage movement more widely respected.

- Tens of thousands of women joined The Women's Land Army to free men for military service.
- Eight million women volunteered for the American Red Cross. They took on varied tasks, which ranged from making surgical dressings to volunteering as nurse's aides in veterans' hospitals.
- Over 10,000 female drivers joined the Motor Service and acted as messengers.
- Evangeline Booth, daughter of William Booth who founded the Salvation Army, formed the National War Board for the welfare of soldiers. She was reportedly asked to "send over some lassies." The "lassies," armed with coffee and donuts, went to the front line where the American Expeditionary forces were serving.
- Librarians supplied books and magazines to American service members.
- Seven thousand women applied to be "Hello Girls." They were switchboard operators who worked for the US Army Signal Corps. Over 200 of them were sent overseas, some near the front lines.

Why was Source 1.45 published at this time?

KEY TERM

Enfranchisement Being given the right to vote in elections.

SOURCE 1.45

A poster issued by the National Woman Suffrage campaign (the term "enfranchisement" means being given the right to vote in elections)

> **AS A WAR MEASURE**
>
> **The Country is Asking of Women Service** AS
> FARMERS
> MECHANICS
> NURSES and DOCTORS
> MUNITION WORKERS
> MINE WORKERS
> YEOMEN
> GAS MAKERS
> BELL BOYS
> MESSENGERS
> CONDUCTORS
> MOTORMEN
> ARMY COOKS
> TELEGRAPHERS
> AMBULANCE DRIVERS
> ADVISORS TO THE COUNCIL OF NATIONAL DEFENSE
> AND
> **The Country is Getting it!**
>
> **Women Are Asking of The Country**
>
> **ENFRANCHISEMENT**
>
> **Are The Women Going To Get It?**

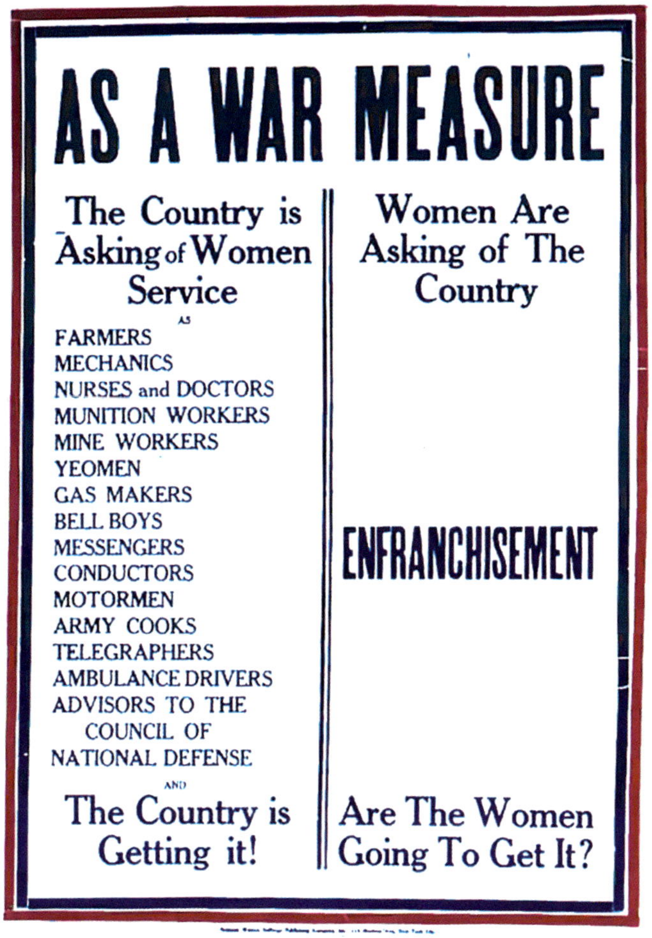

President Wilson eventually came to recognize the contributions of these women. He was horrified by the idea of women going on hunger strike to achieve the vote and finally joined his leading suffragist daughter, Jessie Woodrow Wilson Sayre, in publically supporting the campaign for female suffrage. At the end of September 1918, Wilson addressed Congress, "We have made partners of the women in this war. Shall we admit them only to a partnership of suffering and sacrifice and toil and not to a partnership of privilege?"

SUMMARY DIAGRAM

Aims and policies of the Progressive Movement

Eliminate political corruption	Regulate business practices	Improve society	Improve equality
• Limit power of party machines • Make government more efficient • The role of the muckrakers	• Legislation to curb trusts • Legislation to protect consumers • Regulating child labor	• Temperance and Prohibition • Pressure for change from WCTU and key leaders • Anti-Saloon League	• Votes for Women • Pressure for change from suffrage associations and their key leaders • Reasons for changing political attitudes

Figure 1.4 The main aims and policies of the Progressive Movement

1.3 How successful was the Progressive Movement up to 1920?

Achievements and limitations of the progressive presidents

There were three US presidents between 1901 and 1921. Roosevelt and Taft were Republicans and Wilson was a Democrat. All three were progressive in outlook and between them, they attempted to regulate business, improve social justice, and bring about political reform. How far they succeeded in doing this was, and still is, a matter for debate.

Theodore Roosevelt's "Square Deal"

Theodore Roosevelt served as president for two terms from 1901 to 1909, taking office upon the assassination of President McKinley.

> **KEY FIGURE**
>
> **Theodore Roosevelt** (1858–1919) Theodore "Teddy" Roosevelt was born into a wealthy New York family in 1858. He graduated from Harvard in 1880 and started at Columbia Law School but dropped out to run for office. He was elected to the New York Assembly as a Republican in 1881. Between 1889 and 1896, he served on the US Civil Service Commission and became head of the New York Police Board. After a stint as Assistant Secretary of the Navy, he took part in the Spanish-American War, leading the Rough Riders and gaining a reputation as a national hero. He was elected Governor of New York in 1890. His progressive tendencies were already clear and, as governor, he supported civil service reform and a new tax on corporations. According to some accounts, the old guard of the Republican Party found his energy and determination to bring about change so irritating that they proposed him for the vice presidency, a position they hoped would sideline him. However, the assassination of President McKinley catapulted Roosevelt into the spotlight he loved so much. At 42, he was the youngest person to become president. He had a growing family and was a charismatic and engaging character who challenged some of the traditional ideas about the role and power of an American president. In 1904, he was elected in his own right but decided not to stand for a third term in 1908. In 1912, he stood as presidential candidate for the Progressive Party.

Roosevelt's terms in office demonstrate his commitment to progressive ideas.
- He understood the need to regulate trusts.
- He was concerned about social inequality and favored reform.
- He believed in transparent, accountable government.
- He believed the president should have the power to act in the national interest.

Roosevelt pursued an active and energetic foreign policy which is discussed in detail in Chapter 2. However, he was equally active in domestic policy and his domestic program, known as the "Square Deal," consisted of the "Three Cs": consumer protection, control of corporations, and conservation.

In his first term of office, Roosevelt was aware that he had not become president by design. He was cautious at first and claimed that he would respect McKinley's aims. He also wanted to avoid ruffling the feathers of senior Republicans, some of whom were definitely more conservative than progressive. However, he initiated several important interventions.

In 1902, in a move that shocked Wall Street, Roosevelt invoked the Sherman Antitrust Act (page 36) against the Northern Securities Company. This was a giant railroad company that involved the banker JP Morgan, along with railroad magnates James Hill and EH Harriman. Between them, they controlled most of the railroad shipping across the United States. As far as Roosevelt was concerned, the company was an "illegal combination acting in restraint of trade." Morgan was shocked to receive a telephone call telling him that the Attorney General was filing a lawsuit against Northern Securities. He hurried over to the White House. He was even more shocked when Roosevelt made it clear that he would not accept Morgan's proposal to fix the situation. Roosevelt told him plainly that the courts would resolve the issue. In 1904, the Supreme Court ruled that Northern Securities was illegal.

As seen earlier (page 23), in 1902 Roosevelt intervened in the Pennsylvania Coal Strike on behalf of the miners. His intervention in the strike was controversial and the mine operators accused him of assuming powers that were not sanctioned by the Constitution. His reflections on the strike illustrate his attitude toward his position as president, a feature of his tenure that marked him out from others.

SOURCE 1.46

From President Roosevelt's autobiography, published in 1913

The most important factor ... was my insistence upon the theory that the executive power was limited only by specific restrictions and prohibitions appearing in the Constitution or imposed by the Congress under its constitutional powers. My view was that every executive officer was a steward of the people bound actively and affirmatively to do all he could for the people ... I declined to adopt the view that what was imperatively necessary for the nation could not be done by the president unless he could find some specific authorization to do it. My belief was that it was not only his right but his duty to do anything that the needs of the nation demanded unless such action was forbidden by the Constitution or by the laws. Under this interpretation of executive power I did and caused to be done many things not previously done by the president and the heads of the departments. I did not usurp power, but I did greatly broaden the use of executive power. In other words, I acted for the public welfare, I acted for the common well-being of all our people, whenever and in whatever manner was necessary, unless prevented by direct constitutional or legislative prohibition. I did not care a rap for the mere form and show of power.

> What can you learn from Source 1.46 about Roosevelt's attitude to presidential power?
>
> Think about this in the context of the 1902 Coal Strike. How do the inferences you have made from the source help to explain Roosevelt's actions in trying to bring the strike to an end?

In 1903, the Bureau of Corporations was established. This did not gain the extensive power that Roosevelt had hoped for, as it was only able to investigate rather than enforce.

Although Roosevelt was known as a trust buster, his aim was to regulate big business rather than destroy it. The concentration of industry in ever fewer hands represented not just a threat to fair markets, but also to democracy, as wealthy industrialists consolidated power in their own hands. The Justice Department initiated 42 additional antitrust cases during his presidency. However, his actions were not one-sided. Although Roosevelt had used the Sherman Act in favor of the miners in 1902, he also sent in federal troops to break up labor disputes in Arizona, Colorado, and Nevada.

During Roosevelt's second term, he continued to take steps to regulate business. He saw this as the right way to provide the "Square Deal" he had promised to the people during his election campaign. He supported laws like the 1906 Hepburn Act, which regulated the railroads and set out the maximum rates they could charge. Further legislation against large corporations was passed in 1906, in the shape of the Pure Food and Drug Act and the Meat Inspection Act (page 37).

Another lasting impact of Roosevelt's presidency was the conservation of the nation's natural resources. He encouraged Congress to create several new national parks, set aside sixteen national monuments, and established more than 50 wildlife reserves and refuges on 230 million acres of public land. The new Bureau of Fisheries and the National Forest Service were established to help manage resources and protect the land from businesses that wanted to exploit it for mining or oil. In 1908, Roosevelt honored a promise he had made in 1904 not to stand for a third term and withdrew from politics.

- What is the message of Source 1.47?
- Using your knowledge of Roosevelt's policies, do you think this is an accurate representation of Roosevelt? Explain your answer.

SOURCE 1.47

A cartoon of President Roosevelt, published in 1904. (Mollycoddling means to treat someone in an overprotective or indulgent manner)

NO MOLLY-CODDLING HERE

Taft's economic policies

KEY FIGURE

William Howard Taft (1857–1930) William Howard Taft served as US president from 1909 to 1913 and became the tenth chief justice. He served in that position from 1921 until just before his death and is the only person to have held both offices. Taft was born in Ohio and, after Yale, became a lawyer and was appointed as a judge at an early age. In 1901, President McKinley appointed Taft as civilian governor of the Philippines and, in 1904, Roosevelt made him Secretary of War (a position which his father had also occupied). Roosevelt was impressed with Taft's administrative ability and proposed him as the Republican presidential candidate in 1908. He had never run for office before but easily defeated William J Bryan in the 1908 election. However, Taft's presidency led to divisions within his party and he lacked the political skill and charisma of Roosevelt. He came third in the 1921 election.

What is the message of Source 1.48?

SOURCE 1.48

The front cover of *Puck* magazine in 1906, showing Roosevelt introducing Taft as his "crown prince"

In some ways, Taft appeared to be governing in the same way that Roosevelt had.
- During his presidency 90 antitrust prosecutions were launched and in two cases in 1911, against Standard Oil and American Tobacco, the Supreme Court ordered that the corporations should be broken down into smaller companies.
- In line with an interest that Roosevelt had professed, an eight-hour workday was introduced for those working on federal government contracts.
- The Mann-Elkins Act of 1910 extended the scope of the Hepburn Act and strengthened the Interstate Commerce Commission (ICC) by defining the extent of the government's power more clearly. The Hepburn Act gave the ICC the power to change a railroad rate to one it considered "just and reasonable." Under the Mann-Elkins Act, railroad companies had to demonstrate that a set rate was reasonable. With these new powers, the ICC gained almost complete control over rail rates, and therefore much of rail competition. This led to a lowering of rates, which was in line with demands by progressive groups such as the Populists.
- The establishment of national forests in the East began after President Taft signed the Weeks Law in 1911.

However, not all of Taft's legislation was well received and he struggled to win over unconvinced Republicans.

KEY TERM

Tariffs Taxes imposed by the federal government on specific imported goods.

- The Payne-Aldrich Act reduced **tariffs** but was considered by many Progressives to have not gone far enough. The Act lowered the general tariff rate from 46 to 41 percent and increased rates on items such as animal skins and coal. Tariffs were lowered on 650 items, raised on 220 and over 1,000 remained untouched. Taft found himself under attack from Progressives for doing too little. He was disappointed but thought the Act was an improvement and signed it into law. However, Taft's comment that this was "the best tariff bill the Republican Party ever passed" showed a lack of tact and angered his Republican colleagues and the Democrats.

Roosevelt, although supposedly having retired from politics, became frustrated by Taft's slow pace of reform. The Ballinger-Pinchot controversy brought things to a head. Taft disappointed conservationists by appointing Richard Ballinger, a lawyer and former mayor of Seattle, to head the Department of the Interior in 1909. Ballinger believed that Roosevelt had no right to transfer large tracts of public land to reserve status. Ballinger opened Alaskan coal fields in a reserve area to private mining interests. When Gifford Pinchot, the Chief Forester and longtime friend of Roosevelt, became involved, public concerns were raised. Congress conducted investigations and Ballinger was exonerated. Pinchot, who had openly criticized Ballinger and Taft, was dismissed. The dispute highlighted the deep divisions in the Republican Party, and its impact on the friendship between Taft and Roosevelt can be seen in the cartoon below.

> Why was Source 1.49 published at this time?

SOURCE 1.49

A cartoon published in a British magazine in 1912. It was entitled "Auld Lang Syne." Uncle Sam observes the "scrap" between Taft and Roosevelt and says, "Well, I guess old friends are the best"

ACTIVITY

This is focused on comparing sources and explaining reasons for the differences between them.
- Compare Source 1.49 with Source 1.48.
- What differences can you see between these two sources? Support your answer using details from the source.
- Use the information in this chapter about what happened between 1909 and 1912 to explain why these two sources are different.

The outcome was that Roosevelt decided to stand as presidential candidate in 1912 for the recently formed Progressive Party, also known as the Bull Moose Party due to Roosevelt's frequent boasts that he was as "strong as a bull moose." He campaigned under the banner of a "New Nationalism" which stood for:
- a strong federal government
- an activist presidency

- balance between public and corporate interests
- support for progressive reform causes, which included women's suffrage, abolition, and greater corporate regulation.

In a four-cornered fight between Taft (Republican), Roosevelt (Progressive), Gompers (Socialist), and Wilson (Democrat), Roosevelt and Taft succeeded only in splitting the Republican vote. Democrat Woodrow Wilson swept to victory.

> **KEY FIGURE**
>
> **Woodrow Wilson** (1856–1924) Wilson spent his early career as an academic, teaching history and political science. In 1902, he became the president of Princeton University. In 1910, he was elected as Governor of New Jersey and in 1912 won the presidential election. Between 1913 and 1916 he concentrated on a wide-ranging program of economic and social reforms. His leadership style was quite different from that of Roosevelt. He was a well-respected academic, but quite aloof and reserved, and kept his colleagues at arm's length. He was narrowly reelected for a second term in 1916. His policy of keeping the US out of the war in Europe had gained support during the election campaign, but in April 1917, he led America into the First World War (see page 97).

Wilson's "New Freedom"

Wilson's program when he started his campaign for office was quite vague, but he quickly established his "New Freedom" agenda, which featured the following policies:
- regulating the banks and big businesses
- lowering tariff rates
- aiding farmers through rural credits
- increasing competition.

At this stage, he was most interested in economic reform. As far as Wilson was concerned, social and welfare reform was the priority of state legislatures rather than the federal government.

In April 1913, Wilson called a special meeting of Congress where he outlined his plans to address the tariff question. This resulted in the Revenue Act of 1913, also known as the Underwood-Simmons Tariff Act. This lowered tariff rates across the board to around 26 percent, fifteen percent lower than they had been under Taft, and abolished tariffs on more than 100 imports. These were the first significant cuts in tariffs since the Civil War. To offset the potential loss of revenue, and based on the recent ratification of the Sixteenth Amendment (page 60), a federal income tax was reintroduced. Married couples who earned $4,000 or more, and single people who earned $3,000 or more, were required to pay a one percent graduated income tax.

The Federal Reserve Act, passed later in 1913, regulated the banking industry and established a federal banking system. It was designed to remove power over interest rates from the hands of private bankers. Twelve Federal Reserve Banks were set up and government funds were deposited in those banks. They were privately owned but regulated by a presidentially appointed Federal Reserve Board. The Board regulated the interest rate at which reserve banks loaned money to other banks around the country. This meant that if the economy went into **recession**, interest rates could be lowered to encourage more borrowing. This put more currency in circulation for people to spend or invest. Interest rates could also be increased; for example, to reduce inflation.

> **KEY TERM**
>
> **Recession** Recession in relation to the economy refers to a period of less economic activity, often in line with high unemployment rates, resulting in low production. A recession is longer than a period of a few months. When the economy is in recession for too long, it can become economic depression.

Wilson completed his New Freedom agenda by passing the Clayton Antitrust Act (page 37) and inaugurating the Federal Trade Commission (FTC). The Clayton Act strengthened the power of the original Sherman Antitrust Act (page 36). The FTC helped to enforce the Clayton Act. By 1914, Wilson was pleased with his progress and had achieved what he set out to do in terms of economic regulation. However, many Progressives were unhappy that little had been done to address social issues, and criticized Wilson for not doing enough to restrict big business or help farmers. Their complaints grew as there was a serious recession in 1913–14. In the mid-term elections in 1914, the Democrat majority in the House fell by two-thirds. This reflected public dissatisfaction with Wilson's policies.

> Do you think the cartoonist supported Wilson's economic policy? Explain your answer using details from the cartoon.

SOURCE 1.50

A cartoon showing Wilson and his legislation, published in June 1914

By 1916, Wilson had achieved his limited New Freedom agenda and his focus had already shifted to foreign affairs after war broke out in Europe in 1914 (see page 94). However, the 1916 election was approaching fast, and it began to look as though Wilson did not have the support of the majority of the population. This situation led many contemporaries, and historians since, to question Wilson's motives for introducing further reforms in 1916. Was he reforming out of a genuine conviction that social reform was needed, or was his main interest in maintaining his position as president?

The reforms included:
- the Federal Farm Act, which provided oversight of low-interest loans to farmers
- the Keating-Owen Act (page 39), which restricted child labor
- the Adamson Act, which brought in an eight-hour workday for railroad workers
- the Kern-McGillicuddy Workmen's Compensation Act of 1916, which enabled workers to collect compensation for injuries sustained in the workplace. The 1911 Triangle Shirtwaist Fire in New York City encouraged a number of states to introduce workers' compensation laws. Some state laws, such as those passed in New Jersey in 1911, were comprehensive and effective. Other states had much weaker laws and the Act of 1916 brought a level of standardization.

Reasons for constitutional reforms and their impacts

When the US Constitution was written, the Founding Fathers accepted that it may need to be modified in the future. However, they made the process of amending the Constitution complicated, so that it could not be changed without clear support in the House of Representatives and the Senate, or without the support of most of the states. Article V of the Constitution sets out two methods of proposing and ratifying amendments to the Constitution. The usual method has been for two-thirds of each house of Congress to propose the amendment and the state legislatures in three-quarters of the states to ratify. The exception to this was the Twenty-First Amendment, which repealed prohibition. Ratification can be a lengthy process and Congress sets a time limit. Four amendments were passed between 1913 and 1920, and these are regarded as progressive amendments.

Sixteenth Amendment

- **Date:** proposed July 2, 1909, ratified February 3, 1913.
- **What changed?** Congress was allowed to levy income tax on individuals and corporations.
- **Reasons for the Amendment:** Government revenue was partly dependent on indirect taxes such as tariffs on imported goods. As the role of the federal government expanded, it needed more revenue to fund its programs. To achieve this, business leaders suggested raising tariffs. However, as seen on page 30, the Populists wanted to introduce a graduated form of income tax. Progressives believed that tariffs were unfair to consumers, as they raised prices and this disproportionately impacted poorer Americans. Income taxes had been levied before, such as during the Civil War. In 1894, Congress introduced a two percent tax on incomes over $4,000 which was struck down by the Supreme Court. In 1909, Progressives in Congress attached a provision for an income tax to a tariff bill. In response, conservative members of Congress proposed a constitutional amendment. It is quite likely that they believed that the states would not ratify such an amendment. Support for income taxes was much stronger in the Southern and Western states, where the cost of living was rising steeply and made worse by tariffs. However, it was less popular in the Northeast. Despite that, by 1913 the required three-quarters of states had ratified the Act.
- **Impact:** In 1913, less than one percent of the population paid income taxes at the rate of one percent of net income. However, this Amendment did not introduce a permanent set level of income tax. Instead, it allowed Congress to create further legislation. Progressives were pleased by the introduction of graduated income tax, which meant people with higher incomes had to pay a larger percentage of their earnings than those with lower incomes.

Seventeenth Amendment

- **Date:** proposed in June 1912, ratified on April 8, 1913.
- **What changed?** Senators were to be elected directly. The Seventeenth Amendment restates the first paragraph of Article I, Section 3 of the Constitution, and provides for the election of senators by replacing the phrase "chosen by the Legislature thereof" with "elected by the people thereof." In addition, it allows the governor or executive authority of each state, if authorized by that state's legislature, to appoint a senator in the event of a vacancy, until an election occurs.
- **Reasons for the Amendment:** The Constitution required that senators be elected by state legislatures. However, these often had close ties with large corporations. Progressives argued that senators should be chosen to respond to the people, not the power of big business. After the Civil War, disputes between state legislators over elections to the Senate meant some Senate seats were vacant for prolonged periods of time. For example, Delaware had no representation in the US Senate for two years. Reformers called for a change to the system of elections. Publisher William Randolph Hearst, an advocate of direct elections, hired novelist and muckraker David Graham Phillips to write about the issue. His work, *The Treason of the Senate*, was largely fiction and painted a lurid, and undoubtedly exaggerated, picture of senators in the pay of big business. However, it was influential in attracting public support for reform.
- **Impact:** In July 1913, Augustus Bacon of Georgia became the first senator directly elected under the terms of the Seventeenth Amendment. In 1914, all senatorial elections were held by popular vote.

Eighteenth Amendment

- **Date:** proposed on December 18, 1917, ratified on January 16, 1919, came into effect on January 17, 1920.
- **What changed?** According to the text of the Amendment, "the manufacture, sale, or transportation of intoxicating liquors within, the importation thereof into, or the exportation thereof from the United States … is hereby prohibited." In contrast to

earlier amendments to the Constitution, there was a one-year time delay before it came into operation. Congress also passed the National Prohibition Act, better known as the Volstead Act, in October 1919. The Act defined terms such as "intoxicating liquor." It also gave responsibility for the enforcement of prohibition to the US Treasury Department.

- **Reasons for the Amendment:** See page 42 for a detailed discussion of the Temperance Movement. By the time the Amendment was passed, many states had passed prohibition laws. The momentum for national prohibition was partly provided by the war. It was argued that using wheat to make liquor was wrong at a time of national crisis. It was thought that, as many brewers were German, the enemy in the war, it was unpatriotic to drink.
- **Impact:** The Amendment was in effect for 13 years and was repealed in 1933 by ratification of the Twenty-First Amendment. This was the only time in American history that a constitutional amendment was repealed in its entirety. There is a detailed section in Chapter 2, which considers the impact of prohibition in the 1920s (pages 114–118).

Nineteenth Amendment

- **Date:** passed on June 4, 1919, ratified on August 18, 1920.
- **What changed?** Women were granted the right to vote.
- **Reasons for the Amendment:** See page 48 for a detailed discussion of the women's suffrage movement. The Amendment was first introduced in Congress in 1878. By 1912, nine Western states had adopted female suffrage. By 1916, most suffrage organizations agreed that federal action in the form of a constitutional amendment was needed. New York adopted female suffrage in 1917 and, partly in response to women's contribution to the war effort, President Wilson changed his position to support an amendment in 1918.
- **Impact:** Women (and men) continued to campaign on a range of social, civil rights, and political issues. Organizations turned their attention to educating women voters. These included the League of Women Voters and the National Association of Colored Women. The NWP (page 53) continued to campaign for full legal equality for women. Issues relating to women were accorded higher status. In 1921, Congress passed the Sheppard-Towner Act, introducing federal support to reduce levels of maternal and infant mortality, especially in more rural areas. In 1922, both men and women from the International Uplift League campaigned for legislation to be passed to prevent lynching (page 69). They were narrowly defeated. However, many women of African American descent and other minority groups were unable to vote because of discriminatory state voting laws. Their struggle to be able to exercise their rights is covered in Chapters 3 and 4.

> What is the message of Source 1.51?

SOURCE 1.51

"Senatorial Deadlocks," a cartoon by Clifford Berryman, February 1911. The bear is a symbol used to represent Roosevelt and he appears in many of Berryman's cartoons

Limits of the Progressive Movement and their impacts

The degree to which the Progressives addressed the problems of the age (including urban conditions)

In some areas, the Progressives had a positive impact.

They raised awareness of:
- social injustice
- poverty
- problems of urbanization.

They highlighted the importance of health and safety for industrial workers by:
- showing there were practical ways to help the poor
- working at local, state, and national levels
- encouraging businessmen to take better care of their consumers.

They encouraged politicians to be accountable to the electorate by:
- establishing a principle of public intervention to improve society
- showing that decisions in business and government should be ethical and not just for the benefit of the few.

Despite some progress, the Progressives did not solve all the problems of the age. Some of the most notable shortcomings were that:
- big business continued to influence government
- the courts still had control over social welfare issues
- agencies that were established to provide social welfare services often lacked resources.

However, the greatest failure of the Progressive Movement was its passive approach to the legal and violent disenfranchisement of African Americans. Few progressive reformers joined African American leaders in their fight against lynching (page 69). Some even endorsed the introduction of literacy tests and other methods that were used to prevent African Americans from voting.

Urban conditions

Improving urban conditions was closely linked to municipal (local) reform and the way that cities had traditionally been run. The usual form of government was to have a mayor, city council, and elected officials. The main issue with this system, as the Progressives saw it, was that officials were generally chosen for their party link rather than their ability. Different forms of government were tried and these included the

Commission plan: created in the aftermath of the devastation of Galveston by a hurricane in 1900. Over 6,000 inhabitants were killed and much of the city destroyed. A group of wealthy businessmen suggested a commission should be elected to govern the city during the rebuilding period. Each elected commissioner was placed in charge of one aspect of district affairs. The success of the plan inspired another 400 cities to adopt this form of government.

City government plan: started in Virginia in 1908. Rather than giving control of the city to a member of a political party, an expert such as an engineer or business manager was given control on the expectation that they would remain neutral in city politics.

These changes made it easier to make improvements in infrastructure, building, and sanitation. Some Progressives questioned the Galveston plan as giving too much power to business interests rather than the working class. However, the plan was endorsed by Presidents Roosevelt and Wilson and supported by Progressive newspapers.

The role of individual mayors was also important in bringing about changes in urban conditions in the progressive era. Two of the leading examples were businessmen who developed an interest in local politics.

Tom Johnson of Cleveland: fought for district ownership of public utilities such as water and against the streetcar companies to lower fares. He oversaw the building of public bathhouses and expanded the city's park system. Under his leadership, the Group Plan Commission was formed to plan a new design for public buildings and spaces.

Samuel Jones of Toledo: a Welsh-born immigrant who rose from poverty to become successful in the oil business where he gained a reputation as a progressive employer. Once Mayor of Toledo, he opened free kindergartens, developed a park system, built public baths, introduced an eight-hour day for city workers, and reformed the city government.

Progressive state governors also played a significant reforming role. Possibly the most prominent was Robert La Follette who was the state governor of Wisconsin from 1900 to 1906. During his time in office he introduced a wide range of reforms from regulating the railroads to limiting hours of work for women and children.

Promoted the "Wisconsin Idea." This meant state government collaborated with experts from the University of Wisconsin who provided evidence on economic and social problems and advice about methods to address them.

Impact of Social Darwinism

In 1859, Charles Darwin published his work *The Origin of Species*. It is considered to be the beginning of evolutionary biology and Darwin developed a theory about the ways that animals adapt over millennia. The philosopher Herbert Spencer applied this theory to society. He argued that in order to make progress, humans, like animals, needed the survival of the fittest. Spencer claimed that government intervention to support weaker members of society went against the laws of nature, as it interfered with survival.

White supremacists used these arguments to justify their poor treatment of, and racist attitudes toward, African Americans. Differences in skin tone and racial origin were interpreted to signify that some groups were less intelligent, lazier, and all-round inferior to white Americans. Attitudes like this meant it was easier to bring about segregation.

However, Social Darwinist ideas were not only applied to African Americans. In 1901, Theodore Roosevelt spoke out on how he thought the US government should treat Native Americans.

> **KEY TERM**
>
> **White supremacists** The belief that white people are superior to those of other races and should dominate them, and the promotion of policies and systems that favor white people.

> What Social Darwinist ideas can you identify in Source 1.52? Why do you think this speech was delivered at this time?

SOURCE 1.52

From Roosevelt's First Annual Message, December 1901

In my judgment, the time has arrived when we should definitely make up our minds to recognize the Indian as an individual and not as a member of a tribe. The General Allotment Act is a mighty pulverizing engine to break up the tribal mass. Under its provisions some 60,000 Indians have already become citizens of the United States. We should now break up the tribal funds, doing for them what allotment does for the tribal lands; that is, they should be divided into individual holdings. A stop should be put upon the indiscriminate permission to Indians to lease their allotments. The effort should be steadily to make the Indian work like any other man on his own ground.

In the schools the education should be elementary and largely industrial. The need of higher education among the Indians is very, very limited. The ration system, which is merely the corral and the reservation system, is highly detrimental to the Indians. It promotes beggary, perpetuates pauperism, and stifles industry. It is an effectual barrier to progress. The Indian should be treated as an individual, like the white man.

Continuing challenges to political equality

The Fifteenth Amendment was passed in 1870 and stated that no man should be denied the right to vote based on color, race, or for having previously been enslaved. However, after the end of Reconstruction in 1877, the federal government left it to the states in the South to uphold the amendments that had granted citizenship rights to formerly enslaved people. Many states did not interpret the amendments to the Constitution in the way they were intended and this made life for African Americans in the South very difficult. The main problem was that Reconstruction had not challenged or changed the Southern belief in white supremacy. Many Southern whites were unwilling to accept that those who were previously enslaved should have political and civil rights. Southern states started to find ways of preventing African Americans from exercising their rights and having access to educational and economic opportunities.

In the 1880s, many African Americans voted and some held political office. In the presidential election of 1880, 70 percent of those African Americans who were eligible to vote in South Carolina did so. However, in the presidential election of 1896, only eleven percent voted. This pattern was repeated across the former Confederate states. States employed a number of methods to prevent African Americans from voting.

- More states introduced the requirement to register to vote. Some included an "understanding clause" where a voter had to explain part of the Constitution to the satisfaction of the Registrar. The clauses chosen often varied in difficulty. The difficulty of a clause a person was asked to explain was often dependent on color. The states were keen not to disenfranchise poorly educated white voters.
- In Georgia in 1877, a tax of $2 was introduced as part of the registration process. This was beyond the means of many African American voters.
- A literacy test was introduced in Mississippi in 1890. At this time, schools attended by African Americans were often poorly resourced, leading to lower literacy rates. Therefore, this test had a disproportionately negative impact on African Americans.
- In 1898, Louisiana developed the notorious "grandfather clause," which was later adopted by several other states across the South. The clause worked on the basis that if your grandfather was eligible to vote before January 1, 1867 (so before African Americans were entitled to vote) then you, your father and brothers would not have to take a literacy test as part of the registration process. Again, this development favored illiterate white voters at the expense of African Americans.
- Violence and intimidation, although not part of official policy, were also used to deter African Americans from voting. This is discussed in more detail in the following section.

Being barred from voting had several negative impacts. It prevented African Americans in the South from being involved in politics and made it difficult for them to have representation at local, state, or national levels. It also meant that there was little support for educational or social welfare initiatives that would benefit the African American community, and it reinforced ideas about white supremacy. Added to this, African Americans in the South faced tough economic circumstances which meant progress out of poverty was difficult to achieve.

Race relations in the Progressive Era

The impacts of segregation

In 1892, Homer A Plessy, a free person of color from a French-Creole family, brought a test case against an 1890 Louisiana state law that required railroad companies to provide separate facilities for white and "colored" (the term was used at the time in segregated facilities) customers. He boarded a train with a valid ticket and sat in the "whites only" carriage. When challenged, he refused to leave the train and was arrested. When the case came to court, Plessy argued that his rights under the Fourteenth Amendment had been violated. A local judge (Ferguson) ruled against him. Four years later, the case went to the Supreme Court, which did the same. They argued that separation was not a mark of inferiority and that, in any case, the Fourteenth Amendment applied to state legislatures and the federal government, and not to organizations or individuals. The Court also pointed out that "separate but equal" facilities were within the law. One judge disagreed, however, and voted against the decision. He was John Harlan, interesting because of his background as a Southerner and former slaveowner.

"Harlan did not support the idea of separate but equal." Find three pieces of evidence in Source 1.53 that support this statement. Are you surprised that Harlan held these views? Explain your answer.

SOURCE 1.53

From a speech made by John Harlan in 1896. It came to be known as "Harlan's Great Dissent"

In the eye of the law, there is in this country no superior, dominant, ruling class of citizens. There is no caste here. Our constitution is colorblind, and neither knows nor tolerates classes among citizens. In respect of civil rights, all citizens are equal before the law. The humblest is the peer of the most powerful. The arbitrary separation of citizens on the basis of race, while they are on a public highway, is a badge of servitude wholly inconsistent with the civil freedom and the equality before the law established by the Constitution. It cannot be justified upon any legal grounds.

What can more certainly arouse race hate, what can more certainly create and perpetuate a feeling of distrust between these races, than state enactments, which, in fact, proceed on the ground that colored citizens are so inferior and degraded that they cannot be allowed to sit in public coaches occupied by white citizens? That, as all will admit, is the real meaning of such legislation.

The judgment in *Plessy v. Ferguson* clearly flew in the face of the 1875 Civil Rights Act which guaranteed "full and equal enjoyment of public accommodations." It became obvious that "equal" meant anything but that. During the 1880s and 1890s, a series of local laws and state statutes were issued to further restrict the freedoms of African Americans in the South. These became known as the "Jim Crow Laws." In 1899, education was segregated. African American schools were underfunded, students were not able to access the best teaching or achieve their potential, and ideas about inferiority were reinforced.

Race riots and lynching of African Americans, Hispanic Americans, Asian Americans and Native Americans

In 1900, there were two major race riots. One took place in New York City's Tenderloin District, and the other in the city of New Orleans—at least 106 Black people were lynched. In 1906, there were race riots in Atlanta and in 1908 in Springfield. Race riots often followed a similar pattern.

The New York City riot began with a misunderstanding between Arthur Harris, an African American newcomer to New York, and a white undercover policeman, Robert Thorpe. Harris thought that Thorpe was making inappropriate advances toward his female friend. When Harris approached Thorpe, an argument broke out. Thorpe hit Harris with his truncheon. Harris stabbed Thorpe, who died of his wounds several days later. On the day of Thorpe's funeral, race rioting broke out in the Hell's Kitchen district. For four days, around 10,000 young whites, including members of the city police force, attacked every African American they encountered. Many were injured and one African American man was killed.

The 1906 riot in Atlanta broke out for a number of reasons. The city had seen a growth in tension between whites and African Americans due to:
- population growth especially among African Americans
- pressure on the city's public services
- competition for work
- fear of the growth of an educated African American elite
- an increase in fears of **miscegenation**, partly caused by the press which peddled images of African Americans as degenerate.

The white elite tried to control the African American population in the usual ways:
- They imposed severe restrictions on public conduct.
- They increased segregation through the "Jim Crow Laws" in transportation and housing.

Things were made worse by the campaigns conducted by candidates who wanted to stand for Governor of New York. The candidates competed to provoke white anger against African Americans. Both political parties secretly supported a campaign in the newspapers that made unsubstantiated claims of African American men attacking white women. On September 22, 1906, one newspaper published four of these stories. Almost immediately, a mob formed which raided African American businesses, killed several barbers, stopped streetcars and beat and killed African American men and women. Eventually, the state militia was summoned to calm the violence.

Alongside the violence inflicted through race riots, there was extreme violence against individuals which was rarely punished. Lynching was usually carried out by a group of vigilantes who claimed they were delivering "justice" in the best interests of society. Victims, usually African Americans but not exclusively so, were often accused of violating the racial hierarchy of the South or of attacking white women. They were often taken from their homes at night (and sometimes even from prison) and beaten and murdered. Between 1889 and 1918, 2,558 African Americans were lynched. Some whites were also lynched, often for trying to support African Americans. Although the victims of lynching were often left

> **KEY TERM**
>
> **Miscegenation** Sexual relations or reproduction between people considered to be of different races.

hanging in plain sight as a warning to others, the police and the courts in the South simply refused to investigate these crimes. Very few of the murderers were ever brought to justice, as Ida B Wells explains in Source 1.54, below. Note that Wells uses the term "negro" to refer to African Americans. Although this was common usage at the time she was writing, it is outdated and would be considered offensive now.

> Why do you think Ida B Wells wrote this account at this time? Think about the context in which she was writing, who she was (page 71) and what she wanted to achieve.

SOURCE 1.54

An extract from *The Red Record*, written by Ida B Wells in 1895

Not all nor nearly all of the murders done by white men, during the past 30 years in the South, have come to light, but the statistics as gathered and preserved by white men, and which have not been questioned, show that during these years more than 10,000 Negroes have been killed in cold blood, without the formality of judicial trial and legal execution. And yet, as evidence of the absolute impunity with which the white man dares to kill a Negro, the same record shows that during all these years, and for all these murders only three white men have been tried, convicted, and executed. As no white man has been lynched for the murder of colored people, these three executions are the only instances of the death penalty being visited upon white men for murdering Negroes.

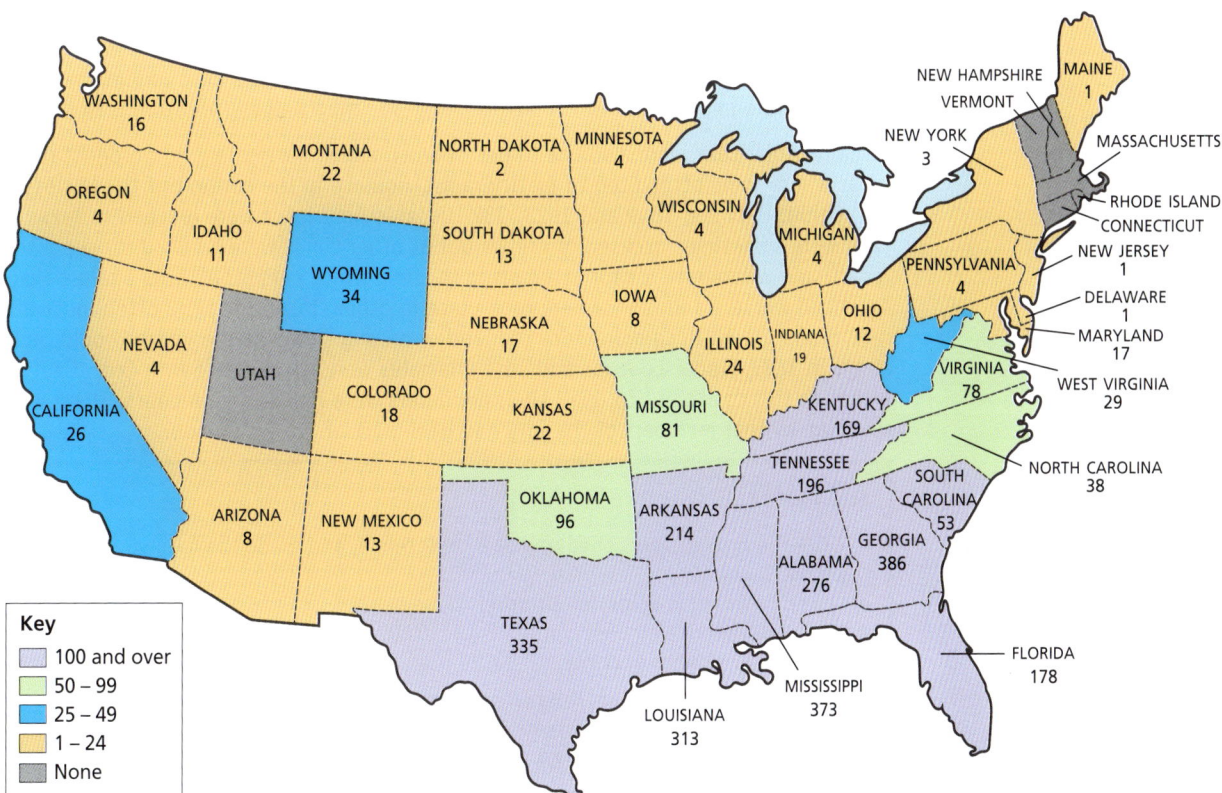

Figure 1.5 A map showing the incidences of lynching between 1889 and 1918. The map was compiled for the NAACP for a book which they published entitled "Thirty years of Lynching."

Lynching was most frequent against African Americans. According to the NAACP in the book published above, 3,224 people were lynched in the period between 1889 and 1921 of whom 2,552 were African American (described as "colored" by the NAACP) and 702 were white. The definition of "white" was a wide one and included Asian Americans, Native Americans, and Hispanic Americans. However, these figures do not include the people killed in race riots such as those in Atlanta in 1906 or the Chinese immigrants who were lynched in riots in California in 1871 and 1880.

As the map shows, most of these murders took place in the former Confederate States. Most of the victims (2,522) were men but 50 females were also lynched. One horrific example was

Ballie Crutchfield in Tennessee. In 1901, her brother allegedly found a lost wallet and kept the money it contained. He was about to be lynched by a mob but managed to escape. The mob then turned on his sister, who had not been involved in the crime, and lynched her in his place.

Other groups were also targeted. At least 137 Native Americans are known to have been lynched (although the figure is likely to be much higher). For example, in April 1890, a group of ranchers from Banning, California, pulled a Native American man named Tacho from a boxcar at the local railroad depot. They dragged him down a track and hanged him from a telegraph pole. Tacho was alleged to have stolen a horse and cattle and was described by a local newspaper as "a desperado of the worst type" which suggests some local support for his lynching.

In California between 1850 and 1935, there were 350 instances of lynching, carried out against Native and Hispanic American and Chinese immigrants. In 1871, a fight broke out between some Chinese immigrants in the Chinese quarter of Los Angeles. Two police officers became involved, one was injured, and a white civilian was killed. To avenge the death of the civilian, a mob of 500 ransacked the Chinese quarter, lynching 19 men, including a respected physician and a teenage boy. The number killed was ten percent of the Chinese population of L.A. at the time and only one of those murdered had been involved in the original dispute. In common with African Americans, Native Americans, Asian immigrants, and Hispanic Americans were barred from testifying against whites in the courts of California. This meant that attacks on Chinese people generally went unpunished. Although nine men were imprisoned for the attacks in 1871, they walked free from prison a year later.

Hispanic Americans were also the target of lynch mobs, particularly in border states such as Texas where some attempted to justify racist violence in the context of the lawlessness of the region. Between 1849 and 1928, 232 Hispanic Americans were lynched in Texas alone. They were sometimes accused of crimes but at other times were lynched for supposedly "practising witchcraft" or for attempting to sue a white person. Attacks against Hispanic-American workers and landowners took place in other states and were often motivated by racism and greed. Once murdered, the land or mining rights of the victim would be taken away. In 1877, Francisco Arias and José Chamales were lynched in Santa Cruz, California. Although this case went to trial, their murderers were not named in court. There was speculation that members of the jury had been part of the lynch mob.

> **ACTIVITY**
>
> In 1909, Ida B. Wells was speaking at a conference, and made the following claims about lynching.
> - First: lynching is **color-line** murder
> - Second: violence against women is the excuse not the cause
> - Third: it is a national crime
>
> Working in a group of three, take one of these claims each. Use the evidence from this section to assess the claims made here.
>
> What evidence can you find to support the claim? Can you find evidence to challenge the claim?
>
> Work together to devise a short presentation to show to the rest of the class about how far you agree with Wells' comments.

> **KEY TERM**
>
> **Color-line** The social and/or legal barriers that segregate people of color from white people.

Civil rights activism

Walter White was an eyewitness to the rioting described in Atlanta on page 68. White helped his father defend their home and family against the mob. The intensity of the brutality that he witnessed made him highly conscious of the need to protect the rights of African Americans and the need to fight against hatred. In 1916, he worked to organize a chapter of the National Association for the Advancement of Colored People (NAACP), which had been founded in 1909. Later, White would go on to become the secretary of the NAACP.

Booker T Washington (1856–1915)

Booker T Washington was born an enslaved person in Virginia and became the most well-known leader of African Americans in the Progressive Era. He realized the importance of education and struggled through poverty to attend college. In 1881, he established the Tuskegee Institute in Alabama. It became a model for education and vocational training for African Americans. Washington was also involved in setting up the National Urban League, which helped African American workers adapt to urban life. He believed that if African Americans worked hard and achieved financial success, discrimination against them would diminish. In his book *Up from Slavery*, he argued that change would come slowly.

> Why do you think that some African Americans might disagree with Booker T Washington?

SOURCE 1.55

From Washington's Atlanta Exposition Speech, September 1895

The wisest among my race understand that the agitation of questions of social equality is the extremest folly, and that progress in the enjoyment of all the privileges that will come to us must be the result of severe and constant struggle rather than of artificial forcing. No race that has anything to contribute to the markets of the world is long in any degree ostracized [isolated for any length of time]. It is important and right that all privileges of the law be ours, but it is vastly more important that we be prepared for the exercises of these privileges. The opportunity to earn a dollar in a factory just now is worth infinitely more than the opportunity to spend a dollar in an opera house.

Ida B Wells (1862–1931)

Like Washington, Wells was born into enslavement. After the Civil War, she was encouraged by her parents to take an interest in politics and to attend college. She was a teacher, journalist, civil rights activist, and founding member of the NAACP. In 1884, Wells sued a train car company in Memphis that had removed her from a train despite her having a ticket. She won the case, although the ruling was overturned by a federal court. After the lynching of three of her friends, she started to write about mob violence against African Americans. Her article so incensed the locals in Memphis that her printing press was destroyed and she was driven out. Wells traveled to Britain where she wrote articles that were critical of the Southern states and tried to raise awareness of discrimination in the South. She confronted women in the suffrage movement who ignored lynching and was often criticized for her views on Southern "chivalry." An example of her writing is on page 69.

WEB Du Bois (1868–1963)

A free man, born in the North, Du Bois had a different life from Booker T Washington. He gained degrees from three universities, including Harvard, and became an academic, lecturing in sociology. Originally, he agreed with Washington that change would come slowly for African Americans. However, his position shifted and he argued that more active resistance against discrimination was necessary. He participated in organizing the Niagara Conference in 1905 (see below), was influential in setting up the NAACP, and edited the *Crisis*, which was the official publication of the organization. However, Du Bois became so frustrated by the slow pace of change that he moved to Ghana. An example of his writing can be seen on page xx.

Marcus Garvey (1887–1940)

Garvey was an Afro-Jamaican political activist. He was the founder and first president-general of the Universal Negro Improvement Association and African Communities League (usually referred to as the UNIA), which he founded in 1914. In 1916, he moved to the US where he established a branch of the UNIA in Harlem, New York. Garvey was committed to the Back-to-Africa movement. However, his separatist views, and his relationship with white racists such as the Ku Klux Klan (who also believed in separatism), caused a rift with other civil rights activists, such as Du Bois, who promoted racial integration. Although a controversial figure, he undoubtedly influenced later civil rights organizations.

The Niagara Movement

In 1905, a group of prominent African American intellectuals, led by WEB Du Bois, met near Niagara Falls to form an organization calling for civil and political rights for African Americans. With its comparatively aggressive approach to combating racial discrimination and segregation, the Niagara Movement served as a forerunner to the NAACP and the civil rights movement.

As discussed earlier, the promises of equality offered by the Fourteenth and Fifteenth Amendments fell far short of what African Americans had hoped for. Booker T Washington advocated a slow transformation to equality (page 70). However, others questioned this approach. WEB Du Bois and William Monroe Trotter, founder of the activist newspaper the *Boston Guardian*, invited twenty-nine men from fourteen states to a meeting at the Erie Beach Hotel in Ontario, near Niagara Falls in July 1905.

At their initial meeting, members of the Niagara Movement adopted a constitution and drafted a "Declaration of Principles" that dedicated the group to fighting for political and social equality for African Americans.

> How do the ideas in Source 1.56 contrast with what you read in Source 1.55 by Booker T Washington?

SOURCE 1.56

Extracts from the Declaration of Principles of the Niagara Movement, 1905

Suffrage: At the same time, we believe that this class of American citizens should protest emphatically and continually against the curtailment of their political rights.

Protest: We refuse to allow the impression to remain that the Negro-American assents to inferiority, is submissive under oppression and apologetic before insults. Through helplessness we may submit, but the voice of protest of ten million Americans must never cease to assail the ears of their fellows, so long as America is unjust.

Color-Line: Any discrimination based simply on race or color is barbarous; we care not how hallowed it be by custom, expediency or prejudice ... discriminations based simply and solely on physical peculiarities, place of birth, color of skin, are relics of that unreasoning human savagery of which the world is and ought to be thoroughly ashamed.

By 1906, the Niagara Movement had 170 members in 34 states. In August 1906, it held its first public meeting in Harpers Ferry, the site being chosen in commemoration of John Brown's raid in 1859. The movement had some success at state level and lobbied against the legalization of segregated railroad cars in Massachusetts. However, it failed to gain widespread support. Booker T Washington and his supporters were opposed to the movement and it had limited financial resources. There was also a disagreement between Du Bois, who wanted to admit women to the movement, and Trotter, who did not.

The National Association for the Advancement of Colored People

The NAACP was formed in 1909 when progressive white Americans joined forces with WEB Du Bois and others from the Niagara Movement. The NAACP initially focused on ending the practice of lynching, with Walter White working as an undercover agent. Although lobbying efforts did not persuade Congress to pass antilynching laws, the 1919 publication of the NAACP report entitled *Thirty Years of Lynching in the United States* convinced President Woodrow Wilson and other politicians to condemn mob violence.

By 1913, in common with other activist groups of the Progressive Era, the NAACP had established branch offices in such cities as Boston, Baltimore, Kansas City, and Washington DC. Membership increased to almost 90,000 by 1919, a ten-fold increase from 1917.

The NAACP quickly established a reputation as an important legal advocate for African Americans. In 1910, the Association won an important victory against voting restrictions based on the grandfather clause in Oklahoma. The Association developed its own newspaper, the *Crisis*, which was founded by WEB Du Bois in 1910 and rapidly became one of the most widely read periodicals about social injustice and race.

The full story of the activities and achievements of the NAACP is covered in the later chapters of this book.

> Why do you think the NAACP chose this image for the front cover?

SOURCE 1.57

The front cover of the NAACP publication the *Crisis*, July 1920, featuring a portrait of young graduate Eva R. Marshall.

The Universal Negro Improvement Association

The Universal Negro Improvement Association (UNIA) was founded by Marcus Garvey in 1914 in Jamaica. However, it was more influential once Garvey moved to Harlem, New York in 1916. The UNIA dedicated itself to fostering racial pride, encouraging economic self-sufficiency, and working toward the formation of an independent Black nation in Africa. The Association appealed to working-class African Americans in urban ghettoes. The UNIA was credited with giving many African Americans a sense of belonging. However, Garvey would not tolerate dissent and insisted on having the complete loyalty of UNIA members. Inevitably, this approach caused tension and there was a high turnover in the leadership of the Association.

Garvey established a number of business ventures under the auspices of the UNIA.
- The Black Star Line was a steamship company operated by Garvey from 1919 to 1922. It was designed to promote worldwide commerce among Black communities.
- The Negro Factories Corporation was the finance division and was designed to support businesses that would employ African Americans and produce goods to be sold to Black consumers.
- The Negro Factories Corporation took over the management of a Harlem steam laundry and opened a Universal Tailoring and Dress Making department.

Many African American leaders in the US criticized Garvey, especially when he announced himself as the provisional president of the Empire of Africa. Garvey's leadership of the UNIA ended in 1923, when he was indicted and convicted of fraud in his handling of funds raised to establish the Black Star Line.

Resistance of and calls for reform among Native American groups

During the Progressive Era, Native people were forcibly assimilated under the Dawes Act and through the boarding school system (page 27). Many Progressives shared the view that indigenous people should learn the value of land owning and have their ways eradicated. However, there were some who campaigned for Native American rights.

In 1879, Helen Hunt Jackson, a writer and activist, attended a lecture in Boston by Chief Standing Bear (Oglala Lakota Sioux), of the Ponca Tribe. Standing Bear described the forced removal of the Ponca from their Nebraska reservation. Jackson was upset by what she heard about their treatment and the harsh conditions they faced. In the manner of the muckrakers some years later, she began to investigate and publicize the misconduct of the government toward Native Americans. In 1881, she wrote a book entitled *A Century of Dishonor*, which was a scathing attack on state and federal policy. She sent it to every member of Congress with a message on the front cover quoting Benjamin Franklin, "Look upon your hands! They are stained with the blood of your relations."

In 1882, the Indian Rights Association was founded in Philadelphia. Formed by non-Native people, this group argued that Native Americans should be given full citizenship and worked to protect their status and rights. For example, in 1901, the Association protested the establishment of the Grand Canyon Forest Reserve, which cut across the traditional lands of the Havasupai.

However, Native Americans began to protest on their own behalf and campaign for their rights. In the period from the 1890s to the 1920s, many Native Americans used the education they were forced to receive in the boarding schools to campaign for their rights. Ohiyesa (also known as Charles Eastman, Santee Dakota) attended the Santee Normal Training School in Nebraska. He went to college and was only the second Native American to train as a doctor in Western medicine. He wrote and gave public talks to challenge the narrative that Native people were "uncivilized and disappearing." In common with other elements of the Progressive Movement, there were disagreements between activists about how best to achieve their aims. Ohiyesa attracted some criticism from contemporaries, as he worked for the Bureau of Indian Affairs and favored assimilation.

In 1911, the Society of American Indians (SAI) was established in Ohio. It was a progressive group made up in the first instance of 50 Native Americans, most of them middle-class professional men and women, and included Ohiyesa and Standing Bear. The aim of the society was to address the problems faced by Native Americans, such as ways to:
- improve health and welfare
- improve education
- secure civil rights
- achieve local government.

The SAI was the first pan-Native American reform organization in the US during the Progressive Era. By 1913, it had been joined by 230 people who, between them, represented 30 Native American tribes. After the initial meeting of the Society, it announced its intention to hold a National Indian Conference. The reasons for holding that conference are described in Source 1.58.

Study Source 1.58 and work with a partner to answer the questions which follow.
Use your knowledge of this topic to explain what is meant by these phrases:
- "bring the Native Americans into modern life"
- "a race consciousness"
- "a century of dishonor."
What were the aims of the SAI?
How did they intend to achieve those aims according to this source?
How useful is this source as evidence about race relations in the Progressive Era?

SOURCE 1.58

From the public announcement made following the establishment of the Society of American Indians

The highest ethical forces of America have been endeavoring on a large scale and in a systematic way to bring the Native Americans into modern life. It is well to see whether these efforts have brought results.

The time is come when the Indian should be encouraged to develop self-help. This can be achieved only with the attainment of a race consciousness and a race leadership. We cannot predict the race leader, the gathering of the educated, aggressive members of all the tribes is a prerequisite to discuss discovery.

The Indian has certain contributions of value to offer to our government and our people. These contributions will be made more efficiently if made in authorizing collectively. They will, at least they may, save us immense losses from mistaken policies which we might otherwise follow.

The white man is somewhat uncomfortable under a conviction that a century of dishonor has not been redeemed. If in any degree he can convince himself and his red brother that he is willing to do what he can for the race whose lands he occupied, a new step toward social justice will have been taken.

Between 1911 and 1923, the SAI worked tirelessly. A journal was published, legal assistance was given to Native individuals and tribes, and Congress and the Office of Indian Affairs were lobbied. The main aim of the organization was to deliver a unified voice to obtain citizenship for Native Americans and allow Native American nations to access the US court system. The SAI had scant resources and there were disagreements between Native and non-Native activists, so the Association was dissolved. However, the 1924 Indian Citizenship Act was, in part, evidence of their work.

ACTIVITY

Using the sources and information in this chapter, copy and complete a table like the one below to show how successful the Progressives were in helping different groups in society.

Group	Helped?	How? Which legislation/ actions would have helped?	Limitations? How far was this group helped?
Industrial workers			
Business leaders			
African Americans			
City dwellers			
Women			
Child laborers			
Native Americans			
Farmers			
Immigrants			
Voters			
The poor			

Having completed the table, ask yourself whether the Progressives brought about positive changes to American politics and society.

SUMMARY DIAGRAM

Progressive changes to the American political landscape

Progressive Presidents
- Roosevelt's "Square Deal"
- Taft's economic policies
- Wilson's New Freedom

Constitutional Amendments
- 16th Amendment
- 17th Amendment
- 18th Amendment
- 19th Amendment

Race relations and activism
- Segregation
- Formation of the NAACP
- Formation of the SAI

Progressivism: Success or failure?

Figure 1.5 A summary of the changes brought to the American political landscape by the Progressives

CHAPTER SUMMARY

In the late 1800s the USA became the greatest industrial nation on Earth. This was due to large amounts of natural resources, entrepreneurship, and developing technology. This allowed certain individuals to amass great wealth. However, it also caused urban growth and increased immigration, which created new problems for Americans to solve. There were opportunities for work, but conditions were often poor and the economy went through periods of depression. Those living in the rapidly expanding towns faced challenging living conditions. New Immigrants and African Americans faced discrimination and prejudice. In rural areas, farmers faced hardship due to falling crop prices. In the West, Native Americans lost their traditional way of life.

Americans responded to these challenges by forming labor unions, political parties, and civil rights groups. They conducted campaigns on a wide range of issues to bring about political, social, and economic change. Early twentieth-century presidents pursued progressive policies that addressed some of the problems facing Americans. Reforms were introduced at state and federal levels and the Constitution was amended to address some of the major issues. However, not all issues were addressed, or even accorded significance, and by 1920 the United States had been involved in a world war which required a change in priorities.

REFRESHER QUESTIONS

1. Why did the US experience rapid urbanization between 1870 and 1900?
2. What challenges did New Immigrants face?
3. Were the main industrialists "robber barons" or "captains of industry"?
4. Why did industrial workers form labor unions?
5. What challenges faced Native Americans in this period?
6. What were the aims of the Populist Party?
7. Why was prohibition introduced?
8. Were women given the vote because of their campaigning or because of their role in the war?
9. Which of presidents Roosevelt, Taft, and Wilson was the most progressive?
10. Why was the NAACP formed in 1909?

Study skills

Writing using sources

Understanding and interpreting sources

In an assessment you may be asked to:
- review two sources and compare them to find similarities and differences or
- evaluate how far a number of sources support a particular view.

Comparing Sources

In cases when you are asked to make a judgment about how far two of the sources agree and disagree regarding evidence about or attitudes toward a historical person, event, or issue, you will need to identify points of similarity and difference by analyzing the sources and providing evidence from the sources to back this up.

First, read the question carefully:
- Identify the subject of the question—who or what is the question asking you to consider?
- Does the question want you to consider attitudes toward, evidence about, or responses to, events?
- Remember, it is important to keep focused on the issue in the question.

Be careful to compare the correct sources.

Tip: write the two source letters down clearly at the start of your plan and double-check them with the question before you start writing your response.

Then, read each source carefully. Take notice of the overall message of the source to understand the argument or point of view of the author. This means that the source should be viewed as a whole rather than divided into individual sentences which, taken alone, might convey different ideas from that of the whole source.

There are four sources below and examples of questions which use those sources.

SOURCE A

Chinese immigrant Lee Chew describes the situation he found in America in 1882

I came to San Francisco before the Exclusion Act. When I got there, I was half-starved but a few days' living in the Chinese quarter made me happy again. I found work as a house servant with an American family, and they were kind to me.

Men of other nationalities are jealous of Chinese immigrants because we are more faithful workers. They have raised such an outcry about Chinese laborers that they have shut them out of working on farms or in factories or building roads. He cannot practice any trade and his opportunities to do business are limited to his own countrymen. The treatment of the Chinese in this country is all wrong and mean. The Irish fill the poorhouses, alehouses and prisons. Yet they are let in, while the Chinese who are sober, law abiding, educated and industrious are shut out. Many Chinese have become sincere Christians. Many of us would become citizens and be patriotic Americans if we were allowed. But how can we make this country our home? Chinese immigrants are not allowed to bring wives here from China, and if they marry American women, there is a great outcry.

SOURCE B

From a Congressional Report on Immigration, February 1892

The popular demand for legislation excluding the Chinese from this country is urgent and almost universal. Their presence here is hostile to our institutions and a source of danger. They live in the most miserable manner, in crowded tenement houses, surrounded by dirt and corruption. Gambling houses and opium joints abound. As a rule, they have no families here:

all are men. They have no attachment to our country and never assimilate with our people, our manners, tastes, religion or ideas.

In San Francisco, Chinese immigrants have invaded almost every branch of industry. They work as farmhands, miners and in all departments of manual labor, for wages at which white men and women could not support themselves and their families. If we do not act, a war between the races will begin, several times violence has broken out and bloodshed has followed.

Sample question

Read Sources A and B. Compare these two sources as evidence of the lives of Chinese immigrants to the United States in the late nineteenth century. [15]

This question asks you to compare two sources. To do this you need to:
- Identify and explain similarities using details from the sources.
- Identify and explain differences using details from the sources.

Work through the sources first and decide what the similarities and differences are between them.

Sample answer 1

The sources have some similarities. For example, both agree that Chinese immigrants are mainly men. Source A explains that "Chinese immigrants are not allowed to bring their wives" and Source B supports this by saying that "they have no families here: all are men." Another similarity is that Chinese immigrants face difficulties. Source A describes the behavior toward the immigrants as "mean" and suggests that other immigrant groups, such as German people, are not treated in the same way.

However, there are differences between the sources. In Source A, Lee Chew says that it is difficult to get work because Chinese laborers have been shut out of many jobs. He says, "They have raised such an outcry … limited to his own countrymen." In contrast, Source B says that Chinese immigrants are employed in many different jobs and that they are undercutting wages. Source A does not mention the wages though. Source B complains that the Chinese live in squalor and dreadful conditions and makes out that they spend all their time in opium dens and gambling. Source A counters this by saying that the Chinese are hardworking and that it is other immigrants who live in poor conditions. Lee Chew also says he would like to be an American and has become a Christian. This goes against what Source B says about having "no attachment to our country" and not adopting American religion or ideas.

Sample answer 2

Chinese immigrants first came to the United States in the Gold Rush of the 1840s and many came to help build the Pacific Railroad. The Chinese built the western end of the railroad and Irish workers started at the other end. There was conflict between Irish and Chinese immigrants and not liking the Irish is mentioned in Source A.

These sources are not the same, as one was written by a Chinese immigrant and the other was part of a congressional report. They were also written around ten years apart. These sources are totally different. Source A supports Chinese immigrants and says good things about them. For example, they are "sober, law-abiding and industrious." However, Source B hasn't got a good word to say about them!

ACTIVITY

Compare the two answers above.

Write a list like the one below to assess the strengths and weaknesses of these answers.
- Does the answer make a clear connection between the sources?
- Does the answer compare details or messages, or make inferences that are relevant to the question?
- Are comparisons like for like?
- Do they answer the question?
- Is there appropriate support from each source?
- Is the use of the sources brief and focused?
- Which of the answers do you think is more effective and why?
- What steps can you identify that would help the writer of the weaker answer to improve it?

Write a checklist to remind yourself of the features you need to include in response to a comparison question.

Next, consider the attribution of the sources:
- the nature (what type of source it is)
- the origin (who wrote or produced the source)
- the purpose of each source (what the intended impact of the source was)
- the dates of each source (what was happening at the time or what happened in the gap between the sources).

This will help you suggest reasons for similarities and differences. You will need to use your contextual knowledge to make this judgment.

Sample answer 3

The sources are more different than similar. I think that Source A is probably the most reliable. Lee Chew was a Chinese immigrant and so he knew first-hand what he was talking about and probably had no reason to say anything other than the truth. Source B is probably a whole lot less reliable, as it was a report for Congress and would say what Congress wanted to hear. Therefore, I would say Source A was a better source for a historian.

Sample answer 4

There are similarities and differences between the sources. One of the similarities is that Chinese immigrants faced prejudice and bad treatment. Source A refers to the Exclusion Act, which was passed in 1882 to limit Chinese immigration and there had been violence against Chinese workers, for example in the 1870s in Los Angeles. In 1885, there was a massacre of Chinese immigrants at Rock Springs. At least 28 Chinese miners were killed and no one was ever prosecuted for their murders. This is an example of the violence discussed in Source B and this helps to explain the similarities between the sources.

ACTIVITY

Explaining similarities and differences
- Which of these responses explains reasons for the similarities/differences?
- How has that been done?

Add the effective features from these responses to your checklist.

Considering how far sources support a view

Questions like this are asking you to make a considered judgement about the extent to which all the sources support and/or challenge a particular view that is stated in the question. You will need to judge "how far" they do so. Some sources might be nuanced and both support and challenge said view. You must make careful use of all of the sources and evaluate them to come to a judgment about which side of the argument is stronger—do the sources mostly support or challenge the view in the question?

Practice question

Read all of the sources. "Restricting immigration was popular with Americans." How far do the sources support this view? [25]

SOURCE C

From a speech made by President Cleveland to veto the proposed 1896 Literacy Test, March 1897

We have welcomed all who came to us from other lands. We have encouraged those coming from foreign countries to cast their lot with us and join in the development of our vast country, securing in return a share of the blessings of American citizenship. A century's stupendous growth, largely due to the assimilation and thrift of millions of immigrants, attests to the success of our policy. A contemplation of its grand results cannot fail to arouse sentiments in its defense.

It is said, however, that the quality of recent immigrants is undesirable. The time is quite within recent memory when the same thing was said of immigrants who, with their descendants, are now numbered among our best citizens.

SOURCE D

A cartoon published in the United States in 1916. It was entitled "The Americanese wall, as Congressman Burnett would build it." Uncle Sam looks over the wall and says, "You're welcome in—if you can climb it!"

Writing your response

You need to consider all four of the sources provided. You will have already looked at two of these in-depth when planning your response to the comparison question.

Make sure you read the question carefully.

Planning your answer:
- Create a **brief** plan listing sources A–D.
- Make brief notes as you analyze them.
- How does the source connect with the view given in the question?
- Does it agree or disagree?
- Where is the evidence in the source?
- Which sources strongly support or challenge the view and which have more subtle or nuanced arguments?

In some cases, the source will be nuanced. This means that the source could be used to both support and challenge the view in the question. This could be implicit or explicit in the text or image, and you may need to use your contextual knowledge to recognize the nuance in the source. This might come from your knowledge of key individuals or important events that may have affected the reason for the view in the source.

ACTIVITY

Planning your answer

Firstly, look in detail at the question and identify its focus. Then, look at Sources A, B, C, and D. Make a copy of the table below. You will see that one part has been done for you. Now fill the rest in for the other sources.

Source	What does the source say about the view in the question?	What evidence from the source shows this?
A		
B	There is widespread support. Congress must have asked for this report to find out whether more restrictions should replace the Exclusion Act when it ended. There has been violence between American and Chinese laborers and the writer complains that Chinese workers refuse to fit in.	"The popular demand for legislation excluding the Chinese from this country is urgent and almost universal."
C		
D		

Based on what each source shows about the view mentioned in the question, group the sources.
- Which sources support the view in the question?
- Which sources challenge the view in the question?
- Is there a source that is nuanced, and both supports and challenges the view in the question?
- Is contextual knowledge used to explain the arguments in the sources?

Comparing sample answers

Sample answer 5

All the sources support the view in the question.

Source A shows that restricting immigration is popular because people have not been pleasant to immigrants. The source refers to the Exclusion Act, which shut out immigrants. They have also competed for jobs with American workers and therefore been barred from certain occupations. This must mean that people do not want immigrants taking their jobs.

Source B is very reliable, as it is a government report and it certainly shows that people wanted immigration to end. It says that "a war between the races will begin" and most people would want to avoid that situation.

Source C says that "the quality of recent immigrants is undesirable" and this shows that immigrants are not welcome and that people would like restrictions to be put in place. In any case, this is by the US president, and he appears to be vetoing immigration in this speech.

Source D also shows that Americans want to restrict immigration. They have built a huge wall along the beach to keep the immigrants out. Uncle Sam says they can come in if they can climb the wall, but it is far too high.

Therefore, all the sources support the view in the question.

Sample answer 6

Sources B and parts of Sources A and C support the view in the question and Source D, Source C, and even Source A partly challenge it.

Source B clearly supports that people would like to see restrictions on immigration. The report starts with the idea that support for restrictions on Chinese immigration is "almost universal" and gives lots of reasons, such as undercutting American workers and failure to assimilate, as to why this should happen. Source A also supports the view in the question to some extent, although Lee Chew does not think this is right. He mentions the Exclusion Act, which was passed in 1882 and forbade the immigration of Chinese laborers for ten years. He says other workers are jealous of Chinese immigrants and that their treatment is "all wrong and mean." This seems to suggest that other immigrants and Americans do not like Chinese workers and would like to reduce their numbers.

On the other side of the argument, Source C is a speech by President Cleveland, who was about to veto the idea that there should be a literacy test for new immigrants. He talks about how much immigrants have contributed to the development of America when he says that, "A century's stupendous growth, largely due to the assimilation and thrift of millions of immigrants attests to the success of our policy." He dismisses arguments that new immigrants are undesirable by saying that the same argument was used recently but those people are "now numbered among our best citizens." He does recognize that some people want to restrict immigration but he does not agree with this and will stop their attempts to change the law. Source D also challenges that there should be restrictions on immigration. The artist portrays the people who have just arrived as very small next to the great big wall that has been constructed. If they cannot climb the wall like Uncle Sam says, they will be washed away by the tide. Even Uncle Sam seems to have a sad look on his face. However, this cartoon was published when war was happening in Europe. The pens that represent the literacy test look like guns. Maybe this shows that the US did not want to be involved in the war and did not want people coming from Europe with radical ideas and trying to change the political views of people in the US. Source A partly supports the idea that Americans wanted restrictions on immigration and that the family that Lee Chew worked for were kind to him. However, the argument is mainly that Chinese immigration should be restricted. Lee Chew complains that other immigrants, such as the Irish, behave much worse than the Chinese but are still allowed in. That must mean that they're not opposed to all immigration.

Strong answers will demonstrate the following:
- sources used to support and challenge the view in the question
- use of source content to develop points
- an explanation of how the evidence answers the question
- nuanced source use if this is possible from the sources
- use of contextual knowledge to help interpret the sources.

Evaluating sources considering provenance and in context

Once you have planned a balanced answer to support and challenge the view in the question, you need to think about the element of the answer that asks "how far" the sources support or challenge the view.

To do this you need to think about the attributions of the sources and how you can evaluate the sources to assess their relative weight in response to the question.

You might find that you have been given sources which are of different types. These may include written extracts, such as speeches or memoirs, or visual sources such as cartoons, posters, and photographs. Each source needs to be analyzed carefully to decide if it is a stronger or weaker piece of evidence in response to the question.

You need to avoid making assumptions based on the type of source. For example, you might assume that all diaries are reliable because the person involved in the historical events wrote them, or all newspaper articles are unreliable because the journalists want to sell papers, or all records of conversation are useless because the person might not remember the exact words. Your response needs to be tailored to the specific source rather than be a stock standard response to the type of source. All sources need to be viewed with a critical eye, and not accepted at face value.

The table below shows a range of questions that you can use to help you evaluate the sources.

Who created the source?
When was it created?
Why was it created?
Who is the intended audience?
What are the main points in the source? (focused on the question)
What is the tone and emphasis of the source? Does it use "loaded language" which shows a particular view?
How likely is it to be a reliable source of information? What might make it unreliable?
What is the context? What do you know from your contextual knowledge about what was happening when this source was created?
Do you recognize the name of the creator of the source? If so, what would you expect their opinion to be? Does the content of the source match your expectations?

ACTIVITY

Use the questions in the table above to analyze Sources A through D.
- What is the weight or value of this source as evidence in response to the question?
- What opinion is held? Does it strongly support one side over another?
- Is this a stronger or weaker source of evidence in response to the question?

Analyzing visual sources

You may be presented with a visual source to evaluate. These should be analyzed and evaluated in the same way as written sources, but you will need to make inferences based on the way the image presents information.

Many visual sources used are cartoons, although photographs could also be used. The nature of visual sources means that you will have to ask yourself some different questions in order to consider context and provenance.

ACTIVITY

Look at the visual sources on pages 17, 18, 40, and 42. Use the table below to analyze these sources, looking at their content and provenance.

Who created the source?
When was it produced?
Why was it produced?
What was its purpose?
Who is the intended audience?
Was a visual source created for a particular reason rather than a written source?
Was it aimed at local people or those abroad?
What are the main points in the source? (focused on the question)
Are there captions on the image? What is their message?
What is the tone and emphasis of the source?
What is the focal point of the image?
Is it satirical?
How does the portrayal of people or events show this?
Are there symbols or messages in the portrayal?
Are features or clothing emphasized for effect?
Why?
How likely is it to be a reliable source of information?
What might make it unreliable?
For example, is it a staged photograph or a re-enactment after the event?
What is the context?
What do you know from your own contextual knowledge about what was happening when this source was created?
Do you recognize the name of the creator of the source?
If so, what would you expect their opinion to be?
Does the content of the source match your expectation?

ACTIVITY

Evaluating sources to reach a supported judgment

Compare the answers below.
- Do you think one answer does a better job of evaluating the sources than the other?
- Why do you think this answer is stronger?
- What areas for improvement can you see in the weaker answer?
- With a partner, go back to your checklist of features required for an effective response to a question where you are required to use sources to test a prompt. What would you add to this list?

Sample answer 7

Most of the answers support the view in the question – Americans wanted restrictions on immigration. There were lots of reasons why this was the case. There was fear that immigrants would take American jobs, and this was especially important at times when there was an economic depression. There were a few times in the 1880s and 1890s when there was a depression in trade, and this would likely have made people start to worry about their jobs. They would feel aggrieved if they thought immigrants were undercutting their wages.

Some of the sources are not very reliable. Source D is a cartoon that was probably just published to entertain people. Source A is from a Chinese immigrant. He knew what things were like, but he was only one person so maybe other people did not have the same experience. Source B is probably the most reliable as it is from a governmental report and a lot of research would have been done in putting this together.

Sample answer 8

I think that, on balance, all the sources support the view in the question. Source B was a report which argued that Chinese immigration should be restricted. The Exclusion Act had been passed ten years earlier (as mentioned in Source A) and people did not want the restrictions to be lifted. The 1880s saw its fair share of economic problems and that supports the source's idea that there was competition for jobs. Also, there was violence between different sets of immigrants and the military had to be sent to Seattle and Tacoma to stop riots. The report does seem to be strongly in favor of immigration, but the facts support what it argues, making it a stronger piece of evidence. Source D does not seem to support the view in the question, but the source would not have been produced if not for Congressman Burnett's support for immigration restriction. Source C shows Cleveland had fought off a literacy test, but twenty years later it was made law. All of this shows that these sources support the view in the question.

2 American Imperialism, the First World War, and the 1920s

> **Introduction**
>
> In the late nineteenth century, attitudes to America's role in the world began to change. When opportunities arose, America began to acquire an empire. When war broke out between the great European powers in 1914, the US aimed to stay neutral. By 1917, this was no longer viable and the US declared war on Germany and its allies. The war had far-reaching consequences. It was an important factor that influenced the prosperity enjoyed by many Americans in the 1920s. In addition, many social changes occurred in the decade following the war.
>
> This chapter will consider America's relations with other countries in the late nineteenth and early twentieth centuries and how this impacted America in the 1920s by examining the following questions:
> - ▶ What were the causes and consequences of US territorial expansion in the late nineteenth and early twentieth centuries?
> - ▶ Why did the US enter the First World War and how did the war impact Americans?
> - ▶ What were the causes and impacts of economic and cultural changes in the 1920s?

▶ KEY DATES

1898	Spanish-American War
1901	Theodore Roosevelt becomes president, following McKinley's assassination
1901–03	Insular Cases
1904	US begins to build the Panama Canal
1907–09	Voyage of the Great White Fleet
1917	US enters the First World War
1918	Armistice ends fighting in the First World War
1919	First Red Scare; Red Summer
1920	Prohibition begins
1921	Warren Harding becomes president
1921	Emergency Quota Act
1923	Calvin Coolidge becomes president on the death of Warren Harding
1924	Snyder Act
1925	The Scopes Trial
1929	Herbert Hoover becomes president

2.1 What were the causes and consequences of US territorial expansion in the late nineteenth and early twentieth centuries?

In the late nineteenth century, there was a debate among American politicians about US relations with neighboring countries. During the previous decades, ideas of American national identity had changed. American citizens had settled the entirety of the US lands, including those acquired by war and treaty. The economy had also changed, and continued growth would only be achieved by developing new markets abroad. The actions of presidents Theodore Roosevelt, Taft, and Wilson were driven by circumstances and changing attitudes. In addition, events such as wars contributed to the changing of America's outlook on the rest of the world. America actively acquired more territory and took a greater role in global events.

Economic, cultural, and nationalist motivations for territorial acquisitions

As they spread across the continent, European Americans gained confidence that their economic and cultural values were superior to others they encountered. They began to consider acquiring new territories beyond the borders of the US.

Was this a continuation of existing trends or did it mark a change in attitudes, ideas, and beliefs about the US? Explaining why the US became more active in foreign policy requires an investigation of the reasoning Americans used at the time to justify their actions. It requires an understanding of the motives and attitudes that underpinned these actions. It also requires an understanding of the changing circumstances of the period, especially the diminishing power of imperial Spain.

Manifest Destiny and the closing of the frontier

The ideas associated with **Manifest Destiny** had existed, to some extent, since the early seventeenth-century European settlement of America. Over the years, there had been government statements limiting westward expansion by the settlers. However, each time further moves west became attractive, whether due to the abundance of farmland or mineral wealth, or to gain freedom from religious persecution, the needs and values of European Americans were prioritized over those of the Native Americans. The phrase "Manifest Destiny" was used and developed from the mid-1840s. It cemented the idea that European American culture was superior to that of indigenous Americans. This process of expansion had been completed by the time of the Civil War and Reconstruction.

By 1890, a new version of Manifest Destiny had emerged. It focused on the importance of dominance of the seas and unlimited economic competition as the means to promote progress. The government used thoughts from multiple academics to guide and justify policies. Frederick Jackson Turner, of Wisconsin University, stated that the American frontier was now closed. He explained that this would have an impact on the economy and American society. His work implied that further economic and cultural growth would have to take place overseas.

New Manifest Destiny also incorporated the mission of spreading Christianity alongside American cultural values, as this was considered a superior morality. By the 1890s, the primary mission of spreading these values to Native and African Americans gave way to overseas missions in the Caribbean and the Pacific. By 1900, there were about 5,000 American missionaries overseas, aiming to educate and convert to Christianity those whom they regarded as uncivilized. These developments were all driven by the confident assumption that the "American way" was beneficial and suitable for everyone. The ideas and attitudes of New Manifest Destiny help to explain what motivated imperialist Americans to extend their influence abroad.

> **KEY TERMS**
>
> **Manifest Destiny** The idea that European Americans had the God-given right to expand across the whole continent, imposing their ideas of democracy, capitalism, and Christianity.
>
> **New Manifest Destiny** From the late 1890s, the definition of Manifest Destiny was expanded to justify the imposition of the USA's political, social, economic, and religious values abroad. In some situations, this involved the colonization of other countries.

Explain the message of Source 2.1, using details from the cartoon and your knowledge.

SOURCE 2.1

A cartoon published in 1901 titled "It's "up to" Them." Uncle Sam is saying to the Filipinos, "You can take your choice; – I have plenty of both!"

Desire for new markets and resources

By the 1890s, the industrialized Northern states dominated the American economy. Internal markets had developed, making goods cheaper and more readily available to all Americans. Developments in transportation, communication, and production created a new kind of economy based around consumption. The wealth of America and Americans depended on economic growth. Growth depended on the import of goods, such as rubber, that could not be produced in the US and, more importantly, on the export of manufactured goods. To achieve this, America needed safe and efficient transportation routes beyond its borders, and trade agreements with other countries. Since Americans generally believed that their economic system of capitalism, and the growth that fed it, was superior to other economic systems, the needs of the economy became a strong driving force in the conduct of foreign policy.

In the years following the Civil War, overseas trade increased enormously and the balance of trade changed so that the value of US exports exceeded those of imports. Trade agreements could be made most readily with countries that had not experienced an industrial revolution. This was because, apart from Great Britain, economically developed countries had strict tariff systems that protected their manufacturing industries from foreign competition. Conversely, less industrialized countries wanted to buy goods that they could not manufacture.

Although previous US policy had been to avoid intervention in other countries, attitudes were changing in the 1890s. The needs of business, influenced by the idea that the economy must grow and by the problems created by the depressions of the 1880s, came to dominate decision-making. The influence of big business on government was such that earlier ideas about non-intervention in other countries were set aside when business interests were threatened.

The US had always traded with China, but the situation was unsatisfactory. China was not a consistently wealthy economy, markets fluctuated, and Europeans had established bases in China which put them at an advantage over the US. The Philippines seemed a useful trading base for Sino-American trade. As Spanish influence there weakened, American business leaders urged their government to take control.

- Explain the message of this cartoon, using details from the source and your knowledge.
- Compare Sources 2.1 and 2.2 as evidence of the reasons for American territorial expansion.

SOURCE 2.2

A cartoon published in 1900. The caption reads, "And, after all, the Philippines are only the stepping-stone to China"

AND, AFTER ALL, THE PHILIPPINES ARE ONLY THE STEPPING-STONE TO CHINA.

Trade also developed to the south, with the islands of the Caribbean and the countries of South America. When there was political instability in these countries, US business leaders urged the government to intervene to protect their interests.

Political interest and military motivations for overseas expansion

Political leaders backed increased overseas influence for reasons already cited: economic and cultural. They also claimed to be acting as anti-imperialists by freeing the peoples of the lands they gained from European imperialists. China was a country of particular concern to America because of its potential for trade. By the late nineteenth century European imperial powers had established trading bases there, trading freely. However, the Chinese government was weak and unstable. American politicians feared that China would soon be divided among the European powers just as Africa had been. The Europeans were beginning to do this by establishing exclusive spheres of influence. In response, Secretary of State John Hay issued **Open Door Notes** to the European powers to protect existing free trade as well as China's territorial integrity.

The expansion of the US Navy was identified as an essential way of protecting American interests. Captain Alfred Thayer Mahan, a lecturer in naval history and the President of the United States Naval War College, researched the question, "What makes a country great?" His studies of the seventeenth and eighteenth centuries pointed to British, and later French, naval strength as the essential precursor to economic power and political dominance. He concluded that lessons from his research could be applied to the US in the late nineteenth century. This idea influenced politicians who were keen to expand American influence overseas and who saw a strong navy as essential in protecting American trading interests. In addition, America needed a military presence in important locations. It established several bases following the Spanish-American War.

KEY TERM

Open Door Notes were a series of notes written by Secretary of State John Hay. In them, Hay tried to secure agreement to the US policy of an unrestricted and open market for trade in China. The other countries Hay sought agreement from included Great Britain, France, Germany, Japan, and Russia.

Causes and impacts of the Spanish-American War, April–December 1898

The beginning of America's overseas empire came with the Spanish-American War of 1898. The great Spanish Empire of the sixteenth century had already been reduced to a few islands in the Caribbean and the Far East. Spain's control over these last outposts of empire was weakening. Unrest against Spain's colonial rule in America's neighbor and trading partner Cuba had been ongoing since 1895.

To sell newspapers, two rival newspaper barons, Joseph Pulitzer and William Randolph Hearst, reported the events sensationally, encouraging the American public to side with the Cubans against tyrannical Spanish rule. A US navy ship, the USS *Maine*, was sent to Havana harbor in Cuba to protect American business interests. On February 15, 1898, there was an explosion on the ship and it sank. Rumors spread about how this happened and who was responsible. In the weeks that followed, the "yellow journalism" of Pulitzer and Hearst inflamed public opinion by blaming the Spanish, and this in turn influenced political decisions. President McKinley pushed Congress to secure Cuban independence on the basis that it was potentially damaging to American trading interests to have civil unrest on an island so close to America. In April 1898, unwilling to give in to US demands, Spain declared war on the US and the US declared war on Spain. A series of naval engagements followed, in which the US was victorious. US troops were dispatched to support Cubans fighting for their liberty from Spain. Spain lost control of its colonies in the Caribbean and the Pacific, and this was confirmed in the Treaty of Paris in December 1898.

> **KEY TERM**
>
> **Yellow journalism** A style of journalism using sensational, eye-catching headlines to attract readers. The term originated in the 1890s, with the rivalry between two New York City newspapers, the *Journal* and the *World*, owned by William Randolph Hearst and Joseph Pulitzer respectively.

The outcome was significant. The US gained Guam and Puerto Rico, and purchased the Philippines. The Treaty of Paris also guaranteed Cuban independence, which was achieved ten years later, with benefits to the US, such as a perpetual lease on Guantanamo Bay. America had begun to acquire overseas colonies and was now a power in the Pacific. Not surprisingly, given US views of colonialism and the prospect of gaining many new culturally diverse citizens, politicians were divided on this outcome. The Treaty was ratified in the Senate by only one vote. Meanwhile, the war highlighted the importance of the navy for defense. Theodore Roosevelt, Assistant Secretary to the Navy at the beginning of the war, was convinced that the US needed to build up its fleet. The war also provided an opportunity for the US to formally annex Hawaii, and use it as a naval and economic base. This helped safeguard America's interests in Asia and the Pacific.

The impact of the idea of the "white man's burden"

In 1899, the fears of anti-imperialists were realized. The Treaty of Paris had just been signed when a nationalist rebellion erupted in the Philippines. The US had agreed to purchase the Philippines from Spain for the sum of $20 million. Philippine nationalists rebelled against their new colonial overlords. The same year, the British writer Rudyard Kipling wrote a poem in response to the difficulties America was experiencing in achieving its military takeover of the Philippines. "The White Man's Burden" is about the responsibilities of the colonial power and its role in ruling over reluctant native peoples. The poet, echoing the sentiments of the period, encourages the US to accept the role of civilizing the Philippines but warns about the cost involved. This "burden" was immediately apparent with the cost far higher for the Filipinos than the Americans. In the three years it took to subdue the rebellion, over 4,000 Americans and 20,000 Filipino soldiers were killed. As many as 250,000 civilians died from diseases and starvation caused by the war. The fighting initially took the form of conventional engagements between the relatively well-equipped US army and the Filipino rebels. Later in the war, when the Filipinos used guerrilla tactics, they were more successful but by this time they had little support. The US gradually prevailed. In 1901, President William McKinley appointed future president William Taft as Civil Governor of the Philippines. William Taft implemented a new approach named a "policy of attraction." This involved:
- introducing social reforms
- promising economic development
- promising some self-rule
- creating schools, hospitals, and transport infrastructure
- introducing legislative reform.

The approach was more effective in securing peace.

In 1902, with fighting mostly over, President Theodore Roosevelt offered a general amnesty and by 1907, the first elections were held. America had taken on the role of the benevolent colonizer recommended by Kipling, "The White Man's Burden."

> **ACTIVITY**
>
> Using information in this section, find evidence to support the view that business interests were the reason for American expansion overseas.

> Why does Kipling think that ruling the Philippines will be a burden for America? Explain your answer using details from Source 2.3.

SOURCE 2.3

Take up the White Man's burden—
   Send forth the best ye breed—
Go bind your sons to exile
   To serve your captives' need;
To wait in heavy harness
   On fluttered folk and wild—
Your new-caught, sullen peoples,
   Half devil and half child.

Extract from "The White Man's Burden" by Rudyard Kipling, published in 1899

Role of Theodore Roosevelt

Theodore Roosevelt's foreign policy ideas signified a break with the past. They are indicated in the phrase he repeated on many occasions, "speak softly and carry a big stick; you will go far." It meant forward thinking to anticipate problems, acting justly, and allowing a defeated enemy to save face, and ensuring that any threat was meant and that any action was backed by force.

The governing principle underpinning Roosevelt's actions is known as the Roosevelt Corollary to the Monroe Doctrine. This justified a more active foreign policy, serving the interests of America. It notably included management of the Panama Canal project and the development of the US navy to protect American economic and political interests. The dominance of the Eurocentric international system policed by the European imperial powers was beginning to diminish. Roosevelt involved America in international agreements such as those formulated by the Hague Conferences and the Algeciras Conference. America acted as a peace-broker in the Russo-Japanese War of 1904–05, hosting the signing of the treaty that ended it in Portsmouth, New Hampshire.

> **KEY TERM**
>
> **Corollary** A proposition that follows from one already proven. The Roosevelt Corollary followed from the Monroe Doctrine.

Major events in President Theodore Roosevelt's foreign policy

- Hague Conferences (1899 and 1907). The US took part in these conferences which were a forerunner to the League of Nations. They established a means of resolving international disputes independently of the European great power system.
- Venezuelan Debt Controversy (1902). When Venezuela defaulted on debts owed to European powers, Roosevelt stepped in to resolve the crisis without allowing further European influence. The crisis was averted in 1903 and led Roosevelt to develop his corollary.
- Dominican Republic Crisis (1902–04). Political turmoil led to US troops being sent to the Dominican Republic on several occasions. In February 1905, the US and Dominican Republic agreed on US responsibility for the Dominican Republic's debt and customs duties.
- Portsmouth Treaty (1905). Roosevelt accepted an invitation to mediate a settlement between Japan and the Russian Empire to end their war. The resulting treaty was signed at the US naval base in Portsmouth, New Hampshire.
- Algeciras Conference over Morocco (1906). The US took part in a conference in Spain to establish the role of France in Morocco.

The Roosevelt Corollary

KEY TERM

Interventionism A political approach characterized by readiness on the part of the government to be involved in political matters abroad and economic policies at home.

The Roosevelt Corollary marked a change from the guiding principles known as the Monroe Doctrine of 1823. This doctrine had been used to justify American annexation of Texas and the war against Mexico in the 1840s. It had also been used to justify American intervention in the Spanish-American War of 1898. After 1904, Theodore Roosevelt's so-called corollary to this doctrine was the new rule on which US foreign policy was based.

The Roosevelt Corollary was developed in response to the Venezuelan debt controversy. At first, Roosevelt had been sympathetic to the European powers. Venezuela defaulted on the debt payments that had been agreed. However, the **interventionist** reaction of the European powers who were owed money by Venezuela persuaded Roosevelt to change his mind.

The corollary allowed the US to intervene in other American countries to ensure that they paid the debts they owed to their international creditors. In theory, this intervention would be a last resort. Action would be taken by America, provided it did not encourage foreign aggression toward any of the nations of the Americas. In practice, the corollary was used by America to ensure political stability in the Americas. It was used to justify intervention in Cuba, Nicaragua, Haiti, and the Dominican Republic. The corollary became associated with President Roosevelt's favorite proverb, "speak softly and carry a big stick; you will go far." The image of America wielding a big stick in its dealings with other countries was often used in political cartoons of the period.

SOURCE 2.4

A cartoon from 1904, illustrating Roosevelt's foreign policy. The title is "The Big Stick in the Caribbean Sea"

> Explain the meaning of Source 2.4 using details from the cartoon and your knowledge of the historical context.

The construction of the Panama Canal, May 1904–August 1914

The Isthmus of Panama was a major obstacle to shipping and therefore to trade (see Figure 2.1). An overland route across the isthmus had long been used to transport people, as they could make the short distances that were not navigable by ships. Posters during the California gold rush of 1849 advertised this "land route" as faster and safer than the trails across the Rockies. The idea for a canal had been considered for many centuries and a French company had started work on it in 1879. In the early twentieth century, the French tried to sell the project and the company's assets to the US. The US purchased the French company at a much-reduced price in 1902. The US began to negotiate with the government of Colombia to agree on terms for building the canal. When the Colombian government rejected the terms, President Roosevelt used "big stick" diplomacy, sending warships to both ends of the proposed canal location in support of Panamanian independence. The Panamanians successfully created an independent state under the French engineer Philippe Bunau-Varilla. He and Secretary of State, John Hay, signed a canal treaty in 1903, giving the US very favorable terms. America gained a ten-mile-wide strip of land on which to build the canal, in exchange for a $10 million payment, an annual sum of $250,000 starting in 1912, and the promise to guarantee independence for Panama. This treaty remained in force until a gradual handover of control between 1977 and 1999.

Building the canal was a major feat of engineering. The design eventually chosen rejected the idea of a sea-level canal in favor of one including locks operated by water from three lakes and several rivers on the route. It included the construction of a massive earthen dam across the Chagres River, which created a large artificial lake. Ships sailed its twenty-mile length as part of the route. Challenges for the canal workers included the unstable terrain and the climate. Temperatures often exceeded 100°F. Several chief engineers came and went. The canal was eventually opened on August 15, 1914. The benefits for trade and for the US navy were significant. It eliminated the two-month voyage of over 9,000 miles around Cape Horn for both merchant shipping and the US Atlantic and Pacific fleets.

Figure 2.1 A map showing the route of the Panama Canal, completed in 1914

Expansion of the US Navy and the Great White Fleet

In his 1897 address to the Naval War College of Newport, Rhode Island, Theodore Roosevelt proposed a strong and growing navy as a key part of America's defense plans, and stated that Spain was a certain rival in the Caribbean and possibly in the Pacific. The US navy was deficient in every class of ship when compared with Spain. Roosevelt's experience as Assistant Secretary to the Navy coincided with the sinking of the USS *Maine* in Havana harbor and the outbreak of the war. When he resigned his naval post to take part in active service in Cuba, Roosevelt had already achieved much through the proposals he made and the improvements to the fleet that he instigated. This work was taken further when he unexpectedly became US president in 1901.

As president, his greatest contribution to the development of the navy was the fourteen-month voyage of the "Great White Fleet." The fleet of sixteen new white-painted battleships of the Atlantic Fleet set out in December 1907, returning to the US in February 1909. The voyage was an important show of sea power. It coincided with a naval arms race between Germany and Great Britain and was an indication of America's capability to defend its overseas interests. The ships began their journey in Virginia. They sailed south to the Caribbean and along the east coast of South America before rounding Cape Horn and sailing the length of South America and Mexico's west coasts. They arrived in San Francisco in May 1908. From there they sailed west, to Hawaii, New Zealand, Australia, Japan, China, and the Philippines. The last leg of the voyage went through the Suez Canal and included visits to Egypt, Italy, and Gibraltar. They arrived back in Virginia in February 1909. Besides demonstrating the US's naval strength to the major world powers, the fleet also showed the humanitarian side of US involvement overseas. While the fleet was in Egypt, there was a severe earthquake on the Italian island of Sicily. The fleet sailed across the Mediterranean to offer its assistance.

Direction of US foreign policy, 1909–21

Under President William Taft (1909–13) and President Woodrow Wilson (1913–21), US foreign policy continued to evolve. Both presidents had ideas about what the priority should be. Taft's guiding principle was the primacy of economic growth. In terms of foreign policy, he therefore wanted to promote trade to benefit American business and industry. Woodrow Wilson's ideas were rooted in his academic background as president of Princeton University. He believed in doing what was right. By this, he meant promoting the values on which America was founded. He wanted to do this by establishing good relations with other countries of the Americas. He was against involvement in the imperial disputes of the European powers because America came into existence in response to Britain's imperial tyranny. He believed each nation had the right to self-determination and that values such as democracy and free enterprise should be encouraged. Like many politicians, these presidents discovered that guiding principles can be difficult to apply. To what extent were they able to follow their ideas when faced with reality?

Dollar diplomacy under President Taft

During William Howard Taft's presidency, foreign policy priorities changed. For Taft, America's interests lay in the development of investment and trading links that benefited American business. He believed that American investment in the Caribbean and Latin and South America would bring prosperity to America and stability to the surrounding area. This focus led to his policies being called **dollar diplomacy**.

Despite his encouragement of trading links, sometimes with the support of the US military, Taft's policies did not increase trade, especially with China. His attempt to use dollar diplomacy to penetrate the Chinese market were unsuccessful. American banking was not capable of operating independently in this international market and Taft antagonized the great European powers who had already established markets in China, as well as destabilizing the Chinese government, leading to a revolution in 1911. Meanwhile, he reversed Roosevelt's conciliatory policy toward Japan, causing that country to extend its influence around the Pacific to the detriment of the US.

Although Taft succeeded in stabilizing the regimes in some neighboring countries, dollar diplomacy also unsettled America's southern neighbors, causing them to convene the Pan-American Conference to find ways of reducing American economic and political influence and interference.

Moral diplomacy under President Wilson

The foreign policy of President Woodrow Wilson was governed by **moral diplomacy**. Decisions about when and how to act were made according to American beliefs about what was right and wrong in government. The assumption was that the American way was right, not only for America but also for every other country. Wilson believed that democracy was the right form of government. This was clear in his public statement of March 1913, made a week after his inauguration. He declared, "One of the chief objects of my administration will be to cultivate the friendship and deserve the confidence of our sister republics of Central and South America ... We hold, ... that just government rests always upon the consent of the governed."

Wilson's commitment to moral diplomacy can be used to explain his reluctance to take sides when the First World War broke out in 1914. He saw the war as a battle between European colonial powers. Imperialism offended his ideas of justice and national self-determination. There were countries on both sides with limited or no commitment to democracy, a form of government he regarded as morally right. When he finally asked Congress to declare war on Germany, he was able to justify siding with France, Great Britain, and Russia on the grounds

---

ACTIVITY

Find evidence in this section to support the view that Theodore Roosevelt's foreign policy marked a break with the past.

KEY TERM

Dollar diplomacy A foreign policy used by the United States to achieve its goals in Latin America and east Asia by using economic power instead of military force.

KEY TERM

Moral diplomacy A principle of international relations that emphasized that the US would only intervene if this served to promote American democratic values and rights.

that the autocratic tsarist regime in Russia had recently been overthrown. From February to October 1917, Russia was ruled by a provisional government that was committed to holding democratic elections.

Wilson's moral diplomacy extended to his proposals for settling the peace at the end of the First World War. He wanted a fair and lasting peace, avoiding the diplomatic mistakes that had contributed to the outbreak of war four years earlier. His guidelines, known as the Fourteen Points, included freedom of the seas, self-determination for nationalities in Europe, and moves toward self-rule for the colonial holdings of the European powers. Wilson also suggested open agreements between nations and an international organization to prevent wars by solving disputes between countries and overseeing disarmament. Regardless of his good intentions, Wilson lacked understanding of the mood in both the US and Europe, and of the international situation. Some of his ideas were implemented, but so poorly that they caused further problems. Others were abandoned. Having lost the Democratic majority in the US Senate, Wilson personally presented the peace treaty for approval. His feeble performance did not receive an enthusiastic response. In an unprecedented move, the US Senate refused to ratify the peace treaty. America did not join the League of Nations. During the 1920s, America followed a policy of isolationism, although there was far more involvement and intervention in world events than this name suggests.

US occupations and interventions in Latin America and the Caribbean

The dollar diplomacy and moral diplomacy of presidents Taft (1909–13) and Wilson (1913–21) led to many interventions in Latin America and the Caribbean.

> **ACTIVITY**
>
> Use the information that follows to decide which president's ideas were more influential. Do this in the following way:
> - Identify what each president, Taft and Wilson, did.
> - Decide which actions were most influential—you will need to decide what criteria make an action influential.
> - Write a paragraph explaining the influence of either Taft or Wilson.

Cuba

The Platt Amendment of 1903 gave the US considerable power in Cuba, specifically to maintain its independence from foreign intervention. As a result, the US military occupied Cuba from 1906 to 1909 after ousting the regime of President Palma. They did so again from 1917 to 1922, to protect American-owned sugar plantations.

Dominican Republic

The US intervened indirectly in 1914 to secure the ousting of General José Bordas Valdez. Bordas Valdez had won a presidential election through fraud and suppression of the opposition. There was an uprising against his government and when the US government withdrew its support for him, he was forced to resign.

Haiti

By the early twentieth century, the US was Haiti's largest trading partner, with American businesses aiming to take over the country. In 1909, despite opposition from the Haitians, American bankers, backed by the State Department, moved to take over Haiti's banks. The US occupied Haiti in 1915, imposing martial law. Forced labor was used to build infrastructure projects. Most Haitians continued to live in poverty under US rule that violated their rights on numerous occasions, for example using Haitians as forced labor and taking money from the Haitian national bank to New York.

Mexico

US Ambassador, Henry Lane Wilson, was involved in the *coup d'état* of February 1913, which deposed and assassinated democratically elected President Francisco I Madero and his vice president. Woodrow Wilson was appalled to learn of Henry Lane Wilson's involvement and recalled him as Ambassador. General Victoriano Huerta became president, but Woodrow Wilson refused to recognize his government, which was known for human rights abuses. In April 1914, Wilson ordered the US navy to occupy the port city of Veracruz after an incident in which US sailors were arrested. Huerta resigned to the landowner and politician José Carranza, whom Wilson did recognize as president. In 1916, there was a border incident when a rival of Carranza sent an expedition into New Mexico. Woodrow Wilson retaliated with an incursion into Mexico, but withdrew rather than initiating a war.

The actions of Henry Lane Wilson and Woodrow Wilson help to explain the US reaction to the Zimmermann Telegram of 1917 (page 102). While there is no indication that Mexico was tempted by Germany's offer, the danger seemed real in the US.

Nicaragua

Mexico and the US competed for political influence in Nicaragua. In 1911 and 1912 the US intervened, claiming that the aim was to ensure good government. Good government meant the protection of US political and commercial interests. In 1912 US troops occupied Nicaragua during the "Banana Wars." Having quelled an anti-American uprising, they continued to occupy Nicaragua for over 20 years.

Panama

The US maintained control of a ten-mile-wide strip of land on either side of the Panama Canal from 1902 until 1977. This enabled the US to protect its investment in the canal project.

Debates over imperialism

By the end of the nineteenth century, many European empires were at their height. Although the Spanish Empire was in terminal decline, those of Britain and France extended into every continent other than Antarctica. The European powers that had come late to the acquisition of colonies competed for the last remaining territories in the Scramble for Africa. Control of the seas was key to controlling an empire and led to a naval arms race between Germany and Great Britain. America had prided itself on its isolation from European imperial rivalries. However, in 1898 the US acquired its first overseas territories in the Treaty of Paris that ended the Spanish-American War. This gave rise to heated public debate about the rights and wrongs of imperialism. The press took advantage of the controversy by publishing letters and articles. Politicians voiced their views. Well-known figures, such as the author Mark Twain, joined the debate.

Imperialism was controversial because, as anti-imperialists pointed out, it went against the fundamental precepts of the Constitution. Arguments for the acquisition of overseas territories emphasized the good that American rule and culture would bring to the autochthonous (indigenous) people of the colonies.

Anti-imperialist movement

Anti-imperialism was a fundamental principle of the US. As the thirteen colonies of Britain, the original states had suffered intolerable levels of taxation and other interference in the mid-eighteenth century. The colonies had been ruled in the interests of the colonial power but not of the American colonists. The US was founded based on objections to being under British colonial rule. The Constitution is a statement by "we the people" about how they wish to be governed. This implies that how they wish to be governed is the will of the people, not a system of rules forced on them. The Constitution specified how land ceded by Native Americans or acquired from other countries could work toward statehood. It did not

> **KEY TERM**
>
> **Scramble for Africa**
> The period between 1870 and 1915 during which major European powers competed to colonize as much of Africa as possible.

allow the annexation of land that was not attached to the US. Anti-imperialists used this to argue that America was not and should not be a colonial power.

Many notable American citizens were proponents of anti-imperialism. Horrified by the outcome of the Spanish-American War, a group of them formed the American Anti-Imperialist League in June 1898. Its aim was to challenge the American annexation of the Philippines. The League included in its membership Andrew Carnegie, Henry James, William James, and Mark Twain. The League's statement of intent made clear that colonialism was:
- evil
- anti-liberty
- likely to lead to militarism
- incompatible with America's goal of promoting life, liberty, and the pursuit of happiness.

The League also believed that colonialism undermined the values of the Declaration of Independence and of the American Constitution, and amounted to "criminal aggression." It was disrespectful to the intentions of the Founding Fathers.

In addition, the views of the time meant that there was opposition to the annexation of the Philippines from those who thought that it might lead to Filipinos having a role in the American government and labor market.

Arguments of the pro-imperialists

Pro-imperialists had different priorities. The promotion and safeguarding of trade and commerce, and the spread of American values, all featured in their arguments.

The prolonged depression of the mid 1890s persuaded American business leaders that America's economic interests required business expansion overseas. This could be achieved through an **open door policy** but still included acknowledgment of formal colonies and the existence of protectorates. The argument for empire also allowed that US troops may need deploying if there was no other way to protect American business interests.

Pro-imperialists also argued that the increase of America's influence would benefit the peoples of the protectorates and colonies by spreading American values. They firmly believed that these values were superior and that they had a duty to educate the inhabitants, whom they regarded as ignorant, to be democratic, just, and Christian. The pro-imperialists used the arguments of New Manifest Destiny and Social Darwinism (see page 66), applying them to the events and circumstances in which America became embroiled.

Discussion of citizenship and status of territories

Discussion of citizenship arose because it related to the status of territories that the US had essentially annexed, and therefore to the status of the people who lived there. Acts passed in the early twentieth century gave citizenship rights but only limited political rights to those living in America's territorial acquisitions.

This marked a change from earlier procedures for US territories in mainland North America to be incorporated into the union as states. The Northwest Ordinance of 1789 had governed the series of steps to be taken by a territory in moving toward acceptance. The main criterion was population size, although the admission of Utah was delayed because its polygamy laws contravened US federal law.

The Supreme Court judgment in the Insular Cases meant that the Northwest Ordinance no longer applied universally. This judgment applied to the newly acquired islands ("insular" means "relating to islands,") including Puerto Rico, Guam, Hawaii, and the Philippines. The judgment was important in developing the concept of citizenship rights. It established that there were two different kinds of US territories and that the rights of their residents should be different. The ruling was that some constitutional rights are fundamental and applied in all territories owned by the US. However, in incorporated territories where US laws were unfamiliar, the rights of the inhabitants were limited and it was the role of Congress to decide what rights to grant. This left scope for continued debate, since Congress could bestow different rights in each territory.

> **KEY TERM**
>
> **Open door policy** A US foreign policy in 1899 and 1900. It aimed to set up equal trading rights for all nations trading with China, hoping that this would prevent China being split into smaller colonized states.

On March 2, 1917, the Jones Act was made law. Puerto Rico became a US territory and Puerto Ricans were given American citizenship. A form of government that resembled that of the US was established with separate executive, judicial, and legislative branches. The Act provided civil rights to the individual and created a locally elected two-part legal structure. However, laws passed by the Puerto Rican legislature could be overridden by the US Governor or Executive. Puerto Ricans did not have the right to vote in elections for US Congress unless they lived on the mainland and registered to vote there. As a result of this Act, over 40,000 Puerto Ricans emigrated to the US in the following decade. Most settled in New York state.

ACTIVITY

Which of the causes of US territorial expansion was the most important in your opinion? Write a paragraph to explain your choice.

Create a presentation as an overview of this section. What changed and what stayed the same in terms of US relations with other countries between 1890 and 1921?

SUMMARY DIAGRAM

US territorial expansion

What were the causes and consequences of US territorial expansion in the late nineteenth and early twentieth centuries?

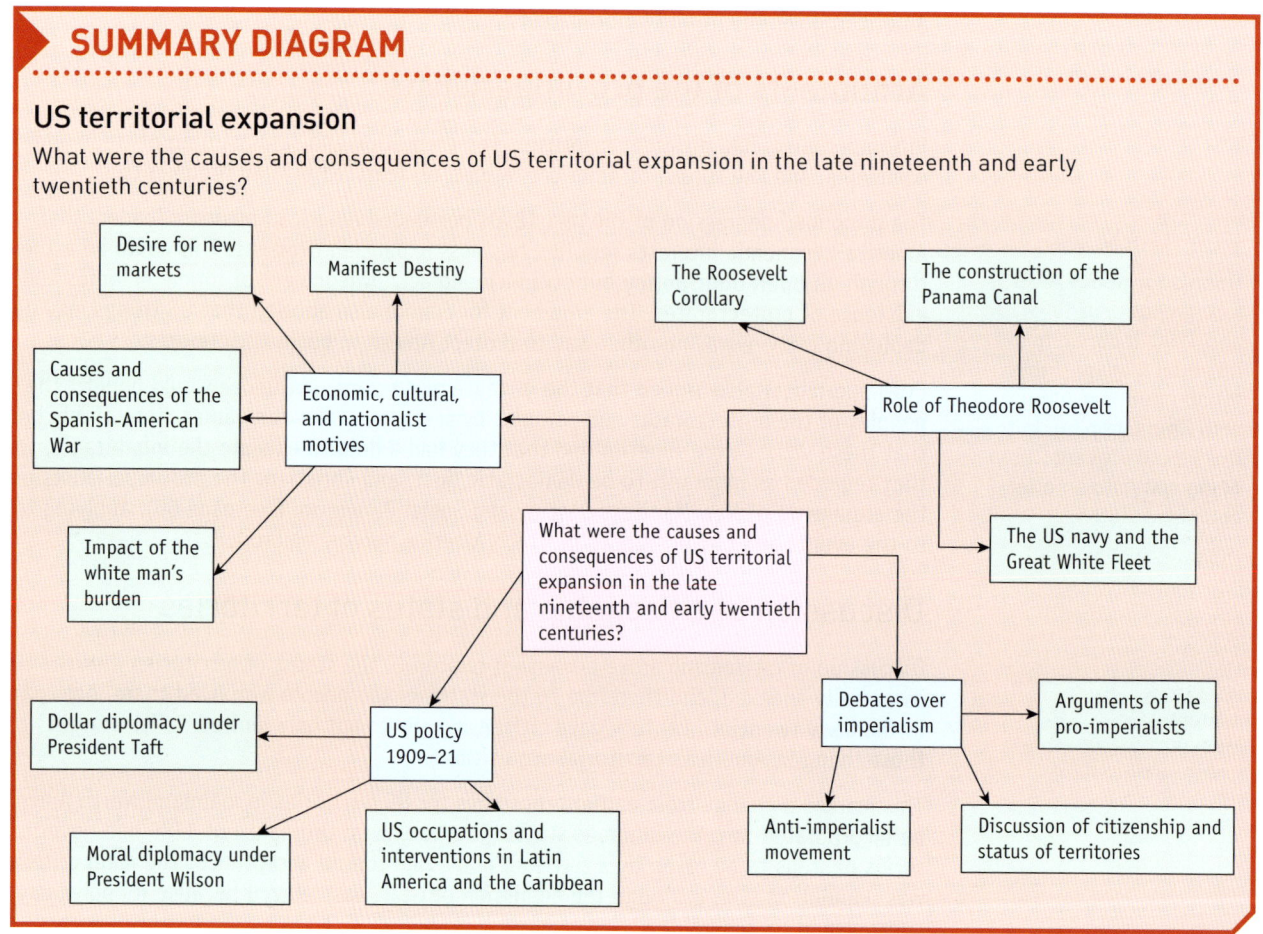

2.2 Why did the US enter the First World War and how did the war impact Americans?

When the First World War began in 1914, the US government was dominated by men of European origin. They and their ancestors had rejected life in Europe for a range of reasons and they chose to distance themselves from a war that seemed to have its origins in imperial disagreements between European countries. President Woodrow Wilson's position of neutrality at the outset of the war reflected the views of the people that this was in America's best interests. However, America was still involved. Loans and sales of supplies to the combatants abounded. The war was fought at sea as well as on land, and this made US shipping vulnerable, whether it carried goods related to the war or not. With suggestions of a German alliance with Mexico and issues around shipping, views began to change. In early April 1917, the US declared war on Germany. The war had already benefited industries that supplied war materials to Europe. Now, all aspects of American life were affected by the adjustments needed for fighting a major war overseas. Inevitably, this was associated with an increased role for federal government. Intervention was wide-ranging. Conscription built up the armed forces and led to adjustments to, and control of, the workforce. Censorship and propaganda aimed to make the population loyal to the US by controlling and manipulating information. There were greater opportunities for women in employment and in the armed forces. Some aspects of life did not change. Segregation in the armed forces was maintained, leading to varying experiences for different races. On the domestic front, the war led to the migration of African Americans from the South to Northern cities where job opportunities in industry had developed as migration from Europe diminished because of the war.

Early reactions of the US to the outbreak of the First World War

> **KEY TERMS**
>
> **Central Powers** In the First World War, Germany and Austria–Hungary were known as the Central Powers.
>
> **Entente Powers** Great Britain, France, and the Russian Empire (also known as the Allies).

Americans of European descent came from a wide range of countries. Inevitably, there were people with historical ties to countries on different sides in the First World War—the Central Powers and the Entente Powers. About ten percent of Americans identified as ethnic Germans. Many others were from neutral Scandinavian countries, such as Sweden or from the Entente countries. Ethnic origin would not necessarily determine allegiance. Some immigrants had actively rejected the political, ethnic or religious stances of their countries of birth. Others were more closely linked to European countries—for example, through return migration or religious affiliation. The reactions to the outbreak of the First World War after the first hostile moves in late July 1914 were varied. However, the overwhelming sentiment was to avoid involvement on the grounds that the disagreements that led to war were of no concern to the US. The American government declared its neutrality on August 4, 1914. Despite this, the largest demonstrations in the world at the outbreak of war took place in Times Square, New York City. The press stirred up feelings; the German-language press was sympathetic to the Kaiser, Yiddish (a Germanic language used by East European Jews and written in Hebrew text) papers suggested that the Austro-Hungarian government was facing the consequences of its repressive policies, while the Irish hoped that war would herald independence for Ireland from what they saw as British misrule. Such was the fervor and potential for violence that the mayor of New York City banned processions of hostile sympathizers. Meanwhile, American businesses looked for new commercial opportunities. Investment bankers JP Morgan & Co. immediately recognized that there was scope to make money. Eventually, the bank became the American broker for funding all the Entente Powers, making over $200 million in profits over the course of the war.

Wilson's desire to keep the US out of the war

Woodrow Wilson had traditionally been portrayed as a president who was more interested in the domestic issues of the Progressives than in foreign policy. His official biographer, Ray Stannard Baker, quoted a conversation in 1913 when Wilson had remarked, "It would be the irony of fate if my administration had to deal chiefly with foreign affairs."

Appealing to the Senate on August 19, 1914, in an address which he ordered to be published, Woodrow Wilson stated, "The United States must be neutral in fact as well as in name during these days that are to try men's souls. We must be impartial in thought as well as in action, must put a curb upon our sentiments as well as upon every transaction that might be construed as a preference of one party to the struggle before another."

The reasoning behind this statement was the varied allegiances likely held by Americans. Almost one in seven Americans had been born in a country that, by late 1914, was involved in the hostilities. Any official involvement meant choosing one side and rejecting the other, a course of action fraught with danger for internal stability. At a personal level, Wilson was peace-loving. This may have been a result of his Christian upbringing or of his academic background in politics. Certainly, he was no expert in foreign affairs.

In his address to the Daughters of the American Revolution in October 1915, Wilson further explained his position, "Neutrality is a negative word. It is a word that does not express what America ought to feel … We are not trying to keep out of trouble; we are trying to preserve the foundations on which peace may be rebuilt."

Rather than becoming caught up as a participant, Wilson hoped to offer the services of the US as a peace-broker. This idea was rejected by the participants. Wilson also made efforts to force peace through intervention in the financial markets. He stepped in to limit loan-raising on Wall Street, despite the enormous profits being made by American banks and brokers. He hoped that if the combatants were starved of finance, they would be forced to negotiate peace. Again, he was unsuccessful. As the war developed, remaining neutral became more difficult.

Impact of unrestricted submarine warfare on the US

The First World War, known as the Great War at the time, involved countries in every inhabited continent. Another sense in which the war was worldwide was naval warfare. Germany and Britain had been engaged in a naval arms race from the late nineteenth century. From 1906, this had been focused on a new class of battleship known as the dreadnought. However, it was submarine warfare that proved most controversial and significant in drawing America into the war. The first relevant incident occurred on May 7, 1915, when the British passenger liner RMS *Lusitania* was sunk by a German torpedo with the loss of almost 2,000 lives, including those of 128 American citizens. One of the dead was Alfred Gwynne Vanderbilt, head of the Vanderbilt railway empire. Besides its passengers, the liner was carrying a cargo of about 173 tons of rifle ammunition and shells destined for the Entente war effort. Germany had warned that it intended to attack the ship, which was seen as a valid target because it was British and because of its cargo. The captain and most passengers had not taken this warning seriously.

> How does Source 2.5 contribute to an explanation of the increase in anti-German sentiment in the US during the early years of the First World War?

SOURCE 2.5

A page from the *New York Times*, May 30, 1915. It shows images of a mass burial in Ireland for some of those who drowned when the Lusitania sank, and a group survivors

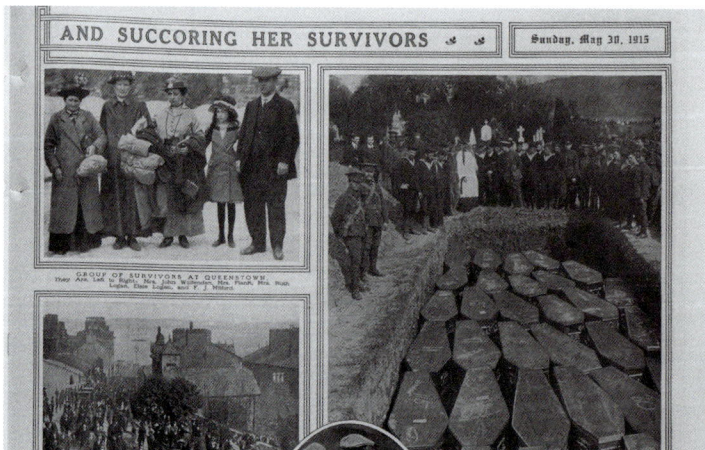

Press reports suggest public horror at this act of war, but the official US response was muted. The US government sent a note to the German government, condemning the principles of their submarine warfare. Two further notes followed but nothing more. Germany agreed not to attack passenger vessels and the US remained neutral.

By early 1917, the situation had changed in Europe. Britain was using its navy to blockade German ports, thus preventing supplies from reaching Germany. Besides this, the manpower needed for war, poor weather, and inefficient transport within Germany meant that people in the cities were very hungry. Germans called the winter of 1916–17 the "turnip winter" as root crops normally used for animal feed were substituted for potatoes and other more nutritious foods. Thousands relied on soup kitchens and the German government faced discontent. The situation was no better in Austria–Hungary, where there were instances of starvation and the army was unable to attack, as ethnic tensions and poor leadership undermined morale and the will to fight. The example of Russia, where a revolution in February 1917 overthrew the imperial government, emphasized the strain that war was placing on the old order in Europe. However, the fall of Russia's government represented an opportunity for the Central Powers to defeat their enemies, as the Russian army refused to go on the offensive under its new provisional government. The German government recognized that it must seize the initiative. To win, they would focus their forces on the Western Front to defeat Britain and France. However, this would only be possible if they could avoid revolution at home by ensuring supplies reached Germany through the North Sea ports. Germany declared an all-out war, including **unrestricted submarine warfare**. The Germans knew that this would bring America into the war, but assumed that they could win before American soldiers could affect the outcome of the land war in Europe. The German campaign was very successful. They had increased their submarine fleet from twenty to 140 during the war.

In April 1917, 430 Allied and neutral ships totaling 852,000 tons were sunk, but the level of destruction was declining. While American shipyards worked hard to replace the shipping lost, Britain introduced a convoy system, with naval vessels protecting groups of merchant ships as they crossed the Atlantic. On April 1, a German submarine torpedoed and sank the American steamship *Aztec*. Among the dead were ten American crew members. News of this broke in America on April 2, the very day that Wilson was proposing to Congress that war should be declared.

As anticipated, attacks on all ships carrying war goods were followed by the American declaration of war on Germany and its allies. Although the declaration cited submarine warfare, including the loss of American lives on the *Lusitania*, it was not the only factor referenced as precipitating direct American involvement in the war. There was also a potential threat to the USA itself, both within and without. Relatively few Americans were directly affected by unrestricted submarine warfare. Why, then, was it important in prompting the American declaration of war on Germany?

Growth of anti-German sentiment

By 1914, there were over eight million people of German origin in the US. They ranged from people whose ancestors emigrated in colonial times to those who were German-born. German was the most widely spoken language after English. There were many German-language newspapers. There was some existing anti-German feeling originating in trade rivalry and confrontation over the Philippines in the early years of the century. When war broke out in Europe in August 1914, thousands of Germans rushed to their consulate, seeking to enlist in the German army. The vast majority, however, identified primarily as American. German Americans were not viewed as a threat to national security. As the war progressed, attitudes to Germany and Americans of German origin began to change. British propaganda portrayed the Germans as barbaric, with shocking headlines about German treatment of vulnerable people in Belgium, the first country invaded by Germany. Although the German press tried to counter this, the sinking of the *Lusitania* in 1915 reinforced the negative image of Germany. In some parts of the US, there were moves against the use of the German language in education. Suspicions about whether German Americans were loyal to the US began to develop. In February 1917, Germany's declaration of unrestricted submarine warfare cemented anti-German sentiments. Even before the US declared war, the government had

> **KEY TERM**
>
> **Unrestricted submarine warfare** Submarine attacks on any ships that were considered to be involved in the war effort, whether naval or merchant, including ships bearing the flags of neutral countries.

> **ACTIVITY**
>
> Explain why unrestricted submarine warfare caused the US to declare war on Germany.

begun to intern Germans as enemy aliens. The US declaration of war on Germany seemed a natural progression.

The Zimmermann Telegram

The German government knew that unrestricted submarine warfare would lead to an American declaration of war, so they made plans to ensure that America would not be able to deploy its full military might in Europe. In January 1917, the German foreign minister, Arthur Zimmermann, sent a telegram to the German Ambassador to Mexico with a proposal to be conveyed to the president of Mexico. It said that in the event of a US declaration of war on Germany, Germany would offer to help Mexico attack the US and reconquer the territory lost in the war of 1846–48. The telegram was encoded, but it was intercepted by the British and its contents communicated to Walter Page, the US Ambassador to London.

Page had been Ambassador since 1913 and he was known to be very sympathetic to the British cause. Indeed, he had been criticized for doing too little to defend American interests and too much to support what he saw as Britain's fight for democracy. Consequently, when the decoded telegram was received in Washington, officials thought it was a fake. The British had indicated that although they were willing to share the contents of the telegram, they would not reveal how they had intercepted it, or how they had been able to decipher the code. Was this a genuine message? Was it a ploy by Britain and Page to draw America into the war? While the press inflamed public opinion as each new development occurred, Washington hesitated. In any case, the level of threat posed by a possible Mexican attack was limited.

On March 29, over a month after news of the telegram became public, the authenticity of the telegram was corroborated. Zimmermann made a speech in the Reichstag (the German legislature) confirming the contents. In his appeal to Congress to support the declaration of war, Wilson referenced the telegram. He explained its threat to America as part of the undercover German efforts to undermine America. The telegram had an important role in rousing enthusiasm for war among the American public. That enthusiasm would be necessary to persuade them to accept participation in a war which they had previously been told did not concern America. Public support would also be necessary if Americans were to tolerate the financial costs and the range of measures needed to enable America to fight the war. The Zimmermann telegram has been described as a catalyst in bringing America into the First World War.

US entry into the war

Woodrow Wilson was very clear in August 1914 that America should not become involved in a war between the blocs of European imperial powers. Yet by April 2, 1917, he had changed his mind and asked Congress to declare war on Germany. Why did this happen? And why did Congress declare war on April 6, 1917? To answer these questions, we must consider what had changed during the two-and-a-half-year period since war broke out in Europe.

Firstly, although the government declared neutrality, from early in the war US financiers and traders had links with the Entente Powers. They brokered loans in the US financial markets. They sold food and other goods with the potential for use in the war effort to Britain and its allies, including (from 1915) Italy. Although public sentiment remained anti-war, the US was involved and committed to the victory of the Entente Powers.

Under international law, Germany could stop and search ships suspected of carrying war materials. The Germans had initially side-stepped the requirement to stop and search before attacking ships. The US ignored this until the sinking of the *Lusitania* in 1915. The press stirred up public opinion but there was little likelihood of war at this stage, since after this, Germany changed its policy to comply with shipping law.

The situation changed again early in 1917. At this point, the US began its slide to war against Germany. The turning point was the note sent by the German Ambassador to the US to Secretary of State, Robert Lansing. The note gave notice of Germany's intention to resume unrestricted submarine warfare on February 1. On February 3, Wilson told Congress that the US had broken off diplomatic relations with Germany.

KEY TERM

Catalyst A person or event that quickly causes change. In chemistry a catalyst is a factor that affects chemical reactions.

ACTIVITY

Construct a flow chart to show the steps leading to the US declaration of war on Germany. Include the Zimmermann telegram.

Wilson still had to consider public opinion before asking Congress to declare war. His election slogans of 1916 showed he was proud of his neutral stance. Wilson appealed to voters with, "He kept us out of war" and "America First." His Republican opponent, Charles E Hughes, criticized Wilson's neutrality. However, this did not appeal to the public, who were generally anti-war. The sinking of several US ships carrying goods to Europe gave Wilson the ammunition he needed. This was clear proof of Germany's hostility to a neutral power, which could be presented as evidence that America was declaring war in self-defense.

Since early in the war, the US public had been subject to British propaganda aimed at encouraging American entry into the war. The emphasis was on tales of German atrocities against civilians, especially in neutral Belgium. It aimed to shock the American public, dehumanize the Germans and focus hatred on the Kaiser. It is impossible to gauge the influence of such propaganda, but it would have encouraged the public to identify the Central Powers as the enemy and to support their government in the war effort.

Wilson's appeal to Congress to declare war in defense of democracy does not seem convincing nowadays. By today's standards, none of the countries involved was democratic. In citing this reason for fighting, Wilson noted that the recent revolution in the Russian Empire had made that country democratic. The new provisional government which replaced the autocratic tsarist regime, had committed to democratic elections. This removed one of the objections to fighting on the side of the Entente Powers, since Britain and France were already more democratic than the Central Powers.

In the days after Wilson's speech to Congress, the press whipped up anti-German sentiment. Wilson's appeal, referencing the threat to American lives and shipping, the threat of Mexican aggression and the danger of traitors in America, aligned with the public image of evil-intentioned, anti-democratic Germans. There was concrete evidence of most of these elements: ships had been sunk, the Germans were willing to support America's neighbor (Mexico) in an attack on the US, and German troops had allegedly committed atrocities, especially in neutral Belgium. When war was declared on April 6, 1917, it seemed to have widespread approval.

ACTIVITY

Choose one of these factors:
- the Zimmermann Telegram
- anti-German sentiment.

Then, write a paragraph to explain why it was a cause of the US entering the war. Explain whether you think the factor you have explained here was more or less important than unrestricted submarine warfare.

SOURCE 2.6

From Woodrow Wilson's address to the Democratic Convention, accepting the party's nomination as its presidential candidate, September 2, 1916

We have been neutral not only because it was the fixed and traditional policy of the United States to stand aloof from the politics of Europe and because we had had no part either of action or of policy in the influences which brought on the present war, but also because it was manifestly our duty to prevent, if it were possible, the indefinite extension of the fires of hate and desolation kindled by that terrible conflict and seek to serve mankind by reserving our strength and our resources for the anxious and difficult days of restoration and healing which must follow, when peace will have to build its house anew.

Compare Sources 2.6 and 2.7 as evidence of Woodrow Wilson's attitude to American involvement in the First World War.

SOURCE 2.7

From Woodrow Wilson's address to a joint session of Congress, April 2, 1917

With a profound sense of the solemn and even tragical character of the step I am taking and of the grave responsibilities which it involves, but in unhesitating obedience to what I deem my constitutional duty, I advise that the Congress declare the recent course of the Imperial German Government to be in fact nothing less than war against the government and people of the United States; that it formally accept the status of belligerent which has thus been thrust upon it.

Mobilization for war

To ensure victory in the war, the American government needed everyone to focus on winning. Of course, men were needed to fight, but it was also important that those who remained at home produced what was needed to fight the war. An industrial-scale war also required that women be involved, both in paid work and in the home. Food and industrial production had first and foremost to serve the needs of the country. One consequence of this was the expanded role of federal government. The Committee of Public Information published propaganda, the Selective Service Act introduced **conscription**, while the War Industries Board coordinated purchases for the armed forces. War bonds were issued to finance the war and the government took on powers to control those who opposed the war, using the Espionage Act of 1917 and its amendment, the Sedition Act of 1918.

Propaganda

America declared war on Germany in April 1917. Americans had been subject to wartime **propaganda** for nearly three years. From April 1917, the government joined other organizations in publishing propaganda. Their purpose was two-fold:
- Some propaganda focused on persuading people to hate the enemy.
- Other campaigns aimed to modify behavior in support of the war effort.

Most Americans did not regard the First World War as "their" war. A major conflict between the European imperial powers had become a world war as troops from throughout the European empires became involved. America and its growing overseas interests were not involved in the fighting on land and were only occasionally affected by naval hostilities. Few Americans volunteered to join the army when war was declared and many of German descent sympathized with America's enemies.

One week after America declared war, the Committee of Public Information was established to persuade Americans that they all needed to contribute to the war effort. Journalist George Creel was appointed head of the Committee. It employed large numbers of people and even greater numbers of volunteers. These included 75,000 speakers, known as the Four Minute Men, who made, on average, ten short speeches each in 5,000 towns and cities over eighteen months—reaching an audience of 300 million people, according to Creel's own report.

Propaganda was successful in persuading people to do their bit for the war effort by growing their own food. This was presented as an important way of helping the country defeat the enemy, with people encouraged to "sow the seeds of victory," and participants described as "soldiers of the soil," working in their "backyard munitions plants." By late 1918, over five million "Victory Gardens" had been sown to offset the cost of war and encourage the consumption of local produce.

KEY TERMS

Conscription Using a law to force people to join the armed forces. This was done by means of the draft: the compulsory enlistment of individuals into military service.

Propaganda Information presented to promote a point of view.

> Use details from Source 2.8 and your contextual knowledge to explain the message of this poster.

SOURCE 2.8

A government poster published in 1917

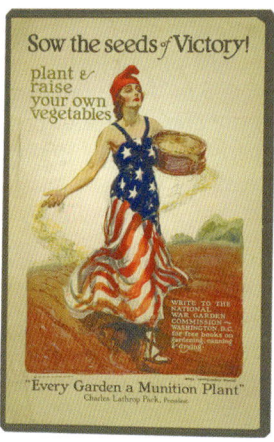

George Creel also attempted to gain the support of working men for the war. In this, he was less successful. He formed the American Alliance for Labor and Democracy, with union leader Samuel Gompers as president, to win working-class support. It had branches in 164 cities, but most working-class people were unenthusiastic. The socialist view of the war was that it was a conflict in defense of the interests of upper-class imperialists, using the working class as cannon fodder.

Newspapers continued to publish stories to persuade their readers of the evil intentions of the Germans. The most famous was the *New York Tribune*'s series of articles, published in November 1917, entitled "The Rape of Belgium." The articles recounted the alleged atrocities committed by the German army that invaded neutral Belgium in August 1914. The articles were accompanied by graphic illustrations which aimed to shock the public.

Rationing

Fighting a war meant adjustments to the economy. The most obvious change for the workforce was the need for large numbers of people, mainly men, to be involved directly in fighting the war. The combatants could not be supplied with basics such as food from the resources of the countries where they were fighting. America had to supply the food and other essentials, sending what the troops needed by sea to Europe. The agricultural workforce diminished, but the same numbers had to be fed. The US Food Administration was set up to address this issue.

Food was not rationed in the US during the First World War. Instead, there were two parallel campaigns to encourage the efficient use of food and to maximize production. The two-pronged campaign used propaganda to persuade civilians to:
- self-ration by serving smaller portions
- avoid serving beef and wheat so that these products could be used for soldiers' rations, including through "meat-free Mondays" and "wheat-free Wednesdays"
- use substitute foods to replace those needed by soldiers in Europe
- reduce food waste by canning and bottling
- grow their own food.

These actions were presented as a means of preserving democracy and defeating the Kaiser. They served to unite the country in waging war. As a result, those who flouted the guidelines were shamed or brought to the attention of the authorities. By the end of the war, food consumption had dropped by fifteen percent.

At the same time, producers were:
- instructed to maximize food production
- told to bring more land into food production
- encouraged to use tractors rather than horses

- forced to replace foodstuffs in short supply with alternatives for the civilian population
- not allowed to sell meat or meat products on Tuesdays.

The first three of these measures were successful in increasing food production. The use of tractors, while limited because of the cost to the farmer, meant that less land was needed to grow fodder for horses. It allowed more land to be brought into production of food for people and reduced the workforce needed for food production. This was also a benefit at a time when many farm workers joined the armed forces. Food exports increased three-fold during the war. The preservation of perishable foodstuffs improved because of the need to ship supplies for the armed forces across the Atlantic. American GIs might have complained about the quality of their rations, but compared to soldiers from other countries they were very well fed.

There were, however, negative long-term effects associated with these changes. While many farmers benefited during the war, they were encouraged to take out loans to increase the size of their farms. These loans remained when the war ended and food prices fell as demand from abroad decreased. Mechanization of farming also reduced the need for farm workers, which impacted those looking to return to farm work after the war. Increased production had lasting environmental impacts too, especially in regions prone to drought and high rates of soil erosion.

Conscription

Woodrow Wilson's administration had recognized for some months that America could not avoid entering the First World War. The National Defense Act of 1916 authorized an increase in the size of the army, but increase in numbers was slow. The First World War was similar to the Civil War in that vast numbers of soldiers were pitted against industrial weapons. This was an uneven contest, which resulted in large numbers of dead and wounded. The US army, numbering around 121,000 men in 1917, needed to recruit thousands of men to go to Europe to fight. Wilson hoped that the shortfall could be made up with volunteers. Only 73,000 men volunteered in the first six weeks after the declaration of war, so the government drafted a conscription law which was introduced in late April. Some politicians opposed conscription, but they were overruled and the law was enacted on May 18, 1917. Men aged 21–30 were required to register for military service. The following year, the age range was extended to men aged 21–45. By the time conscription ended, with the signing of the armistice in November 1918, two million had volunteered and 2.8 million had been drafted.

> ### KEY DATES
>
> | | |
> |---|---|
> | April 1917 | 127,500 officers and soldiers in the US army |
> | May 1917 | Draft begins, men aged 21–30 |
> | June 1917 | First US troops arrive in Europe |
> | October 1917 | First Division enters the trenches, supporting British and French troops |
> | May 1918 | First United States victory |
> | August 1918 | Draft extended to men aged 21–45, volunteering banned |
> | November 1918 | Four million men + 800,000 in other military service branches |
>
> Casualties: The US suffered more than 320,000 casualties in the First World War, including over 53,000 killed in action and 204,000 wounded. The remainder died of diseases, mainly Spanish flu.

The new recruits needed to be trained. America also needed to organize the transfer of men and equipment to Europe. There were few troop ships, so cruise liners, captured German ships and borrowed Allied ships were used to transport soldiers and equipment. At first, US troops were used in support of British and French troops on the Western Front. By the late spring of 1918, the army, commanded by General Pershing, was an effective fighting force in its own right.

Some men refused to fight. If they did so on religious or ethical grounds they were known as "conscientious objectors." Mennonites and members of the Society of Friends were among those who would not fight. Conscientious objectors were allowed to join the military in noncombatant roles, such as stretcher bearers, if their beliefs permitted this. Later in the war, because of labor shortages, they were allowed to work on farms or in relief work in France. Around 2,000 men refused to cooperate in any way and were imprisoned in military prisons where they often suffered physical and mental abuse.

Limitations on civil liberties

Being at war meant the government introduced controversial measures. The First Amendment grants freedom of speech, but the government wanted to suppress the publication and dissemination of any material that challenged America's participation in the war. Woodrow Wilson expressed his fears about treason and espionage as early as his State of the Union address in December 1915.

> What can you learn from Source 2.9 about Wilson's attitude toward immigrants? Support your answer using details from the source.

SOURCE 2.9

Part of Wilson's State of the Union address to Congress, December 1915

I am sorry to say that the gravest threats against our national peace and safety have been uttered within our own borders. There are citizens of the United States, I blush to admit, born under other flags but welcomed under our generous naturalization laws to the full freedom and opportunity of America, who have poured the poison of disloyalty into the very arteries of our national life; who have sought to bring the authority and good name of our Government into contempt, to destroy our industries wherever they thought it effective for their vindictive purposes to strike at them, and to debase our politics to the uses of foreign intrigue.

These ideas were reflected in inflammatory press reports. Every industrial accident was reported as an act of sabotage by people with evil intent toward the state. Any residents of America who were born in enemy countries and were not naturalized American citizens were considered "enemy aliens." This also applied to American-born wives of "enemy alien" men. When war was declared, they became subject to many restrictions, such as being barred from owning firearms or from living or working in certain areas. Such was the fear of spies that from November 1917, all "enemy aliens" had to register with the authorities. Almost half a million Germans registered, 200,000 residence permits were issued and 6,300 "aliens" were arrested on presidential warrants.

The Espionage Act of June 1917 placed severe restrictions on the freedom of speech. It restricted the information that could be collected, criminalizing those who took pictures or copied documents if the authorities believed that these might be used to harm the country or advantage their enemies. No one was allowed to speak out against conscription by obstructing enlistment or by showing disloyalty to military personnel. The penalties were severe. Postmasters were made responsible for preventing material deemed harmful from being mailed. This was so strictly enforced that 74 newspapers were denied mailing privileges.

In May 1918, the terms of the Espionage Act were extended by the Sedition Act. Any speech critical of the war was illegal. The punishments were as severe as those for publications.

The most famous case challenging the restrictions on freedom of speech was *Schenck v. United States* (March 1919). Charles Schenck, the General Secretary of the Socialist Party of Philadelphia, was authorized by the Executive Committee to print and distribute 15,000 leaflets challenging the draft. The leaflets challenged the draft on the grounds that it imposed involuntary servitude on those conscripted. This violated the Thirteenth Amendment and the socialists argued that the draft should not, therefore, be obeyed.

ACTIVITY

Discuss with a partner whether the American administration was justified in the measures it took to mobilize the country for war.

Schenck and his associate Elizabeth Baer were convicted under the Espionage Act. The leaflets were judged likely to disrupt the draft. They were intended to result in the crime of draft dodging and the court ruled that it was likely that they would influence people to do so. Those responsible for producing the leaflets therefore violated the Act. When Schenck and Baer appealed against this judgment on the grounds that the Espionage Act violated the First Amendment, the Supreme Court judges unanimously upheld the original verdict. They ruled that the state has the right to curtail freedom of speech in the interest of protecting itself and the public from danger. In other words, the citizen's rights in relation to the First Amendment are restricted during times of war.

Using propaganda and restricting their right to freedom of speech, the government took more control over its citizens than ever before.

Experiences of Americans during the First World War

All Americans were affected by the First World War, but their experiences varied according to factors such as gender, race, and wealth. The government expected that all its citizens would pull together in the war effort. Generally, they did so, but with mixed experiences and rewards. Shortly after the war ended, women were granted the right to vote in federal elections, and Native Americans gained citizenship rights in 1924. However, there was no political will to enforce civil rights for African Americans.

Role of women at home and in the war

The war affected every woman in the US. For some, new roles marked a change from the past. In other cases, women built on their existing skills. Many women played an active part—for example, as:
- factory workers
- farmworkers
- office workers, including switchboard operators
- voluntary workers in support of the war effort
- armed forces personnel in the navy and Marine Corps, and Army Nurse Corps
- Red Cross nurses.

KEY TERM

Home front The civilian population and activities of a nation during wartime, focusing on support for the military effort.

On the **home front** women of all social classes were involved in the war effort. In the workplace, women replaced men who had been conscripted. Employment rates among women of working age almost doubled as they took on a range of jobs. Besides peace-time factory work, there was additional employment in munitions factories and other defense industry work. Farmwork was particularly important, since food production was an important part of the war effort. Troops overseas needed to be fed and surplus food was exported to America's European allies.

Women were central to the campaign to use food more efficiently. Middle-class women taught classes on preserving methods such as canning. They publicized the campaign and checked guidelines were followed. Women were also central in raising funds for the war through liberty loan drives. Many of these women were utilizing the skills they had learned in other campaigns, such as the Temperance Movement and women's suffrage associations (page 48). The mainstream suffragists decided to focus their efforts on the war rather than on their battle for the vote. Arguably, by doing so, they gave a stronger case for politicians to give women the vote.

This was the first war in which women were admitted to the armed forces. Over 100,000 joined the navy and Marine Corps. They performed non-combatant roles—for example, as drivers, mechanics, and switchboard operators. This freed up men for active combat. Women also joined the army. They worked in communications in the Army Signal Corps and in other non-combatant roles.

The Army Nurse Corps was formed in 1901. In 1914, it comprised only 403 active nurses. It enrolled only unmarried white women as nurses. By the end of the war, it employed 21,480 nurses, over 10,000 of whom had served overseas.

In 1914, there were also about 8,000 American Red Cross nurses. Many of them served in Europe, caring for wounded soldiers in France and Belgium in the three years before America joined the war. In addition, Red Cross nurses worked alongside army nurses in the reserve hospitals established in America before the war broke out. When war was declared, they were transferred to Europe, arriving before the American combat troops.

Segregation of the US military

The US military operated segregated units for African Americans. They were not permitted to join the Marine Corps. The US navy employed them as cooks, stewards, and construction workers, but not in combatant roles.

Some politicians objected to expanding opportunities for African Americans in the military, but they were included in the draft, representing almost ten percent of those registered. When African Americans registered, their Selective Service forms were marked to indicate their ethnicity, ensuring that they would be assigned to segregated units. These were the first African Americans to be deployed in a European conflict. Most African American soldiers were employed in menial construction work, building roads and handling freight, based on racist assumptions that they would be incapable of operating effectively in combat, despite their integral contributions to the US military as far back as the Revolutionary War. There were undoubtedly also concerns that giving African Americans equal treatment to European Americans in the military would lead to increased demands for more equal treatment in all other parts of society.

African Americans were discriminated against at all points in their service. In some training camps, they were left with poor clothing and accommodation. Discriminatory behavior went unpunished. The training of African American officers was initially segregated. However, the training provided was so poor that only one class graduated. Thereafter, officers were trained in the same camps, although it was left to each camp to decide whether to integrate the training of white and Black officers. The authorities were reluctant to intervene because they did not want to cause trouble that would distract from the primary task of training troops and officers to fight in Europe. Attitudes among white soldiers varied and the people in charge did not try to change discriminatory attitudes.

The African American soldiers hoped that their service would be rewarded with better treatment when they returned to America after the armistice was signed. Instead, they were met with hostility. Some white Americans feared that they would use their military skills to force the granting of rights. Racial tension increased, as did lynchings of African Americans.

Differing experiences of US soldiers abroad

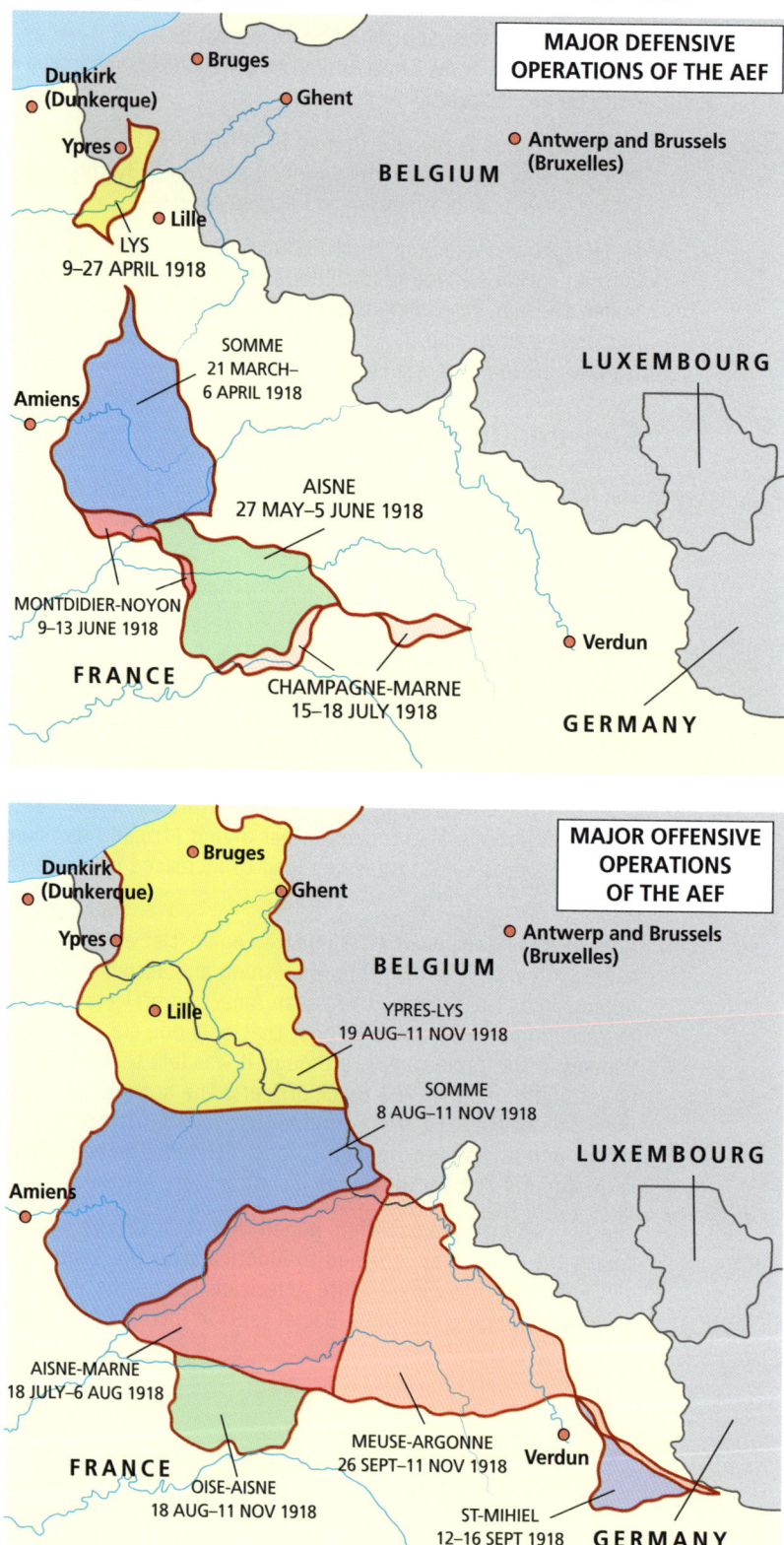

Figure 2.2 Maps of defensive and offensive operations of the American Expeditionary Force (AEF) on the Western Front

> **KEY TERM**
>
> **Trench warfare** The main way the First World War was fought on land. This involved each side digging trenches into the land and shooting at the other side while they tried to make advances. Fights were often lengthy and cost a great number of lives, and the winning side was usually the side with most men left at the end.

American soldiers served on the Western Front in Europe. It took time to recruit, train, and transport soldiers, so the first soldiers arrived in Europe in June 1917, three months after war was declared in the USA. They did not arrive in significant numbers until October. American divisions usually supported the British and French units, adding to their numbers in the **trench warfare** that formed much of the fighting. They did not operate independently until May 1918. By July, the French were being assigned to support American operations. In the spring of 1918, the stalemate of the Western Front turned into a war of movement. At first, the Germans made significant advances. However, they were unable to sustain this and were gradually pushed back. By the fall, the American Expeditionary Force, under its commander, General Pershing, was on the move. It contributed to the Allied counterattack that began in the second week of August with the British victory in cooperation with the French at the Battle of Amiens. In September and October, successful offensives in the Battles of St-Mihiel and Meuse-Argonne involved up to a million French and American soldiers. More than 200 square miles of French territory was recovered in these battles. Americans were also involved in other sections of the front. In the 100 days it took to push the Germans to sign the armistice, the US army suffered 127,000 casualties. Overall, the US suffered more than 320,000 casualties, including over 53,000 killed in action, and 204,000 wounded.

African American soldiers

The only two African American infantry units were the 92nd and 93rd Infantry Divisions. The former did not do well in active service, being disadvantaged by never having trained together and being given inadequate preparation, equipment, and information. However, it is difficult to assess their performance since Lieutenant General Robert Bullard, commander of the American Second Army, was known to hold views which could be considered racist and took every opportunity to spread negative reports about them. He wanted them to fail. The French, with whom they worked, decorated several of their number. The successes of the 93rd Infantry Division (the Harlem Hellfighters) are clearer. This division, despite never reaching full strength, worked with the French Army. The French, having brought Senegalese troops from their empire, treated the members of this division as equals and decorated them with military awards when merited for bravery and valor. Their experience working alongside the French gave the African Americans a taste of equality. Sadly, on their return to the US, they found that racial discrimination was growing rather than diminishing.

Hispanic American soldiers

Hispanic and Native American troops were not segregated. Only US citizens were subject to the draft, but this included Puerto Ricans who had been granted US citizenship in March 1917. However, the 200,000 Hispanic and Latino soldiers that were mobilized were discriminated against. Like African American troops, many were confined to menial heavy labor. Anyone with a Spanish-sounding name was liable to be targeted. In addition, many Hispanics were forced to spend time in the US at special training centers to improve their English language skills before they were allowed to join military units. Since the US was involved in the war for a relatively short time, few Hispanics were sent to Europe. Puerto Rican soldiers were mostly used to guard the Panama Canal against enemy attack.

Native American soldiers

Most Native Americans were not citizens of the US until 1924; regardless, they were considered eligible for the draft. In addition, many volunteered to fight. The 12,000 Native American servicemen served in regular units but were often assigned roles that reflected racial stereotyping, such as scouts and snipers. These dangerous roles might account for the relatively high casualty rate among Native American troops. They were also used as code talkers, with messages transmitted in Native American languages that were unintelligible to the enemy. Like the African American troops, they hoped that fighting for their country, for the cause of democracy, would help them achieve civil rights. Although Native Americans were granted citizenship rights six years after the end of the war, many states continued to effectively prevent Native Americans from voting through electoral restrictions, and the US government continued putting pressure on Native Americans to assimilate into US society and culture, which included undermining Native American land rights and practices. All the same, the experiences of the war meant some veterans took on leadership roles within the growing Native American civil rights movement.

Great Migration of African Americans

The Great Migration of African Americans from the rural South to the cities of the North began before the First World War, in about 1910. The first wave of migration ended when the Great Depression began in the late 1920s. Explaining why so many African Americans moved North at this time involves looking at the push and pull factors. The context is also significant. The circumstances created by the First World War are one of the factors that caused this development.

The situation of African Americans in the South had deteriorated since the end of Reconstruction in 1877. By the early twentieth century, cotton farming was not profitable. Not only were African Americans tied into **sharecropping**, but also the decline in world cotton prices, the ravages of the cotton borer weevil, and flooding combined to keep African Americans in poverty. In addition, Southern legislatures found ways to exclude African Americans from politics and segregate them socially using "Jim Crow Laws." Lynching was common but was not a specific federal crime distinguished from murder. This meant that if state law enforcement did little to prosecute those responsible for lynching, as was often the case in Southern states, the federal government could not do much about it. These factors meant that African Americans were pushed away from the South.

The Northern cities provided pull factors and these were accentuated by the conditions created by the First World War. Labor shortages in the North increased when the war led to a decline in European immigration. The annual number of European immigrants went from 1.2 million before the war to around 300,000 during each war year. When conscription began, further job opportunities appeared. In addition, Northern businesses employed agents who came South to seek out African American workers. These workers were offered help with transportation and housing costs. African Americans went North to work in steel mills, automobile factories, meatpacking plants, and on the railroads.

Such a large influx of migrants caused tensions with groups of immigrants such as the Irish, who arrived in the years preceding the war. The largest increases in African American populations occurred in Philadelphia, Detroit, Chicago, Cleveland, Baltimore, and New York City. Competition for jobs, housing, and status contributed to rising resentment. The American Federation of Labor pushed for segregation in the workplace to ease the tensions generated largely by European workers. This had the opposite effect, as African American workers objected. A critical example of violence was the East St Louis Illinois Riot of 1917. This led to greater activism from the NAACP, starting with a silent march of 10,000 people in Harlem, New York. A further consequence of urban migration was the emergence of the New Negro Movement, a cultural movement later known as the Harlem Renaissance (page 129).

Strikes and the creation of the National War Labor Board

The First World War came toward the end of the Progressive Era, a period in which the difficult living and working conditions of urban industrial workers had been highlighted, and to some extent addressed by the federal government. The war changed the economic environment for American businesses even before the US entered the war.
- The supply of workers from Europe decreased.
- Exports of industrial goods to Europe increased.
- Food exports increased.
- The US financed loans to European states and invested heavily in Latin America.

The first two of these changes had a direct bearing on the labor market and the bargaining power of workers in labor disputes. A shortage of immigrant workers gave greater bargaining power to industrial workers in the Northern cities. As a result, more of them joined labor unions. The number of strikes recorded doubled in 1916 compared with 1915, as workers aimed to take advantage of the situation. Their dissatisfaction with their pay and conditions was made worse by the influx of African American workers, and this caused so many strikes that the federal government acted. The US Commission on Industrial Relations, established in 1912, took evidence about workers' conditions and concluded that workers' organizations and collective bargaining were the best ways to resolve the issues. The report also identified the disparity of wealth as a serious issue and criticized the systems employed in large agricultural holdings.

ACTIVITY
Create a table looking at why African Americans moved North. Add two columns, one titled Push Factors and one titled Pull Factors, and compile the factors you can find in this section into the table.

KEY TERM
Sharecropping An agricultural system that was dominant in the southern US states until the introduction of machinery in the 1930s and 1940s. Sharecroppers (farmers) were tenants on the land they worked in return for a share of the crops they grew. Over the season, they would accumulate debt covering the costs of food, equipment, and animals. At the end of the season a share of the crop would be used to pay this debt. Often there was no money left after the season's debts had been paid, and sharecroppers sruggled to gain financial freedom.

When America entered the war, it became even more important to ensure that productivity levels were maintained and manufacturing was not interrupted by strikes. It is difficult to gauge the success of the systems set up by federal government to achieve this, since they were relatively short-lived. It was clear that these were wartime, not permanent, measures. Nevertheless, entry into the war saw a further increase in strike action. Not only were there more strikes, but they involved more workers. In the first six months that America was at war, there were over 3,000 strikes; at least 67 involved more than 10,000 workers each. Rapid changes in the available workforce, together with higher food prices and rents, fueled worker discontent and sometimes led to sympathetic general strikes in towns or racially motivated unrest.

The increase in strikes did not help the government's priority of responding to the high demand from the US military and America's allies. As a result, the National War Labor Board was established in April 1918, to make recommendations in labor disputes. Nine in every ten of the 1,245 cases investigated arose from worker complaints. Of these, the Board presented formal findings in 520 cases. Although they heard both sides of the argument, the Board generally favored the workers' positions. They based their findings on the premise that workers had the right to organize and bargain collectively. However, they favored informal groups of workers organized within individual workplaces rather than the wider labor unions. When the war ended, government intervention was scaled back, but strikes and other worker unrest continued.

ACTIVITY

- Find evidence from this section to support and challenge the statement, "Americans supported involvement in the war."
- To what extent do you agree with the statement?

SUMMARY DIAGRAM

America and the First World War
Why did the US enter the First World War and how did the war impact Americans?

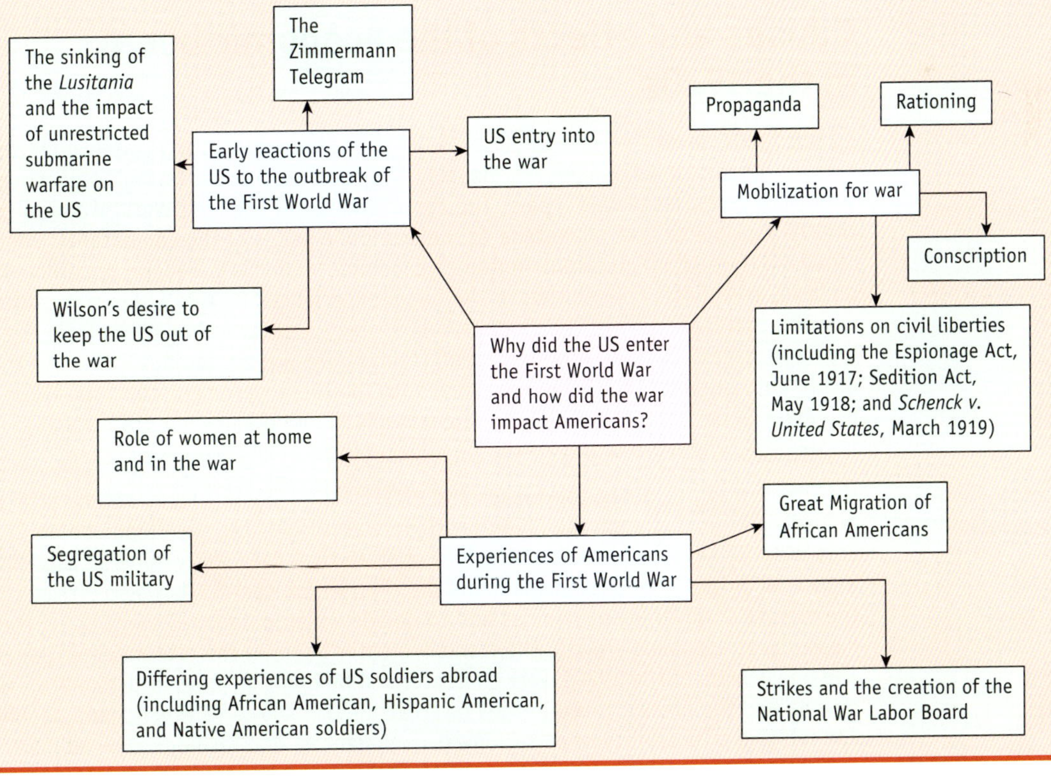

2.3 What were the causes and impacts of economic and cultural changes in the 1920s?

The 1920s was an exciting decade in the USA. The economy grew in new ways. There were periods of greater economic growth at the end of the previous century, but these were based on heavy industry and infrastructure projects. By 1920, investment and levels of disposable income were high and credit was readily available. The development of new ways of working more efficiently meant that goods were produced in greater numbers and more cheaply. Advertising techniques were developed to attract consumers. Economic growth in the 1920s focused on consumer goods that changed the lives of many Americans, although the labor-saving domestic appliances promised more than they delivered in terms of creating additional leisure time. Cars, telephones, radios, and other domestic appliances powered by electricity became commonplace. Social norms were challenged, particularly by the "New Woman." Cultural changes included widespread access to the cinema and the fairytale world of Hollywood, as well as new phases in the development of African American culture through the Harlem Renaissance and the popularity of jazz.

There were also negative sides to the 1920s. The Eighteenth Amendment, which banned the manufacture, importation, transportation, and sale of intoxicating liquor at a national level came into effect in January 1920. Despite substantial support for prohibition, it heralded an age of unprecedented crime and mob violence, founded on illicit trade in alcohol. The 1920s also witnessed a reaction against modernity. This was epitomized by the trial of Tennessee science teacher John Scopes for teaching the Darwinian theory of evolution, which had been banned because it conflicted with Christian creationism. The "New Woman" was criticized for being immodest and immoral, rather than praised for being liberated. African American culture, especially jazz and dance crazes such as the Charleston and Black Bottom, were considered immoral by traditionalists. In the 1920s, racial prejudice extended to many groups. Fear of socialism in all its forms was widespread. There were also concerns about the scale of immigration and its impact on the politics and ethnic makeup of America. This led to strict **quotas** being imposed on immigration based on national origin, as well as the famous conviction and execution of two Italian anarchists, Sacco and Vanzetti.

Causes and effects of the economic boom in the 1920s

By the 1920s, America's economy was the biggest in the world. Historians point to many reasons for this. Developments in industry and commerce in the late nineteenth and early twentieth centuries played a part. The circumstances of the First World War and the way that the US was able to take advantage of the economic needs of the combatants, while its lands remained unscathed, also contributed to economic supremacy. Federal government policy on taxes and tariffs contributed to the boom experienced by new industries. Although the wealth generated was not evenly distributed, many Americans benefited from the country's prosperity. Mass consumerism developed from its pre-war beginnings, based on the ready availability of credit in a banking system with limited government controls. However, the economic boom did not make all Americans rich. Farming and some traditional industries did not benefit, and more than half the population lived below the poverty line.

Historians disagree about the causes and effects of economic change. Some economic historians even challenge the idea that there was a significant economic boom in the 1920s. This is partly because of the unreliability of statistical data concerning all aspects of trade, industrial output, personal income, and distribution of wealth. It is also difficult to gauge the effects of government policies and to decide which data is relevant. Using the usual measures of economic growth, there was a greater boom in the late nineteenth century. The boom years of the 1920s were characterized by great displays of personal wealth. The cinema and the press created images of an affluent lifestyle to which many people aspired. The relative affordability of cars, domestic appliances, and fashions allowed many people to experience a new freedom.

> **KEY TERM**
>
> **Quota** A fixed restriction on quantity. This can be a minimum or maximum, e.g. a maximum number of immigrants that a country will accept or a minimum number of attendees required for an event.

Legacy of the First World War

The American economy benefited from the First World War. America emerged from the war as the wealthiest and most developed industrial country in the world. America's relative wealth was helped by the enormous financial cost of fighting the war being borne by the great European powers, as well as the cost to them in lives and material damage. American wealth increased through selling food and war materials to the Entente Powers. These sales were financed by loans brokered by American finance companies. For example, the investment bank JP Morgan & Co. underwrote $1.5 billion in war loans to London over the course of the war. Later, France and Russia also financed their war on Wall Street. JP Morgan profited by over $200 million in commission on the loans. When the war ended, the Allies owed vast sums of money to the US. Repayment was so difficult for the European countries that the US had to step in twice during the 1920s to prevent the collapse of European government finances.

The need to produce food and industrial goods for export encouraged the mechanization of US agriculture and the development of mass production methods in industry. This contributed to lower consumer prices in the post-war years. The decline in immigration caused by the war was an additional factor discouraging the reliance on a large, cheap labor force.

This legacy was disastrous for agriculture. Farmers had been encouraged to invest heavily in expensive machinery such as tractors and combine harvesters. They had also been encouraged to bring additional marginal land into food production. These investments were financed by loans. At the end of the war, European agriculture recovered quickly and demand fell for US imports.

On the other hand, industries that made household goods could now mass-produce items at a lower cost. This fed the consumer boom of the 1920s. Some industries, such as those making cotton textiles, were in decline by the 1920s. This was because their products were being replaced by cheaper alternatives, such as synthetic fabrics that came through scientific developments. War can hasten such developments, but it is not the sole cause.

The transition to a peacetime world economy was problematic and was one reason for an economic depression in 1920–21. At the end of this short depression, many sectors of the American economy were well-placed to prosper although farming remained depressed.

"Return to normalcy" and *laissez-faire*

During the First World War, the US had taken a more active role in world affairs than ever before. The war had also built on the Progressive Era increase in federal government involvement in the lives of ordinary Americans. By 1920 there was a reaction based on the idea of restoring American values. These included:
- A policy of isolationism, not seeking active involvement in world events. Congress refused to ratify the Paris Peace Treaties that ended the First World War and the USA did not join the League of Nations.
- Supporting private enterprise over government direction of production. Though the government had supported farming in expanding food production during the war, it did not come to its aid in adjusting to peacetime circumstances.
- Reduced interference in relations between employers and employees. For example, Ford Motor Company employees were not allowed to join labor unions.
- Focus on making America prosperous, not on helping other countries. America imposed high import tariffs and demanded repayment of war loans from its allies.

In the 1920 presidential election, Republican candidate **Warren Harding's** statement that "America's present need is not heroics but healing, not **nostrums** but normalcy, not revolution but restoration" held great appeal for the electorate. He won by a greater margin than any previous candidate, polling 60.4 percent of the popular vote to Democrat James Cox's 34.1 percent.

Harding's election marked a reduction in federal government involvement in the economy, despite calls for help from sections of the economy that were suffering. This was driven by Harding's opinion that government intervention in the economy should be kept to a minimum and that businesses should be allowed to function independently. This marked

> **KEY TERM**
>
> **Nostrum** A medicine prepared by an unqualified person that is not considered effective.

a "return to normalcy" in that it reflected the fundamentals of American ideology. It was closer to the *laissez-faire* values of the Gilded Age, with its emphasis on the growth of business. For most of the 1920s, this approach allowed some elements of the economy to prosper. However, as was the case in the Gilded Age, much of the shine of the 1920s boom was superficial and insecure.

Although his critics accused him of being lazy and lacking understanding of the situation, others regarded Harding as shrewd. His statement, "We want less government in business and more business in government," resonated with his Republican supporters and was reflected in his appointment of millionaire banker **Andrew Mellon** as Secretary of the Treasury. Harding's ideas were reflected in policy as he:
- repealed high wartime taxes
- returned to a policy of high tariffs
- did not enforce antitrust laws
- supported employers in industrial disputes.

When Harding died in 1923, Vice President **Calvin Coolidge** took his place and Republican policies continued.

Calvin Coolidge, known as "Silent Cal," believed in minimal government. He wanted to maintain a booming economy. He regarded tax-cutting and light regulation of business as the way to achieve this, on the grounds that wealth would trickle down from the rich to the less well-off. The growth of the economy provided the evidence to justify his policies. Coolidge's Commerce Secretary was Herbert Hoover. His ideas were less laissez-faire than those of Harding and Coolidge. However, he had limited influence. He created the "Own Your Own Home" program. This encouraged the construction industry to build more houses and allowed federally chartered banks to lend to house purchasers, to enable more individual home ownership.

> ### KEY FIGURES
>
> **Warren G. Harding (1865–1923)** Harding was born in Ohio. He was staunchly Republican, had a good speaking voice and allowed leading industrialists to influence his policies. This led to success in politics in Ohio and in securing the Republican nomination for the 1920 presidential election. The "Ohio gang" continued to influence him when he entered the White House in 1921. Harding's lack of control over his so-called friends meant that scandal was emerging by the time he died in August 1923.
>
> **Calvin Coolidge (1872–1933)** Coolidge was born in Vermont and rose to political prominence in Massachusetts where he was a lawyer. He was selected as vice-presidential candidate in 1920, having won admiration among Republicans for his anti-strike stance. He was not associated with the scandals of the Harding presidency and easily won the Republican nomination and the presidential election of 1924. As Harding's vice president he was known as "Silent Cal" as he rarely spoke in Senate or in cabinet meetings. In contrast, as President he was a very public figure, engaging in press conferences, radio broadcasts, and photo opportunities.
>
> **Andrew Mellon (1855–1937)** Andrew Mellon was appointed Secretary to the Treasury by President Warren Harding and remained in that post under Coolidge and Hoover. His ideas on the way to achieve economic prosperity for the nation were behind government policy. He believed that the Treasury should aim to reduce government debt and to balance the budget. He thought that low taxes on businesses would allow the profits of business to be transferred to the nation. These ideas appeared to work well until the Great Crash of 1929. After this he was increasingly criticized and he left the Treasury in 1932.

Federal policies: low taxes, high tariffs, and widespread availability of credit

To what extent did 1920s federal policies reflect a "return to normalcy" and *laissez-faire* government? The cost of the First World War for the American government far exceeded that of every other war it had fought. It necessitated high levels of taxation. The Sixteenth Amendment, ratified in 1913, allowed federal government to collect income tax. The levels at which this was collected increased significantly when America joined the war. In 1917, anyone earning more than $2,000 a year had to pay income tax at two percent. Previously, the limit had been $20,000. The top bracket of tax, for those earning over $2 million, was increased from fifteen to 67 percent. In 1918, those earning over $1 million had to pay 77 percent tax. In 1918, nearly $4 billion, representing 60 percent of federal income, came from income tax. These levels of taxation could be justified during wartime but not in peacetime. During the 1920s, the rates were gradually lowered. The top tax rate was reduced to 58 percent in 1922, 25 percent in 1925, then to 24 percent in 1929. The proportion of the country's Gross National Product paid in income tax declined. Despite these cuts, federal government receipts from income tax increased. The rise in wages was so great that revenues rose from $719 million in 1921 to $1.164 billion in 1928.

> **KEY TERM**
>
> **Gross National Product**
> The total value of all goods and services produced within a country.

Tariffs were a controversial means of manipulating international trade. The main aim of the American government was the protection of American companies and jobs. They wanted to ensure well-paid employment for demobilized service personnel. One effect of America's wealth was that high wages made home-produced goods more expensive to make than the equivalent foreign-produced goods. To protect American businesses from cheap imports, the government raised tariffs. The Fordney–McCumber Tariff of 1922 was a law that raised American tariffs on many imported goods to protect factories and farms. Tariffs were set on average at fourteen percent, with much higher rates for some manufactured goods. They were calculated using a complex system. The tariff related to the cost of the American equivalent product rather than the price of the imported product. While this had the desired effect of protecting American industry, it meant that consumers paid more. The price of food, as well as manufactured goods, was inflated. Not surprisingly, other countries introduced their own tariffs in retaliation, so American goods were more expensive abroad. France raised its tariffs on cars from 45 to 100 percent, Spain raised its tariffs on American goods by 40 percent, and Germany and Italy raised their tariffs on wheat. The result was that American goods were less attractive to foreigners and people who relied on exports, such as farmers, suffered. The American Farm Bureau estimated that the tariffs lost American farmers $300 million a year. This was made up of lost sales and the increased cost of equipment. Henry Ford argued that his industry did not need tariffs since Ford cars were sufficiently low priced that Americans would buy them regardless of foreign competition and his company would do better if sales abroad were not handicapped by foreign tariffs.

A further feature of the 1920s that certainly promoted economic growth was the widespread availability of credit. The level of business and personal debt that existed by the late 1920s set the economy on fragile foundations. "Buy now, pay later" was the message for businesses and individual consumers. Real estate developers took out loans and banks offered mortgages for house purchase for the first time. Installment plans for the purchase of consumer goods were common. In the late 1920s, the speculative boom extended to the purchase of shares on Wall Street. Inexperienced investors saw this as a means to make money, buying shares with a ten percent deposit "on the margin." Consumer debt doubled in the 1920s and borrowing to finance business expansion was the norm. In 1929, debts amounted to over $200 billion. To place this in context, the nation's entire annual income was $87 billion.

The fiscal and financial policies favored by the Republican administrations of the 1920s allowed some parts of the economy to flourish. They also sowed the seeds for the Wall Street Crash and the Great Depression.

> **ACTIVITY**
>
> Working in a group, pick one each of these factors that contributed to the economic boom:
> - *laissez-faire* policies
> - the Fordney-McCumber Tariff
> - availability of credit
> - low taxes
> - the impact of the First World War.
>
> Take turns to explain how your factor contributed to the boom. Then discuss the following:
> - What links are there between these factors?
> - Is one factor more important than the others? Why?
>
> Compare your ideas with other groups in the class.

Increasing standards of living and the development of modern consumerism

Living standards for many Americans rose during the 1920s. They could afford better food, more of them had access to electricity to light their houses and power domestic appliances, they bought more consumer goods, and they were promised more leisure time. This was a consequence of the boom and it also fed it.

Technological advances produced new devices for the home. In 1920, 35 percent of households had electric power. By 1929, 68 percent had electricity. Electric-powered refrigerators, washing machines, irons, and vacuum cleaners were among the labor-saving devices that made household chores easier and less time-consuming. These products were all expensive, but their modern appeal meant that consumers did not want to wait to save for them. They did not need to, as stores offered installment plans; a downpayment was made and the remainder paid in regular installments. This created a high level of demand. About 60 percent of furniture and 75 percent of radios were bought on credit offered by the store where they were purchased.

Women typically carried out the domestic chores in the 1920s and these advances meant they could now do their housework faster. The cleaning and laundry might be done more frequently. More elaborate meals could be prepared using an electric stove that did not need to be fed with solid fuel. It is unclear, however, if this meant more leisure time for women. Alternatively, the woman of the house might find employment outside the home.

Home entertainment was also popular. The percentage of households with radios increased from 19 percent in 1925 to between 35 and 40 percent in 1929. In 1922, $60 million was spent on radios. In 1929, the sum was $843 million.

Automobile ownership rapidly increased as prices fell relative to wages. In 1919, there were 6.7 million cars in America. By 1929, there were 23 million cars on the road. In 1916, a Model T Ford car cost two years' average salary. By 1924, it was less than three month's salary. In 1916, the car cost $390 and in 1924, it cost $290.

A new style of advertisement popularized these products. The consumer was encouraged to identify themselves as the owner by picturing themselves using their purchase in an idealized environment. Advertisements might show families in cars, enjoying a day out in the countryside, or happy women using household appliances.

> What can you learn from this image about attitudes in the 1920s?

SOURCE 2.10

An advertisement published in 1920

ACTIVITY

Explain how each of the problems shown in Figure 2.3 contributed to farmers' poverty.

Economic difficulties in the 1920s

Not everyone benefited from the boom of the 1920s. Using the measures in place at the time, about 60 percent of the population lived at or below the poverty line. These people were unable to benefit from the boom because of barriers to prosperity. These barriers were caused by occupations and ethnicity.

Farmers suffered very badly. By 1928, half of all farmers were living in poverty. Farming income fell from $22 billion in 1919 to $13 billion in 1929.

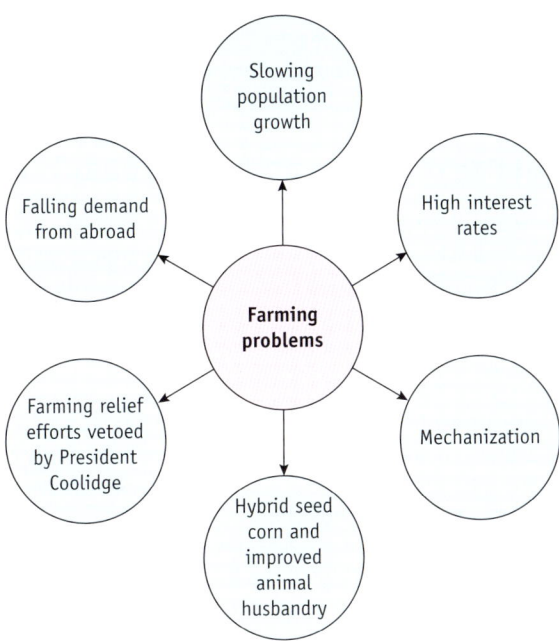

Figure 2.3 Causes of farming problems in the 1920s

Many poor farmers were African American. African Americans in the South were small-scale sharecroppers growing crops that were no longer in demand. Cotton was replaced by synthetic fibers such as rayon for clothing. The price of cotton dropped from 38 cents a pound in 1919, to seventeen cents a pound in 1920, and by 1932 it was five cents a pound. An insect, the cotton boll weevil, devastated crops in some areas. Tobacco prices also fell. Three-quarters of a million African American agricultural workers became unemployed during the 1920s. If they moved North in search of factory work, they were employed in low-skill, low-paid jobs. Immigrants, who often had poor levels of English, were also disadvantaged, and were paid the least. They were resented because they would work for low wages and so kept wages low for other workers. Prejudiced views of African Americans and recent immigrants prevented most from sharing in the prosperity of the 1920s.

Traditional industries failed to prosper. Electricity and oil replaced coal as a household and industrial fuel. Although coal could be used to generate electricity, it was only one of several options. Surplus production kept prices and miners' wages low. Shipbuilding was also in decline as demand decreased. Wages barely increased in the construction industry, despite the boom in buildings. New synthetic textile production needed fewer workers than cotton or wool. Workers in traditional industries were trapped in poverty.

ACTIVITY

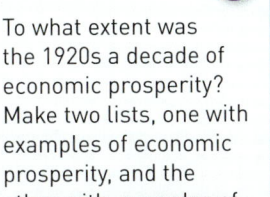

To what extent was the 1920s a decade of economic prosperity? Make two lists, one with examples of economic prosperity, and the other with examples of poverty and economic stagnation. Use your lists to help you decide whether prosperity or poverty was more widespread.

Impacts of prohibition and the rise of organized crime

The Eighteenth Amendment, enforced by the Volstead Act, came into effect on January 16, 1920. It marked the triumph of the Temperance Movement, as it extended prohibition to the whole of America. The manufacture, importation, transportation, and sale of intoxicating liquor was banned. The only exemptions were for religious and medicinal use, and, consequently, sales for these purposes increased massively. Poison was added to alcohol needed for industrial purposes, but much of this alcohol went missing and was then responsible for hundreds of deaths. The consumption of alcohol was not made illegal.

When drinking clubs, known as speakeasies, were raided it was the owners who were prosecuted rather than their clients. Supplying intoxicating liquor to the numerous people who had no intention of giving it up turned existing mobsters into finely tuned and organized criminal gangs. Many at the top of politics and society, including President Harding, who was a keen whiskey drinker, continued to consume alcohol. Underpaid law enforcement officers were open to bribes from criminals. There were also far too few of these officers and they were too spread out to make much difference. Bootlegging, protection rackets, prostitution, gambling rings, and shoot-outs—all were within the remit of the gangs, which were often based on the ethnic divisions of cities. One of the difficulties for the mobsters was concealing their illegal earnings. Some managed to invest their money in legitimate businesses. For others, such as Al Capone, it was financial crimes that led to their downfall at the hands of the tax authorities. These unintended outcomes of prohibition overshadowed the benefits anticipated by the Temperance Movement.

Life under prohibition and speakeasy culture

Prohibition was not universally popular. Alcohol continued to be produced in homes across the country. **Moonshine** spirits were produced in illegal "stills." Home-distilled "bathtub" gin was made in such tall bottles that they had to be filled in the bath as they would not fit in the sink. In 1930, government agents seized 282,122 illegal stills. The products of home distilling were often unpleasant and sometimes deadly. They were poisonous and could cause blindness.

In cities, drinking clubs were rife. They were known as **speakeasies**—perhaps because customers needed to speak quietly to avoid detection or because a password needed to be spoken to gain entry to the club—or because of the effect of the alcohol on the clients. Speakeasies were more numerous than saloons had been before prohibition. By 1930, there were estimated to be 250,000 speakeasies across the country, including 32,000 in New York City. The first was known simply as the Back of Ratner's. Famous actors of stage and screen, as well as notorious gangsters, drank there. Clubs where alcohol was freely available included the Cotton Club in Harlem and later the 21 Club in Manhattan. The Cotton Club was famous for its African American entertainers but exclusively white clientele. It was operated by the New York gangster Owney Madden and sold his "#1 Beer." By the late 1920s, the 21 Club was frequented by members of high society. Elaborate efforts were made to hide the liquor in case of raids by emptying the shelves in the bar using a series of levers and creating a secret hidden section of the cellar. The speakeasies sold bootleg alcohol imported from Canada or the Caribbean. This included "The Real McCoy," unadulterated rum shipped from the Bahamas by Captain William McCoy, a famous **rum runner**.

Reasons for the rise of organized crime

A combination of factors led from the well-intentioned ban on alcohol to the proliferation of organized crime.
- The trade in alcohol was now illegal but there was still demand. **Outlawing** a widely consumed and popular beverage was an invitation to criminals to set up supply chains and provide what many people wanted.
- There was a ready supply of criminal gangs to do this work. They had previously operated in limited areas of cities, mainly based in specific neighborhoods which were dominated by specific ethnic groups such as Polish, Italian, Jewish, and Irish. There they engaged in moneylending, extortion, sex work, and gambling. The most successful gangs were those operated by corrupt city bosses, securing votes and intimidating their political opponents in exchange for being allowed to operate their criminal operations. They soon developed into organized criminal gangs under bosses such as Al Capone and Charles "Lucky" Luciano.
- The illegal liquor trade operated between states and internationally. This required high levels of organization and planning. Small-time local criminal gangs needed to develop into well-organized enterprises. They had to cooperate to organize the trade. They had to pay off or eliminate anyone who got in their way.
- The **bootleggers** made vast profits. They needed to conceal this money so they had to employ lawyers and accountants who could make this happen. They needed to purchase the means to carry out their business and hide their profits from the authorities. This all required a level of organization that far exceeded earlier mobster activity.

KEY TERMS
Moonshine Illegally distilled liquor.
Speakeasy An illicit club selling alcohol.

KEY TERM
Rum runner A person who illegally brought alcohol ashore or across land borders.

KEY TERMS
Outlawing Banning or making something illegal.
Bootlegger A person who illegally produced, transported, or distributed alcohol

ALPHONSE "SCARFACE" CAPONE (1899–1947)

Al Capone was the son of Italian immigrants. He was born in Brooklyn, New York in 1899. Leaving school after the sixth grade, he was allowed to join Johnny Torrio's street gang. One of the other members of the gang was Charles Luciano. In his early twenties, Capone moved to Chicago where he was a bodyguard for Torrio, head of a bootlegging enterprise. After a gang war with another group, Torrio retired and Capone became boss of "The Outfit." Capone's relationship with Mayor William Hale Thompson and the Chicago Police Department made him immune from law enforcement, despite rising levels of gang violence. He allegedly made a $250,000 donation to Thompson's reelection campaign and bribery of the police meant that his alcohol trade with Canada and business concerns in Chicago went unchallenged. His charitable donations turned him into a popular hero, as witnessed by the spectators' cheers when he attended baseball games. The level of gang violence in Chicago became increasingly shocking. His downfall came after the Saint Valentine's Day Massacre. Although he could not be linked to the murders, the tide of public opinion turned against him. A group of federal agents, including Prohibition Bureau Agent Eliot Ness, was formed on the orders of recently elected President Hoover, to bring an end to the reign of "Public Enemy Number One." After a series of arrests for a range of crimes, including 5,000 violations of the Volstead Act, Capone was eventually sentenced to eleven years in jail for federal tax evasion. This ended his years of notoriety. He was already suffering the symptoms of syphilis (a sexually transmitted disease that can cause brain damage if not treated) and by the time he was released from jail, he was judged to have the mental capacity of a twelve-year-old.

A police photo of Al Capone, taken in 1931

ACTIVITY

What reasons for the power of organized crime can you identify in the information about the gang leaders Al Capone, Charles Luciano, and Bugs Moran?

CHARLES "LUCKY" LUCIANO (1897–1962)

Charles Luciano was born in Sicily in 1896 and moved to New York City with his parents at the age of ten. He immediately began to commit petty crimes, such as mugging and shoplifting. His first jail term came at the age of twenty for selling heroin. By the time prohibition started, he was working for Arnold Rothstein, an early bootlegger. After becoming New York City's top bootlegger, Luciano was soon a multimillionaire. His position depended on working with the leaders of all five of New York City's crime families. Inevitably, there were rivalries, suspicions, and plots. Having ordered the murder of his boss, Joe Masseria, he found out that Masseria's successor was plotting to kill him. He then had his new boss, Salvatore Maranzano, killed. The new-style organization that followed involved cooperation among all the crime chiefs in a nationwide grouping known as the Commission. Luciano managed to control this from his prison cell between 1936 and 1945, and continued to do so after he was deported to Italy the following year.

GEORGE "BUGS" MORAN (1893–1957)

Bugs Moran was born in St Paul, Minnesota in 1893, the child of French immigrants. He moved to Chicago in 1912 and quickly became involved in petty crime, spending several short terms in prison. His ascendancy coincided with the start of prohibition. His gang of bootleggers controlled distilleries and breweries in Chicago's North Side. Inevitably, this put him in conflict with rival gang leaders Johnny Torrio, Charles Dion O'Bannion, and Al Capone. At first, agreements led to peaceful coexistence. However, violence soon started. O'Bannion was assassinated by Capone and Torrio. Moran, together with the remains of O'Bannion's gang, went to war. There were several assassination attempts on Torrio and Capone. After a narrow escape, Torrio retired, leaving Capone as leader. There was a short-lived truce between Moran and Capone, but isolated shootings then turned to full-scale violence again. When two of Capone's closest associates were murdered, he vowed to kill Moran and executed the Saint Valentine's Day Massacre (page 122). When prohibition ended, Moran's fortunes declined. He continued in a life of crime, ending his days in 1957 while serving a lengthy prison sentence for bank fraud.

The pre-existence of criminal gangs, and corrupt politicians, combined with the nature of the liquor trade and the vast profits it generated, meant that the Eighteenth Amendment triggered a frenzy of organized crime.

The power of organized crime and the bootlegging industry

Why was organized crime powerful in the prohibition era? Gangster bosses and their families made personal fortunes and controlled wide-ranging business interests. Not only did they control these great enterprises, but they also held power over politicians and police chiefs by association and bribery. These establishment figures often purchased alcohol from bootleggers. Chicago boss Al Capone paid $500,000 a month in bribes to police to allow him to carry on his trade. These bribes were a small proportion of the $100 million he was reputed to earn each year.

The main centers of organized crime were the cities of Chicago and New York. Immigrants of Italian, Polish, Irish, and Jewish origin dominated poor areas in these cities. Prior to prohibition, the gangs were run by leading families from these communities. Prohibition-era gangs differed from earlier criminal groups in that they crossed ethnic divides and relied on cooperation between large numbers of criminal gangs. However, at times, rivalries caused violence between different factions. Over 1,000 mobsters were killed in New York gang clashes during prohibition. In the Chicago "Beer Wars" of the mid-1920s, 475 mobsters were killed: 315 by gang members and 160 by the police. The most infamous murders took place on February 14, 1929; members of Al Capone's gang dressed as policemen and gunned down seven of rival gang leader Bugs Moran's men. There was insufficient evidence to link Capone to the Saint Valentine's Day Massacre, as it became known.

The power of the leading gangsters is unsurprising. The bootlegging trade required high levels of organization. Bootleg liquor was imported and rum runners brought bottles by ship from the Caribbean. Other bootleggers imported liquor from Canada by ship or by road. All aspects of transportation, from the ships themselves to the crews and captains, were in the control of the gangs. Gangsters also controlled production at distilleries and breweries in the US. They controlled what happened to the liquor, whether it was sold in the condition in which it was imported, adulterated, or simply watered down. They controlled the speakeasies where it was sold and paid protection money to the authorities to avoid raids and investigations. Border patrols and customs officials were all on the payroll of the gangsters. Gangsters employed armed protection to defend their assets and destroy their rivals. The demand for bootleg liquor was huge and hence the profits were enormous. The chances of being caught were low. Prohibition caused a crime wave on a scale until then unknown.

The federal response to organized crime

Prohibition was a major problem for the agencies of law enforcement. Before national prohibition, liquor smuggling had been an issue—for example, on the Canadian border with Alaska. The **Bureau of Investigation (BOI)** worked with the Canadian authorities to stop this. The BOI had also been involved during the First World War in efforts to keep American soldiers alcohol-free so they were fit to fight. When national prohibition was introduced, the work of enforcement escalated. Enforcement of prohibition was the responsibility of the Treasury Department's Bureau of Internal Revenue, but the workload was so great that the BOI had to help.

Law enforcers dealt with hundreds of cases of violation of the Volstead Act. They often found that the crimes they investigated were linked to many others. Liquor might be transported in stolen vehicles, for example. The crimes could be very large-scale. In Savannah, Georgia, 142 arrests were made regarding a conspiracy to violate prohibition laws. More than 50 BOI agents were involved in the case.

Sometimes, the BOI had to arrest state law enforcement officers. In a Michigan sheriff's office, a group of deputies had seized bootleg alcohol smuggled in from Canada for their own business. Six deputies and former deputies were fined and imprisoned.

> **ACTIVITY**
> Draw a diagram to show how factors linked together to cause the rise of organized crime. Choose one of the factors and explain why it caused the rise of organized crime.

> **KEY TERM**
> **Bureau of Investigation (BOI)** A federal law enforcement organization and the predecessor of the Federal Bureau of Investigation (FBI).

Since law enforcement officers were not particularly well-paid, there was always the danger that they would be tempted by the bribes handed out by gangsters. The most notorious of these corrupt agents was Gaston Means. He already had a poor record when he became a BOI agent in 1921. He had been accused of spying for Germany during the war and of forging the will of a rich widow and then murdering her so that he could inherit her fortune. As an agent, he received payments from bootleggers, promising to get them out of jail. In 1924, J Edgar Hoover was appointed head of the Bureau and Means was sacked.

In 1927, a new law enforcement body was created, making the policing of prohibition separate from the BOI. This was the Bureau of Prohibition, a branch of the Department of Justice. From the outset, it was overwhelmed with work. Agents such as Eliot Ness struggled to find the evidence to implicate the gangsters. Although his most famous target was Al Capone, it was the Internal Revenue Service, not the Bureau of Prohibition, that secured Capone's conviction.

Law enforcement was inevitably a challenge in a large country with too few officers. The Prohibition Bureau employed between 1,500 and 2,000 agents. Despite being poorly paid, some of them were driven to work by chauffeurs. Their lifestyles did not match their pay grade. Nevertheless, only twelve were ever sacked for corruption.

Izzy Einstein and his partner Moe Smith were among the successful BOI agents. Their strategy was to use disguises to deceive the crooks. Their arrest and conviction rates were impressive, but the fame that this brought them came at a price. It is unclear what the BOI's phrase "for the good of the service" meant when it fired them in 1925. There were stories in the press suggesting that their superiors were unhappy about the publicity they received. This might have been because of their amusing disguises or possibly because their names were better known than those of their bosses. Einstein's version of events was that he was asked to transfer from New York City to Chicago and he resigned because he wanted to stay.

A more surprising agent was Richard "Two-Gun" Hart. Born into an Italian family who moved from Sicily to New York City, he distanced himself from his background and left the city to work for a traveling Wild West show. During the First World War, he served in France. During prohibition, he worked first as a BOI agent, then for the Bureau of Indian Affairs. The high levels of alcoholism on the reservation where he was based in North Dakota meant bootleggers had many willing customers for liquor. Hart gained a fearsome reputation. In one successful raid, he removed 25 gallons of alcohol from the reservation. Hart had an unusual secret: the family he had left behind in New York City included several brothers, one of whom was Al Capone. In the years that followed, he never acknowledged the relationship, although when work was harder to find in the years of the Great Depression, he occasionally asked his brother for financial help. In 1951, he was called to testify in the trial of another of his brothers and the truth emerged.

On December 5, 1933, the ratification of the Twenty-First Amendment overturned the Eighteenth Amendment and ended prohibition. This fulfilled one of Franklin Roosevelt's 1932 election promises. Prohibition was widely unpopular and widely flouted. In the context of the Great Depression, the following all contributed to this decision:
- the tax revenue that alcohol sales would bring
- the employment opportunities provided by a legitimate liquor trade
- the hope of ending mob violence.

"Modernity" vs. "Tradition"

> **KEY TERM**
>
> **Flapper** A fashionable young woman, often someone who wanted to go against conventional behavior.

The popular image of 1920s culture is deceptive. The boom time, fast-living, Hollywood-style glamour of the flapper, the jazz club, and the speakeasy were not typical. Some changes were more far-reaching in society. The new domestic appliances, car ownership, and changing opportunities for women affected more people. In the 1920s, some characteristics of a more modern lifestyle began to develop. At the same time, there was a reaction against change. Some aspects of this were rooted in fundamentalist religious beliefs or ideas about gender roles. The division between modernity and tradition often fell along the urban-rural divide. To a lesser extent, the split was generational. Understanding the 1920s involves recognizing the presence and influence of both sets of views.

KEY TERM

Christian fundamentalist A religious movement that emerged in the late nineteenth century rejecting attempts to align Christianity with the latest scientific developments, instead focusing on a literal interpretation of the Bible.

Fundamentalism vs. evolution and the Scopes trial

America had long been the refuge of those with Christian religious views outside the mainstream. The values of some of these Christian fundamentalist groups fed into many aspects of life. The Temperance Movement was largely driven by Christian women who thought that the social problems they identified were caused by alcohol consumption and that the solution was to ban alcohol. As we have seen (page 120), the success of the Temperance Movement had unintended and negative consequences. During the 1920s, with traditional morality under challenge, Christians were on the defensive. In 1925, the state of Tennessee passed the Butler Act. It was a law that banned public school teachers from denying the account of the creation of humans found in the Bible in the book of Genesis. The law also forbade the teaching of the evolution of humans from more primitive primates, as implied by Charles Darwin in *On the Origin of Species*. The spread of public schooling meant that this law offered an opportunity to limit the attack on traditional beliefs. It was designed to reassure the people of conservative states that schooling was a good choice that did not present a challenge to their values.

In 1925, there was a famous court case challenging the Butler Act. The American Civil Liberties Union (ACLU)'s offer to come to the defense of any teacher accused of violating the Butler Act was taken up in Dayton, Tennessee. To demonstrate the folly of the Act, and its insistence that fundamentalist beliefs should prevail over science, a local businessman advertised for a teacher willing to state he had taught evolution. Science teacher John Scopes was persuaded to stand trial, despite not being sure he had taught the theory. The case caught the eye of the media and became a national press and radio spectacle. The stars of the trial were the lawyers who enjoyed the drama and publicity. Scopes was represented by Clarence Darrow, an experienced and well-known defense lawyer. He was not a Christian believer. In contrast, the lawyer for the state of Tennessee, William Jennings Bryan, believed the Bible should be taken literally and that evolution was a dangerous theory. The trial became an argument about the validity of Biblical creationism and Darwinian evolution rather than a test of the law of Tennessee. The colorful language of the lawyers made for good entertainment. Bryan described Darwin's theory as "millions of guesses strung together." Darrow stated that the creation account in the Bible was "fool ideas that no intelligent Christian on earth believes." Scopes was found guilty and a fine imposed, but there were no further trials for violating the law until 1967. The fundamentalist movement had been mocked for being foolishly unscientific and did not want to draw further attention.

> What can be learned about the Scopes trial from this photograph?

SOURCE 2.11

Spectators on the courthouse lawn listening to the Scopes trial court proceedings through speakers, July 1925

Changes in gender roles and the development of the "New Woman" and feminism

Social and economic changes in the 1920s affected all women. These changes had begun before the First World War, but had increasing impact during the 1920s. Changes in attitudes and circumstances meant the lives of women changed significantly. These changes were greater for some women than others. Young, unmarried women in urban areas had more opportunities and freedom to become educated, to live independently by working to support themselves, to demonstrate that they were not physically or mentally weak and to socialize with men as equals. In doing so, they met the criteria to be "New Women." The lives of rural and older women changed less.

Women had been at the forefront of social and political campaigning for many years before the First World War. War posters encouraged them to aspire to active service and thousands did so. The ratification of the Eighteenth and Nineteenth Amendments marked the success of two important pre-war campaigns. A new decade meant a realignment of aims for the women's movement in the context of a changing world. Some aimed for an equal opportunities amendment but it was difficult to achieve unity. Despite the attractiveness of the concept, working class women feared this would undermine the protection women had, for example, in legislation on working hours and wages.

When women were granted the vote in national elections, politicians passed various laws to appeal to female voters. They established clinics for women and infants, and child labor laws were passed. Women were guaranteed the right to sit on juries and hold public office. However, most women who exercised their right to vote, voted the same way as their husbands or fathers. Politicians had little to gain from introducing measures that benefited women. Further issues emerged as the decade progressed.

- During the Red Scare, feminists became associated with foreign radicals.
- Opposition from conservatives in the Catholic Church and the Southern states meant the child labor amendment was not ratified.
- Congress did not provide funding for the health care clinics that had been established.
- The Supreme Court judged the minimum wage law for women to be unconstitutional.
- Gender roles changed very little during the 1920s.
- Most of the eight million women in paid employment were in poorly paid jobs. Domestic work, support work in offices, and work in factories on the shop floor were the norm.
- Very few women progressed in their professions, despite better access to university education. Where women did progress, it was in traditionally female areas such as education and nursing.

It might appear that feminism had done little to support the reality of the "New Woman." However, the image persisted. In magazine literature widely read by middle-class women, the heroines matched the "New Woman" ideal. The same was true of advertising and the cinema. Women of all ages were encouraged to purchase the products that would transform them into modern women. Female movie stars were presented as role models. The idea of the "New Woman" had become deeply embedded.

The "New Woman" was more apparent in social settings. The fashions of the time, popular entertainment venues and the opportunities offered by the motor car contributed to allowing women more freedom than at any time in the recent past. As we will see in the next section, the flapper personified these social changes.

Flapper lifestyle and new fashions

Flappers are one of the most enduring images of the 1920s. Their fashions, carefree attitudes and wild behavior typify the idea of the "Roaring Twenties." Does the image reflect reality, and how widespread was the phenomenon?

The term "flapper" originated in the late nineteenth century. The word was first used to denote immoral women, and by 1900 to describe young women who wore their hair loose because they were not yet married. In the 1920s, the name was given to young women whose lifestyles and attitudes shocked more traditional social groups.

Flappers symbolized changes in the lives of women. For example, they:
- pursued their own interests
- wore short dresses and skirts cut in a way that allowed freer movement
- cut their hair short in a bob
- smoked, drank illegal alcohol, and partied
- participated in nightlife by going to jazz clubs, vaudeville shows, and speakeasies
- rejected the idea that women should conform to traditional norms of chastity, modesty, and temperance
- married at a later age and had fewer children.

There were relatively few real-life flappers. The image depends as much, if not more, on the fictional young women of authors such as F Scott Fitzgerald and the daring females of some Hollywood films. Many women cut their hair short as a practical measure. Simpler, less constricting clothing had a widespread appeal. The wildest excesses, however, were not universally embraced. Most women were not able to afford to live the carefree, pleasure-oriented lifestyle of the flapper. Economic necessity meant that the reality for most lay in juggling the multiple demands of marriage, motherhood, housework, and paid work.

> What impression of flappers does this image create?

SOURCE 2.12

Flappers dancing during a Charleston dance competition at the Parody Club, January 1926

Opposition to feminism and the flapper lifestyle

In 1920s America, there was a strong desire to return to what was "normal," following the upheavals of the war years. In foreign policy, this meant isolation from events abroad. In domestic politics, the popular phrase was "return to normalcy." Consequently, there was a negative reaction to the young women who represented social change, especially since their lifestyles were so alien to the traditional and idealized American way of life. Feminism challenged the patriarchal and misogynistic values that dominated politics, the workplace, and society as a whole. Flappers challenged traditional morality.

Objections to feminism and flappers came from a number of quarters. Fundamentalist Christians, such as Baptist preacher John Roach Straton, railed against the culture of the 1920s in general. The commercialism and liberalism of the times clashed with his interpretation of the Bible. The "New Woman" and the flapper were both at odds with his preaching.

Charlotte Perkins Gilman wrote about new opportunities for women, including the concepts of the kitchen-less home and equal shares of housework for men and women. However, she rejected the sexual morality of the flapper, recognizing a place for women in the home and as mothers.

Lillian Symes's article in the May 1929 edition of *Harper's Magazine* bemoaned the results of 1920s feminism. She used examples to show how men had taken advantage of "New Women." Despite contributing equally to the household income, women did more than their fair share of housework. The option of divorce left them susceptible to being abandoned for a new, younger woman.

Writer Dorothy Parker published a satirical poem entitled "The Flapper." The poem illustrates how the flapper cares only about being noticed, rather than about her reputation.

> Identify and explain two examples of satire in this poem. Satire means holding up human vice or foolishness to ridicule.

SOURCE 2.13

"The Flapper" by Dorothy Parker, written in 1922

The Playful flapper here we see,
The fairest of the fair.
She's not what Grandma used to be,—
You might say, au contraire.
Her girlish ways may make a stir,
Her manners cause a scene,
But there is no more harm in her
Than in a submarine.

She nightly knocks for many a goal
The usual dancing men.
Her speed is great, but her control
Is something else again.
All spotlights focus on her pranks.
All tongues her prowess herald.
For which she well may render thanks
To God and Scott Fitzgerald.

Her golden rule is plain enough—
Just get them young and treat them
Rough.

Feminism and the flapper lifestyle were seen in the cities of the Northern US, but made little impact on the lives of women in rural areas or in the South. Poverty, lack of opportunity for education or well-paid employment, and traditional attitudes all limited change for most American women.

> ## ACTIVITY
>
> Make two lists: examples of modernity and examples of traditional values in the social landscape of the 1920s. Work with a partner; one should write a paragraph arguing that modernity was dominant and the other should write a paragraph arguing that traditional values were dominant. Which argument do you find more convincing?

Race relations and activism in the 1920s

America and its allies won the First World War. This did not lead to confidence in the future, as might be expected. Repeated waves of the Spanish flu epidemic that originated in America and caused more deaths worldwide than the war were frightening. The economic dislocation caused by the end of the war also contributed to a sense that America should prioritize its own well-being. The war did nothing to liberalize ideas about race. Instead, old prejudices came to the fore and went largely unchallenged. Waves of immigration in the late nineteenth and early twentieth centuries had made American-born whites of European origin worry that the culture of their country was changing. Resistance to further immigration grew. The quotas set in successive immigration acts made clear the racial and political prejudices of the lawmakers. Meanwhile, African Americans continued to suffer discrimination that was increasingly legalized in "Jim Crow Laws," following the landmark

Supreme Court judgment on the case of *Plessy v. Ferguson* in 1896. The Ku Klux Klan was resurgent and attitudes to Native Americans were scarcely better, although they were granted a measure of citizenship in 1924. A wave of unrest sweeping across cities in the immediate post-war years further demonstrated the racist views of many Americans. The trial and execution of Sacco and Vanzetti illustrate the prejudice against recent immigrants and the fear of left-wing political ideas following the triumph of Bolshevism after the Russian revolutions of 1917.

The growth of intolerance and the rise of the Second Ku Klux Klan

In the post-war years, nativism was the driving force of thinking on race (page 10). Chinese immigration had been halted since 1882. New European immigrants from southern and eastern Europe were Roman Catholic Christians or Jewish. White Anglo-Saxon Protestants (WASPs) assumed these immigrants had been influenced by socialist ideas such as communism and anarchism, ideas that ran counter to the American ideals of unfettered capitalism.

New theories of race (see page 62) were used to support nativism. The idea that there was a hierarchy of races, with "Anglo-Saxons" at the top, was used to justify prejudice and discrimination. This helps to explain the introduction of new laws restricting immigration. The 1921 Emergency Quota Act was a turning point. For the first time, numerical limits were set and quotas were based on the National Origins Formula. Applicants also had to pass a literacy test. The laws, aiming to "keep America American," were passed with minimal opposition in Congress.

- The Emergency Quota Act (1921) stipulated that immigration from European countries was restricted to three percent of American residents born in each country, as recorded in the 1910 census.
- The Johnson-Reed Act (1924) altered the National Origins Formula for Europeans to two percent, based on the 1890 census. It completely excluded Asian people.
- The National Origins Formula was changed to be based on the 1900 census in 1930.

Changes to the quota allocations meant that from 1925 to 1930 Germany had the largest share of the quota, with the United Kingdom a close second. From 1930, the United Kingdom had 42 percent of the quota and Germany only sixteen.

Fears of un-American political ideals were compounded when the Bolsheviks seized control of Russia in October 1917, re-organizing Russia's government along socialist lines, nationalizing production and dispossessing the middle- and upper-classes of their property. The arrest, conviction, and subsequent execution of two Italian immigrants for robbery and murder has come to symbolize the political intolerance of the 1920s that was manifested in the First Red Scare. Socialism in all its forms was regarded as un-American. It went against market-based, capitalist economic ideals. Some socialists, including the Bolsheviks in Russia, believed in the violent overthrow of all systems based on capitalism, which meant encouraging revolution in countries like the USA. A wave of strikes in the US after the First World War reinforced the fear of socialism and started the Red Scare of 1919–21. Labor unions such as the Industrial Workers of the World were thought to be hotbeds of communism. Strikes in coal mines, steel mills, and even the police force often became violent as employers, encouraged by the government, used force against the workers.

The press hyped up hysteria when well-known figures were the subject of bombing campaigns. Thirty-six letter bombs were intercepted at a New York City post office, including one addressed to John D Rockefeller. On June 2, 1919, an anarchist bomb exploded, blowing up the front of Attorney-General Mitchell Palmer's house in Washington DC, as well as the perpetrator. This was one of eight bombs that exploded simultaneously. This led to the Palmer Raids in which between 4,000 and 6,000 suspected communists were arrested across the country and 556 suspect "aliens" were deported.

In 1921, Nicola Sacco and Bartolomeo Vanzetti were tried for the murder of Alessandro Berardelli and Frederick Parmenter, during an armed robbery in Braintree, Minnesota. The evidence was circumstantial or based on testimony from unreliable witnesses. The district attorney emphasized their radical, anarchist views. Sacco and Vanzetti's poor English made it difficult for them to understand the proceedings. In July 1921, Sacco and Vanzetti were

> **KEY TERM**
>
> **National Origins Formula** Measures used to limit immigration based on quotas of immigrants for each country of origin (the country immigrants are migrating from).

convicted by the jury of murder. They did not have a fair trial. In 1927, despite a series of legal appeals, the protests of the Industrial Workers of the World labor union, and demonstrations in cities around the globe, they were executed. Their guilt has been hotly debated ever since. What is not in doubt is that their conviction was based on their national origins and political leanings, rather than evidence that could prove their guilt.

Racial intolerance was also evident in the resurrection of the Ku Klux Klan (KKK). The Klan had been outlawed during Reconstruction. DW Griffith's infamous and popular film *Birth of a Nation* glorified the KKK and reignited support and enthusiasm for it. By the 1920s, the Klan was in the ascendant, encompassing an extended range of prejudices. The original Klan was a rural Southern phenomenon that had aimed to keep emancipated African Americans in subservient roles using violence and intimidation. The new Klan expanded to urban industrial areas where immigrants were clustered, creating competition for jobs in industry. By the early 1920s, membership stood at two million mostly white males. By 1925, it is estimated to have had between 2.5 and 4 million adherents. It targeted Catholics, Jews, socialists, and immigrants, in addition to African Americans. All were accused of taking jobs and diluting the imagined "racial purity" of WASPs. These ideas combined the traditional racism of the KKK with the theories of Social Darwinism. This also fed into attempts to eliminate "undesirable elements" through enforced sterilization of certain people who were considered unsuitable to have children because of their moral or physical traits. Thirty-two states passed laws allowing this and 64,000 people were sterilized as a result.

Membership of the KKK waned in the late 1920s. The conviction of Indiana Grand Dragon David C Stephenson for rape, kidnapping, and second-degree murder led people to question the values of the Klan. There were other examples of immorality, as well as infighting for the leadership of this extremely wealthy organization. With a flawed leadership that certainly did not meet the values of the Klan, membership declined. While many of its ideas can be seen to recur later, the level of violence and hypocrisy meant many walked away from it.

The Red Summer of 1919 and racial violence of the 1920s

In 1919, violence broke out in at least 26 cities across the US. This was the "Red Summer." Unlike the Red Scare, this "red" was not a reference to socialism but to the amount of African American blood spilled. This violence was given the label "Red Summer" by James Weldon Johnson, an NAACP field secretary.

African American veterans had experienced more equal treatment in Europe, but were attacked when they returned to the US after the First World War. They had hoped for some improvements in their civil rights, having been told they were fighting for democracy. Instead, there was renewed violence against them. The worst incident occurred in Elaine, Arkansas where between 100 and 200 African Americans and twenty of their attackers were killed. A white mob attacked a meeting of African American farmers who wanted to organize a union. The violence was not confined to the South. Chicago was the scene of a week of violence in late July and early August. This began after an African American teenager, Eugene Williams, drowned in Lake Michigan after being hit by rocks thrown by white people because the teenager was swimming near a "white-only" beach. The police did not arrest those responsible. Twenty-three African Americans and fifteen whites died in the riots that followed. Millions of dollars' worth of property was damaged. In a riot in Tulsa, Oklahoma in 1921, estimates suggest that between 50 and 300 people were killed.

In the Jim Crow South, thousands of African Americans were hanged, burned to death and tortured in other ways. The white perpetrators were rarely prosecuted. The federal government persisted in refusing to make lynching a separate crime (page 107). Migration from the South to the North continued because opportunities in the North outweighed the problems there, while life in the South held few attractions for African Americans.

The Harlem Renaissance and "New Negro" Movement

During the 1920s, there were two positive developments for African Americans. Both the Harlem Renaissance and the "New Negro" Movement were initiated and driven by African Americans. For the first time, the African American voice was widely heard and there was new momentum in the drive for rights. Although racist views were challenged, they were not yet eroded. However, involvement in both movements built the self-confidence of African

Americans. Harlem in New York City fostered and gave a platform to an African American cultural movement encompassing all forms of artistic expression. Through the arts, African Americans defined what it meant to be Black in America. American culture began to enter the mainstream. The "New Negro" Movement abandoned the compliance and patience of Booker T Washington's assumption (see page 70) that rights would come eventually. Instead, it took an active role in challenging the unconstitutional Jim Crow state laws by supporting legal cases where African Americans were discriminated against. WEB Du Bois and the NAACP were important advocates of this "New Negro" Movement. Many of the leading figures were involved in both movements—they were mutually supportive. Eventually, both strands had important consequences for African Americans.

The Harlem Renaissance, as its name suggests, developed in New York's Manhattan. Harlem was one of the most popular destinations for African Americans who migrated from the South to the North. Living in such a small, densely populated area fired a social and artistic movement that helped to put African American musicians, stage performers, artists, and writers at the center of 1920s culture. There were numerous notable authors. The poetry of Claude McKay told African Americans they ought to stand up for their rights. Jean Toomer wrote a poem and a novel with the title "Cane," which explored the lives of African American women in the South, as well as the acceptance of people of different races in each other's culture. Langston Hughes's poetry was written in the distinctive rhythms of African American musical genres. These are just a few examples of the many writers whose works came to prominence. The movement also had its own magazines. The NAACP magazine the *Crisis*, edited by WEB Du Bois, published the work of Harlem Renaissance writers. It had a circulation of over 100,000. The magazine of the National Urban League, *Opportunity*, also published the work of Harlem writers. Both magazines offered literary prizes. The Amy Spingarn Contest in Literature and Art was sponsored by Joel Spingarn and his wife, Amy. Joel was the first Jewish leader of the NAACP. Walter White, later head of the NAACP, published his first novel, *Fire in the Flint,* in 1924 based on his experiences investigating cases of lynching in the South.

> Explain the imagery of this book cover.

SOURCE 2.13

The front cover of Walter White's novel *The Fire in the Flint*, published in 1924. The novel is about the experiences of a young African American doctor who returns to his native Georgia after training in the North. He expects to be treated as a professional but discovers that prejudice there is deep-rooted

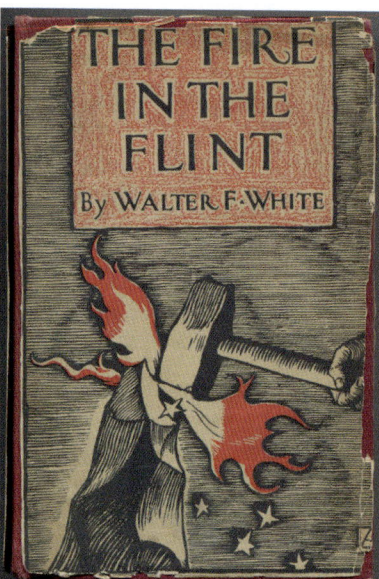

Music was an important part of the Harlem Renaissance. The imposition of prohibition did not close the clubs in which African American musicians popularized jazz and blues music. These genres originated in the Deep South but became forever associated with venues such as New York's Cotton Club. Jazz was very popular. Its style fit the mood of the "Roaring

Twenties." It was unconventional in its instrumentation, rhythms, and improvisations. Dancing in jazz venues was unrestrained and individualistic. "Jazz fever" popularized artists such as Duke Ellington, Bessie Smith, Jelly Roll Morton, and Louis Armstrong.

The Harlem Renaissance continued into the 1930s, but the impact of the Great Depression weakened it, with many of the early contributors moving away from New York. In 1935, a race riot in which three people died, hundreds were injured, and extensive property was damaged, marked its end.

The Harlem Renaissance depended on the "New Negro" Movement. Without its publications, editorial advice, and financial support the literary works would not have had their widespread success. Besides its support for the arts, the "New Negro" Movement was heavily involved in the campaign to bring justice to African Americans by challenging instances where they were denied their constitutional rights. Under Jim Crow, many states found ways of preventing voter registration by using grandfather clauses or literacy tests. Racial stereotyping and prejudice meant that juries were predisposed to convict African Americans and reluctant to find white perpetrators guilty.

The NAACP appealed the conviction of African Americans who had been found guilty by an all-white jury, with twelve receiving the death sentence and 67 long prison terms for their part in the Elaine, Arkansas riots. In 1923, the Supreme Court overturned the convictions on the grounds the trials were mob-dominated and therefore violated the due process of law granted by the Fourteenth Amendment. This was a landmark ruling, leading to more decisions being reversed.

Further examples of NAACP initiatives include investigations of lynchings, challenges to a law in Texas barring African Americans from primary elections, and successful petitioning on behalf of African American soldiers who had been convicted and punished after they were provoked by police brutality in Houston, Texas. The NAACP lobbied aggressively but unsuccessfully for a federal law to ban lynching, and they challenged the legality of segregation ordinances and restrictive covenants. They used the Ossian Sweet case in Detroit to advance the case against residential segregation.

When the NAACP met at their annual conference in Cleveland Ohio in 1929 to mark their twentieth anniversary, there was much to celebrate.

Native Americans' conditions and status

In 1920, the European American notion of what it meant to be an American citizen did not include Native Americans. The Constitution stated that "Indians not taxed" could not be counted in the voting population of states. Native American land use, customs, and beliefs were regarded as primitive. When there was a conflict of interest between European Americans and Native Americans it was, therefore, acceptable to override the Native Americans in favor of the "superior" European American value system. In 1870, the Senate Judiciary Committee ruled that, "the Fourteenth Amendment to the Constitution has no effect whatever upon the status of the Indian tribes within the limits of the United States," although Native Americans were subject to the law. A report from 1921 showed that most Native American land was being farmed by European Americans. Land allotments for Native Americans were generally small and of poor quality. Farming these allotments could not support a family.

Reservation land with natural resources such as coal was developed by white businessmen together with the Indian Office without compensation. Native Americans were further exploited in Montana, where they had to pay for the coal mined on their land while European American settlers received it free of charge. Living conditions on reservations and in many of the Native American boarding schools were shocking. The physical results included short life expectancy, disease, and malnutrition. John Collier, the executive secretary of the Indian Defense Association, publicized the economic disparity between Native Americans and the rest of the population. The Meriam Report of 1926 recommended changes to the Indian school curriculum and boarding requirements. By the end of the 1920s, some of the recommendations were being adopted.

Along with African Americans, the Native American soldiers must have anticipated that, when the First World War ended, they would be granted the citizenship rights granted to other native-born Americans. However, by 1924, 125,000 of the 300,000 Native Americans were not yet citizens. The Snyder Act of 1924 granted voting rights, but not full protection of these rights. Individuals were granted citizenship; they did not have to apply for it. Individual states were allowed to impose conditions on voting for Native Americans just as they already did for African Americans. New Mexico and Arizona did so until 1948 and these rights were not properly protected until the 1965 Civil Rights Act.

The Snyder Act allowed Native Americans and Alaska Natives to retain tribal citizenship in addition to holding American citizenship. This clause was necessary to meet the conditions of tribes' communal landholding. Most Native Americans accepted this dual citizenship. Some objected because it ran counter to the eighteenth-century treaties that had recognized native tribes as nations.

By the end of the 1920s, there was official recognition of the dire conditions of many Native Americans. Progress was being made in supporting them. Nevertheless, laws that forced indigenous people to give up their culture in exchange for rights were not completely removed.

ACTIVITY

Create a table like this. Look back over the chapter to fill in as many factors as you can to explain the most important reasons for cultural changes in the 1920s.

Possible cause	How it contributed	Evidence against	Links to other factors

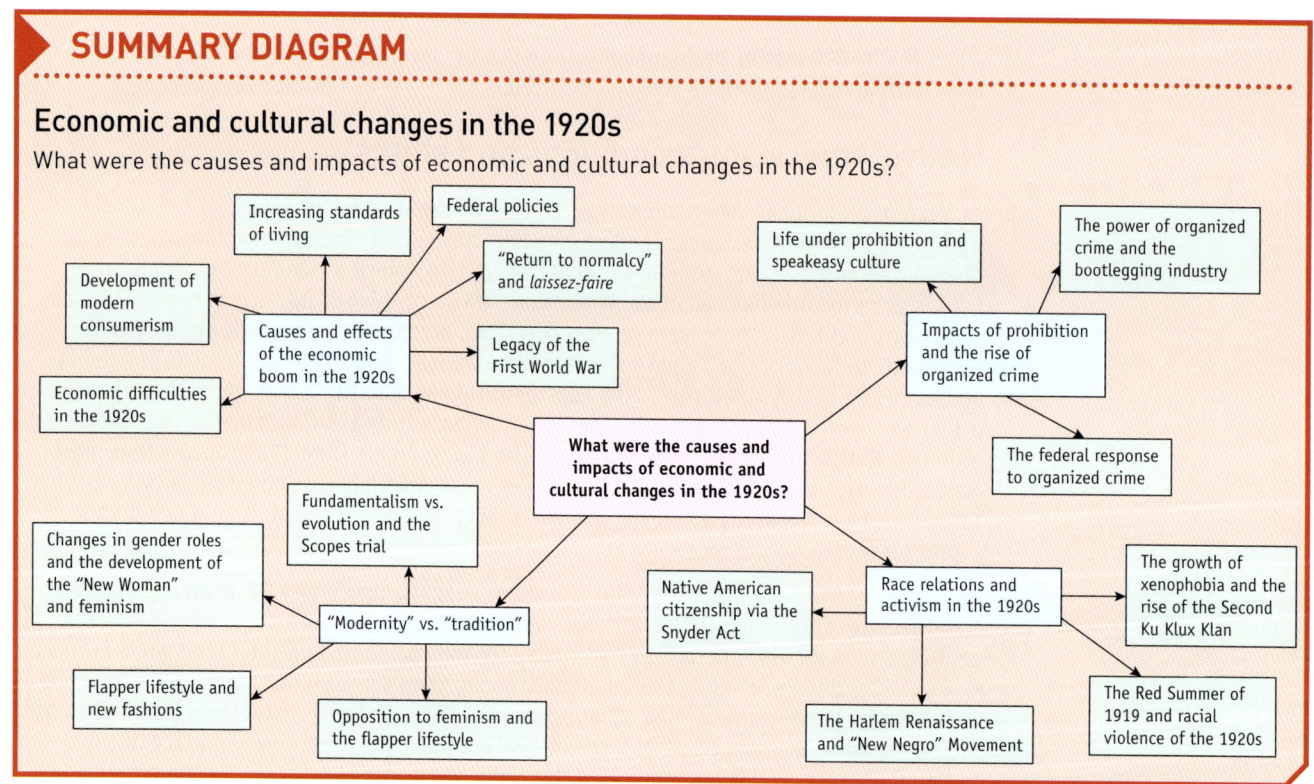

SUMMARY DIAGRAM

Economic and cultural changes in the 1920s
What were the causes and impacts of economic and cultural changes in the 1920s?

CHAPTER SUMMARY

The world position and outlook of America changed out of all recognition between 1890 and 1929. An increasingly interventionist foreign policy based on economic imperatives and changing attitudes about America and its values presented great opportunities. Combined with the effects of the First World War on the European imperial powers, America emerged as a great economic power with increasing global influence. America also began to lead in cultural developments. The darker side of that culture reflected the tension between the old and the new:

- the impact of traditional religion in bringing about prohibition and the wave of organized crime it created
- the opportunities available to women, set against traditional values and expectations
- the popularity of African American cultural developments in the context of a country where racial segregation and prejudice were the norm and often legalized
- attempts by Christian fundamentalists to deny the march of scientific knowledge.

Debates about all these issues were carried out publicly and heatedly. The issues that had come to the fore were unresolved when the decade ended with the Wall Street Crash and its consequences.

REFRESHER QUESTIONS

1. Why did the US gain new territories after 1890?
2. Why was the Panama Canal important?
3. How did dollar diplomacy differ from moral diplomacy?
4. Why did the US enter the First World War?
5. Why were some Americans anti-imperialist?
6. Why were American civil liberties limited during the First World War?
7. To what extent did the impact of the First World War challenge social norms in America?
8. Why was the availability of credit important in the 1920s boom?
9. Why was prohibition unenforceable?
10. How far-reaching were changes in society in the 1920s?

Study skills

Guidance on answering essay questions

Understanding the task and planning your writing

This section is designed to support your ability to write in an organized and clear way. To explain the causes of an event, you will need to show your understanding of the reasons why a specific event occurred or why someone adopted a particular course of action. You should focus on the key issue of causation, analyzing a range of factors to show how they are connected and reach a supported conclusion about why something happened.

When a question asks you to "explain," the focus is on causation. This means that you will need to identify and explain a range of causes.
- You need to show detailed knowledge and understanding of the reasons why a specific event occurred or why someone adopted a particular course of action.
- This will be the combined effect of several factors, both long- and short-term.
- Useful ways to categorize causes include:
  - underlying causes
  - short-term causes
  - triggers or catalysts.
- Another way to categorize causes, depending on the question, could include:
  - circumstances and events
  - actions and motives
  - attitudes, beliefs, and ideas.

Planning your response
- First, you have to select the questions you are going to answer. Make sure you read all the questions through carefully. Try not to pick a question just because you like the look of one aspect of it, as it may come with other parts that you will need to respond to as well.
- Think carefully about how much time you have to write each part of your answer.
- Devise a time plan so you do not spend too long on any part.
- Plan your answer by writing a quick list of causes that you can explain in turn.
- It is helpful to think in terms of one cause for each paragraph.

> **ACTIVITY**
>
> **Think about this question**
>
> **Explain why the United States went to war in 1917.** [10]

Going to war was an action taken by the United States government despite Woodrow Wilson's boast that he had kept America out of the war in his election campaign of 1916. This suggests that you need to explain how the changes that took place between November 1916 and April 1917 caused the declaration of war.

First, make a list of causes. You need to explain how more than one of these causes led to war. Choose two or three causes that you know and understand the best. Write a paragraph about how each of these caused the US to go to war.

Your list could look like this:

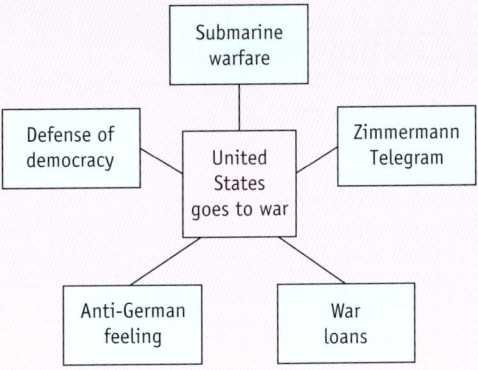

What makes an effective paragraph in a causal explanation?

Sample paragraph 1

The United States went to war because the Germans had declared they would resume unrestricted submarine warfare. In January 1917, the German government made the decision that their submarines would attack any ship they suspected of carrying war goods to their enemies, regardless of who owned the ship or whether it carried passengers. The United States immediately broke off diplomatic relations with Germany. A policy of neutrality was no longer possible if American shipping and civilians were in danger of attack. When Woodrow Wilson asked for Congress's approval to declare war, unrestricted submarine warfare was an important reason. This action by Germany was, therefore, an important step toward America declaring war.

Sample paragraph 2

In 1917, the Germans resumed their policy of unrestricted submarine warfare, as they wanted to defeat the Allies by starving them of food and other supplies. They had stopped this policy when the Americans complained about the sinking of the *Lusitania* but they restarted it in 1917. The Germans thought they could still win the war even if America did join in. They thought the British and French would soon run out of everything. Using submarines to sink their ships made the Americans angry. They wanted to be able to sell food and other goods to Britain as this was good for trade. It made the United States want to go to war with Germany.

The list below shows what examiners are looking for:
- two or three **relevant** factors to be considered
- factors to be **explained** rather than described
- a clear **link** to be made between the factor and the event
- supporting information to be **accurate** and **relevant**
- consideration of the **relationship** between factors.

ACTIVITY

Read Sample paragraph 1 and think about these questions.
- Can you tell what the question is just by reading the paragraph?
- What cause(s) are mentioned in this paragraph?
- Is the paragraph an explanation (this cause led to this event because) or does it just describe what happened?
- How many supporting details does the paragraph use?
- Are these details accurate?

ACTIVITY

Working with a partner, compile a list of the features of an effective paragraph. Then, read Sample paragraph 2.
- Does this paragraph have the features of an effective paragraph?
- How would you improve this paragraph?

> **ACTIVITY**
>
> ### Assessing a sample answer
> - Use the checklist on page 135 and your ideas about the features of effective paragraphs to assess the response below.
> - Working on your own, decide what you think are the strengths and weaknesses of this answer.
> - Discuss your ideas with a partner.
> - Work out how you would advise this learner to improve their response.

Sample answer 1

There are several reasons for the United States going to war with Germany in 1917. These include unrestricted submarine warfare, the Zimmermann Telegram and the defense of democracy.

Unrestricted submarine warfare meant that a ship could be attacked by German submarines (known as U-boats) even if the ship does not belong to an enemy country. The Germans wanted to starve the British, just like the British were starving them, and to do this they had to stop any supplies getting to Britain and France. They thought that even if this made the United States join the war against them, it would not matter because it would take so long for American soldiers to arrive in Europe that Germany would be able to win the war before that happened. This was not the case, as the Americans quickly mobilized their forces.

The Zimmermann Telegram annoyed the United States because it was Germany asking Mexico to attack the United States. The Germans told Mexico they would get back the land they had lost in 1848. When they found out about the telegram, the Americans wanted to fight Germany.

When President Wilson asked Congress to back him up in going to war against Germany, he said the United States should defend democracy. This was because Germany and its ally, Austria–Hungary, were very undemocratic. France and Britain were more democratic although not very. Russia was about to have elections, as they had a provisional government instead of an emperor.

All these reasons made the United States go to war against Germany in April 1917.

Question practice

Practice planning and writing well-focused paragraphs to answer this question.

Explain why life changed for American women during the First World War. [10]

3 The Great Depression, the Second World War, and the Early Cold War

> **Introduction**
>
> The 1930s were dominated by the Great Depression. In the US, there were major social and economic consequences including high unemployment, homelessness, and bank failures. From 1933, President Franklin Roosevelt's New Deal used federal laws to address its problems. The economy had not yet recovered when the Second World War began. As that war ended, tensions between the Union of Soviet Socialist Republics (USSR) and the US, began to harden into the Cold War. The post-war period in America was dominated by the fear of nuclear war but also by increasing wealth, and social and cultural changes and tensions. This chapter will consider these themes by asking the following questions:
>
> ▶ What were the causes and impacts of the Great Depression and New Deal?
> ▶ Why and how did US foreign policy evolve between 1935 and 1959?
> ▶ Why and how far did US society change in the 1940s and 1950s?

KEY DATES

1929	The Great Crash
1932	Franklin D Roosevelt elected president
1933	New Deal measures introduced
1935	Neutrality Act
1935–36	Second New Deal
1941	Lend-lease
	America enters the Second World War
1945	First atomic bombs detonated
	End of the Second World War
1948	Berlin blockade and airlift
1950–53	Korean War
1950–54	McCarthyism
1955–56	Montgomery Bus Boycott
1956	Suez Crisis

3.1 What were the causes and impacts of the Great Depression and New Deal?

The rapid economic growth of the 1920s "boom" came to a sudden end with the Great Crash (also sometimes known as the Wall Street Crash) of October 1929. It was followed by a long period of significant economic depression which challenged the assumptions and practices of the American government and caused it to change. The Great Depression can be explained in different ways. The economic cycle of boom and bust had happened before but the depression of the 1930s was more serious. Everyone was affected in some way, but those who suffered most were the people on low incomes and those whose backgrounds had already left them disadvantaged. High levels of unemployment led many men to leave home in search of work. The federal government was not able to help. The separate responsibilities of federal and state administrations limited how much the federal government could do to ease poverty. However, during the presidency of Franklin D Roosevelt (sometimes referred to as FDR), ways were found to reduce some of the effects of the Depression. What the president called a "New Deal" for the American people promoted relief, recovery, and reform. Roosevelt's unprecedented level of intervention had many critics on both the right and the left of politics. Arguably, the impact of the Great Depression was still not over when the economy had to adjust to fight another war.

The causes and impacts of the Great Depression

Capitalist economies experience cycles of prosperity and depression. Economic historians have two main approaches to explaining why depressions happen. Some historians focus on the money supply. They consider the amount of money available for businesses to invest and how much money consumers spend. The government and the banks have some control over this. The government can print money, and the central bank (which, in the case of the US, is the Federal Reserve, established in 1914) can fix the base interest rate for lending money. Consumer spending is affected by income and the amount people can borrow. Alternatively, other historians explain fluctuations in the economy by focusing on the supply of and demand for goods and services. The price of many goods decreased relative to wages in the 1920s. Food was cheap because of over-supply, while more efficient production methods reduced the unit price of manufactured goods. In the 1920s, American presidential administrations had a *laissez-faire* approach to the economy, but the tariffs they used to protect American manufacturers limited the availability of cheaper goods from abroad. See page 116 for reasons why Republican presidents favored high tariffs and their impact on foreign trade. The 1920s administrations' failure to support the farming industry left millions of Americans stuck in poverty. Economic historians are unclear of the impact of high tariffs on the US economy.

In the twentieth century, the economies of the capitalist countries of the world were increasingly interdependent. International loans made to fund the First World War were still being repaid and renegotiated during the 1920s. American investors might invest their money abroad if interest rates were more favorable than returns in America. Other countries responded to American import tariffs with retaliatory tariffs on American exports. These tariffs made it harder for manufacturers to export their products.

> **KEY TERM**
>
> **Hoovervilles** Improvised towns built during the Great Depression by people who had lost their homes. Named for the then president, Herbert Hoover, who was blamed for many of the problems of the Depression.

By 1929, the economy was fragile. Although some analysts were aware of this, they had no idea how serious the consequences could be. After the Great Crash of 1929, the economy spiraled into a depression so deep that it lasted until the Second World War. Businesses and government were ill-equipped to respond. Many banks and businesses closed, meaning people lost their savings and jobs. The social impact was widespread and severe. Charities attempted to support the unemployed. Food lines, soup kitchens, **Hoovervilles**, and men traveling the country in search of work are all characteristics of the Great Depression. Herbert Hoover's administration began to plan a response, but, for many voters, it amounted to "too little, too late." In 1932, Democrat Franklin Delano Roosevelt was elected as president on the promise of "a New Deal for the American people."

Varied causes of the Great Depression

While the results of the Great Depression are obvious, its causes are not. In retrospect, it is clear there were many and varied problems in the economy during the 1920s. One of these problems was that more goods were produced than could be sold at a profit. This was certainly the case in the farming industry, as discussed in Chapter 2 (page 115). During the First World War, farmers had been encouraged to maximize production by farming more land and using expensive modern machinery that could do the work of many men. They produced more food than Americans could eat and sold the surplus to the war-torn European countries whose farm laborers were needed in the armed forces. The expectation that food farming would continue to export its surplus and make profits allowed farmers to borrow money to buy additional land and new machinery. To repay their creditors farmers needed to increase their productivity and run at a profit. Unfortunately, this was impossible. By the early 1920s, food exports were no longer needed in Europe and retaliatory tariffs made American food expensive abroad. American consumers had a limit to how much they could eat. The more the farmers produced, the more the prices fell and the lower profits sank. The situation was no better for cotton farmers. World prices fell because synthetic fibers were overtaking natural ones in popularity. Some traditional industries also produced a surplus throughout the decade which caused prices and, hence, profits and wages to stagnate or decrease. Cotton textiles and coal are two examples.

There is more debate concerning consumer goods. The demand for consumer goods is more elastic than that for food. Unit prices decreased during the 1920s as manufacturing became more efficient. Advertising persuaded people they needed to purchase consumer goods. However, poverty meant that over half of the US population could not afford the more expensive household items, such as cars and refrigerators. Relatively high wages in the US made home-produced goods more expensive than the equivalent from overseas. To protect domestic manufacturing, tariffs were applied to imports. Retaliatory tariffs meant that the overseas market was not accessible to American goods. By the middle of the decade, the construction industry was stagnant. By the end of the decade, sales of cars and steel production were declining and company profits were diminishing.

The easy availability of credit was an additional flaw in the economy. Loans and installment plans allowed consumers to buy now and pay later. This was a new phenomenon. It led to high levels of sales but also high levels of personal debt. Consumers continued to make purchases even as wages began to stagnate in 1928–29. In addition, banks, stockbrokers, and increasing numbers of ordinary people invested in the Stock Exchange, borrowing up to 90 percent of the money needed to buy shares. Neither they nor the financial institutions making loans understood the consequences. There was little regulation of banking, especially of smaller banks. Many were operated by incompetent people who did not understand the need to limit loans in relation to reserves. The instability of the banking industry worsened during the 1920s but this was not apparent until late 1929.

Speculation in stock market and real estate

In the 1920s, the economy appeared to many people to be doing well. Prices of **stocks** and **shares** on the New York Stock Exchange (Wall Street) rose throughout the 1920s. The dividends paid on shares meant returns were higher than the interest rates offered by banks. Investors assumed this would continue. Increasingly, ordinary people with spare cash decided to buy company shares. Stock market investment always carries an element of risk but the risks taken in the 1920s were extreme, based on a combination of over-optimism and ignorance. Some stockbrokers expected a quick profit and invested heavily. Small and large investors borrowed money to buy shares. They put down a ten percent deposit and borrowed the rest of the money. This was known as "buying on the margin." It meant that investors were vulnerable. If the value of shares fell more than ten percent, they would lose their entire investment and would have an outstanding debt and no way to pay it. The banks which eagerly lent money were also vulnerable. If a bank was thought to have too many **bad debts**, depositors would withdraw their cash in case the bank failed, in what was known as a "bank run." If the bank did not have enough money to pay them, it would go bankrupt. By 1929, the boom was beginning to slow and there were rumors of trouble ahead.

ACTIVITY

As you read the section on the causes of the Great Depression, construct a diagram to show how the factors interrelate. Choose one of the factors and write a paragraph to explain why it was a cause of the Great Depression.

KEY TERMS

Stocks The ownership certificates of a company; divided into shares.

Shares Part of a stock. Shares allow a company to have many owners, and they are traded according to changes in their value.

Bad debt Debt that a business is unable to pay back. A bank having "bad debts" means that the businesses the banks loaned money to are unable to pay the bank back.

An alternative area for investment was in real estate. The real estate market boomed in the early 1920s as house ownership increased and, as more people started to own cars, middle-income earners moved to the suburbs. As a result, developers and investors bought land in anticipation of further demand. Their optimism was misplaced, as demand peaked in the mid-1920s. One state that was hit particularly hard was Florida. Purchase of holiday homes for those wanting to enjoy the sunshine (for the first time, suntanned skin became a sign of wealth rather than of having to work outdoors in all weathers) generated a real estate boom here in the early 1920s. However, a series of hurricanes in 1926 and 1928 made holidaying in the Sunshine State less popular and the real estate bubble burst. Citrus fruit growing had also gained in popularity but there were insufficient sales for it to be profitable. Real estate values plummeted and speculators lost out.

Availability of easy credit

Money supply is an important element in a capitalist economy. Everything depends on the availability of **capital**. By the 1920s, banks where money could be deposited and which made loans to individuals and companies had existed for centuries. However, economic understanding was in its infancy. American banks were largely unregulated because the American government did not interfere in business. The Federal Reserve had been established in 1914, giving some power to leading banks to hold quantities of gold in reserve to support the economy in difficult times. By 1927, the Federal Reserve Bank of New York held ten percent of the world's stock of monetary gold. This would allow the bank to intervene in controlling the money supply if necessary. Although there was some understanding of the need for loans to be guaranteed by reserves, small banks did not get the relationship between the two elements right. Overall, the Federal Reserve had too little regulatory power and when it intervened to raise interest rates in 1929, it made the situation worse by reducing the money supply at a time of decreasing demand.

Bank failures and the Great Crash

Some analysts focus on the money supply as the driving force of the economy. From the spring of 1929, economists warned that it was too easy to borrow money, which was causing an increase in borrowing that was impossible to maintain. On March 25, the Federal Reserve issued a warning about excessive **speculation**. This led to a short-lived rush of share-selling. Share prices fell, but an intervention by the National City Bank to stop the slide in the value of shares was successful. In August, the Federal Reserve decided to make borrowing less attractive. It raised interest rates from five to six percent. Paying the interest on loans became more expensive and the amount of money available to invest and make purchases decreased. An already fragile market was easily destabilized.

The Great Crash began in late October. Once share prices began to decrease, the effect was catastrophic. The value of shares was reduced by 25 percent in two days (October 28–29). The drop in share prices was not evenly spread. Companies that were most prominent in the boom years were hardest hit. Shares in General Electric, United States Steel, and the Radio Corporation of America plummeted in value. There was a brief improvement but it did not last. Despite the reassuring statements of President Hoover, the US economy was not strong and resilient. Because of the recession that had begun in mid-1929, share prices continued to fall. When other countries began to move their currencies off the **gold standard** (Britain was the first to do so in 1931), recovery became more difficult.

> **KEY TERM**
>
> **Capital** Wealth; this can be money, but also valuable assets such as real estate or art.

> **KEY TERM**
>
> **Speculation** A risky financial choice. Also used to mean "guessing," which was often what made speculation risky.

> **KEY TERM**
>
> **Gold standard** From 1870 to 1932 (and again from 1944 to 1971) the gold standard defined the value of currencies in terms of the value of gold reserves of a country. It was a useful tool for stabilizing the world economy because it prevented governments from issuing and spending too much money. However, during the Great Depression, governments realized that recovery required substantial government investment. The use of the gold standard limited how effective this investment could be. Once Britain abandoned the gold standard, other countries followed. The economies of countries that did not do so were disadvantaged.

One of the immediate effects of the Great Crash was a run on the banks. Recognizing that many banks had bad debts, account holders rushed to withdraw their money. However, badly run banks had insufficient reserves and they began to fail. By 1933, thousands of smaller banks, representing between a third and half of the total number, had failed with losses of over $3 billion (worth around $73 billion in 2025). The banking industry helped to cause the Crash. The impact of the Crash on the banks is one reason that it was followed by the Great Depression. Learning from the damage their reckless lending had caused, the remaining banks did not make as many loans. Instead, they kept money in reserve. As a result of this, and Federal Reserve policies at a time of deflation, far less money was available to invest. Faced with reduced demand and high interest rates on loans, businesses stopped investing. They laid off workers and reduced the pay of those they kept.

Rising unemployment rates among different groups of Americans

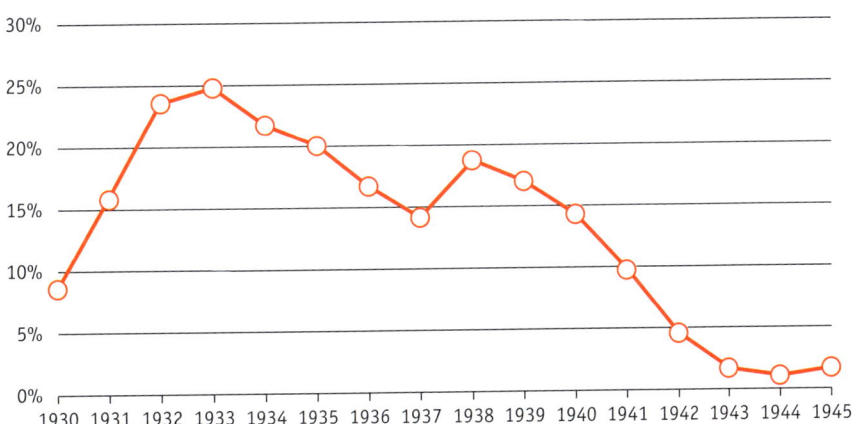

Figure 3.1 The US unemployment rate, 1930–45

In 1929, the unemployment rate in the US was 3.2 percent. It was low but rising, as the economy went into recession. In 1933, it reached a peak of 25 percent. This meant that 12,830,000 people were unemployed. Those who had jobs were often working reduced hours for reduced wages. Wage income for workers fell by 42.5 percent from 1929 to 1933.

These overall figures do not tell everything. In Northern cities, 25 percent of white men were unemployed. The figure for African American workers was far higher. They generally had low-paid, unskilled factory jobs before 1929. During the Great Depression, they were far more likely to lose their jobs and found it more difficult to find new ones. Many jobs no longer existed, and many employers preferred to give the remaining jobs to white workers. The unemployment rate among African Americans rose to 50 percent in Chicago and Pittsburgh and 60 percent in Philadelphia and Detroit. It was worst in the South with 70 percent of African Americans unemployed in Atlanta.

Many African Americans in the South were sharecroppers. The problems of agriculture meant they were already living in poverty and debt. During the Depression thousands of them were evicted by landowners, abandoned their land and headed to the cities, joining the ranks of the unemployed.

America did not have a national welfare system. There was no unemployment benefit. The unemployed and their families had to rely on local welfare or charity. The local welfare was organized by city governments which relied on local taxes for funding. As the Depression hit, the amount of tax collected dropped. Some city councils, such as Chicago, were declared bankrupt and could no longer finance welfare. Bread lines and soup kitchens were set up by charities, but such was the demand that they could not provide for everyone. There was no system for advertising job vacancies. The unemployed had to walk the streets looking for companies that were advertising work. When there was no work in a town, the unemployed had to look for work elsewhere. They boarded freight trains, hitching a free ride in search of work. In 1930, there were 6,000 men on the streets of New York City trying to survive by selling apples.

Records from New York show the direct effects of unemployment on the health of the population. One-third of New York's children were malnourished. In 1931, the hospitals listed starvation as the cause of around 100 deaths. Many other people died of diseases that were a direct result of their poor diets. This was a serious situation in a country where the president had boasted in his election campaign only four years earlier that, "We in America today are nearer to the final triumph over poverty than ever before in the history of this land."

Homelessness, migration, and family separation

Homelessness was an increasing problem during the Depression. By 1940, the homeownership rate had fallen to 44 percent, the lowest in the twentieth century. Unemployment or reduced pay meant that, as the Depression began to bite, many people could not pay their mortgages. By 1932, 250,000 households were unable to pay. This led to repossession by the lender, which was usually a bank. The owner became homeless. Those who were unable to pay their rent were evicted. Shanty towns sprang up on the outskirts of towns as the homeless used any building materials they could find to erect shelters. Corrugated iron and even cardboard boxes were used to create the shacks. Not surprisingly, there were no sewers or other utilities. These townships were known as "Hoovervilles" (page 138).

The high level of borrowing in farming meant that, by 1933, almost 45 percent of farmers could no longer pay the interest on their debts. They were faced with the lender foreclosing and making them homeless. The degraded soil from years of intensive farming created a **dustbowl** in the Midwest in the middle of the decade, which made matters worse. Three million people left their farms and headed West.

> ### KEY TERM
>
> **Dustbowl** In the 1930s, a combination of natural causes and poor farming practices caused a dustbowl in the prairies. The soil was exposed by cultivation which removed the prairie grasses. Intensive cultivation degraded it, then dry weather turned the topsoil to dust and winds blew it away. With no topsoil, no crops could be grown.

Men seeking work traveled the railroads in search of employment. They were known as "hobos" (a term considered derogatory today) and they lived in tents or in freight wagons. By 1932, there were estimated to be two million of them. Such was the level of discomfort that some of them deliberately got arrested—a night in jail was preferable to a night in the open air. These men had left their families behind. Statistics reveal significant impacts on family life. Marriages were delayed. The birthrate fell below the replacement level for the first time since records began. The divorce rate also fell. The cost of paying a lawyer and living in two separate households was more than couples could afford.

African American sharecroppers left the land in their thousands. Hispanic Americans were in an even more precarious position. Discrimination prevailed. Public officials wanted to reserve jobs for unemployed white Americans. A major **repatriation** of people of Mexican descent began across the whole country. They were rounded up in informal raids and deported regardless of their status. A million of the 1.8 million deported were US citizens. Their rights were ignored; there was no recourse to legal process. In Los Angeles, hospitals were cleared of Hispanic Americans, regardless of how ill they were. Families were split up. The legacy of insecurity lasted for many years, even after the **Bracero Program** was introduced in 1942, which gave employment contracts to Mexican farm and railroad workers.

KEY TERMS

Repatriation The return of someone or something to their country of origin. Unlike deportation, repatriation can be voluntary.

Bracero Program An initiative set up by the US and Mexican governments to bring temporary guest workers from Mexico into the United States for farm labor.

ACTIVITY

"Unemployment was the most serious consequence of the Great Depression." To what extent do you agree?

Work with a partner. One of you selects evidence to support the statement and the other selects evidence to challenge it. Discuss your findings, then write a paragraph that sums up your answer to the question.

Responses of the Hoover administration

> ## HERBERT HOOVER (1875–1964)
>
> Hoover was a self-made man. He acquired a poor reputation for being uncaring toward those suffering during the Depression, but this misrepresents him. He was born into a Quaker family in Iowa in 1874 and was brought up in Oregon. The son of a blacksmith, he worked his way through college to pay his fees, graduating from Stanford as a mining engineer. He worked in California's gold mines, then abroad in Australia and China before settling in London as a mining consultant.
>
>
>
> He earned a reputation as "the great humanitarian" during the First World War. Aged 40, Hoover wanted to do more than earn a good living and looked for opportunities to contribute to the welfare of people. He performed charitable work during and after the war in Europe. First, he responded to a request from the American Consul General to organize the repatriation of 120,000 Americans
>
> Herbert Hoover, 1928
>
> who were in Europe when the war broke out. Next, he helped to feed the victims of the war in Belgium, a neutral country invaded by Germany in August 1914. When the US entered the war in 1917, President Woodrow Wilson appointed him head of the Food Administration. He ran this so successfully that when the war ended, he was made head of the American Relief Administration. He organized food for millions of hungry Europeans. In 1921, he extended the relief to famine-struck Soviet Russia, putting the needs of the starving people above the country's Bolshevik politics. He served in the administrations of Harding and Coolidge as Secretary of Commerce before being picked as the Republican candidate in the 1928 presidential election.
>
> During the Great Depression, Hoover used federal government powers to support the economy. Unfortunately, his actions were inadequate in providing relief and insufficient to bring about recovery. The 1932 election was a landslide victory for his Democrat opponent, Franklin D Roosevelt.
>
> In the post-Second World War era, Hoover served under both Truman and Eisenhower, heading a commission to reorganize the Executive Department. In this role, he successfully introduced many economies. He died, aged 90, in 1964.

During Hoover's election campaign of 1928, a group of New York businessmen, "Republican Business Men, Inc.," ran a campaign slogan on his behalf promising "a chicken for every pot." Hoover's campaign focused on his record during and after the First World War. A "Hoover home" relied on his stability, vision, integrity, and experience. As Secretary for Commerce, Hoover might have been aware of weaknesses in the American economy, but he thought that they could be overcome with wealth gradually filtering down to the poor. Within a year of taking office, Hoover was faced with an unprecedented economic collapse. There were no plans for addressing economic problems on this scale. The structure of the government, with specified powers for federal government, limited the scope for presidential action. Did Hoover do the best possible in very difficult circumstances or did his attitudes further hinder him?

Attitude of rugged individualism

Hoover believed that Americans should be self-supporting. This was an attitude that had its origins with the first European settlers. Adversity was inevitable and it was "character-building" to face it and overcome it. Hoover thought that almost everyone could support themselves and that the government's role did not include helping those who could help themselves. This is the meaning of the phrase "rugged individualism," which is associated with Republicans and with Herbert Hoover in particular. Hoover often used the phrase and it has been taken to mean that he lacked compassion. Nevertheless, his role during and after the First World War shows that he believed in helping people who were suffering through no fault of their own. In America, the provision of welfare was the responsibility of local government at state and city levels. Charities helped to provide for the poor and sick. Hoover provided support for these organizations by making funds available and helping them to coordinate their efforts. Hoover's "rugged individualism" did not mean leaving the poor to starve.

Attempts at relief

Hoover focused on helping businesses. His opinion was that this would help workers because it would protect jobs. Unfortunately, his policies were not enough to prevent the economy declining further. Some had the opposite effect to that intended. While focusing on businesses, Hoover also allowed loans to local government and charities providing help for the poor, and helped them to coordinate their efforts.

Help for businesses

The Hawley-Smoot Act of 1930 increased import tariffs on manufactured goods by 50 percent. It aimed to help American industry sell more home-produced goods. However, it damaged manufacturing because retaliatory tariffs made it more difficult for American manufacturers to sell their products abroad.

Hoover cut personal and business taxes by $130 million to stimulate investment. However, people were struggling to pay for the basics and hoarded any spare money rather than buying consumer goods. Businesses were not sufficiently confident to invest in growth. In 1932, taxes were increased on businesses to help balance the budget.

The Reconstruction Finance Corporation (RFC) was established in 1932. It provided loans totaling $1.5 billion to rescue businesses, banks, and insurance companies. It did not help enough businesses to make a difference.

The Banking Act of 1932 allowed the Federal Reserve to purchase large quantities of **government securities**. This policy ended **deflation** but was discontinued in June 1932.

Help for workers

Hoover encouraged voluntary agreements between employers and their workforces to keep wages steady. This did not prevent some companies from cutting wages.

Tax reductions on workers' wages in 1930 gave them more money, but not enough to boost consumer confidence.

The Boulder Canyon Project was established in 1928. It extended over several states, so did not contravene states' rights. It was funded by the RFC and led to the construction of the Hoover Dam. The dam was completed in 1935. The project brought important infrastructure to the area and controlled flooding on the Colorado River.

The RFC funded further infrastructure projects that created jobs. In July 1932, the Emergency Relief Construction Act allowed the RFC to loan $1.5 billion for public works projects.

Help for homeowners

Hoover persuaded Congress to pass the Home Loan Bank Act of July 1932. This established Federal Home Loan Banks to help prevent people from losing their homes by providing low-cost funds for banks to use for mortgage lending. The banks that joined the scheme were centrally regulated. This had limited impact by the time of the election of November 1932.

Help for state governments and charities

In 1931, the President's Organization for Unemployment Relief (POUR) was set up. The aim was to coordinate local welfare agencies without spending government money. The impact was limited because the organizations could not function effectively without more money. The scheme ended in June 1932.

> **KEY TERMS**
> **Government securities** Loans to the government in the form of bonds that the government guarantees to repay.
> **Deflation** A general decline in prices for goods and services. It occurs when an economy has less money and credit available.

Hoover's policies did not make a significant difference. During his term in office:
- industrial production fell by 45 percent
- home construction fell by 92 percent
- 5,000 banks failed
- in New York 10,000 out of 29,000 manufacturing firms closed.

Response to the Bonus Army, July 1932

Frustrated that the government appeared unable to control the economy and help the destitute, some turned to violence. There were strikes and clashes across many cities because wages were too low to support people. A demonstration in front of the White House in March 1930 gives an indication of the depth of feeling because it was so unusual. Thousands of people, white and black together, gathered to demonstrate against both racial injustice and unemployment. Many of them were members of the Communist Party. The president watched as police broke up the demonstration with clubs and tear gas.

The biggest protest was the Bonus Army March of 1932. First World War veterans had been promised a bonus that would not be payable until 1945. In desperation, thousands who were unemployed marched, some with their families, to Washington DC to demand that the bonus be paid immediately. In May, they settled around the city with at least 15,000 in an improvised settlement on Anacostia Flats across the river from and within view of the Capitol.

Their case was debated in Congress. Although the House agreed on a bill to pay them immediately, in June the Senate voted against the bill. The Bonus Army protesters remained encamped in the city until July. Hoover's reaction was harsh and helps to explain how he gained a reputation for being callous. He later claimed they were "communists" and "hoodlums." The DC police were ordered to remove the protesters but when they arrived to do so, a riot ensued. Two protesters were shot dead and the army was called in to restore order. Tanks, armed troops, cavalry, and tear gas were deployed by General **Douglas MacArthur**. MacArthur exceeded his orders, crossed the river, and moved into the camp on Anacostia Flats. Not surprisingly, injuries resulted, including those of children, and two babies were killed. DC's hospitals were inundated with the wounded.

The military operation was a success, but the political fallout was a disaster for Hoover—just months before the presidential election. Even the pro-Republican press expressed horror at what had happened. With the economy still in decline, Hoover's reelection was unlikely.

> **KEY FIGURE**
> **Douglas MacArthur**
> (1880–1964) General Douglas MacArthur was a career soldier. In 1930, President Hoover appointed him to the top army job, the Chief of Staff. Leading the army in forcibly removing Bonus Army encampments from Washington DC in 1932 damaged his reputation. In the Second World War, he retreated to Australia on Roosevelt's orders when the Japanese invaded the Philippines, famously asserting, "I will return." He was true to his word. On September 2, 1945, he presided over the Japanese surrender. He commanded the UN forces in Korea (1950–51) but was relieved of his command after disobeying direct orders.

> What can you learn from Source 3.1 about the Bonus Army and the response of the authorities? Use details from the source to explain your answer.

SOURCE 3.1

"Bonus Marchers" and police battle in Washington DC, July 1932

The policies and impacts of Franklin D Roosevelt's "New Deal"

Between Roosevelt's election in November 1932 and his inauguration in March 1933, the economy had deteriorated significantly. During that period, he had appointed his Cabinet along with an unofficial group of advisers referred to as the "Brains Trust." They worked to give substance to the promises he had made before the election, sometimes using plans already drawn up but not yet implemented by Hoover. Roosevelt (often referred to by his initials, FDR) had spoken with great confidence as a candidate, giving the impression that he understood what America needed. As president, he continued to communicate with the American people in radio broadcasts known as "fireside chats," explaining how his policies would improve their lives. The "New Deal" really was new. It was far more interventionist than any previous president's actions. It pushed the boundaries of what was possible for the federal government within the confines of the Constitution. When the laws encroached on the states' rights, Roosevelt was forced to alter his approach, introducing a Second New Deal. Nevertheless, his aims remained constant—to use the powers of government to mitigate the effects of the Depression and bring about a stronger, fairer economy. The success of the New Deal is difficult to measure. The only real indicator is the "Roosevelt recession" of 1937–38, which showed that, despite promising indicators, government support for the economy was still necessary. Before Roosevelt's work was complete, the Second World War began. The American economy focused on supplying the needs of a warring world. The country returned to full production and full employment.

> **ACTIVITY**
>
> Write a paragraph defending Hoover's response to the Great Depression. Do you think Hoover's reputation as a heartless, reactionary conservative is justified?

SOURCE 3.2

From Roosevelt's radio broadcast to the nation, May 7, 1933

It is wholly wrong to call the measure that we have taken government control of farming, control of industry, and control of transportation. It is rather a partnership between government and farming and industry and transportation, a partnership in planning and partnership to see that the plans are carried out.

We are working toward a definite goal, which is to prevent the return of conditions which came very close to destroying what we call modern civilization. The actual accomplishment of our purpose cannot be attained in a day. Our policies are wholly within purposes for which our American Constitutional Government was established 150 years ago.

> What evidence is there in Source 3.2 that FDR expected the New Deal to face criticism? Explain your answer using details from the source and your knowledge.

The three Rs—relief, recovery, and reform—and the First Hundred Days

Roosevelt's goals can be summed up as the "three R's": relief, recovery, and reform. He aimed to provide relief from the effects of the Depression, to promote the recovery of the economy, and to reform the way that banks and businesses operated to prevent a repeat of the Depression.

In his first hundred days in office, numerous pieces of legislation were passed, establishing a range of agencies that each targeted one or more of these aims.

> **ACTIVITY**
>
> Make a chart showing Roosevelt's actions during the First Hundred Days. Use the headings of relief, recovery, and reform to show how he addressed each aim.
>
> | Relief | Recovery | Reform |
> |---|---|---|
> | | | |
> | | | |
> | | | |

The Banking Crisis

During Hoover's "lame duck" months, between the 1932 election and Roosevelt's inauguration, the banking system in the US had come close to collapse. In his inaugural address, Roosevelt had said, "the only thing we have to fear is fear itself." This was certainly true of banking. So many banks had collapsed that people thought it was safer to keep their money hidden at home than to deposit it in a bank. This hindered recovery because the money could not be invested in businesses. Three days before Roosevelt's inauguration, a crisis was reached. The Federal Reserve reported that gold reserves had fallen below the legal limit set by the Federal Reserve Act of 1913. The banks needed to close while a solution was found. Hoover refused to act. Consequently, on Roosevelt's first day in office, he was forced to declare a Bank Holiday.

> **KEY TERM**
>
> **Lame duck** An elected official or leader whose term is nearing its end and who has either chosen not to run for reelection or is not allowed to do so. This person often has reduced influence or power because they are no longer accountable to voters.

March 6	Banks all forced to close while officials drew up a plan.
March 9	Roosevelt recalled Congress which agreed to the government plan: • Category A banks, which were considered sound, would be allowed to reopen immediately. • Category B banks could reopen if they were reorganized to be solvent. • Category C banks were so insolvent they would never reopen. • The Emergency Banking Act put this plan into operation. To stabilize the currency, the link between the dollar and the gold standard was abandoned. Banks were hurriedly assessed and decisions were made about their futures.
March 13	Banks began to open their doors.
March 15	Banks controlling 90 percent of banking resources had opened; 4,000 banks never reopened.

In the following days, more money was deposited than was withdrawn. Roosevelt's measures had restored confidence in the banking system.

The remainder of Roosevelt's first hundred days in office were taken up with introducing a series of bills into Congress. The House and Senate, which had a slim Democrat majority, seemed relieved to have a president who acted decisively. There was no difficulty in passing the bills into law.

Here are some of them and what their aims were:
- The Economy Act reduced the salaries of federal workers and cut benefit payments to veterans. The aim was to reduce the federal deficit.
- The Civilian Conservation Reforestation Relief Act created jobs for unemployed single men aged 18–25 (later extended to 17–28) in the Civilian Conservation Corps (CCC). The men lived in camps and did outdoor manual work. They were provided with accommodation, food, and clothing. They had to send most of their earnings to their families.
- The Agricultural Adjustment Act (AAA) aimed to raise the prices of farm products. This could only be done by reducing output. Farmers received subsidies in return for producing less.
- The Federal Emergency Relief Act (FERA) established the Federal Emergency Relief Administration to organize public works that created jobs for the unemployed.
- The Tennessee Valley Authority Act created the Tennessee Valley Authority (TVA), which addressed the problems of the Tennessee Valley area which extended over eight states. It used regional planning powers to develop an area that suffered from a lack of infrastructure and had been hit particularly badly during the Depression. Public works comprised electricity generation, navigation, flood control, and fertilizer production.
- The Securities Act established ways of preventing excessive speculation on the Stock Exchange using the Securities Exchange Commission.
- The 1933 Glass-Steagall Act built on Hoover's 1932 Glass-Steagall Act by establishing the Federal Deposit Insurance Corporation. It was widely debated, as it restricted the banks by separating commercial banking from investment banking in order to make deposits more secure.

- The National Industrial Recovery Act (NIRA) helped to promote fair practice in business. It aimed to stabilize prices and ensure workers' rights regarding their wages and membership of labor unions. It established the National Recovery Administration (NRA) to enforce fair competition codes that companies signed up to, setting hours of work, rates of pay, and fixing prices to earn the blue eagle badges that indicated their compliance with the NIRA's standards. It also created self-governing bodies within industrial sectors such as steel, glass, and automotive manufacturing, in which businesses agreed to minimum prices and production quotas. The NRA was hailed as an important initiative in fair business practice, but enforcement proved difficult because codes were voluntary and ultimately found to be unconstitutional. The NIRA also created the Public Works Administration (PWA), which created jobs by instigating a major program of public works.
- The Home Owners Loan Act set up the Home Owners Loan Corporation. The corporation refinanced mortgages on urban housing. In total, a fifth of mortgages were refinanced, allowing homeowners to avoid being evicted for defaulting on their mortgages.

The policies of the First New Deal (1933–34)

The policies of the First New Deal were many and varied. They addressed some of the most serious effects of the Depression. However, they were not all well-planned or considered. While they were well-intended and had some success, there were also drawbacks and problems. There was overlap and confusion.

The new agencies and administrations all had some success. However, they also had flaws which their critics were quick to point out. Did their achievements outweigh their drawbacks?

ACTIVITY

As you read about the work of the agencies, complete a chart like the one below to help you assess the New Deal.

Agency	Agency (full name)	Achievements	Problems
CCC	Civilian Conservation Corps		
AAA			
TVA			
NRA			
PWA			

The CCC provided thousands of young men with work and ensured that their families benefited. Between 1933 and 1942 nearly three million men participated in the work camps. They received food, clothing, and a small wage. Most of their wages ($25 out of the $30 earned) had to be sent to their families. Most were from urban areas, so while rural areas benefited from the work done, urban communities had increased spending power. It is likely that the physical work and regular meals had health benefits for the workers. They learned skills that would help them gain work after their six months at a CCC camp. Some people saw the CCC as providing cheap labor. There was a separate organization for Native Americans. The camps were run by individual states with their own priorities, and many discriminated against African Americans. African Americans found it more difficult to get placements and camps were increasingly segregated even though the regulations forbade this. Quotas were set according to the balance of the population. This did not take account of the higher unemployment rate among African Americans. The She-She-She camps for women, championed by **Eleanor Roosevelt**, did not have widespread appeal, and only 8,500 women were enrolled.

KEY FIGURE

Eleanor Roosevelt (1884–1962) Eleanor Roosevelt married FDR in 1905. During his presidential election campaigns, she traveled the country, speaking on his behalf and she used her position as First Lady to advocate for civil and human rights.

Eleanor focused on groups poorly supported by the New Deal. She used her influence to secure the appointment of Frances Perkins as the first woman to head the Department of Labor. She supported the work of the Federal Council on Colored Affairs, an unofficial group of African American advisers to the president, convened by the famous African American educator Mary McLeod Bethune.

> Why was Source 3.3 published at this time? Use details from the photograph and your knowledge to explain your answer.

SOURCE 3.3

Eleanor Roosevelt and Dr Mary McLeod Bethune visiting George Washington Carver Hall, a men's dormitory for African Americans in Washington DC, May 1943

The Farm Credit Administration made loans to a fifth of farmers so they would not lose their land. Together with the AAA, they raised farm prices which reduced the number of people leaving rural communities. Between 1933 and 1939, farm incomes doubled. Production was decreased: ten million acres of cotton plants were plowed up. The government purchased and slaughtered six million piglets. This was a waste of food, since only a small proportion was canned and given to households in poverty. However, it did succeed in the aim of steadying and then increasing food prices. Work on conservation and drought management helped landowners. But there were drawbacks. The measures helped farm owners. However, fewer laborers were needed so sharecroppers and other laborers, a disproportionate number of whom were African American, became unemployed. Some jobs were seen as relatively worthless and merely a way of occupying people and giving them a little money.

The TVA is generally seen as a success. Although economic growth in the Tennessee Valley region was less than anticipated, the TVA was very productive. Thirty-three dams were built to control river flow and generate hydroelectric power, which provided cheap electricity for businesses and households. Employment was created in the area along with health and welfare facilities. There was consultation with people in the local area to plan the scheme.

The NRA drew up codes for each industry and encouraged employers to sign up. The codes gave workers protection by limiting hours, setting minimum wages, and allowing workers to join unions. They also banned child labor. Prices were fixed for goods produced. Employers were encouraged, not forced, to sign up for the codes. The NRA established federal government controls on businesses, though these were optional. These federal controls on businesses were what caused the Supreme Court to rule that the NRA was unconstitutional in 1935. According to the Constitution, the regulation of businesses that operated within one state was not within the jurisdiction of the federal government.

The PWA did not employ people directly. Instead, it awarded government contracts to companies to build public infrastructure. They, in turn, employed skilled workers on much-needed projects. The agency spent $7 billion on building dams, roads, bridges, sewage systems, houses, hospitals, and schools. Rural America was provided with electricity. Since the usefulness of the projects was clear, this was not a controversial use of government money. For every worker employed on a PWA-funded project, two further jobs were created.

The policies of the Second New Deal (1935–36)

The "Second New Deal" was a series of acts passed from 1935 to 1936. It represents a continuation of Roosevelt's First New Deal, but with some change of emphasis and a corrective to some of its flaws. To what extent did the Second New Deal show continuity with the first, and to what extent did it contain new ideas?

A second series of acts was passed. These included the Emergency Relief Appropriation Act, which allowed money to be spent on job-creation programs. The PWA and CCC were granted more funds. In 1935, the Works Progress Administration (WPA) was established to provide job opportunities to people who had previously been neglected by the PWA, which only awarded contracts needing skilled workers. The WPA provided employment for to up to two million people a year on projects such as roads, public buildings, tunnels, and the planting of windbreak trees to prevent dustbowls. More controversially, it spent seven percent of its money on cultural projects, giving work to artists, musicians, writers, and actors. Some people thought that these jobs would not benefit the economy and that government should not fund them.

The National Labor Relations Act (Wagner Act) aimed to continue the work of the NRA, which had been declared unconstitutional. It concerned the relations between workers and private sector employers, which had deteriorated in 1933–34. After a wave of strikes and factory takeovers in 1933–34, the federal government was keen to establish workers' rights to form and join labor unions. The Act applied to organizations whose activities extended across state boundaries other than airlines, railroads, agricultural companies, and government agencies. It provided arbitration services where disputes between employers and workers could not be resolved. Like the NIRA, this agency was challenged in the Supreme Court, but this time the act was designed to ensure that it was constitutional and the challenge was defeated. The result was a large increase in labor union membership.

The Social Security Act of 1935 introduced old-age pensions and support for people with disabilities and dependent children. This marked a change in attitude, as previously everyone had been expected to provide for themselves and their future needs. Unemployment insurance was also proposed, to be organized and funded by state governments, with financial support from federal government.

Opposition to the New Deal and its impact

FDR won two elections in the 1930s, with significant majorities in the popular vote and almost complete victory in the electoral college. The level of support for him as president was enormous. Nevertheless, his policies attracted many vocal critics and some of his legislation was challenged as unconstitutional. Some people on the political right criticized his measures on the grounds that they were socialist and very close to being communist. They thought that he was taking on the characteristics of the Soviet dictator Joseph Stalin. These critics thought the USA should be a nation of people who were self-reliant and self-sufficient, and they felt that Roosevelt's policies undermined this. They thought that the federal government was taking on roles that should be the responsibility of the individual. In contrast, critics on the political left thought that his policies did not go far enough to support poor, unemployed, and disadvantaged people. They thought that Roosevelt was protecting business owners at the expense of the workers. They favored federal government intervention to reduce the gap between rich and poor to make America a more economically equal society.

There were also legal challenges to the New Deal. The Constitution limited the powers of the federal government. The wording of the Constitution meant that it was open to interpretation. The role of the Supreme Court was to decide whether a federal law met the criteria set out in the Constitution. In several cases, the Supreme Court found elements of the New Deal unconstitutional.

While political opposition from the right barely affected Roosevelt's popularity, critics on the left had the potential to attract Democrat voters. The Second New Deal went some way to addressing their concerns. The judgments of the Supreme Court meant that the executive had to realign the focus of later New Deal laws to meet its aims.

KEY FIGURE

Joseph Stalin

(1879–1953) Joseph Dzhugashvili was born in Georgia in the Russian Empire. By the early 20th century, he was a committed Marxist. In 1913 he took the name Stalin, meaning "man of steel." After the death of Lenin, the first Bolshevik leader of Russia, he outmaneuvered other prominent Bolsheviks to become leader of the USSR. He ruled from 1928 until his death. He was a ruthless and paranoid man who did not hesitate to eliminate anyone he regarded as a threat to his power. His policy of "Socialism in One Country" aimed to modernize the Soviet economy and to protect the Soviet Union from outside threats.

Opposition from both sides of the political spectrum

Opposition from the liberal left

> **KEY TERM**
>
> **Left wing and right wing**
> The two sides of the political spectrum which span from the extreme left of anarchism and communism to the extreme right of fascism. In the US, the major political parties span the central section of this spectrum, from liberal left to conservative right.

Among a broad range of opponents of the New Deal on the liberal **left wing**, some individuals stood out because of their vocal campaigns and widespread appeal.

Senator Huey Long was a popular politician. He campaigned with policies that were much more left-wing than other Democrats. As Governor of Louisiana in the 1920s, he spent a lot of taxpayers' money modernizing his state and fighting big business on behalf of ordinary people. In 1932, he won a seat in the US Senate where he became a vocal critic of the New Deal, arguing that it was not bold enough. Long's plans involved the redistribution of wealth. Incomes above $1 million and personal wealth above $5 million would be taxed at 100 percent and the proceeds shared across the population. His promises attracted significant support. They included an annual income of $2,500 for every household, a car, a radio, a right to homeownership, pensions, a bonus for veterans, and free college education. There was a strong element of fantasy in his promises, as his proposed taxes could not generate enough revenue to give every family the income and possessions he promised. Nevertheless, Long formed an organization called the Share Our Wealth Society. It claimed a membership of seven million. It was funded by Long's supporters, but also by Roosevelt's enemies. They supported his campaign because they hoped that Long would split the Democrat vote and that this would enable a Republican presidential candidate to be elected.

Another politician who opposed the New Deal was a priest and radio presenter, Father Coughlin. He initially supported left-wing policies and in the 1932 election, endorsed Roosevelt. He drew an income of $500,000 from his listeners and in the 1932 election endorsed Roosevelt. However, he thought the New Deal did not go far enough in alleviating poverty and turned against Roosevelt. Instead, he formed an organization called the National Union for Social Justice. Over time his broadcasts became more right-wing and started to contain antisemitic conspiracy theories. He falsely believed that there was a Jewish-Communist conspiracy that controlled use of gold to underpin the currency; this influenced a lot of his criticisms and suggestions.

Francis E Townsend also had radical ideas about how to improve the economy. He advocated giving $200 a month to everyone aged over 60, on condition that all the money was spent by the end of each month. He thought that the spending power of these older people would stimulate demand and hence create jobs in manufacturing. The idea started with a published letter and within a year had attracted interest across the country. By 1935, his movement had ten million supporters. If the New Deal had been more successful in alleviating poverty, Townsend's support would have been far less.

Opposition from the conservative right

The American Liberty League brought together Roosevelt's **right-wing** opponents. It included prominent Democrats as well as Republicans and business owners. It was formed in 1934, ahead of the mid-term elections, to rally those who did not approve of the New Deal. At its height, it achieved a membership of 125,000.

The basis of the American Liberty League's criticism of the New Deal was that it was socialist and therefore anti-business. They accused Roosevelt of being too dictatorial, like the Soviet Union's Joseph Stalin. They claimed that the New Deal took away people's liberties. Whatever the validity of the League's criticisms, it was unlikely to garner significant support. Most Americans preferred the New Deal to any alternative. Roosevelt had gained their trust and the way the League presented its ideas did not convince the public that it had their interests at heart.

Rulings of the Supreme Court

The role of the Supreme Court is to uphold the Constitution. This includes ensuring that all legislation passed complies with the Constitution. In several cases, the judges decided that the New Deal was unconstitutional. The most famous judgment was in the case of *Schechter Corp. v. United States*, commonly known as the "sick chickens case." This case revolved around a poultry firm, Schechter Poultry Corporation, operating in New York state. It had signed up to NRA codes but was found to have sold a chicken that was not safe for humans to eat which violated the code. The company was at fault but appealed to the Supreme Court on the saying that the NIRA violated the Constitution. They said that the federal government could not make rules about issues that were within state governments' authority without violating the Constitution. The Supreme Court found unanimously in favor of the Schechter Corporation. It ruled that Congress delegated too much power to the president and industrial groups, and that the NIRA's codes affected more than just interstate commerce. As a result, 450 NIRA codes were found to be illegal. The NRA collapsed. The National Labor Relations Act of 1935 which replaced it was acceptable to the Supreme Court.

In 1936, the AAA was also found to be in breach of the Constitution. The Supreme Court ruled that the system used to generate government subsidies paid to farmers who reduced their yields did not comply with the Constitution. The judgment was a technical one, depending on the definition of "tax." The case against the AAA was also upheld on the grounds that the federal government exceeded its permitted role by paying farmers to cut production. Although the judgment was not unanimous on this occasion, the AAA had to be replaced.

Roosevelt's responses to opposition

Roosevelt saw Senator Huey Long as a real threat. By 1935, the Democrats calculated that he commanded eleven percent of the vote. If this continued into the election year of 1936, the Democrat vote would be split, increasing the chance of a Republican presidency. Roosevelt gave aid to Long's enemies in Louisiana and started an Internal Revenue Service investigation of his finances. This soon turned into an investigation of the alleged corruption in Louisiana with which Long had been associated for some time. In September 1935, Long died after being shot. His challenge to FDR was brought to an abrupt end.

Like Long, Father Coughlin had engaged in suspicious financial dealings. His opinions about the evils of basing the currency on the value of gold and the benefits of using silver instead were based on antisemitic conspiracy theories. His financial activities and antisemitism caused his career to end. He had invested money in silver futures, and his policies would have made this investment more valuable. The Vatican decided to discipline him for his antisemitic campaigning. He was thoroughly discredited.

Of all the left-leaning critics, Francis Townsend seemed the most legitimate. A retired doctor, his ideas may have been eccentric, but they were popular. Roosevelt countered this threat to his support by adopting some of Townsend's ideas. Older people did not receive $200 a month but Roosevelt did introduce old-age pensions in the Social Security Act of 1935.

The critics from the conservative right did not warrant much attention, as they posed little threat to Roosevelt's popularity. Roosevelt's 1936 campaign team mocked the Liberty League, as the way they described the president was nothing like his reputation as a "man of the people." The conservatives labeled him a "traitor to his class" because he came from a privileged political background, but his long-cultivated image as the people's friend was impossible to shift. They attacked his policies and personality, but their appeal was limited. Although some leading politicians were involved, Herbert Hoover, a staunch critic of the New Deal, refused to join them. The opposition from the right was never significant in electoral terms, as was demonstrated by the strength of support for Roosevelt in the 1936 election.

The opposition from the Supreme Court was incontestable. Roosevelt responded by finding other legislative routes to provide the relief, recovery, and reform that had been declared unconstitutional. Some of the acts of the Second New Deal, regarding agriculture and workers' conditions and rights, show how he changed his approach.

He also considered a more radical approach. He proposed changing the rules for membership of the Supreme Court so that judges had to retire at the age of 70. If they failed to retire, the president could add another judge to the bench. Since judges often voted according to the policies of their political party, interpreting the law in a way that matched the president who had appointed them, this rule change would quickly change the Supreme Court to one dominated by Roosevelt appointees. This "court-packing plan" was contained in the Judicial Procedures Reform Bill of 1937. It was very controversial. Roosevelt believed that he had the right to appoint additional justices, as the Constitution did not stipulate the number of Supreme Court judges. However, his opponents claimed that, because this plan would make it very difficult to challenge Roosevelt's laws on the grounds that they were unconstitutional, it would make him into a dictator like the Soviet leader, Stalin, or the German chancellor, Adolf Hitler. Before a crisis point was reached, another Supreme Court judgment was made on a case relating to wages in Washington state. The judgment was five to four in favor of the New Deal law that the case challenged. One judge had decided to change his voting pattern and indicate that he was no longer prepared to undermine New Deal laws. The precise sequence of events is not clear, as the judgment was reached before the Judicial Procedures Reform Bill was introduced. Nevertheless, after considerable delay the bill was eventually stopped. The Democrats in Congress were worried that the bill might be unconstitutional. Roosevelt was very popular with the public but there were limits to his powers.

SOURCE 3.4

A political cartoon from February 1937. The caption reads 'Do we want a ventriloquist act in the supreme court?'

> What can you learn from this cartoon about opinions on the "court-packing" plan?

The legacy of the New Deal

The New Deal changed the American politics. Both the main national parties, Republicans and Democrats, represented a wide range of people and views. The conservative Democrats of the South, often long-standing Congressmen, were natural opponents of Roosevelt's style of Democrat politics. They disliked change and feared that he would undermine white dominance in the South and "American values." Liberal Republicans agreed more with Roosevelt's policies and were more likely to vote for them. Roosevelt succeeded in winning over a broad range of support. He won over the Southern Democrats by not addressing issues of racial discrimination and gained the support of labor unions and a range of religious and ethnic groups in the North, including Catholic, Jewish, and African American people. This grouping, known as the New Deal Coalition, dominated federal government until the last decades of the twentieth century. While Roosevelt was president, there was political maneuvering to establish the composition of the alliance. The severity of the Depression and the Republican failure to address these problems convinced some traditionally Republican cities of the North to vote in Democrat mayors. Pittsburgh, for example, was built on business and strongly Republican. The Depression and the mobilization of minority ethnic groups to the Democrat cause changed Pittsburgh's politics. The provision of jobs and relief persuaded voters that it was the Democrats who best served their interests. To secure the working class and minority ethnic vote, Roosevelt ensured that the Second New Deal served the interests of these new Democrat voters. These loyalties remained long after Roosevelt's presidency.

To address the nationwide problems of the early 1930s by providing relief, aiding recovery, and introducing reforms, Roosevelt had to expand the scope of federal government. In 1937, when he decided that reducing the budget deficit should be a priority, he found that his New Deal measures had yet to create a self-sufficient economy. A sharp decline in production and employment meant that he had to start spending again. A federal government with expanded powers became a permanent feature of the United States. As historian Eric Foner wrote in 2005, "Before the 1930s, national political debate often revolved around the question of *whether* the federal government should intervene in the economy. After the New Deal, debate rested on *how* it should intervene."

ACTIVITY

The New Deal aimed to provide relief, recovery, and reform. How successfully did it do this for the following groups?
- industrial workers
- farmers
- the unemployed
- homeowners
- women
- African Americans

SUMMARY DIAGRAM

The Great Depression and New Deal

What were the causes and impacts of the Great Depression and New Deal?

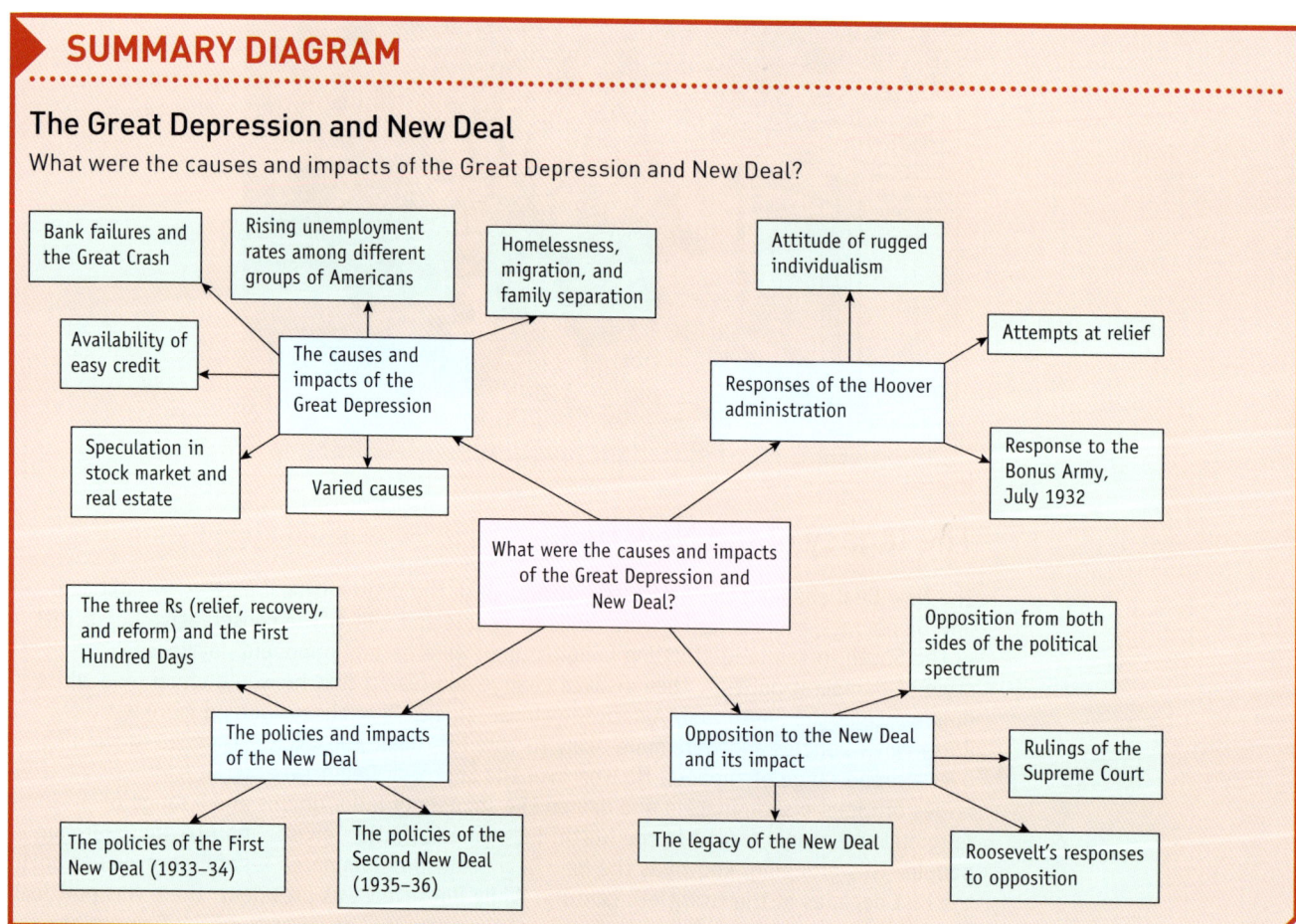

3.2 Why and how did US foreign policy evolve between 1935 and 1959?

By the mid-1930s situations were developing around the world that would eventually combine into the worldwide conflict that was the Second World War. In 1935, the US was hardly involved in these events. It had not joined the League of Nations, the international forum dominated by Britain and France. When Japan, Italy, and Germany began to take over other sovereign nations, the US was only slightly involved in the imposition of economic sanctions against them. War broke out in Europe on September 1, 1939, after Germany invaded Poland. Meanwhile, Japan was increasing its control of east Asia. The US remained neutral. This changed in December 1941, when the Japanese Air Force attacked the American naval base at Pearl Harbor in Hawaii. For the next four years, America was at war with the **Axis Powers**. As it became clear that **the Allies** would win the war, the leaders of the three main Allied powers met face-to-face to establish guidelines for peace. This was an uneasy alliance and tensions were unavoidable. By the time the war ended these tensions had developed into a "Cold War" which dominated American foreign policy for over 40 years. Capitalist America was worried by the spread of communism in eastern Europe and in Asia. The US positioned itself as the "champion (protector) of the free world." The invention, deployment, and increased building of nuclear weapons added further to the tension. Involvement of the two sides in other areas of conflict, such as the Middle East, added another dimension. The level of tension varied as American presidents and Soviet premiers came and went. By 1959, it was clear that Cold War incidents could occur anywhere in the world.

> **KEY TERMS**
>
> **Axis Powers** The US's opponents in the Second World War, principally Germany, Italy, and Japan.
>
> **The Allies** Allies of the US in the Second World War, principally Britain and the USSR.

Early US reactions to the outbreak of the Second World War and reasons for US entry

The prospect of the US becoming involved in the Second World War divided American opinion. Many of the big global events happened far away from America: Japanese military incursions into China from 1931, German expansion in Europe, which broke the terms of the Treaty of Versailles (1919), and Italy's attempt at gaining an overseas empire by conquering and colonizing Abyssinia (Ethiopia). Americans who thought their country should avoid involvement in the conflicts of distant countries favored neutrality. They did not want to take part in a war that did not directly involve them, as in 1917. On the other side were people who thought that the US should not ignore violations of international treaties and the invasion of a weaker country by a militarily stronger one. President Roosevelt was reluctant to involve America directly in war, but he also thought that America should make clear that military incursions into other countries by fascist dictatorships would not be tolerated. Laws were altered to allow the US to sell weapons to the Allies. When France was defeated by Nazi Germany in June 1940, Britain stood alone against Hitler's Germany. Sales of arms to Britain increased but desperate British pleas did not persuade Roosevelt that America should fight. Public opinion was generally anti-war. This changed in December 1941, when Japanese territorial expansion led to an attack on the US naval base at Pearl Harbor in Hawaii. Intelligence reports show that that the attack was not unexpected. However, the location was. America had expected to be attacked in the Philippines. It is possible that British intelligence was deliberately withheld so that America would have to become involved. On December 8, 1941, the United States declared war on Japan. Japan's allies, Germany and Italy, then declared war on the US.

Neutrality Acts, 1935–39

US foreign policy in the interwar period is often referred to as isolationist. Isolationism did not mean that the US had nothing to do with other countries. It became involved in international affairs when they affected their interests. The Washington Naval Conference of 1921 discussed placing limits on the size of countries' navies and the situation in the Far East. Three treaties were drawn up. Although the US was not a member of the League of Nations, the US was still tied to the European powers as a result of the international loan system that financed the First World War. During the 1920s, the US stepped in twice to reschedule German reparations payments, setting them at a more manageable level with the Dawes Plan of 1925 and the Young Plan of 1929.

KEY FIGURES

Adolf Hitler (1889-1945) Born in Austria-Hungary, Hitler moved to Germany in 1913 and served in the German army during the First World War. After the war he joined what would become the Nazi Party, and soon became its leader. He used people's economic fears to become popular, blaming minority groups, including Jewish, Romani and disabled people, for Germany's problems. In 1933, as Chancellor, Hitler transformed Germany into a single-party fascist state. His policies included the mass-murder of millions of people, including six million Jewish people. His expansionist foreign policy led to the outbreak of the Second World War. On the December 11, 1941 Hitler declared war on the U.S.

Winston Churchill (1874–1965) Winston Leonard Spencer-Churchill was a British politician who was Prime Minister from 1940 to 1945 and 1950 to 1955. His mother, the New York socialite Jeanette Jerome, gave him firm ties with America. His long career in the army, as a journalist and, from 1908, a member of the British parliament meant he had wide experience. In the 1930s, unlike many politicians, he recognized that Hitler's Germany posed a serious threat to peace. After the Second World War, his warnings about communism were therefore influential.

As the Great Depression spread around the world in the 1930s, some countries elected extremist governments that promised to solve their problems by rearming and using their military might to prove their power. The Japanese army controlled the imperial government. Japan already had considerable influence over China but began to take military control in 1931. After electoral success, **Adolf Hitler** was appointed chancellor of Germany, but then took on dictatorial powers. He gradually expanded Germany, first by reoccupying the Rhineland, then forming a union with Austria before invading Czechoslovakia in 1938–39. The Italian fascist leader, Benito Mussolini, who had already established a form of dictatorship, decided to invade Abyssinia (Ethiopia) to distract from the problems of the Depression in Italy. The response of the League of Nations was weak. When persuasion failed, it imposed economic sanctions on countries that had violated international boundaries. The US had subscribed to this policy in the Kellogg-Briand Pact of 1928. However, the Depression made it difficult to persuade countries to impose economic sanctions and the US felt it was not required to do so. The US government thought that another war in Europe was likely. The Japanese conquest of China was ongoing.

In the mid-1930s Congress passed Neutrality Acts. The first of these Acts reflected the isolationist view that the US should stay out of wars that did not affect it. The counter-argument of the internationalists was more in line with Woodrow Wilson's "moral diplomacy" (page 94). Internationalists thought that America should support countries threatened with aggression. Initially, the isolationists had the most influence. The Neutrality Act of 1935 made it illegal for Americans to sell or transport arms or other war materials to countries that were at war. This Act was extended until May 1937. The 1937 Act specified that the Neutrality Act applied to all warring countries including those where there was a civil war, such as Spain. Arms manufacturers had to apply for export licenses. In addition, Americans were not allowed to make financial deals with countries that were at war. The transport of munitions to warring countries in American ships was banned even if the arms were produced elsewhere. These Acts were not supported by the president, but he agreed to them because public opinion was so strongly anti-war. The public thought that the First World War had only benefited bankers and other rich people, not ordinary Americans. The only concession to Roosevelt in the 1937 Act was that countries could purchase non-war materials on a "cash and carry" basis. They had to pay for goods in cash (upfront, rather than through loans) and carry the goods on their own ships. This favored Britain and France, as they were the only countries with the resources to pay cash and to ship supplies. The definition of "non-war materials" was critically important. Oil, as it was used by civilians as well as militaries, was classified as "non-war" which meant it could be exported for cash.

The policy began to change in 1939, in the months before the outbreak of war. It was clear that there was a danger of fascism taking over Europe. By 1939, Spain's democratically elected Republican government had been defeated by the forces of the fascist dictator General Franco, who received support from Italy and Germany, while the Republicans were supported by Soviet Russia. In 1936, Germany and Italy, both with fascist dictators, signed a defense agreement known as the Rome–Berlin Axis. Roosevelt had never wanted the Neutrality Act, and in March 1939, after Germany seized Czechoslovakia, he suggested amending it. At first, Congress voted against FDR's wishes. After the German invasion of Poland on September 1, 1939, they finally agreed that nations involved in conflicts could purchase munitions from the US. Again, "Cash and carry" conditions were applied and, again, they favored Britain and France, who had both declared war on Germany on September 3, in defense of Poland. Loans to warring countries were still banned. The isolationists recognized that neutrality was no longer possible.

Lend-Lease Program, 1941

Like Woodrow Wilson in 1916, Roosevelt promised in the 1940 election campaign to keep America out of the war. He stated, "I have said this before, but I shall say it again and again and again: your boys are not going to be sent into any foreign wars." However, it was difficult to ignore the new British prime minister, **Winston Churchill**, or the territorial gains of the Axis Powers. The Axis Powers were fascist dictatorships. Since America was opposed to dictatorship, the government favored those fighting against them. Initially, this meant France and Britain. In June 1940, the French government surrendered to German invaders. Britain stood alone against Nazi Germany and fascist Italy. The British were desperate for more allies. Still, Roosevelt hesitated. The American public did not want to become involved in another European war.

After the Royal Navy suffered significant losses, Churchill asked for ships. Instead, in September 1940, Roosevelt signed a "Destroyers for Bases" agreement, giving the British obsolete ships in exchange for 99-year leases on territory that would make useful US military bases. Two months later, Britain was running out of cash. The proposed solution was "lend-lease," by which Britain would continue to receive supplies and could pay for them later.

Eventually, Congress agreed to the Lend-Lease Act. The policy protected American defense interests by aiding the defeat of the Axis Powers without America having to fight. Eventually, lend-lease agreements were reached with 30 countries. War supplies could be lent or leased to any country considered to be vital to US defense. The agreement led to a range of support. This included revoking portions of the Neutrality Acts regarding the arming of merchant shipping and its uses. Britain's Royal Air Force had lost a lot of pilots and it was difficult to train replacements in a country under attack from the Luftwaffe (the German air force). The solution was to train the pilots abroad in friendly countries. One example was the use of Falcon Field in Mesa, Arizona where the climate was ideal for initial pilot training. The airfield opened in September 1941, later training US and British pilots together.

Most importantly, the Act bought time. The government knew that America would be drawn into the war. They knew that they were unprepared. Lend-Lease delayed their entry into the war.

Japanese attack on Pearl Harbor, December 1941

Figure 3.2 Japanese expansion, 1931–42

> **KEY TERM**
>
> **Puppet state** A country which appears independent, but is controlled by another nation.

As the government anticipated, America was eventually drawn into the war. Until 1941, America was mainly concerned about the spread of fascism in Europe. A secondary threat came from Japanese expansion around the Pacific. After invading Manchuria (a region in north-east China) in the early 1930s, Japan set up a **puppet state** in the region. The state, Manchukuo, was officially ruled by the last Emperor of China, Puyi. He abdicated his throne as a child during the revolution. Japan hoped that Puyi would make Manchukuo appear to be more legitimate. However, in reality, Puyi had little to no power, and Japan controlled Manchukuo completely. Manchukuo was just the start. Japan built up its military and in 1937 began to invade the nationalist-run Republic of China. Progress was slow and probably convinced the Americans that Japan was not a big threat. When France and the Netherlands fell to Germany and Britain was fighting the war alone, Japan turned its attention to French and Dutch colonies in southeast Asia as well as British colonies. American colonial possessions, such as the Philippines, Guam, and Hawaii also became targets. Britain and the US both knew from intelligence reports that a Japanese attack was likely and anticipated that it would occur in Thailand. There is a conspiracy theory which claims that Britain's Churchill knew about the attack and shared the intelligence with Roosevelt. Allegedly, Roosevelt chose not to tell anyone about the attack plans hoping that the attack would force the US to declare war. This theory is untrue. Japan had planned multiple attacks: first on Pearl Harbor and simultaneously on Hong Kong, Malaya (Malaysia), and the Dutch East Indies (Indonesia). It was a bold plan, carried out in radio silence, and was largely successful. On December 7, 1941, 360 Japanese aircraft were launched undetected from aircraft carriers to attack Pearl Harbor. In the surprise attack, all eight US battleships stationed there were hit, as were various other ships. Over 180 US aircraft were destroyed and others were damaged; 2,330 troops were killed and 1,140 wounded. Luckily, the three aircraft carriers of the Pacific Fleet escaped as they were at sea on maneuvers.

On the same day, December 7, Japan attacked the Philippines, beginning a highly successful campaign in which they seized large areas of southeast Asia. This culminated in the defeat of the British base at Singapore in February 1942, where they captured 90,000 British and British Empire troops. The attack on Pearl Harbor was an act of war. Roosevelt had no alternative but to ask Congress to sanction a declaration of war and Congress did not disagree. There was only one dissenting vote, that of Jeannette Rankin, a committed pacifist who was the first woman elected to Congress. The declaration came on December 8, the day after the attack on Pearl Harbor.

> **ACTIVITY**
>
> - Draw up a list of the steps by which America became involved in the Second World War.
> - "Without the Japanese attack on Pearl Harbor, the US would not have fought in the Second World War." Work in a pair. One person finds evidence to support the statement and the other finds evidence to challenge the statement. Look at each other's evidence. Write a paragraph to show whether you agree or disagree with the statement.

The growth and development of the Cold War

The Allied nations were very different, and were united only by their shared enemy: the Axis Powers. The US had been cooperating with Britain since the early months of the war. In June 1941, there was a significant change. Having failed in its attempts to break Britain, Germany invaded its former ally, the Soviet Union. This meant that when Germany and Italy formed an alliance with Japan and declared war on America, Roosevelt was drawn into an alliance with the world's only communist power. American and Soviet values were almost complete opposites, but their common cause against the Axis Powers forced them to work together. When Truman became president near the end of the war and began establishing a peace settlement, tensions increased. Before long, the uneasy alliance became open hostility. There were numerous misunderstandings and much posturing and provocation on both sides. Historians debate who was most to blame for the development of the Cold War. There can be no consensus on such a controversial question.

Tensions between the Allied powers at the Yalta Conference (February 1945) and Potsdam Conference (July 1945)

The Allied leaders of the US, USSR, and Britain met face-to-face on three occasions during the Second World War. The first meeting was in Tehran in late 1943. By this stage it was clear that Germany was in retreat, but not ready to admit defeat. There was discussion of the need for a "second front," which would involve the Western Allies invading German-occupied Europe from the west to take pressure off Soviet forces in the east. Although the Western Allies agreed to this, the invasion of France was delayed until June 1944. By the time the "Big Three" met again at Yalta in February 1945, Germany was about to be defeated. The allies agreed that Germany must surrender unconditionally. It would be divided into zones of occupation, de-Nazified and war criminals punished. Stalin wanted a "buffer zone" of friendly states on his western border to prevent a future invasion. In June 1941, Germany's invasion of the USSR had been sudden, unexpected, and initially very successful. The war in the Soviet Union was brutal: over twenty million people died. Compromises were reached, but they came with long-term consequences.

> **KEY TERM**
>
> **denazification** The removal of Nazis and Nazi culture from German and Austrian society.

> How accurate is the impression of the relationship between the "Big Three" in this photograph? Use your knowledge to explain your answer.

SOURCE 3.5

Winston Churchill, Franklin Roosevelt, and Joseph Stalin at the Yalta Conference, February 1945

The final meeting of the Allies was held at Potsdam in July 1945, two months after the war in Europe had ended. The dynamic had changed. Truman, Roosevelt's vice president, had been sworn in after Roosevelt died in April. He was very anti-communist. Toward the end of the conference, Clement Attlee replaced Churchill as British prime minister, Churchill having lost his majority in a general election. Stalin remained the leader of the USSR. The new situation and leaders made for tense negotiations. A provisional plan for Germany was agreed though many issues were not resolved. To maintain Soviet support, Roosevelt had promised Stalin substantial reparations, but Truman was less generous. He did not want to repeat mistakes made after the First World War. Drawing new boundaries for Poland was difficult because each leader had a different idea of what a "democratic government" for Poland should be. The Soviet Union had not declared war on Japan, but agreed to do so. The US and Britain agreed that only unconditional surrender from Japan would be acceptable. During the conference, Truman learned that the first successful atomic bomb test had taken place. He hinted at terrible consequences if Japan did not surrender, but Stalin did not seem very surprised. Truman was unaware that Stalin already knew about the bombs from his spies. The conference was conducted in a tense atmosphere; everyone was suspicious and nobody trusted each other. Within weeks, the USSR had declared war on Japan and America had dropped two atomic bombs on the country. Japan's unconditional surrender was accepted by General MacArthur on the USS *Missouri* on September 2, 1945.

Increasing tensions in a divided Europe

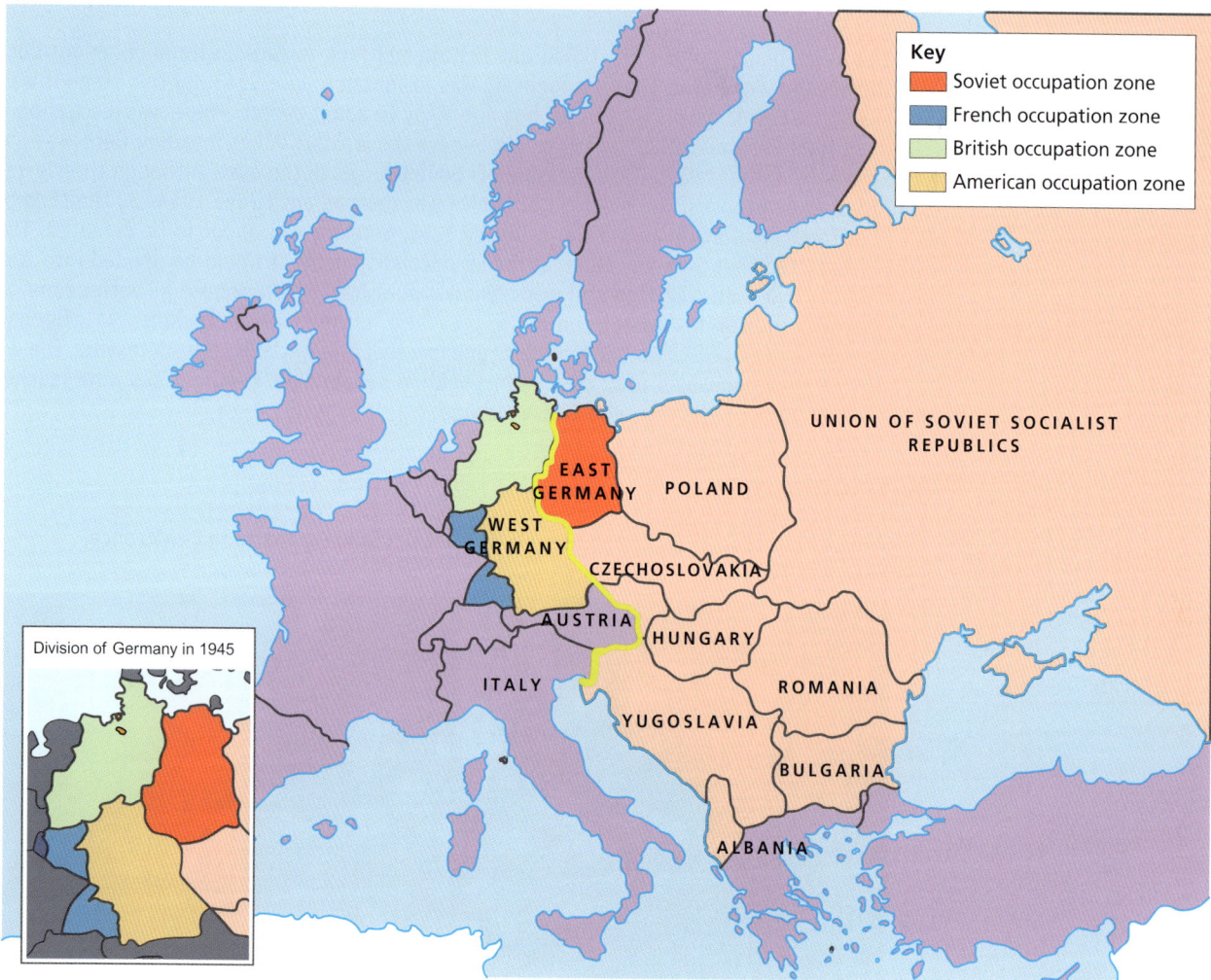

Figure 3.3 Post-war Europe and its divisions

By the time Germany surrendered, the land that had been controlled by Germany was occupied by two invading armies. The Soviet Red Army invaded from the east while the Americans and British advanced from the west. When the war ended, the Western Allies, and especially America, wanted to withdraw their armies at the earliest opportunity. The Soviet Red Army stayed. The lands occupied by the Red Army were regarded as a "Soviet sphere of influence." This had been agreed on at the Yalta Conference. They created a buffer zone that Stalin regarded as necessary to protect the USSR from future invasions. Tensions arose among the Allies over what had actually been agreed concerning these countries. The Western Allies had understood that the governments of these countries would be democratically elected. Stalin's understanding of democratic elections was elections in which the communists would win. He made sure this was the case by removing politicians who were uncooperative with him. Truman felt that Roosevelt had not been firm enough with Stalin about the terms of the agreement. Stalin thought Truman was trying to change what had already been agreed. Since the Red Army was still the occupying force, communist-leaning governments were chosen. Poland was particularly controversial because during the war the Polish government had been in exile in Britain, and expected to return to rule Poland, but the Soviets made sure the Polish government in exile was discredited. Meanwhile, in Germany there was still disagreement between the Allies about how to create a new democratic government, the extent of reparations, and the punishment of war criminals. These tensions were exacerbated by the large number of displaced ethnic Germans moving to Germany from eastern Europe. By 1946, the boundary between the communist East and the free West of Europe had been drawn. It was what Winston Churchill referred to in his speech of March 1946 as an "Iron Curtain." He described a grave situation in Europe in which an Iron Curtain had descended across Europe from Stettin in the Baltic to Trieste in the Adriatic. Behind the Iron Curtain, he said, lay the historic capitals of the central and eastern European states. They were all subject to a high level of control from Moscow. In some cases that level was increasing. The misunderstandings between the Soviets and the Western Allies over Europe were an important source of the tension that was the Cold War.

> What is Churchill's message? Use your contextual knowledge to explain why Churchill made this speech.

SOURCE 3.6

Extract from a speech made by former British Prime Minister, Winston Churchill, at Westminster College, Fulton, Missouri, March 1946

It is my duty to place before you certain facts about the present position in Europe.

From Stettin in the Baltic to Trieste in the Adriatic an iron curtain has descended across the Continent. Behind that line lie all the capitals of the ancient states of Central and Eastern Europe. Warsaw, Berlin, Prague, Vienna, Budapest, Belgrade, Bucharest and Sofia, all these famous cities and the populations around them lie in what I must call the Soviet sphere, and all are subject in one form or another, not only to Soviet influence but to a very high and, in some cases, increasing measure of control from Moscow.

Whatever conclusions may be drawn from these facts – and facts they are – this is certainly not the Liberated Europe we fought to build up. Nor is this one which contains the essentials of permanent peace.

If the Western Democracies stand together in strict adherence to the principles of the **Charter of the United Nations**, their influence for furthering these principles will be immense and no one is likely to molest them. If, however, they become divided or falter in their duty and if these all-important years are allowed to slip away then indeed catastrophe may overwhelm us all.

[https://www.nationalarchives.gov.uk/education/resources/cold-war-on-file/iron-curtain-speech/]

> **KEY TERM**
>
> **Charter of the United Nations** The Charter of the United Nations was its founding document. It was signed by 50 countries in San Francisco, California in June 1945.

The impact of the dropping of the atomic bomb and nuclear proliferation

On August 6, 1945, the first atomic bomb used as a weapon of war exploded in the air over Hiroshima in Japan. The death toll was enormous: it is estimated at between 90,000 and 166,000 by the end of the year. Hiroshima was flattened and incinerated. A second bomb was detonated at Nagasaki three days later. The Japanese, who were already on the point of surrender, conceded defeat.

Why were the bombs used and what were the consequences?

In the context of the Cold War, the bombs were significant. The USSR, which had declared war on Japan on August 8, did not have the opportunity to conquer land controlled by Japan before its surrender. They demonstrated the destructive power of the US's new weapon to the USSR and the rest of the world. The USA had made its military power very clear.

The impact of the radiation on the site and the survivors was horrific, and is one reason why the world's nuclear powers have never again used a nuclear device against an enemy.

Over the next few years, the US and USSR spent huge amounts of money on the development of nuclear weapons. There were those in the US who thought that the imbalance of military capability in the US's favor was wrong. In 1949, with the help of their espionage, the Soviets detonated their first atomic bomb. In 1950, a top secret US national security document known as NSC-68 stated that the US must engage in a massive build-up of conventional and nuclear weapons to counter the Soviet threat. By 1952, Britain also had nuclear weapons. In 1954, the US launched the world's first nuclear-powered submarine and two months later carried out the first hydrogen bomb test. Only two years after this, the USSR announced it had developed a hydrogen bomb. In the late 1950s, the US began deploying nuclear missiles in Britain.

Nuclear weapons were developed in immense secrecy, yet sophisticated espionage meant the designs were shared. They did not make either side feel safer. By the late 1950s, the US had become paranoid about the number of missiles held by the USSR and was convinced that there was a sizeable gap in capability in favor of the Soviet Union. This was used to justify continued high levels of defense spending. In contrast, recognizing the immense danger to the future of the human race, there were also calls for nuclear test bans and limits to proliferation.

The Truman Doctrine and the Marshall Plan

The US had entered the Second World War reluctantly. Most of its three million troops were swiftly withdrawn from Europe when the war ended, with plans to leave about 340,000 there to oversee the US occupation zones in Germany and Austria. By the end of 1945, there were protests by service personnel and their families because demobilization was happening too slowly. Public opinion wanted an end to war and involvement abroad.

The contents of **George Kennan**'s "Long Telegram," followed by the "Iron Curtain" speech given by Winston Churchill at Fulton, Missouri about the dangers of Soviet expansion in Europe, caused a change in US policy toward Europe. The administration's interpretation of Kennan's telegram and Churchill's speech supported Truman's instinct to take a firm stance against communism. Developments in Iran and Turkey the previous year, together with Stalin's rejection of the Baruch Plan for international control of nuclear energy and arms, had reinforced Truman's distrust of Stalin. He now believed that peaceful coexistence with the USSR was impossible. The British announced that, from the end of March 1947, they would no longer be able to support the Greek government, who were fighting Greek communists in a civil war. At the time, the US government believed that the Soviet Union was supporting the Greek communist war effort and worried that if the communists won, the Soviets would ultimately influence Greek policy. In fact, Stalin had deliberately refused to support the Greek communists and had forced the Yugoslav prime minister, Josip Tito, to follow suit.

KEY FIGURE

George Kennan (1904–2005) Kennan was a career diplomat specializing in the Soviet Union. In early 1946, while in charge of the American Embassy in Moscow, he received a query from Washington about why the Soviets were being difficult regarding the World Bank. His response was the "Long Telegram." It contained a detailed analysis of Soviet government mentality regarding the rest of the world. In 1947, he published an article in the journal *Foreign Affairs*, developing these ideas. Kennan's analysis was understood by his readers largely in military rather than psychological terms. The US administration's response was the policy of containment.

On March 12, 1947, Truman spoke to Congress, asking for their permission to provide assistance to Greece and also to Turkey, another country in the region that Britain had been helping. Soviet influence in Turkey would, Truman argued, undermine the Middle East, which was an area of strategic importance for the US. He asked for $400 million of aid for Greece and Turkey, as well as the deployment of military and civilian personnel. When Congress agreed, it became US policy to "support free peoples who are resisting attempted subjugation by armed minorities or by outside pressures." This policy of **containment** was central to what became known as the Truman Doctrine.

KEY TERM

Containment The idea that communism should not be allowed to spread any further, but should be contained within the countries that already had communist governments. This idea was embodied in the Truman Doctrine.

Why did President Truman make this speech to Congress? Use details from Source 3.6 and your knowledge to explain your answer.

SOURCE 3.7

An extract from President Truman's speech to a joint session of Congress, requesting aid for Greece and Turkey, March 12, 1947

At the present moment in world history nearly every nation must choose between alternative ways of life. The choice is too often not a free one.

I believe that it must be the policy of the United States to support free peoples who are resisting attempted subjugation by armed minorities or by outside pressures.

I believe that our help should be primarily through economic and financial aid which is essential to economic stability and orderly political processes.

The seeds of totalitarian regimes are nurtured by misery and want. They spread and grow in the evil soil of poverty and strife. They reach their full growth when the hope of a people for a better life has died. We must keep that hope alive.

The free peoples of the world look to us for support in maintaining their freedoms.

If we falter in our leadership, we may endanger the peace of the world—and we shall surely endanger the welfare of our own nation.

Great responsibilities have been placed upon us by the swift movement of events.

I am confident that the Congress will face these responsibilities squarely.

- How accurate is the cartoonist's view of Stalin's actions?
- What can you learn about American perceptions of Soviet aims from this cartoon?

SOURCE 3.8

A cartoon from 1946 illustrating the American view of Soviet involvement in Greece. The caption on the cartoon is "Joseph Stalin lands a prize catch and threatens the West through Soviet meddling in Greece"

The Marshall Plan, named for Secretary of State, George Marshall, followed. The Economic Recovery Act of 1948 offered aid on the basis that western European countries were in grave danger of becoming communist because of their poverty following the war. Aid was offered to any country that would guarantee free elections and trade with the US. $13.3 billion was given to Europe over the following four years. The aid was offered to all the countries of Europe, including the USSR. However, the conditions of the Act precluded communist governments from accepting the aid. Of these, only Yugoslavia, a communist state that rejected Stalin's Soviet controls, accepted it.

The plan was clearly anti-communist and Stalin knew this. The conditions required for the granting of aid made American claims that it was open to any country unconvincing. Both the Truman Doctrine and Marshall Plan demonstrated American hostility to communism and this is how Stalin interpreted them. They both contributed to the development of the Cold War.

ACTIVITY

List reasons for the development of the Cold War. Put the reasons into three groups: reasons based only on ideas (communism or liberal democracy/capitalism); reasons that are the result of actions or events; and reasons that relate to ideas and actions or events.

Write a paragraph to explain why you agree or disagree with the statement "The Cold War was the result of differences between American and Soviet ideas."

The Berlin Blockade and Airlift

The flashpoint for tensions in Europe was always going to be Berlin. The British, French, and American sectors of Berlin were an isolated pocket of capitalism in the middle of the communist-controlled Soviet zone of Germany. Like Germany itself, Berlin was split into four. The sectors were controlled by France, Britain, America, and the USSR. Access to West Berlin (the sectors controlled by the Western Allies) was by canal, road, rail, and air. The German citizens of Berlin were allowed access to the four sectors through checkpoints.

The Allies' aim for post-war Germany had been to support its development into a single democratic state. Since the Soviets were uncooperative, France, Britain, and America worked together without them. In 1946, they combined the administration of their three zones and in 1948 worked to establish a single state. Without telling the Soviets, they introduced a new currency, the Deutschmark, into their zones of Germany and their sectors of Berlin. Stalin saw this as anti-communist provocation. A parallel currency, the Ostmark, was introduced in the Soviet-controlled parts of Germany and Berlin. Stalin decided to take a stand, using West Berlin as a pawn. In June 1948, over the course of a few days, all the transport links from western Germany into Berlin were blocked. The Western Allies could no longer bring in the power and other supplies needed by the population. Stalin's plan was to make it impossible for them to remain in control. The Western Allies were not prepared to accept this and organized an airlift of all the supplies needed to support the people living in West Berlin. The situation was tense. Transport planes were vulnerable to anti-aircraft fire. However, shooting down the planes would be an act of war and Stalin did not want to provoke hostilities. The airlift became an efficient enterprise that could be maintained indefinitely. In May 1949, the Soviets relented and reopened the land and canal links from western Germany to West Berlin. The Federal Republic of Germany was established, with West Berlin as a separately administered entity. Located in the Soviet-controlled German Democratic Republic, it continued to be a potential flashpoint for Cold War confrontation. In 1958–59 another crisis began (page 198).

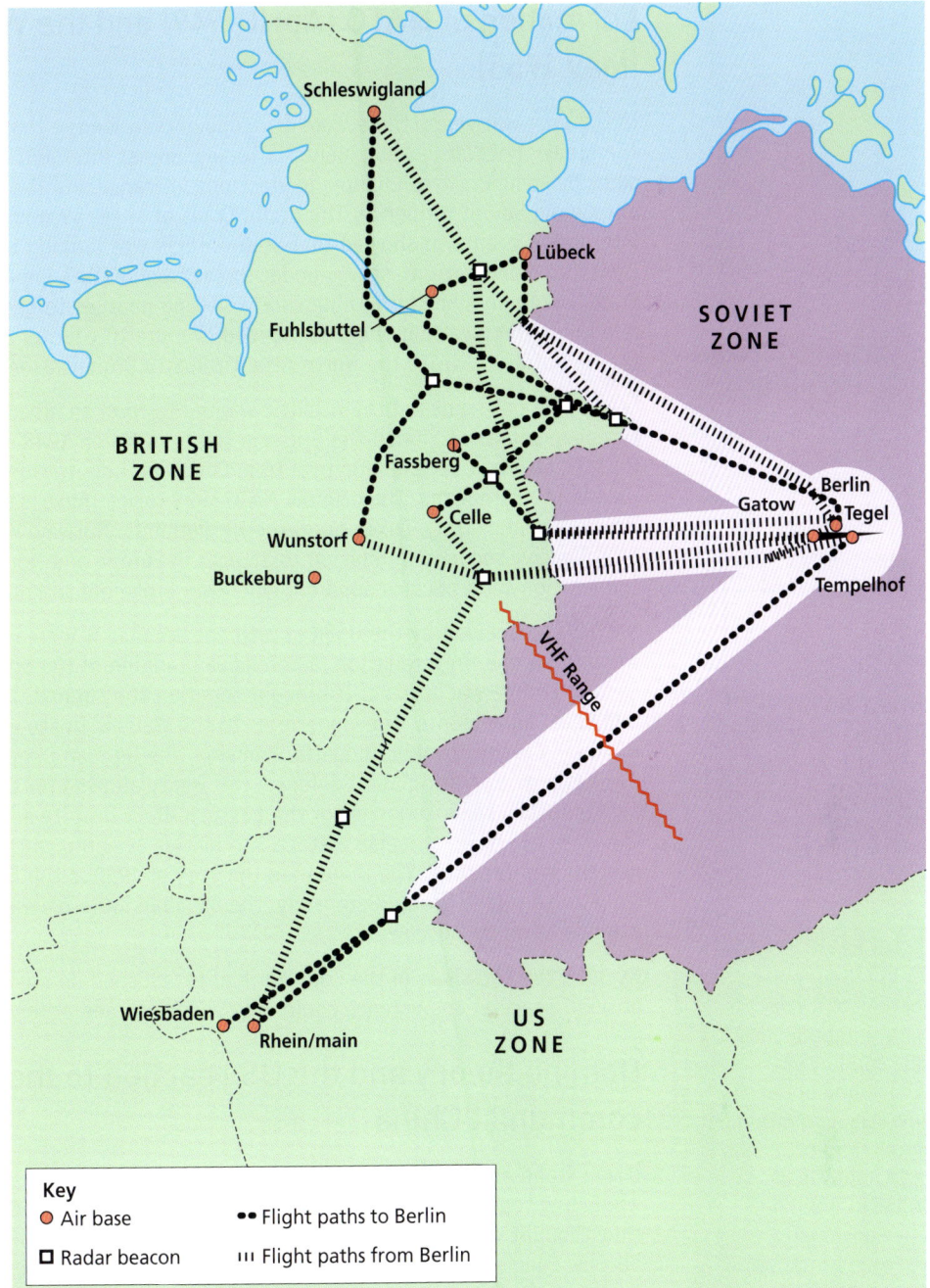

Figure 3.5 A map showing the routes used during the Berlin Airlift. Radar beacons were used to manage the aircraft and prevent accidents on the flight paths

The US and communism in the 1950s

In the 1950s the world became used to living with the constant threat of war or nuclear war. The US hoped to maintain peace by making sure their military power and defensive alliances were so strong that the enemy would not test them. This was expensive but Truman and Eisenhower, who was president from 1953–61 both felt it was essential. Many of the countries of Western Europe had been keen to enter an alliance with America. During the 1950s this led to the deployment of large numbers of US troops and weapons in Europe. There were setbacks elsewhere in the world. Communism continued to spread, in Asia rather than Europe. China grew in strength but the US still refused to recognize the Chinese Communist Party (CCP) as the rightful government. From 1950–53, encouraged by support from both the USSR and China, North Korea tried to extend communism to the south. Although this was not successful, it showed that communism remained a force to be reckoned with.

Formation of NATO (April 1949) and the Warsaw Pact (May 1955)

In the post-war years, there were developments in Europe that were worrying for the US. The Greek Civil War, developments in Turkey, Soviet intervention in Czechoslovakia, and the gains by communist candidates in elections in France and Italy all contributed to a sense of growing Soviet influence. The Berlin Crisis of 1948–49 was the culmination. As the US interpreted events, it showed that Stalin's USSR was looking to expand. It showed that the capitalist democratic West was under threat from Stalin's imperial ambitions. It showed that Stalin would do almost anything short of firing missiles to get what he wanted. Above all, it reinforced the idea that the West needed to unite to counter the Soviet threat. This led to the formation of NATO, the North Atlantic Treaty Organization, in April 1949.

Leaders on both sides of the Atlantic wanted to form an alliance. Representatives of five European countries signed the Brussels Treaty in March 1948, agreeing to collective security. Once Truman had secured approval from Congress, negotiations took place between the US and the Europeans. The original NATO signatories (America, Canada, Belgium, Denmark, France, Iceland, Italy, Luxemburg, the Netherlands, Norway, Portugal, and the UK) agreed on collective security in relation to attacks in Europe and North America. The need for cooperation soon became apparent when war broke out in Korea.

NATO was perceived by the USSR as a threat because it increased the military presence in Western Europe. In retaliation, a defensive grouping of the Soviet-dominated states of Eastern Europe was formed. It brought together the countries with which the USSR had individual agreements. The signatories to the Warsaw Treaty were the USSR, Poland, Hungary, Czechoslovakia, Bulgaria, Romania, the German Democratic Republic, and Albania. Besides providing for mutual defense, the Treaty allowed for the group to address the rising civil unrest in some countries of the **Eastern Bloc**. Despite assurances of non-interference in the internal affairs of member states, collective action could occur if these events destabilized the bloc. The Hungarian Uprising of 1956 is the first example of discontent suppressed by the group. Ostensibly, the members were partners. In practice, all its actions were dictated by Moscow.

By 1955 the two sides in the Cold War had established defensive alliance systems that ensured peaceful coexistence could only be maintained at enormous military cost.

Domino theory and the US reaction to the rise of communist China

If you stand a row of dominoes on end in a line, and push one over onto the next, then the whole line topples over. This was the image used by the US administration to illustrate what they thought would happen when one state becomes communist. The neighboring states become communist too. This idea was known as **domino theory**. It was used by President Truman to justify sending US troops to Greece and Turkey. It became better known when President Eisenhower applied it to the states of southeast Asia. It was famously used to justify US involvement in the Vietnam War.

Fear of the spread of communism after the Second World War is easy to understand. From 1917 until 1945 the only communist state was the USSR. Suddenly, East European countries were either absorbed into the USSR or so strongly under its influence that they could not avoid having governments that followed the Moscow line. On October 1, 1949, another large country joined the Communist Bloc. Mao Zedong declared the formation of the

> **KEY TERM**
>
> **Eastern Bloc** An unofficial group of communist states aligned with the USSR, mostly in Central and Eastern Europe.

> **KEY TERM**
>
> **Domino theory** A geopolitical theory which suggested that if one country in a region came under the influence of communism, surrounding countries would follow in a domino effect. The term was initially used by Eisenhower in reference to Indochina in a news conference in 1954, but it formed a key part of US foreign policy under successive administrations.

People's Republic of China (PRC). This had been a long time in the making. The nationalist government of Chiang Kai-shek, despite financial support from the US from the late 1930s, had been unable to withstand Japanese occupation of China. This was partly because Chiang was more concerned with suppressing the rise of the Chinese Communist Party than with fighting the Japanese. Eventually, an uneasy alliance between the nationalist government and the Communist party was formed against the Japanese. At the end of the Second World War, China again descended into civil war. Mao's communists prevailed and Chiang fled to Taiwan with the last of his supporters.

Truman's critics saw this as a failure of his administration. Truman had taken the view that the US should not intervene in the Chinese Civil War. When the nationalists fled, Truman's critics claimed that he had "lost" China. The relationship with the People's Republic of China was complicated by Chiang's nationalist government in Taiwan. This gave the unrealistic impression that the revolution was incomplete and might be reversed. It was not possible to recognize both governments as legitimate since both claimed to rule China. For 22 years, until 1971, the US government refused to acknowledge the People's Republic of China as the government of China. Instead, they supported the Nationalist Republic of China, based in Taiwan.

The Korean War reinforced the US opinion of the PRC as an aggressive, expansionist power. This view was cemented by the role of the PRC in the Vietnam War (page 201).

Causes of the Korean War and reasons for US involvement, June 1950–July 1953

> **KEY TERM**
>
> **38th parallel** Short for 38th parallel north, a line of latitude that circles the Earth 38 degrees north of the equator. Used to mark the border between North and South Korea before the Korean War. The post-war border is in a similar location, but does not follow it precisely.

Korea was part of Japan's empire from 1910. When Japan surrendered at the end of the Second World War, the empire was lost. Most countries returned to their pre-war governments, but Korea had no such rulers. There were two distinct groups of Korean exiles who laid claim to rule: the Marxists and the ultranationalists. The Soviets and Americans agreed that, for administrative purposes, the country would temporarily be divided at the **38th parallel**. The long-term stated aim was to reunite the region. However, as was the case in Germany, the Soviets and Americans pursued contradictory policies and could not agree. They had different aims for the country and, with the 700,000 Japanese occupiers repatriated, it was difficult to establish a viable government. Soviet-supported Kim Il-Sung was establishing a power base in the north. At the same time, the US built up a Korean police force to keep order in the south. In 1947, President Truman persuaded the newly created United Nations (UN) to take over control of the country and in 1948, US troops started to withdraw.

The US had not factored Korea into its defense strategy for east Asia. Seeing this and the defenselessness of the south, Kim Il-Sung's army attacked the south in June 1950. They were so successful that they took control of almost all of Korea.

The American military was redeployed to Korea to support the defense of the south. They were representing the UN and were later joined by forces from other countries. The US-led forces under General MacArthur were initially successful. Having pushed Kim's forces back to the 38th parallel, they were permitted to invade the north, again with the aim of reuniting Korea. This provoked a Chinese-backed counterattack in which the south's capital, Seoul, was retaken by the communists. Again, the UN forces, with a new commander, moved north from Chosin. The war then reached a stalemate. Truman decided that it was better to negotiate a ceasefire than to provoke a more widespread conflict, given that both the PRC and the USSR were backing the communist north. When MacArthur challenged this policy, he was dismissed from his role commanding forces in Korea.

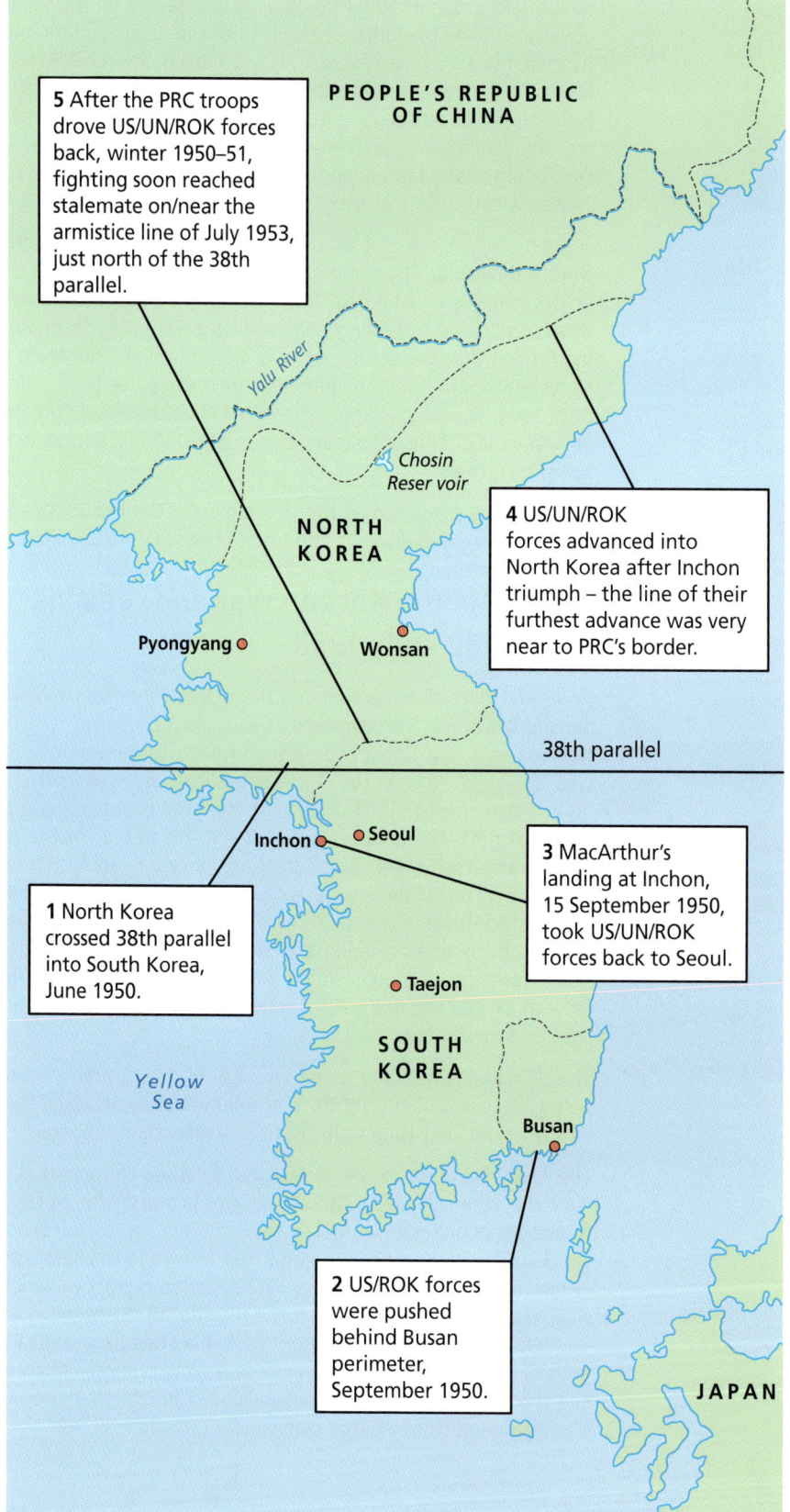

Figure 3.6 The course of the Korean War: MacArthur's advance to Chosin, defying orders, meant he was relieved of his command

Impacts and outcomes of the Korean War

The Korean War ended with a ceasefire in July 1953. By this time, America had a new president, Dwight D Eisenhower. A military man, he assessed the situation in Korea, recognized that it was not possible to win the war without excessive cost in men and materials, and decided to negotiate. Korea remained divided as it had been before the war. Technically, the war is ongoing as the two sides have never signed a peace treaty. The end of the war demonstrated that Eisenhower was a realist. Although, like Truman, he was opposed to communism, he was also committed to balancing the needs of defense against what America could afford.

The war also showed the world that the US would uphold its commitment to the UN and to defending countries from aggression. This gave the US more authority in its dealings with its NATO allies in Europe. The need for US intervention also strengthened the commitment within the US to building up its arsenal of both nuclear and conventional weapons.

ACTIVITY

Draw a graph to show how the level of Cold War tension changed during the early 1950s. The x-axis should have the dates evenly spaced. You decide the scale for the level of tension. Plot the events onto the graph according to how great the tension was. When was the most tense or dangerous time? You could add to this graph when you have studied the Cold War in the Eisenhower years to 1959.

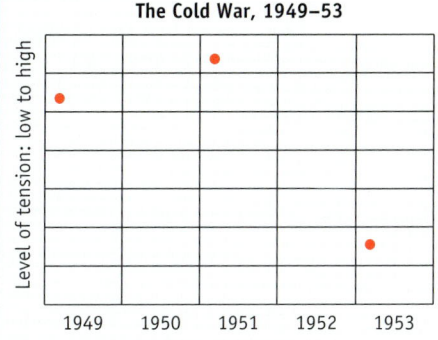

The Cold War, 1949–53

The Cold War policies of the Eisenhower administration

The change of president from Truman to Eisenhower marked a change of policy in the Cold War. Eisenhower was equally anti-communist, but he changed the focus of defense spending and recognized that the spread of communism went beyond the invasion and installation of compliant governments. In addition, the death of Joseph Stalin in March 1953 created uncertainty. It took two years for the members of the Presidium, the Soviet executive committee, to finalize the succession with Nikita Khrushchev establishing his position as leader. In 1956, Khrushchev's Secret Speech denouncing Stalin suggested that a change of style was planned. While Khrushchev was generally more accommodating than Stalin, he took advantage when he sensed weakness in the American government.

Eisenhower's "New Look"

When Eisenhower took office as president in 1953, the Korean War was about to end and America had a large army in Europe. Eisenhower's strategy was different from Truman's. The National Security Council Paper he ordered set out his priorities.

These were to:
- cut spending on conventional forces and weapons of the army and navy
- focus on developing and building nuclear weapons
- build up the air force, especially its bombing capacity
- develop capacity for a flexible response to aggression

- meet military obligations without undue strain on the economy
- increase covert operations (spying) to undermine Soviet influence and control
- strengthen ties to US allies
- actively seek good relations with non-aligned countries.

This was Eisenhower's "New Look." This policy change was unpopular with some sections of the armed forces. However, the Korean War showed a lack of public support for the deployment of large forces, especially in remote locations that seemed to have little strategic importance.

Changes in Soviet leadership: Khrushchev and "peaceful coexistence"

> **KEY FIGURE**
>
> **Nikita Khrushchev**
> (1894–1971) Born in a village in western Russia, Khrushchev worked as a metal worker and political officer during the Russian Civil War. He worked his way up the Soviet hierarchy and was sent to govern Ukraine in 1938. After Stalin's death in 1953 a power struggle brought Khrushchev to the role of First Secretary of the party and leader of the USSR. He was forced out of office in October 1964 and lived the rest of his life in Moscow where he died in 1971.

In March 1953, Soviet leader Joseph Stalin died. The members of the Presidium moved to establish who would be the next leader. Rivalries and old grudges came to the fore. In December, Lavrenti Beria, who had expected to take control, was executed for anti-party and anti-state activities. Georgy Malenkov, who initially took power, was more conciliatory to the West than Stalin had been. However, by 1955 **Nikita Khrushchev** had outmaneuvered Malenkov and the other members of the Presidium, and established his primacy. Khrushchev's manner, personality, and approach were very different from those of Stalin. The differences in approach were made clear at the Twentieth Party Congress in 1956, when Khrushchev shocked his audience, and later the world, with a secret speech denouncing many of Stalin's policies. He did not, however, criticize the policies that he had been directly involved in.

In contrast with Stalin's assumption that war with the West was inevitable, the foreign policy elements of Khrushchev's speech indicated that he advocated "peaceful coexistence" with the West. When the US administration received a transcript of the speech from Israeli intelligence, they were initially skeptical of its authenticity. The reality proved that although there were times of tension and confrontation (for example, over the U2 incident and the Cuban Missile Crisis, pages 190 and 191), Khrushchev was seeking a more cooperative approach. The communist leaders in China and Vietnam were unimpressed.

The speech had a destabilizing effect on the Soviet-controlled states in Europe. In Poland, demonstrations were harshly suppressed. In Hungary, month-long protests were put down when the Soviets took back control and removed the Hungarian leader, Imre Nagy. Despite being offered safe passage out of Hungary, Nagy was later tried and executed. The American government was shocked but did nothing.

The Suez Crisis, October–November 1956

The Suez Canal was completed in 1869 and links the Red Sea and the Mediterranean. It is an important shipping route through Egypt, especially for Middle Eastern oil. It was constructed by the French and British, and in 1956 was still owned by the British-French company that built it. The British retained control of the canal zone after Egypt gained independence, maintaining a military presence there. In 1953, Secretary of State John Foster Dulles had assured Nasser, the most prominent of Egypt's military rulers, that the US supported the withdrawal of British forces from the Suez Canal zone and would help to fund the Aswan Dam project on the Nile. Nevertheless, America's support for Egypt was not secure, as Egypt had been courting Soviet support—for example, by making an arms deal with the USSR. When America and Britain went back on their promise to fund the Aswan Dam project, Nasser nationalized the Suez Canal, seizing it from the company that owned it. The only way for Egypt to fund the dam project was from the tolls paid by ships using the Suez Canal.

The US wanted a negotiated solution, but this did not satisfy the French and British. Instead, they secretly negotiated with Israel for a joint invasion of Egypt. This began in

> **KEY TERM**
> **United Nations**
> An international organization founded at the end of the Second World War and designed to support governments to avoid further conflicts.

late October. The Israelis were successful and there was also a joint British and French invasion force. The US and USSR demanded a ceasefire and, in the United Nations, the US also demanded all foreign forces withdraw from Egypt. A UN force supervised this. The British and French left. Israel was eventually forced to return all the Egyptian land seized.

Figure 3.7 The Suez Crisis, 1956, showing the location of the canal and the extent of Israeli incursion into Egypt

As a result of the crisis:
- Britain and France lost influence in the area and were humiliated
- Nasser gained standing in the Arab world
- relations between the US and its allies Britain and France were strained
- the UN assumed a larger peacekeeping role
- Soviet influence in the Middle East increased, especially in Syria
- the US established better relations with Egypt
- the role of the US as mediator meant that it was later drawn into the unresolved disputes in the Middle East.

1956 proved to be a significant year, with the move toward "peaceful coexistence" between the US and the USSR, and the US's unequivocal stance against old-style European colonialism.

The Eisenhower Doctrine

The Eisenhower Doctrine was formulated in January 1957 and passed by Congress in March.
- It was similar to the Truman Doctrine in that it continued the policy of containment of communism. It continued to commit America to using political, economic, and military methods to prevent the further spread of communism.
- It built on the Truman Doctrine by extending this approach to the Middle East.

The Middle East was and is strategically important. The non-aligned countries of the region, which were not allied to either the US or USSR, had become adept at using this importance to their advantage by accepting aid from both sides in the Cold War. The aim of the Eisenhower Doctrine was to convince those nations to ally with America. After the Suez Crisis and the expulsion of the British and French from the region, America feared that Gamal Nasser, as a result of his increased standing with other Arab states, would become the dominant force. Given his pro-Soviet leanings, this could open the whole area to Soviet influence. Eisenhower thought that the power vacuum opened up when the British and French were forced out would be exploited by the Soviets. American involvement in Lebanon in 1958 was intended to demonstrate commitment to the Eisenhower Doctrine.

The race to successfully launch a satellite into orbit

The so-called space race was symbolic of the rivalry between the two sides in the Cold War. It was a public display of the technological rivalry between the US and the Soviets. The nuclear arms race, in contrast, was swathed in secrecy. Testing nuclear devices was so dangerous that, in May 1955, the UN brought together the nuclear powers to negotiate an end to nuclear weapons testing. US scientists were persuaded of the necessity for this in 1959, when radioactive deposits were found in wheat and milk in the Northern states. Scientists and the public demanded that the moratorium on testing that had begun in 1958 be extended. The Partial Nuclear Test Ban Treaty was ratified in 1963. Meanwhile, the arms race had begun to explore and make use of space. The first goal was the successful launch of a human-made satellite to orbit the Earth. Both sides worked on the rocket technology needed to launch the satellites, a rocket technology that could also be used to launch nuclear weapons in the event of war.

The first country to launch a satellite was the USSR. In 1957, Sputnik 1, a telecommunications satellite whose name meant "fellow traveler," was launched. The speed with which Soviet scientists and engineers had caught up with the American space program was a shock to the US. The USSR now knew how to build a rocket capable of carrying an intercontinental ballistic missile. A month later, a second satellite was launched. Khrushchev had insisted on a date in November to coincide with the fortieth anniversary of the Bolshevik revolution. A dog called Laika was placed in the capsule so that scientists could monitor the effects of the flight on a mammal. This was an important precursor to human space flight.

The space race continued with the USSR's Luna 1 in 1959, the first human-made object to orbit the sun. The US launched Pioneer 4 to fly past the moon. The Soviets countered with Luna 2, launched at the moon. The first satellite equipped with a spy camera was America's Discovery XIV in 1960. American rockets were launched with much publicity while Soviet ones took off in secrecy from Baikonur Cosmodrome in the Kazakh SSR. American accidents were public while information about Soviet ones was suppressed. Both nations worked under time pressure, which made errors likely, and there were some disasters. Nevertheless, the space race provided each side in the Cold War with a competition to demonstrate and develop its technological and scientific prowess without engaging in warfare.

Draw up a timeline of all the events in Section 3.2. Color code them to show events in different areas of the world (Europe, Asia, and the Middle East).

SUMMARY DIAGRAM

US foreign policy, 1935–59

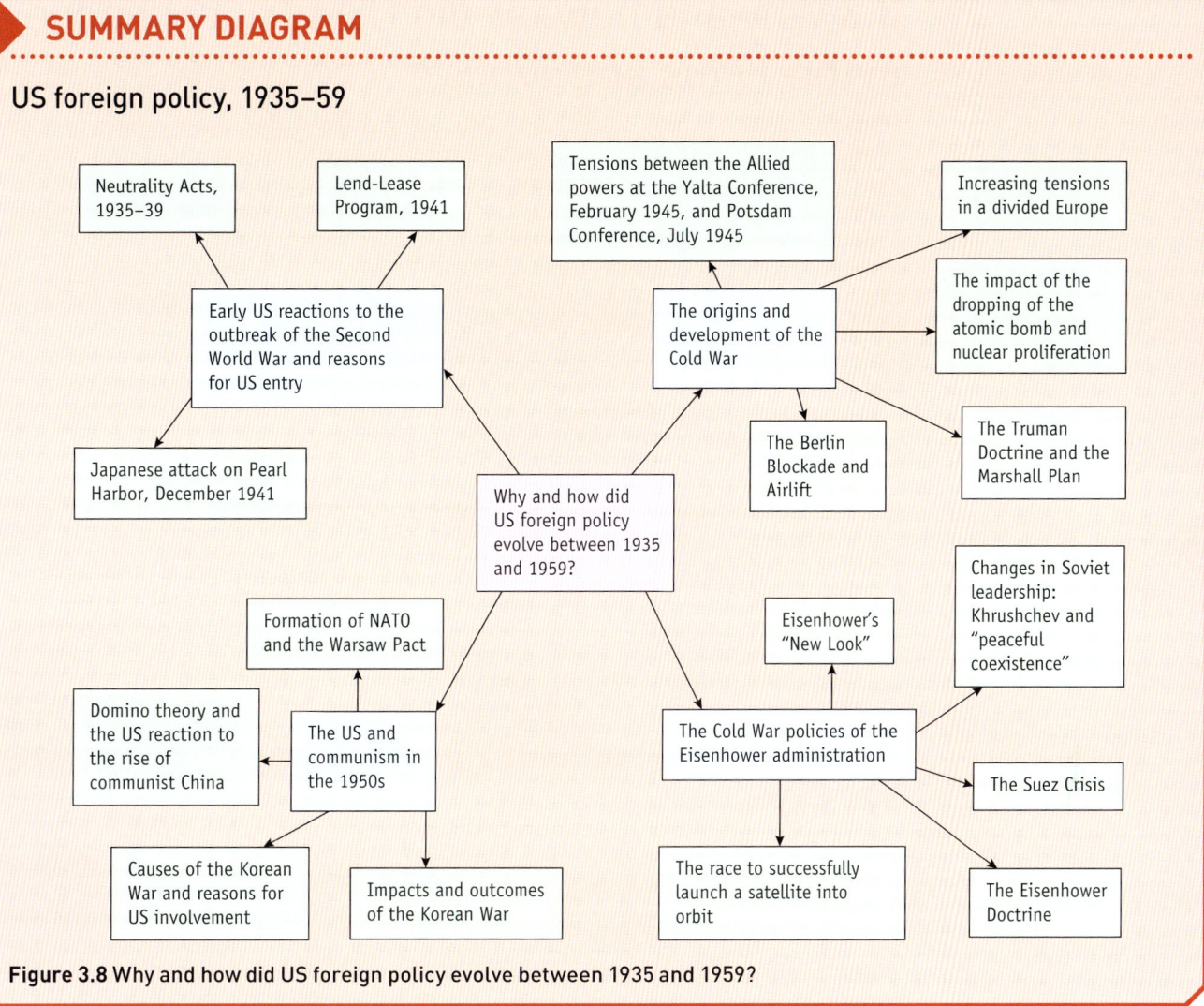

Figure 3.8 Why and how did US foreign policy evolve between 1935 and 1959?

3.3 Why and how far did US society change in the 1940s and 1950s?

Economic change can be measured using data. Social change can also be measured to some extent. Changing social attitudes are more difficult to gauge. Historians study the changes and try to explain the extent of the changes and why they occurred. In the 1940s and 1950s, the average income of Americans rose significantly and a consumer culture developed in which ownership of products, and replacing them with more sophisticated versions, was a prime driver of economic growth. The growth of home ownership and suburbia and the consequences of this can be observed. Statistics show the prevalence of churchgoing, and getting married and having children at a young age. The conformity of the immediate post-war years and the reaction against this are also accepted, but the evidence is more anecdotal and impressionistic. Studying what is typical can mask the continuing poverty of some sections of the population and the reasons they were not party to mainstream prosperity and values.

Underlying the prosperity and social conservatism, there was fear and uncertainty. Propaganda made Americans fearful of communism. This encouraged conformity but also allowed the witch hunt that was McCarthyism to take hold. McCarthyism subsided only when its accusations were demonstrated to be absurd. The Civil Rights Movement challenged accepted norms, especially, but not exclusively, in the South. Reactions to it showed the depth of prejudiced resistance to change. These reactions made the activists more determined to push for their rights, but, by 1959, they had made limited progress partly because federal government was reluctant to stir up old sectional antagonisms.

Economic developments and their impact on society, 1945–59

In his 1941 State of the Union address, Roosevelt identified four freedoms as the key to protecting democratic government. They were freedom of speech, freedom of religion, freedom from fear, and freedom from want. In the post-war years, the last of these moved closer. A consumer society dominated. This was driven by factors such as the opportunities offered by the GI Bill and government policies. The growing middle classes moved to the suburbs. Prosperity created a baby boom, which in turn created more consumers. Despite the worrying developments of the Cold War and social tensions, the economy of the late 1940s and 1950s gave rise to optimism.

Impacts of the GI Bill

In 1944, the Roosevelt administration anticipated the end of the Second World War, which would mean the demobilization of millions of service personnel. The First World War measure of providing bonuses had led to a range of issues including the Bonus March of the Depression era. Instead, an act was passed that aimed to give ex-servicemen the opportunity to better themselves through education and business loans. The American Legion had advocated for this and Harry Colmery, its former chairman, made the proposal.

The results were far-reaching. Over two million ex-service personnel took advantage of finance for college courses and cheap loans for homes and businesses. This created a major boost for the economy. The route to prosperity via a college course, whether academic or technical, was established. The influx of students, often with their families, as many GIs were married, meant the growth of suburbs around the colleges. These students could not be accommodated in the usual student dormitories. This contributed to the housing boom. Not many GIs needed the weekly payments offered to those who were unemployed.

The administration of the GI Bill was carried out at state level. This might be the reason it reflected the racial discrimination that was still a feature of American life. Many colleges were segregated. Those that admitted African Americans were less well-equipped to expand and accommodate the influx of GIs. Housing discrimination meant fewer mortgages approved for African Americans, with all-white suburbs the norm in some cities. Although many African Americans did receive a college education and loans, the proportion who did so was the lowest of any ethnic group.

The program ended in 1956, but was replaced by new ones for the veterans of later wars.

The growth of consumerism

The capitalist economy of the twentieth century grew because it turned people into consumers. This was apparent in the 1920s, but in the post-Second World War era consumerism became embedded in the American way of life. A reaction to the uncertainty of the Depression, which had discouraged spending, and the sparsity of goods during the war, consumerism was driven by increasing wealth, the invention of new products and the development of old ones. These factors combined to generate aspirational consumerism beyond what was needed for basic survival. Each year, from the end of the war until 1950, a million new homes were built. All needed to be furnished and provided with appliances. Spending on household goods increased by 240 percent each year. Even poorer families spent more than they had in the past. The most popular new gadget was a television.

The consumer boom reflected more sophisticated sales and marketing techniques. Women were the primary targets, since they made 75 percent of all purchases. The advertisements featured homes that were aspirational. The image matched that of the ideal middle-class family and home of the 1950s. These images were now seen not just in magazines but also on the television. The products had built-in obsolescence. The latest version of the appliance was more sophisticated, with additional features. Therefore it was more desirable.

Buying American-produced goods was associated with patriotism. It created jobs and kept American wealth in the country to make it more prosperous. Between 1945 and 1949, Americans purchased 20 million refrigerators, 21.4 million cars, and 5.5 million stoves. These were not luxury items, signifying a decadent lifestyle. They were everyday items that contributed to homemaking. They reflected homespun, traditional American values and created the impression that poverty belonged to the past.

Impact of the baby boom

During the post-war baby boom, which lasted until the early 1960s, 76 million babies were born in the US. There were several reasons for this. Birth rates had been falling since the beginning of the century. The era of the Depression and the circumstances of war had contributed to this fall. The relative wealth and optimism, high levels of employment and high wages combined with early marriage and the prevalence of the "American dream" household, with a stay-at-home mother and several children, all contributed.

At the time, there was an impact on the need for housing and schools. Families chose to move to the suburbs. The resulting housing boom generated the need for shopping malls and for increased car ownership, as private transport was the most convenient way to travel in the vast suburban housing areas.

Business owners took advantage of the opportunity presented by the unprecedented number of children living in prosperous homes. They developed clothing lines, toys, games, and food targeting children's tastes. As they grew into adolescence, the baby boomers had spending power of their own. Magazines, music, and films were produced for their consumption.

Later there would be other impacts. For example, the growth in demand for college enrolment in the 1960s. There was a new focus on teenagers and these began to be seen as a group with a distinct identity, including groups of dissatisfied youngsters who reacted against the complacent consumerism of their parents' generation. This was the counterculture of the late 1950s and 1960s. The effects continued to be felt as the baby boomer generation reached retirement and old age. In 1959 this was still in the future.

> What information does this graph provide about the post-war baby boom?

SOURCE 3.9

Graph of baby boom figures

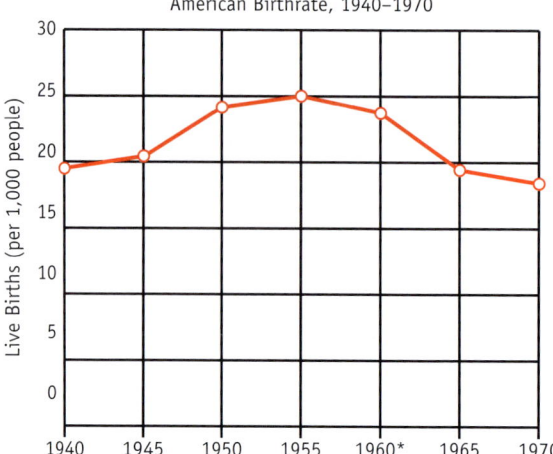

*First year for which figures include Alaska and Hawaii.

Migration and the development of the suburbs

The post-war era, with its increasing prosperity, marked a move from city centers to suburbs. The quest for security that had been lacking before the war was a leading factor in the growth of home ownership. The proportion of American families living in their own homes rose from 43.6 percent in 1940 to almost 62 percent by 1960. They lived in new homes built on the outskirts of cities. Richer citizens had chosen to live away from city centers in the past, but this was a mass exodus based on automobile ownership. Cheap loans available through the GI Bill were often used to pay for these homes. Housebuilder William Levitt was the first to take advantage of new construction techniques, which allowed prefabricated houses that could be erected in a day. Starting in New York, "Levittowns" were built in numerous locations. Restrictive clauses in the contracts ensured that these would be white-only suburbs.

There were other negative effects. Families needed two cars, one for each adult. This caused traffic congestion. A massive road-building program followed at city, state, and federal levels. Roads were needed to allow commuters to get to work and citizens to go about their everyday business and visit the increasing number of out-of-town entertainment venues. This took money away from other services, including public transport. In city centers, poor or marginalized communities were demolished to accommodate new roads. The reduction in the tax-paying population in city centers meant city governments were short of cash. Public services in the inner cities declined. With the decline in population, political representation in the House was reduced.

The prosperous suburbs, with their limited range of house designs, symbolized the best of post-war America. They also represented a conformity against which young people began to react and rebel.

> What can you learn from Source 3.8 about Levittowns and those who lived in them?

SOURCE 3.10

An aerial photograph of a Levittown in Pennsylvania, taken around 1959

> **ACTIVITY**
> Make a chart to show the benefits and drawbacks of the growth of the suburbs. To what extent do you agree that the growth of the suburbs benefited America?

Roles of federal government economic policies and programs in stimulating the economy

The post-war period was generally prosperous. There were two minor recessions in the 1950s, but in total the economy grew by 37 percent and unemployment was low. The role of federal government in the economy was two-fold. It set federal taxes and spent them.

Truman had liberal ideas about the role of the state. In 1949, referencing Roosevelt's New Deal, he proposed a "Fair Deal." This would involve further support for Americans in terms of health, social security, housing, and education, as well as anti-discriminatory employment laws and a rise in the minimum wage. In the context of the Cold War, these ideas appeared too socialist to some. Nevertheless, Congress agreed to raise the minimum wage, and 800,000 houses were built for the poor.

Eisenhower rejected "big government" at the level of intervention seen in the New Deal and proposed by the Fair Deal. He also rejected the demands of right-wing Republicans to roll back the state. He focused on balancing the federal budget while spending on infrastructure projects that would benefit the economy by allowing it to grow.

Overall spending increased, as did the proportion of the federal budget spent on domestic projects. However, because the economy grew so much, the proportion of GDP spent by the government decreased. Taxes were reformed to make them more equitable. When the economy entered a recession, the federal government was able to increase spending to stimulate the economy.

Eisenhower's most notable project was the Federal-Aid Highway Act of 1956. In total, over 41,000 miles of interstate highways were built, funded by fuel tax. This provided construction jobs, allowed the trucking industry to develop, promoted the growth of suburbs, and eased travel for private individuals.

The US partnered with Canada in the construction of the St Lawrence Seaway. This encouraged international travel.

In 1954, the Atomic Energy Act was passed, giving the power industry further access to nuclear technology. This led to the development of various types of nuclear power plants. The first large-scale plant went into operation in 1957, supplying electricity to the Pittsburgh area.

Return to traditional, conservative family norms after the Second World War

When the Second World War ended, many Americans longed to return to normality. This meant aspiring to the "American dream" of families with children living idealized lives in prosperity. This aspiration can be seen in the cultural trends of middle-class America in the late 1940s and 1950s.

Women who had been needed in the wartime workforce lost their jobs because so many men who were drafted returned to their pre-war jobs. Religion was growing in popularity—by the late 1950s, over half of Americans attended church.

Role of women in the Second World War

All women were called on to support the war effort, whether by entering employment or by avoiding waste in the home or by fundraising. The demands of fighting a world war required that women take on traditionally male jobs in factories, including the defense industry, as well as white collar jobs in the armed forces. They were not sent into combat, but they freed men to fight by doing jobs in offices and workshops.

To encourage women to do the jobs usually associated with men, there was a government campaign. A character called "Rosie the Riveter," practical yet glamorous, was created. The catchy campaign song told how, by working on the assembly line riveting aircraft fuselage, she was helping her boyfriend Charlie, a marine, as well as her country. Some factories even offered make-up lessons to women workers so they could look like Rosie.

> What is the message of Source 3.9 and what can you learn from it about the role of women in the Second World War?

SOURCE 3.11

A recruitment poster featuring Rosie the Riveter

> **ACTIVITY**
> Listen to a recording of the song "Rosie the Riveter." How does the song add to your understanding of the role of women in the war? Consider the lyrics and the musical style.

The number of women in the workforce increased and the range of jobs they did changed. A third of the women working in defense were mothers who balanced childcare, housework, and paid work. Eleanor Roosevelt was instrumental in persuading her husband to pass legislation to provide childcare facilities and in encouraging employers to provide nurseries.

About 350,000 women joined the military. Some performed traditional female roles, such as nursing and clerical work. Others learned new skills including truck driving and repairing aircraft. Those who were already licensed commercial pilots went into the WAFS (Women's Auxiliary Ferrying Squadron) and flew planes from factories to airbases. Others were trained to become pilots under the WASP (Women Airforce Service Pilots) scheme, which enabled them to fly military aircraft so that male pilots were released for overseas combat. Thousands were employed in the Manhattan Project, developing the atomic bomb.

Many African American women exchanged domestic service for low-paid factory work, which had been the preserve of white women. Meanwhile, white women took on more skilled jobs. Women gained greater spending power as a result, but, regardless of the work, they were paid less than a man doing the same job. There was negativity toward the women from some quarters. They experienced sexual harassment and those from minority ethnic groups were subject to racism. When police recorded more juvenile delinquency it was blamed on mothers who were doing paid work rather than supervising their children. This gave ammunition to politicians when they passed legislation such as the Veterans Preference Act, which allowed companies to fire women workers so that ex-servicemen could be employed.

Increased popularity and diversity of religion during the 1950s

Church membership grew from 57 percent of the US population in 1950 to 63 percent in 1960. The events of the Cold War, both at home and abroad, along with the emphasis on family life, combined to produce this anomaly in the generally downward trend of faith allegiance. The range of Christian denominations with a presence in each town meant that there was a church to suit everyone. This diversity also created bitter clashes over local issues such as schooling.

As the decade progressed, the range of religious experience broadened. Spirituality became popular. Evangelical preachers such as Billy Graham drew enormous crowds and many converts. The certainties of evangelical Christianity appealed in an age of international uncertainty, fear of communism at home and abroad, and increasing challenges to societal norms, especially regarding race.

The Civil Rights Movement was strongly associated with Christian churches; for example, the Southern Christian Leadership Conference (SCLC) civil rights organization was formed in 1957. At the other extreme, the Southern Baptist Church continued to put forward an interpretation of the Bible that upheld segregationist views.

By the end of the decade, the counterculture movement had developed interests in other forms of belief. Roman Catholic Thomas Merton developed ideas linking his spiritual and contemplative life with those of Tibetan Buddhism. Interest in Zen Buddhism was developing. Space exploration led some people to believe that UFOs were the work of extra-terrestrial beings. The religious conformity that mirrored the social conformity of the era was breaking down. It seemed that Roosevelt's freedom of religion had been attained.

Mass evangelism and televised church services

High levels of participation in religious worship led to large-scale religious events. The most famous was Billy Graham's crusade in the summer of 1957 at New York's Madison Square Garden. During the sixteen weeks of the crusade, nearly 2.4 million people attended meetings and over 61,000 were converted. They were responding to Graham's simple message of salvation in exchange for repentance of sin. The event was well-planned. Anyone who went forward in response to the call to become a born-again Christian was immediately spoken to by a counselor and handed literature to take away.

Television could reach even larger audiences. Many evangelists used this new medium, building on the work of the radio priests of earlier decades. The styles and messages were varied. Some programs consisted of televised sermons. Others were more like chat shows. Some were inspirational but with limited theological content. Others had a clear sociopolitical message. The broadcasts of Granville Oral Roberts were devoted to faith healing. His prosperity gospel theology was no doubt attractive because it was so clearly aligned with the values of the time. He taught that faith, expressed through positive thoughts and statements, along with donations to the church, generates well-being in the form of health, wealth, and happiness. One of the necessities for this new format was fundraising, as television filming was a relatively expensive way to broadcast. Later, this would highlight the greed that was one of the weaknesses of the brand.

Return to conservative gender norms

The conservative social values of the post-war era, together with higher wages, meant that many families could afford to emulate the image depicted in advertisements. Although women had a large part in the wartime workforce, mothers had a difficult time because childcare arrangements were inadequate. Once the war ended, employers, supported by the law, favored men over women.

Social conformity was important in post-war society. Men aspired to have a stay-at-home wife. The demands of looking after their new houses, husbands, and children meant women had little time for paid work. Since men's wages were high and rising, one salary was sufficient to support a family. Many women appeared content to be homebuilders and child raisers. Producers of consumer goods were delighted that, although women as a whole made up a third of the workforce, the middle-class women at whom they aimed their advertisements were likely to be at home or socializing with friends all competing to have the ideal home. The image of the home created by the advertisers made these women eager consumers. This eagerness drove a significant proportion of these women to work part-time to pay for the latest gadgets.

> What do you learn from this source about the American Dream of the 1950s?

SOURCE 3.12

A PERSONAL VOICE CAROL FREEMAN "As dissatisfied as I was, and as restless, I remember so well this feeling [we] had at the time that the world was going to be your oyster. You were going to make money, your kids were going to go to good schools, everything was possible if you just did what you were supposed to do. The future was rosy. There was a tremendous feeling of optimism... . Much as I say it was hateful, it was also hopeful. It was an innocent time."—quoted in The Fifties: A Women's Oral History

Conformity was apparent in the age of first marriages, which went down to twenty-three for men and twenty for women. It was also the norm to have children soon after marriage. Religious organizations disapproved of birth control. Conformity was so prevalent that people were willing to follow the rules of their neighborhood. These might prohibit on-street car parking or even dictate the type of clotheslines that were permitted.

Conformity for men meant being the breadwinner, taking the lead in strong decision-making in the family, and being a role model for their sons. This reinforced gender stereotyping. The conformity lasted until the baby boomers became teenagers. Their reaction to, and rejection of, conformity is reflected in the works of writers, artists, filmmakers, and musicians.

Resistance to conservative family norms in youth culture

Conformity did not suit everyone. The "Beat Generation" rejected many of the values of their parents. The leading figures led unconventional lives, criticized those who accepted what they viewed as wrong in American society, and questioned its values. They looked to other cultures for inspiration. Materialism, defense industry spending, racism, poverty, and above all conformity and repression were reviled by them. The movement is associated with Columbia University students, including the writers Allen Ginsberg and Jack Kerouac. The Beat Generation wrote fictional works that mocked corporation employees. The film *Rebel without a Cause* and JD Salinger's coming-of-age novel *The Catcher in the Rye* were shocking because the delinquent protagonists were from "good" families. This was an intellectual challenge to carefree, self-satisfied mainstream consumer culture.

Teenagers were exposed to these ideas through music and film. As they reached their later teenage years they learned to drive and had their own automobiles. Cars were essential to their social lives. They met their friends at drive-in movies, soda bars with jukeboxes, and drive-in restaurants. They had broken free from parental control. The rock and roll music of Buddy Holly, Chuck Berry, and Elvis Presley encouraged emotions and cravings that were judged unbecoming by conformists. For the first time, popular music was targeted at young people. It referenced a range of African American music styles, including jazz and rhythm and blues, as well as country music. It appealed to both African American and white teenagers, which helped to break down racial barriers and fueled the increasingly active Civil Rights Movement.

The products of this social and artistic movement were an affront to middle-class America. In 1955, the film *Blackboard Jungle* was released. It was banned in many places. The subject matter of juvenile delinquency in a high school, the rock and roll soundtrack, and the multi-racial cast were all too shocking.

> ## ACTIVITY
> - Make two lists about society in the post-war era. In the first list, note changes that had taken place. In the second list, note what stayed the same as in earlier decades.
> - "American social life in the 1950s was very different from that in the 1930s." Use the points in your lists to write two paragraphs, one supporting the statement and one challenging it.

The impacts of the Second Red Scare, 1946–53

In twentieth-century America, there were periodic episodes of intolerance. The Red Scare of the 1920s is one of these and the Second Red Scare, orchestrated by Senator Joseph McCarthy, is another. There are various explanations for the Second Red Scare, some psychological and some rooted in the emerging Cold War. Two of Roosevelt's freedoms were eroded. Americans were not "free from fear." Indeed, the Second Red Scare encouraged an anti-communist hysteria that was traumatic and destructive for individuals accused of links to communism. The impact on the civil rights of all Americans was damaging. Roosevelt's "freedom of speech" was severely curtailed. The impact on the State Department was serious.

Beliefs of and role of Joseph McCarthy

In the early Cold War, the US feared the activities of Soviet spies. In 1949, the Soviets had exploded their first atomic bomb well ahead of the projected schedule. This was possible only because classified secrets from the Manhattan Project had been passed to the USSR. In January 1950, Alger Hiss, who had worked for the State Department, was convicted of perjury in a case involving espionage. He had almost certainly been involved in giving away information, but had not been found guilty in jury trials. Such was the determination to punish him that a different route had to be taken. Other examples of Soviet infiltration of government in the 1930s were emerging. In the context of the rise of communist China and the Korean War, the West was seemingly under threat. In this uneasy and untrusting landscape, it seemed that anyone and everyone was a potential traitor. Consequently, when Senator **Joseph McCarthy** claimed in February 1950 that 205 communists had infiltrated the State Department, his accusations seemed convincing.

> ### KEY FIGURE
> **Joseph McCarthy** (1908–57) McCarthy was a Wisconsin lawyer. In 1947, he was the surprise nomination at the Republican Convention, beating Robert La Follette Jr, son of the famous Wisconsin Progressive governor. He served as a Senator for Wisconsin until his death at the age of 48 in 1957 from hepatitis, exacerbated by alcoholism. In a speech in Wheeling, West Virginia in February 1950, he claimed that the State Department had been infiltrated by 205 communists. This started a period in which increasingly wild, unsubstantiated claims were made against individuals and even the US army. The investigations of the Senate Committee on Government Operations, which he chaired from 1952, were televised, raising him to national fame. McCarthy was finally discredited and condemned for conduct "contrary to Senate traditions" in December 1954.

When McCarthy was called upon to provide evidence to the Senate Committee on Foreign Relations of who these 205 people were, he was unable to name any of the alleged card-carrying members of the Communist Party. Nevertheless, the publicity surrounding his accusations made headlines and he became famous. As Chairman of the Senate Committee on Government Operations, his aggressive interrogations were broadcast on TV. The style of questioning meant it was almost impossible for the accused to avoid the traps he lay. The slightest suggestion of any links with communism or association with a known communist was regarded as self-condemnation. To challenge McCarthy was to denounce oneself as a communist.

McCarthy investigated institutions and professions in turn. When he started to investigate the US army and the presidential administration itself, President Eisenhower knew he had to be stopped. Eisenhower was unforgiving of traitors. He did not hesitate to approve the execution of the married couple Julius and Ethel Rosenberg for theft of atomic secrets in 1953. However, in May 1954, Eisenhower ordered that no one in the administration or any executive employees should respond to an order to testify. McCarthy was powerless. His fellow senators turned against him and passed a motion of condemnation of him.

The role of the House Un-American Activities Committee (HUAC)

HUAC was the institution used to investigate private citizens, public employees, and organizations that were suspected of disloyalty. It was set up in 1938, at a time of growing suspicions about Soviet espionage. If HUAC found evidence of disloyalty, those accused were sent for trial. During the early 1950s, HUAC investigated numerous individuals. Its investigations extended beyond government employees and departments to labor unions, academia, and, most famously, the entertainment industry. Those called to testify experienced social isolation and professional difficulties. Anyone could be suspected through association with them.

Investigating the influence of communism in Hollywood, HUAC questioned "the Hollywood Ten." The group included the famous writers Bertolt Brecht and Arthur Miller. All ten had been members of the Communist Party; this was not illegal. Despite being subpoenaed, they refused to answer questions about their membership of the Party on the grounds that HUAC had no right to ask these questions. They were convicted of contempt of Congress and sentenced to prison. A better defense would have been to invoke the Fifth Amendment, which protects people from being forced to testify against themselves. The strength of feeling against communism was great, but the importance of upholding constitutional rights would probably have outweighed those feelings. Hollywood then refused to employ anyone who had refused to testify to the Committee, giving rise to the "Hollywood blacklist."

Anti-communist congressional legislation and its impacts

Laws that ban membership of a political party are controversial in a democracy. They deny an individual the right to free association and possibly freedom of speech. Nevertheless, the perceived threat from communism was so great that laws were passed restricting that freedom in America. Even liberal politicians agreed that they were needed.

Truman's first move to eliminate communist sympathizers fell short of a legal ban. The Loyalty Order, introduced in 1948, let the FBI investigate all federal employees. If enough "derogatory information" was found, the FBI could begin a full investigation. A list of organizations was drawn up and if the federal employee was associated with one or more of them, this could be grounds for dismissal. Several hundred of the five million employees who were reviewed were dismissed. Several thousand resigned.

The campaign against communist sympathizers was characterized as morally necessary. The leaders began to associate their definition of "political deviance" with what they classified as "immoral" sexual preferences. It developed into a campaign that also targeted LGBT people. This "Lavender Scare" became official policy when Eisenhower's Executive Order 10450 of 1953 banned the employment of LGBT people by the federal administration and its contractors. LGBT people were erroneously seen as a security threat, underwent intrusive and irrelevant questioning about their private lives, and were fired. The impact of EO 10450 extended beyond government employment, certainly to the arts, and no doubt beyond, as it legitimized discrimination on the grounds of sexuality.

In 1950, there were moves to introduce a law banning membership to the Communist Party on the grounds that it was undemocratic. Rather than add an amendment to the Internal Security Act of 1950, a new bill was drawn up and was passed in 1954 as the Communist Control Act. The first Act targeted communists in the labor unions. It was passed by Congress despite President Truman vetoing it. The second Act went much further. Members of the Communist Party were banned from holding office in labor organizations. Unregistered members of the Communist Party were punished with large fines and imprisonment. The Communist Party was regarded as un-American because it aimed to undermine liberal democracy and because it was an international organization. However, in the later 1950s, some aspects of the Acts were weakened. For example, only those with access to classified and sensitive information were subject to the Loyalty Order.

Politicians did not dare to challenge the passage of the 1954 Act. They were being asked to take a stand against communism and any hesitation would likely end their careers. It was introduced quickly, which might explain the ambiguities that would make its enforcement difficult. Both Acts impacted a range of organizations. Labor unions were a focus, but any organization that challenged the status quo might be considered for investigation. One of these was the NAACP.

The Second Red Scare's impacts on political discourse

The events of the Second Red Scare constituted a massive attack on civil liberties. Those who made that attack justified it as a means of protecting America and its way of life. Those who disagreed with it did not dare to speak out. They would be unemployed and unemployable. Their families and friends would be ostracized because of their association with the person who challenged the received wisdom of the attacks on those suspected of communist sympathies.

ACTIVITY

Explain why people interrogated by HUAC found it difficult to defend themselves.

In addition, the Red Scare had an adverse impact on social and welfare schemes for the disadvantaged. It removed officials who advocated for policies to distribute wealth more evenly. These policies were intended to strengthen democracy by giving more people a stake in the US. Instead, they were interpreted as socialist and therefore dangerous. The Red Scare did not make any distinction between loyal, socially minded capitalists and internationalist communists or anarchists who aimed to undermine American democracy.

The Civil Rights Movement, 1939–59

The New Deal did little to support African Americans and, in some instances, policies actively discriminated against them. Roosevelt did not want to invite criticism by singling them out for help, despite the disproportionate impact of the Great Depression on African American farmers and industrial workers. In addition, Mexicans were deported whether they were US citizens or not because their labor was not needed. Many Mexicans returned through the Bracero Program when labor was short during the war. When Japan attacked Pearl Harbor, Japanese Americans were imprisoned in concentration camps regardless of their citizenship status. These groups struggled to achieve freedom from fear and want.

During and after the war, racial injustices in America were increasingly brought to the fore by well-organized groups with focused campaigns. The minorities who seemed to be excluded from the American dream began to be heard. Truman was sympathetic but also aware that he could only act within the parameters allowed by the Constitution and needed to maintain Southern Democrat support. Eisenhower explained his intervention, for example at Little Rock, Arizona in 1957, as necessary to enforce law and order. Nevertheless, his reluctance to intervene was noted and gave strength to opponents of integration. By the end of the 1950s, government had outlawed some forms of discrimination, but the open defiance of more conservative Americans persisted.

KEY TERM

Disenfranchise Prevent someone from using their right to vote, or deprive them of that right.

Race relations and civil rights during the Second World War

An irony of the Second World War was that America asked its citizens to fight an enemy because that enemy was anti-democratic and openly racist. Although the US did not aim to eliminate any races, Jim Crow Laws and other methods continued to be used to **disenfranchise** African American citizens, and there was widespread and open hostility against some races. During the war, Japanese Americans were singled out as a potential threat, despite there being no evidence to support this and much to contradict it, and interned in appalling conditions. Prejudice against them continued after they were released.

Despite Jim Crow Laws in the South and other discriminatory practices elsewhere, many African Americans joined the armed forces. A campaign begun by the *Pittsburgh Courier* newspaper called on them to fight for two victories—one against America's foreign enemies and one at home, against racism. This was the "Double V Campaign."

Instead of encouraging Americans to unite for a common cause, the relocation of African American troops and workers into white areas often resulted in hostility from the white inhabitants. There were riots in Detroit, Harlem, and Beaumont. Complaints about the treatment of African Americans in the US army, especially around bases in the South, were so serious that James Farmer and Walter White of the NAACP were asked to investigate. Their recommendations were influential post-war.

Mexican Americans had been expelled in the thousands during the Depression. The draft created a shortage of farm laborers. The solution was the Bracero Program, which allowed them to work in the US. There was prejudice against them and as a means of establishing their own identity, the youths began to wear "zoot suits." This led to riots in Los Angeles over several days in June 1943, when shore-leave sailors attacked Mexicans wearing zoot suits. The baggy suits were seen as unpatriotic in that they were wasteful of fabric at a time of austerity. The real cause was more deep-seated, rooted in the long-term prejudice against Mexicans which associated them with crime, illegal migration, and delinquency.

The most serious wartime racial discrimination was reserved for Japanese Americans. Shortly after war broke out, Roosevelt signed Executive Order 9066, which gave the War Department the power to remove anyone they identified as a threat from military areas and relocate them. Italian and German Americans were interned if they had connections to fascist organizations or espionage. In contrast, on the West Coast, the military targeted all Japanese immigrants and Japanese Americans. Two-thirds of these were American citizens. 127,000 people were rounded up in assembly centers with inadequate facilities before being taken to internment camps inland. Those interned displayed remarkable resilience in the harsh conditions. Families were separated, most of their possessions had been left behind and conditions in the camps were overcrowded. The inmates organized their lives to include work, education, and leisure activities. However, it was a traumatic time for a group that a government-commissioned study found would likely be loyal to the US. The overreaction was afterward acknowledged to have been a mistake. Prejudice against the Japanese continued after they were allowed to return to their homes in January 1945. Wartime propaganda against Japanese people reinforced existing hostilities. Many were not accepted back into their communities.

Impact of key civil rights groups

Organization was the key to achieving civil rights. Faced with Southern white determination to deny them their constitutional and legal rights, African Americans realized that even with federal law on their side, they must fight to exercise these rights.

The NAACP was formed in 1909 with the aim of using the law to fight for equality. By the 1940s, its focus was on desegregation, especially in education. While *Plessy v. Ferguson* in 1896 (page 67) had established the principle of "separate but equal," the reality was quite different. In Mississippi in 1949–50, for example, expenditure on each Black school student was $32.55, whereas $122.93 was spent on each white student. Desegregation was the only way to achieve equal access to education.

In the 1940s and 1950s, the NAACP refined its strategy. It identified circumstances where white supremacists were likely to put up a robust fight, and where politicians and law enforcement officials were likely to resort to extreme measures to support them. In these cases, adverse publicity for the racists, as well as the law, would support their cause. The Montgomery Bus Boycott and high school integration in Little Rock, Arkansas are prime examples of this tactic.

The Congress of Racial Equality (CORE) was founded in Chicago in 1942, by an interracial group of students led by James Farmer. Its chosen method was **non-violent resistance**. This was a particularly effective method in the face of the violent retaliation of white supremacists. The group's first sit-in was at a Chicago coffee shop which refused to serve African Americans. They would not leave until served or forcibly removed. They started a trend. They moved on to organize sit-ins in Washington DC to bring about the desegregation of public places. By the late 1950s, they turned their attention to the South where they challenged public segregation and encouraged the voter registration of African Americans.

Like CORE, the Southern Christian Leadership Conference (SCLC) advocated non-violent protest. It was formed following the Montgomery Bus Boycott victory of January 1957 in Atlanta, Georgia with Dr Martin Luther King Jr its first president. This organization was an affiliation of individual Christian churches and community groups. There was significant resistance to its approach from groups who might have joined. Firstly, many organizations were reluctant to take direct action because they were afraid of reprisals from white supremacists. Secondly, their more educated leaders were accustomed to speaking on behalf of their members and were reluctant to allow mass participation. Many church pastors preferred to focus on the spiritual needs of their congregations rather than the social injustices they faced. After a slow start, the SCLC became more prominent in the 1960s.

The role of leading African Americans

The Civil Rights Movement would not have been possible without the contributions of thousands of ordinary Americans. However, there were key individuals whose leadership was of great importance. They determined the way in which African Americans would fight for their rights and inspired the whole movement.

> **KEY TERM**
>
> **Non-violent resistance**
> A method of protest used to achieve political ends by mass collective action without violence. This strategy was used by the Indian leader Mahatma Gandhi to highlight the injustices of British colonial rule in India. His example inspired similar methods elsewhere.

> **ACTIVITY**
> - Draw a Venn diagram to show the methods used by the leaders of the Civil Rights Movement. How much agreement was there about the methods to use?
> - Draw another Venn diagram showing the fundamental principles of the leaders. How much agreement was there between the leaders?

James Farmer

James Farmer was a star college debater with strong principles. He contemplated a career in medicine, then decided to study divinity. At college, he learned about the teachings of Mahatma Gandhi, the Indian nationalist leader. He subscribed to the same non-violent civil resistance used by Gandhi in India, applying it to the campaign to end racial segregation in the US. In 1942, he organized the first sit-ins in Chicago and founded CORE.

A Philip Randolph

Asa Philip Randolph was a labor unionist who was active in the fight for civil rights. In the 1920s, he led the first successful African American union to victory over equal pay for sleeping-car porters. During the Second World War, his threat of a March on Washington led Roosevelt to end discrimination in the defense industries and, after the war, he successfully advocated for desegregation of the armed forces. In the 1950s, he organized marches, including two protesting the slow integration of schooling. He also continued his union work, fighting racial discrimination within labor unions.

Bayard Rustin

Baynard Rustin was, like James Farmer, a pacifist. In his case, this originated from his Quaker upbringing. He was an organizer who influenced others with his tactics and ideas. He planned the "Journey of Reconciliation" which was a precursor of the later freedom rides of the 1960s. The aim was to challenge the application of state segregation rules on interstate buses. He advocated non-violent resistance. In this, he was an important influence on Dr Martin Luther King Jr.

Thurgood Marshall

Thurgood Marshall was a lawyer who served as the first African American Supreme Court justice from 1967–91. He began his civil rights involvement as a lawyer for the NAACP in 1936. During the 1940s and 1950s, he won almost 30 cases in the Supreme Court challenging civil rights violations, including *Shelley v. Kraemer,* and *Brown v. Board of Education of Topeka*.

Dr Martin Luther King Jr

Dr Martin Luther King Jr became involved in civil rights campaigns as an organizer of the Montgomery Bus Boycott, for which he was arrested and imprisoned. Influenced by the campaign of Mahatma Gandhi in India, he followed a policy of non-violent resistance. He did this because he wanted publicity for the cause and thought that the media would give positive coverage if peaceful pro-civil rights activists were shown suffering violent attacks from white supremacists. To achieve his end, he and other church leaders formed the SCLC.

Responses of the peoples and governments of Southern states

Conservatives in the Southern states saw the demands of African Americans as a challenge to their way of life and values. This clash of values came to national and international prominence in high-profile incidents. White Southerners, out of line with the mood of the nation as well as a world in which independence movements were gaining momentum, attempted to hold back the tide of history. To do this they used the law, law enforcement officers, violence, and the threat of violence. The news reporters of the world descended on the hotspots. Across the world, the footage they recorded demonstrated the limits of freedom in the country that, in Cold War terms, presented itself as the defender and champion of democracy.

In December 1955 in Montgomery, Alabama, **Rosa Parks**'s refusal to give up her bus seat to a white man led to a year-long boycott of Alabama's buses by the African Americans who made up over 60 percent of its passengers. The campaign was carefully managed by the NAACP, who were determined to achieve their aim of desegregation through direct action rather than by appealing to the bus company. The Supreme Court eventually ruled that the bus company was acting illegally by segregating seating. The incident brought the young pastor of Dexter Avenue Baptist Church to prominence. His name was Martin Luther King Jr.

> ### KEY FIGURE
> **Rosa Parks** (1913–2005) By 1955, Rosa Parks was a seasoned civil rights activist. Secretary of the NAACP chapter in Montgomery, Alabama from 1943, in 1954 she re-founded the NAACP youth branch where she met the schoolgirl activist Claudette Colvin.
>
> Parks's role in the Montgomery Bus Boycott was planned. Her arrest for refusing to give up her seat to a white person on a bus was the last in a series of confrontations, including the arrest of Claudette Colvin in March 1955. Parks may have been identified as a tired seamstress, but hers was a deliberate action, designed to provoke a well-publicized campaign.

In 1956, Southern Congressmen drafted a Declaration of Constitutional Principles, which became known as the Southern Manifesto. It was issued in response to the Supreme Court judgment on *Brown v. Board of Education of Topeka* (see page 188), which ruled that racial segregation in public schools was unconstitutional. The statement, signed by nineteen US senators and 82 Representatives from the Southern states, challenged the constitutional right of the Supreme Court to interfere with the way education was provided in a state. Education, it stated, was not mentioned in the Constitution. Public education was a matter for individual states. The manifesto cited the Tenth Amendment in support of its argument that the Supreme Court had abused its judicial powers. The Southern Manifesto's aim was, no doubt, to achieve a reversal of the Supreme Court decision, but the final version did not make explicit reference to this. The manifesto demonstrated to segregationists that their elected representatives would support their efforts to prevent school integration.

Despite the *Brown v. Board of Education of Topeka* ruling of 1954, many states were slow to desegregate schools. It was a sensitive issue that raised strong feelings. Racist white parents who were opposed to integrated education claimed to be protecting their children. In 1957, following a decision by the Little Rock School Board to integrate high schools, the NAACP decided to take a stand. Nine African American teenagers, selected by the School Board from a hundred volunteers on the basis of their grades and attendance, enrolled at Central High. The NAACP coached them in the skills they would need to withstand the resistance they would likely encounter. The NAACP also tried to ensure that the "Little Rock Nine" were able to enter the school safely, despite the baying crowds, some of whom had traveled across state boundaries to oppose the move. Governor Orval Faubus used the National Guard to prevent the nine children from entering. Such was the furor that eventually President Eisenhower intervened, sending in the 101st Airborne Division to restore order and taking the Arkansas National Guard out of Faubus's control. Eventually, the nine students were admitted, but such was the anger this caused that each one had to be assigned a National Guardsman for protection inside the school. In December, one of the students, Minnijean Brown, reacted to provocation in the lunch hall and was expelled. The remaining eight graduated but not before Faubus had closed all of Little Rock's high schools for a whole year from September 1958, in a defiant stand against integration.

These and other events demonstrated the level of determination on both sides of the debate.

SOURCE 3.13

From President Eisenhower's address to the American people, broadcast on September 24, 1957

At a time when we face grave situations abroad because of the hatred that communism bears toward a system of government based on human rights, it would be difficult to exaggerate the harm that is being done to the prestige and influence, and indeed to the safety, of our nation and the world.

Our enemies are gloating over this incident and using it everywhere to misrepresent our whole nation. We are portrayed as a violator of those standards of conduct which the peoples of the world united to proclaim in the Charter of the United Nations. There they affirmed "faith in fundamental human rights" and "in the dignity and worth of the human person" and they did so "without distinction as to race, sex, language, or religion."

And so, with deep confidence, I call upon the citizens of the State of Arkansas to assist in bringing to an immediate end all interference with the law and its processes. If resistance to the federal court orders ceases at once, the further presence of federal troops will be unnecessary and the City of Little Rock will return to its normal habits of peace and order and a blot upon the fair name and high honor of our nation in the world will be removed.

Thus will be restored the image of America and of all its parts as one nation, indivisible, with liberty and justice for all.

Good night, and thank you very much.

What can you learn from Source 3.13 about Eisenhower's priorities? Why did Eisenhower use these arguments in his address to the American people? Explain your answers using details from the speech and your knowledge.

Another protest method employed by civil rights activists was the sit-in. In the 1950s sit-ins occurred at segregated store lunch counters in Baltimore, Maryland, Wichita, Kansas, and Oklahoma City, Oklahoma. Despite their success in bringing about the desegregation of the lunch counters, they were not given widespread attention. Nevertheless, they served as a model for similar direct action at Greensboro in 1960.

Impact of federal actions and Supreme Court cases

While Civil Rights Movement groups demonstrated and acted against America's racial inequalities by various means, civil rights were also impacted by a number of Supreme Court cases and the Civil Rights Act of 1957.

- In *Korematsu v. United States* of 1944, the Supreme Court justices issued three separate decisions. The majority decision, issued by six of the justices, upheld the way the armed forces had implemented Roosevelt's Executive Order 9066 (page 184). They argued that in extreme situations, such as during a war, it was permissible to base decisions about loyalty on race. The dissenting opinions argued that the majority decision legitimized racism. One of the three dissenting justices pointed out that the majority decision violated the Equal Protection Clause of the Fourteenth Amendment. In 2000, the decision was criticized by Justice Antonin Scalia as one of the worst ever made by the Supreme Court.
- Although the segregation of the armed forces was controversial, it was not ended during the Second World War due to FDR's fear of political backlash by Democrats in the South. After the war, President Harry Truman acted, although only in response to widespread lobbying by civil rights groups. On July 26, 1948, Truman signed Executive Order 9981: Desegregation of the Armed Forces. This mandated equality of treatment and opportunity for all armed forces personnel, regardless of race, color, religion, or national origin.
- Housing segregation was widespread. Restrictive covenants were placed on housing. They specified that African Americans were not allowed to purchase or live in a house. These covenants were designed to segregate housing, and hence, social interaction. They were outlawed by the Supreme Court judgment in the case of *Shelley v. Kraemer* of 1948. This judgment held that private racial covenants could not be enforced by the state to evict African American purchasers of homes which were subject to these covenants. The ruling had limited significance. It closed one method of segregating housing, but there were others at the disposal of people who opposed integration.
- In the case of *Henderson v. United States* of 1950, the Supreme Court ruling desegregated dining cars on interstate trains. The judgment did not reject *Plessy v. Ferguson* because it was not a challenge to "separate but equal," instead basing the judgment on the terms of the Interstate Commerce Act. The ruling had little impact, as most transport was within states and therefore not subject to federal judiciaries.
- *Brown v. Board of Education of Topeka* of 1954 is the most famous of all the landmark judgments of the era because it related to education, a topic that was at the heart of the segregation issue. Educating white Southern children to believe that they were superior to African Americans was easier if the children were segregated. The Supreme Court ruling that state laws establishing segregated education were unlawful overruled *Plessy v. Ferguson* and led to high-profile efforts to enforce the judgment, including that at Little Rock.
- *Browder v. Gale* of 1956 is another case that appears to mark a civil rights victory. It ruled that segregation on Alabama's buses was unconstitutional. All appeals were rejected. As a result, the Montgomery Improvement Association, which had promoted the boycott, voted to call off their action. However, like many such "victories," the principle could only be applied where the relevant agencies were made to enforce the law.
- During the Cold War, America was the champion of democracy. This could easily be challenged. In the South, various methods were used to hamper voter registration by African American citizens. The Civil Rights Act of 1957 sought to address this. It established the Civil Rights Section of the Justice Department, giving its prosecutors the right to obtain injunctions against anyone who interfered with the right to vote. The Act had little impact because it failed to outlaw the discriminatory methods used to prevent African Americans from voting, such as literacy tests. In addition, there was little effort to enforce the law. It simply made clear that further legislation and commitment from those in authority was needed.

ACTIVITY

To what extent do you agree that the Civil Rights Movement had made little progress by 1959? Working with a partner, find examples to support and challenge this statement. Write a paragraph summarizing and explaining your conclusion.

Overall, the period from 1944 to 1959 saw the government giving little, if any, practical support to the Civil Rights Movement. Some Supreme Court judgments upheld discrimination and those that did not had little practical impact. The Civil Rights Act of 1957 was too weakly worded and too weakly enforced to bring change. By 1959, the Movement had developed effective strategies, but with little impact on the lives of those subjected to racial discrimination.

SUMMARY DIAGRAM

Change and continuity in American society in the 1940s and 1950s

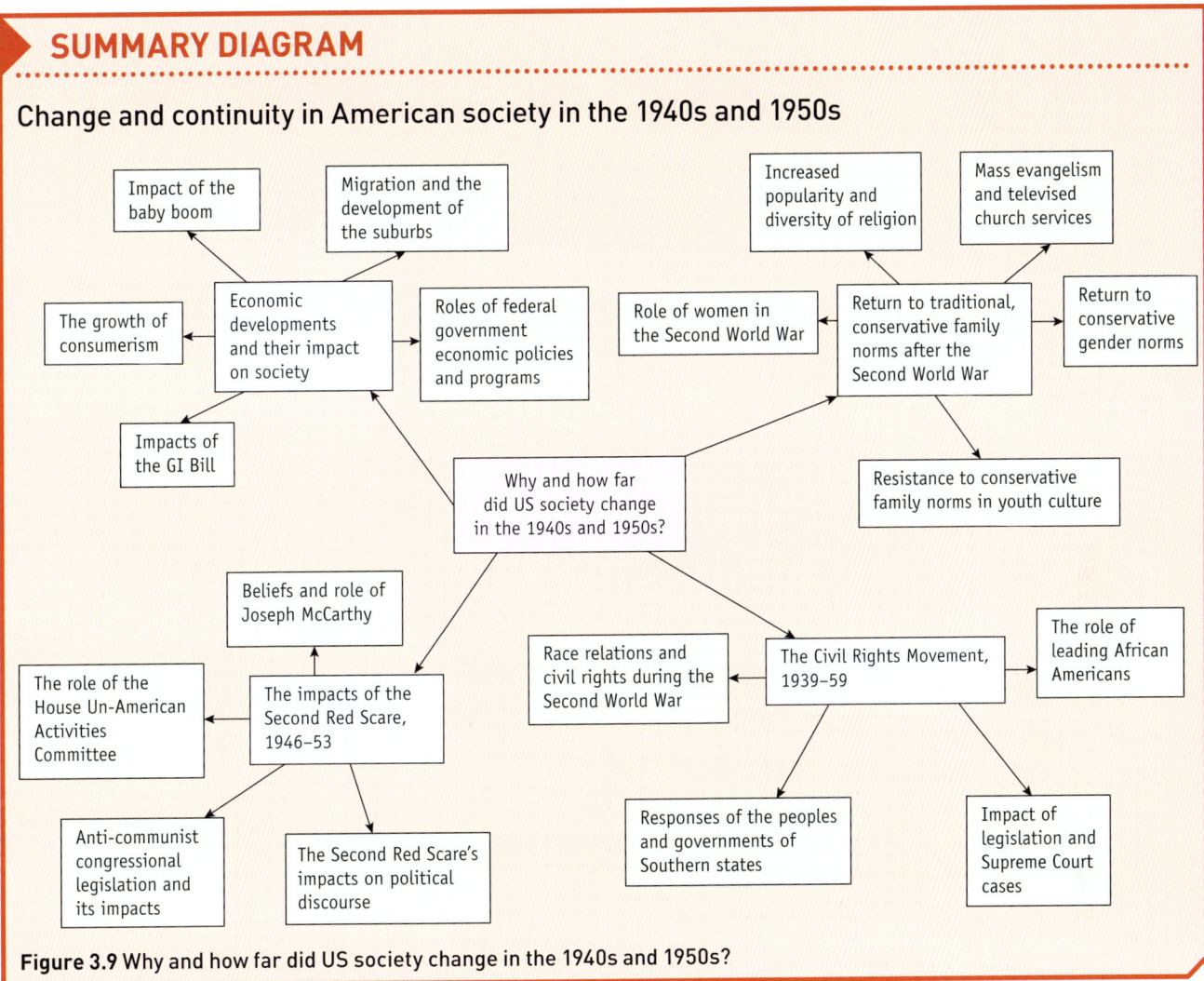

Figure 3.9 Why and how far did US society change in the 1940s and 1950s?

CHAPTER SUMMARY

The key questions in this chapter cover a period of severe economic hardship followed by growing prosperity in America and, in foreign policy, the change from isolationism to the world center stage. Events, actions, and the attitudes of the period all had a part to play, some causing changes, while others were the consequences of those changes. The role of federal government in economic issues, and the extent to which it was involved in upholding or challenging discrimination, were controversial. The impact of the Cold War on domestic and foreign policy, and the extent to which it affected the lives of ordinary Americans, is an issue that began as the Second World War ended and which we will continue to consider when we move on to study the 1960s and beyond. As you review the events of the period 1930 to 1959, consider which changes were most significant, what stayed the same, and what were the main drivers of change. In doing this, you will be thinking like a historian.

REFRESHER QUESTIONS

1. What were the main causes of the Great Depression?
2. Do you agree that Hoover did "too little, too late" in response to the Great Depression?
3. Why was Roosevelt popular with the electorate?
4. Which of Roosevelt's opponents had the greatest impact on him?
5. Why was the situation in Europe important in the early years of the Cold War?
6. How did nuclear and space technology impact the Cold War?
7. Identify the similarities and differences between Truman and Eisenhower's approaches to foreign policy.
8. Explain why consumerism grew in the post-war period.
9. Why was religion popular in 1950s America?
10. Why was Joseph McCarthy influential?

Study skills

Guidance on answering long essay questions

Understanding the task and planning your writing

When you need to answer longer essay questions, often the focus will be on a specific historical issue and you may be asked to consider its significance, weigh the relative importance of causal factors, or assess the failure or success of policies or institutions. You will need to make a supported judgment to address any "to what extent" or "how far" elements of the question.

- Answers must address the question rather than the topic.
- A balanced answer which shows support and challenge for the issue is essential.
- Carefully selected and accurate knowledge is necessary to support the answer.
- It is important to be analytical rather than simply tell the story.

Understanding the question

Let's consider the following question:

"Speculation on the stock market was the main cause of the Great Crash." How far do you agree with this view? [20]

To answer this question, you would need to consider the following issues:
- The question contains a statement: what does it claim?
- What points and evidence support the statement?
- What other factors were at play in causing the Crash? These might include:
  - the policies enforced by the Republican presidents
  - availability of easy credit to Americans
  - overproduction of consumer goods and increased desire to spend money.

Planning an answer

Once you have understood the demands of the question, the next step is planning your answer. The plan should outline the structure of your response. Therefore, you need to think about what arguments you are going to include before you start writing. This will help you to maintain a consistent line of reasoning throughout your answer. It also means that your plan will be a list of factors about the issue or issues mentioned in the question, which will ensure an analytical response. Simply having a list of dates would encourage you to write a narrative or descriptive answer; instead, you will need to be analytical. However, you will need to use your contextual knowledge to support your arguments.

Planning an answer will help you focus on the actual question and not simply write about the topic. It is easy to forget the importance of planning and just to start writing, but this will usually result in an essay that does not have a clear line of reasoning, or changes its line of argument halfway through, making it less convincing.

Consider the question above. Your plan should be structured around issues like:
- the impact of stock market speculation on share prices including the Great Crash
- the impact of wider share ownership and inexperienced investors
- the impact of weaker sales and growth
- the role of rumors and ideas about weaknesses in the American economy.

A plan for this essay might take the following form:

Speculation	Other factors
Inexperienced investors	Share prices inflated
High levels of borrowing	Market saturation
Investor nervousness	Overproduction
	Rumors and ideas about future profits and high levels of debt

Characteristics of effective responses

Sample answer 1

The Great Crash of October 1929 was a disaster waiting to happen. Before the crash, people had been buying shares "on the margin" so they were massively in debt. When share prices began to fall, they panicked and sold their shares. If they sold them for less than what they had borrowed, they still owed the bank money and they were in big trouble. Some of them lost so much money they threw themselves off skyscrapers. Everyone was now panicking, so the stock market crashed.

Sample answer 2

Speculation on the stock market played a part in causing the Great Crash of October 1929. Speculators created demand for shares which pushed up the prices. Many ordinary people with some spare cash decided to invest in shares as a way of making money. Many bought shares "on the margin" meaning that they borrowed 90 percent of the share price. This speculative buying helped to cause the Great Crash because when some share prices began to fall, these investors panicked and sold their shares. As demand for shares fell, so too did share prices. This led to the Great Crash, as so many shares were sold and there were so few buyers that the prices kept falling.

However, there were other factors at play that led to the Great Crash. For example, the fact that lots of people had bought things they could not really afford using credit. This was a problem because the banks had not been strict enough in offering credit only to people who could really afford to pay the banks back. This meant that lots more people couldn't afford to pay back what they owed. This led to high levels of debt among people and contributed to the Great Crash.

> **ACTIVITY**
> ## Comparing sample answers
> Compare the two extracts given in sample answers 1 and 2.
> - What are the strengths and weaknesses of each answer?
> - Which answer do you think is more effective?
> - What can you learn from this activity about writing effectively for longer essay answers?
> - What advice would you give to the writer of each answer to help them improve?

The opening sentence of each paragraph

One way that you can avoid a narrative approach is to focus on the opening sentence of each paragraph. A good opening sentence will offer a view or idea about an issue relevant to the question, not describe an event or person. With a very good answer, you should be able to read the opening sentence of each paragraph and see the line of argument that has been taken in the essay. It is therefore worth spending time practicing this skill.

ACTIVITY

Look at the following seven opening sentences. Which of these offer an idea that directly answers the question on page 191 and which simply give facts?

- The Stock Exchange crashed because investors became so nervous, they panicked and sold their shares as quickly as possible.
- The prices of shares fell rapidly, with some, including General Electric, US Steel, and General Motors, doing very badly.
- Bankers tried to help by buying shares, so the prices did not fall so far.
- On October 24, 13 million shares were sold and on October 29 16.5 million shares were sold.
- The increase in the value of shares was far greater than was justified by the increase in the productivity of companies.
- By the late 1920s, companies were making less profit, as it was becoming more difficult to sell consumer goods.
- High levels of borrowing to finance share purchases meant the market was fragile.

Answering different types of questions

The first question you considered asked for a discussion of the relative importance of factors. The following practice question is different, as it asks you to assess the impact of an event.

"The Second World War brought significant changes to the lives of women in the period up to 1959." How far do you agree with this view? [20]

What does the difference in this question mean for how you might plan your answer?

The statement in this question accepts that women's lives were changed by the Second World War. It asks you to make a judgment about how significant these changes were.

You will need to start by identifying changes that took place. This part of your plan will be a list. You will also need to decide which criteria you will use to judge the significance of a change. This might be:
- What proportion of women were affected?
- Did the changes affect all women regardless of age?
- How long-term were the changes?

Your plan might look like this:

Long-term significance	Significance at the time	Little significance
Fewer African American women in domestic service	Replaced men in the workforce	Return to gender norms after the war
Women had proved they could perform all kinds of work	Roles in the military	Employment discrimination post-war
	Role in Manhattan Project	

Of course, you might want to add points or categorize them differently. Like all questions that historians ask, there are no right or wrong answers. You will need to include evidence to support all the points that you make.

ACTIVITY

Assessing a sample answer

Read the following sample response to the question above. Use this checklist to assess the answer:
- Does the answer show awareness of a range of relevant issues?
- Is it relevant to the question?
- Does it contain relevant, accurate knowledge?
- Are points explained and linked to the question?
- Are there sections of narrative?
- Is there a clear structure?
- Does the answer achieve a balance?

Sample answer 3

During the Second World War, women's lives were affected in many ways. They were encouraged to play their part at home and in the workforce. Although the post-war period marked a return to conservative gender norms, some changes could not be reversed.

During the war, women had far more job opportunities because men were needed in combat roles. For example, they were employed in non-combat roles in the military. The Rosie the Riveter campaign glamorized traditionally male jobs. There were posters and a song which featured a lady called "Rosie the Riveter." The campaign emphasized the importance of women taking on these roles to release men to fight. Women were portrayed as mechanics and aircraft builders. They were shown images of women in clean overalls and perfect makeup, to encourage them to take on these jobs. Some employers encouraged this image by offering "Rosie the Riveter" makeovers. Many African American women left domestic service to work in factories. Overall, the working lives of women changed significantly.

There was a big campaign to improve nutrition during the Second World War. The government knew that during the Great Depression the diets of many Americans were poor, and they knew that people could work better if they were properly fed. Seven basic types of foods were listed as important. The recommendations were based on the diet of New Englanders and did not take into account the needs of different racial groups. Women had to put up with food rationing as well. This was confusing as the rationed foods often changed. Luckily, there were maximum prices for some foods. Sugar was in short supply because the Japanese captured the Philippines. This all made shopping and cooking difficult for American women during the war and had a significant effect on their lives.

During the post-war period to 1959, many of these changes were reversed. The changes in employment were only short-lived, so had little significance. In the post-war years, employers gave preference to men over women in engineering and construction work. This was encouraged by laws. Many women preferred to return to their traditional roles as housewives and mothers. However, when the baby boomer generation reached adulthood, all this began to change. The experience of the Second World War demonstrated that women could do the same work as men. In the 1960s and 1970s, the women's liberation movement built on this to demand equality of opportunity for women.

In conclusion, the Second World War had a significant impact on the lives of women. They had to work and look after their families at the same time. This was very difficult for them. It is not surprising that most of them did not want to carry on working after the war ended.

ACTIVITY

- Working on your own, decide what you think about the strengths and weaknesses of this answer.
- Discuss your ideas with a partner.
- How would you advise this learner to improve their response?

4 The Development of the US in the 1960s and 1970s

Introduction

In the 1960s and 1970s, many Americans tried to improve their positions, leading to social progress which was often met with significant resistance. Internationally, in the 1960s, the Cold War escalated into the Cuban Missile Crisis, bringing the world to the brink of nuclear war. The USA also engaged in a proxy war in Vietnam. By the 1970s, America moved toward a policy of negotiation with the USSR and normalization of relations with China. This chapter will examine these decades by considering the following questions:

▶ Why and how did US approaches to the Cold War change between 1961 and 1979?
▶ Why and how did politics in the US evolve between 1960 and 1979?
▶ Why and how far did the position of minorities improve in the US between 1960 and 1979?

▶ KEY DATES

April 1961	Bay of Pigs invasion
August 1961	Berlin border closed
October 1962	Cuban Missile Crisis
1963	President Kennedy assassinated
1964	Civil Rights Act passed
August 1964	Gulf of Tonkin incident
1965	Operation Rolling Thunder begins
1968	Tet Offensive begins
January 1969	Richard Nixon becomes president
June 1969	Stonewall Uprising
May 1972	SALT I
June 1972	Watergate break-in
1974	Nixon resigns
1975	Helsinki Agreement
1979	SALT II

4.1 Why and how did US approaches to the Cold War change between 1960 and 1979?

In the 1960s, US foreign policy featured multiple confrontations with the USSR, some direct, such as the Berlin Crisis, and some by proxy conflicts like the Vietnam War. After Vietnam, the US became more interested in avoiding conflict with the USSR. There were many reasons for the escalation and easing of aggression in the US approach to the Cold War. This section will focus on three key topics: foreign policy under John F Kennedy, the impact of the Vietnam War, and the role of **détente**.

Foreign policy under Kennedy

In Kennedy's inaugural speech in 1961, he said, "Let every nation know ... we shall pay any price, bear any burden, meet any hardship, support any friend, oppose any foe, in order to assure the survival and the success of liberty." Kennedy was committed to the containment of communism. However, he believed that Eisenhower's Cold War policy relied too heavily on massive retaliation. He recognized the importance of the USSR's nuclear threat and the threat to US interests posed by "**wars of liberation**." His focus on these issues led to the development of the "flexible response" policy.

Flexible response March 1961–November 1963

Eisenhower's New Look discouraged direct attack by the USSR, but it did little to deter Soviet involvement in revolutions in developing countries. Kennedy abandoned the policy of massive retaliation in favor of a policy of flexible response. This aimed to enhance deterrence by providing the president with a range of nuclear, conventional (non-nuclear), and non-military options to deal with a variety of crises. A key aspect of the policy was the theory of **mutually assured destruction**.

Flexible response gave the US a variety of options to use when responding to a crisis. These included:
- Diplomatic options, like maintaining and developing relationships with existing and potential allies and conducting negotiations.
- Political options, like including the press more in foreign policy dialogue.
- Economic options, like withdrawing or increasing financial aid to other countries.
- Military options, like modernizing missile fleets and increasing conventional weapon stocks.

Flexible response had mixed success. Negotiation, economic sanctions, diplomacy, and military threats did help to resolve some of the crises faced by the Kennedy administration, such as the Cuban Missile Crisis, but it proved less successful in other situations, such as the Bay of Pigs invasion and the Berlin Crisis.

> **KEY FIGURE**
> **John F Kennedy**
> (1917–63) Born into a wealthy and well-connected Massachusetts family, Kennedy was the 35th president of the United States. After serving as both a Congressman and a Senator for Massachusetts, he took office as president in 1961. He was assassinated in Dallas, Texas on November 22, 1963.

> **KEY TERMS**
> **détente** A French word meaning relaxation; the relaxation of tensions between superpowers in the 1970s.
>
> **Wars of liberation** Refers to the wars and rebellions fought during the decolonization movement, which saw mainly developing countries seek to gain political and economic independence from Western nations. Some of these wars were supported by the USSR, which claimed to be an anti-imperialist power.
>
> **Mutually assured destruction** An understanding that the use of nuclear weapons against a nation also armed with nuclear weapons will result in the nuclear annihilation of both attacker and defender.

KEY DATES

Timeline of the Bay of Pigs invasion

April 15, 1961	Eight bombers launch the first airstrike and miss most of their targets, leaving Cuba's air force intact. Kennedy cancels the second airstrike.
April 17	Invasion force lands at the Bay of Pigs and comes under heavy fire.
April 18–19	Cuban troops advance on the beaches, supported by the Cuban Air Force.
April 19	Kennedy authorizes six US fighter planes to help defend the invaders. The planes arrive an hour late and are quickly shot down.
April 20	Invasion is defeated.

The Bay of Pigs invasion and its impact, April 1961–June 1961

In March 1952, Fulgencio Batista, a Cuban general, led a coup in Cuba, declared himself president, and established a dictatorship. The corrupt Batista regime allowed US companies to gain a significant foothold in the Cuban economy, especially in sugar cane plantations. Various groups within Cuba opposed Batista with armed rebellion. From 1956 to 1959, **Fidel Castro** led a guerrilla campaign against the Batista government known as the Cuban Revolution. This resulted in Batista's resignation, after which he and many of his followers were exiled. In February 1959, Castro's chosen candidate, Manuel Urrutia Lleó, took over as president of Cuba and Castro took on the role of prime minister.

> **KEY FIGURE**
>
> **Fidel Castro** (1926–2016) Born to a wealthy farming family, Castro developed left-leaning ideals while studying law at the University of Havana. After participating in uprisings against right-wing governments in the Dominican Republic and Colombia, he practiced law in Cuba before joining the Cuban Revolution. He served as prime minister of Cuba from 1959–76 and then as president from 1976–2008 before handing the presidency to his brother, Raúl. He died on November 25, 2016 at the age of 90.

> **KEY TERM**
>
> **Huber Matos affair** In October 1959, Huber Matos, a Cuban army commander, resigned over what he saw as increasing communist influence within the Castro government. Castro ordered Matos's arrest, and accused him of helping the CIA and Cuban opposition plan a counter-revolution. The Matos affair marked a turning point as Castro began to assert more personal control of the revolutionary government.

The revolutionary regime began a program of widespread reform, taking much of Cuba's land into state ownership and redistributing it through the Institute of Agrarian Reform (INRA). This concerned some members of the government who saw it as an overly socialist step. After the **Huber Matos affair**, Castro confirmed that Cuba would continue to move in a socialist direction. He ordered the country's US-controlled oil refineries to process crude oil from the USSR. When they refused to do so, Castro nationalized them, leading the US to cancel imports of Cuban sugar. In retaliation, Castro nationalized most of Cuba's US-owned assets, including sugar mills and banks. In October 1960, the US launched an economic embargo blocking most exports to Cuba. Castro retaliated again by nationalizing and seizing the assets of US companies and private-run businesses in Cuba, including Coca-Cola and Sears Roebuck.

By 1960, many in the US saw Castro as a threat to US national security, a sentiment that only intensified as he strengthened the country ties to the USSR following the economic embargo. In March 1960, Eisenhower approved a program to train Cuban exiles to launch an invasion of their homeland. This aimed to overthrow the government and establish a non-communist, US-friendly government. The US assumed that the Cuban people and military would support such an invasion. In early 1961, Kennedy authorized the plan, selecting the Bay of Pigs as the invasion site.

The plan called for two airstrikes on Cuban air bases, followed by a surprise attack by a 1,400-man force in the dead of night. The invasion launched on April 15, 1961 and was defeated by Cuban forces by April 20, 1961 (see timeline, page 196). Those invaders who did not manage to escape were rounded up and imprisoned. Photos of the US-owned planes, which had been painted to look like Cuban Air Force planes, quickly revealed US involvement in the invasion.

The US initially denied involvement, but the failed invasion was an embarrassment for the US and strengthened the position of Cuba's government. The invasion had significant consequences for future US Cold War policy.
- The Cuban administration pursued closer ties with the USSR and embraced communism (which Castro had rejected before the invasion). Cuba also requested military assistance from the USSR, which alarmed the US.
- The Bay of Pigs incident had a lasting impact on US-Cuban relations. It deepened the mistrust and hostility between the two countries. This strained relationship has continued long after the conclusion of the Cold War.
- The reputation of the US was damaged at home and abroad. Many in Latin America, the Global South, and the USSR saw this failure as a sign of American weakness. It showed that the US was unable to manage or combat communism and emboldened the USSR. This made it more challenging for Kennedy to navigate the next Cold War standoff: the Berlin Crisis.

Figure 4.1 A map of Cuba showing the location of the Bay of Pigs and Soviet missile sites, 1962

The Berlin Crisis and its impact, June 1961–November 1961

In the late 1950s and early 1960s, the question of Berlin flared up again, leading to a crisis that would change the city and the lives of its residents for the next 30 years.

In 1958, Soviet Premier Nikita Khrushchev demanded that the US withdraw its forces from West Berlin within six months. Talks between Eisenhower and Khrushchev made some progress, but relations deteriorated after the USSR shot down a US spy plane over Soviet territory in 1960. Talks resumed on June 4, 1961, a few months after Kennedy became president. Khrushchev again demanded that the US withdraw from West Berlin and set a deadline of December 1961. The US refused, and tensions grew. In July 1961, Kennedy announced his intention to increase military spending, triple the draft, and call up reserves. He stated, "We seek peace—but we shall not surrender."

Since early 1961, the East German government had been looking for a way to stop its citizens from leaving for the West. They began to secretly stockpile material to build a wall. This activity was well known, but the US and its allies were unwilling to engage in warfare over it. Although Kennedy's July speech angered Khrushchev, he was also not willing to risk a war over Berlin at that time.

On August 13, 1961, residents of Berlin awoke to find that, overnight, a barbed wire fence separating East and West Berlin had been built. It quickly grew into a concrete panel wall with guard towers and became known as the Berlin Wall. The Wall provoked instant outrage in West Berlin. To calm the anger, Vice President Lyndon B Johnson traveled to West Berlin and Kennedy sent more US troops over.

In October 1961, a military standoff at checkpoint Charlie, a diplomatic checkpoint along the Wall, led to one of the tensest moments of the Cold War up to that point. The US accused the East German government of preventing Americans from crossing to the East, leading to the US and Soviet militaries positioning tanks at Checkpoint Charlie. The tanks remained locked in a standoff at the checkpoint for eighteen hours before Kennedy and Khrushchev agreed to withdraw them. Kennedy was not happy about the Wall, but he was pragmatic, stating, "It's not a very nice solution, but a wall is a hell of a lot better than a war."

The Berlin Wall restricted movement and became a defining image of the Cold War. It stood, dividing the city, until 1989. In the Berlin Crisis, both sides faced heavy criticism and both sides claimed victory. Khrushchev's critics at home saw his actions as impulsive. This incident and the Cuban Missile Crisis were key factors in Khrushchev ultimately being forced out of power in 1964. The US faced extensive criticism from the West German government and West Berliners for its lack of action, effectively isolating West Berlin within the Soviet bloc.

The US claimed victory by maintaining control of West Berlin. The Wall offered the US a propaganda victory of sorts. Kennedy argued that if communism was so great, why would the USSR need to build a wall to prevent East Berliners from moving to the capitalist West? The USSR claimed victory because the Wall prevented the flow of migrants to the West. Moscow also saw the West's lack of response to the Wall as a further sign of weakness. Berlin was a key factor in the escalation of the Cold War during the early 1960s. The perceived weakness demonstrated by the Bay of Pigs and the lack of action in Berlin contributed to the escalation of the situation in Cuba, which resulted in the Cuban Missile Crisis.

> What does Source 4.1 tell you about why the US accepted the existence of the Berlin Wall?

SOURCE 4.1

Forces from the US army's Berlin Command face off against police from East Germany during one of several standoffs at Checkpoint Charlie in 1961

The Cuban Missile Crisis and its impact, October 1962

The Cuban Missile Crisis of October 1962 was a direct confrontation between the US and the USSR. It was the moment that the two **superpowers** came closest to nuclear conflict during the Cold War. After failing at the Bay of Pigs, the Kennedy administration launched Operation Mongoose, a covert operation planned by the CIA. It aimed to overthrow the Cuban government. Operation Mongoose armed, trained, and funded **terrorist** attacks in Cuba and planned assassination attempts against Castro.

After the Bay of Pigs invasion, the Castro government strengthened its relationship with the USSR. In late 1961, Castro asked Khrushchev for SA-2 anti-aircraft missiles, which Khrushchev initially ignored. Angry at the rejection, Castro criticized the USSR and started to speak to China about economic aid. There were also rumors of a second US invasion of Cuba. This worried Khrushchev, so in April 1962, he sent SA-2 missiles and a regiment of Soviet troops to Cuba.

The Bay of Pigs and the Berlin Crisis gave Khrushchev the impression that Kennedy was weak and indecisive. By May 1962, Khrushchev decided he needed to counter the US's growing lead in developing and deploying strategic missiles. The USSR believed that the US had "first strike" capability due to the missiles it had stationed in Turkey. The proximity of these missiles meant that, if launched, they could destroy the USSR before it had a chance to react. Khrushchev wanted to restore balance. In July 1962, Khrushchev agreed to secretly place strategic nuclear missiles in Cuba. He took this decision based on his concern over first-strike capabilities, his desire to bring West Berlin under Soviet control, and his growing worry about US efforts to overthrow the Castro government. He believed that this would establish the principle of mutual assured destruction, show the USSR's support for Cuba, and

KEY TERMS

Superpowers Extremely powerful nations able to influence events on a global scale.

Terrorism The use of violence against non-combatants to achieve political or ideological aims. It usually refers to intentional violence against civilians during peacetime or violence against civilians during war.

provide a threat or bargaining chip to force the withdrawal of the US from West Berlin. In October 1962, the crisis began when the US government saw photos of the missiles in Cuba.

From the outside, the Cuban Missile Crisis looked like a victory for the US. Khrushchev agreed to withdraw missiles from Cuba in exchange for a promise from the US not to invade the island state. In reality, after a flurry of letters between Kennedy and Khrushchev, they struck a deal that saw the US withdraw its missiles from Turkey in exchange for the removal of missiles from Cuba. However, this part of the deal was kept secret for 25 years. Publicly, the world saw Khrushchev back down in exchange for a promise from the US not to invade Cuba.

The arms race did not end with the withdrawal of missiles, but tensions between the superpowers eased. Negotiation and diplomacy had averted nuclear war and, at least publicly, Kennedy had secured a victory after the failure of the Bay of Pigs and perceived failure in Berlin. In the aftermath of the crisis, a telephone hotline was set up between Moscow and Washington to enable direct communication between leaders and help to avoid the **brinkmanship** that had led to the crisis. In July 1963, the US and the USSR agreed to the Partial Nuclear Test Ban Treaty, hoping to decrease the diplomatic tension. The treaty prohibited the testing of nuclear weapons above ground. In June 1963, Kennedy delivered a speech with a message that was very different from his inaugural address. In it, he said, "In the final analysis, our most common basic link is that we all inhabit this small planet ... and we are all mortal."

> **KEY TERM**
>
> **Brinkmanship** The policy of trying to achieve a successful or advantageous outcome by pushing dangerous situations to the brink of active conflict.

> **KEY DATES**
>
> ### Timeline of the Cuban Missile Crisis
>
> | | |
> |---|---|
> | 14 October 1962 | Photos taken by a U2 surveillance flight show missile bases under construction in Cuba. President Kennedy is informed. |
> | 16 October | Kennedy is presented with three options: negotiation, a naval quarantine of Cuba, or an airstrike. |
> | 22 October | Kennedy orders a naval quarantine of Cuba. He writes to Khrushchev demanding removal of the missiles. |
> | 23–26 October | Letters are exchanged between Khrushchev and Kennedy. Kennedy demands the removal of the missiles, Khrushchev refuses. |
> | 26 October | Khrushchev appeals to Kennedy to work together to de-escalate the situation. |
> | 27 October | Khrushchev demands withdrawal of US missiles from Turkey. Attorney General Robert Kennedy secretly agrees to this demand. |
> | 28 October | Khrushchev writes an open letter promising to remove missiles from Cuba. |

> ### ACTIVITY
>
> Examine the list of causes of the Cuban Missile Crisis below. Work in groups or pairs to explain each cause, then divide them into long-term (underlying or preconditions) and short-term (triggers) causes of the crisis and discuss the links between them.
>
> - Cuban Revolution, 1959
> - Castro's support for communism
> - Khrushchev's view of Kennedy
> - Bay of Pigs, 1961
> - Berlin Crisis, 1961
> - Nuclear competition/arms race
> - Operation Mongoose
> - Placement of Soviet missiles in Cuba
> - US blockade of Cuba

The impacts of the Vietnam War

The Vietnam War fundamentally changed the way Americans saw their country and their government. Lasting almost twenty years, Vietnam was one of the Cold War's many **proxy wars**. Proxy wars acted as theatre stages on which a greater superpower conflict was played out and Vietnam was perhaps the most significant of these conflicts.

KEY TERM

Proxy war A conflict in which one or more states directly or indirectly support other states or non-state actors to influence the outcomes of domestic conflicts and advance their own interests. Proxy wars enable major powers to avoid direct confrontation while competing for influence and resources.

Figure 4.2 Map of Vietnam, Laos, and Cambodia in 1972 showing the division between North and South Vietnam

KEY FIGURE

Ngo Dinh Diem (1901–63) Born into a prominent Catholic family, his father was a high-ranking official for the Vietnamese Emperor during the colonial era. Diem pursued a career in the civil service progressing rapidly in Emperor Bao Dai's court and becoming Interior Minister in 1933. He resigned this position after three months and denounced the Emperor as a tool of France. After several years in exile in Japan, he returned and Bao Dai appointed him Prime Minister. He deposed the Emperor in 1955 and declared himself President. In 1963, he was assassinated in a military coup and buried in an unmarked grave.

Origins of the Vietnam War and reasons for US entry into the conflict

The origins of the Vietnam War stretch back to the 1940s and 1950s when nationalist groups sought to overthrow colonial rule. Vietnam had been a colony of France from the nineteenth century until it was invaded by Japan during the Second World War. In 1941, **Ho Chi Minh** established the Viet Minh, an anti-Japanese resistance movement advocating for Vietnamese independence. After Japan's surrender in 1945, Ho Chi Minh launched a revolution and declared Vietnam an independent nation. One month later, French forces overthrew Ho Chi Minh's government and reinstated French control in Vietnam.

KEY FIGURE

Ho Chi Minh (1890–1969) Born in French Indochina (part of the French Empire; Vietnam, Laos, and Cambodia), Ho Chi Minh received a French education before working overseas. In 1920 he was a founding member of the French Communist Party before returning to Vietnam in 1941. He founded the Viet Minh and, in 1945, led the August Revolution against the Vietnamese monarchy. After Vietnam was divided, he became President of North Vietnam. He died of heart failure in Hanoi on September 2, 1969.

By 1946, the conflict between the French and the Viet Minh had become a full-scale war. In 1950, China and the USSR formally recognized Ho Chi Minh's Democratic Republic of Vietnam, based in Hanoi, as the legitimate government of the country. Soon after, the US and its allies recognized the French state, led by the former emperor, Bao Dai, and based in Saigon, as the legitimate government. In May 1954, France surrendered and, at the Geneva Conference in the same year, signed a treaty dividing Vietnam. This created two countries: North and South Vietnam. Ho Chi Minh governed the North and Emperor Bao Dai governed the South. In 1955, Bao Dai was pushed out and the strongly anti-communist **Ngo Dinh Diem** became president of South Vietnam.

> **KEY TERM**
>
> **Viet Cong** The name given initially to the opposition movements against Diem in South Vietnam. The term eventually came to refer to the armed movement across Vietnam, Laos, and Cambodia led by the National Liberation Front.

In 1955, Eisenhower promised support to South Vietnam and sent equipment, military advisers, and CIA operatives to train local forces. With this support, Diem launched a crackdown against Viet Minh supporters in the South, whom he referred to as the "Viet Cong," arresting, torturing, and executing large numbers of people. By 1957, the Viet Cong and other groups opposed to Diem's regime were fighting back and, in 1960, they formed the National Liberation Front (NLF). The US assumed that the NLF was a puppet organization of Hanoi, although the group claimed to be autonomous and many of its members were not communists.

When Kennedy took office in 1961, he sent a team to report on conditions in South Vietnam. The report advised building up US military, economic, and technical aid to help Diem fight the Viet Cong threat. Kennedy was a strong believer in domino theory and increased US aid. However, he refused to commit to a large-scale military intervention. By 1962, there were around 9,000 US military personnel in South Vietnam.

Johnson's escalation of the war, including the Gulf of Tonkin Resolution and Operation Rolling Thunder

In November 1963, Diem was overthrown and executed in a coup launched by some of his own generals. This created huge political instability in South Vietnam, as military-led governments toppled one another in quick succession. In the chaos, Hanoi increased its support for the Viet Cong guerrilla fighters. During his time as vice president, **Lyndon B Johnson** did not have much involvement with the war in Vietnam. Once Johnson took office, he immediately turned his attention to the war. Recognizing that the situation was rapidly deteriorating, he began to increase US military and economic support.

> **KEY FIGURE**
>
> **Lyndon B Johnson** (1908–73) Born in Stonewall, Texas in August 1908, Johnson worked as a high school teacher and congressional aide before being elected to the House of Representatives in 1937. He was elected as a Senator for Texas in 1949 and served in that role for twelve years before becoming Kennedy's vice president in 1961. When Kennedy was assassinated in 1963, Johnson became president and won the 1964 election by a landslide; but he served just one term, withdrawing from the 1968 primary and retiring to his ranch in Texas, where he died in January 1973 at the age of 64.

In August 1964, the USS *Maddox*, on an intelligence mission in the Gulf of Tonkin off the coast of North Vietnam, allegedly fired on some North Vietnamese torpedo boats that had been following it. Two days later, torpedo boats apparently attacked the *Maddox* and another US navy vessel, the *Turner Joy*, again. The ships fired on radar targets and claimed that they sunk two torpedo boats; however, no wreckage was ever found, and it is unclear whether any Vietnamese ships were even in the area. After this alleged second attack, the US began retaliatory airstrikes on North Vietnam and, on August 7, 1964, Congress approved the Gulf of Tonkin Resolution, granting the president power to "take all necessary measures to repel any armed attack against the forces of the United States and to prevent further aggression." Johnson relied upon this resolution for the authority to increase US involvement in Vietnam.

> **KEY TERM**
>
> **Guerrilla warfare** A form of unconventional warfare in which small groups of irregular military (such as rebels, armed civilians, paramilitaries, or militias) use ambush, terrorist, raid, and hit-and-run tactics in a war against regular military, police, or other forces. Tactics avoid head-on confrontations, typically due to inferior weapons or manpower.

US military leaders were dissatisfied with the retaliatory airstrikes following the Gulf of Tonkin incident and demanded a wider, more aggressive campaign. In February 1965, the Viet Cong attacked a US airbase in South Vietnam, and in response on March 2, 1965, the US launched a bombing campaign against North Vietnam codenamed Operation Rolling Thunder. Johnson's officials hoped to reduce North Vietnam's ability to produce and transport supplies to the Viet Cong. They believed that a heavy and sustained bombing campaign would encourage North Vietnamese leaders to accept the South Vietnamese government. Johnson also believed that the bombing campaign would boost South Vietnamese morale while destroying the communists' will to fight.

Shortly after the start of Operation Rolling Thunder, Johnson sent ground troops to Vietnam, and by July 1965 around 82,000 US troops were stationed there. As the war escalated, Johnson sent a further 100,000 troops in July 1965 and another 100,000 in 1966. Simultaneously, he expanded Operation Rolling Thunder in both range and intensity.

US bombers attacked military and industrial targets across North Vietnam with only the cities of Hanoi and Haiphong deemed off-limits for bombing raids.

Between 1965 and 1968, the ground war in South Vietnam raged. The Viet Cong fought using mostly **guerrilla** tactics. The US forces, led by General William Westmoreland, pursued a policy of attrition. The aim was to kill as many enemy troops as possible. By 1966, large portions of South Vietnam had been declared "free-fire zones." This meant, in theory, that all civilians had been evacuated from these areas and only enemies remained. These areas remained uninhabitable due to heavy bombing and shelling by US forces. Throughout this period, North Vietnam delivered manpower and supplies to the Viet Cong via the "Ho Chi Minh Trail," a military supply route that ran from North Vietnam through Laos and Cambodia to South Vietnam.

> What does Source 4.2 tell us about why Congress passed the Gulf of Tonkin Resolution?

SOURCE 4.2

Extract from the Gulf of Tonkin Resolution, August 7, 1964

To promote the maintenance of international peace and security in southeast Asia.

Whereas naval units of the Communist regime in Vietnam, in violation of the principles of the Charter of the United Nations and of international law, have deliberately and repeatedly attacked United States naval vessels lawfully present in international waters, and have thereby created a serious threat to international peace; and

Whereas these attackers are part of a deliberate and systematic campaign of aggression that the Communist regime in North Vietnam has been waging against its neighbors and the nations joined with them in the collective defense of their freedom; and

Whereas the United States is assisting the peoples of southeast Asia to protect their freedom and has no territorial, military or political ambitions in that area, but desires only that these people should be left in peace to work out their destinies in their own way: Now, therefore be it

Resolved by the Senate and House of Representatives of the United States of America in Congress assembled, That the Congress approves and supports the determination of the President, as Commander in Chief, to take all necessary measures to repel any armed attack against the forces of the United States and to prevent further aggression.

Impact of the Tet Offensive on US strategy and on US public opinion

In January 1968, North Vietnamese and Viet Cong forces launched coordinated attacks on targets across South Vietnam. They believed successful attacks on major cities might force the US to negotiate or withdraw. The attacks took place over the Vietnamese Lunar New Year festival known as Tet, which is traditionally a time of truce, and consequently became known as the Tet Offensive. The US and South Vietnamese militaries initially sustained heavy casualties and, while they eventually repelled Viet Cong forces, attacks on major cities had a profound psychological impact. The Tet Offensive proved that the Viet Cong were not as weak as the US had claimed.

At the end of the Offensive, both sides declared victory. The Tet Offensive was a key turning point in domestic US attitudes toward the Vietnam War. Johnson was rapidly losing popularity and extensive news reporting of the Tet Offensive seemed to prove to Americans that, despite what their government said, victory in the war was not imminent. News broadcasting of the Tet Offensive gave the US public cause to challenge not only US involvement in the war, but also the conduct of US soldiers. Incidents such as the massacre at the village of My Lai in 1968, in which US soldiers killed around 300 civilians including children, severely tarnished American domestic opinions of the war. Public figures began to speak out against the war. In the aftermath of the Offensive, the CBS News anchor Walter Cronkite pleaded on air for a negotiated settlement.

As a result of his declining popularity and the souring of US attitudes to the war in an election year, Johnson halted the bombing campaigns in North Vietnam and promised to spend the rest of his term seeking peace in Vietnam. On March 31, 1968, Johnson told the nation that he would not be seeking reelection and called for peace talks.

> What does Walter Cronkite's broadcast suggest about how domestic US attitudes to the Vietnam War had changed following the Tet Offensive?

SOURCE 4.3

Excerpt from Walter Cronkite's CBS evening news broadcast on February 27, 1968

To say that we are closer to victory today is to believe, in the face of the evidence, the optimists who have been wrong in the past. To suggest we are on the edge of defeat is to yield to unreasonable pessimism. To say that we are mired in stalemate seems the only realistic, yet unsatisfactory, conclusion. On the off chance that military and political analysts are right, in the next few months we must test the enemy's intentions, in case this is indeed his last big gasp before negotiations. But it is increasingly clear to this reporter that the only rational way out then will be to negotiate, not as victors, but as an honorable people who lived up to their pledge to defend democracy, and did the best they could.

> What does this picture tell us about the importance of news media in the Vietnam War?

SOURCE 4.4

CBS anchor Walter Cronkite conducts an interview with an American officer during the Tet Offensive, February 1968

Nixon's "Vietnamization"

In 1968, **Richard Nixon**, the Republican candidate, won the presidential election. When he took office in January 1969, he knew that honorably ending the Vietnam War was key for him to be successful as President. To this end, Nixon and his advisors developed the policy of "Vietnamization."

Vietnamization was a program to equip, train, and develop the South Vietnamese military and gradually hand over combat roles to them while the US withdrew its troops. In June 1969, Nixon announced the first withdrawal of US troops. These withdrawals were accompanied by an increase in bombing of North Vietnamese bases and, in 1970, Nixon secretly authorized the bombing of supply lines in Cambodia.

Simultaneously, the US was engaged in peace talks to end the war. Alongside the increased bombing of North Vietnam and neighboring nations, Nixon offered conciliatory terms in negotiations and put diplomatic pressure on the USSR to encourage their North Vietnamese allies to agree to terms. It soon became clear that these talks, which were public, served as propaganda theatre for both sides. As a result, the US began to hold private talks with the North Vietnamese leadership alongside the public negotiations. Throughout this period North Vietnamese forces launched several offensives into South Vietnam to test Nixon's resolve and cast doubt on the Vietnamization program. These offensives often demonstrated that the South Vietnamese troops were still heavily reliant on US air power.

KEY FIGURE

Richard M Nixon (1913–94) Born to a Quaker family in Southern California, Nixon graduated from Duke Law School in 1937 and practiced law before being elected to the House of Representatives in 1946. He served as a Senator for California and as Eisenhower's vice president. Nixon first ran for president in 1960, narrowly losing to Kennedy. After losing an election to be Governor of California and announcing his political retirement, he decided to run for president once more in 1968. He won the election and served as president until resigning in 1974 over the Watergate Scandal. He died in April 1994.

Paris Peace Accords (January 1973) and the outcome of the Vietnam War

The private and public negotiations between the US and North Vietnam continued until January 1973, when a peace agreement was reached. The Paris Peace Accords required the US to withdraw its remaining troops from Vietnam within 60 days in exchange for an immediate ceasefire, the return of US prisoners of war, and North Vietnamese recognition of the South Vietnamese government.

The Paris Peace Accords effectively removed the US from the situation in Vietnam, but the war continued. The agreement was largely ignored by both the North and South Vietnamese governments and North Vietnam expanded into the South steadily throughout 1973. Nixon had secretly promised the South Vietnamese leadership to support them with US airpower, but in August 1973, Congress passed an amendment forbidding further US military involvement in the region without congressional approval. In 1975, North Vietnam launched its final offensive. Congress refused to provide military assistance for South Vietnam and, in April 1975, Saigon was conquered by North Vietnamese troops as the US rapidly evacuated its remaining personnel.

The Vietnam War changed the way the US saw itself both militarily and morally. Public anger at the Vietnam War led to Congress replacing the military draft with an all-volunteer force and restricting the president's ability to send troops into combat without congressional approval. Johnson's escalation of the war caused a split within the Democratic Party. The difference between the government message that victory was imminent and the footage being broadcast into American homes by the news caused many Americans to lose trust in their government.

The failure to achieve outright victory, alongside the high number of deaths and visibility of atrocities, left the American public and politicians with a very low desire for military intervention abroad. This aversion to military involvement overseas became known as "Vietnam Syndrome." US military morale was significantly undermined and the Vietnam War was a key factor in Nixon's drive for *détente* with the USSR in the 1970s.

ACTIVITY

"The Tet Offensive was the main reason US public opinion turned against Vietnam."

Working in pairs, look through the previous and following sections and find points that support and challenge this view.

In the first column, write down evidence that you can find which shows that the Tet Offensive damaged US public opinion and why.

In the second column, record evidence which shows that other factors were to blame for US public opinion turning against the war.

The Tet Offensive was the main reason	The Tet Offensive was not the main reason

Discuss which of the points for and against are the most important and why.

Role of *détente*

In the 1970s, the US tried to improve relations with both the USSR and China through a policy approach known as *détente*. During this period, the superpowers signed treaties limiting nuclear weapons, and promoting peaceful settlement of disputes, scientific cooperation, and human rights. For a while, the Cold War looked to be de-escalating and relations between the US and the USSR improved.

> **KEY TERM**
>
> **Sino** A prefix used to indicate something related to China.

Reasons for seeking *détente* under Nixon

After the Cuban Missile Crisis, the US and the USSR recognized how close the world had come to nuclear conflict. The Test Ban Treaty of 1963 was a tentative step toward acknowledging the dangers nuclear weapons posed. Negotiations took place intermittently between 1963 and the formal beginning of *détente* in 1972. The main reasons for seeking *détente* related to fear of nuclear war, domestic factors, economic factors, and **Sino**-Soviet relations.

Fear of nuclear war

The Cuban Missile Crisis caused paranoia and fear among the public in the USSR and the US. In the period after the crisis, the superpowers came under international pressure to reduce their stockpiles of nuclear weapons. There was also growing pressure from groups such as the Campaign for Nuclear Disarmament (formed in 1957) and Greenpeace (formed in 1971). This led to the superpowers and Great Britain signing the Non-Proliferation Treaty in 1968, which limited the spread of nuclear weapons while working toward disarmament.

Domestic factors

In the early 1970s, both superpowers were tackling challenges at home that drew their attention away from foreign policy. Widespread opposition to the Vietnam War limited the president's ability to engage in military conflict elsewhere. In 1972, the Watergate Scandal (page 220) began, and Nixon became preoccupied with this until his resignation in 1974. In the USSR, falling crop yields, internal opposition, and discontent within the wider Soviet bloc resulted in a rollback of Khrushchev's liberal reforms, the empowerment of the KGB (Soviet secret police), and a tightening of censorship.

Economic factors

The arms and space races were expensive endeavors for both superpowers. The US had significantly increased its national deficit through its involvement with the Vietnam War and an oil embargo in 1973 led to disruption of oil supply, increased fuel prices, and a stock market slump. The Soviet economy, which had grown rapidly in the 1950s and 1960s, began to stall, leading to increased food prices. The cost of propping up communist regimes with military intervention was also becoming a significant economic burden for the USSR. These issues meant that continuing the arms race at the same intensity was economically unsustainable for both sides.

Sino-Soviet relations

In the early years of the Cold War, the USSR and China enjoyed good relations. **Chairman Mao**, the leader of China, had a good relationship with Stalin but disagreeed with both Khrushchev and his successor, Leonid Brezhnev. In 1969, this came to a head with border clashes between Soviet and Chinese soldiers. Nixon saw the potential benefits of widening this split and began to establish relations with China with the aim of making the USSR worry that China would turn against them.

> **KEY FIGURE**
>
> **Mao Zedong** (1893–1976) Born to a peasant family in Hunan, China, Mao adopted Marxism while working as a librarian in the University of Peking. In 1921 he was a founding member of the Chinese Communist Party (CCP). He became the leader of the CCP in 1935 and, in 1949 after China's civil war, he proclaimed the founding of the People's Republic of China, a one-party state controlled by the CCP. Despite increasing ill health, he ruled China until his death at the age of 82 on September 9, 1976.

Nixon and *détente* policies in China and the USSR

Nixon believed the deterioration of Chinese-Soviet relations presented an opportunity. Nixon wanted the USSR to worry about a US-Chinese alliance against them. In 1967, Nixon signaled his interest in opening relations with China in an article entitled "Asia after Vietnam" published in the journal *Foreign Affairs*. This article suggested that the US could begin a new relationship with China and begin to withdraw from Vietnam. Once Nixon became president in 1969, he set both of these policies in motion.

In the early 1970s, Henry Kissinger, Nixon's National Security Advisor, began secret talks with Beijing. While he was on a visit to Pakistan in 1971, he secretly traveled to Beijing to meet with representatives from the Chinese government. During this meeting, he secured an invitation for Nixon to visit China. While there were significant challenges to the US-Chinese relationship, most notably the questions of Vietnam and Taiwan, in June 1971,

Nixon surprised the world by announcing that he would travel to China and meet with Chairman Mao.

The visit went ahead in February 1972. Nixon and Mao undertook a series of talks which resulted in the Shanghai Communiqué. This was a joint statement in which both nations pledged to work toward full normalization of diplomatic relations. The Communiqué also committed the Nixon administration to ending its official recognition of the Taiwanese government and withdrawing its troops from the island. While this concerned the Taiwanese government, the Communiqué was a key step on the road to the normalization of relations with China, which was finally completed in 1979.

Nixon's visit to China sparked an almost immediate improvement in US relations with the USSR. In May 1972, Nixon made a state visit to Moscow to meet Brezhnev. On this visit, they undertook extensive meetings, signing trade agreements and two treaties to reduce arms manufacturing: the Strategic Arms Limitation Treaty (SALT I) and an Anti-Ballistic Missiles Treaty.

> What impact do you think Source 4.5 would have had on US-Soviet relations and why?

SOURCE 4.5

President Nixon shakes hands with Chairman Mao during his visit to China in 1972. This photo appeared on the front page of a Chinese newspaper

SALT, May 1972 and SALT II, June 1979

The SALT talks began in 1967 after President Johnson announced that the USSR was building an anti-ballistic missile (ABM) defense system around Moscow. An ABM system challenged the mutual assured destruction principle, as it would allow one side to launch a first strike while preventing the other from retaliating. The SALT talks aimed to take control of the ABM race.

Nixon believed in the aims of the SALT talks and negotiations continued after he was elected. Over the next two-and-a-half years the sides argued and haggled. Finally, in May 1972, SALT I was signed. In the Treaty, both sides agreed to limit the number of nuclear weapons in their arsenals, limit the number of deployment sites protected by an ABM system, respect principles of non-interference, and promote economic, scientific, and cultural ties.

> **KEY TERMS**
>
> **MIRV systems** A type of ballistic missile containing several warheads, each of which can be aimed to hit a different target.
>
> **Intercontinental ballistic missile (ICBM)** A ballistic missile with a range greater than 3,400 miles, primarily for nuclear weapons delivery.

Soon after the signing of SALT I, negotiations began for SALT II. SALT I left several questions unanswered, and these became the focus of talks for SALT II. SALT II talks reached an interim agreement in 1974, which included limits on strategic nuclear delivery vehicles, limits on Multiple Independently Targeted Re-entry Vehicle (MIRV) systems, a ban on new land-based intercontinental ballistic missile launchers, and limits on deployment of new types of strategic offensive weapons. Despite these agreements, there were still two outstanding issues from SALT I: the number of strategic bombers and the total number of warheads in each arsenal. After another five years of talks, the parties reached an agreement on these issues and SALT II was signed on June 17, 1979. However, due to suspicion of the USSR's crackdown on dissent and the Soviet invasion of Afghanistan in December 1979, the US Congress never ratified SALT II.

Helsinki Agreement

The Helsinki Conference had initially been suggested by the USSR in 1954, but it wasn't until the shift toward *détente* that Western leaders were prepared to consider participating. The Conference on Security and Cooperation in Europe (as it was officially called) began in July 1973. Intensive negotiations took place from 1973 to 1975. In August 1975, participants met again for the final time in Helsinki to sign the Helsinki Agreement.

The Agreement was far-reaching and dealt with a variety of issues which were divided into four broad chapters.

Political and military

This chapter set out ten principles to which participants should adhere, including territorial integrity, the definition of borders, peaceful settlement of disputes, and the implementation of confidence-building measures between opposing militaries. It also highlighted the link between international security and human rights.

Economic

This chapter focused on the rising need for economic, scientific, and environmental cooperation. It aimed to facilitate a move toward market economies, lessen economic disparities between participating nations, and combat economic and environmental threats to security.

Human rights

This chapter identified the protection of human rights and fundamental freedoms as one of the basic purposes of government. It also affirmed that recognition of these rights and freedoms constitutes the basis of freedom, justice, and peace.

Implementation

The final section highlighted the importance of the signatories developing a schedule to meet and maintain the Conference proceedings.

The Helsinki Agreement was initially unpopular in the West, but it served as an important turning point in the Cold War. It was regularly cited by dissidents in the Soviet bloc, particularly the third section on human rights, as a means of criticizing Soviet governments. The regular schedule of follow-up meetings also led to greater cooperation between Eastern and Western Europe.

> **KEY TERM**
>
> **Mujahideen** In this book, "mujahideen" refers to the Islamic guerrilla movement against the communist government of Afghanistan in the late 1970s. The term has referred to many different groups throughout history and is still in use today.

US reaction to the Soviet invasion of Afghanistan, December 1979

In December 1979, the USSR sent troops into Afghanistan. Following a coup in 1978, Afghanistan was led by a communist government. Most Afghans rejected this regime as its atheism was at odds with the strong Islamic majority in the country. The communist government imprisoned, tortured, and killed religious leaders, sparking insurgencies across the country carried out by religious and tribal groups known collectively as the Mujahideen.

After a power struggle, Hafizullah Amin became head of the communist regime. Under his leadership, the insurgency worsened. On December 24, 1979, the USSR invaded, killing Amin and replacing him with a pro-Moscow leader. Over the coming ten years, the USSR poured billions of dollars into the war in Afghanistan, which quickly settled into a stalemate with Soviet troops controlling most urban centers and the Mujahideen having free rein in the countryside.

The invasion prompted the end of *détente*. President **Jimmy Carter** immediately recalled the US Ambassador to the Soviet Union, asked Congress not to approve the SALT II treaty, and began to support the Mujahideen. The US halted key exports to the USSR, including grain and new technologies, and boycotted the 1980 Moscow Olympics. Carter announced that the US was prepared to use force to stop any country from gaining control of the oil-rich Middle East and the policy of containment was expanded to this region.

KEY FIGURE

Jimmy Carter (1924–2024) Born in Plains, Georgia, Carter's support for the Civil Rights Movement led him to join the Democratic Party and, in 1963, he was elected to the Georgia State Senate. After serving as Governor of Georgia from 1971 to 1975, Carter won the Democratic nomination and narrowly defeated Gerald Ford in the 1976 election to become president. He lost the 1980 election and went on to establish the Carter Center to promote and expand human rights, for which he won the Nobel Peace Prize in 2002.

In 1980, Carter lost the presidency to Ronald Reagan. Reagan was much more opposed to communism than Carter. He fully abandoned *détente* and the containment policies that had defined so much of American Cold War policy.

▶ SUMMARY DIAGRAM

US approaches to the Cold War, 1961–79
Why and how did US approaches to the Cold War change between 1961 and 1979?

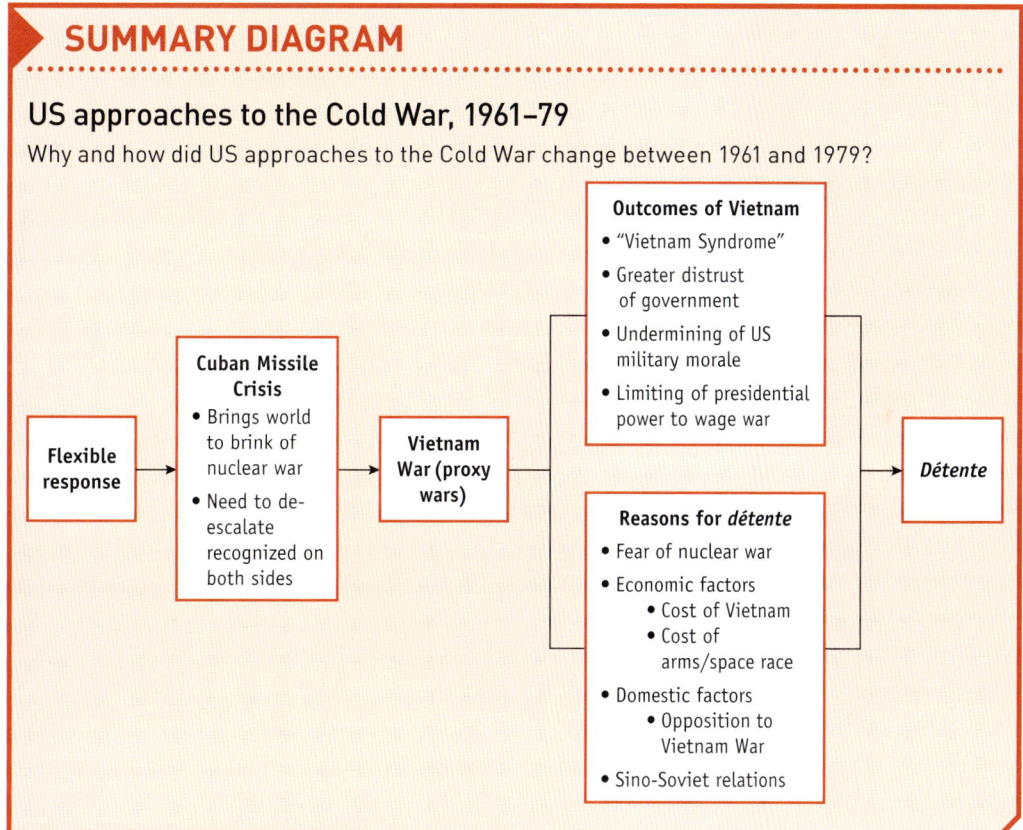

ACTIVITY

What were the main causes of *détente*? Which do you think was the most important reason?

In pairs or groups, create a presentation as an overview of this section. What changed in US foreign policy between 1961 and 1979 and what stayed the same?

The Development of the US in the 1960s and 1970s

4.2 Why and how did politics in the US evolve between 1960 and 1979?

The 1960s saw a socially progressive, increasingly popular left wing; counterculture movements grew, and student movements became influential in mainstream politics. By the late 1960s, anti-war protest was splitting the Democratic Party and fueling support for the right which resulted in Nixon's election in 1968. Conservative policies and ideas gained further traction under Jimmy Carter's troubled presidency, culminating in the election of Ronald Reagan in 1980.

Changing domestic policies of the presidents from 1960 to 1979

The Kennedy and Johnson administrations embarked on a war on poverty and made large advances in civil rights. However, economic challenges, including high inflation and high unemployment, plagued their administrations. In response, Nixon focused on lowering inflation and unemployment and protecting the dollar from international interference. However, his policies caused an increasingly difficult economic climate for the **Ford** and Carter administrations.

Kennedy's "New Frontier"

Kennedy's "New Frontier" was a package of policies for reform and change. He intended for the New Frontier to be a grand, far-reaching plan that encouraged Americans to be optimistic about the future and tackled poverty, inequality, and injustice. Despite a Democratic majority in Congress, opposition from many Southern Democrats prevented Kennedy from achieving many of his aims before his assassination. The New Frontier did however manage to make some progress in the realms of poverty, healthcare, and education.

Poverty

Kennedy had some successes in alleviating poverty. Some of these successful policies included:
- increasing minimum wage from $1 per hour to $1.25 per hour
- increasing social security benefits to provide more support to older and unemployed people
- passing a housing act that enabled people in economically deprived areas to access loans for home improvements
- creating a pilot "food stamp" program for Americans in poverty
- making funds available to businesses to buy new technologies and train their workforces.

Success in this area was limited and often did not go far enough, and policies faced congressional opposition. Congress opposed a tax cut designed to stimulate economic growth, and the Housing Act was limited and did not account for the fact that those in poverty could not afford to repay the loans.

Healthcare

Kennedy made mental health a priority of his healthcare policy. He provided federal funding for community mental health centers and research facilities. This was a great success, rapidly increasing the number of Americans making use of mental health centers. Kennedy also established federal grants for health services for migrant workers, provided for the vaccination of millions of children and improved prenatal care for women from low-income families. In 1961, he began to look at proposals for providing free healthcare for people over 65. This proposal was blocked by Congress and did not pass under Kennedy's administration.

KEY FIGURE

Gerald Ford (1913–2006) Born in Nebraska, Ford began his political career as a congressman representing Michigan. He served in this role for 25 years. When Nixon's vice president resigned in 1973, Ford became vice president under the 25th Amendment's rules of succession. He became president following Nixon's resignation in 1974. Ford lost the 1976 election but stayed active in the Republican Party, although his moderate views increasingly put him at odds with the party. He died in 2006, aged 93.

Education

Around one-third of all major New Frontier programs had some form of education policy within them. The New Frontier increased funding for libraries, school lunches, provisions for teaching disabled and gifted children, and vocational education. Measures were also introduced to aid educational television, medical education, and community libraries. Kennedy established the Peace Corps, an organization that sent volunteers to less economically developed countries. Volunteers worked as teachers, doctors, nurses, and technical advisors. The program was incredibly popular with young Americans.

Johnson's "Great Society"

After Kennedy's assassination, Americans felt great empathy for Johnson and the tragic circumstances of his presidency. Johnson was an incredibly astute political operator and took advantage of this sympathy to push through several key elements of Kennedy's legislative agenda. He was committed to continuing and expanding the progressive work Kennedy started, aiming to create a "Great Society" to end poverty and racial injustice in America. In the end, Johnson's legacy was overshadowed by the Vietnam War, but he succeeded in pushing through some key policies to make the US a fairer and more equal place.

The war on poverty

In 1964, Johnson called for a "war on poverty" and, after winning the 1964 election with a substantial mandate, he appropriated $1 billion for that purpose with a further $2 billion spent by 1966. The war on poverty was extensive. Some of its key programs were as follows:
- The Job Corps provided work and training to young people.
- The Neighborhood Youth Corps provided work and training specifically to young people from impoverished urban neighborhoods.
- Volunteers in Service to America (VISTA) was a domestic version of the Peace Corps.
- The Model Cities Program provided funding for urban redevelopment.
- Upward Bound assisted poor students to go to college.
- The Food Stamp Act expanded the federal food stamp program.

Perhaps the most controversial aspect of the war on poverty was the Community Action Agencies. Johnson believed that the key to uplifting impoverished Americans was to involve poor and marginalized citizens in the administration of poverty programs. This was known as "maximum feasible participation." Depending heavily on volunteers, Community Action Agencies (CAAs) operated a variety of grants from federal, state, and local sources. The boards of CAAs were initially composed mostly of members of the community they served. Many of the Agencies faced significant challenges. Local political authorities sometimes felt threatened by the empowerment of residents and these power struggles eventually caused the decline of citizen participation. A congressional amendment gave two-thirds of seats on Agency boards to elected city officials and private sector representatives instead of local citizens, effectively ending community control of CAAs.

Healthcare

Perhaps the two most significant policies of the Great Society were Medicaid and Medicare. Medicare provided federal funding for the medical costs of older Americans. Although the American Medical Association opposed it, Medicare was passed in the Social Security Act of 1965. The same Act created Medicaid, a health insurance program for those on limited incomes. Both Medicaid and Medicare continue to operate today.

Education

To ensure that every child had a chance of succeeding in life, Johnson launched Head Start. The Head Start program initially provided eight-week summer camps for children aged three to five. By 1966, it grew into a year-round child development program to help communities meet the needs of disadvantaged preschoolers.

Perhaps the most important piece of education legislation was the Elementary and Secondary Education Act. This guaranteed federal funding for education in school districts where most students were from low-income families. It also funded preschool programs, school libraries support for disabled students, and textbooks and materials for schools.

Environment

To combat worsening water pollution, Johnson signed the Water Quality Act in 1965 to set national water quality standards. The administration also passed the Motor Vehicle Air Pollution Control Act, forming the first vehicle emissions standards. Laws were also passed to protect wildlife and rivers, and to form a network of trails between historic landmarks.

Not all Americans were happy with the New Frontier and the Great Society. Conservatives resented what they saw as government handouts and believed that the government was overstepping its bounds. Republicans made major gains in the 1966 mid-term elections by challenging the war on poverty. Despite this and a lot of opposition in Congress, Johnson managed to pass 226 out of the 252 major legislative requests he made during his presidency.

> What does this source tell you about Johnson's intentions for the Great Society and his presidency?

SOURCE 4.6

An extract from Johnson's remarks at the University of Michigan announcing the Great Society

"…For in your time we have the opportunity to move not only toward the rich society and the powerful society, but upward to the Great Society.

The Great Society rests on abundance and liberty for all. It demands an end to poverty and racial injustice, to which we are totally committed in our time. But that is just the beginning.

The Great Society is a place where every child can find knowledge to enrich his mind and to enlarge his talents. It is a place where leisure is a welcome chance to build and reflect, not a feared cause of boredom and restlessness. It is a place where the city of man serves not only the needs of the body and the demands of commerce but the desire for beauty and the hunger for community.

It is a place where man can renew contact with nature. It is a place which honors creation for its own sake and for what it adds to the understanding of the race. It is a place where men are more concerned with the quality of their goals than the quantity of their goods.

But most of all, the Great Society is not a safe harbor, a resting place, a final objective, a finished work. It is a challenge constantly renewed, beckoning us toward a destiny where the meaning of our lives matches the marvelous products of our labor…"

ACTIVITY

Match this list of Great Society policies with the correct description.

Policies
- Volunteers in Service to America
- Upward Bound
- Food Stamp Act
- Community Action Agencies
- Water Quality Act
- Elementary and Secondary Education Act
- Social Security Act of 1965

Descriptions
- created Medicare and Medicaid
- assisted poor students to attend college
- set national water quality standards
- established a domestic version of the Peace Corps
- expanded federal food stamp program
- operated grants for local communities through community participation
- guaranteed federal funding for education in low-income school districts

Nixon's "New Economic Policy" and Southern Strategy

When Nixon took office, his primary domestic interest was the economy. In an address to the nation in 1971, Nixon said, "The time has come for a new economic policy ... it targets unemployment, inflation, and international speculation."

At the time of this speech, the unemployment rate in America was around six percent and the inflation rate was just under six percent. Nixon's response to these challenges centered on three key actions:
- suspending the convertibility of the dollar to gold and stopping foreign governments from exchanging their dollars for gold
- imposing a 90-day freeze on wages and prices to counter inflation
- imposing a ten-percent import surcharge to ensure that US products would not be disadvantaged by changes in exchange rates.

This was the first time since the Second World War that the US government enacted wage and price controls. The import surcharge was dropped within three months as part of a wider reevaluation of key international currencies. In March 1973, the fixed exchange rate system was replaced by a **floating exchange rate system**. Under this system, the value of the dollar fell by a third during the 1970s. Politically, and in public opinion, Nixon's policies were successful. However, they unleashed huge speculation against the dollar, leading to greater inflation and worsening the economic picture overall.

The rapid progress made by the Civil Rights Movement in the 1950s and early 1960s had caused a great deal of disquiet among white conservative voters in the South. The rise of the Black Power Movement (see page 230), anti-Vietnam protests, and the growing visibility of countercultures and drug-taking scandalized many Americans.

To appeal to these voters, Nixon ran his 1968 campaign on states' rights and law and order. This was widely understood to symbolize objections to civil rights progress. For the midterms and 1972 elections, the so-called "Southern Strategy" involved painting Democratic candidates as permissive liberals. In 1972, Nixon won 79 percent of the white Southern vote. He was the first Republican presidential candidate to win the entirety of the South. In recent years, historians have come to question the concept of a "Southern Strategy," suggesting that the strategy is perhaps more accurately described as a "suburban strategy."

> **KEY TERM**
>
> **Floating exchange rate system** A type of exchange rate system in which a currency's value is allowed to change in response to the foreign exchange markets. In the modern world, most currencies are floating.

> **KEY DEBATE**
>
> **WAS THERE A "SOUTHERN STRATEGY"?**
>
> Scholarship on the Southern Strategy has typically emphasized the role of racial backlash in the realignment of Southern voters. However, some argue that racial issues took a back seat to demographic change. This argument suggests that the "Southern Strategy" model does not account for the fact that Nixon won 49 of 50 states in 1972, postulating that he operated a successful national rather than regional strategy, as well as the fact that the Republican Party remained relatively weak at local and state level across the South for decades. This argument suggests there was more of a "suburban strategy" rather than a "Southern Strategy," appealing to disaffected white voters across the country, not just in the South.

Economic challenges under Ford and Carter

Nixon's economic policies failed to decrease inflation or unemployment. In fact, the devaluing of the dollar only worsened inflation. After Gerald Ford took office, he made a speech to Congress offering a solution known as "Whip Inflation Now" or "WIN."

The WIN program called on businesses to maintain or cut prices and on citizens to spend less and save energy. Ford put in place a temporary five percent tax surcharge on corporations and high-income individuals. In response to rising oil prices, he set a goal of reducing oil imports by one million barrels a day. Policymakers and economists had doubts about Ford's plan. They did not think there was any traction in asking small business owners, who operated on tight margins and had no control over the prices charged by their suppliers,

KEY TERMS

Stagflation A set of economic circumstances in which the inflation rate is high or increasing, economic growth is slow or slowing, and unemployment is steadily high. Stagflation is a challenge for policymakers, as traditional measures for reducing inflation can also increase unemployment.

Tax credits The benefit granted to some taxpayers allowing them to claim on their tax return to reduce the total amount of tax owed to the state.

to voluntarily forego price increases. The critics were correct. WIN was not able to reduce inflation and the policy soon became the subject of many jokes among Americans. In 1975, the program was scrapped.

By 1977, Jimmy Carter inherited a very troubled economy. Inflation remained high and the economy was in recession—a situation known as "**stagflation**." Carter announced that his primary domestic goal was job creation. He passed an Economic Stimulus Appropriations Act, which provided tax reductions to low- and middle-income workers, expanded the number of jobs in the public sector, and launched a public works program. The program lasted a year and helped to create 9.3 million jobs. However, it also created another spike in inflation which made the challenges of stagflation worse.

The 1970s also saw a significant oil crisis. Since 1973, the Organization of Petroleum Exporting Countries (OPEC), the association of oil-exporting nations in the Middle East, had reduced oil output. This sparked a period of very high oil prices which forced higher prices, slowed the US economy and caused energy shortages through 1977. When Carter took office, he developed a plan to address the energy crisis. He provided **tax credits** for energy conservation, taxed domestic oil production and gasoline consumption, and mandated conversions from oil and natural gas to coal power.

In 1979, the US faced another energy shortage, causing queues at gas stations and frustrating motorists across the country. Carter asked Congress to deregulate the price of oil and imposed a windfall tax on profits for energy companies which would return around half of the new profits from deregulation to the US government. Carter's policies contributed to a decrease in per capita energy consumption and cut oil imports by half from 1979 to 1983.

ACTIVITY

In groups or pairs, make a list of the economic challenges facing the US between 1970 and 1979. Consider how these challenges affected US politics in this period. Select one economic challenge and make a presentation explaining the issue and how it impacted US politics in this period.

What does Source 4.6 tell us about the likely impact of the energy shortage on Carter's popularity?

SOURCE 4.7

Photograph showing long lines of cars at a gas station waiting for fuel, June 15, 1979

Evolution of the political spectrum in the mid-twentieth century

The start of the 1960s saw growing left-wing movement in the US. Progressive governments, coupled with the rise of student organizing, led to a political focus on social injustice. By the end of the 1960s, however, the influence of student groups and growing discontent over Vietnam had led to significant divisions within the Democratic Party.

Rise of the "New Left"

The New Left was a broad political movement that emerged from the countercultures of the 1960s. The New Left was a global phenomenon. In the US, it grew out of socialist student activism and intersected with, and was inspired by, the Civil Rights Movement. As the war in Vietnam escalated, opposition to the war became one of the major focuses of the movement.

The movement reached its peak in 1968 when a wave of radical protest swept across the world. From protests at the Democratic Convention in Chicago and anti-Vietnam protests in London to student action against the authoritarian government in Mexico, workers, students and disadvantaged people across the world took to the streets in 1968. Even the Soviet bloc saw student protests in Poland, Czechoslovakia, and Moscow. These protests had various aims in their domestic contexts, but many in the US, Canada, Japan, and Western Europe focused on opposition to Vietnam. Across the Global South, anti-authoritarianism and the challenges of poverty and inequality were also common themes.

The New Left splintered and declined after the protests of 1968, many of which were met with violence by governments, but key lines of continuity remained between the New Left and new social movements that came into focus in the 1970s, such as environmentalism.

Role of student organizations in perpetuating ideals

The 1960s saw an explosion in the number of young people attending university. There were two main reasons for this. First, this was the "baby boom" generation. There were simply more young people than in the previous generation. Second, the post-war economic boom meant more young people of this generation had privileges their parents did not, including access to university education.

The sudden mass of students descending on universities changed the institutions themselves. They became larger, more institutional, and more bureaucratic. They often had insufficient facilities for the number of students, which led to many students living off campus. These student communities were often in inner cities, sometimes living on the edge of inner-city ghettos. This shed a stark light for many students on the difference between the way they had been raised (often in affluent neighborhoods and suburbs), and the realities of life for many Americans. The realization that what they took for granted was denied to others led many to a greater interest in fixing social injustices.

> **KEY TERM**
>
> **Participatory democracy**
> A form of government in which citizens participate individually and directly in political decisions and policies that impact their lives. It is an alternative to representative democracy (the form practiced in most Western countries), in which decisions are made by elected representatives on behalf of citizens.

The main organization of the New Left in the US was the Students for a Democratic Society (SDS). Founded in 1959, the SDS published its political manifesto, known as the Port Huron Statement, in 1962. The Port Huron Statement set out a vision of **participatory democracy** based on non-violent civil disobedience. It outlined racial issues and Cold War-induced alienation as the major problems for the US and demanded reform of the Democratic Party, calling for Democratic liberals to support Southern voter registration and African American political candidates. The Statement set out a divide between this movement and the parts of the left that had developed strong anti-communist attitudes after the McCarthy hearings. The SDS rejected the hardline anti-communist attitude to foreign policy.

The Port Huron Statement issued a call to action which became a key part of the discussion around anti-war activism and college campus activism. Perhaps most importantly, it also informed the conversations being had within the Democratic Party which went on to create the Great Society.

> What does Source 4.7 tell you about what the SDS saw as the main problems in US society?

SOURCE 4.8

Extracts from the Port Huron Statement, 1962

First, the permeating and victimizing fact of human degradation, symbolized by the Southern struggle against racial bigotry, compelled most of us from silence to activism …

We would replace power rooted in possession, privilege, or circumstance by power and uniqueness rooted in love, reflectiveness, reason, and creativity. As a social system we seek the establishment of a democracy of individual participation, governed by two central aims: that the individual share in those social decisions determining the quality and direction of his life; that society be organized to encourage independence in men and provide the media for their common participation …

In such a setting of status quo politics, where most if not all government activity is rationalized in Cold War anti-communist terms, it is somewhat natural that discontented, super-patriotic groups would emerge through political channels and explain their ultra-conservatism as the best means of Victory over Communism … But actually "anti-communism" becomes an umbrella by which to protest liberalism, internationalism, welfarism, and the active civil rights and labor movements. It is to the disgrace of the United States that such a movement should become a prominent kind of public participation in the modern world.

Divisions within the Democratic Party

Kennedy and Johnson's push for progress on civil rights combined with the escalation of the Vietnam War continued to cause significant divisions within the Democratic Party during this period. The pursuit of civil rights legislation split the Party largely along regional lines, with Southern Democrats often opposing civil rights legislation. Most famously, this came to a head in 1964 when Southern Democratic (and some Republican) senators conducted a record-setting, if ultimately failed, **filibuster** to try to stop the passage of the Civil Rights Act.

> **KEY TERM**
>
> **Filibuster** A political tactic in which members of a legislative body exploit the rules of a debate to delay or prevent a decision or vote being taken on legislation, typically by speaking for as long as the rules allow.

> **KEY TERM**
>
> **Blue-collar** Used to describe jobs involving manual labour and working with tools or hands, and the workers who do these jobs. White-collar typically refers to office, administrative, and managerial roles.

The division over civil rights caused turmoil within the Party; however, it was the Vietnam War that caused the greatest conflict. The Vietnam War was unpopular from the start among counterculture and pacifist groups. In the mid-1960s, a sense that the draft unfairly targeted and drew from minority and lower- and middle-class communities grew. This alienated many **blue-collar** Democrats who became opposed to conscription. As Americans saw footage, images, and increasing numbers of returning casualties, opposition to the war increased among other groups.

The split in the Democratic Party over Vietnam played out most clearly in the primary elections and 1968 Democratic National Convention. After Johnson stepped aside in 1968, three major candidates remained in the running for nominee: Eugene McCarthy, **Robert Kennedy**, and Hubert Humphrey. Initially, the anti-war vote was split between McCarthy and Kennedy. However, after Robert Kennedy was assassinated in June 1968, anti-war support rallied behind McCarthy. By the time of the Convention in August 1968, it was clear that Humphrey, the continuity candidate, would win the nomination, despite having not competed in any of the primary elections. Angered by this, anti-war activists and McCarthy supporters planned mass protests at the Convention in Chicago. The protests were met with an extreme police response and the Convention was overshadowed by televised riots in the streets of Chicago to the sound of anti-war protestors chanting "the whole world is watching." The events of the 1968 Convention laid the divisions within the Democratic Party out for the world to see. In the aftermath, the Party launched the McGovern–Fraser Commission to examine and reform the nominating process to ensure that primaries, not the Convention, were the most important factor in choosing nominees. Prior to 1968, state conventions were used to select convention delegates in two-thirds of states. After the McGovern–Fraser Commission, over three-quarters used primary-election processes.

KEY FIGURE

Robert F. Kennedy (1925–68) The brother of President Kennedy, Robert was a prominent member of the Democratic Party. Initially a lawyer at the Justice Department, Robert resigned to manage his brother John's Senate campaign in 1952. He gained national attention as chief counsel of the Senate Labor Rackets Committee for challenging corrupt union practices. He ran Kennedy's presidential campaign in 1960 and was appointed Attorney General in Kennedy's administration where he advocated for civil rights and fought against organized crime. He was elected to the Senate in 1964 and ran in the 1968 presidential primary. Shortly after winning the California primary on June 5, 1968, he was assassinated.

The development of counterculture and its impact

"Counterculture" was an anti-establishment movement formed of many different groups. It was often synonymous with cultural liberalism (the freedom of individuals to choose whether to conform to cultural norms) and the wider social changes of the 1960s, from civil rights to anti-war movements.

In the early 1960s, events such as the Bay of Pigs, the Cuban Missile Crisis, and Kennedy's assassination, led many Americans, especially young Americans, to lose trust in government. The growing importance of social issues such as civil rights, gender inequality, anti-nuclear movements, and environmentalism fueled the growth of a larger countercultural movement. The FDA's approval of the birth control pill in 1960 sped a growing sexual revolution in which recreational sex, unencumbered by unwanted pregnancy, became more common. These rapid changes led to the development of new subcultures that celebrated experimentation, individuality, and a rejection of traditional US lifestyles.

The most famous counterculture group was known as the "hippies." Successors to the Beatniks and bohemians of the 1950s, hippies rejected established institutions and middle-class values. They were opposed to nuclear weapons, were often pacifists and embraced many aspects of Eastern philosophy. The movement championed sexual liberation and promoted the use of psychedelic drugs (such as LSD). The hippy movement really came to prominence with the Summer of Love in 1967. In 1967 as many as 100,000 young people, mainly hippies and other counterculture groups, descended on the Haight-Ashbury district of San Francisco. Music, hallucinogenic drugs, anti-war sentiment and free love were the way of life for the young people who traveled to San Francisco in the summer of 1968.

Music was a key part of the counterculture movement. Psychedelic rock, folk, and protest music were prevalent genres. Late Beatles albums such as *Sgt Pepper's Lonely Hearts Club Band* and musicians like Jimi Hendrix were prime examples of the growing psychedelic rock movement. Taking inspiration from folk and blues music, Bob Dylan, Joan Baez, and Janis Joplin sang protest songs containing anti-war sentiment, highlighting injustice, and giving voice to intergenerational tensions. The height of the counterculture movement is often seen to be the Woodstock Festival in 1969. Woodstock was a large music festival held in Bethel, New York. It attracted more than 460,000 attendees and became a defining image of the counterculture movement in the 1960s.

ACTIVITY

Find and listen to Bob Dylan's song "The Times They Are a-Changin'." Discuss what the song tells you about how the youth felt about American society in the 1960s.

The rise of counterculture had two main impacts. It laid the groundwork for the women's rights and gay people's liberation movements of the 1970s, and sparked wider debates around sexual freedom and drug use. It also provoked resistance and concern from older generations and more conservative Americans. Fears over increasing drug use, anti-war protests and inner-city unrest led to greater interest in law and order. Older generations often saw the counterculture movement as self-indulgent and childish, and an intergenerational rift formed between parents who had lived through the Depression and served in the Second World War, and their children who had grown up with greater privilege, education, and time to engage with issues of identity.

What does this image tell you about the popularity and impact of counterculture in the 1960s?

SOURCE 4.9

An aerial view of the crowd and stage at the Woodstock festival, August 17, 1969

The Republican Party and the "silent majority"

The term "silent majority" has a long history, but in the late 1960s it was used as a rallying call for Nixon's Vietnam policies and a means to moderate the renewed anti-war movement.

Nixon first used the phrase in a speech in 1969. The popularity of anti-war protests in October 1969 left him feeling besieged. He made an address on national television outlining his plan to end the war. He ended the speech by saying, "And so tonight, to you, the great silent majority of my fellow Americans—I ask for your support." Public reaction to the speech was very favorable.

Nixon's "silent majority" referred mainly to older Americans, but it also described some younger people in the Midwest, West, and South, many of whom ended up serving in Vietnam. The term tended to refer to blue-collar, white, often suburban, ex-urban, and rural voters who did not usually actively participate in politics. The "silent majority" shared Nixon's concern that rapid social changes and the seemingly growing permissiveness of society threatened to erode the "normality" of American lives.

In his speech, Nixon contrasted the silent majority with the "idealism" of the "vocal minority." He claimed that following the demands of the anti-war movement to withdraw all troops from Vietnam immediately would be disastrous for world peace. After his speech, Nixon's approval rating sky-rocketed from around 50 percent to 81 percent across the nation and 86 percent in the South.

Nixon's use of the "silent majority" term was contentious. Many thought it formed part of the Southern Strategy, while some claimed it was merely a way of dismissing anti-war protests. What is certain is that citing the "silent majority" divided Americans into two groups and formed part of the divide-and-rule strategy Nixon favored for resolving political conflicts. Whatever the rationale for the term, Nixon was vindicated by a landslide election victory in 1972. The term has continued to appear in Republican Party rhetoric since then. It featured in Ronald Reagan's presidential campaign in 1980, the New York City mayoral campaigns of Rudy Giuliani in the 1990s and Michael Bloomberg in the 2000s, and Donald Trump's presidential campaign in 2016.

Role and impact of mass media, including the anti-war movement

In the 1950s, television arrived in people's homes and, almost immediately, became the main medium for communication. In the 1960s, newspaper and magazine journalists began to change their main sources of information from government press conferences and press releases to academic research and first-hand interviews. Suddenly, people were able to see images and read first-hand accounts of events abroad and at home, many of which appeared to contradict what they were being told by government sources.

Importance of television to the anti-war movement

Vietnam was the first "television war." For the first time, the effects of war were something Americans could see in their own homes. News networks strived to have the most attention-grabbing stories, and this often meant on-the-ground coverage of the war. The censorship of media that was common during the Second World War had lapsed by the 1960s, and journalists could report directly from combat zones. This gave Americans a more realistic glimpse into the lives of their soldiers and the activities they were undertaking. Many Americans did not like what they saw.

Coverage of the Tet Offensive showed US soldiers killing Vietnamese civilians and destroying ancient monuments. It demonstrated to many Americans that the war was far from over or even winnable. Growing distrust in government and disgust at both the actions of US soldiers and the conditions in which they were living, fed into a growing disquiet about Vietnam. For some, it was enough to prompt them to join anti-war movements.

Television also provided a platform for anti-war activists and critics. Prominent figures such as Dr Martin Luther King Jr and Senator Robert F Kennedy (President Kennedy's brother) used television appearances to express their opposition to the war. These appearances influenced public opinion and galvanized the anti-war movement. The coverage of anti-war protests on television brought them to the attention of more Americans nationally. The visibility of protests was something of a double-edged sword. It drew more Americans to the movement, but it also drove opposition from those who believed anti-war protests were disrespectful to American troops.

> What does Source 4.10 show about the impact images of the Vietnam War had on American public opinion?

SOURCE 4.10

A US soldier burns the village of My Lai after the massacre of its citizens in 1968. Most of the victims were women, children, and elderly people. The massacre was reported in the US in 1971, and 26 US soldiers were charged with criminal offenses for their actions. Only one was convicted

The credibility gap, the Pentagon Papers, and Watergate

The term "credibility gap" refers to what happens when the public senses that their government is lying to them. It was initially used in relation to Johnson's handling of the escalation of Vietnam, but later events, particularly the release of the Pentagon Papers in 1971 and the Watergate Scandal, confirmed public suspicions that there was a significant difference between what their government was telling them and reality.

The Pentagon Papers, officially called the *Report of the Office of the Secretary of Defense Vietnam Task Force*, was commissioned by Secretary of Defense Robert McNamara in 1967. He wanted to write a history of the war so future administrations could learn from policy errors. In 1971, sections of the papers were released to the *New York Times* by Daniel Ellsberg, one of the contributors to the study. The Pentagon Papers revealed that the US government secretly enlarged the aim of its actions in Vietnam, Laos, and Cambodia without telling the media or the public. Not only that, but every administration since Truman had misled the public about their intentions in Vietnam. The Department of Justice fought the release of the Papers in the courts, and it took a majority vote from the Supreme Court to free the newspapers to continue publishing the Papers.

The release of the Pentagon Papers embarrassed Nixon, who was facing reelection in 1972, and widened the credibility gap. Nixon was so distressed by the leak that he authorized unlawful efforts to discredit Ellsberg, including breaking into the office of Ellsberg's psychiatrist. Ellsberg was initially charged with conspiracy, espionage, and theft of government property, although these charges were later dropped after Nixon's unlawful attempts to discredit him came out.

The Watergate Scandal had a similarly long-lasting impact on how Americans perceived their government. The name came from Nixon's attempt to conceal his involvement in a break-in at the Watergate Hotel, where the Democratic National Committee was headquartered. Five people were arrested for the break-in and the Department for Justice connected funds found on the perpetrators to the Nixon campaign's fundraising organization. In the investigations that followed, witnesses testified that Nixon had sanctioned plans to cover up his administration's involvement in the break-in and that he kept a tape-recording system in the Oval Office. As a result of these revelations and Nixon's attempts to impede the investigation, the House of Representatives initiated **impeachment** proceedings against him. The Supreme Court forced Nixon to surrender the Oval Office tapes that revealed his complicity in the cover-up and, on August 9, 1974, after the articles of impeachment against him were approved, Nixon resigned.

> **KEY TERM**
>
> **Impeachment** The process by which a legislative body brings charges against a public official for misconduct. In the US, impeachment is a two-stage process. The House of Representatives can impeach by a majority vote but conviction and removal from office requires a two-thirds vote in the Senate.

The connection between the break-in and Nixon's reelection committee was emphasized in the media. Investigative reporting in the *Washington Post* by Bob Woodward and Carl Bernstein revealed information indicating that knowledge of the break-in and a cover-up went high up in the White House, Justice Department, FBI, and CIA. The media coverage and televising of Senate hearings on the Scandal increased publicity of the incident and the legal and political consequences for those involved.

These scandals widened the credibility gap and led to an increased belief in the duplicity of the Johnson and Nixon administrations. Disgust at the events of Watergate had a substantial impact on the 1974 mid-term results, and Ford's decision to pardon Nixon played a part in his defeat to Jimmy Carter in 1976.

What do Sources 4.11 and 4.12 tell us about the impact of the Watergate Scandal?

SOURCE 4.11

"Nixon Hanging between the Tapes," a political cartoon by Herblock published in the *Washington Post* on May 24, 1974 during the Watergate trial. The cartoon shows Nixon hanging between two reels of tape referencing the White House tapes which, when released, had many key parts missing

SOURCE 4.12

Extract from Nixon's resignation speech, August 8, 1974

In all the decisions I have made in my public life, I have always tried to do what was best for the Nation. Throughout the long and difficult period of Watergate, I have felt it was my duty to persevere, to make every possible effort to complete the term of office to which you elected me.

In the past few days, however, it has become evident to me that I no longer have a strong enough political base in the Congress to justify continuing that effort. As long as there was such a base, I felt strongly that it was necessary to see the constitutional process through to its conclusion, that to do otherwise would be unfaithful to the spirit of that deliberately difficult process and a dangerously destabilizing precedent for the future.

But with the disappearance of that base, I now believe that the constitutional purpose has been served, and there is no longer a need for the process to be prolonged …

… I have never been a quitter. To leave office before my term is completed is abhorrent to every instinct in my body. But as President, I must put the interest of America first. America needs a full-time President and a full-time Congress, particularly at this time with problems we face at home and abroad.

The concept of the "imperial presidency"

In 1973, American historian Arthur Schlesinger wrote a book titled *The Imperial Presidency*. The book highlighted two key concerns: that the Office of the President was out of control, and that it had breached the limits set by the Constitution. The "imperial presidency" as a concept can be defined by a few key features:

- An increase in the number of staff in the executive office, who are typically appointed by the president. These appointments lack accountability to the checks and balances of the Constitution.
- The creation of new executive agencies alongside main Cabinet departments. This implies the declining influence of the Cabinet and the rise of a "court" around the president.
- Unlike Cabinet appointments, appointments to the executive office of the president are not confirmed by the Senate. This removes a key area of accountability.
- The power the president holds over foreign policy is vast. It is constitutionally unclear where this power comes from.
- The only accountability for presidents is at election time or through impeachment proceedings.

Schlesinger highlighted the unlawful actions of some of Nixon's staff as an example of the way in which presidents had become surrounded by "courts" which sometimes acted in contravention of acts of Congress.

The theory of the imperial presidency is controversial. Those opposed to the idea suggest that, after Watergate, several executive controls were introduced. They argue that the executive office is a relatively small part of the federal bureaucracy and that, since members of the office change with every president, there is no continuity of individuals in executive roles. Critics also suggest that, where presidents have acted illegally in the past, they have typically been forced to resign.

Questions over the use of "imperial" power by presidents have continued since the 1970s. Using vetoes to reject congressional legislation, carrying out foreign policy without the approval of Congress, and issuing executive orders are all ways presidents have bypassed congressional checks and balances. Concerns about the increasing use of such tactics have persisted throughout the late twentieth and early twenty-first centuries.

Impact of the anti-war movement on political discourse

The anti-war movement had a significant impact on political discourse. In the foreign policy space, mass protest against the Vietnam War contributed to Nixon's decision to make withdrawal from Vietnam a key aspect of his foreign policy and changed the discourse around US military involvement abroad. Domestically, the anti-war movement contributed to a split within the Democratic Party, the election of Nixon, and, in the longer term, the rise of the right and some of the polarization visible in US politics today.

The strength of the anti-war movement curtailed Johnson's ability to escalate the war further. In 1967, anti-war sympathizers in the House of Representatives held hearings urging Johnson to request an emergency session of the UN Security Council to consider proposals for ending the war. Johnson's declining approval ratings after the Tet Offensive led to him not seeking a second term. Nixon understood the need to remove the US from the conflict in Vietnam, but there is little doubt that the threat of domestic unrest caused by the anti-war movement played a part in pushing him to follow through with enacting a plan.

The anti-war movement played a part in changing the way Americans viewed military engagement abroad. The horrors Americans saw on their televisions, anti-war protests, and the economic cost for little reward led to an aversion to sending US military personnel into foreign wars. In 1973, after overriding Nixon's veto, Congress passed the War Powers Resolution, which limited the president's authority to wage war without congressional approval.

Televised anti-war protests and the violence at the 1968 Democratic National Convention concerned many Americans. Most of the violence at the Convention was perpetrated by the police, but many Americans turned their interest to law-and-order policies anyway. To many older and more socially conservative Americans, anti-war protests and wider countercultural movements illustrated that the American way of life they knew was being destroyed. These individuals, particularly blue-collar Democrats, began to turn to the Republican Party. Nixon's silent majority speech put the anti-war movement in opposition to "normal" Americans, categorizing the left wing of the Democratic Party and anti-war and social justice activists as "other."

What does Source 4.13 tell us about popular feeling concerning the Vietnam War?

SOURCE 4.13

Anti-Vietnam War protestors during the March on the Pentagon demonstration. The protesters were standing on the National Mall near the Lincoln Memorial, October 21, 1967

ACTIVITY

Create a list of direct and indirect consequences of US involvement in the Vietnam War. These consequences can be domestic and international. Draw a diagram using arrows to show the links between the direct and indirect consequences.

SUMMARY DIAGRAM

US domestic politics, 1960–79
Why and how did politics in the US evolve between 1960 and 1979?

New Frontier
- Increased minimum wage
- Increased social security for elderly and unemployed
- Housing Act offering loans to deprived homeowners
- Pilot food stamp programme
- Funding for training and technology adoption for businesses
- Funding for community health and research
- Improved health services for migrants
- Increased vaccination
- Improved prenatal healthcare for low-income women
- Funding for libraries, school lunches, and vocational education
- Increased provision for disabled and gifted children
- Aid for education television, medical education, and community libraries
- Peace Corps

Great Society
- War on poverty
  - Job Corps
  - Neighborhood Youth Corps
  - Volunteers in Service to America
  - Model Cities Program
  - Upward Bound
  - Food Stamp Act
  - Community Action Agencies
- **Medicaid**—health insurance for limited-income individuals
- **Medicare**—healthcare for the elderly
- **Head Start**—helping communities to meet the needs of disadvantaged preschoolers
- **Elementary and Secondary Education Act**—federal income for low–income school districts
- **Water Quality Act**—national water quality standards
- **Motor Vehicle Air Pollution Control Act**—vehicle emissions standards

"New Economic Policy"
- Implemented floating exchange rate
- Introduced 90-day freeze on wages and prices
- 10% import surcharge
- Suspended convertibility of the dollar to gold
- Stopped foreign government exchanging dollars for gold

Economic challenges for Ford and Carter
- "Whip Inflation Now"
- Stagflation
  - Economic Stimulus Appropriations Act
- Oil Crises, 1977 and 1979
  - Energy tax credits
  - Domestic oil production tax
  - Conversion from oil and natural gas to coal
  - Taxing gasoline consumption
  - Deregulating price of oil
  - Windfall tax on energy company profits

4.3 Why and how far did the position of minorities improve in the US between 1960 and 1979?

The 1960s and 1970s saw the growth of movements for social justice and equality. Feminism, civil rights activism, and gay liberation movements all gained traction during this period. Progress in these areas, however, was met with resistance. Anti-feminist movements and the religious right also developed during this time. This section will focus on three key movements—women's rights, civil rights, and gay rights—as well as resistance against them and the limits to their success.

Growth and impact of feminism and passage of Title IX

After the Second World War, women's role in US society changed. By the 1960s, more women were entering the paid workforce than ever before. There was increasing dissatisfaction about the huge gender disparity in pay and advancement, and a culture of sexual harassment in many workplaces. In the 1960s, frustration began to translate to activism.

Betty Friedan and *The Feminine Mystique*, 1963

The Feminine Mystique by **Betty Friedan** is widely credited with sparking a resurgence in American feminism. The phrase "feminine mystique" described the assumption that women would be fulfilled by their housework, marriage, and children. The book suggests that the prevailing attitude that women who were truly feminine should not want to work, get an education, or have political opinions was false. Friedan set out to prove that women were unsatisfied but unable to voice their dissatisfaction and to urge women to break free of the "feminine mystique."

> **KEY FIGURE**
>
> **Betty Friedan** (1921–2006) Betty Friedan was a leading figure in the US feminist movement. In 1963, she published *The Feminine Mystique*, which is often credited with sparking the second wave of American feminism. In 1966, she co-founded the National Organization for Women (NOW). She remained active in politics and activism until the 1990s. She died on February 4, 2006, her 85th birthday.

Immediately after its publication, the book received criticism for its focus on the plight of middle-class, white women and for not giving enough attention to the struggles of women from differing economic backgrounds and races. Despite these criticisms, the book drew large numbers of white, middle-class women to the feminist cause. Many women did relate to the unvoiced dissatisfaction Friedan outlined, and the book distilled the work of psychologists, economists, and political theorists, combined it with personal stories and translated it into powerful, relatable reading. *The Feminine Mystique* and Betty Friedan were key influences in the formation of the National Organization for Women (NOW) in 1966.

Formation of the National Organization for Women (NOW), 1966

The Feminine Mystique was not the only influence in the founding and rise of NOW. In 1961, President Kennedy established a Commission on the Status of Women. Chaired by Eleanor Roosevelt until her death in 1962, the Commission issued a report in 1963 criticizing the inequalities facing women, documenting women's status in the US, and making recommendations. In 1966, a group of women attending the Third National Conference of Commissions on the Status of Women (the successor to Kennedy's Commission) founded NOW. Betty Friedan was one of the founders and co-authored NOW's Statement of Purpose.

The founders of NOW were frustrated that the federal government was not enforcing the new anti-discrimination laws. Under the Civil Rights Act of 1964, employment discrimination on the grounds of race, sex, religion, or national origin was prohibited. Despite this, by 1966, employers were still discriminating against women in hiring and in pay. The founders of NOW worried that without a feminist pressure group like the NAACP, women would not be able to challenge these issues. NOW aimed to mobilize women, give women's rights activists the power to put pressure on the government and employers, and promote full equality of the sexes.

In 1968, NOW drew up a Bill of Rights advocating the passage of the Equal Rights Amendment (see below), enforcement of the employment discrimination title of the Civil Rights Act, maternity leave rights, and the right of women to equal education and training opportunities and to control their reproductive lives.

NOW helped women get equal access to banking services, protesting against individual banks and eventually driving the passage of the Equal Credit Opportunity Act, which made it unlawful for creditors to discriminate against applicants on the grounds of race, religion, sex, marital status, or age.

In August 1970, on the 50th anniversary of the ratification of the Nineteenth Amendment, which granted women the right to vote, NOW sponsored the Women's Strike for Equality. Around 10,000 women took to the streets of New York City and about 500,000 women participated in events across the US. The Strike had three stated goals: free abortion care, 24/7 childcare centers, and equal opportunities in jobs and education. Despite dismissal in some media, with spectators calling demonstrators anti-feminine, "ridiculous exhibitionists," and even communists, in the weeks after the event NOW's membership rose by 50 percent.

The women's liberation movement and the fight for the Equal Rights Amendment (ERA)

NOW was just one of many branches within the feminist movement in this period. NOW's members were mostly middle-class, middle-aged women, but the women's liberation movement was formed of racially and culturally diverse groups. These groups questioned the validity of patriarchy and the social and sexual hierarchies used to limit the legal and personal independence of women. They believed women needed to work together to free themselves from the control and oppression of men instead of seeking legal equality with them.

The women's liberation movement particularly appealed to younger women. Perhaps the most famous piece of direct action by the women's liberation movement was the protest at the Miss America Pageant by the New York Radical Women in September 1968. The protest aimed to highlight the way the pageant and society exploited women and women's bodies. The protesters crowned a sheep Miss America and threw instruments of female oppression, such as high-heels, curlers, bras, and girdles, into a "freedom trash can." This protest was mistakenly reported by media outlets as a "bra-burning" protest, although no bras were actually burned.

Another key group in the movement was the Combahee River Collective, an African American feminist organization that argued neither the white feminist movement nor the Civil Rights Movement addressed the needs of Black women and, more specifically, Black lesbians. In 1977, the group published the Combahee River Collective Statement. The Statement argued that the liberation of Black women could only occur once all systems of subjugation were removed, which would, by default, lead to the absence of oppression for all marginalized people.

One significant fight for the women's liberation movement was the attempted passage of the Equal Rights Amendment (ERA). Initially drafted in the 1920s, the ERA was a proposed amendment to the US Constitution that would explicitly prohibit sex discrimination. While groups and individuals lobbied for the passage of ERA throughout the twentieth century, the fight gained traction in the 1960s and 1970s. NOW and other groups lobbied for the passage of the ERA by undertaking marches, rallies, petitions, pickets, and other acts of civil disobedience. They were initially successful, and the ERA was passed by both houses of Congress. Despite continued protest and lobbying, however, they were not able to persuade enough states to ratify the Amendment, so it did not become part of the Constitution.

What does Source 4.14 tell us about the popularity of the feminist movement by 1977?

SOURCE 4.14

First Lady Rosalynn Carter, former First Ladies Ladybird Johnson and Betty Ford, Coretta Scott King, and Susan B Anthony II attend the First National Women's Conference in Houston, Texas, September 19, 1977

Advances in gender equality through Congress and Supreme Court rulings

Between the late 1940s and 1963, little progress was made on gender equality through legislation or the courts. In 1963, Congress passed the Equal Pay Act, promising equality of pay for equal work regardless of race, religion, national origin, or sex. This was followed in 1964 by the Civil Rights Act (page 233). The Civil Rights Act contained Title VII, which included a prohibition against employment discrimination based on sex, race, national origin, or religion. In theory, this ended discrimination in hiring and pay; however, the federal government failed to enforce the legislation.

The lack of enforcement of Title VII led to several landmark cases being taken against companies engaging in discriminatory hiring and pay practices. The first sex discrimination case to reach the Supreme Court was *Phillips v. Martin Marietta* in January 1971. At this time, the Martin Marietta Corporation had a policy of not hiring mothers of preschool-aged children because they believed they would be unreliable employees. Ida Phillips, a mother of preschool-aged children, applied for a job at the company and was denied because of her parental status. Phillips sued the company under Title VII and the Supreme Court unanimously held that the Marietta Corporation had discriminated based on sex.

In June 1974, a further case concerning employment discrimination was brought to the Supreme Court. *Corning Glass Works v. Brennen* claimed that Corning was discriminating against its female workforce because men could work the higher-paid night shifts, while women were only allowed to work on day shifts, which were paid less. The company argued that there was no pay inequality because the jobs were different, but the Supreme Court held that the "working conditions" of day and night shifts were similar enough to allow the claim.

The 1970s also saw landmark legislation and court rulings on equality of education, legal standing, and reproductive rights. In 1972, Congress passed Title IX of the Education Amendments. Title IX prohibited sex-based discrimination in any school or education program that received funding from the federal government. It is probably best known for its impact on high school and college sports, but it covered all sex-based discrimination in educational contexts including on scholarships, facilities, and curriculum offers. The most visible impact of Title IX was a considerable increase in the number of female students participating in organized sports in schools and colleges. It also led to greater activism concerning sexual harassment in educational institutions and sparked the beginning of the argument that sexual harassment of female students deprived them of equal access to education and, therefore, counted as illegal sex-based discrimination.

In 1971, a case was taken before the Supreme Court challenging an Idaho state code which specified that, when appointing the administrators of estates, "males must be preferred to females." In the *Reed v. Reed* case, a separated couple was in conflict over who would be named administrator of their deceased son's estate. Under the Idaho code, the husband was appointed administrator. The case argued that, under the Equal Protection Clause of the Fourteenth Amendment, the Idaho code was discriminatory. The Supreme Court upheld that the code was arbitrary and unconstitutional. This landmark decision ruled for the first time that the Equal Protection Clause prohibited differential treatment based on sex and, therefore, that sex-based discrimination was, in fact, unconstitutional.

Perhaps the most contentious Supreme Court decision concerning women's rights in this period was *Roe v. Wade*. In January 1973, "Jane Roe" (a legal pseudonym) was pregnant with her third child and Texas law prohibited her from having an abortion. Roe brought a case against her local District Attorney, Henry Wade, arguing that the Texas abortion law was unconstitutional. This case made its way to the Supreme Court, and on January 22, 1973, the Court ruled that women in the US had a fundamental right to access abortion without excessive government restrictions. *Roe v. Wade* found the Texas abortion law unconstitutional and ruled that the US Constitution generally protected the right to abortion.

Supreme Court rulings were a major source of progress in women's rights during this time. While Congress passed several key acts relating to equality, they were often poorly enforced by federal government. Taking cases to the courts, particularly the Supreme Court, was a way to ensure greater enforcement of congressional acts and to define the limits of these pieces of legislation.

ACTIVITY

Complete a chart like the one below on the changing position of women in the US between 1960 and 1979.

Factor	What improved?	What did not improve?
Discrimination in employment		
Discrimination in education		
Other sex-based discrimination		
Reproductive rights		

Discuss which of the points for and against are the most important and why.

Growth and impacts of civil rights activism

The Civil Rights Movement made significant progress in the 1960s. The work of key individuals led to the passing of various civil rights acts and Supreme Court rulings to end segregation of African Americans. The 1960s also saw the spread of the Civil Rights Movement to focus on the inequality faced by other cultural minorities in the US, including Latino Americans, Native Americans, and Asian Americans.

Role of key leaders

The Civil Rights Movement was made up of many groups and activism was very much a collective endeavor. There were also some key individuals whose work drove progress and around whom civil rights groups were built and developed. This section will explore the work of some of them.

Dr Martin Luther King Jr

Dr Martin Luther King Jr had been a key figure in the Civil Rights Movement since the Montgomery Bus Boycotts. In the 1960s, King was a strong unifying figure and played a vital part in organizing civil rights groups into mass actions. Perhaps the most famous of these was the March on Washington for Jobs and Freedom in 1963. King worked with the NAACP and other civil rights organizations to organize a rally for the civil and economic rights of Black Americans. Around 250,000 people descended on Washington and, in front of the Lincoln Memorial, King delivered his famous "I Have a Dream" speech. This event played a part in pressuring the government to pass the Civil Rights Act in 1964 and King was awarded a Nobel Peace Prize for his work.

In 1965, King worked with other civil rights groups to organize 54-mile protest marches from Selma, Alabama to the state capital, Montgomery, to protest voting restrictions on Black Americans in the South. Marchers endured attacks by police, which were televised across the country. The Selma Marches pressured the government into passing the Voting Rights Act later that year. In the latter half of the 1960s, King's focus broadened to include the Vietnam War and economic issues and, in 1968, he went to support striking workers in Memphis. He was assassinated on the balcony of his Memphis hotel on April 4, 1968. King's influence was so great that President Johnson called for a national day of mourning for his death.

> **ACTIVITY**
>
> Find and listen to King's "I Have a Dream" speech. Discuss why you think this speech has had such a lasting impact.

What does Source 4.15 tell you about the influence of Dr Martin Luther King Jr and the Civil Rights Movement in the 1960s?

SOURCE 4.15

Crowds of African American and white people gather at the National Mall during the March on Washington for Jobs and Freedom political rally in Washington DC, August 28, 1963

Stokely Carmichael (aka Kwame Ture)

Stokely Carmichael started out as a student activist. In 1961, he went on a **Freedom Ride** and was arrested for entering a "whites only" waiting room. In 1964, he joined the Student Nonviolent Coordinating Committee (SNCC) and became a field organizer for the group. At this point, Carmichael was committed to King's non-violent philosophy of activism.

As the 1960s progressed, Carmichael became frustrated with the slow pace of change. He grew tired of enduring acts of violence, brutality, and humiliation at the hands of white police officers. By 1966, when he was elected national chairman of the SNCC, he had lost faith in non-violent methods. He took the SNCC in a radical direction. In June 1966, the activist James Meredith was shot by a sniper during a solidarity march. The SNCC, King and other civil rights organizations decided to continue the march in his honor. Carmichael was arrested during the march and, on his release, gave a speech in Greenwood, Mississippi. Enraged by his experience, he said, "We been saying freedom for

> **KEY TERM**
>
> **Freedom Ride** In 1961, civil rights activists rode interstate buses into segregated Southern states to protest the non-enforcement of two Supreme Court rulings that deemed bus segregation to be unconstitutional. These were known as Freedom Rides.

six years and we ain't got nothing. What we got to start saying now is Black Power. We want Black Power!

This represented a break from King's doctrine of non-violence and the term Black Power caught on among younger, radical civil rights activists. Black Power was associated with Black separatism and proved incredibly controversial, provoking fear in many white Americans and exacerbating divisions in the Civil Rights Movement.

Malcolm X

When Malcolm Little was a child, his family was targeted by the Ku Klux Klan and forced to flee their home. He was arrested for robbery in 1946 and converted to Islam in prison, changing his name to Malcolm X. When he left prison in 1952, he joined the Nation of Islam, a Black nationalist group led by Elijah Muhammad. The Nation of Islam believed that Black people should abandon existing structures and create their own social, economic, and political power structures.

Malcolm X believed in achieving civil rights by "any means necessary." He attracted the attention of the FBI, who put him under regular surveillance from the time he was released from prison. In the early 1960s, he left the Nation of Islam and, in June 1964, founded the Organization of Afro-American Unity. The Organization was more moderate, suggesting that racism, not the white race, was the enemy of justice. These more moderate beliefs particularly influenced the SNCC.

In February 1965, Malcolm X was assassinated at an Organization of Afro-American Unity rally in New York City. The assassination remains controversial, and, while three men were imprisoned for the murder at the time, no consensus exists on who the real assassins were and two of the three were exonerated in 2021.

Cesar Chavez

Cesar Chavez was born to a Mexican American family in 1927. As a child, he worked as a migrant farmworker enduring long hours of back-breaking labor for extremely low wages. In 1944, he joined the navy, but his experiences as a farmworker shaped his life and, after he was discharged, he joined the Community Service Organization (CSO), a Latino civil rights group, and became a powerful leader in the group.

In 1962, Chavez left the CSO to establish the National Farm Workers Association (NFWA) with Dolores Huerta. The NFWA organized farmworkers' strikes, using non-violent tactics including pickets and boycotts to pressure farm owners to give in to demands. In 1965, working with a Filipino workers group, the Agricultural Workers Organizing Committee (AWOC), the NFWA engaged in a strike of grape pickers in Delano, California for higher wages. Chavez worked with left-wing activists, particularly students, to ensure that picket lines were constantly populated. By 1966, a protest camp with its own medical clinic and nursery had been established in Delano. From 1965 to 1970, strikers engaged in protests and organized a successful consumer boycott of purchasing grapes. In 1970, the farm owners relented and signed new labor contracts with strikers. This was the first major victory won by migrant workers. By this time, the NFWA and AWOC had merged to form the United Farm Workers union (UFW).

Chavez was a controversial figure during his lifetime and his legacy is still contested. He was soft-spoken and his leadership of the UFW was influenced by his devout Catholicism. His commitment to non-violence won him supporters but also critics among the movement. His deputy, Dolores Huerta, was a tougher figure with great attention to detail and a direct approach.

Dolores Huerta

Huerta grew up in a diverse community. She did well in school but was frustrated by the low societal expectations for Mexican American women. She was a feminist but believed that the feminist movement did not address deeper social issues such as poverty and racism. She joined the CSO in 1955, where she met Cesar Chavez. She directed the consumer boycott during the Delano grape strike and lobbied tirelessly for laws to improve the lives of farm workers.

She secured disability insurance for farm workers and was instrumental in the passing of California's Agricultural Labor Relations Act in 1975. This legislation gave farmworkers in California the right to unionize and engage in collective bargaining. Huerta's influence was evident when, in 1968, she stood alongside Robert Kennedy on the speakers' platform as he delivered his victory speech after winning the California primary. She has received numerous awards and recognitions for her work on labor and women's rights and increased the visibility of Latina women in political activism.

Dennis Banks

Born on an Indian reservation in Minnesota, Dennis Banks was taken to a federal Indian boarding school at the age of five. He joined the US air force at seventeen and was stationed in Japan. When ordered to shoot Japanese citizens who were protesting the presence of US bases, he went absent without leave and was dishonorably discharged from the military.

In 1968, Banks co-founded the American Indian Movement (AIM) with the goal of protecting the civil rights of Native Americans living in urban areas and protesting the treatment of Native Americans in the US. In 1969, he participated in an occupation of Alcatraz to highlight Native American issues and promote Indigenous sovereignty in their own lands. In 1972, Banks helped to organize the "Trail of Broken Treaties" (see page 232).

In 1973, Banks was asked by a Lakota Sioux civil rights organization to come to Wounded Knee (the site of the last major conflict in the "American Indian Wars" in 1890) to help engage with law enforcement in nearby border towns who, they believed, were failing to prosecute crimes committed against Native Americans. Banks and other AIM activists occupied the area, leading to a 71-day siege by armed federal law enforcement which resulted in the injury of a US marshal and the death of two Native activists. Resident families returned to the village to find that their homes and businesses had been destroyed by federal agents. Banks was arrested and charged with incitement to riot.

Banks played a pivotal role in raising awareness of Native American issues. His work with AIM resulted in important changes to policy to improve the quality of life for Native Americans.

Emergence of different activist groups and ideas

In the 1960s, the Civil Rights Movement expanded. Disillusionment with the slow pace of change made some, especially younger people, lose faith in the non-violent tactics of the early Civil Rights Movement. This led to the rise of more radical groups, including some with separatist ideals. The movement also grew to include other cultural minorities. In this period, new groups emerged representing Native Americans, Latino Americans, and Asian Americans.

The Black Power movement

In the 1950s, non-violence was the dominant tactic of the Civil Rights Movement. This began to change in the 1960s as new groups with more radical and militant tactics emerged.

Non-violent resistance did not come to an end with the diversification of the Civil Rights Movement. In February 1960 four African American students sat down at the lunch counter of the Woolworth's in Greensboro, North Carolina to protest the store's policy of refusing service to non-white customers. This was the first sit-in protest of the 1960s and it sparked a movement. Within a week 300 students had joined the Greensboro sit-in and, by the end of March 1960 sit-in protests were occurring in over 55 cities in 13 states. At the end of July 1960, the Greensboro Woolworth's integrated its lunch counter.

In 1961, the Congress of Racial Equality (CORE) set out to protest the segregation of interstate buses by organizing Freedom Rides. In May 1961, 13 Freedom Riders left Washington, D.C. on a Greyhound bus. They traveled through Virginia and North Carolina with minimal public attention but in South Carolina three Freedom Riders were violently attacked as they tried to enter a whites-only waiting area. Violence followed them into Alabama where an angry mob prevented the bus from stopping in Anniston, blew out the bus's tires and fire-bombed it. The Freedom Riders escaped but were attacked by the mob.

ACTIVITY

Assemble a list of key similarities and differences between the ideas of Dr Martin Luther King Jr, Stokely Carmichael, and Malcolm X. In pairs or groups, evaluate the pros and cons of the three sets of ideas and decide which you think had the greatest impact on civil rights in the US.

The Freedom Rides drew widespread media attention and continued into the fall of 1961 when the Interstate Commerce Commission, under pressure from the Kennedy administration, prohibited segregation in interstate transit terminals.

SOURCE 4.16

> How do you think images like this appearing in the media influenced American public opinion of the Civil Rights Movement?

Freedom Riders sit beside a Greyhound bus they had ridden which was burned by a mob of white people on the highway near Anniston, Alabama, May 14, 1961

The Black Power movement became popular in 1966 after Stokely Carmichael used the term in a speech, but it had existed in some form since the founding of the Nation of Islam in the 1930s. Malcolm X is often credited with the movement's rise in popularity in the 1950s, but it wasn't until the mid-1960s that it really gained traction. In 1965, a series of riots in LA, known as the Watts Riots, sparked by anger at the racist practices of the Los Angeles police, led to the SNCC formally breaking with the mainstream Civil Rights Movement. They argued that Black people needed to build their own power structures rather than seek accommodations from those power structures already in place and began to establish ties with other radical student groups such as the SDS.

The Black Panther Party

In 1966, the Black Panther Party was founded. Using open-carry gun laws, the Party organized armed patrols to protect their communities and challenge the excessive force used by police against Black communities. In 1967, the SNCC began to fall apart due to policy disputes among its leadership. Many left the organization and joined the Black Panther Party. In the late 1960s, the Party staged rallies and disrupted the California State Assembly with armed marches. By 1969, the Party and its members were prime targets for the FBI and many of its leaders had been arrested. Despite this, membership numbers soared. In 1970, the Party formed the Black Liberation Army to continue a violent revolution alongside the Party's reform movements. By the early 1970s, several Panther officials fled the US, others were imprisoned, and chapters of the movement were beginning to shut down. The movement continued to exist and undertake violent actions until the 1980s, but its popularity declined throughout the 1970s.

The Rainbow Coalition

In 1969, a multicultural, working-class anti-racist movement was founded in Chicago. The Rainbow Coalition, as it was known, was initially an alliance between the Black Panthers and two Chicago-based organizations, the Young Patriots Organization and the Young Lords. The Young Patriots was a left-wing organization mostly of white Southerners living in Chicago. It promoted Southern culture and used the Confederate flag as its symbol but focused primarily on the challenges of poverty and discrimination faced by Southern migrants in urban centers. The Young Lords fought for neighborhood empowerment and self-determination for Puerto Ricans. The Coalition eventually grew to include various other radical socialist groups and, later, was joined by the SDS and AIM. The Rainbow Coalition focused on issues of poverty, racism, corruption, police brutality, and substandard housing. The participating groups supported each other in protests, strikes, and demonstrations for common causes.

The Chicano/a movement

The Chicano/a movement was a Mexican American movement influenced by the Black Power movement. They both had similar aims of community empowerment and liberation and called for black-brown unity in the face of white supremacy. Much like the Black Power movement, Chicano organizations faced heavy state surveillance, infiltration, and repression. In addition to the work of the NFWA, the Chicano movement involved student action including protests and marches. In 1968 around 20,000 high school students walked out of their LA schools in protest at their segregation from white students, poor quality facilities, curricula that did not include Latino content, and teachers who could not speak Spanish. Ultimately, the movement did win reforms, from improved conditions for migrant farm laborers to the creation of bilingual and bicultural education programs in Southwest US.

The American Indian Movement (AIM)

In 1968, Dennis Banks co-founded AIM. AIM sought to create a housing program for Native Americans, improve education, increase Native American employment, and improve communications between Native Americans and the rest of American society. Toward the end of the 1960s, AIM turned to more radical protest methods. In November 1969, 89 Native Americans set out to occupy Alcatraz Island on the grounds that, since the Federal Penitentiary on the island was due to be closed, the property was now surplus government land. Under the Treaty of Fort Laramie (1868), surplus land could be claimed by the Sioux. The occupation lasted 19 months and, at its height, 400 people were living on the island. Although AIM was not involved in organizing the occupation, they learned a lot from it. It sparked greater cooperation between AIM and other civil rights organizations, with the Black Panthers helping to deliver food and essentials to the island.

The occupation motivated Native Americans across the country and, in 1972, AIM organized the Trail of Broken Treaties, a group of caravans of Native American activists traveling from the West Coast to Washington to demand compensation for years of destructive polices. The group drafted a paper demanding the recognition of Native American sovereignty and the restoration of Indigenous rights as guaranteed by treaties. This paper guided the Native American rights movement to come. The caravan had planned meetings with a number of government officials. However, these were cancelled without notice. In response, demonstrators staged a sit-in at the Bureau of Indian Affairs (BIA) building which turned into an occupation. Demonstrators occupied the building for the following week. Unfortunately, the occupation and damage caused to the BIA building overshadowed their demands in the press and the Trail of Broken Treaties did not achieve what its organizers had hoped.

These protests increased public awareness of Native American concerns and, in 1975, Congress passed the Indian Self-Determination and Education Assistance Act which authorized some government agencies (particularly the Secretary of Health, Education, and Welfare) to enter into contracts with and make grants to federally recognized Indian tribes. The tribes would have authority over administration of the funds which gave them greater control over their welfare.

By the end of the 1970s, Native American activists had developed a clear and effective message identifying Native American sovereignty as the solution to discrimination against them. In 1978, they organized the Longest Walk campaign. The Walk set out in February from Alcatraz Island on a five-month pilgrimage to Washington, D.C. When they arrived in July 1978 around 2000 supporters marched through the city. Over the next week, they held rallies, marches, and religious ceremonies before Congress, the White House, and the Supreme Court. Unlike the marchers on the Trail of Broken Treaties, the Longest Walk was almost welcomed by the government. The National Park Service cleared the way for demonstrators to camp on Greenbelt Park and the National Guard provided logistical assistance. This radically different welcome demonstrated the impact of the work AIM and

> **KEY TERM**
>
> **Chicano/a** A term used by Mexican Americans who identify with their Indigenous Mexican heritage. Originally a racial slur, it was reclaimed in the 1940s and then again in the 1960s in the building of a movement toward political empowerment and ethnic solidarity. It was used distinctly from "Mexican American" identity.

other Native American activists had undertaken across the country in the six years between the two events.

The Asian American Political Alliance

The Asian American Political Alliance (AAPA) was formed in Berkeley, California in 1968. It aimed to unite all Asian Americans to push for political and social action. The AAPA identified as an anti-imperialist organization seeking liberation and self-determination for Asian Americans. It was involved with the Black Power movement and in the anti-Vietnam movements. It also supported the NFWA in the Delano grape strike. The AAPA was short-lived; by 1969, the two main chapters had disbanded. However, it had a strong influence in inspiring Asian Americans to participate in political organizing and the fight for social change.

> What does this source tell you about the scale of support for the Trail of Broken Treaties in the US?

SOURCE 4.17

Dennis Banks and Carl McIntire on the Trail of Broken Treaties. The Trail of Broken Treaties received a visit from Fundamentalist Preacher Carl McIntire who pledged support for them. November 4, 1972

Key legislation and its impacts

The 1960s gave rise to some very important legislation that enshrined key aspects of civil rights into law. Legislation during this time prohibited segregation in public spaces, employment discrimination, and racial discrimination in voting, and abolished the de facto discrimination against Asian people and southern and eastern Europeans in immigration policy.

Congress passed two acts called "Civil Rights Act" in the 1960s. The first, in 1960, was concerned with voting rights. It established federal inspections of local voter registration polls and introduced penalties for obstructing anyone's attempt to register to vote. It prevented the discriminatory practices common in the South, where Black and Latino Americans had been essentially disenfranchised since the late nineteenth century.

The Civil Rights Act of 1964 outlawed discrimination based on race, religion, color, sex, or national origin. The Act prohibited unequal application of voter registration requirements, racial segregation in public spaces and schools, and employment discrimination. The Act divided both the Republican and Democratic parties and received opposition from white business owners who claimed that Congress did not have the constitutional authority to ban segregation in public spaces. The Act was a significant achievement for both the civil and women's rights movements, but the powers it gave for enforcement were weak. Numerous court cases were taken to the Supreme Court under the Act, which helped to tighten enforcement and set out its parameters.

Since the end of the Civil War, states often sought to disenfranchise minorities and, by the 1960s, this often took the form of literacy tests for voting. Literacy rates among African American communities during this time were often poor and being forced to take a literacy test they were likely to fail was a way of disenfranchising African Americans. In 1965, Congress passed the Voting Rights Act to prevent voter registration discrimination. The Act banned the use of literacy tests, provided federal oversight of voter registration in areas where less than 50 percent of the non-white population was registered to vote, and authorized the Attorney General to investigate the use of poll taxes in state and local elections. Again, enforcement measures for the Act were weak. Nevertheless, the Act vastly improved voter turnout among African Americans.

In the 1920s, the US established the National Origins Formula as a key part of its immigration policy. The Formula was a series of quotas on immigration that restricted immigration from Asia, and eastern and southern Europe. The Formula increasingly came under attack in the 1960s for being racially discriminatory and, in 1965, the Immigration and Nationality Act abolished the Formula. The passage of this Act led to an increase in immigration to the US from Asia, Africa, the West Indies, and Central and Latin America.

The legislation passed during the 1960s radically changed the legal standing of some minorities in the US. However, it was often poorly enforced during this time. Provision for enforcement was weak and movements were angry that the federal government failed to enforce effectively.

Important Supreme Court cases and their impacts

The 1960s also saw significant progress in civil rights made through the courts. The Supreme Court confirmed rights to legal counsel and interracial marriage and the constitutionality of **affirmative action** policies. These judgments had a sizeable impact on the court system, as well as individual people's lives.

In 1963, Clarence Earl Gideon, accused of burglary, appeared in court alone as he was unable to afford a defense lawyer. The court refused to appoint legal counsel for him, forcing him to defend himself and, after he was convicted, he appealed on the grounds of his Sixth Amendment right to legal counsel. The Supreme Court decided unanimously in his favor, confirming the right to counsel if desired and confirming that this ruling was also binding on states. The decision in *Gideon v. Wainwright* created a need for public defenders who were properly trained in criminal defense. Prior to the ruling, public defenders were rare. The ruling had a huge impact on the legal aid system in the US and ensured, for the first time, that everyone could access legal aid regardless of their race or financial position.

In the 1950s, several states had laws prohibiting interracial marriage. In 1959, an interracial couple, Richard and Mildred Loving, were sentenced to prison for violating Virginia's law against interracial marriage. They appealed their case to the Supreme Court, and in 1967 the Court ruled unanimously in their favor. This decision prohibited all race-based marriage restrictions in the US. Although several states retained such laws on their books, they were now unenforceable. *Loving v. Virginia* also set the precedent for the argument for allowing same-sex marriage in 2015.

The Supreme Court had outlawed educational racial segregation with *Brown v. Board of Education of Topeka*. However, the question of affirmative action policies as a means of providing greater access to minorities was not addressed. In 1977, Allan Bakke (a white man) tried to get into medical school. After being rejected by the University of California, Davis twice (partially because he was deemed too old to begin medical school), Bakke brought a challenge against the university's affirmative action program on the grounds that it violated the rights of white applicants. The 1978 *Regents v. Bakke* case was contentious and the Supreme Court penned six opinions, none of which had the full support of a majority of

KEY TERM

Affirmative action Programs designed to address historical imbalances and encourage fair consideration of all groups in society.

justices. In a plurality opinion, the Court struck down UC Davis's affirmative action program. Four justices supported this and four dissented but joined them in finding that affirmative action programs were sometimes permissible, and that race could be considered during admissions processes. Overall, the case ruled that affirmative action was constitutional and, practically, most affirmative action programs continued unchanged.

Supreme Court rulings in the 1960s and 1970s expanded and guaranteed access to legal counsel, prohibited discrimination against, and criminalizing of, interracial marriage, and, to an extent, upheld the validity of affirmative action programs. These rulings, alongside the legislation made during this time, helped to ensure that, at least on paper, minorities in the US had the same opportunities and rights available to them as white Americans.

ACTIVITY

Complete a chart like the one below to summarize progress on civil rights from 1960 to 1979. Assess the effectiveness of relevant legislation and court rulings. What changed and what stayed the same?

Legislation/court ruling	Evidence of success	Evidence of failure	Judgment on impact of measure

Growth and impact of the gay rights movement

The gay rights movement saw some progress in the early 1960s as a few states began to remove their anti-sodomy laws. Despite this, LGBT people were routinely subjected to harassment and persecution in public spaces. Bars would sometimes deny service to them, or throw them out completely, for fear of being shut down. Others would refuse to let them socialize. The late 1960s saw a more organized gay rights movement start to evolve.

The Stonewall Uprising, June 1969

In the 1960s, the Stonewall Inn was a clandestine gay club in Greenwich Village, New York City which offered dancing and an opportunity to drink and socialize affordably. On June 28, 1969, New York City police raided the Stonewall Inn. The raid did not go as planned. Patrons refused to go with officers or produce identification and those who were not arrested refused to leave, instead waiting outside where a crowd started to gather.

As the first detainees were being loaded into police wagons, bystanders began to shout "gay power" and to sing "We Shall Overcome." When police tried to restrain the crowd, violence broke out. The crowd tried to overturn police cars and wagons and started to throw beer cans at police, eventually cornering them inside the Stonewall Inn. When the Tactical Patrol Force arrived to free the police in the club the violence escalated, with buildings, including the Stonewall Inn, set alight and further clashes between police and patrons. Protests and violence continued around the Stonewall Inn for a further five days.

The Stonewall Uprising was a key moment in the gay rights movement. It was remembered one year on by a march from the Stonewall Inn to Central Park. At the time, this was known as "Christopher Street Liberation Day," but it became America's first gay pride event. The official chant of the march was "Say it loud, gay is proud."

> What does this source tell you about the arguments for gay rights in the 1960s?

SOURCE 4.18

Handwritten chalk text on a boarded-up window of the Stonewall Inn after the riots, June 28, 1969. The text refers to bribes paid to police officers by the gangs who operated then-illegal gay bars

Formation of the Gay Liberation Front (July 1969) and other similar organizations

Immediately after the Stonewall Uprising in July 1969, the Gay Liberation Front (GLF) was formed. The GLF provided a voice for the newly radicalized gay community and a meeting place for activists who would go on to form other gay rights groups. From the start, the GLF stated that its aim was to confront all forms of sexism and male supremacy, which it believed was the source of LGBT oppression, and to form coalitions with other radical groups.

The GLF organized a march protesting the coverage of gay people in local New York City media. It took an anti-capitalist stance, attacked the concept of the nuclear family and traditional gender roles, denounced racism, and supported the Black Panther Party. In the coming years, it would continue to protest the portrayal of gay people in the media.

In December 1969, a group of dissident GLF activists formed the Gay Activist Alliance (GAA). Unlike the GLF, the GAA sought to work solely toward gay and lesbian rights. They declared themselves politically neutral and wanted to work within the political system. They published a newspaper, organized protests against police raids of gay bars, and executed raucous public demonstrations designed to embarrass public figures or celebrities to call attention to the issue of their rights.

The GLF had several associated and spin-off organizations. In 1970, some women from the group formed the Radicalesbians, a lesbian activist organization. Radicalesbians' first protest was at the NOW Second Congress to Unite Women. They protested NOW's exclusion of lesbians and lack of support for lesbian issues. Also in 1970, Silvia Rivera and Marsha P Johnson, two drag queens, formed the Street Transvestite Action Revolutionaries (STAR). STAR was a radical political collective that provided housing and support to LGBT youths and sex workers, as well as seeking to achieve recognition for trans individuals in society and the gay liberation movement.

Increased visibility and activism by the LGBT community led to several victories during the 1970s. In 1977, the Supreme Court ruled that a transgender woman could play at the US Open tennis tournament in the women's competition and, in 1978, Harvey Milk, running on a pro-gay rights platform, became the first openly gay man elected to political office in California.

National March on Washington for Lesbian and Gay Rights, October 1979

The first attempt to organize a national gay and lesbian march on Washington occurred in 1973, but it never came to fruition. In 1978, a conference was organized aiming to revive the idea of a march on Washington. Although this committee was dissolved, Harvey Milk, one of its members, moved forward with organizing the march, but was assassinated on November 27, 1978. His assassination motivated the subsequent organizers, and another conference was organized in February 1979, which decided the event would take place in 1979, marking the ten-year anniversary of the Stonewall Uprising.

The march had five demands:
- to pass a comprehensive lesbian and gay rights bill in Congress
- to pressure the president to issue an executive order banning discrimination based on sexual orientation in the federal government and the military
- to repeal all anti-gay laws
- to end discrimination against lesbian mothers and gay fathers in custody cases
- to protect gay and lesbian youth from laws used to discriminate against them in homes, schools, jobs, or social environments.

The march took place on October 14, 1979 and drew more than 100,000 people. Activists succeeded in meeting with senators and representatives alongside the march to discuss gay rights legislation. The march was another galvanizing moment for the movement. However, any progress was cut short by the AIDS crisis of the 1980s (page 287).

Resistance to social change

While minorities made significant progress through legislation and the courts in the 1960s and 1970s, this was not universally accepted as a benefit, nor did progress end inequalities. Resistance to social change grew over the decades. Anti-feminist movements and the religious right grew in numbers during this time and inequalities in social and economic opportunities persisted, especially for racial minorities.

Anti-feminist movement

Opposition to the feminist movement, particularly in the 1970s, was led by **Phyllis Schlafly**. Schlafly was an attorney and conservative activist. She campaigned throughout the 1960s for women to maintain the conservative values of the pre-war era, reject feminism, and embrace being homemakers. She also spoke out against abortion.

> **ACTIVITY**
>
> In pairs or groups, choose a minority group (for example, women, African Americans, Latino Americans or LGBT people) and create a presentation on what was achieved by and for your group between 1960 and 1979. Assess whether the changes were far-reaching or long-lasting.

> **KEY FIGURE**
>
> **Phyllis Schlafly** (1924–2016) Born in St Louis, Missouri, Schlafly ran for Congress in 1952, losing to the incumbent Democratic candidate. In 1964 she self-published a book called *A Choice is not an Echo* in support of the Republican candidate Barry Goldwater. She was an avid anti-feminist campaigner and an opponent of the ERA. She died on September 5, 2016.

In 1972, Schlafly began a campaign against the Equal Rights Amendment (ERA). By this point, the Amendment had been passed and ratified by 28 of the required 38 states. Schlafly began the STOP ERA campaign, which argued that the ERA would take away the gender-specific privileges enjoyed by women, including "dependent wife" social security benefits, gender-segregated bathrooms, and exemption from the draft. STOP ERA organized a group for each state, often using churches to promote its campaign and raise funds.

After the STOP ERA campaign began, seven further states ratified the ERA, but five also rescinded their ratifications. The ERA was narrowly defeated, with only 35 of the necessary 38 states ratifying it by 1982.

The religious right

The Christian or religious right wing in the US was opposed to the feminist movement, as well as to LGBT rights, aspects of reproductive autonomy, and drug-taking. The visibility of countercultures in the 1960s, combined with the rapid pace of change in women's rights and the growing movement around gay liberation, led the religious right to claim that America had stopped being a Christian nation. In response to these changes, the religious right began to form itself into a more coherent movement.

Spurred by Supreme Court rulings banning state-sponsored school prayer in the 1960s, and *Roe v. Wade* in 1973, the religious right began to organize politically. They found a home in the Republican Party where they worked for the inclusion of prayer and Christian teaching in schools, anti-abortion policies, "traditional family values," and religious freedom. They opposed movements they saw as a risk to traditional family values such as feminism and the LGBT movement.

The religious right actively engaged in politics, endorsing and campaigning for candidates who supported their agenda. They gained a great deal of political influence throughout the 1970s. The vote of the religious right was key for Jimmy Carter, a "born again" Baptist. Their support for Carter, however, was short-lived; when he supported the ERA and other socially liberal policies, they turned on him. The religious right also played a crucial role in Ronald Reagan's electoral victory in 1980.

Race riots of the late 1960s

In the 1960s, a wave of civil unrest took hold of cities across the US. Starting in 1964 and running through to 1968, the disturbances were mostly unplanned, and the violence caused a slowdown in civil rights progress. The unrest peaked in the summer of 1967 with riots in Newark and Detroit. These resulted in the creation of the Kerner Commission.

In August 1965, violence broke out in the Watts area of Los Angeles. On the night of August 11, police pulled over an African American man for drunken driving. His mother and brother were also at the scene and, after a police officer pushed his mother, the incident escalated with the man being struck in the face by police and all three eventually being arrested. The arrest drew a crowd that refused to disperse, throwing rocks and pieces of concrete at police. This incident was the beginning of six days of violent unrest. The day after the first arrest, a community meeting held by leaders in the area descended into a barrage of complaints about the treatment of the African American community by police. Overnight, crowds fought with police, set fire to buildings and cars, and looted area stores. By the third day, 50 square miles of Los Angeles were affected by rioting and the National Guard was called. The violence continued for three more days with sniper fire on police and Guardsmen, raids by police on cars and houses, and rioters throwing Molotov cocktails. A total of 34 people died in the Watts riots, mostly African American citizens, but also two policemen and a firefighter.

Like the Watts riots, the Newark riots in July 1967 began with a police traffic stop. Two white officers pulled over a Black taxi driver, beat him and arrested him on the charge of assaulting an officer. Residents of a nearby public housing project saw the man being dragged away by police and rumors spread that they had beaten him to death, causing a large crowd to gather outside the police precinct. Accounts of what happened next vary from the crowd rushing the police station to police confronting the crowd and being met with thrown bottles and rocks, but small-scale violence broke out. The violence continued for four more days with rioters looting and setting fires. The Newark riots resulted in 26 people being killed and 700 injured. The days of rioting also resulted in over 1,400 arrests, with State Troopers and the National Guard being called in to help local police.

Less than a week later, rioting broke out in Detroit, this time in response to a police raid on a Black nightclub. The police arrested everyone in the club and a large crowd gathered outside. As the police took the patrons away, looting broke out and the riots began. The violence lasted five days during which the National Guard was called, and, on the third day, President Johnson authorized the use of federal troops, who occupied the city. Thirty-seven Black people were killed, mostly by the police and military.

Social unrest in Black communities in the mid-to-late 1960s was, perhaps, not surprising. Despite inroads made by the Civil Rights Movement, police brutality and racial injustice persisted. Writer and activist James Baldwin perhaps summed the feeling up most effectively when he stated, "To be a Negro in this country and to be relatively conscious is to be in a rage, almost all the time."

Informal segregation in services such as housing, discriminatory policing, and disproportionate economic hardship meant that African Americans were still denied many of the rights and opportunities available to white Americans. The boiling over of tension in the summer of 1967 caused significant concern among white Americans, as well as officials and the government. In response to the violence, President Johnson launched the Kerner Commission to investigate the causes of the riots saying, "The only genuine, long-range solution for what has happened, lies in an attack, mounted at every level, upon the conditions that breed despair and violence."

> How do you think images like this impacted public opinion on race in the US?

SOURCE 4.19

Armed police stand by as rioters lie face down in the street during the Watts riots in Los Angeles, California, August 1965

The Kerner Report, February 1968

While the riots described here were the three largest, there were in fact around 150 riots across the US in 1967. Johnson felt that he had to do something to react to the events and, in July 1967, he launched the Kerner Commission. The Commission, chaired by Governor Otto Kerner of Illinois, was tasked with investigating the causes of the riots and providing recommendations to prevent a recurrence of the violence.

After seven months of work and investigation, the Commission published the Kerner Report in February 1968. It became an instant bestseller, selling over two million copies across the US. The Report's main finding was that the riots stemmed from Black communities' frustration at a lack of economic opportunity and the way "white society," particularly the police, treated them. The Report highlighted failures of both federal and state governments in housing, education, and social services policy. It concluded that white racism was the main cause of the violence and that white America bore much of the responsibility for Black rioting.

The report received widespread media coverage and responses were mixed. Conservatives disliked that white Americans were blamed and felt that the Report did not place enough culpability on the rioters themselves. Others were happy that racism was being formally acknowledged, while some were frustrated that the Report had no new findings, instead reporting what most Black people already knew. Johnson's administration mostly rejected the Report on the grounds that the funding it called for was unrealistic. Johnson also felt that, given the scale of the rioting, there must be some conspiracy involved, but the Report had found no evidence of this.

The rioting and the Kerner Report highlight that, although significant progress had been made in civil rights through legislation and the courts, the lived experience of Black people in the US was still marked by racism, discrimination, and obstacles not faced by their white counterparts.

SUMMARY DIAGRAM

The position of minorities in the US, 1960–79

Why and how far did the position of minorities in the US improve between 1960 and 1979?

Women
- Formation of NOW-1966
- NOW Bill of Rights
- Women's Strike for Equality
- Women's liberation movement
  - Miss America protests
  - Combahee River Collective
  - Fight for ERA (unsuccessful)
- Equal Pay Act – promised equal pay for equal work
- Title VII of the Civil Rights Act - prohibition of employment discrimination on the basis of sex
  - *Phillips v. Martin Marietta*
  - *Corning Glass Works v. Brennan*
- Title IX of the Education Amendments – prohibited sex-based discrimination in schools and education programs funded by the federal government
- *Reed v. Reed* – upheld that sex-based discrimination was unconstitutional
- *Roe v. Wade* – constitutionally protected the right to abortion

Civil rights
- Key leaders:
  - Martin Luther King Jr.
  - Stokely Carmichael
  - Malcolm X
  - Cesar Chavez
  - Dolores Huerta
  - Dennis Banks
- Key Groups:
  - Black Power Movement
  - Black Panther Party
  - Rainbow Coalition
  - Chicano Movement
  - AIM
  - Asian American Political Alliance
- Civil Rights Act 1960 – prevented discriminatory practices in voting registration
- Civil Rights Act 1964 – outlawed discrimination based on race, religion, colour, sex, or national origin
- Voting Rights Act 1965 – prohibited discriminatory practices in voter registration
- Immigration and Nationality Act 1965 – abolished discriminator National Origins Formula
- Indian Self-Determination and Education Assistance Act 1975 – authorized government agencies to enter into contracts with and make grants to Native American peoples

Civil rights
- *Gideon v. Wainwright* – confirmed the right to legal counsel
- *Regents v. Bakke* – confirmed constitutionality of affirmative action
- *Loving v. Virginia* – ruled laws against inter-racial marriage unconstitutional
- Founding of the National Farm Workers Association 1962 – organised Delano grape pickers' strike 1965
- Formation of the United Farm Workers union 1966
- California's Agricultural Labor Relations Act 1975 – gave farmworkers the right to unionize and engage in collective bargaining in California
- Founding of AIM 1968
  - Occupation of Alcatraz 1969
  - Trail of Broken Treaties 1972
  - Occupation of Wounded Knee 1973
  - Longest Walk 1978
- Founding of the Asian American Political Alliance

LGBT Rights
- Stonewall Uprising – 1969
- Christopher Street Liberation Day (first gay pride event) – 1979
- Formation of Gay Liberation Front – 1969
- National March on Washington for Lesbian and Gay Rights – 1979

Persisting inequalities
- Race riots – Watts, Newark, Detroit
  - Persistence of police brutality
  - Informal segregation
  - Discrimination in services
- Kerner Commission and Kerner Report
  - Concluded that riots stemmed from African American communities' frustration at lack of economic opportunity and poor treatment from white society

Resistance to social change
- Phyllis Schlafly and STOP ERA
- Rise of the Christian right
- Opposition to *Roe v. Wade*
- Support for "traditional family values"
- Opposition to LGBT movement

CHAPTER SUMMARY

The 1960s and 1970s saw significant change for the US in both foreign and domestic affairs. After bringing the world to the brink of nuclear war in the early 1960s, the superpowers moved away from direct confrontation to engage in proxy wars, before embarking on a period of *détente* and trying to normalize relations. Domestically, the period saw the beginning of the polarization that has gone on to dominate US politics. A period of progressive, left-leaning government which moved toward equality between races and sexes was met with resistance from certain sections of society. Driven partially by fear of perceived societal disintegration through countercultural values, race riots, and anti-war protests, and partially by concerns about the economy, the right wing of US politics came to the fore with Nixon's election in 1968. The right grew in power and popularity throughout this period thanks to growing organization among those opposed to the liberalization of social policy. The legalization of abortion and liberalization of sexuality and gender roles led to the rise of the religious right. Using its developing organizational acumen, the religious right played a part in the election of Carter before turning on him, and the Democrats more generally, for his liberal social views, leading to the election of Reagan in 1980.

REFRESHER QUESTIONS

1. How did Kennedy's "flexible response" differ from Eisenhower's Cold War policy?
2. What was the Gulf of Tonkin Resolution?
3. What was the impact of the Vietnam War on US foreign policy?
4. Why did Nixon pursue *détente* policies?
5. What were the key policies of the war on poverty?
6. How did the Republican Party appeal to the "silent majority"?
7. Why was television so important in giving rise to the anti-war movement?
8. What impact did Supreme Court decisions have on the position of minorities between 1960 and 1979?
9. What key legislation was passed concerning civil rights between 1960 and 1979?
10. What was the impact of the Kerner Report?

Study skills

Guidance on answering essay questions

Explaining causation

This section is going to consider how you can develop your answers by building on the skills you practiced in Chapter 2.

To recap: this section will focus on answering questions that focus on *causation*. This means that you will need to identify and explain a range of causes.
- You need to show detailed knowledge and understanding of the reasons why a specific event occurred or why someone adopted a particular course of action.
- This will be the combined effect of several factors, both long- and short-term, and may include different types of causes, such as political and economic.

To develop your answer fully, consider the following:
- You will need to show how these factors are connected.
- Think about how important a cause was—without it, would the event/issue have taken place?
- Be analytical. Show how the causes are linked together or assess their relative importance. Avoid writing a narrative about what happened.
- Produce a short but reasoned conclusion to your answer.

> ### ACTIVITY
> #### Planning an answer
> Using the techniques covered in Chapter 2, plan an answer to this question:
> **Explain why the Cuban Missile Crisis occurred in October 1962.** [10]
> What issues do you need to consider for this question?
> - What were the key events in the build-up to the missile crisis?
> - Why did Khrushchev place missiles in Cuba?
> - What was the relationship between Cuba and the US?
> - Why had this relationship deteriorated in the 1950s?
> - What was the role of ideology?

What makes an effective paragraph in a causal explanation?

> #### Sample paragraph 1
> One of the causes of the Cuban Missile Crisis was Khrushchev's perception of Kennedy. After the failed Bay of Pigs invasion and Kennedy's weak response to the Berlin Crisis, Khrushchev believed that Kennedy was weak and would be unwilling to stand up to Soviet provocation in the Caribbean. As such, in July 1962, when Khrushchev decided that he needed to counter the US's lead in the arms race, he believed he could level the playing field by agreeing to Castro's demands to place missiles in Cuba without incurring a reaction from Kennedy. This incorrect assumption which led to Khrushchev placing missiles in Cuba led to the US responding by blockading the island. This brought the superpowers into direct conflict and acted as a catalyst for the Cuban Missile Crisis.

> ### ACTIVITY
> Using the checklist you made in Chapter 2, read this paragraph in response to the question above.

Read the paragraph carefully. Do you think it meets the criteria in the list below?
- Are relevant factors considered?
- Are the factors explained rather than described?
- Is it clear how the factor caused the event?
- Is the supporting information accurate and relevant?

Developing your answer to the question

Once you have honed your skills in planning answers and writing effective paragraphs, you need to think about the following:
- How do the factors in your answer link together?
- Is one factor more important than the others—would the event have happened at all without it?

Below is a list of factors which caused the Cuban Missile Crisis:
- Khrushchev placing missiles in Cuba
- the Cuban Revolution
- ideological conflicts between the US and USSR
- the Bay of Pigs incident
- the Berlin Crisis
- the US blockade of Cuba
- the arms race.

Are these long-, medium- or short-term causes?

If you removed one of these causes, would the Cuban Missile Crisis still have happened?

Assessing a sample answer

In Chapter 2 you saw that strong answers contain the following features:
- two or three relevant factors are considered
- factors are explained rather than described
- a clear link is made between the factor and the event
- supporting information is accurate and relevant
- there is consideration of the relationship between factors
- a supported conclusion is reached.

> ### ACTIVITY
>
> Read the following two responses to the question. For each response, ask yourself:
> - Does this answer meet your criteria for effective paragraphs?
> - Does it meet the criteria that strong answers demonstrate
>
> Now compare the two responses:
> - Which answer is more effective?
> - How could the other answer be improved?

Sample answer 1

The Cuban Missile Crisis was caused by the Soviet Union putting missiles in Cuba in 1962. On October 14, 1962, a US plane took photos of Soviet missiles in Cuba, which led to Kennedy blockading the island. This brought the superpowers into direct conflict which was resolved by Kennedy and Khrushchev making a deal in which the blockade would be lifted if the missiles were removed.

Another cause of the Cuban Missile Crisis was Castro's support for communism. After the Cuban Revolution, Castro, the leader of Cuba, took control of the island. He nationalized American-owned businesses and supported the USSR. This made the US nervous because Cuba is very close to Florida, and they did not like having a communist regime so close by.

Sample answer 2

The causes of the Cuban Missile Crisis stretch back to the Cuban Revolution of 1959. After the Revolution, Fidel Castro took control of Cuba and nationalized many American-owned businesses, including sugar mills and banks. This led to increased tension between the US and Cuba and, in retaliation, the US launched an economic embargo of the island. Now cut off from US imports, Cuba turned to the USSR for economic support and embraced communist ideals. This led to significant tensions between the US and Cuba since the US was very concerned about having a communist regime so close to its shores.

By 1962, Khrushchev perceived Kennedy as a weak and ineffective leader. The failure of the Bay of Pigs invasion and Kennedy's lack of response to the Berlin Crisis had led Khrushchev to believe that Kennedy did not have the expertise or power to resist Soviet military build up in the Caribbean. At the same time, Khrushchev became concerned about the US's growing nuclear superiority. Therefore, he decided to agree to Castro's demands for military assistance and place missiles in Cuba. This was the immediate trigger which sparked the Cuban Missile Crisis. Khrushchev's assessment of Kennedy turned out to be incorrect and, when the US discovered the missiles, Kennedy launched a blockade of the island and demanded removal of the missiles.

Overall, the most important cause of the Cuban Missile Crisis was the ongoing arms race between the superpowers. By 1962, the superpowers had enough nuclear firepower to wipe each other out completely. However, the US was much better armed with around 6,800 nuclear warheads compared to the Soviet Union's 500. The US had begun to station missiles in Turkey. Khrushchev felt that the US had superior "first strike" capability and, partly because he believed Kennedy to be weak, decided to place missiles in Cuba to level the playing field. If the superpowers had not been so determined to maintain the policy of mutual assured destruction, it is unlikely that Khrushchev would have agreed to put missiles in Cuba, sparking the crisis.

Question practice

Using this question, practice planning an answer that shows the links between different factors.

Explain why Nixon introduced the policy of Vietnamization. [10]

5 The Modern US, 1980 to 2008

Introduction

The late twentieth century brought many changes for the US, both internationally and domestically. The reescalation and eventual end of the Cold War ushered in a new, more globalized world with greater international cooperation and new challenges and dangers. At home, US politics grew more divided and political discourse turned toward economics and "culture wars." Globalization and technological advances brought new challenges as countries became more multicultural and political engagement more popularized through social media. This chapter will examine these decades by considering the following questions:

▶ Why and how did the global role of the US evolve between 1980 and 2008?
▶ Why and how did US politics change between 1980 and 2008?
▶ Why and how far did US society change between 1980 and 2008?

▶ KEY DATES

January 1981	Ronald Reagan takes office
November 1989	Fall of the Berlin Wall
December 1991	Collapse of the Soviet Union
April 1992	LA race riots
January 1993	Bill Clinton takes office
February 1993	Bombing of the World Trade Center
December 1993	Signing of NAFTA
November 1993	Establishment of the European Union
January 1995	Establishment of the World Trade Organization
January 2001	George W Bush takes office after a contested election
September 2001	Attack on the World Trade Center and the Pentagon (9/11)
March 2003	Invasion of Iraq
January 2009	Barack Obama takes office

5.1 Why and how did the global role of the US evolve between 1980 and 2008?

During this period, the Cold War intensified again before coming to an abrupt end in 1991, with the collapse of the USSR. The collapse brought radical change to global geopolitics. It resulted in the rise of a more united Europe, greater international engagement, free trade, and the rise of new threats. This section will focus on four main areas:
- the reescalation and end of the Cold War
- the impacts of globalization
- post-Cold War developments
- the impacts of the 9/11 attacks and the War on Terror.

Reescalation and end of the Cold War

The last phase of the Cold War involved a sharp increase in hostility between the superpowers. President **Ronald Reagan** rejected the earlier strategies of both containment and *détente* in favor of the Reagan Doctrine (see below). By the mid-1980s, leadership in the USSR had become unstable and the economy was failing. In 1985, **Mikhail Gorbachev** became the USSR's fourth leader in five years. He took a more conciliatory approach to the West and a less hardline approach domestically, allowing the countries of Eastern Europe to move away from the communist system if they wished.

> **KEY FIGURES**
>
> **Ronald Reagan** (1911–2004) Reagan started his career as a sports broadcaster before becoming an actor. In 1966, he was elected as Governor of California and unsuccessfully challenged Gerald Ford in the 1976 Republican primary. He ran for president in the 1980 election and won by a landslide victory over Jimmy Carter. Famous for his implementation of "Reaganomics" (page 265), he left the presidency in 1989 before dying in 2004.
>
> **Mikhail Gorbachev** (1931–2022) Born to a peasant family of Russian and Ukrainian heritage, Gorbachev grew up under Stalin's rule. He worked on a collective farm before joining the Communist Party and studying at Moscow State University. He was a keen supporter of Khrushchev's de-Stalinization policies. He was elected General Secretary of the Party and leader of the USSR in 1985. After the fall of the Berlin Wall, Gorbachev was re-elected but by November 1990 calls for his resignation increased. After a failed coup attempt, Gorbachev resigned in favor of Boris Yeltsin in December 1991. He lived in Moscow and became a critic of Vladimir Putin's government. He died at the age of 91 on August 30, 2022.

Reagan's abandonment of *détente*

Reagan was a committed anti-communist. He referred to the USSR as the "evil empire" and believed that it was the US's responsibility to save the world from Soviet repression. During his first term, he returned to a confrontational approach. He aimed to combat the USSR by:
- diminishing Soviet resources (including depressing the value of Soviet commodities)
- increasing US defense spending to strengthen its negotiating position
- forcing the USSR to devote more of its economic resources to defense.

He set out the "Reagan Doctrine," promising aid and assistance to right-wing, often repressive, regimes and guerrilla movements opposing Soviet-supported governments. Under the Reagan Doctrine, the CIA trained, equipped, and led Mujahideen (see p.208 Key Term) forces against the Soviet army.

Reagan increased US defense spending by $32.6 billion. One of his key proposals was for the Strategic Defense Initiative (SDI). Known as "Star Wars" by its critics, the SDI was a speculative program involving research into an array of advanced weapons concepts. These included lasers, particle-beams, and ground- and space-based missiles, as well as the sensor and computer systems required to control a system of satellites spanning the globe. Critics believed the plan to be fanciful science fiction (hence the nickname "Star Wars") and the SDI plan was never realized.

In addition to the SDI, under Reagan the US military produced a neutron bomb. The USSR described the neutron bomb as a "capitalist weapon" because it was designed to kill people but leave buildings and property intact. Originally developed in the 1950s and 1960s, Reagan authorized production of the bomb in 1981. It remained part of US arms stockpiles until it was retired in 1992.

Reagan's harsh language and hardline attitude toward the USSR marked much of the early years of his presidency. The Reagan Doctrine resulted in the US supporting and allying with regimes across the world that had poor human rights records, including Ferdinand Marcos's dictatorship in the Philippines and South Africa's apartheid government. It also led to covert US involvement with violent guerrilla movements in Angola, Nicaragua, and Afghanistan. In contrast, during his second term, Reagan's attitude toward the USSR relaxed, largely thanks to the conciliatory policies of his Soviet counterpart Mikhail Gorbachev.

The impacts of the policies of Gorbachev and his relationship with President Reagan

Mikhail Gorbachev became leader of the USSR following four years of turmoil within the leadership. After Brezhnev died in 1982, Yuri Andropov became leader through his connections as head of the **KGB**. He tried to eliminate corruption and inefficiency but suffered from ill health and died in February 1984. He was succeeded by 71-year-old Konstantin Chernenko. Also in poor health, suffering from lung disease, he attempted to reduce the Communist Party's micromanagement of the economy, but in March 1985, also died after just a year in office.

By this time, the USSR was also struggling economically. The economy had not grown for nearly twenty years by the 1980s; shelves in shops were often empty and queues for food and other necessities were common. Following Chernenko's death, Gorbachev became leader of the USSR. As the first Soviet leader born after the 1917 revolution, Gorbachev came to power with very different ideas from his predecessors. Although still committed to preserving the Soviet state and communist ideals, he believed the only route to the USSR's survival was significant, far-reaching economic and political reform. Domestically, he implemented two key reforms: *glasnost* and *perestroika*.

> **KEY TERMS**
>
> **KGB** The Committee for State Security (KGB) was the main security agency for the USSR from 1954 to 1991. It carried out internal security, counterintelligence, foreign intelligence, and secret police functions.
>
> *Glasnost* Meaning "openness," the *glasnost* program aimed to deliver increased transparency in government institutions and activities. It reflected a commitment to the citizens of the USSR to allow public discussion of the challenges of their system and potential solutions. At its heart, this translated to greater freedom of speech and of the press domestically.
>
> *Perestroika* Literally meaning "restructuring," perestroika was an attempt to end the stagnation of the Soviet economy and political system. It allowed greater independent action from government ministries and introduced key market-like reforms to the Soviet command economy (an economy in which the government decides levels of production and prices).

Alongside his policy of increased openness in domestic government, Gorbachev got along with other world leaders, and, over time, he and Reagan developed a bond. Reagan and Gorbachev wrote many letters back and forth and undertook four key summits in three years, including one in Geneva in 1985 and one in Reykjavik in 1986. Aware that he would never be able to out-spend the US, Gorbachev cut spending on nuclear weapons and resumed the Strategic Arms Reduction Talks (START), a continuation of the SALT Program. This resulted in a deal to limit the production of intermediate-range nuclear missiles in 1987.

Gorbachev's reforms and ability to get along with other world leaders led to a stabilization of superpower relations toward the end of the 1980s. When asked in 1988 if he still considered the Soviet Union the "evil empire," Reagan responded, "No, that was another time, another era." It is difficult to say how much of this shift in attitude was down to the personal relationship between Reagan and Gorbachev, but Gorbachev's willingness to meet Reagan halfway certainly helped.

The fall of the Berlin Wall

Gorbachev's increased openness in the USSR encouraged similar changes across the Eastern Bloc countries. In June 1989, Poland held free elections and in August a protest on the border between Austria and Hungary began to dismantle the barbed wire barrier between the two countries. This set in motion a chain of events that reshaped the political geography of Europe.

When Gorbachev did not respond to the dismantling of the Austrian-Hungarian barriers, refugees from across the Bloc began to travel to Hungary to cross the border. Many also went to the West German embassy in Prague, Czechoslovakia. In September 1989, after negotiations with East Germany and the USSR, the West German foreign minister visited Prague to tell those in the embassy that they were allowed to travel to West Germany.

On November 9, 1989, an East German Communist Party spokesperson announced new policies on border crossing, which would allow East Germans to apply for permission to cross from East to West and allow for permanent crossing. When asked when these changes would come into force, he said, "As far as I know ... effective immediately." As news spread, East Germans gathered at checkpoints along the Berlin Wall chanting, "Open the gates." After making panicked calls to their superiors and receiving no clear response, the overwhelmed border guards opened the gates.

Over the following weekend, individuals knocked away chunks of the Wall with sledgehammers and chisels while cranes and bulldozers tore down other parts. Initially, the East German border guards tried to stop people from attacking the Wall, but they quickly gave up. In December 1989, the Brandenburg Gate was opened and the West German chancellor met with the East German prime minister to announce visa-free travel.

The fall of the Berlin Wall was the first step toward German reunification, but not all of Europe was happy about this. British prime minister Margaret Thatcher and French president François Mitterrand opposed reunification, with Thatcher privately confiding in Gorbachev that she wanted him to try to stop it. Despite these objections, the fall of the Berlin Wall is often considered the moment that marked the beginning of the end of the Cold War.

> What does Source 5.1 tell us about the attitudes of Berliners to the Berlin Wall by 1989?

SOURCE 5.1

A man attacks the Berlin Wall with a sledgehammer following the opening of the border. The area around the hole was later secured by West German police and the East German border guards attempted to repair it

The impact of the collapse of the USSR and its satellite states

After the Berlin Wall fell, events escalated rapidly. Within two years, the whole Soviet system had unraveled. Throughout 1989, communist regimes in the Eastern Bloc fell, starting with Poland in June 1989. This was quickly followed by the fall of the regimes in Czechoslovakia in November 1989, Romania in December 1989, and Hungary and Bulgaria in 1990. By the summer of 1990, almost all the Eastern Bloc countries had democratically elected governments, although not all these transitions were peaceful.

In 1990, the Communist Party of the USSR voted to end one-party rule, and in June 1991, **Boris Yeltsin** was elected president of the new Russian republic. Yeltsin had been a member of the Communist Party until 1990 when he resigned. He ran in the 1991 election independently and was associated with liberalism. In July 1991, the Warsaw Pact was dissolved, and in December 1991, the Soviet Union was formally dissolved.

> ### KEY FIGURE
>
> **Boris Yeltsin** (1931–2007) Born in present-day Kazakhstan, Yeltsin studied at the Ural State Technical University before working in construction and joining the Communist Party. He criticized Gorbachev's reforms as being too moderate. In 1987 he was the first member to resign from the Politburo. This made him a popular anti-establishment figure. He was elected President of Russia in 1991 and remained in office until his resignation in December 1999. His presidency was marked by political and economic crises and corruption scandals. Throughout his time in office, Yeltsin suffered from poor health and his alleged alcoholism was often the subject of media discussion. He maintained a low profile following his resignation and died on April 23, 2007 aged 76.

The fall of the USSR left the US as the world's only major superpower. This freed it from the constraints imposed by the threat of a powerful rival. In 1989, **George HW Bush** had taken over from Reagan and, when Yeltsin came to power, the US quickly recognized the new republics from the Eastern Bloc and established relations both with them and the new Russian republic. Yeltsin and Bush met in Camp David, the US president's official country retreat, in February 1992, followed by a state visit to Washington DC in June. In 1993 they signed the START II treaty, which amounted to a 50 percent reduction in nuclear weapons.

> ### KEY FIGURE
>
> **George HW Bush** (1924–2018) Bush served as a pilot in the US Navy Reserve during the Second World War before moving to Texas and establishing a successful oil company. He was elected to the House of Representatives in 1966. Following his defeat by Reagan in the 1980 Republican primary, he became vice president before winning the presidential election in 1988. When he lost the 1992 election, he spent his time working on humanitarian activities. He died on November 30, 2018 at the age of 94.

The removal of the USSR as an opposing power allowed the US to intervene in other countries with no fear of major retaliation or pushback. However, this situation also highlighted cracks in the relationships between the US and its allies. The fall of the USSR brought about greater interaction between states and people. This accelerated the process of globalization and changed the way nations communicated and negotiated. This led to expanded global commerce and more foreign direct investment to developing nations, but also led to new conflicts, crises, and wars in places previously controlled by the interests of the US or the USSR.

> ### ACTIVITY
>
> In groups or pairs, using the information in this chapter, make a list of the consequences of the fall of the Berlin Wall. Divide this list into short-, medium-, and long-term consequences and discuss how the consequences link to each other.

The Iran-Contra affair

Figure 5.1 Nicaragua's location in Central America

Reagan won the 1980 election, but the Republican Party could not maintain this electoral enthusiasm. In the 1982 mid-terms, they lost the majority in both the House and the Senate. After they took control of Congress, the Democrats passed the Boland Amendment. This restricted the activities the CIA and Department of Defense could carry out in foreign conflicts.

The Boland Amendment was aimed at the Reagan administration's involvement in Nicaragua. Nicaragua is a Central American nation often considered by the US to be part of its sphere of influence. In July 1979, the US-friendly government was overthrown by the Sandinista National Liberation Front (or the **Sandinistas**). Various rebel groups, known collectively as the "**Contras**" arose to oppose the Sandinistas. Under the Reagan Doctrine, the US Government provided the Contras with military and financial aid. This was despite the Contras' documented terrorist tactics and human rights abuses. The Boland Amendment was designed to stop this support to the Contras.

> **KEY TERMS**
>
> **Sandinistas** The Sandinistas were a left-wing political party in Nicaragua. After overthrowing the government in 1979, they ruled Nicaragua until 1990. They operated a form of participatory democracy, implementing literacy programs, land reform, significant healthcare programs, and nationalization. They were criticized by the international community for human rights abuses, including the oppression of indigenous communities.
>
> **Contras** The collective term for the right-wing rebel groups that were active between 1979 and 1990 in opposition to the Sandinista government. Largely based in Honduras, the Contras used terrorist tactics and committed numerous human rights violations within Nicaragua. From an early stage, they received financial and military support from the US government.

A few months after the Sandinista revolution, a group of Iranian students in the Middle East stormed the US Embassy in Iran and took 52 Americans hostage. In response, President Carter imposed an arms embargo on Iran which Reagan publicly refused to lift when Iraq invaded Iran in September 1980.

In the mid-1980s, seven Americans were taken hostage in Lebanon by an Iranian-backed organization. Reagan was desperate to secure the release of the hostages. Therefore, when Iran approached the Reagan administration in 1985 to buy weapons, he agreed to the sale, and undermined the embargo. The secret sale of arms to Iran provided the CIA with funds which they secretly sent to the Contras. Not only did this violate the embargo and the Boland Amendment, but also Reagan's own commitment never to negotiate with terrorists.

In 1986, a Lebanese newspaper broke the story about the US–Iran arms deal. The US Attorney General, Edwin Meese, launched an investigation into the sales and found that some of the money Iran had paid was unaccounted for. Lieutenant Colonel Oliver North, a member of the National Security Council, came forward to say that he had diverted the missing money to the Contras with the full knowledge of Reagan's National Security Advisor, Robert McFarlane, and presumably Reagan himself.

Reagan was hounded by the press over the scandal for the remainder of his presidency. In 1987, a televised congressional investigation secured testimony from those involved, including Reagan. The Tower Commission, set up to investigate the administration's involvement, concluded that the scandal occurred due to Reagan's lack of oversight. Fourteen people were charged with crimes related to the affair, although Reagan was not among them. The scandal did not have a particularly negative impact on Reagan's popularity.

Impacts of globalization on US foreign policy

Globalization refers to the political, economic, and cultural exchanges between people and nations that make the world more interconnected and interdependent. The integration of newly independent Eastern Bloc countries into the global market economy led to increased trade, investment, migration, and cultural exchange. New alliances and trading groups emerged, and this brought new challenges for international relations and geopolitics.

> **KEY TERM**
>
> **Globalization** The process of increasing interaction and integration of the world's economies, markets, societies, and cultures. It is often characterized by the free movement of goods, people, capital, skills, and ideas across borders.

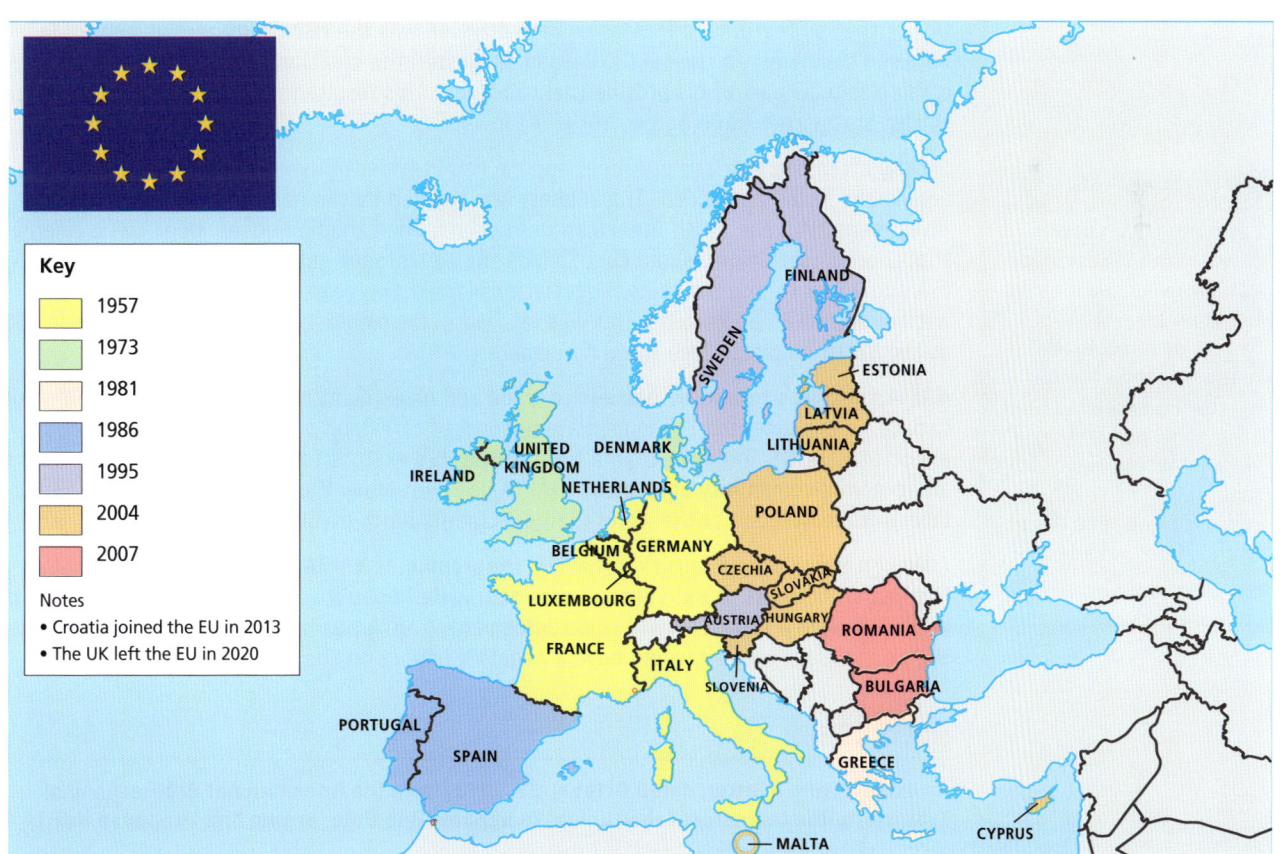

Figure 5.2 Map of Europe showing the EU nations by the year they joined, up to 2007

Rise of the European Union

Although Eastern Europe had been isolated for much of the twentieth century, after the Second World War, European integration started to be seen as a solution for the extreme nationalism many saw as the cause of the conflict. Several organizations had been formed between 1948 and 1993 to facilitate European integration, including the European Economic Community, which established a customs union. Over the 1970s and 1980s, the Community grew steadily, resulting in the Maastricht Treaty, which came into force in November 1993, forming the European Union (EU).

The EU initially brought together twelve nations: the UK, France, Germany, Spain, Ireland, Portugal, Italy, Greece, Denmark, Luxembourg, Belgium, and the Netherlands. It secured European cooperation on issues of the economy, society, the environment, foreign and security policy, and international crime. The EU created a single market, guaranteeing free movement of goods, services, people, and capital across member states and the European Economic Area (including Norway, Iceland, and Liechtenstein, which are not EU member states). In 1995, Austria, Sweden, and Finland also joined the EU. In 1996, the **Schengen Agreement** abolished internal border checks between almost all member states and the EU began to discuss the creation of a single currency (although this would not come into existence until 2002).

The rise of the EU changed the global economic and geopolitical dynamic again. After the fall of the USSR, the US had been the only major economic and political superpower. With the expansion and formalization of European integration, this began to change. Soon, the US and EU dominated world trade and played leading roles in international diplomacy and security. While not exactly a superpower, the EU created a counterbalance to US power, albeit a friendly one. Ideological alignment has not, however, prevented disagreements; the US and EU have held very different political, economic, and social agendas over the years.

Signing of the North American Free Trade Agreement, December 1993

One of the key features of increasing globalization was the rise of interest in free trade between countries. In the 1980s, Reagan suggested the creation of a North American free trading zone as part of his presidential campaign. This resulted in the signing of the Canada–United States Free Trade Agreement (FTA) in 1988.

Shortly after, the Mexican president approached President Bush to propose a similar agreement including Mexico. This request was sparked by the need to increase foreign investment after the **Latin American debt crisis**. The Canadian government was concerned that these negotiations would cost Canada the advantages gained through the Canada–US FTA and asked to join the talks. Negotiations lasted two years and, in 1992, the three nations signed an agreement. This was ratified in December 1993, coming into force in 1994 as the North American Free Trade Agreement (NAFTA).

NAFTA's goal was to remove barriers to trade and investment between the US, Mexico, and Canada. It implemented the immediate removal of tariffs on more than half of Mexico's exports to the US and more than a third of the US's exports to Mexico. While deliberately not an economic-community agreement (NAFTA does not allow the free movement of people or labor), it created one of the world's largest trading blocs by GDP.

Although it began as Reagan's initiative, the signing of NAFTA (page 270) was one of the first major victories of Bill Clinton's presidency. He hoped it would encourage other nations to work toward a broader world trade agreement. NAFTA was not universally popular in the US, as critics believed it would have a negative impact on the US manufacturing sector.

SOURCE 5.2

An extract from a letter, dated October 27, 1993, from the International Brotherhood of Teamsters (the teamsters labor union) to Senator Bob Dole, urging him to oppose NAFTA

NAFTA is bad for working people on both sides of the border and poses new threats to highway safety. It will cost good American jobs, while locking Mexican workers into $4-a-day conditions.

KEY TERM

Schengen Agreement the Schengen Agreement established free movement between the countries that signed up to it. The original member states included Germany, France, Belgium, Luxemburg, and the Netherlands.

KEY TERM

Latin American debt crisis In the 1980s, many Latin American countries (most notably, Brazil, Argentina, and Mexico) found that their foreign borrowing exceeded their earning power, so they were unable to repay their debt. The resulting crisis is often referred to as the "Lost Decade."

It will encourage more employers to demand cuts in our standard of living. It will also cost the American taxpayer and add billions of dollars to the federal deficit because of lost taxes and tariffs, as well as new spending for environmental clean-up and employment benefits.

Fortunately, there is an alternative. Once NAFTA is defeated, President Clinton and the Congress can develop a <u>fair</u> trade policy aimed at raising labor, environmental and consumer standards in other countries instead of lowering them here. That is the only way to increase trade, protect and expand good American jobs, reduce immigration, and stop the exploitation of working people and the environment both at home and abroad …

> What do Sources 5.2 and 5.3 tell us about the arguments for and against NAFTA? What do they show about the different groups who supported and opposed the agreement?

SOURCE 5.3

An extract of the talking points (notes) for President Clinton's speech at the Wall Street Journal Conference, October 28, 1993

By boosting our exports to Mexico, NAFTA creates jobs here in the United States. 200,000 new jobs by 1995. If it didn't, I wouldn't support it.

NAFTA is vital not only because cutting tariffs will foster exports, but because it will help us compete with our rivals around the globe. It will give us an extra edge in our own backyard, and enable our hemisphere to work cooperatively in a way that benefits all our people.

- Consider the auto industry. Today, Mexican law requires that part of each car sold in Mexico be made in Mexico. NAFTA would repeal that rule. This year, the Big Three will sell 1000 U.S.-made cars in Mexico. In the first year after NAFTA, they will sell 60,000. Our competitors will face the same rules of origin as today.
- Consider computers. After NAFTA, computers shipped from the US to Mexico will pay no tariff. Computers shipped from Europe or Japan will continue to pay a 20% tariff. That gives us an immediate 20% cost advantage.
- Our competitors know this. Last week in Mexico, Japan's Deputy Trade Minister complained that NAFTA was unfair to Japan because it gave the US preferential access to the Mexican market.

And it is clear that if we do not take advantage of this opportunity, our competitors may well do so.

Establishment of the World Trade Organization, January 1995

In 1947, 23 countries established a multilateral treaty to promote international trade by reducing barriers such as tariffs and quotas. In September 1986, a renegotiation of this treaty led to the founding of the World Trade Organization (WTO) in January 1995.

The WTO was established to govern world trade. Made up of member states that made decisions by consensus (collective agreement), it facilitated trade in goods, services, and intellectual property. It provided a framework for the negotiation of trade agreements aiming to reduce tariffs, quotas, and other restrictions. It also provided dispute resolution to ensure countries acted in line with trade agreements and resolved trade disputes.

The US was a key player in the creation of the WTO; however, Russia was not one of the founder members. Although it had been in negotiations to join the WTO's predecessor treaty since 1993, these negotiations were not resolved until 2012. The WTO opened markets for US industry, agriculture, and manufacturing, and provided a significant boost to the US economy in the late 1990s.

Rapid economic growth of China

Figure 5.3 World map indicating China (in green).

In 1979, China's government began to implement free-market reforms in its economy. These reforms, combined with the opening of the country to foreign trade and investment in the early 1980s, made the Chinese economy one of the fastest-growing in the world. Foreign firms rushed to build factories there to take advantage of low labor costs. Between 1980 and 2008, China's economy experienced the fastest sustained expansion of a major economy in history, almost doubling its GDP every eight years.

The growth of China as an economic powerhouse also meant that the US's status as the world's only superpower was short-lived. As US businesses began to move their manufacturing to China, China became a major commercial partner of the US through the 1990s and 2000s. This had a challenging effect on the US middle class as America lost factories and manufacturing jobs. The loss of manufacturing was made worse by the signing of an act that led to China becoming a permanent free trade partner of the US. The intention of the act was to normalize relations with China and open a new export market to American businesses; however, as became clear later, this came largely at the expense of the US middle class.

In the 1990s and 2000s, China became an economic superpower to rival the US and the EU. The economic balance of power began to shift throughout these decades because, as US manufacturing declined, the **trade deficit** with China widened and China became the largest holder of US Treasury securities. The two economies became increasingly intertwined during this period. Post-2010, this has led to many concerns about the risk China poses to US national security.

> **KEY TERM**
>
> **Trade deficit** When a country is importing more goods and services than it is exporting.

The role of the G8 nations

In the 1970s, the US, UK, West Germany, Italy, France, and Japan formed the Group of Six. This was an informal grouping of industrialized nations that would meet yearly to discuss matters of economic and political importance. The group widened to include Canada in 1976 and, in 1997, Russia joined to form the Group of Eight (G8).

The G8 met annually, providing a place where leaders of member nations and their finance ministers could openly discuss international issues. In the 1990s and early 2000s, the G8 nations wielded significant power, as their combined wealth and resources constituted roughly half of the global economy. They worked together to help solve global problems, discussing matters such as terrorism, financial and energy crises, and monetary systems.

ACTIVITY

In pairs or groups, discuss the impact on US foreign policy of the establishment of the EU, the WTO, and the G8, and the economic growth of China. Select one of these factors and make a presentation outlining how it changed (or did not change) US foreign policy thinking.

While lacking the legislative or authoritative power of the UN, the G8 held significant sway. It allowed a place for discussion, problem-solving, and increased international cooperation. It recommended policies and plans for member states to work together to implement. However, critics suggested that the G8 operated as a "rich nations club," ignoring the needs of developing and poorer nations. In the late 1990s and early 2000s, the group was also criticized for not including the five key emerging economies of Brazil, India, China, Mexico, and South Africa.

Post-Cold War developments

The end of the Cold War did not bring an end to geopolitical crises. US attention was drawn to conflicts in the Middle East and the republics created as the Eastern Bloc fell were not always culturally or historically logical, resulting in internal conflict. Without the threat of retaliation by the USSR, the US was free to intervene in conflicts across the world. This was not always well received by its allies and these activities provoked a backlash against the US in the mid-1990s.

Expansion of NATO

As the Cold War ended and the USSR collapsed, NATO and its member states had to adapt to a new security environment. The purpose for which NATO had been established was seemingly no longer relevant and questions arose that needed to be addressed: what was NATO's mission in a post-Cold War world, what should its composition be, and what was its role in the new political and economic structures that were growing within Europe?

In the summer of 1990, NATO issued a declaration saying, "Today our Alliance begins a major transformation. Working with all the countries of Europe, we are determined to create enduring peace on this continent." When Germany reunified, it was agreed that the newly reunified nation would continue to be a member of NATO, and after the Warsaw Pact was dissolved in 1991 more former Eastern Bloc nations began to seek NATO membership.

The potential enlargement of NATO was debated widely throughout the 1990s as member states weighed the implications, costs, and likely outcomes of expansion. In 1995, NATO conducted a formal Study of Enlargement and drew up general criteria for membership before announcing that it would be inviting new members in 1996. NATO invited the Czech Republic, Poland, and Hungary to join and in 1999 they became the first ex-Warsaw Pact members to join the Alliance. Many more followed in the early 2000s; by 2009, nine further ex-Eastern Bloc nations had joined NATO.

US interventions in the breakup of Yugoslavia

Figure 5.4 A map of Yugoslavia, showing the individual nations that made up the country as they are today. Kosovo announced its independence from Serbia in 2008, but this status is not universally recognized among UN members

The nation of Yugoslavia was created after the First World War. It broke up under Nazi occupation but reunited at the end of the war when the communist-led force of Josip Tito liberated the country. Although named a communist state, Yugoslavia was not under Soviet influence. However, when the USSR collapsed, the Yugoslav state rapidly followed.

The reasons for the breakup of Yugoslavia range from cultural and religious divisions between ethnic groups, to the memories of atrocities committed by all sides during the Second World War, to growing nationalist sentiments. When Tito, who had ruled Yugoslavia since 1944, died in 1980, the constitution effectively removed power from the Yugoslav federal government and gave this to republics and provinces. This established a collective presidency of eight provincial representatives and a federal government with little control over economic, social, and political policy. The collapse of the USSR ended political stability in Yugoslavia. As the West became less interested in the region, the financial aid it had provided Yugoslavia, which was needed to maintain the rapidly deteriorating state, also disappeared.

Seeing a growing power vacuum in Yugoslavia's leadership, the president of Serbia, **Slobodan Milosevic**, used Serbian ethno-nationalism to provoke conflict in other Yugoslav republics and consolidate his own power. In 1990, Slovenia and Croatia elected non-communist leaderships and declared themselves sovereign, meaning local law took precedence over Yugoslav law. They were rapidly followed by Bosnia-Herzegovina. In 1991, Croatia and Slovenia declared independence. Croatia, however, had a large but minority population of ethnic Serbs who wished to remain united with Serbia. After Bosnia also declared independence in 1992, conflict and persecution in the region escalated into full-scale war.

> **KEY FIGURE**
>
> **Slobodan Milosevic** (1941–2006) Milosevic was born in Serbia in 1941. While studying law at the University of Belgrade, Milosevic joined the League of Socialist Youth of Yugoslavia. He served as an advisor to the mayor of Belgrade in the 1960s and became close to the Serbian leader in the 1970s while acting as a chairman for several large companies. He came to power as President of the League of Communists in Serbia in 1986 and became President of the Republic of Serbia in 1989. In 1999, he was charged with war crimes related to the Bosnian, Croatian, and Kosovo Wars by the International Criminal Tribunal for the former Yugoslavia. He was extradited to the Tribunal in 2001 and his trial for genocide and war crimes began in 2002. He died in prison of a heart attack on March 11, 2006 before the trial could be concluded.

In 1993, the UN intervened in the Bosnian conflict, declaring cities safe zones for persecuted minorities. This had limited success and in 1995 Serbian forces decided to end the war by destroying minority ethnic enclaves in Bosnia. In August 1995, the US and other NATO leaders intervened to defend civilians and began a US-led air-based intervention against Serbian forces in Bosnia. In November 1995, a peace treaty was signed to end the war. From the signing of the treaty until 2004, NATO maintained a peacekeeping force in the region, with most of the troops coming from the US.

Crisis in the Persian Gulf: US reaction to Saddam Hussein's invasion of Kuwait

Figure 5.5 The Persian Gulf, showing the location of Iraq, Kuwait, and Iran

> **KEY FIGURE**
>
> **Saddam Hussein**
> (1937–2006) Born to a Sunni Arab family in northern Iraq, Hussein joined the Ba'ath party of Iraq in 1957. After the July 17 Revolution in 1968 he became vice president of Iraq. Following the President's resignation in 1979 he formally took power, purging the party and becoming a dictator. Following the US invasion of Iraq in 2003 he was captured, tried, and executed on December 30, 2006.

After the war between Iran and Iraq (1980–88) ended, Iraq emerged with an intact state, a renewed sense of national pride, and extensive national debt. In 1988, Iraq's leader, Saddam Hussein, accused its wealthy (but militarily weak) neighbor Kuwait, of syphoning crude oil from the fields along the countries' common border. He demanded Kuwait write off $30 billion of Iraqi debt and began to gather troops along Kuwait's border.

Alarmed by these actions, Egypt initiated negotiations between the two nations to try to avoid intervention by the US or other outside influences interested in the security of oil supply. Hussein ended negotiations and, on August 2, 1990, ordered the invasion of Kuwait, believing other Gulf and Arab nations would do nothing to stop him. This proved to be a grave miscalculation. Two-thirds of the 21 members of the Arab League, a regional organization of the Arab world, condemned the invasion and Saudi Arabia and the Kuwaiti government-in-exile turned to the US and NATO for help.

After condemnation from President Bush, the British and Soviet governments, and a call from the UN Security Council for Iraq to withdraw, the US began to build up air forces in Saudi Arabia in preparation for Operation Desert Storm. These forces were accompanied by troops from other NATO nations, as well as from Egypt, Saudi Arabia, and several other Arab nations.

Early on January 17, 1991, Operation Desert Storm began. The coalition, led by US forces, launched an air offensive against communications networks, weapons plants, oil refineries, and defense infrastructure in Iraq. In February, with the Iraqi air force almost destroyed, focus shifted to driving Iraqi ground forces out of Kuwait. The coalition liberated Kuwait and attacked Iraqi forces to the point of collapse. On February 28, Bush declared a ceasefire, ending the Gulf War.

The coalition succeeded in liberating Kuwait. However, the war had lingering effects. Saddam Hussein was not forced out of power. He continued to run an oppressive regime, suppressing uprisings from different ethnic and religious groups within Iraq, including Iraqi Kurds in the north of the country and Shi'ites in the south. The US-led coalition failed to support these uprisings or prevent their brutal suppression. Tensions in the region continued with Iraqi authorities often refusing to comply with the terms of the ceasefire. The region would become tense again in the early 2000s with the US-led invasion of Iraq (page 261).

UN-sanctioned embargo on trade with Iraq

Four days after Iraq invaded Kuwait, the UN placed a comprehensive set of sanctions on Iraq. They were intended to force Iraq to withdraw from Kuwait, pay reparations, and disclose and destroy any weapons of mass destruction (WMDs). The sanctions banned all trade with Iraq and occupied Kuwait except for medicine and foodstuff "in humanitarian circumstances."

> **KEY TERM**
>
> **Weapons of mass destruction (WMDs)**
> Chemical, biological, radiological, or nuclear weapons that can kill or harm many people or cause significant damage to artificial or natural structures or the environment.

With the collapse of the USSR, the UN Security Council was no longer stopped by the mutual veto power of the US, UK, and France against the USSR and China. This allowed the Council to enter a period of "activism" and undertake measures with unprecedented scope. The sanctions placed on Iraq were the first of such measures. Global sanctions of this kind were almost unenforceable during the Cold War, because if the US imposed sanctions on a country that nation was usually able to turn to the USSR for trade.

After Iraq's defeat in 1991, the sanctions continued with only moderate revisions. In 1995, the Oil for Food Program allowed Iraq to export oil again and use the proceeds for humanitarian goods. The sanctions continued until 2003 and have often been cited as having created a significant humanitarian crisis in the country. Their wide-ranging nature led to resentment from some in the region and, from that point onward, sanctions were rarely as comprehensive.

> **ACTIVITY**
>
> Make a list of the consequences of the Gulf War. Evaluate the impact of each consequence for the US and order the consequences from most to least important from a US perspective.

Motivations for Clinton's attacks on Al-Qaeda bases in Afghanistan

US involvement in Afghanistan, the first Gulf War, and US sanctions on Iraq fostered resentment in the Middle East. Founded in 1988 by Mujahideen veterans of the Soviet-Afghan War, the terrorist organization Al-Qaeda grew during the 1990s under the leadership of **Osama bin Laden**. When Iraq invaded Kuwait, Bin Laden offered his fighters to Saudi Arabia to assist but was rebuffed as Saudi Arabia sought US aid instead. In the late 1980s and early 1990s, Al-Qaeda ran training camps for fighters in Afghanistan and other nations.

> ### KEY FIGURE
> **Osama bin Laden** (1957–2011) Born in Riyadh, Saudi Arabia to an aristocratic family, bin Laden studied at Saudi and foreign universities until he joined the Mujahideen in 1979. In 1988 he founded Al-Qaeda and went on to declare two fatawa against the US in 1996 and 1998. He was killed by US special operations forces on May 2, 2011.

Opposed to the US on ideological grounds, Al-Qaeda was enraged by the presence of US troops in Saudi Arabia. In 1993, a group of terrorists led by an Al-Qaeda-trained operative planned an attack on the World Trade Center in New York City. On February 26, 1993, they parked a van filled with explosives in the car park, set the fuse and fled. The bomb went off, blowing a 100-foot-wide hole in the foundations, cutting the power lines, destroying the emergency lighting system and sending smoke throughout the stairwells and elevators. Six people were killed and around 1,000 injured, mostly during the evacuation of the building. The terrorists mailed letters to New York newspapers before the attack, demanding an end to US aid to and diplomatic relations with Israel, and a pledge from the US to end interference in the affairs of Middle Eastern nations.

In 1996 and again in 1998, Bin Laden issued demands that the US withdraw forces from Saudi Arabia. In August 1998, two almost simultaneous bomb explosions occurred at US embassies in Tanzania and Kenya. A total of 213 people were killed in the blast in Kenya and a further eleven in Tanzania.

> ### ACTIVITY
> Set out a chronology of the key events in US–Middle East relations between 1979 and 2000.

In response to the bombings, President **Bill Clinton** ordered a series of missile strikes on Al-Qaeda targets in Afghanistan and Sudan, citing intelligence that Bin Laden was planning to mount further attacks. While supported by US allies, Cuba, Russia, China, Sudan, Afghanistan, and other Muslim nations condemned the strikes. The strikes contributed to a growing anti-US sentiment in parts of the Middle East that continued to develop throughout the late 1990s and early 2000s.

> ### KEY FIGURE
> **Bill Clinton** (1946–) Born and raised in Arkansas and a member of the Democratic Party, Clinton served as Governor of Arkansas from 1979 to 1981 and again from 1983 to 1992. He ran for the presidency in 1992, defeating George HW Bush. He was comfortably reelected in 1996, but his second term was marked by the Lewinsky scandal (page 271). He left office in 2001 with the joint highest approval rating of any US president.

The impacts of the 9/11 attacks and the War on Terror

The 1990s was a decade of great change. For the US, it is often remembered as a time of prosperity and relative peace. The economy boomed and the threat of nuclear war that had long hung over the population's heads was reduced. The period was not without violence, but for many in the US there was an increased sense of security. By 2008, this had shattered. A direct attack on US soil led to the US becoming embroiled in a second Gulf War. In parts of the globe, the US became seen as an aggressor, causing discomfort among its allies and distrust in unaligned nations.

Outcomes of the terrorist attacks on September 11, 2001

On September 11, 2001, a group of Al-Qaeda-affiliated terrorists hijacked four commercial airliners mid-flight. Two planes were flown into the World Trade Center towers in New York City, and one into the west side of the Pentagon in Washington DC. After passengers and crew fought with the hijackers, the fourth plane crashed into a field in Shanksville, Pennsylvania. The collisions with the World Trade Center led to the collapse of both towers, which in turn destroyed the other five buildings in the complex and caused extensive damage to nearby buildings. Nearly 3,000 people were killed in the attacks in what became known as "9/11."

The attacks were motivated by outrage at the US military presence in Saudi Arabia, its support of Israel, and the sanctions against Iraq following the invasion of Kuwait. They were orchestrated by Osama bin Laden in retaliation for US actions against Muslims across the world.

The outcomes and reactions in the immediate aftermath and over the following years were many and varied. Perhaps the most long-lasting outcome was the declaration of the "War on Terror." First used in a speech given to Congress by President **George W Bush**, the War on Terror came to describe a global conflict spanning multiple individual wars. The first of these was in Afghanistan in pursuit of Al-Qaeda.

> ### KEY FIGURE
>
> **George W Bush** (1946–) The son of President George HW Bush, George W Bush was elected Governor of Texas in 1994, after working in the oil industry and co-owning the Texas Rangers baseball team. He won the 2000 presidential election in a narrow victory, which hinged on a contested result in Florida. He was reelected in 2004, in another close election, and, upon finishing his second term, returned to Texas where he has since maintained a low public profile.

9/11 led to a spate of anti-terrorist legislation across the Western and **Anglophone** world. On September 13, 2001, NATO invoked Article 5 of the North Atlantic Treaty, which commits member states to consider an attack against one as an attack against all. This led to a globalized response to the attacks, with partnership action plans and NATO maneuvers in the Mediterranean to prevent the movement of terrorists and weapons.

Domestically, the National Security Agency was given wide-ranging powers for warrantless surveillance of Americans and non-US nationals across the world. In January 2002, a detention camp at the US naval base in Guantanamo Bay, Cuba was established, operating indefinite detention without trial for supposed enemy combatants. Indefinite detention, as well as reports of torture and abuse, led to Guantanamo Bay being heavily criticized for human rights violations by Amnesty International and other non-governmental organizations.

> **KEY TERM**
>
> **Anglophone** English-speaking. The term can be used to refer to people, countries, or content.

> What do you think Source 5.4 tells us about American perceptions of their own security following 9/11? What impact do you think images like this had on the population?

▶ SOURCE 5.4

United Airlines Flight 175 crashes into the South Tower of the World Trade Center on September 11, 2001

What does Source 5.5 tell us about the role of George Bush in the aftermath of the attacks?

SOURCE 5.5

President Bush visits the site of the collapsed World Trade Center in New York and gives an impromptu speech to firefighters and rescue workers, September 14, 2001

The impacts of the USA Patriot Act (2001) and Homeland Security Act (2002)

In the aftermath of the 9/11 attacks, the US government passed the USA Patriot Act in October 2001. The aim of the Patriot Act was to tighten US national security, particularly relating to counterterrorism. The Act contained three main provisions:
- expanded surveillance options for law enforcement, including the tapping of domestic and international phones
- greater inter-agency communication, allowing federal agencies to effectively use all available resources for counterterrorism
- increased penalties for terrorism and an expanded list of activities that qualified for terrorism charges.

Many of the provisions in the Act had "sunset clauses," according to which they were supposed to expire in 2005. However, Bush reauthorized the Act in 2006. Although initially popular, the Patriot Act became incredibly controversial. It allowed for indefinite detention without trial for immigrants and gave law enforcement officials the right to search property and records without the owner's knowledge or consent. Civil rights groups claimed the law violated citizens' constitutional right to privacy and allowed the government to spy on, search, and detain individuals without due process. Since it was passed, the law has been challenged numerous times in court, often successfully.

In November 2002, Congress passed the Homeland Security Act, establishing the Department of Homeland Security as a new department in the executive branch. This superseded the Office of Homeland Security and housed many services previously provided by other departments. The aim of the Department was to prepare for, prevent, and respond to domestic emergencies, particularly related to terrorism. In 2003, it also absorbed the immigration service, leading to the creation of the Immigration and Customs Enforcement Agency (ICE). Since 2002, the Department of Homeland Security has been criticized for wastage, civil liberty violations, and mail interception.

The Patriot Act was somewhat successful in improving inter-agency communication. However, its success in combating terrorism is a contested subject to this day. In 2004, the FBI director called the Act "extraordinarily beneficial in the War on Terrorism." By contrast,

ACTIVITY

Outline the key provisions of the Patriot Act and the Homeland Security Act. Create a list of the key arguments for and against the Patriot Act.

KEY TERMS

Taliban An Afghan militant movement that ruled most of Afghanistan from 1996 to 2001. This ultraconservative religious and political faction combined strict religious ideology with an equally strict social code, creating a repressive regime that included the near-total exclusion of women from public life, the destruction of non-Islamic relics and art, and harsh punishment of criminals.

Northern Alliance A military alliance of Islamic groups that took control of the city of Kabul in 1992. It disintegrated in 1993, but reformed in 1996 and controlled around ten percent of Afghan territory between 1999 and 2001. Following 9/11, it became the main opposition to the Taliban on the ground in Afghanistan and a key US ally.

Preemptive action A military attack on an enemy in response to the threat of attack rather than an actual attack.

in 2015, the *Washington Post* revealed that the Justice Department had admitted that the FBI could not point to any major terrorism cases solved as a result of the powers allowed under the Act. Court cases and criticism of the surveillance powers granted by the Act have also continued and led to several major scandals in the 2010s.

Attacks on Al-Qaeda and the ousting of the Taliban in Afghanistan

It was determined that the ultimate responsibility for 9/11 lay with Osama bin Laden. Al-Qaeda had established bases in Afghanistan in 1996 and it was believed that the **Taliban** government was harboring Bin Laden there. On September 20, 2001, Bush demanded that the Taliban extradite Bin Laden and other Al-Qaeda leaders to the US or "share in their fate." When the Taliban refused, the US, with UK assistance, launched the first air strikes of Operation Enduring Freedom against Al-Qaeda and Taliban targets on October 7.

The initial airstrikes lasted five days, followed by the deployment of a large international coalition of ground forces, including from Afghanistan's **Northern Alliance**. Initially, the invasion was a great success. The airstrike campaign against key targets had caused significant damage and by mid-November, the coalition had captured almost all major Taliban strongholds, including the capital, Kabul. The official end of Taliban rule in Afghanistan came on December 6, 2001 when Kandahar was captured. The Taliban and Al-Qaeda fled in large numbers to Pakistan, but many remained in the rural and remote mountainous regions of Afghanistan.

At this point, the coalition forces formed a security mission, sanctioned by the UN, aiming to create a new democratic authority in Afghanistan. This initially only covered the Kabul area. The eighteen nations of the coalition helped the Afghans maintain security around the capital. Afghanistan held its first democratic election in 2004 and, for a while, the coalition's focus turned toward peacekeeping and reconstruction.

The invasion of Iraq, 2003

After the end of the first Gulf War, the UN ordered Iraq to destroy its WMDs and began a program of inspections to prevent it from developing more. In 1998, Iraq suspended cooperation with UN weapons inspectors. At this point, the removal of Saddam Hussein's government in Iraq became official US policy. The US and UK funneled aid to democratic opposition organizations in Iraq and launched sporadic airstrikes in the country. After Bush's election in 2000, US policy toward Iraq became more aggressive. After the 9/11 attacks, a strike against Iraq was seriously considered as part of the response.

The "War on Terror" included a willingness to engage in "**preemptive**" military action. On September 12, 2002, Bush began to make the case for an invasion of Iraq to the international community. In October 2002, Congress passed the Iraq Resolution, which authorized the president to use "any means necessary" against Iraq. The question divided NATO. Some key US allies, like the UK, were supportive of invasion, but France and Germany favored continued diplomacy and weapons inspections. A compromise was reached with a UN resolution threatening "serious consequences" if Iraq continued to block weapons inspectors. Saddam Hussein accepted this, and inspections resumed in November 2002. Despite the inspectors finding no evidence of WMDs, the US government undertook a concerted campaign to link the Iraqi regime to WMDs and support for Al-Qaeda.

In March 2003, the US gave Saddam Hussein and his two sons 48 hours to leave Iraq. Almost immediately after they failed to meet this deadline, the US and its allies launched airstrikes against the country and an invasion began. Saddam Hussein went into hiding and the US quickly defeated Iraq's military forces and captured its major cities. In May 2003, in a televised speech on the aircraft carrier USS *Abraham Lincoln* in front of a banner displaying the message "Mission Accomplished," Bush declared the end of major combat operations in Iraq. In October 2005, Saddam Hussein was found and put on trial for crimes against his people. He was found guilty and executed in December 2006. Elections were held and a new constitution implemented that same year. Despite all this, a guerrilla war raged in Iraq until 2011, driven mainly by violence between religious factions within Iraq.

The invasion of Iraq was incredibly contentious. Some of the reasons included:
- Critics challenged the human cost of the war.
- The justification that there were WMDs was questionable. No WMDs were found in Iraq and suggestions from the Bush administration that Iraq supported Al-Qaeda were formally discredited in a 2004 report.
- The legality of the war was questioned. The invasion never received a UN mandate. In 2004, UN Secretary-General Kofi Annan said in an interview with the UK's BBC, "From the [UN] Charter point of view [the war] was illegal."
- Criticism came from the US military community, which questioned the Bush administration's security priorities. They believed the invasion of Iraq and subsequent war took attention from the real threat of Al-Qaeda.

The invasion challenged the international norm of state sovereignty, which had dominated international relations for many years. It undermined the UN Charter's ban on aggressive war and dealt a decisive blow to the rules-based international system of which the US had been a key architect. The invasion caused a rift within NATO, as key US allies favored diplomatic solutions and refused to support the invasion. It was also opposed by most Middle Eastern nations, including US allies like Saudi Arabia, leading to a rise in resentment against the US in the region. The questionable nature of the evidence used to justify the invasion also undermined US credibility within the international community.

Bush Doctrine

The phrase "Bush Doctrine" was rarely used by the Bush administration. It was first used in June 2001, referring to Bush's unilateral withdrawal from the Anti-Ballistic Missile (ABM) Treaty and the Kyoto Protocol on climate change. Post-9/11 it was used to justify the invasion of Afghanistan and became particularly associated with the invasion of Iraq. It broadly refers to three interconnected principles running through the Bush administration's foreign policy. These principles were **unilateralism**, preemptive strikes, and regime change.

Unilateralism

The Bush administration often operated without support or negotiation with other international actors. As evidenced by Bush's surprising withdrawal from the ABM Treaty after 30 years, the US under Bush was happy to act alone in its own interests. This was a shift away from the tone of the Clinton administration, which favored diplomatic solutions and multilateral diplomacy through the UN and other bodies. Although the Bush administration did still attempt to work with multilateral organizations, it was more willing to take on the role of hegemonic superpower and act with or without support from other nations.

Preemptive strikes

The Bush Doctrine called for the use of preemptive attacks, up to and including warfare, against hostile states and terrorist groups. This was the principle used to justify the invasion of Iraq. Under Bush, the US used preemptive strikes as a defensive tactic against perceived future threats. This policy was particularly applied in the Middle East following 9/11. Strikes on Afghanistan, which had not been involved directly in 9/11, were a key demonstration of the preemptive approach to dealing with perceived threats. After the 9/11 attacks, Bush said, "We make no distinction between the terrorists who committed these attacks and those who harbor them." This conflation of terrorist groups and the countries in which they resided allowed any nation containing suspected terrorists to be deemed a hostile threat to the US, thus fair game for preemptive strikes.

Regime change

The Bush Doctrine suggested that the US should actively promote democratic governments, especially in the Middle East, as a strategy against terrorism. The Doctrine believed that resentment of the US and its policies did not exist because of US actions, but rather because the nations from which terrorists emerged were not experiencing the freedom of democracy. It suggested that the US had a responsibility to protect itself by promoting democracy abroad, even to the point of engaging in active regime change.

> **KEY TERM**
>
> **Unilateralism** Any doctrine or agenda that supports one-sided action. The action may be in disregard for other parties or may just refer to action taken alone.

>
>
> **ACTIVITY**
>
> Create a list of the direct and indirect consequences of the 9/11 attacks. Create criteria to make a judgment about how important these consequences were and put them in order of importance. You could consider:
> - the impact of events over time
> - how deeply people's lives were affected
> - how many people's lives were affected.

The Bush Doctrine represented a marked change from Clinton's multilateral, diplomatic foreign policy. It was driven by a desire within part of the Republican Party to embrace the opportunities for security and democracy offered to the US by its position as single superpower. The Doctrine was polarizing both domestically and internationally. It alienated US allies such as France and Germany and, by 2008, had helped to fuel anti-Americanism in various parts of the world. The willingness to use military force unilaterally caused some to look upon the US as an aggressor and to question the legitimacy of the US in the rules-based international order it helped to create.

SUMMARY DIAGRAM

Global role of the US, 1980–2008

Why and how did the global role of the US evolve between 1980 and 2008?

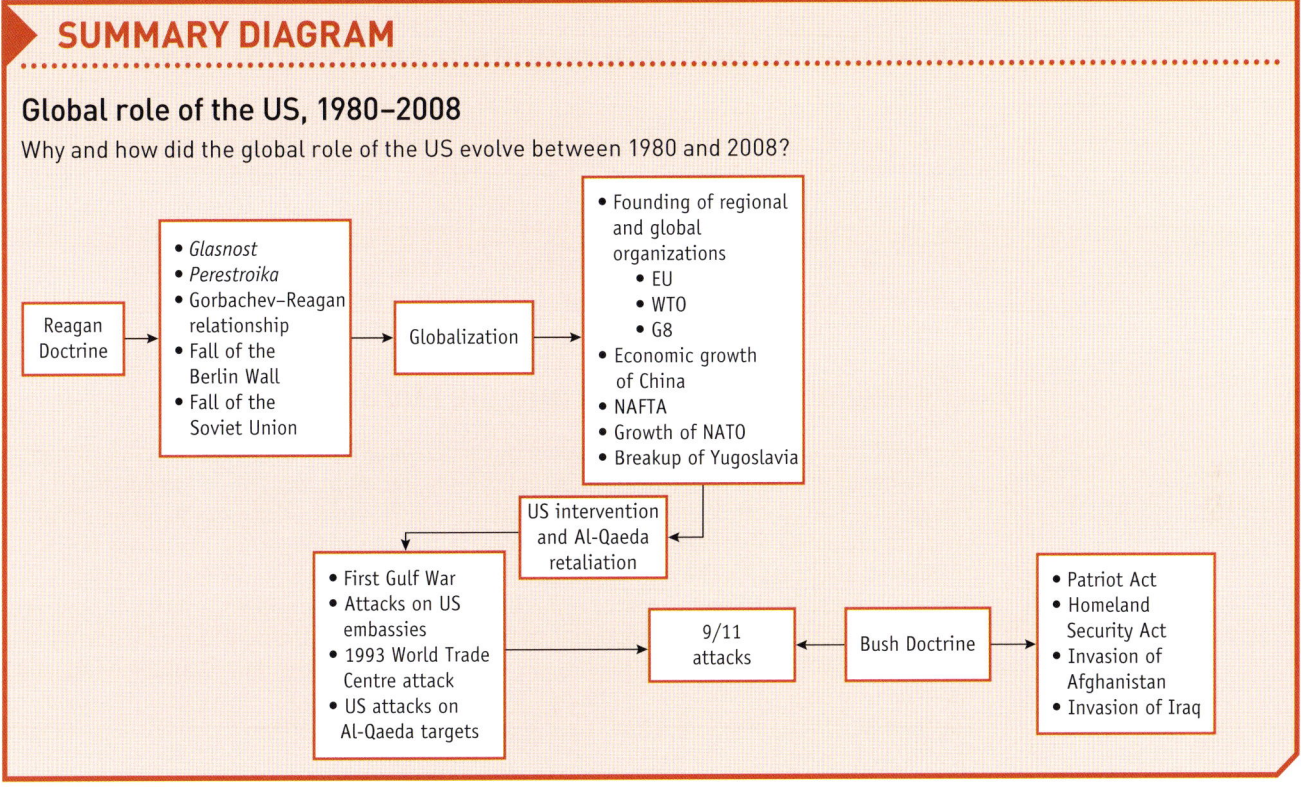

5.2 Why and how did US politics change between 1980 and 2008?

The 1980s brought a backlash against the progressive governments of the 1960s and 1970s through the election of Ronald Reagan and the growing dominance of social and cultural issues within political discourse. The era also gave rise to a new form of economic thinking which has persisted to the current day. By the early 2000s, US domestic politics was deeply divided and, following a short boom in the 1990s, showed potential for catastrophe, which came to fruition with the Great Recession in 2008.

Evolution of political trends from 1980 to 1992

With the election of Reagan in 1980, the right in US politics was growing in power. Building on the gains it made in the 1970s, the New Right aimed to counter what it saw as the "liberal establishment." At its heart lay an objection to the perceived decline in morality illustrated by counterculture movements, civil rights and anti-war protesters, drug use, and liberalizing attitudes to sexuality. The political clash between left and right that resulted from these objections has often been referred to as the "culture wars." Alongside this sat a new economic model, focusing on supply-side or "trickle-down" economic theory and the shrinking of government.

The rise of the New Right and the Moral Majority

The New Right emerged after the presidential campaign of Barry Goldwater in 1964. It had a more populist tone than traditional Republicanism and often focused on "wedge issues." Wedge issues are political or social issues that are controversial or divisive for groups that are typically united. The New Right grew rapidly in the 1960s and 1970s. Nixon was not considered a success for the movement because his economic policy was too progressive and his interest in ending the Vietnam War did not align with New Right priorities. However, he can be considered an early proponent of the social policy of the New Right. Believing that the New Left had captured the nation's education system, the New Right aimed to gain leverage over the nation's ideas by founding a series of think tanks, such as the Heritage Foundation. These think tanks conducted research to shape government policies aligned with New Right thinking.

Throughout the 1960s and 1970s, white, often Protestant, middle-class Americans were frustrated by a perceived decline in morality that they argued was illustrated by rising drug use, open displays of sexuality, rising crime rates, race riots, civil unrest, and anti-war movements. The New Right blamed the nation's ills on "liberalism," which they believed contributed to mismanagement and corruption within the federal government. Newly mobilized Christian conservatives played a key part in driving the rise of the New Right through extensive grassroots and community organizing. This, and the prominence of New Right think tanks, created the policy approach and electoral machine that brought Reagan to the White House.

A key galvanizing force in the development of the New Right was the *Roe v. Wade* decision legalizing abortion. Many Christians fought against the legalization through grassroots political action. Grassroots activity, combined with new religious institutions, helped to turn the anti-abortion issue into part of the New Right movement. In 1979, Jerry Falwell, a Baptist minister and televangelist, formed the Moral Majority. He dedicated the organization to advancing a "pro-life, pro-family, pro-morality, and pro-American" agenda.

The Republican Party steered US domestic politics to the right thanks to the influence of newly mobilized conservatives, think tanks, and religious organizations. The strong grassroots movement and increasing dominance of conservative-funded think tanks led to a radical change in political discourse that persisted well into the 2000s. The polarization of politics that had begun in the 1970s deepened, and cultural and social issues became an increasingly decisive aspect of people's political thinking and voting habits.

> What does this source tell you about the relationship between Reagan and the religious right?

SOURCE 5.6

Jerry Falwell, founder of the Moral Majority, greets Reagan as he arrives to address the National Religious Broadcasters during his campaign, October 1980

The Reagan coalition

In 1980, Ronald Reagan won the election by a landslide, carrying 49 of the 50 states and attracting around 60 percent of the popular vote. This was not possible without a major political realignment in the electorate. The combination of voters that made up this landslide became known as the "Reagan coalition." It included traditional Republican voters, New and Christian Right activists, traditional Southern Democrats, and the so-called "Reagan Democrats."

The two sets of Democratic voters that made up part of the coalition had different motivations. The white Southern Democrats who began to vote Republican under Nixon committed to the switch in their party allegiances and voted for Reagan. They are part of the group addressed by Nixon as the "silent majority," often socially conservative and concerned by civil rights advances. Reagan's campaign continued a form of the Southern Strategy adopted by Nixon, using racially coded rhetoric, attacking the welfare state, and vocally supporting states' rights. By 1980, the Republican Party had firmly become the party of the South.

By contrast, the "Reagan Democrats" were Democrats who voted for Reagan and George HW Bush, but did not continue to vote Republican into the 1990s. They were mostly white, Northern, blue-collar workers who approved of Reagan's social conservatism, **hawkish** foreign policy and economic policy. They felt that the Democrats worked primarily for the benefit of others, such as the very poor and African Americans, and no longer championed their middle-class aspirations. The Reagan coalition began to collapse in 1988, and, by 1992, most "Reagan Democrats" returned to their traditional voting patterns and voted for Clinton.

Reaganomics

A key aspect of what attracted many voters to Reagan was the challenging state of the economy. After a decade of stagflation, the prevailing post-war trust in **Keynesian economics** was beginning to come under attack. In his campaign, Reagan committed to lowering taxes, a significant departure from his predecessors. His economic policy, which became known as Reaganomics, was based on the idea that tax cuts, particularly to businesses, would stimulate economic growth by incentivizing investment and innovation.

KEY TERMS

Hawkish Used to describe a person who favors interventionist, strong, or aggressive military foreign policy (although not necessarily outright war).

Keynesian economics Based on the theories of the early twentieth-century British economist John Maynard Keynes, Keynesian economics centers around the idea that governments should play an active role in their countries' economies instead of allowing the free market to reign. Keynes advocated public spending as a means of mitigating economic downturns and Keynesian economics was the ideological drive behind the New Deal.

Reaganomics had four main policy objectives: reduce government spending on domestic programs, reduce taxes for individuals and businesses, reduce the burden of regulation on businesses, and reduce inflation.

Reduced government spending

Following the trickle-down economic model, between 1980 and 1988 Reagan cut multiple areas of public spending, including Medicaid, social security, the food stamp program, education funding, and job training programs. Despite cutting social funding, over the lifespan of his presidency public expenditure increased. Much of this came from increases in defense spending. The Department of Defense budget rose from $267.1 billion in 1980 to $393.1 billion in 1988 to fund Reagan's anti-communist foreign policy.

Reduced taxes for individuals and businesses

In his first year as president, Reagan significantly lowered federal income tax rates, reducing the top bracket from 70 percent to 50 percent and the lowest bracket from fourteen percent to eleven percent. The same act also cut estate taxes and taxes paid by corporations. After undoing around a third of this initial tax cut in 1982, Reagan introduced an act in 1984 closing tax loopholes and a second in 1986 simplifying the tax structure. The 1986 Tax Reform Act eliminated many tax deductions, and reduced the highest marginal rates and the number of tax brackets. It also set capital gains tax rates at the same levels as income tax rates, with both topping out at 28 percent.

Reduced regulation

Reducing regulation appears to have been the lowest of the four priorities. Economic deregulation had begun under Carter and continued under Reagan, but at a slower rate. Reagan eased or removed price controls on oil, natural gas, cable TV, long-distance telephone services, ocean shipping, and interstate buses. He reduced the scope of antitrust laws and broadened the range of assets in which banks were allowed to invest. The Environmental Protection Agency relaxed its interpretation of the Clean Air Act and opened large areas of federal land to private development. Contrary to his commitment to deregulation, Reagan also substantially increased import barriers.

Reduced inflation

Reagan encouraged the Federal Reserve to continue policies to reduce money supply, which initially resulted in a recession in 1982. This and the Federal Reserve's raising of interest rates to discourage lending and borrowing did go some way toward reducing inflation.

Reaganomics remains controversial and its results are still debated. It brought about an end to stagflation and GDP growth was stronger under Reagan than his predecessors. On the other hand, Reaganomics is often held responsible for widening the income gap, reducing social mobility and creating an overall less equal society. Critics also point out that the national debt tripled during Reagan's presidency. Reaganomics challenged the existing agreement that Keynesian economics was the right approach. It changed economic policy thinking for the first time since the New Deal and brought a new way of thinking about economics into the mainstream.

Domestic policies of the George HW Bush administration

George HW Bush's presidency lasted only one term. It was dominated by international affairs, including navigating the fall of the Soviet Union, the first Gulf War, and the negotiation of NAFTA. Domestically, he faced a Democrat-controlled Congress, a large federal budget deficit, and, in 1990, a mild recession. Preoccupied by international and economic issues, Bush did not propose many major domestic programs. This was not surprising since he was not elected on a change platform, instead promising to maintain the status quo. He offered a limited agenda, including education and environmental reforms, with only two major pieces of legislation: the Americans with Disabilities Act (pages 283–284) and the Clean Air Act Amendments. He made frequent use of the presidential veto and used the threat of veto to influence legislation outcomes.

> **KEY TERM**
>
> **Trickle-down economics** Economic policies that favor wealthy individuals and large corporations in the belief that this will eventually benefit the economy as a whole. The principle is based on the idea that spending by businesses and wealthy individuals "trickles down" to those less fortunate through stronger economic growth.

> **ACTIVITY**
>
> In your own words, write a brief explanation of the following terms: Reaganomics and Keynesian economics. Write a list of the key differences between the two economic models.

Economy

As Bush took office in 1989, the savings and loan industry was beginning to collapse due to risky investments following deregulation. In 1990, Bush negotiated a plan with Congress to bail out the industry. This cost taxpayers over $100 billion and added to the challenging financial environment. During his election campaign Bush had pledged not to raise taxes. However, faced with a soaring budget deficit and a Democrat-dominated Congress keen to raise taxes on the wealthiest, he had no choice but to negotiate and compromise. This resulted in the Omnibus Budget Reconciliation Act of 1990. The Act included deficit reduction measures, including the cutting of government expenditure and increased taxes.

By 1991, the public was increasingly concerned with the state of the economy and increasingly unhappy with Bush's handling of it. The challenging economic climate overshadowed his generally well-received handling of international affairs and, in large part, cost him the 1992 election.

The Clean Air Act Amendments

Bush's drive to improve environmental protections was aided by a large environmental disaster at the start of his presidency. In March 1989, the *Exxon Valdez* oil tanker ran aground near Alaska, spilling ten million gallons of oil into the Prince William Sound. This increased public support for strengthened environmental protections. The 1990 Amendments to the Clean Air Act focused on reducing urban smog, combating acid rain, and removing industrial emissions of toxic chemicals. While critics argued that the cost of the Amendments was too much and would have a negative impact on an already struggling economy, the Amendments passed with significant Congressional support and were signed into law in November 1990.

War on drugs

Since the Nixon administration, the US government had taken a hard line against illegal drugs. Reagan escalated policies against drugs and, when he took office, Bush maintained the zero-tolerance policy. In November 1989, he signed off $3 billion to expand drug treatment facilities and federal prisons, and to increase anti-drug education and law enforcement. In 1991, Congress passed the 1208 Program (later expanded into the 1033 Program) which authorized the Department of Defense to transfer surplus military equipment they deemed "suitable for use in counter-drug activities" to local law enforcement agencies. Bush also began a program calling for states to punish drug offenses, including cannabis use, with 6-month driver's license suspensions. The administration threatened to withhold federal highway funds from states that did not comply. There is minimal evidence to suggest these policies reduced illegal drug use in the US. The 1990s did, however, see the beginning of the over-prescription of legal opioids which led to the opioid epidemic which continues to this day.

Civil Rights Act 1991

In 1991, the Bush administration passed the Civil Rights Act in response to Supreme Court decisions limiting the rights of employees who had sued employers for discrimination. The Act provided the right to trial by jury for discrimination cases, introduced the possibility of emotional distress damages, and limited the amount juries could award. It also expanded the rights of women to sue and collect compensation for sexual discrimination and harassment.

Although remembered most for his foreign policy, Bush's legislative contributions had a wide-reaching impact. The Clean Air Act Amendments have been found to have prevented many premature deaths and decreased hospital admissions for conditions related to airborne pollution.

Prominence of social and cultural issues in party politics

The 1980s and 1990s saw the rise of "hot button" issues, such as abortion, gun rights, recreational drug use, sexual orientation and "family values," on which there existed two distinct, definable polarities. These new fault lines were tied to ideological worldviews and political party identification instead of race, class, or gender.

KEY TERM

Crack cocaine A highly addictive drug derived from powdered cocaine; also known as "crack."

The importance of the evangelical Christians' voting bloc was a key driver of the "culture wars" of this period. They believed that premarital sex, abortion, drug use, gay people, and "irreligious" popular culture threatened American society. This period brought a shift in the tactics of the "War on Drugs." In the 1980s, interest moved away from the hallucinogenic drugs popular in the 1960s and 1970s, toward cheaper street drugs, most prominently **crack cocaine**. Initiatives like the "Just Say No" campaign, launched by Reagan's wife, Nancy Reagan, implied heavily that drug addiction and drug-related crimes were not just lifestyle choices but directly linked to personal morality.

During this time, two Supreme Court decisions narrowed, though did not overturn, *Roe v. Wade*. Arguments around family values also arose following the continued growth of the gay rights movement. The debate about gay people reached a peak in the early 1980s with the onset of the AIDS crisis (page 287), which sparked widespread condemnation of gay people within some circles.

The culture wars were closely entwined with political polarization. Reagan mobilized a strong conservative movement that capitalized on the anxieties of social conservatives and promised a return to traditional values. The liberal response, led by individuals such as Hillary and Bill Clinton, pushed to advance causes like gender equality, healthcare reform, and civil rights. This clash of ideologies shaped the political landscape and created deep divisions which still plague the US today.

> What does this source tell you about the Reagan administration's attitude towards drugs?

SOURCE 5.7

An excerpt from a statement made by Nancy and Ronald Reagan from the White House to launch the "Just Say No" campaign, September 14, 1986

"… As a parent, I'm especially concerned about what drugs are doing to young mothers and their newborn children. Listen to this news account from a hospital in Florida of a child born to a mother with a cocaine habit: "Nearby, a baby named Paul lies motionless in an incubator, feeding tubes riddling his tiny body. He needs a respirator to breathe and a daily spinal tap to relieve fluid buildup on his brain. Only 1 month old, he's already suffered 2 strokes."

Now you can see why drug abuse concerns every one of us – all the American family. Drugs steal away so much. They take and take, until finally every time a drug goes into a child, something else is forced out – like love and hope and trust and confidence. Drugs take away the dream from every child's heart and replace it with a nightmare, and it's time we in America stand up and replace those dreams. Each of us has to put our principles and consciences on the line, whether in social settings or in the workplace, to set forth solid standards and stick to them. There's no moral middle ground. Indifference is not an option. We want you to help us create an outspoken intolerance for drug use. For the sake of our children, I implore each of you to be unyielding and inflexible in your opposition to drugs …"

The role of the Clinton administration

Bill Clinton sought to remake the Democratic Party to effectively undermine the Reagan revolution, prioritizing law and order, individualism, and welfare reform. Clinton's presidency had many successes but was marred by a sexual scandal and impeachment proceedings. Despite this, Clinton improved the fiscal health of the US while retaining Democratic commitments to regulation and social welfare.

Clinton's "third way"

The third way was an international centrist movement that aimed to reconcile the politics of the center-right and center-left by combining liberal economics with center-left social policy. Clinton's third way had three main goals: to bridge the party divide through bipartisan policymaking, to reject the notion that social spending was too expensive by not increasing the budget deficit, and to demonstrate an alternate approach for the Democratic Party.

Clinton had an ambitious domestic agenda centered on economic growth. This was a typical feature of third-way politics, which argued that economic growth was the best way to raise tax revenue. Clinton's economic policy included increasing taxes on higher-income taxpayers. He also expanded earned-income tax credits and reduced defense spending. This led to increased revenue and a decline in spending relative to the size of the economy. Simultaneously, Clinton passed a substantial package of welfare reform.

Clinton's attempts at national healthcare legislation and welfare reform

When Clinton took office in 1993, around twenty percent of Americans did not have health insurance. After the Omnibus Budget Reconciliation Act (page 270) and ratification of NAFTA, healthcare was Clinton's primary legislative focus.

The administration formed a task force led by Bill Clinton's wife, Hillary Clinton, to create a plan to provide universal healthcare. The resulting plan involved extending employer-based health insurance, with the government insuring those without employer-based insurance. The federal government's regulatory role would be expanded. It would include setting a minimum level of benefits that plans could provide. This would prevent insurers from charging different rates based on age and pre-existing conditions.

The plan was controversial. It was supported by many companies who thought it might reduce their own costs. Liberals criticized the plan for not going far enough, while conservatives opposed expansion of the power of federal government. The Health Insurance Association of America was particularly opposed to the plan, alleging that it would lead to healthcare rationing, reduced choice, and increased costs.

With the Republican Party unified in opposition, Democrats divided, and public opinion being targeted by aggressive attack adverts from interest groups, Clinton abandoned attempts to pass the healthcare plan in September 1994. He succeeded in passing some healthcare reform, including the Family and Medical Leave Act, guaranteeing workers up to twelve weeks of unpaid medical leave (including for pregnancy). He also passed an act granting people the right to keep their insurance plan if they changed jobs and a program providing matching funds to states for health insurance for families with children.

Welfare reform

Outside of healthcare, Clinton passed a large package of welfare reform. His strategy was to position reform midway between liberal and conservative stances, building a majority coalition in Congress. Clinton wanted to shift funding from the assistance program for low-income families with children into job training and childcare programs; however, Republicans disagreed. Clinton decided that the Republican reform package was better than no reform, so signed an act ending the original program and creating an alternative in its place. This imposed work requirements and lifetime limits on recipients and transferred the administration of the program to state rather than federal government.

Clinton introduced a Direct Student Loan program, an Early Head Start program for children aged up to three, expanded the Medicare benefit package, and expanded the earned income tax credit to give larger benefits to working families and include childless workers. He also passed a twenty percent increase in the minimum wage, improved nutritional support for low-income families, introduced a child tax credit, and offered welfare recipients vouchers to help them move closer to work.

Clinton's failure to pass his healthcare plan was, undoubtedly, a blight on his social policy record, but his other welfare and healthcare reforms had a sizable impact. However, his administration is more often remembered for its economic record, which saw substantial success.

What does this cartoon show you about the opposition faced by Clinton in implementing his healthcare plan and why he failed?

SOURCE 5.8

A political cartoon published in the *Seattle Post*, October 2, 1993. The cartoon depicts Clinton, representing his healthcare plan, about to be operated on by the American Medical Association and the Republican Party

Economic boom, the North American Free Trade Agreement (NAFTA), and reduction of budget deficits

Clinton oversaw strong economic growth and record job creation. His economic approach encompassed modernization of the federal government and greater devolution to state and local government. He aimed to eliminate the budget deficit and protectionist tariffs, maintain low interest rates, encourage private sector investment, and invest in human capital through education and research.

One of Clinton's goals was to lower the barriers to trade with other nations. This was a break from the policies favored by many of his Democratic Party allies and the trade unions. Clinton believed that free trade would encourage economic growth and influence other nations toward economic and political reform. Clinton negotiated around 300 trade agreements with other countries across his presidency. The largest of these was NAFTA, the North American Free Trade Agreement.

Bush had signed the NAFTA agreement in December 1992 and it was pending ratification when Clinton took office. Clinton complemented NAFTA with the North American Agreement on Environmental Cooperation, which outlined principles and objectives on conservation and environmental protection alongside measures to further environmental cooperation, and the North American Agreement on Labour Cooperation, which created an international discipline of enforcement of domestic labor laws. These additions made NAFTA the first "green" trade treaty and the first to be concerned with national labor laws. NAFTA and other trade agreements formed part of Clinton's **budget deficit** plans.

Clinton's budget and tax legislation (the Omnibus Budget Reconciliation Act, 1993) planned to cut the deficit by $500 billion over five years through reductions in government spending and increased taxes on the wealthiest 1.2 percent of Americans. The budget imposed a new energy tax on all Americans and higher taxes on social security for around 25 percent of recipients. Over the following eight years, Clinton reduced taxes for many small businesses, increased tax deductions for self-employed business owners, reduced some federal taxes (particularly on capital gains), expanded tax credits, and provided tax relief on educational savings and retirement funds.

KEY TERM

Budget deficit A situation in which government spending is greater than what is brought in through tax revenues.

The economy grew throughout Clinton's presidency, breaking the record in 2000 for the longest uninterrupted economic expansion in US history. After the Republicans took control of Congress in 1994, Clinton had to fight to secure spending on education, the environment, and government entitlements. These battles came to a head in 1995 over Congress-proposed cuts to Medicaid, Medicare, and education. Following numerous presidential vetoes of spending bills, Republicans in Congress refused to pass temporary spending authorizations, forcing a partial government shutdown. A compromise budget was finally agreed in April 1996.

All four of Clinton's final budgets (starting in 1997) were balanced budgets with surpluses. These were the only **budget surpluses** the US government experienced in the years 1970–2023. They were attributed to high tax revenues, tax rises for upper-income taxpayers, spending restraints, and increased capital gains revenue from a boom in the stock market.

Clinton has been criticized for failing to reverse growing income and wealth inequalities. He was also heavily criticized for the ratification of NAFTA, which made it cheaper for companies to outsource manufacturing jobs to other countries than to maintain them in the US. Despite this criticism, unemployment rates in Clinton's presidency were the lowest they had been in some time, particularly during his second term.

Clinton's impeachment

In 1994, the Whitewater investigation was launched into the Clinton family's real estate investments. Led by Independent Counsel Kenneth Starr, the Whitewater investigation was looking into real estate investments Bill and Hillary Clinton made in the Whitewater Development Corporation. This investigation was ongoing through the 1990s.

In November 1995, Clinton had an affair with a White House intern called Monica Lewinsky. After the affair ended, Lewinsky told a coworker, Linda Tripp, about it. Tripp secretly recorded conversations in which Lewinsky provided details of the affair. Some years later, in early 1997, lawyers for a woman named Paula Jones, who was suing Clinton for sexual harassment, subpoenaed Lewinsky, who provided an affidavit denying the affair she had with Clinton. Clinton was also deposed in this case and denied the affair.

After both denied the affair, Linda Tripp contacted Kenneth Starr to discuss the tapes she'd made of her conversations with Lewinsky. Based on these tapes, Starr requested to expand his investigation into Whitewater to include the possibility of perjury and obstruction of justice in the Paula Jones sexual harassment case. In January 1998, Lewinsky was questioned and offered immunity if she cooperated with the Whitewater prosecution. The story of the affair broke in the media and Clinton publicly denied the allegations saying, "I did not have sexual relations with that woman."

In August 1998, Lewinsky and Clinton testified before a grand jury in the Whitewater investigation. Contrary to the testimony he had given in the sexual harassment suit, Clinton admitted to having an affair with Lewinsky. Clinton also gave an address to the nation admitting to the affair. Less than a month later, Starr issued his report to the House of Representatives. It outlined a case for impeaching Clinton on eleven grounds and contained explicit details of the affair. On October 8, the House authorized an impeachment inquiry and, on December 11, approved four articles of impeachment. On December 19, 1998, Clinton was impeached by the House of Representatives on two of the articles. On February 12, 1999, the Senate acquitted Clinton on both articles of impeachment.

Polls conducted in 1998 and 1999 suggested that only around a third of Americans supported Clinton's impeachment or conviction. Around 57 percent of Americans supported the Senate's decision to keep him in office and around two-thirds of those polled said the impeachment was damaging to the country. Throughout the impeachment process, Clinton's opinion poll ratings were at an all-time high. However, his poll numbers regarding honesty, integrity, and moral character declined. This led to "moral character" playing a significant part in the 2000 elections.

> **KEY TERM**
>
> **Budget surplus** When government spending is lower than the amount brought in through tax revenues.

> **ACTIVITY**
>
> Using the information in this chapter, in groups or pairs, discuss the arguments for and against NAFTA and the consequences of NAFTA for the US economy. Make a presentation answering the question "NAFTA benefited the US economy. How far do you agree with this statement?."

ACTIVITY

Assess the effectiveness of the Clinton administration. Use the table below to help you organize your thinking.

Issue	Evidence of success	Evidence of failure	Judgment on effectiveness
Economy			
Welfare			
Healthcare			
Foreign policy			

The role of the George W Bush administration

The presidency and legacy of George W Bush, from his initial election to the invasion of Iraq, the growth of the budget deficit to his response to Hurricane Katrina, are profoundly controversial. Despite a unifying moment around the 9/11 terrorist attacks, Bush presided over an ever more divided nation fraught with domestic and international challenges.

Disputed presidential election of 2000

The election of 2000 was highly contested. George W Bush was running against Clinton's vice president, Al Gore. During the campaign, Gallup tracking polls showed nine lead changes with Bush holding a slight lead in the final week and Gore taking the lead on election day itself.

On election night, Bush held 246 **Electoral College** votes and Gore held 250 with 270 needed to win. The election came down to the result in Florida, which carried a decisive 25 Electoral College votes. At around 2:30 am, with 85 percent of the Florida vote counted, television networks declared Bush had won Florida despite the margin being close and the remaining votes coming from Democratic-majority counties. As the count continued, the margin narrowed to 2,000 votes and the networks retracted their declarations of a Bush win. The final result, a Bush lead of just 300 votes, triggered a mandatory recount under Florida law.

Gore requested hand recounts in four counties. Florida's Secretary of State, who had also co-chaired Bush's campaign in Florida, set a deadline for recounts of 5 pm on November 14, 2000. The Florida Supreme Court extended this deadline to November 26, but this decision was vacated (made legally void) by the US Supreme Court, leading to one county abandoning their recount and another failing to meet the deadline. When Bush was subsequently certified as the winner of Florida's electors, Gore contested the result. The Florida Supreme Court ordered a recount of ballots rejected by the counting machines. The next day, the US Supreme Court halted this recount. In the *Bush v. Gore* decision of December 12, 2000, the US Supreme Court ruled that the Florida Supreme Court's ruling requiring a statewide recount of ballots was unconstitutional.

Despite losing the Electoral College vote, Gore won the **popular vote** (the overall number of votes across the whole country), making him the first candidate since the 1880s to win the popular vote but lose the election. The controversy contributed to the growing polarization in US politics. It damaged the reputation of the US Supreme Court, contributing to the feeling many Americans had that judges are partisan actors. It also decreased Americans' trust in the integrity of elections and the electoral process.

KEY TERM

Electoral College In US elections, citizens vote to decide who will be the next president and vice president. In practice, the votes are for an "elector," who forms part of the Electoral College. The electoral college is the group that formally votes in the president and vice president. Electors are usually nominated by the political parties before the election, but the process differs between states. Each state has as many electoral votes as it has Senators and Representatives. A majority of 279 is necessary to elect a president.

KEY TERM

Popular vote The total number of votes in an election. To "win the popular vote," a candidate must receive the most votes. In the US, due to the Electoral College system, winning the popular vote does not guarantee electoral victory.

> What does Source 5.9 tell you about the contested nature of the 2000 election? What does it show about divisions in the US?

SOURCE 5.9

Supporters of George W Bush and Al Gore argue outside the Supreme Court in Washington, D.C. 1 December 2000

KEY TERM

Dot-com bubble When the internet became more widely available in the late 1990s, stock markets predicted that new online businesses would make lots of money, and the value of these companies' shares increased very rapidly. By 2000, many of them had failed to make the money predicted, and their value very rapidly decreased (or "crashed"). A lot of the new companies were unable to continue trading and either went bust or were bought by other companies.

Tax cuts

In 2001 and 2003, Bush implemented a series of temporary income tax relief measures.

The Economic Growth and Tax Relief Reconciliation Act of 2001 aimed to boost the economy during the recession caused by the bursting of the **dot-com bubble**. It included:
- lowering the maximum estate tax rate to 50 percent, with a one percent reduction each year until 2007
- introducing a new tax bracket of ten percent and reducing existing tax brackets from 28 percent, 31 percent, 36 percent, and 39.6 percent to 25 percent, 28 percent, 33 percent, and 35 percent respectively
- increasing the per-child tax credit from $500 to $1,000
- doubling the standard tax deduction for a married couple filing jointly.

The cuts were designed to provide families with more disposable income. The hope was that this would spur spending and bring money into the economy. However, many taxpayers chose to save or invest money instead. Much like Reagan's tax cuts, these cuts provided greater benefits to the top twenty percent of earners than to middle- and lower-income earners.

The Jobs and Growth Tax Relief Reconciliation Act of 2003 provided tax cuts for businesses and accelerated the changes passed in the 2001 Act. It included:
- reducing long-term capital gains tax from eight percent and ten percent to five percent, and from twenty percent to fifteen percent
- accelerating the tax provisions from the 2001 Act, which were due to be phased in gradually
- increasing the amount of income exempt from alternative minimum tax to allow more taxpayers to pay tax at regular income tax rates instead of higher minimum tax rates.

In line with the economic ideas of Reaganomics, Bush hoped that by putting money into the pockets of businesses and investors, investment in the stock markets would be encouraged and more power would be added to economic recovery.

These tax cuts were due to expire in 2008 and 2010 respectively; however, following the 2008 recession they were extended. Evidence suggests that the cuts did little to improve economic growth or pay for themselves. The cuts, coupled with the increased defense spending on the wars in Afghanistan and Iraq, led to a budget deficit from the reduction in tax revenue received by the government.

Growth of the budget deficit

Under Bush's presidency, the US fiscal position worsened. In January 2001, the Congressional Budget Office projected that, assuming no changes in policy or expected economic performance, the US would have $5.6 trillion in annual surpluses for the 2002–11 decade. This proved to be incorrect.

During Bush's presidency, spending was only slightly below that of the Clinton administration, but due to tax cuts and two recessions, revenue coming into the federal government decreased compared to the Clinton years. As a result, the national deficit increased substantially during the Bush years.

While much of the debt increase was linked to defense spending, the tax cuts of 2001 resulted in $1.2 trillion amounting over six years. These cuts and the two wars accounted for around 84 percent of the increase in debt during this time. Following a period of budget surpluses at the end of the Clinton era, when Bush left office the January 2009 forecast from the Congressional Budget Office suggested that the deficit that year would be $1.2 trillion.

> **ACTIVITY**
>
> Make a list of the causes of the growth of the budget deficit during the Bush presidency. Order this list from least to most important and write a brief explanation of the order you have chosen.

Response to 9/11 attacks and an emphasis on homeland security

The foreign policy outcomes of the 9/11 attacks have been discussed earlier in this chapter. On the day of the attacks, after being moved around the country to mitigate security concerns, Bush returned to the White House and delivered a televised address from the Oval Office saying, "Terrorist attacks can shake the foundations of our biggest buildings, but they cannot touch the foundation of America."

A few days later, a state of emergency was declared, giving Bush expanded powers to mobilize the military and target terrorist financing. These two emergency declarations were renewed each year by Bush and subsequent presidents. On September 18, 2001, a series of letters containing anthrax were delivered to newsrooms and Congressional offices, killing five people. As a result, domestic policy interests turned toward the question of homeland security.

The Patriot Act (page 260) was signed into law in October, followed quickly by legislation to create the Transportation Security Administration (TSA). The TSA assumed responsibility for airport security and, in the coming years, rolled out a host of new passenger safety procedures and restrictions, including luggage screenings, full body scanners, shoe removal, pat-downs, restrictions on liquid and personal electronics, and limitations on in-flight movement.

In 2002, the Department of Homeland Security was formed. This was the broadest reorganization of the federal government since the Second World War. The Homeland Security Act centralized more than twenty domestic security functions under the Department of Homeland Security, including immigration and border control, the Coast Guard, the Federal Emergency Management Agency (FEMA), and the Secret Service.

Although it appeared Bush and Congress had formed a united front on national security, once the new Department was created, critics who feared the potential abuse of presidential power and abandonment of civil liberties began to speak out. Bush attempted to reassure people that the changes were constitutional and subject to Congressional oversight. Nonetheless, the administration faced accusations of violating the Constitution and creating a culture of secrecy in the national security space.

Response to Hurricane Katrina

In August 2005, Hurricane Katrina, a category five hurricane, struck the US. It made landfall as a tropical storm over southern Florida before escalating and making a second, catastrophic landfall over Louisiana and Mississippi on August 29. The impact of Katrina was devastating, particularly in New Orleans, where flaws in the flood protection system caused around 80 percent of the city and surrounding areas to be flooded for weeks after the hurricane had passed.

The flooding destroyed most of New Orleans's transportation and communications systems, leaving tens of thousands of people who had not been evacuated without food or shelter. The damages were estimated at around $190 billion and 1,392 people lost their lives. A national and international response was mounted including local, federal, and private rescue operations to evacuate those left in the city. The response from federal, state, and local governments was widely criticized.

In 2005, New Orleans was one of the poorest metropolitan areas. Many people lacked private transportation and this prevented many people from evacuating on their own. The mandatory evacuation called on August 27 made no provision for homeless and low-income individuals, the elderly or the sick, meaning that most of the people stranded in the city were poor, elderly, or ill. More people than predicted turned up to refuges of last resort, quickly depleting supplies. Many deaths resulted from the inadequate evacuation process.

The federal response to Katrina was slow. The day after the hurricane, as the storm surges overwhelmed flood defenses, Bush was on vacation in Texas. He did not return to Washington DC until more than 24 hours after the hurricane. It took until September 2 for Bush to sign a $10.5 billion relief package and order troops to assist with relief efforts. The Mayor of New Orleans expressed frustration at insufficient reinforcements.

Bush was criticized for delays and a perceived insufficient response. He didn't visit the area quickly, saying that he didn't want to disrupt rescue efforts, and the weak federal, state, and local response undermined his reputation for being a decisive and strong crisis manager. Despite widespread condemnation of the FEMA response, Bush praised the FEMA director early in the crisis, leading to him appearing out of touch. His reputation never fully recovered from the response to Katrina. As a result of Katrina and the ongoing involvement in Iraq, Bush's job approval rating in September 2005 had dropped to 42 percent while 57 percent were disappointed in his performance.

SOURCE 5.10

President George W Bush looking out over the devastation in New Orleans from Hurricane Katrina as he flies back to Washington D.C. on Air Force One, August 31, 2005

> What do you think Americans would have felt about Bush's attitude toward the devastation from this image? Do you think this image was a public relations success?

Reasons for the election of Obama in 2008

In 2008, Barack Obama became the first African American president of the US. There were many factors behind his victory. They included his own strengths, the promises made in his campaign, and the weaknesses of his opponent, and wider factors such as the 2008 recession and the ongoing Iraq war.

Obama's personal and political background

Obama was born in Hawaii in 1961 to an American mother and Kenyan father. His father left the family in 1964, and Obama's mother remarried in 1965 to an Indonesian man, moving the family to Indonesia in 1967. In 1971, Obama returned to Hawaii to live with his maternal grandparents. Of his childhood, Obama has said, "I was raised as an Indonesian child and a Hawaiian child and as a Black child and as a white child ... And so what I benefited from is a multiplicity of cultures that all fed me."

After two years at Occidental College in Los Angeles, he transferred to Columbia University in New York City, graduating with a major in political science in 1983. He began his career as a community organizer in Chicago's mostly poor, African American South Side before attending Harvard Law School. He taught constitutional law at the University of Chicago Law School from 1992 to 2004. In the 1992 election, Obama directed Illinois Project Vote, a voter registration drive aimed at increasing African American turnout, and in 1996 was elected to the Illinois State Senate for Illinois's Thirteenth District, covering much of Chicago's South Side.

As a State Senator, he passed campaign finance reform and crime legislation despite being part of a Democratic minority. When Democrats won control of the Illinois Senate in 2002, he became a leading legislator, passing around 300 bills aimed at helping children, labor unions, the elderly, and the poor. He was an early critic of the Iraq War, a stance which worked in his favor as the war became increasingly unpopular.

In 2004, Obama successfully ran for US Senate, securing the largest margin of victory for a Senate candidate in Illinois's history. Obama delivered the keynote address at the 2004 Democratic National Convention. The speech was well received and elevated his status within the party.

Obama's 2008 campaign promises

Obama's 2008 campaign built a significant following at grassroots level based on his charisma, life story, and message of hope and change. The campaign is perhaps best remembered for its unprecedented use of the internet for organizing and fundraising. The campaign rewrote the Democratic platform on issues such as healthcare reform, and garnered significant support from young and minority voters.

Obama campaigned on a platform of withdrawing US troops from Iraq and closing the Guantanamo Bay detention camp, pursuing energy independence, and expanding healthcare, financial regulation, and immigration reform. The issues of Iraq and healthcare were key to helping Obama win the election.

Many Americans were angered by the unfairness of healthcare delivery in the US. By 2008, they were ready to make the issue a priority in voting. The plan Obama set out intended to make affordable health coverage (like that offered to members of Congress) available to all Americans. The plan walked a careful line in fairly and inexpensively offering healthcare to all Americans without the government providing those services.

Obama also promised to repeal the "Don't Ask, Don't Tell" policy for the military (page 288) and deliver immigration reform that would offer some illegal immigrants a path to US citizenship. Although he did not manage to achieve this, the promise of new pathways to citizenship was enough to win Obama a large turnout of Hispanic voters. Obama also made significant promises about financial regulation and cutting taxes. These promises addressed the discontent voters were feeling with the economy following the 2008 financial crash.

Impact of the Great Recession on the 2008 election

In September 2008, Lehman Brothers, a large financial services firm, collapsed. This is often considered the spark that resulted in the collapse and bailout of the banking system in the US and Europe, and the Great Recession that followed. This event took place during the 2008 presidential election, only a few months before Americans were due to go to the polls. Obama's opponent, John McCain, paused campaigning to return to Congress and help work on a response to the financial crisis. The crisis transformed the focus of media coverage in the campaign and, from September 15 onward, the economy and financial crisis dominated media headlines.

In the weeks that followed, three televised debates took place. Obama's calm and confident attitude in these debates impressed voters who were looking for reassurance. His eloquence when discussing his own experiences of growing up in modest circumstances led middle-class voters to believe that he understood the challenges they were facing. Middle-class anger about economic unfairness was growing and Obama's suggested tax cuts, rescue plans for small businesses, and promises of new job creation and reformation of Wall Street (including new regulation of financial markets) appealed to many voters.

Impact of the continuing war in Iraq on the 2008 election

A good deal of the debate during the 2008 campaign centered around the Iraq War. By 2008, the war had been ongoing for almost five years since Bush had declared "Mission Accomplished" on May 1, 2003. By 2007, around one-third of Americans rated the war as an extremely important issue in their voting decision. Popular disillusionment with the war led to negative views of the Republican Party and Obama's long-held anti-war stance gave him the edge over Hillary Clinton in the primaries and over John McCain in the election itself.

Although it cannot be said that the Iraq War was the main reason for Obama's victory, it was certainly a key contributing factor. Centrist swing voters, who decide most elections, were tired of the war and favored withdrawal. Obama's unambiguous messaging and the concrete plan he proposed for withdrawal within sixteen months appealed to weary voters.

Obama's opponents

In addition to Obama's appeal to voters, his electoral victory can also be attributed to the weaknesses of his opponents. The Republican presidential candidate, John McCain, was fighting an uphill battle for the White House in 2008. The Republican Party had run a crowded primary and McCain's victory had come as something of a surprise. The conservative wing of the Republican Party was disappointed with the selection of McCain. In choosing his running mate, McCain selected a candidate designed to unite Republicans rather than widen the appeal of the ticket overall: Sarah Palin.

Palin appealed to conservative voters and was, initially, quite popular. After the announcement, however, her positions, policies, and lack of experience in foreign policy became the focus of intense media attention. Much like the Obama campaign, she made extensive use of Facebook to skirt the media and speak directly to voters. She energized the Republicans' conservative voter base, with 69 percent of Republicans feeling that she had helped McCain's bid. However, while she maintained popularity among Republican voters, she divided public opinion generally.

It has been argued that selecting Sarah Palin as a running mate may have damaged McCain's campaign. A 2010 study undertaken by researchers at Stanford University suggested that Palin may have cost McCain around 2.1 million votes. The impact of the "Palin effect" on the election is still heavily debated, but Palin's impact on the Republican Party is clear. She awoke and mainstreamed the conservative wing of the Republican Party, and her aggressive campaigning style, widespread use of social media, and reliance on disinformation are visible in many of the Republican Party campaigns that followed.

ACTIVITY

List the factors that led to Obama's election in 2008.

Factor	Explanation	Importance on a scale of 1–5	Reason for importance score

SUMMARY DIAGRAM

US politics, 1980–2008

Why and how did US politics change between 1980 and 2008?

Reaganomics
- Cuts to welfare programmes
  - Medicaid
  - Social Security
  - Food Stamps
  - Education
  - Job training
- Increased defense spending
- Lower federal taxes
- Reduced regulation on:
  - Oil
  - Gas
  - Cable TV
  - Long-distance telephone services
  - Ocean shipping
  - Interstate buses
- Reduction of anti-trust laws
- Relaxation of the Clean Air Act
- Opening of federal land to private investment
- Increased import barriers
- Encouraged Federal Reserve to continue money supply reduction policies

George H. W. Bush Domestic Policy
- $100 billion bailout of the Savings and Loans industry
- Cut government expenditure
- Increased taxes
- Clean Air Act Amendments
  - Reduce urban smog
  - Combat acid rain
  - Eliminate industrial emissions of toxic chemicals
- Americans with Disabilities Act
  - Prohibited discrimination based on disability
  - Guaranteed adequate access to business and public venues, transport, and telecommunications
- War on Drugs
  - Expansion of treatment, federal prisons, education, and law enforcement
  - 1208 Program
- Civil Rights Act 1991
  - Right to jury trial for discrimination cases
  - Option of emotional distress damages
  - Limited amount juries could award
  - Expanded rights of women to sue for sexual discrimination and harassment

Clinton's Third Way
- Reduction of the budget deficit
  - Reduction in government spending
  - Increased taxes on wealthiest Americans
  - Energy tax
  - Tax deductions for small businesses and self-employed
  - NAFTA
  - Encourage private sector Investment
  - Invest in education and research
- Welfare Reform
  - Direct Student Loan programme
  - Early Head Start
  - Expansion of Medicare
  - Expansion of earned income tax credit
  - Increased minimum wage
  - Improved nutritional support for low-income families
  - Child tax credits

George Bush Administration
- 2001 tax cuts
  - Lowered maximum estate tax
  - New 10% tax brackets
  - Reduced existing tax brackets
  - Increased per-child tax credit
  - Doubled deduction for married couples
- 2003 tax cuts
  - Reduced long-term capital gains tax
  - Accelerated 2001 provisions
  - Increased amount of income exempt from Alternative Minimum Tax
- Increased budget deficit
- Patriot Act 2001
- Homeland Security Act 2002– formation of the Department for Homeland Security
- Slow response to Hurricane Katrina

Obama's Election
- Obama's personal and political background
  - Mixed-race
  - Worked as a community organizer in the South Side of Chicago
  - Directed Illinois Project Vote
  - Successful career in State Senate and federal Senate
  - Early critic of Iraq war
- Campaign Promises
  - Withdraw from Iraq
  - Close Guantanamo Bay
  - Increase energy independence
  - Expand healthcare
  - Increase financial regulation
  - Immigration reform – routes to US citizenship
  - Repeal Don't Ask, Don't Tell
- Great Recession
  - Obama's calm, confident attitude in the aftermath of the crisis impressed voters
  - Background made voters believe he understood the challenges they faced
- Opponents
  - Challenging Republican primary
  - Palin energized conservative voter base but polarized public opinion

5.3 Why and how far did US society change between 1980 and 2008?

This was a time of rapid technological and social change. From personal computing and social media, to increased multiculturalism and civil rights victories, the world seemed to be completely changed in just 30 years. This brought many advantages and advances for minority groups and businesses. However, it also brought challenges for society, sparking backlashes and increasing social divides. This section will explore the period through four key themes: the impact of new technology; the growth of multiculturalism; civil rights and race relations; and arguments about resistance to social change.

Development and impact of new technology and the digital revolution

The technology of 1980 was almost unrecognizable by 2008. Computers had become smaller and more portable, allowing for them to become prevalent across much of the globe, particularly in the form of smartphones. The internet, first commercialized in the early 1990s, connected the world, changing how people interacted and did business. The popularity of the internet allowed for the rise of social media and, eventually, the robotics revolution and the rise of automation.

Personal computers

In the mid-1970s, the first personal computers (PCs) became available. These early PCs were mostly very expensive, specialized machines that could fit on top of a desk. They were still quite big, compared to the pocket-sized computers of today, but they were much smaller than previous computers, which took up entire rooms. The first commercially successful PC, the Altair 8800, was released in 1974. In 1975 Bill Gates and Paul Allen, who had worked on programming for the Altair, formed Microsoft. It went on to become a key part of the computing revolution. The personal computer industry developed rapidly from 1977 with the introduction of the Apple II. Apple, founded by Steve Jobs and Stephen Wozniak, released the Apple II in April 1977. Unlike its predecessors, it had a keyboard and a colour screen. Apple encouraged programmers to create "applications" for it. A spreadsheet program made it a practical tool for businesses.

Most of the early PCs were designed for business use. However, in the early 1980s, the first home computers were developed. Often these had software for personal productivity, programming, and games. Throughout the 1980s, demand for personal computers grew, particularly in the business world. In 1981, IBM Corporation, the leading computer maker of the time, entered the PC market with the IBM PC. In 1984, the Apple Macintosh was released. It was particularly useful for desktop publishing because it could lay out text and graphics on the screen as they would appear on a printed page. In 1985 Microsoft released Microsoft Windows, an **operating system** that gave Microsoft operating system-based computers many of the same capabilities as the Macintosh. Windows became the dominant operating system for personal computers in this time.

Computers rapidly increased in power, speed, and the variety of functions they performed. A computer could make many tasks much quicker, including bookkeeping, inventory management, and data entry and processing. They increased productivity, making businesses more efficient, and revolutionized sectors such as medical research where the ability to analyze huge data sets quickly and efficiently led to new treatments and improvements in care. PCs also helped to make everyday tasks such as doing taxes, keeping family records, and writing letters quicker and simpler. They revolutionized entertainment in the form of video gaming and allowed for the creation and flourishing of new, multi-million-dollar industries.

PCs created something of a societal revolution on their own, but mostly in the way business operated. The spread of internet access in the 1990s changed the way individuals interacted with each other and, increasingly, the world around them. The connection of computers through the internet was a driver of significant change, not only in the US, but across the world.

> **KEY TERM**
>
> **Operating system (OS)** The core software for using a computer, the operating system manages the hardware (the physical parts of a computer) and runs programs. Microsoft Windows and Apple's Mac OS were, and still are, the most popular operating systems. In the smartphone age, new operating systems have been developed. The most popular are iOS (Apple) and Android (Google).

The Modern US, 1980 to 2008

The development of the internet

The Cold War created the need for a communications system that would not be affected by a nuclear attack. This led to the invention of the internet: a networking technology that allowed computers in separate places to connect and communicate. Initially known as ARPANET (after the Advanced Research Projects Agency), this technology was used within the Department of Defense for some years. However, it was complex and required a lot of technical skill to use. In 1989, Tim Berners-Lee, a British computer scientist, proposed a new, quick, and easy-to-access way to structure and link computer networks. This became the World Wide Web, an easy way to share information using the internet. The "www." part of a web adddress is for "World Wide Web."

With the public launch of web browsers in 1993, activity on the internet increased very rapidly. The number of websites grew from 130 in 1993 to over 100,000 at the start of 1996. The internet and its affiliates, the World Wide Web and email, completely changed day-to-day life for much of the world. It hugely accelerated the process of globalization, enabling instant communication across the world. The internet enabled instant access to news, research, and information, and completely changed how shopping, entertainment, and business happened. With the rise of social media in the 2000s (see below) new challenges and opportunities arose for democracy and activism.

The internet also initially changed the nature of the businesses competing in the market. Between 1997 and 2001, the first internet-related speculative investment bubble occurred. Centered around **Silicon Valley** in Northern California, which had become the home of many computing and software companies, the dot-com bubble was driven by the exceedingly high valuations placed on dot-com companies, as investors rapidly increased stock values. During the bubble, real estate prices in Silicon Valley reached unprecedented levels, and the area became home (briefly) to some of the most expensive commercial real estate in the world. The bubble was followed by a market crash. However, enthusiasm recovered quickly. Silicon Valley is still one of the top research and development centers in the world to this day.

> **KEY TERM**
>
> **Silicon Valley** A region of Northern California that has become the biggest center of technological innovation and manufacturing in the US. It is home to some of the biggest technology companies in the world including Apple, Google, Meta, and Netflix.

Changes in phone technology: cell phones and smartphones

Alongside the revolution in computing that was beginning in the 1970s, a similar change was occurring in phone technology. In 1973, the first call from a mobile telephone was made and, in 1984, the first cell phone went on public sale. It was large and expensive and did not sell particularly well. In the early 1990s, the second generation of cell phone technology arrived and cell phones became a much more common sight. These models were significantly smaller, though still much larger than today's cell phones. They had the capacity to send text messages in addition to making phone calls. The use of cell phones started to extend beyond the world of business as teenagers began to use them.

In 1996, the first handset that was able to access the internet was produced and, with the launch of the Blackberry in 1999, internet-ready phones became more common. At first, these were only really for business use. At first, "internet ready" did not mean phones could access the World Wide Web; mostly the only extra feature an "internet-ready" phone had was the ability to send and receive emails. Internet-ready cell phone technology became truly pervasive with the 2007 launch of the Apple iPhone. This was the first "smartphone." In addition to the typical capacity to make calls, text, and access emails, the iPhone allowed users to access the internet through a browser and play and store music. The second generation of iPhone also introduced the App Store.

As computer chips became smaller, greater and greater capabilities became available to cell phone technology. Now, smartphones are essentially very small, portable computers. Improvements in phone technology changed the way individuals interacted with each other. People were now instantly contactable at any time in any location, which fundamentally changed our interactions with both work contacts and friends and family. Suddenly, it was very challenging to be uncontactable and the expectation became that people should be able to be contacted at any time and in any place. Cell phones, especially once they became fully internet capable, fundamentally remade our attitudes to and expectations of each other both socially and in the workplace.

Rise of social media

In the mid-1990s, online services that functioned as platforms for social interaction started to become popular. The earliest social media web sites included SixDegrees.com and Classmates.com. These allowed people to connect with each other by offering features such as friends lists, school affiliations, and profiles. However, they did not allow for anonymous interaction. Social media use became more widespread with the launch of Friendster in 2002 and Myspace in 2003. By 2005, only around five percent of the US used social media. However, with the public launch of Facebook in 2006, social media use increased rapidly and by 2008, around ten percent of Americans used social media.

The impacts of social media have been many and varied. Social media allowed for new forms of activism and civic engagement. It offered widespread access to information and was used successfully to encourage social awareness and, initially, provided a new voice to minorities and underrepresented groups. For example, in the 2008 election, Barack Obama's presidential campaign made very successful use of social media. It was the first political campaign in the US to do so. Particularly during the primary campaigns, when Obama was a relative outsider; his campaign used social media to bypass traditional media sources (which often overlooked him) and connect directly with supporters. His own website hosted materials that individuals could download and share on social media to spread the message, and he made effective use of crowdsourcing to create and distribute content.

Social media also had negative impacts. For example, it made it easier to spread disinformation and misinformation. Sarah Palin, John McCain's running mate in 2008, is one of the first politicians to participate in the "post-truth" environment. While debate continues about whether social media directly contributed to society's polarization, it certainly made it easier to interact with like-minded individuals and, by extension, cement opinions already held. Overall, social media offered a new way for individuals to engage with each other, with their political representatives, and with the world around them. It provided new ways of organizing and gave a platform to those often ignored, while simultaneously providing a largely unregulated space for the spread of misinformation.

The robotics revolution

When the first industrial robot entered the market in the 1960s it marked a step forward in the **automation** of dangerous and difficult tasks. Initially used in the automotive industry, the first mass-produced robotic arm paved the way for the widespread adoption of robots and robotics in industry, particularly in the manufacturing sector. By the 1980s, advances in sensor technology made basic machine-vision systems possible and it became generally accepted that industrial robots were the future of the manufacturing industry.

In the 1990s, with the rise of the PC era, computer-controlled robots became more common and, as the cost and size of microprocessors decreased, robotics became obtainable for most industries and businesses. Improvements in sensor technology and a higher degree of programmability began to give robots what many thought of as basic intelligence. This allowed for collaborative robotics that provided industry with robots designed to work safely alongside humans, as well as robots that could handle materials with greater delicacy and precision.

The rapid automation that followed these advances caused the displacement of factory workers and, by the 1990s, many factories in advanced economies looked more like places where people helped machines to make things rather than the other way around. In the US, the share of jobs in manufacturing fell from 30 percent in 1970 to ten percent in 2010. This was partially due to automation, but also due to factors such as NAFTA making it cheaper for companies to manufacture abroad. By contrast, for the services sector, advances in computing produced a significant increase in the number of jobs available. The birth and development of the software industry, alongside new services and e-commerce, meant that new service-sector and professional jobs were created. This began to change the economies of many developed nations, resulting in deindustrialization and contributing to social and economic challenges.

> **KEY TERM**
>
> **Automation** The term used to describe a wide range of technologies that reduce human involvement in processes.

> **ACTIVITY**
>
> In pairs or groups, make a list of the impacts the digital revolution had on American society. Discuss whether these impacts were negative or positive, to make a judgment about the impact of the digital revolution.

Development of multiculturalism and an increasingly diverse population

Since 1980, every state in the US has increased in diversity. Racial and ethnic diversity rose rapidly between 1980 and 2008 due to various factors such as immigration, differing fertility rates, and age demographics. After the end of the Cold War, greater migration and growing diversity across the West led to a growing interest in the idea of multiculturalism.

The idea of multiculturalism and its growth

Multiculturalism has a variety of meanings across sociology, political philosophy, and colloquial use. Broadly, it looks to tackle the challenges that arise from cultural diversity, with the idea that distinct identities and cultural groups should be acknowledged, preserved, and supported in society. The trend of international migration following the end of the Second World War lent credence to the idea, but following the collapse of the USSR and the resultant escalation of economic migration, it gained new and renewed interest.

Multiculturalism had been the policy of some Western nations, such as the UK, since the 1970s. Historically, the US has favored the "melting pot" theory, in which immigrant cultures are mixed and amalgamated without state intervention—this theory assumes that individual immigrants and groups of immigrants will settle into American society at their own pace. This differs from multiculturalism, which does not require complete assimilation or integration. By the 1990s, multiculturalism had its supporters in the US; however, it did not form part of formal government policy. This period also saw attempts to bring some of the tenets of multiculturalism into the education system, but this varied by state and was not driven at the federal level.

Growth in minority populations and the 2000 census

From 1980 to 2008, the demographics of the US changed. In 1980, white residents made up around 80 percent of the national population; by 2008 they made up 64.8 percent. The population of Latino/Hispanic and Asian Americans grew significantly in this period. In the 1980 census, Latino/Hispanic Americans made up around 6.5 percent of the population; by 2008 they made up 15.7 percent. Similarly, the proportion of Asian Americans increased from 1.6 percent to 4.6 percent in this time.

The 2000 census highlighted the increased diversity of the US. When it released the results of the 2000 census, the Census Bureau said, "Never have we been so diverse; never have we been so many; never have we been so carefully measured." The census showed that the total national population had grown by 32.7 million since the 1990 census. It also showed that the population distribution across states had changed, with the South and the West of the country experiencing significant population growth. The Constitution dictates that population distribution is the basis for representation in the House of Representatives and, as such, the 2000 census resulted in several Southern and Western states gaining one or two seats while states on the East Coast and in the Midwest lost seats.

The 2000 census also revealed sharp increases in immigration and a falling birth rate among the American-born population. The census suggested that this group had stopped reproducing at the level required to maintain the population; the fact that the US population grew so significantly was more due to a rise in immigration and higher-than-replacement birth rates among foreign-born Americans. A large part of this was tied to the growth in the Latino/Hispanic American population which, the 2000 census revealed, had become the country's largest minority group.

> **ACTIVITY**
>
> Look at the census data on racial demographics. In pairs or small groups discuss what this data shows you about the changing demographics of the US from 1980 to 2000. Discuss how you think this would make different ethnic groups feel about their place in US society.
>
> | Race/ethnic group | 1980 Census | 1990 Census | 2010 Census |
> |---|---|---|---|
> | White | 83.10% | 80.30% | 75.10% |
> | Black | 11.70% | 12.10% | 12.30% |
> | Native | 0.60% | 0.80% | 0.90% |
> | Asian | 1.50% | 2.90% | 3.80% |
> | Hispanic (of any race) | 6.40% | 9.00% | 12.50% |
> | Non-Hispanic White | 79.60% | 75.60% | 69.10% |
> | Other | 3.00% | 3.90% | 5.50% |

Causes of increasing amounts of immigration from Central and South America, the Caribbean, and Asia

At the end of the twentieth century, a series of civil wars, political crises, natural disasters, and other shocks drove substantial migration from Central and South American nations. In the 1980s, several Central American countries, such as El Salvador, experienced civil wars in which the US government was often involved. This led to significant displacement and economic instability, even after the wars ended. The aftermath of these civil wars also saw a rise in gang violence and crime. It is estimated that around one million Salvadorans and Guatemalans fled to the US between 1981 and 1990. Many also fled the region following Hurricane Mitch in 1998 and two large earthquakes in 2001.

South Americans were historically a relatively small group in the US. However, between 1960 and 2010, they grew from around one percent to almost seven percent of the immigrant population. Generally, South Americans were more likely to migrate to the US for economic reasons or to join immediate family members. As a group, they were typically better educated and less likely to come to the US to join refugees. Most of the immigration from South America in this period occurred after 1990 and came from Colombia, Ecuador, Peru, and Brazil.

Between 1980 and 2000, the Caribbean immigrant population in the US increased by more than 50 percent every decade. Part of this was due to a large influx of Cuban immigrants. Many Cubans came to the US on a boatlift run by Cuban exiles after the Cuban government opened one of Havana's ports for Cubans wishing to leave, who could be collected by relatives living abroad. Large-scale migration also occurred from the Dominican Republic, which had suffered a coup, a civil war, and US military occupation in the 1960s. The ensuing economic and social crises drove many Dominicans to migrate to the US. Dominican migration was largely driven by economic interests and the substantial wage disparity between the two countries.

For much of the twentieth century, the US operated exclusionary immigration policies against Asian immigrants, particularly those from China and Japan. After these were lifted in the 1960s, a new wave of Asian immigration began. The end of the Korean and Vietnam wars brought large numbers of people from Korea, Vietnam, Laos, and Cambodia to the US. Some came as dependents of US soldiers returning home, others were part of the waves of refugees that followed the communist takeover of South Vietnam and the ensuing struggles between Cambodia and Vietnam in the 1980s. Asian immigrants during this time were a mix of highly skilled and low-skilled individuals; they frequently entered the US through family reunification and work visas.

The fight for and passage of the Americans with Disabilities Act (ADA) of 1990

The Civil Rights Acts of the 1960s did not include provisions for disabled Americans. By the late 1980s, a movement had developed to rectify this and deliver an act that enshrined disability rights in law. Although it eventually passed with bipartisan support, the Americans with Disabilities Act (ADA) was hard fought for.

The first step toward the ADA was Section 504 of the 1973 Rehabilitation Act, which banned discrimination based on disability by recipients of federal funds. This Section formed the basis for what became the ADA. For the first time, people with disabilities were viewed as a minority population rather than being categorized based on diagnosis. Throughout the early 1980s, disability activists fought to prevent the Reagan administration from "deregulating" (abolishing) Section 504 on the grounds that it was burdensome to businesses. In 1986, the National Council on Disability issued a report in which it examined incentives and disincentives in federal laws toward increasing the independence and integration of people with disabilities into US society. One of the key disincentives identified was large gaps in civil rights coverage for people with disabilities.

In late 1988, the idea of federal legislation extending civil rights legislation to Americans with disabilities gained bipartisan support. In early 1989, both Congress and the newly elected George HW Bush worked separately, then together, to draft legislation to expand civil rights without imposing undue cost on those already in compliance with existing laws. In March 1990, when the ADA seemed to have stalled in Congress, 60 disability activists staged a "Capitol Crawl." They shed their mobility aids and proceeded to crawl or pull themselves up the front steps of the Capitol chanting "ADA now." The impact of the Capitol Crawl is debated, but it certainly made a statement and likely did influence at least some members of Congress to approve the Act.

When it was passed, the ADA prohibited discrimination based on disability in employment, public accommodations, and transportation. It guaranteed adequate access to business and public venues, transport, and telecommunications. The ADA was controversial, drawing criticism from conservatives for the cost and the intrusion of the federal government into the private sector. It also saw opposition from religious groups, since it protected individuals with HIV/AIDS, which was often associated with gay men (page 287). Some religious groups also opposed the Act because it labeled religious institutions as "public accommodations" and would have required churches to make costly structural changes. Furthermore, there was opposition from business groups and companies, who argued that the legislation would impose unaffordable costs on businesses.

Despite the opposition, the ADA did have a big impact on the lives of Americans with disabilities. It led to significant improvements in access to public services, societal understanding of disabilities, and accessibility of the built environment across the US.

> What does this source show about the challenges activists faced in getting the ADA passed?

SOURCE 5.11

A group of disabled people led by 8-year-old Jennifer Keelan take part in the Capitol Crawl, March 1990

Civil rights and race relations from 1980 to 2008

By the 1980s, some Americans believed that racial problems and institutional discrimination were a thing of the past. However, economic and social inequality persisted for ethnic minorities, as did police violence against African American communities. Disparities in economic and social opportunity, and the feeling that race inequality issues had fallen off the national agenda led to renewed social unrest and acts of protest. This period also saw the growth of the LGBT rights movement, as well as further advances for women's rights.

Continuing economic and social inequalities for ethnic minorities

Despite the successes of the Civil Rights Movement in legally ending discrimination on the grounds of race, significant economic and social inequality persisted in this period, particularly between white Americans and African and Hispanic Americans. The difference in educational attainment between white Americans and their African and Hispanic American counterparts began to narrow in the 1980s but remained significant. White Americans were also significantly more likely to hold a bachelor's degree than African and Hispanic Americans. The income of households headed by African and Hispanic Americans remained much lower than of those headed by white Americans. In the mid-1990s, the average income in African American households was around $37,800 compared to $63,600 for white households (Hispanic American households had similar income levels to African American households). While households with higher levels of formal education overall earned higher incomes, the racial income gap persisted across all education levels.

In the 1980s, some economists assumed that racial economic disparity was an anomaly that would narrow as younger African Americans with a higher level of education replaced older African Americans in the workforce. Instead, the policies of Reaganomics around cutting taxes, decreasing domestic spending, and deregulating markets disproportionately benefited white Americans. Automation and offshoring of manufacturing led to significant challenges for African Americans, many of whom worked in blue-collar roles. Many of these roles were replaced by less well-paid and less unionized roles in the service industry. This left African Americans in the workforce particularly economically vulnerable.

The Reagan administration also operated staunch tough-on-crime policies. Laws such as the 1986 Anti-Drug Abuse Act fueled the over-policing of African and Hispanic American neighborhoods. The Act set out sentencing disparities between crimes involving crack cocaine versus powder cocaine. A crime involving 0.18 ounces of crack cocaine received the same sentence as an equivalent crime involving 17.6 ounces of powder cocaine. This disproportionately impacted African Americans; the number of African American people sent to federal prison increased from around 50 in 100,000 adults to 250 in 100,000 adults following the Act, whereas the incarceration rate among white people saw almost no change. Prison sentences could devastate a family economically both through lost income and through the difficulty an offender had in finding employment after receiving a federal criminal record.

Unemployment, economic and social inequality, and over-policing in the 1980s and 1990s drove a rise in social unrest, both violent and in the form of peaceful protest. Recognition of the fact that women of color, and African American women in particular, were especially disadvantaged within society also sparked organized protest by African American women in the 1990s.

Race riots and civil rights marches
Los Angeles Riots

In March 1991, an African American man named Rodney King was severely beaten by police officers from the Los Angeles Police Department (LAPD) during his arrest for driving while intoxicated. A bystander filmed the incident and sent the footage to a local news station. When it was broadcast by news media, the footage caused a public uproar which resulted in the LAPD chief announcing that the four officers involved would be disciplined and face criminal charges. In April 1992, the officers charged with excessive force were acquitted by a jury. This sparked a wave of civil unrest in Los Angeles County which lasted through April and May of 1992, and became known as the Los Angeles Riots or the Los Angeles Uprising. Widespread looting, assault, and arson occurred during the unrest and the situation was only resolved after the California National Guard, the US military, and federal law enforcement deployed forces to end the violence. By the end of the unrest, 63 people had been killed, 2,383 injured, and more than 12,000 arrested. Around $1 billion worth of property damage was also caused.

> What does Source 5.12 tell us about the grievances that led to the LA riots of 1992?

SOURCE 5.12

Rodney King's attorney, Steven Lerman, holds up a photo of his client during a press conference. The photo shows King after his beating by LAPD officers. King's doctor outlined the extent of his injuries for reporters during the conference

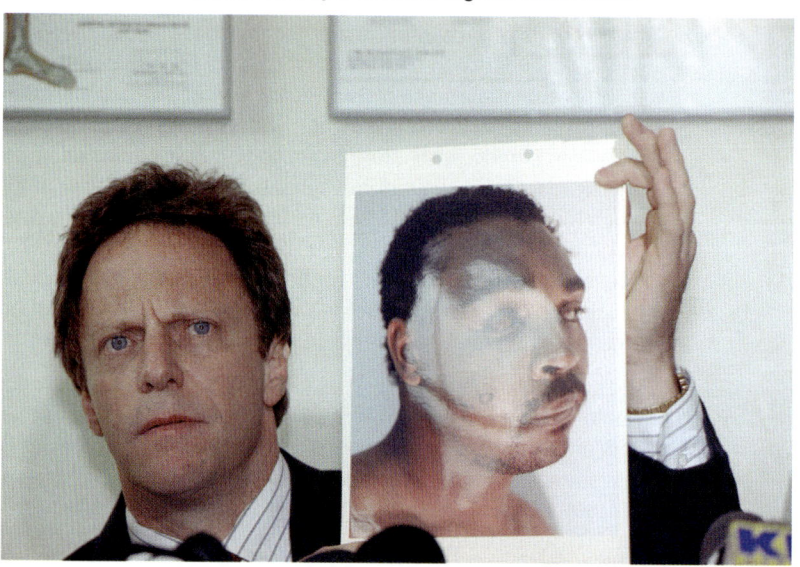

While the spark for this unrest was the acquittal of the officers involved in the Rodney King incident, its causes went far beyond this. Minority community leaders had complained repeatedly about harassment and excessive force against minorities by the LAPD. Widespread gang sweeps by police during the LA Olympics in 1984 were continued in the years that followed, leading to frequent mass arrests of African American youths and allegations of racial profiling. In the years preceding the unrest, there had also been growing racial tension between the African American and Korean communities in LA County. This came to a head in 1991, when a Korean shopkeeper, Soon Ja Du, shot and killed Latasha Harlins, a Black teenager, during an altercation. The shopkeeper was convicted of voluntary manslaughter, but the judge decided against prison time, opting instead for community service, probation, and a $500 fine. This significantly worsened relations between the communities, and Korean-owned shops were a particular target during the unrest, making up around 45 percent of all damages.

Million Man March

In response to the issues exposed in the unrest, as well as high-profile scandals like the OJ Simpson trial and Mike Tyson's conviction for rape, a group of civil rights activists known as the National African American Leadership Summit and the Nation of Islam organized the Million Man March on Washington in October 1995. The broad aim of the March was to place Black issues on the nation's political agenda. Organizers believed that the social and economic issues faced by the Black community were being ignored by politicians, who were instead blaming urban Black Americans for domestic economic challenges. Organizers also expressed a desire to change public perception of African American men, arguing that these men were treated as scapegoats for the sins of all American men.

Despite women being involved in the organization of the March, it received criticism from Black feminists who believed it might spark a resurgence of Black male sexism. They were angered by the exclusion of women from the March and the argument from the Nation of Islam leader that the March was for Black men to "atone" and take their "rightful" place as heads of families and households. The March was accompanied by a "day of absence" in which organizers encouraged Black women to stay home and care for their children.

Million Woman March

Two years after the Million Man March, a protest march for African American women took place in Philadelphia, known as the Million Woman March. The March was organized by **grassroots** activists and bypassed traditional civil rights leaders and organizations. It relied on a network of women's organizations distributing fliers and leaflets, as well as Black-run media, and word-of-mouth. It sought to unite Black women to address the issues of interest to them. These included the economic deterioration of Black communities, their lack of voice in politics and the Civil Rights Movement, and the deficiencies in education, healthcare, and addiction support services. The Philadelphia Police Department estimated a turnout for the March of around 300,000 people (organizers suggested there were as many as 1.5 million participants throughout the day-long event).

While the fight for legal recognition had been largely won, significant differences in economic and social standing for minority ethnic groups and civil rights activism persisted throughout the 1980s and 1990s. The racial wealth gap, income disparity, and inequality in educational attainment, as well as economic return from education, persist in the US to this day.

> **KEY TERM**
>
> **Grassroots** Used to describe movements and activities that originate from the ordinary people, rather than leaders.

> **ACTIVITY**
>
> - Look at this chapter and previous chapters and discuss the changing position of ethnic minorities in American society. Examine social and economic factors and the attitudes and actions of white Americans.
> - Select one minority ethnic group and create a presentation in groups or pairs, examining how the position of that group in American society changed throughout the twentieth century.

The growth of the LGBT rights movement

In the 1980s, LGBT political organizations grew and expanded. Gay activists won support from the Democratic Party in 1980, when the party added non-discrimination based on sexual orientation to its platform. Campaigns by activists urging gay men and women to "come out of the closet" also encouraged them to enter the political area as candidates. The 1980s saw the first openly gay member of Congress, Barney Frank, come out while serving his term in the House of Representatives. However, the 1980s also brought enormous challenges for the LGBT community in the form of the **HIV/AIDS** crisis.

In 1981, the Centers for Disease Control and Prevention published a report about five previously healthy gay men becoming infected with a rare type of pneumonia; this turned out to be the first identification of AIDS. AIDS (Acquired Immunodeficiency Syndrome) was originally falsely identified as a "gay disease," as gay men were one of the first and largest groups afflicted. Parts of the media initially referred in derogatory terms to the disease as "gay men's pneumonia," "gay cancer," and "gay-related immune deficiency." This contributed to the widespread misconception that AIDS only affected gay men.

As cases spread, the Reagan administration did very little to acknowledge the crisis, which sparked an activist response from the LGBT community. In March 1987, the AIDS Coalition to Unleash Power (ACT UP) was formed. In October of the same year, the Second National March on Washington for Lesbian and Gay Rights occurred, prompted by the Reagan administration's lack of acknowledgment of the AIDS crisis and a Supreme Court ruling which upheld the criminalization of sexual relationships between two consenting men. ACT UP argued for greater access to experimental AIDS drugs and a coordinated national policy to fight the disease.

> **KEY TERMS**
>
> **AIDS** Acquired Immunodeficiency Syndrome: a group of life-threatening illnesses that occur after the immune system has been severely damaged by untreated HIV.
>
> **HIV** Human Immunodeficiency Virus: an infection that attacks the body's immune system, making it difficult to fight off other infections. It is mostly spread through unprotected sex, but also in other ways such as breastfeeding and contaminated blood transfusions. AIDS occurs if the virus is not treated.
> HIV is incurable, but in the twenty-first century, treatments have been developed that make the infection untransmittable and prevent it from damaging the body.

By the 1990s, a younger generation of LGBT activists pushed gay rights to the forefront of the political conversation. In his campaign, Clinton had indicated his intention to end the prohibition against gay people in the military; however, this was met with opposition, so a compromise was reached. In 1993, the US military instituted the "Don't Ask, Don't Tell" policy which permitted gay people to serve in the military, while simultaneously banning same-sex relationships and sexual activity and allowing for personnel to be discharged for claiming to be gay or bisexual. In response to "Don't Ask, Don't Tell," as well as increasing hate crime and discrimination against the LGBT community, a third march, the March on Washington for Lesbian, Gay and Bi Equal Rights and Liberation, took place in April 1993.

In 1996, the Defense of Marriage Act (DOMA) banned federal recognition of same-sex marriage and allowed states to refuse to recognize same-sex marriages granted under the laws of other states. Numerous attempts were made to challenge DOMA in court but, before the mid-2000s, all were struck down in federal courts. By the 2000s, gay rights issues were more prominent in the mainstream dialogue. In 2000, Vermont became the first state to legalize civil unions and registered partnerships between same-sex couples. In 2003, the Supreme Court ruled that criminalizing consensual sexual conduct between same-sex individuals was unconstitutional and, in 2004, Massachusetts became the first state to legalize same-sex marriage.

> What can you learn from this source about the priorities of the LBGT movement during the 1980s?

SOURCE 5.13

ACT UP protesters outside the Federal Drug Administration demanding the release of experimental medication for those living with HIV/Aids. October 11, 1988

Impacts of feminism of the 1980s and 1990s

By the 1980s, despite the failure to ratify the ERA in 1982, some believed that the campaign surrounding the legislation had succeeded in changing social attitudes to gender roles. The 1980s saw the first female Supreme Court judge, Sandra Day O'Connor, and the first female nominee for US vice president, Geraldine Ferraro. However, feminism had begun to fall out of favor with younger women and the conservative policies of the Reagan administration slowed momentum toward full gender equality.

> **KEY TERM**
>
> **Head and master law**
> Head and master laws were American property laws that permitted a husband to have the final say regarding all household decisions and jointly owned property without his wife's knowledge or consent.

The women's equality movement did see some successes through the courts in the 1980s. In 1981, the Supreme Court overturned Louisiana's **head and master law** in the *Kirchberg v. Feenstra* decision. In 1974, Joan Feenstra's husband was jailed and, under Louisiana's head and master law, he remortgaged their shared home to pay for his lawyer, despite Joan having fully paid for the property. Feenstra separated from her husband and returned to court to challenge the constitutionality of the law. The Supreme Court held that Louisiana's law violated the Equal Protection Clause of the Fourteenth Amendment and declared it unconstitutional. The ruling marked a commitment to ensuring that laws did not arbitrarily discriminate based on gender.

In 1986, the Supreme Court made a landmark ruling in *Meritor Savings Bank v. Vinson*, which redefined sexual harassment in the workplace. In 1978, having been subjected to three years of sexual harassment by her supervisor, 23-year-old Mechelle Vinson was fired from her job at Meritor Savings Bank, supposedly for excessive use of sick leave. Vinson started a civil lawsuit against her supervisor, arguing that the harassment had created a "hostile work environment" and constituted unlawful discrimination under Title VII of the Civil Rights Act. The Supreme Court upheld that Title VII was "not limited to economic or tangible discrimination" but that the intention of the Act was to "strike at the entire spectrum of disparate treatment of men and women in employment."

The *Meritor Savings Bank v. Vinson* ruling was the first instance of sexual harassment being recognized as "actionable" by the Court. Following the ruling, reported sexual harassment cases grew from ten cases registered per year before 1986, to 624 cases in 1987. Through the 1990s, reporting of cases continued to rise with 2,217 cases reported in 1990 and 4,626 in 1995. In 1991, the televised testimony of Anita Hill, which outlined the sexual harassment she had received from Supreme Court nominee Clarence Thomas, inspired a resurgence in the feminist movement. Despite the 1986 ruling, in the high-profile sex scandals, like the Lewinsky scandal (page 271), and harassment cases of the 1990s, the media often gendered and stereotyped women's experiences. The feminism of the 1990s often tried to question and change the ideas and words that the media transmitted about gender, womanhood, beauty, and sexuality.

Arguments about and resistance to social change

The rise of global immigration and the increased mainstreaming of civil rights ideas, LGBT rights, and ideas of multiculturalism did not take place without resistance. This period saw increased division and debate over immigration, particularly the question of illegal immigration, a rise in opposition to affirmative action programs, and continued opposition to the perceived dissolution of family values represented by the successes of the LGBT rights movement.

Conservative reactions to the AIDS epidemic

When the AIDS epidemic began in the early 1980s, the Reagan administration met the issue with indifference. Despite public health officials becoming aware of AIDS in 1981, the first mention of AIDS by the White House did not occur until October 1982 and, even then, only in response to a question from the White House press pool. In June 1983, Reagan held a meeting with members of his administration and representatives of the LGBT community. This was the first time the administration had met with the community; they discussed concerns about and basic solutions to the AIDS epidemic (such as encouraging condom use to mitigate the spread of the disease).

Reagan found the meeting unsatisfactory, and, in August, he scheduled another meeting on the AIDS epidemic, this time without anyone from the LGBT community. Instead, this meeting included conservative activists such as Ron Goodwin from Moral Majority and the National Director of the Conservative Caucus. Conservative activists were keen that the epidemic only be discussed in the context of gay people's "moral failing." Public health officials and epidemiologists struggled to gain control of the epidemic. Reagan's conservative advisors, who wanted AIDS education to fit into the attitude of social and religious conservatism, claimed that gay men were dangerous and sick. After these meetings in 1983, there are currently no records of internal White House conversations about the epidemic until 1985. In an interview in 2006, Reagan's Secretary of Health and Human Services (1983–85), Margaret Heckler, stated that she was never able to speak to Reagan about the AIDS crisis and the epidemic did not appear on Reagan's highly structured Cabinet meeting agendas during this time.

Assertions that AIDS patients were to blame for their own condition due to being gay were particularly common within the religious right. In June 1983, Catholic newspaper columnist Pat Buchanan wrote in a column, "The poor homosexuals. They have declared war on nature, and now nature is exacting an awful retribution." Later, Buchanan became Reagan's communications director. The Moral Majority proclaimed AIDS to be "the wrath of God." It became clear that heterosexual sex, as well as blood transfusions, needle-sharing, and from mother to child during pregnancy could spread HIV. However, many on the religious right continued to associate the disease primarily with gay men. Even public health campaigns, which did acknowledge the fact that anyone could contract HIVAIDS, still focused on messages of abstinence and the shaming of sexual behavior. Conservative activists often used the AIDS epidemic as a means of promoting messages of abstinence and anti-LGBT discrimination. These activists had access to the Reagan administration, which made it increasingly challenging for public health officials to respond in the early years of the epidemic.

SOURCE 5.14

> What does Source 5.14 tell you about the public response to the AIDS crisis in the US?

A poster published by the Dallas County Health Department. The small print contains information on how to prevent the spread of AIDS

Opposition to the LGBT movement

As with the reaction to the AIDS crisis, influential right-wing Christian organizations were at the forefront of the anti-LGBT movement at the end of the twentieth century. In the 1990s, the religious right began to be more proactive in its opposition to LGBT rights, producing anti-gay laws rather than simply opposing gay rights legislation. The Christian right became increasingly interested in preemptively preventing and protesting same-sex marriage, claiming that being forced to recognize and celebrate same-sex marriages would be a curtailment of religious freedom.

By 1996, more than half of the states considered legislation banning same-sex marriage. This movement to preemptively ban same-sex marriage came to a head with the federal passage of DOMA in 1996. In the late 1990s, Alaska, Nebraska, and Nevada amended their state constitutions to prohibit same-sex marriage. These constitutional changes aimed to take the issue out of the hands of the courts. By the early 2000s, some states had begun to allow same-sex civil partnerships and marriage. In 2008, however, California put forward a ballot proposition known as Proposition 8. This was a state constitutional amendment intended to ban same-sex marriage. It passed in the November 2008 state elections. In 2000, California had adopted Proposition 22, which forbade the recognition or licensing of same-sex marriage. This was challenged in California's Supreme Court and Proposition 8 was put forward by opponents of same-sex marriage to preempt the ruling in the Proposition 22 court case. It contained almost the same wording as Proposition 22 but was put through as a state constitutional amendment rather than a legislative change.

Although Clinton's campaign had made specific commitments regarding LGBT rights, he faced significant opposition to implementing his proposals. His push to lift the ban on gay people in the military was met with stiff, bipartisan resistance from Congress. Congress attempted to enact the existing gay ban into federal law, outflanking Clinton's attempts at repeal. Clinton's call to overturn this was opposed by the Joint Chiefs of Staff, members of Congress, and members of the public. As a result, "Don't Ask, Don't Tell" was implemented as a compromise. "Don't Ask, Don't Tell" did little to promote acceptance of LGBT people in the military. The statute itself concluded that, if openly acknowledged, LGBT people would "create an unacceptable risk to the high standards of morale, good order and discipline, and unit cohesion."

> **ACTIVITY**
>
> In pairs or groups, discuss the impact of the AIDS crisis on progress toward greater LGBT rights. How do you think the crisis emboldened opposition to the LGBT rights movement?

Debates over illegal immigration and increasing nativism

Over the end of the twentieth century and the beginning of the twenty-first century, debates about immigration became louder. A particular point of contention was the question of illegal immigration. In 1986, Reagan signed an immigration law known as the "Reagan Amnesty" which allowed around three million people who were in the US illegally to gain legal status. The intention was to create a new era of strict enforcement, and the amnesty was implemented alongside laws barring employers from hiring workers without legal status and creating more ways to immigrate legally. This new era of immigration enforcement never really came to fruition. George Bush Sr and Clinton both tried to overhaul immigration laws during their time in office.

In 1990, Bush Sr signed the Immigration Act of 1990. Building on the Immigration and Nationality Act of 1965, this increased total overall immigration quotas to allow 700,000 immigrants to enter the US per year from 1992 to 1994. Under the Act, this allowance would then be reduced to 675,000 per year from 1995. The Act created a family-based visa, five employment-based visas, and a diversity visa program with a lottery to admit immigrants from "low admittance" countries. The Act aimed to prevent illegal immigration by opening more routes to legal immigration. The 1990 Act did increase the number of employment-based immigrants; however, it also decreased legal opportunities for low-skilled workers. Unintentionally, this led to an increase in illegal low-skilled workers entering the US.

As the US tipped into recession in the early 1990s, debates about immigration grew again. Lower-income Americans felt that they were competing for jobs with immigrants, particularly illegal immigrants, who were willing to work for lower wages. This led to a resurgence of anti-immigrant feelings and nativist attitudes in the US, and led, in 1996, to Clinton passing the Illegal Immigration Reform and Immigrant Responsibility Act. The Act aimed to "crack down on illegal immigration at the border, in the workplace and in the criminal justice system." The Act increased resources for border enforcement, narrowed criteria for asylum, and increased the income threshold required to sponsor immigrants. It also authorized the deportation of non-citizens from ports of entry without judicial hearings.

Throughout the 1980s and 1990s, a narrative of "Latino threat" began to rise in the media. Increasing income inequality led to a wider sense of resentment toward illegal, often Hispanic, immigrants. While many Americans were particularly concerned with illegal immigration, nativist rhetoric increasingly depicted immigration generally as a "crisis," without making a distinction between legal and illegal immigration. Some politicians seized upon the political benefits that could be found in demonizing illegal immigration. Reagan asserted that it was a question of national security, saying in 1986 that, "Terrorists and subversives are just two days' driving time from [the border crossing at] Harlingen, Texas." This rhetoric turned public opinion more conservative on issues related to immigration.

The terrorist attacks in the 1990s and 9/11 amplified concerns about illegal immigration and, following the immigration act of 1996 and the Patriot Act of 2001, the number of arrests, detentions, and deportations of immigrants rapidly increased.

Opposition to multiculturalism

Alongside the increase in concern about illegal immigration, the 1980s and 1990s saw extensive criticism of the concept of multiculturalism from both the left and the right. A prominent criticism was that multiculturalism undermined national unity, hindered cultural and social integration, and led to society breaking down into ethnic factions. American conservatives were particularly concerned about shared "traditional values" and, throughout the 1990s, challenges to multiculturalist ideas such as university courses in "Ethnic studies" grew.

In the aftermath of 9/11, opposition to multiculturism grew. Soon after the attacks, Lynne Cheney (wife of US vice president Dick Cheney) said that multiculturalism and the idea that Americans needed to learn more about other cultures suggested that, "The events of September 11 were our fault, that it was our failure to understand Islam that led to so many deaths." Since 9/11, some conservatives have argued that teaching and understanding other viewpoints and cultures signals agreement with them and have pushed for a reorientation of education, to focus on the perceived superiority of American values and society. With the creation of the Department of Homeland Security in the aftermath of the attacks, immigration became no longer an economic or social issue, but rather one of national security. Terror was injected into immigration debates, giving increased oxygen to nativist and populist anti-immigration groups.

Opposition to affirmative action

The 1990s and 2000s also saw a growing anti-affirmative action movement. It was argued that affirmative action hurt white men or amounted to discrimination against other racial and ethnic groups (such as Asian Americans). In the 1990s and early 2000s, a series of challenges to affirmative action were made, resulting in several states specifically prohibiting the use of affirmative action.

The first electoral test of affirmative action came in California in 1996 with Proposition 209. California had a history of controversy concerning affirmative action running back to the *Regents v. Bakke* case of 1978 (page 234). In 1996, a campaign to amend the state constitution to prohibit state governmental institutions from considering race, sex, or ethnicity in public employment, contracting, and education began. The Proposition was put on the ballot in 1996 and passed with 55 percent in favor. Initially, enforcement of the Proposition was blocked by the District Court, but this was overruled by a Court of Appeals. Proposition 209 has been the subject of many lawsuits since it came into force, but has withstood legal scrutiny. It instigated a dramatic change in admissions for the University of California. Underrepresented group enrolment fell significantly between 1996 and 2001 but did then start to increase again.

Similar challenges to affirmative action were passed by Washington state in 1998, Michigan in 2006, and Nebraska in 2008. All three of these prohibited all or some forms of affirmative action in public hiring, education, and contracting at state level.

SUMMARY DIAGRAM

US society, 1980–2008
Why and how far did US society change between 1980 and 2008?

Digital revolution
- Personal computers
  - Increased computing power and speed
  - Improved efficiency
  - Increased business productivity
  - Revolutionized entertainment
- Creation of the internet
  - Enabled instant global communication, access to news, research and information
  - Changed the way we shop, entertain ourselves, and do business
- Changes in phone technology
  - Enabled constant communication
  - Changed work expectations
- Rise of social media
  - Enabled activism and civic engagement
  - Rise of disinformation and misinformation
- Robotics revolution
  - Rapid automation
  - Loss of blue-collar manufacturing jobs
  - Deindustrialization

Immigration and race relations
- 2000 census shows major increase in ethnic diversity in the US
- 1980s sees marked increase in immigration from Central and South America, the Caribbean, and Asia
- Ethnic minorities continue to face significant economic and social inequality
  - LA Riots, 1992
  - Million Man March
  - Million Woman March
- Increasing nativism in the 1990s
  - Increased concern about illegal immigration
  - Increase in rhetoric suggesting all immigration is a "crisis"
  - Blurring of lines between legal and illegal immigration
  - Strict immigration enforcement
- Growing opposition to multiculturalism
  - Challenges to ethnic studies programs
  - Focus on shared traditional values
- Growing opposition to affirmative action

LGBT rights and opposition
- Growth in LGBT activism in response to AIDS crisis
- Establishment of ACT UP
- Campaign to end the prohibition against gay people in the military
- Campaign for same-sex marriage
- Vermont recognizes civil unions, 2000
- Imposition of "Don't Ask, Don't Tell" policy
  - March on Washington for Lesbian, Gay, and Bi Equal Rights and Liberation, 1993
- Defense of Marriage Act, 1996
- Conservative reactions to AIDS crisis
  - Sought to frame AIDS education in the context of painting gay men as dangerous or sick
  - Moral Majority—AIDS is the "wrath of God"
  - Promote abstinence and anti-LGBT+ feeling
- Propositions to prevent same-sex marriage

Feminism and women's rights
- Feminism had begun to fall out of favor with young women
- Reagan administration slowed momentum on gender equality
- *Kirchberg v. Feenstra*
  - Declared "head and master" laws a form of discrimination and unconstitutional
- *Meritor Savings Bank v. Vinson*
  - Ruled that sexual harassment constituted discrimination
  - Recognized sexual harassment as "actionable"
- Increased interest in questions of sexual harassment
  - Spurred by Lewinsky scandal and Anita Hill's testimony against Clarence Thomas
- Continued gendering and stereotyping of the experiences of women in the media
- Feminist movement sought to question and redefine how the media wrote about gender, womanhood, and sexuality

CHAPTER SUMMARY

Between 1980 and 2008, the world changed dramatically. The fall of the Berlin Wall and subsequent collapse of the USSR transformed both geopolitical power and the physical map of Europe. It left the US as the sole global superpower while Europe rebuilt and unified. During this period, rapid technological development and increasing migration led to an increasingly globalized world. This brought with it challenges relating to management of and opposition to migration and increased automation in work. The period saw further achievements in civil, LGBT, disability, and women's rights. However, economic and social inequalities persisted and resistance to these changes grew, leading to increasing division within US society and politics. The 9/11 attacks marked a significant turning point for the US. Where the 1990s had seemed like a time of optimism for many, the post-9/11 2000s felt fraught, plunging the US into the long-running War on Terror and changing how the US interacted with not only its enemies, but also its allies and its own citizens. America's unhappiness at this shift in mood, coupled with Obama's team's effective use of social media and his own personal appeal, led to the election of Barack Obama as the first Black president in 2008.

REFRESHER QUESTIONS

1. What were the key elements of Gorbachev's reform policies, *glasnost* and *perestroika*?
2. What was the purpose of the World Trade Organization?
3. What were the consequences of the first Gulf War?
4. What were the key aspects of the Patriot Act?
5. What was the Bush Doctrine?
6. What was Reaganomics?
7. Why did Clinton's attempts at healthcare reform fail?
8. What factors contributed to Obama winning the 2008 election?
9. What is the theory of multiculturalism?
10. How did conservatives react to the AIDS crisis?

Study skills

Guidance on answering long essay questions

Understanding the task and planning your writing

Some questions will ask you to respond in longer essay format. The question will be focused on a specific historical issue and you may be asked to consider its significance, consider relative importance of causal factors, or assess the failure or success of policies or institutions. You will need to make a supported judgment to address any "to what extent" or "how far" elements of the question.

The question requires you to be more analytical, to create a balanced argument, and reach a reasoned conclusion.
- Answers must address the question rather than the topic.
- A balanced argument is essential.
- Carefully selected and accurate knowledge is necessary to support the answer.
- It is important to be analytical rather than simply tell the story.
- A clear argument and supported conclusion are important for a good answer.

Understanding the question

Let's consider the following question:

"The Iraq War was the most important factor in Barack Obama's election as US president in 2008." How far do you agree with this view? [20]

To successfully answer this question, you need to consider different ways to judge significance.
- Assess the Iraq War as a factor in Obama's election:
  - Importance—how important was Iraq to people's voting patterns?
  - Profundity—how much were people affected by the war?
  - Quantity—how many people voted for Obama because of Iraq?
  - Durability—how long were people's lives impacted by the Iraq War?
- You also need to think about other factors that may have affected Obama's election:
  - Obama's personality and political background
  - campaign promises
  - the Great Recession
  - Obama's opponents
  - effectiveness of the campaign (use of social media/internet).

Planning an answer

Once you have understood the demands of the question, the next step is planning your answer. The plan should outline your argument. You need to think about what you are going to argue before you start writing. This will help you to be consistent in your argument throughout your answer. It also means that your plan will be a list of factors about the issue or issues mentioned in the question. This will help you write an analytical response. Simply having a list of dates would encourage you to write a narrative or descriptive answer: this would only show that you understood what happened. Doing this does not answer the question. Instead, you will need to be analytical and think about why it happened. You will need to use your contextual knowledge to support your arguments.

Planning an answer will help you focus on the actual question and not simply write about the topic. Under pressure, such as during an examination, it is easy to forget the importance of planning and just start writing, but this will usually result in an essay that does not have a clear argument, or one that changes its argument halfway through, making it less convincing.

Consider the question on page 294. A plan for this essay might take the following form:

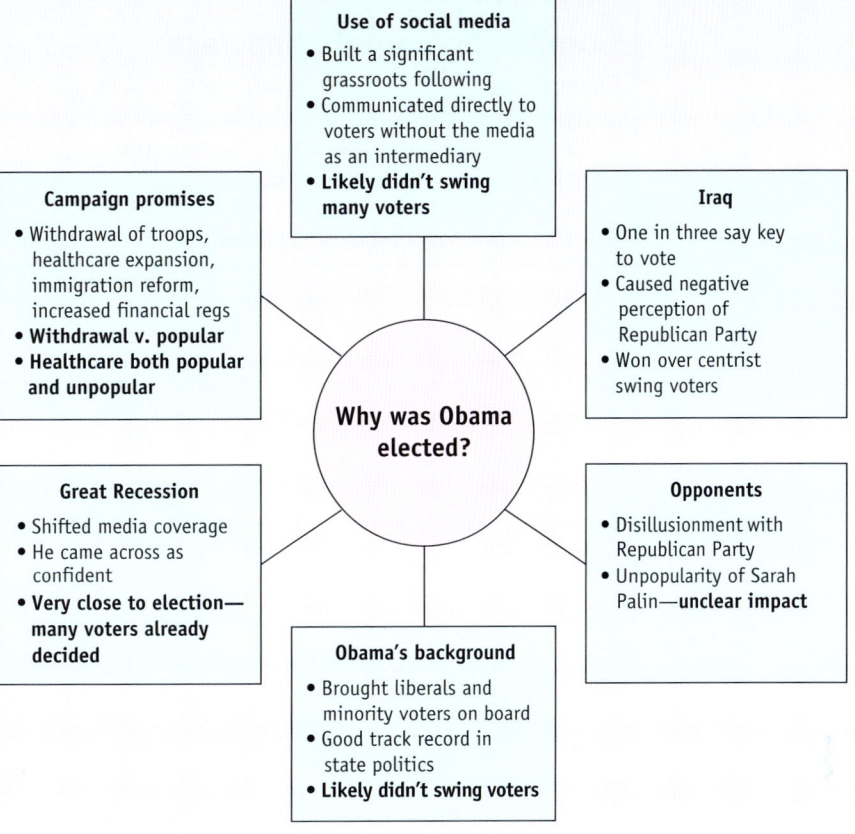

Characteristics of effective responses

Sample answer 1

The Iraq War had gone on since 2003 and, by 2008, many Americans were unhappy with the war. Obama did not agree with the war in Iraq, and this made him popular with Americans who did not like the war. Therefore, this was the most important reason he was elected.

Sample answer 2

The Iraq War was the most important factor in Obama's election. By 2008, the war had been raging for around five years since Bush had declared "Mission Accomplished." Americans were tired of the war and popular disillusionment with the war had led to negative opinions of the Republican Party. By 2007, around one in three Americans rated the Iraq War as an extremely important issue to their vote. Obama had been vocally opposed to the Iraq War since the beginning and, in 2008, his long-held anti-war stance gave him a significant edge over John McCain. His unambiguous messaging was a significant factor in turning centrist swing voters to his campaign, leading to his victory in the 2008 election.

> **ACTIVITY**
>
> In Chapter 4, you considered the features of an effective response. To the right, there are two sample answers to the question at the start of this section. Compare these two answers.

> **ACTIVITY**
>
> **Comparing sample answers**
>
> Compare sample answers 1 and 2 by answering the following questions:
> - What are the strengths and weaknesses of each answer?
> - Which answer do you think is more effective?
> - What can you learn from this activity about writing effectively for extended essay answers?
> - What advice would you give to the writer of each answer to help them improve?

Writing an introduction

A good introduction can set the scene for your answer. However, it needs to be short and focused with an outline of your argument. This means you need to think about what you are going to argue before you start your answer, which is another good reason to plan carefully.

Planning an answer to a different type of question

Consider this question:

To what extent was Reaganomics successful? [20]

The first question you considered asked for a discussion of the relative importance of factors. This question is different, as it asks you to assess the success of a policy.

What does this difference mean for how you might plan your answer?

Here are some clues:
- Highlight the need to establish criteria for measuring success.
- Suggest ways that the answer can analyze different impacts for different people.

You will need to establish some criteria for "objectively" measuring success. This means analyzing the policy against its stated aims and priorities and deciding whether it met these aims and to what degree.

To do this you can consider:
- The stated aims of the policy—did it achieve its own aims? Were there targets it set— did it or did it not achieve these?
- The scope of the policy—could more have been achieved? Was the policy delivered as intended or planned?
- Negatives—were there any aspects of the policy that worked against its stated aims, or that prevented the policy from being successful?

You can also consider the impact the policy had on individuals and groups. This is a more subjective analysis. To answer the question in this way, you will be looking at whether the policy improved the lives of different groups or individuals or made them worse. To answer questions in this way you can consider the following:
- The impact of the policy on different groups, for example:
  - low-income individuals
  - minority groups
  - the middle class
  - businesses.
- The improvement the policy brought to the lives or positions of different groups, for example:
  - Were the financial burdens of low-income individuals lifted (did their disposable income increase)?
  - Were minority groups given more equality within society?
  - Did the disposable income of the middle classes increase?
  - Were regulatory burdens on businesses eased?

When answering questions in this way, consider what the groups you're thinking about would consider improvement in their lives, as well as what might constitute an improvement for society. For example, less regulation may be in the best interests of business, but may create challenges for wider society.

Sample introduction

In the 2008 election, Democrat Barack Obama was standing against Republican John McCain. Obama became the candidate after defeating Hillary Clinton in the primary campaign. Surprisingly, since he was a relatively unknown politician and something of an outsider in the Democratic Party, Obama won the election. There were many reasons why he won, including his personal story, his campaign promises, the weakness of his opposition, his strong campaigning tactics, the Great Recession, and the Iraq War. Of these, the Iraq War was the most important. In this essay I will explain why the Iraq War was the most important factor in Obama's election.

- This introduction has some strong elements as well as some unnecessary background and weaker elements.
- First, this introduction is overly long. The initial background of who Obama had defeated in the primary, and who his Republican opponent was, is not necessary in the introduction.
- Highlighting why it was surprising that Obama won the election (the fact that he was an outsider in the Democratic Party and, initially, not very well known outside of Illinois) provides useful background to the election.
- It is useful in the introduction to outline the other factors and highlight which you will be discussing as the main factor. However, only list the factors you will be discussing in the essay. There is no reason to outline all relevant factors if you will not be discussing them further.

Ending your introduction with a strong statement of your argument (Iraq was the most important factor in Obama's victory) effectively sets expectations for what the rest of the essay should explain.

Writing a conclusion

A good conclusion will reach a judgment. It will summarize the relative importance of different factors, bringing in interim conclusions from previous paragraphs.

Sample conclusion

In conclusion, there were many reasons why Obama won the 2008 election, but the most important one was growing disillusionment with the war in Iraq. The effectiveness of the campaign, particularly the use of social media, ensured that people got to know Obama and his story. However, it is unlikely that this impacted on many voters who were not inclined to vote for Obama already. Similarly, his policies on healthcare were very popular among Democrats and liberals but were equally unpopular among conservative voters, who saw them as an unnecessary expansion of government. By contrast, Obama's anti-war policies won over centrist swing voters who had grown tired of the war in Iraq. Similarly, the ongoing perceived failure in Iraq had embedded disillusionment with the Republican Party into voters, leading them to be more inclined to vote Democrat. Overall, the fact that one in three Americans cited Iraq as a key issue to their vote highlights how many voters the anti-war policy is likely to have won over, leading to Obama's victory.

What makes this a good conclusion?
- This conclusion highlights the argument made throughout the essay (that Iraq was the most important factor in Obama's victory) and provides a strong overview of both why this was the case and why the other factors were less important.
- It offers a clear argument for what caused the Iraq War to be the most important factor (disillusionment with Republicans, one in three Americans saw it as key to their vote, the importance of swing voters) and ends with a clear link back to the question.

What are the features of an effective essay?
- good understanding of the scope of the question
- analysis rather than description
- relevant and accurate details that are carefully selected to support the argument
- a well-structured response that deals with issues clearly
- a balanced approach
- a reasoned conclusion that reaches a judgment in response to the question.

> **ACTIVITY**
>
> **Assessing a sample answer**
> Read the sample response given below.
> Working on your own, decide what you think about the strengths and weaknesses of this answer. Discuss your ideas with a partner.

Sample answer 3

Reaganomics was a program of economic policies enacted by President Reagan between 1980 and 1988. The program had four main aims: to reduce government spending, to reduce taxes for individuals and businesses, to reduce regulatory burdens on businesses, and to reduce inflation. In this essay, I will argue that Reaganomics was only partially successful. While it did reduce individual and business taxes and bring an end to stagflation, public expenditure increased under Reagan and the national debt nearly tripled.

Measured against its aim to reduce taxes for individuals, Reaganomics was relatively successful. Between 1980 and 1988, Reagan introduced a number of acts to reduce income and estate taxes, as well as corporation taxes. These included reducing the top tax bracket from 70 percent to 50 percent and reducing the highest marginal rates. As such, the amount of tax most individuals paid did go down throughout Reagan's presidency. However, these tax reductions mostly helped the highest earners and corporations, who saw disproportionate tax reductions compared to their lower-income counterparts. For example, the lowest tax bracket was only reduced by three percent compared to twenty percent for the highest bracket.

Reagan also encouraged the Federal Reserve to continue its policies for reducing money supply. This, along with raising interest rates, did reduce inflation somewhat. In this, Reaganomics was successful.

On the other two primary aims of Reaganomics, Reagan was less successful. Although Reagan did cut multiple welfare programs during his presidency, including Medicaid, social security, food stamps, and education funding, overall public expenditure increased between 1980 and 1988. Most of this increase was caused by increases in defense spending. During this period, defense spending rose by $126 billion. As this shows, Reaganomics did little to achieve its aim of reducing government expenditure.

In the space of regulation, Reaganomics did reduce regulations in some industries. He removed price controls on oil and natural gas, as well as relaxed the interpretation of the Clean Air Act. However, he also increased import barriers, which was against his deregulation policy.

Overall, Reaganomics had mixed success. It lowered taxes for many individuals and corporations, but it also increased government spending and did not prioritize deregulation. While inflation fell, this was more because of Federal Reserve policy rather than Reaganomics. Reagan also tripled the national debt. In conclusion, Reaganomics was more unsuccessful than successful.

Further reading

General texts

MA Jones, *The Limits of Liberty, American History, 1607–1992* (Oxford University Press, 1995)

EC Hoffman, EJ Blum and J Gjerde, *Major Problems in American History, Volume II: Since 1865* (Cengage Learning, 2011)

Chapter 1 The Gilded Age and Progressive Era

L Fink (Ed), *Major Problems in the Gilded Age and the Progressive Era* (Houghton and Mifflin, 2001)

J Addams, *Twenty Years at Hull House* (Macmillan, 1911)

WEB Du Bois, *The Souls of Black Folk* (Oxford University Press, 2008)

JG Neihardt, *Black Elk Speaks* (University of Nebraska Press, 2014 [1932])

E Wharton, *The Custom of the Country* (Penguin, 2019 [1913])

DK Goodwin, *The Bully Pulpit* (Simon and Schuster, 2013)

C Postel, *Equality: An American Dilemma, 1866–1896* (Farrar, Straus and Giroux, 2019)

PJ Giddings, *Ida: A Sword Among Lions* (Harper Collins, 2008)

Chapter 2 American Imperialism, the First World War, and the 1920s

S Zeiger *In Uncle Sam's Service: Women Workers with the American Expeditionary Force* (Cornell University Press, 2019)

T Britten, *American Indians in World War I: At Home and at War* (University of New Mexico Press, 1997)

K Boyer Sagert, *Flappers: A Guide to American Subculture* (Bloomsbury Publishing, 2009)

P Clements, *Prosperity, Depression and the New Deal: The USA 1890–1954* (Hodder Education, 2008)

AG Hopkins, *American Empire: A Global History* (Princeton University Press, 2019)

DG Gutiérrez, *Walls and Mirrors: Mexican Americans, Mexican Immigrants, and the Politics of Ethnicity* (University of California Press, 1995)

AA Kling, *The Red Scare* (Greenhaven Publishing LLC, 2011)

SB Gluck, *Rosie the Riveter Revisited: Women, the War, and Social Change* (Penguin Books USA, 1988)

Chapter 3 The Great Depression, the Second World War, and the Early Cold War

DM Kennedy, *Freedom from Fear: The American People in Depression and War, 1929–1945* (Oxford University Press, 2005)

S Terkel, *Hard Times: An Illustrated Oral History of the Great Depression* (New Press, 2012)

G Robinson, *A Tragedy of Democracy: Japanese Confinement in North America* (Columbia University Press, 2010)

JL Gaddis, *The United States and the Origins of the Cold War, 1941–1947* (Columbia University Press, 2000)

O Edwards, *The USA and the Cold War, 1945–1963* (Hodder Education, 2002)

ML King Jr, *Stride Toward Freedom: The Montgomery Story* (Harper, 1958)

E Lindhop, *America in the 1950s* (Twenty-First Century Books, 2009)

JD Salinger, *The Catcher in the Rye* (Penguin Books, 1994 [1951])

Chapter 4 The Development of the US in the 1960s and 1970s

JL Gaddis, *The Cold War: A New History* (Penguin Press, 2005)

R Roberts and JS Olson, *Where the Domino Fell: America and Vietnam 1945–1995,* Revised 6th edition (Wiley-Blackwell, 2013)

JM Hanhimaki, *The Rise and Fall of Détente: American Foreign Policy and the Transformation of the Cold War* (Potomac Books, 2013)

JA Andrew, *Lyndon Johnson and the Great Society* (Ivan R. Dee, 1998)

E Black and M Black, *The Rise of the Southern Republicans* (Harvard University Press, 2003)

AM Schlesinger, *The Imperial Presidency* (Houghton Mifflin Harcourt, 2004)

C Carson, DJ Garrow, G Gill, V Harding and DC Hine, *The Eyes on the Prize Civil Rights Reader: Documents, Speeches and Firsthand Accounts from the Black Freedom Struggle* (Penguin Books, 1991)

R Rosen, *The World Split Open: How the Modern Women's Movement Changed America* (Penguin, 2000)

Chapter 5 The Modern US, 1980 to 2008

S Miles, *Engaging the Evil Empire: Washington, Moscow and the Beginning of the End of the Cold War* (Cornell University Press, 2020)

SJ Walker, *The Day that Shook America: A Concise History of 9/11* (University Press of Kansas, 2021)

J Engel, *Into the Desert: Reflections on the Gulf War* (Oxford University Press, 2014)

KJ Heineman, *The Reagan Revolution and the Rise of the New Right* (ABC-CLIO, 2021)

K Kenski, BW Hardy and K Hall Jamieson, *The Obama Victory: How Media, Money and Message Shaped the 2008 Election* (Oxford University Press, 2010)

R Farley and J Haaga, *The American People: Census 2000* (Russell Sage Foundation, 2005)

R Shilts, *And the Band Played On: Politics, People and the AIDS Epidemic* (Souvenir Press, 2011)

D Baker, *The United States since 1980* (Cambridge University Press, 2007)

Glossary

38th parallel Short for 38th parallel north, a line of latitude that circles the Earth 38 degrees north of the equator. Used to mark the border between North and South Korea before the Korean War. The post-war border is in a similar location, but does not follow it precisely.

Affirmative action programs Programs designed to address historical imbalances and encourage fair consideration of all groups in society.

AIDS Acquired Immunodeficiency Syndrome: a life-threatening illness that occurs after the immune system has been severely damaged by HIV.

Alderman A member of the governing body of a town or city.

The Allies The Second World War alliance of Britain, the USSR, and the United States.

Anarchism An ideology that believes that an ideal society would not have a government of any kind.

Anglophone English-speaking.

Anthracite A hard form of coal containing a lot of carbon and few impurities; it is ideal for use in industry and for domestic heating.

Arms race When nations compete with each other for military advantages.

Assimilate Assimiliation is the complete incorporation of an individual or group of people into an existing society and their customs and traditions are adopted.

Attribution See "Provenance"

Automation Using technology to reduce human manual intervention in processes.

Axis Powers The Second World War alliance of Germany, Japan, and Italy. Opposed the Allies.

Bad debt Debt that a business is unable to pay back. A bank having "bad debts" means that the businesses the banks loaned money to are unable to pay the bank back.

Blue-collar Used to describe jobs involving manual labor and working with tools or hands, and the workers who do these jobs.

Bootlegger A person who illegally produced, transported, or distributed alcohol.

Bracero Program An initiative set up by the US and Mexican governments to bring temporary guest workers from Mexico into the United States for farm labor.

Brinkmanship The policy of trying to achieve a successful or advantageous outcome by pushing dangerous events to the brink of active conflict.

Britain Formally known as the United Kingdom of Great Britain and Northern Ireland (UK). Includes England, Northern Ireland, Scotland, and Wales. In 1922, Ireland left the UK, with the exception of Northern Ireland.

Budget deficit A situation in which government spending is greater than what is brought in through tax revenues.

Budget surplus When government spending is lower than the amount of money generated by taxes.

Bureau of Investigation (BOI) A federal law enforcement organization and the predecessor of the Federal Bureau of Investigation (FBI).

Capital Wealth; this can be money, but also valuable assets such as real estate or art.

Catalyst A person or event that quickly causes change. In chemistry a catalyst is a factor that affects chemical reactions.

Central Powers In the First World War, Germany and Austria–Hungary were known as the Central Powers.

Charter of the United Nations The document that officially founded the United Nations. It was signed by 50 countries in San Francisco, California in June 1945.

Chicano/a Originally a racial slur, used by Mexican Americans who identify with their Indigenous Mexican heritage.

Christian fundamentalism A religious movement that emerged in the late nineteenth century rejecting attempts to align Christianity with the latest scientific developments, instead focusing on a literal interpretation of the bible.

Color line The social and/or legal barriers that segregate people of color from white people.

Communism An ideology in which all property is owned by the community, and each person contributes and receives according to their ability and needs.

Conscription Using a law to force people to join the armed forces.

Containment Preventing communism from spreading beyond countries that already had communist governments.

Contras Right-wing rebel groups that were active between 1979 and 1990 in opposition to the Sandinista government in Nicaragua. From an early stage, they received financial and military support from the US Government.

Coolie A racial slur directed toward people of Asian descent.

Corollary A statement is proven by another, already proven statement e.g. "It is snowing, therefore it must be cold."

Crack cocaine A highly addictive drug derived from powdered cocaine; also known as "crack."

Deflation A general decline in prices for goods and services. It occurs when an economy has less money and credit available.

Denazification The removal of Nazis and Nazi culture from German and Austrian society.

Détente A French word meaning relaxation; the relaxation of tensions between superpowers in the 1970s.

Disenfranchise Prevent someone from using their right to vote, or deprive them of that right.

Dollar diplomacy A US foreign policy using economic power to achieve its goals in Latin America and East Asia.

Domino theory A geopolitical theory which suggested that if one country in a region came under the influence of communism, surrounding countries would follow in a domino effect.

Dot-com bubble When the internet became more widely available in the late 1990s, stock markets predicted that new online businesses would make lots of money, and the value of these companies' shares increased very rapidly. By 2000, many of them had failed to make the money predicted, and their value very rapidly decreased (or "crashed".) A lot of the new companies were unable to continue trading and either went bust or were bought by other companies.

Dumbbell tenement Blocks of housing built in New York during the 1890s, named for their central air shafts which created a building shape resembling a dumbbell weight.

Dustbowl 1930s; an area of the south central United States where drought and intensive farming practices inappropriate for the prarie landscape led to dust storms. These blew away the topsoil, making the land impossible to farm.

Eastern Bloc An unofficial group of communist states aligned with the USSR, mostly in Central and Eastern Europe.

Electoral College The group that formally votes in the president and vice president.

Emigrant Someone who has moved away from their home country.

Enfranchisement Being given the right to vote in elections.

Entente Powers In the First World War, the United Kingdom, France, and the Russian Empire (also known as the Allies).

Exodusters African Americans who left the South in the late 1870s. Many set up home in Kansas.

Filibuster A political tactic in which members of a legislative body exploit the rules of a debate to delay or prevent a decision or vote being taken on legislation, typically by speaking for as long as the rules allow.

"Five Civilized Tribes" A colonial term grouping together the Cherokee, Chickasaw, Choctaw, Creek, and Seminole peoples.

Flapper Slang for a fashionable young woman, often someone who wanted to go against conventional behavior.

Floating exchange rate system An exchange rate system in which a currency's value is allowed to change in response to the foreign exchange markets. In the modern world, most currencies are floating.

Freedom Ride In 1961, civil rights activists rode interstate buses into segregated Southern states to protest the non-enforcement of two Supreme Court rulings that deemed bus segregation to be unconstitutional. These were known as Freedom Rides.

Glasnost Russian, meaning "openness;" describes USSR policies aiming to deliver increased government transparency and greater freedom of speech and the press.

Globalization The process of increasing interdependence and integration of the world's economies, markets, societies, and cultures. It is often characterized by the free movement of goods, people, capital, skills, and ideas across borders.

The gold standard When the value of a currency is linked to the value of a country's gold reserves.

Government security A loan to the government in the form of a bond that the government guarantees to repay.

Grassroots Used to describe movements and activities that originate from the ordinary people, rather than leaders.

Greenbacker A member of a political party opposed to a reduction in the amount of paper money in circulation.

Gross National Product (GNP) The total value of all goods and services produced within a country.

Guerrilla warfare A form of unconventional warfare in which smaller groups of independent forces such as rebels, civilians, or militias, engage with a much larger or better-equipped foe.

Hawkish Used to describe a person who favors interventionist, strong, or aggressive military foreign policy (although not necessarily outright war).

Head and master laws American property laws allowing a husband to make decisions about the household and jointly owned property without his wife's knowledge or consent.

HIV Human Immunodeficiency Virus: an infection which attacks the body's immune system, making it difficult to fight off other infections. It is mostly spread through unprotected sex, but also in other ways such as breastfeeding and contaminated blood transfusions. AIDS occurs if the virus is not treated.

Home front The civilian population and activities of a nation during wartime, focusing on support for the military effort.

Hoovervilles Improvised towns built during the Great Depression by people who had lost their homes. Named for the then president, Herbert Hoover, who was blamed for many of the problems of the Depression.

Horizontal integration The owner of one business buys out its competitors, thus creating a monopoly.

Huber Matos affair In October 1959, Huber Matos, a Cuban Army commander, resigned over what he saw as increasing communist influence within the Castro government. Castro ordered Matos' arrest, and accused him of helping the CIA and Cuban opposition plan a counter-revolution. The Matos affair marked a turning point as Castro began to assert more personal control of the revolutionary government.

Immigrant Someone who moves to a country to become a permanent resident.

Impeachment The process by which a legislative body brings charges against a public official.

Inflation When prices increase and the purchasing value of money decreases.

Intercontinental Ballistic Missile (ICBM) A ballistic missile with a range greater than 3,400 miles, primarily for nuclear weapons delivery.

Interventionism Government involvment in political matters abroad and economic policies at home.

Keynesian economics The economic theories of John Maynard Keynes, centered around the idea that governments should take an active role in their countries' economies.

KGB The main security agency for the USSR from 1954 to 1991. Also known as the "Committee for State Security."

Laissez-faire French, meaning "allow to do." A doctrine where a government has minimal interference in the economy, with few laws controlling businesses.

Lame duck An elected official or leader whose term is nearing its end and who has either chosen not to run for reelection or is not allowed to do so. This person often has reduced influence or power because they are no longer accountable to voters.

Latin American debt crisis Often referred to as the "Lost Decade," in the 1980s, many Latin American countries (most notably, Brazil, Argentina, and Mexico) found that they were unable to repay their debts to other counntiers, creating a crisis.

Left wing and right wing Two ends of the political spectrum spanning from the extreme left of communism to the extreme right of fascism.

Lobbying To attempt to influence the decisions of a government.

Lynching The murder of someone by an angry mob of people. In the US, lynchings were predominantly racially motivated.

Manifest Destiny The idea that European Americans had the God-given right to expand across the whole continent, imposing their ideas of democracy, capitalism, and Christianity.

Migrant Someone who moves to another country temporarily. Also, someone who moves within their own country.

MIRV systems A type of ballistic missile containing several warheads, each of which can be aimed to hit a different target.

Miscegenation A perjorative (insulting) term for sexual relationships between people of different ethnicities.

Monopoly A person or a company having sole control or possession of something, in this context often a commodity such as steel.

Moonshine Illegally distilled liquor.

Moral diplomacy A principle of international relations that emphasizes that the US would only intervene if this served to promote American democratic values and rights.

Mujahideen In this book, "mujahideen" refers to the Islamic guerrilla movement against the communist government of Afghanistan in the late 1970s. The term has referred to many different groups throughout history and is still in use today.

Mutually assured destruction A military strategy which asserts that the use of nuclear weapons against a nation also armed with nuclear weapons would result in the nuclear annihilation of both attacker and defender.

National Origins Formula Measures used to limit immigration based on quotas of immigrants for each country of origin (the country immigrants are migrating from).

National Society of the Daughters of the American Revolution A non-profit, volunteer organization founded in 1890 for women who were directly descended from someone who was involved in the American Revolutionary War.

Nativism An ideology based on the idea that people born in a country are more important than people who have moved there. Applied to policies, ideas and people as "Nativist."

"New immigrants" People who emigrated to the US during the period from the end of the Civil War up until the 1920s.

New Manifest Destiny 1890s; an expansion of Manifest Destiny seeking to justify the USA imposing its values on other nations, sometimes including the colonization of other countries.

Non-violent resistance A method of protest used to achieve political ends by mass collective action without violence.

Northern Alliance A military alliance of Islamic groups that controlled around 10 per cent of Afghan territory between 1999 and 2001. Following 9/11, it became the main opposition to the Taliban in Afghanistan and a key US ally.

Nostrum A medicine prepared by an unqualified person that is not considered effective.

"Old immigrants" People, mainly from northern Europe, most of whom emigrated to the US before the Civil War.

Open door policy A US foreign policy in 1899 and 1900. It aimed to set up equal trading rights for all nations trading with China, hoping that this would prevent China being split into smaller colonized states.

Operating System The core software for using a computer, the operating system manages the hardware (the physical parts of a computer) and runs programs.

Outlawing Banning or making something illegal.

Participatory democracy A form of government in which citizens participate individually and directly in political decisions and policies that impact their lives. It is an alternative to representative democracy (the form practiced in most Western countries) in which decisions are made by elected representatives on behalf of citizens.

Party machines Political party organizations headed by single bosses or small groups that held enough votes to maintain political and administrative control of cities, counties, or states.

Patent medicine: An over-the-counter medicine which could be purchased without a prescription from a qualified doctor. Often these contained dangerous substances and were marketed misleadingly as "cure-alls."

Perestroika Russian, meaning "restructuring." *Perestroika* was an attempt to end the stagnation of the Soviet economy and political system. It allowed greater independent action from government ministries and introduced key market-like reforms to the Soviet command economy.

Popular vote The total number of votes in an election. To "win the popular vote," a candidate must receive the most votes. In the US, due to the Electoral College system, winning the popular vote does not guarantee electoral victory.

Pre-emptive action A military attack on an enemy in response to the threat of attack rather than an actual attack.

Prohibition A ban on the manufacture, sale, and transportation of alcohol.

Propaganda Biased communications designed to promote a specific point of view, often containing half-truths or lies.

Provenance The origin or source of a document or artifact.

Proxy war A conflict in which powerful states offer support to opposing sides of a conflict in order to pursue their own competing interests while avoiding direct confrontation.

Puppet state A country which appears independent, but is controlled by another nation.

Quota A fixed restriction on quantity. This can be a minimum or maximum, e.g. a maximum number of immigrants that a country will accept or a minimum number of attendees required for an event.

Ratification The process of making a policy part of the law.

Recession A period of decreased economic activity, often including high unemployment rates and low levels of production. A recession is longer than a period of a few months.

Repatriation The return of someone or something to their country of origin. Unlike deportation, repatriation can be voluntary.

Robber barons Wealthy and powerful industrialists who dominated businesses, equivalent to the billionaires of today.

Rum runner A person who illegally brought alcohol ashore or across land borders.

Sandinistas A left-wing political party in Nicaragua. They ruled from 1979, when they overthrew the previous government, until 1990.

Scramble for Africa The period between 1870 and 1915 during which major European powers competed to colonize as much of Africa as possible.

Separate spheres An ideology prescribing gender roles, confining women to the "private sphere" of domestic duties and childcare within the home. Men were confined to the "public sphere": the world of business, politics, and law.

Share Part of a stock. Shares allow a company to have many owners, and they are traded according to changes in their value.

Sharecropping An agricultural system that was dominant in the southern US states until the introduction of machinery in the 1930s and 1940s. Sharecroppers (farmers) were tenants on the land they worked in return for a share of the crops they grew.

The Schengen Agreement A treaty that established free movement between the countries that signed up to it. This meant that almost all border checks between Germany, France, Belgium, Luxemburg, and the Netherlands were removed.

Silicon Valley A region of Northern California that has become the biggest center of technological innovation and manufacturing in the US.

Sino A prefix used to indicate something related to China.

Socialism An ideology that advocates that the economic system should be changed so that major industries are owned by the workers, rather than by private businesses or corporations. It is different from capitalism, the basis of the American economy, where private individuals, such as business owners and shareholders, own the means of production.

Speakeasy An illicit club selling alcohol.

Speculation A risky financial choice. Also used to mean "guessing," which was often what made speculation risky.

Spoils system When, following an election, officials reward friends, family, and supporters with government jobs.

Stagflation When the inflation rate is high or increasing, economic growth is slow or slowing and unemployment is steadily high.

Stock The ownership certificates of a company; divided into shares.

Suffrage The right to vote in political elections.

Superpowers Extremely powerful nations able to influence events on a global scale.

Taliban An Afghan militant movement that ruled most of Afghanistan from 1996 to 2001 and regained power in 2021. An ultraconservative religious and political faction, they combine strict religious ideology with a strict social code, creating a repressive regime that excludes women almost completely from public life.

Tariffs A means for the government to raise revenue by setting taxes to be paid on imported goods.

Tax credits The benefit granted to some taxpayers allowing them to claim on their tax return to reduce the total amount of tax owed to the state.

Temperance Choosing to not drink alcohol.

Terrorism The use of violence against non-combatants to achieve political or ideological aims.

Trade deficit When a country is importing more goods and/or services than it is exporting.

Trench warfare The main way the First World War was fought on land. This involved each side digging trenches into the land and shooting at the other side while they tried to make advances. It often became a fight of attrition, in which the winning side was the side with most men left at the end.

Trickle-down economics Economic policies that favor wealthy individuals and large corporations in the belief that they will drive economic growth, and that the impact of this growth will "trickle down" to the rest of the population.

Trust An arrangement in which multiple shareholders transfer shares in a business to a named party or group to manage so that they become the single largest body. The members of the trust benefit from the combined earnings of the group. Modern "antitrust" laws work against the monopolies held by Trusts in businesses to preserve competition.

United Nations An international organization founded at the end of the Second World War and designed to support governments to avoid further conflicts.

Unilateralism A doctrine or agenda that supports one-sided action. The action may be in disregard for other parties or may just refer to action taken alone.

Unrestricted submarine warfare Submarine attacks on any ships that were considered to be involved in the war effort, whether naval or merchant, including ships bearing the flags of neutral countries.

Vertical integration When a business owns all parts of the manufacturing process, from raw materials to distribution.

Viet Cong The name given initially to the opposition movements against Diem in South Vietnam. The term eventually came to refer to the armed movement across Vietnam, Laos, and Cambodia led by the National Liberation Front.

Wars of liberation Conflicts fought during the decolonization movement.

Weapons of mass destruction (WMD) Chemical, biological, radiological, or nuclear weapons that can kill or harm many people or cause significant damage to artificial or natural structures or the environment.

Web browser A software application that allows users to access websites and navigate the internet by entering information into search engines.

Yellow journalism 1890s; a style of journalism using sensational headlines to attract readers.

Index

38th parallel 167

A

affirmative action programs 234–5, 289
Afghanistan 208–9, 247, 256–9, 261–2, 274
AIDS 287, 289–90, 293
alderman 34
Allies 99, 135, 155, 159–60, 164
American Imperialism 86–135
anarchism 10, 12, 128, 151
Anglophone 259
anthracite 24
anti-war movement 217–19, 222, 241, 264
arms race 172, 200, 206, 242–4
assassination 9, 121
    Harvey Milk 237
    Kennedy 210
    Malcolm X 229
    McKinley 56
assimilate 10, 14, 25, 74, 78, 82, 111
attribution 5, 79, 83
automation 279, 281, 285
Axis Powers 155–8

B

bad debt 139, 141
Bay of Pigs invasion 195–7, 199, 244
Berlin Wall 198–9, 245–6, 248–9, 263, 293
blue-collar 216, 218, 222, 265, 285, 293
bootleggers 120–3
Bracero Program 142, 183–4
brinkmanship 200
Britain 8–9, 71, 94, 96, 100–3, 135–6, 140, 155–62, 164, 170–1
budget deficit 154, 267–8, 270, 272, 274, 278
budget surpluses 271, 274
Bureau of Investigation (BOI) 122
Bush. George W 245, 259, 272
see also terrorism; Taliban

C

capital 2, 140, 251–2
Carnegie, Andrew 16–17
catalyst 35, 102, 134, 242
Central Powers 99, 101, 103
Charter of the United Nations 161, 187, 203
Chicano/a 232
Chinese Communist Party (CCP) 165, 167, 206
Christian fundamentalism 124, 132
Churchill, Winston 156, 160–2
Civil War 3, 8–10, 29, 43–5, 48, 63, 71, 156, 162, 167, 283
Cold War 155, 158, 161, 164, 169, 172–3, 188–90, 195–9, 205–6, 208–9, 245–6, 255
color-line 70, 72
communism 10, 128, 151, 155–6, 162, 164–6, 169, 172, 174, 179, 181–3, 197
Communist Party 145, 167, 181–3, 246–7, 249
conscription 99, 104, 106–7, 112–13, 216
containment 162, 209, 246
Contras 250–1
Coolidge, Calvin 86, 116
coolie 12
corollary 91–2, 98
crack cocaine 268, 285
Cuban Missile Crisis 170, 195–6, 198–200, 206, 209, 217, 242–4

D

Dawes Act 1, 25, 74
deflation 141, 144
Democratic Party 205, 209, 215–17, 222, 258, 268, 270, 287, 297
denazification 159
détente 196, 205–6, 208–9, 241, 246
digital revolution 279
disenfranchise 37, 65, 67, 184, 234
dollar diplomacy 94–5, 98, 133
domino theory 166, 173, 202
dot-com bubble 273, 280
dumbbell tenement 5–6
dustbowl 142, 150

E

Early Cold War 137–93
Eastern Bloc 166, 248–9, 251, 255
Eisenhower Doctrine 172
Electoral College 150, 272
embargo 197, 244, 257
emigrant 3, 14
enfranchisement 55
see also disenfranchise
Entente Powers 99, 102–3, 115
Exodusters 28–9, 32

F

Federal Bureau of Investigation (FBI) 122, 182, 220, 229, 231, 261
filibuster 216
First Gulf War 257, 261, 263, 266, 293
First Red Scare 86, 128
First World War 86–136, 138–9, 143–5, 155–6, 159
Five Civilized Tribes 25
flapper 123, 125–7, 132
floating exchange rate system 213
Freedom Rides 186, 228, 230–1

G

Gilded Age 1–2, 15, 18, 32, 48, 116
glasnost 247, 263, 293
globalization 245–6, 249, 251–2, 263, 280
gold standard 140, 147
Gorbachev, Mikhail 246–7
government security 144
grassroots 264, 276, 287, 295
Great Depression 112, 117, 123, 131, 137–43, 146, 154, 156, 190, 194
Great Recession 264, 277–8, 294–5, 297
Greenbackers 30–1
Gross National Product (GNP) 117
guerrilla warfare 202

H

Harding, Warren G. 116
hawkish 265
head and master law 289, 293
Helsinki Agreement 195, 208
Hitler, Adolf 153, 156
HIV 287, 290
home front 108
Hoovervilles 138, 142

horizontal integration 16–17
Huber Matos affair 197
Hussein, Saddam 256–7, 261

I

immigrants 2–3, 8–12, 14–15, 20–1, 23–4, 78, 80–2, 85, 99, 112, 119, 122, 128–9, 291–2
    African Americans 119
    Asian 70, 283
    Chinese 9, 12–13, 69–70, 77–9, 85
    Cuban 283
    European 112
    French 121
    German 9–10
    illegal 276, 291
    Irish and German 10
    Italian 121, 128
    Japanese 13, 184
    new 7, 9–10, 12, 15, 21, 76, 82
Immigration and Nationality Act 234, 240, 291
impeachment 220, 271
industrialization 3, 9, 25, 31, 33, 40, 48
inflation 30, 61, 213–14, 266, 298–9
intercontinental ballistic missile (ICBM) 172, 208
Interventionism 92
interventionist 92, 133, 146, 265
Iraq War 276–8, 294–5, 297–8

K

Kennedy, John F 196
Keynesian economics 265–6
KGB 206, 247
King Jr, Martin Luther 185–6, 219, 228, 230, 240
Korean War 137, 167–70, 173, 181
Ku Klux Klan (KKK) 71, 128–9, 132, 229

L

laissez-faire 3, 37, 115–17, 132, 138
lame duck 147
Latin American debt crisis 252
left wing and right wing 151
lobbying 13, 18, 34, 72, 225
lynching 37, 64–5, 68–72, 109, 112, 129–31

M

Malcolm X 229, 231, 240
Manifest Destiny 87, 98
McCarthy, Joseph 181, 189–90
Mellon, Andrew 116
Monroe Doctrine 91–2

N

NATO 166, 173, 255–7, 259, 262–3
Nazi Germany 155–6
New Manifest Destiny 87, 97
non-violent resistance 185–6, 230
Northern Alliance 30, 261
nostrum 115
nuclear war 137, 165, 195, 206, 209, 241, 258

O

Old Immigrants 9
open door policy 97
operating system 279
outlawing 120

P

Paris Peace Accords 205
participatory democracy 215, 250
party machines 33–4, 55
patent medicine 39–40
Peace Corps 211–12, 223
Pearl Harbor 155, 157–8, 173
perestroika 247, 263, 293
popular vote 35, 63, 115, 150, 265, 272
preemptive action 261–2
prohibition 19, 42–5, 47–8, 57, 64, 114, 119–23, 130, 132–3, 226, 288, 293
    Bureau of Prohibition 123
    employment discrimination 240
    ended 123
    era 122
    impacts 64, 119, 132
    laws 43–5, 64, 122
    legislative 57
    national 47, 64, 122
    National Prohibition Act 64
    nationwide 46
    speakeasy culture 120, 132
propaganda 46, 99, 103–5, 108, 113, 174
provenance 5, 83–4
proxy war 195, 201, 241
    Vietnam 195
puppet state 158

Q

Al-Qaeda 258–9, 261–2
quota 114, 128, 148, 234, 253
    Emergency Quota Act 86, 128
    immigrant 128, 234
    immigration 291
    production 148
    tariff 253

R

ratification 35, 63–4, 123, 125, 225, 237, 270
Reagan, Ronald 209–10, 218, 238, 245–6, 264–5, 268
Reaganomics 246, 265–6, 273, 278, 285, 293, 298–9
recession 61, 140–1, 177, 214, 266, 273–4, 276, 291
see also Great Recession
repatriation 142–3
Republican Party 56, 60, 210, 213, 218, 222, 238, 250, 263–5, 269–70, 277, 295, 297
robber barons 15, 76
Roosevelt, Franklin D 137–8, 143, 146
Roosevelt Corollary 91–2
rum runner 120, 122

S

Saint Valentine's Day Massacre 121–2
same-sex marriage 234, 288, 290–1, 293
Sandinistas 250
Schengen Agreement 252
Scramble for Africa 96
Second World War 137–67, 171, 173–5, 177–9, 183–5, 187–9, 193–4
separate spheres 48, 50
share 15–17, 117, 139–40, 191–3, 273
sharecropping 112
Silicon Valley 280
Sino 206
    American trade 88
    Soviet 206, 209
smartphone 279–80
Social Darwinism 66, 97, 129
socialism 10, 114, 128–9
    communism 128
Soviet Union 150, 158–9, 162, 209, 243–5, 247, 249, 263, 266
speakeasy 120, 132
speculation 139–40, 147, 154, 191–2, 213
speech, freedom of 107–8, 174, 181–2, 247
spoils system 35
stagflation 214, 223, 265–6, 298
Standard Oil 16–17, 37–8
stock 16–17, 139
Suez Canal 93, 170
suffrage 44, 50, 53, 72
    African American 50
    American Woman Suffrage Association (AWSA) 48, 50, 52
    International Woman Suffrage Alliance (IWSA) 53

National Association Opposed to Women Suffrage 51
women 7, 48, 53–4
superpowers 196, 199–200, 205–6, 241–4, 246, 252, 254

T

Taliban 261
tariffs 60–1, 63, 88, 114, 117, 138–9, 252–3
tax credits 214, 278
temperance 42, 44–5, 55, 64, 126
terrorism 199, 254, 260, 262
terrorists 199, 202, 251, 258–9, 262, 291
trade deficit 254
trench warfare 111
trickle-down economics 266
trust 15–17, 32, 36–9, 55–6, 151, 205, 217, 268
antitrust laws 116, 266
Beef Trust 39–40
Clayton Antitrust Act 61
Sherman Antitrust Act 1, 16, 23, 37–8, 56, 61
July 37
trustees 16–17
see also Standard Oil Company

U

unilateralism 262
United Nations 161, 167, 171, 187, 203
unrestricted submarine warfare 100–3, 135–6

V

vertical integration 16
Viet Cong 202–3

W

wars of liberation 196
Watergate Scandal 204, 206, 220–1
weapons of mass destruction (WMD) 257, 261–2
web browser 280
Wilson, Woodrow 1, 61, 96, 99–100, 102–3, 107, 134–5, 156
World Trade Center 245, 258
World Trade Organization (WTO) 245, 253, 255, 263, 293

Y

yellow journalism 90

Photo credits

The Publishers would like to thank the following for permission to reproduce copyright material:

p.5 © Public Housing Administration (1903). Hester Street, New York City [Lantern slide]. National Archives and Records Administration / NAID: 3854683; **p.6** t. © New York (State). Legislature. Tenement House Commission., De Forest, R. W. (Robert Weeks). (1901). Advance sheets of part of the report of the Tenement House Commission. / Cornell University via Hathi Trust; **p.6** b. © Jacob Riis via Preus Museum on Flickr; **p.10** © Unknown Artist. (1916). The Melting Pot: the great American drama. University of Iowa Libraries Special Collections Department, Redpath Chautauqua Collection / MSC0150; **p.11** © Billy Ireland Cartoon Library and Museum, The Ohio State University; **p.13** The only one barred out, (Frank Leslie's Illustrated Newspaper, 1882) [Cartoon]. Library of Congress Prints and Photographs Division / LC-USZC2-780; **p.17** © GRANGER - Historical Picture Archive / Alamy Stock Photo; **p.18** J. Ottmann after drawing by J. Keppler. The Bosses of the Senate. (Puck, 1889) [Lithograph]. Library of Congress Prints & Photographs division / LC-USZC4-494; **p.19** The blast furnaces of Pittsburgh at night (Harper's Weekly, New York, 1883) [Engraving]. University of Michigan, via Hathi Trust; **p.23** De Thulsrup, T. The Anarchist Riot in Chicago - A Dynamite Bomb exploding among the police (Harper's Weekly, New York, 1886) [Wood engraving]. Library of Congress Prints and Photographs Division / LC-USZ62-796; **p.24** Ohio State Journal/Shaw, A. (18971907). The American monthly review of reviews. New York: Review of Reviews. / via Internet Archive https://archive.org/details/sim_review-of-reviews-us_1902-11_26_154/page/543 a; **p.26** © B Christopher / Alamy Stock Photo; **p.28** © Everett Collection Historical / Alamy Stock Photo; **p.30** American Oleograph Co. (c 1875). I feed you all! [Lithograph]. Library of Congress Prints and Photographs Division / LC-DIG-pga-00025; **p.36** Nast, T. The real lesson of the fall elections (Harper's Weekly, New York, 1886) [Wood engraving]. University of Michigan, via Hathi Trust; **p.40** © North Wind Picture Archives / Alamy Stock Photo; **p.42** © History and Art Collection / Alamy Stock Photo; **p.44** Morton, S. B. The Ohio whiskey war (Frank Leslie's Illustrated Newspaper, 1874) [Wood Engraving]. Library of Congress Prints and Photographs Division / LC-USZ62-90543; **p.46** © GRANGER - Historical Picture Archive / Alamy Stock Photo; **p.49** © The Reading Room / Alamy Stock Photo; **p.50** © Collection of the Massachusetts Historical Society; **p.51** National Association Opposed to Woman Suffrage / https://commons.wikimedia.org/wiki/File:Household_Hints.jpg /http://creativecommons.org/licenses/by/4.0/; **p.55** © Poster US 5083, Poster collection, As a war measure, the country is asking of women service as farmers, mechanics, nurses and doctors ... and the country is getting it! Women are asking of the country enfranchisement. Are the women going to get it?, Hoover Institution Library & Archives; **p.58** © GRANGER - Historical Picture Archive / Alamy Stock Photo; **p.59** © Chronicle / Alamy Stock Photo; **p.60** Raven-Hill, Leonard, Punch Magazine / https://commons.wikimedia.org/wiki/File:For_Auld_Lang_Syne_-_Leonard_Raven-Hill.jpg / http://creativecommons.org/licenses/by/4.0/ ; **p.62** Berryman, C. (1914). Priming (Washington Evening Star, Ed.) [Engraving]. National Archives and Records Administration / NAID: 306143; **p.64** Berryman, C. Untitled (Washington Evening Star, 1914) [Engraving]. National Archives and Records Administration / NAID: 6010878; **p.73** The Crisis Staff / https://commons.wikimedia.org/wiki/File:The_Crisis,_special_education_number,_cover,_July_1920.jpg / http://creativecommons.org/licenses/by/4.0/ ; **p.80** Evans, R. O. The Americanese wall - as Congressman Burnett would build it (Puck, 1916) [Photomechanical print]. Library of Congress Prints and Photographs Division / LC-USZ62-52584; **p.88** Keppler, U. It's "up to" them (Puck, 1901) [Chromolithograph]. Library of Congress, Prints & Photographs division / LC-DIG-ppmsca-25583; **p.89** Emil Florhi / https://commons.wikimedia.org/wiki/File:Flohri_cartoon_about_the_Philippines_as_a_bridge_to_China.jpg / http://creativecommons.org/licenses/by/4.0/ ;

p.92 William Allen Rogers / https://commons.wikimedia.org/wiki/File:Tr-bigstick-cartoon.JPG / http://creativecommons.org/licenses/by/4.0/ ; **p.100** Some of the sixty six coffins buried in one of the huge graves in the Queenstown churchyard (New York Times, New York, 1901) [Photograph]. Library of Congress, Serial and Government Publications Division / sn78004456; **p.105** Flagg, J. M. & National War Garden Commission, 1918. (n.d.). Sow the seeds of victory [Lithograph]. Library of Congress Prints and Photographs Division / LC-USZC4-10234; **p.118** © GRANGER - Historical Picture Archive / Alamy Stock Photo; **p.121** Chicago Bureau (Federal Bureau of Investigation) - Wide World Photos / https://commons.wikimedia.org/wiki/File:Al_Capone_in_1930.jpg / http://creativecommons.org/licenses/by/4.0/ ; **p.124** © Courtesy Tennessee State Library & Archives; **p.126** © Hulton Archive / Getty Images; **p.130** Retreived from:https://www.abebooks.com/signed/Fire-Flint-WHITE-Walter-F-Alfred/31150595203/bd; **p.143** Portrait of Herbert Hoover (Underwood & Underwood, Washington, D.C., c 1928.) [Photograph]. Library of Congress Prints and Photographs Division / LC-USZ62-24155; **p.145** © Niday Picture Library / Alamy Stock Photo; **p.149** © CORBIS/Corbis via Getty Images; **p.153** © Fotosearch / Getty Images; **p.159** Courtesy of the Franklin D. Roosevelt Library archives. https://creativecommons.org/licenses/by/2.0/deed.en; **p.163** Berryman, C. Untitled (Washington Star, 1946) [Engraving]. National Archives and Records Administration / NAID: 6012362; **p.177** Photograph of Suburban Growth. (U.S. Information Agency, Press and Publications Service, c 1959). National Archives and Records Administration / NAID: 595663; **p.178** We Can Do It! Rosie the Riveter. (War Production Co-Ordinating Committee, 1942) Library of Congress / 2021669753; **p.199** © Universal Art Archive / Alamy Stock Photo; **p.204** U.S. Marine Corps. (1968). Vietnam. Walter Cronkite and a CBS Camera crew. [Photograph]. U.S. National Archives / NAID: 532454; **p.207** President Richard Nixon Shaking Hands with Chairman Mao Tse-tung. (1972). [Photographs]. Richard Nixon Library via National Archives and Records Administration / NAID: 194759; **p.214** Leffler, W. K. (1979). Gasoline lines [Photograph]. Library of Congress Prints and Photographs Division / LC-DIG-ppmsca-03433; **p.218** © Dick Kraus/Newsday via Getty Images; **p.219** Ronald L. Haeberle /https://commons.wikimedia.org/wiki/File:Burningdwelling2.jpg#Licensing / http://creativecommons.org/licenses/by/4.0/ ; **p.221** © A Herblock Cartoon, © The Herb Block Foundation; **p.223** © Wolfe, Frank, White House photographer/ U.S. National Archives and Records Administration ID 192605; **p.226** White House Staff Photographers (1977) Rosalynn Carter with Betty Ford and Lady Bird Johnson at the National Women's Conference. [Photograph]. Jimmy Carter Library via National Archives and Records Administration / NAID: 176924; **p.228** Leffler, W. K., photographer. (1963) View of the huge crowd from the Lincoln Memorial to the Washington Monument, during the March on Washington. Washington D.C, 1963. [Photograph] Library of Congress, Prints & Photographs Division / LC-DIG-ds-04417; **p.231** © Bettmann / Getty images; **p.233** © Bettmann / Getty images; **p.236** © Fred W. McDarrah/MUUS Collection via Getty Images; **p.239** © Hulton Archive / Getty images; **p.248** © Tom Stodart / Getty images; **p.259** © Spencer Platt / Getty images; **p.260** White House Staff Photographers (2001) 911: President George W. Bush Visits New York. [Photograph]. George W. Bush Library via National Archives and Records Administration / NAID: 5997294; **p.265** © Bettmann / Getty Images; **p.270** © Steve Greenberg, 1993; **p.273** © TANNEN MAURY / AFP via Getty Images; **p.275** © Paul Morse/White House via Getty Images; **p.284** © Associated Press / Alamy Stock Photo; **p.286** © Associated Press / Alamy Stock Photo; **p.288** © Mikki Ansin/ Contributor via Getty Images; **p.290** Courtesy of the U.S. National Library of Medicine;